ISBN 978-0-428-70675-3
PIBN 10841034

REPORTS

OF

CASES

ARGUED AND DETERMINED

IN THE

Court of Common Pleas,

AND

OTHER COURTS,

FROM HILARY TERM, 55 GEO. III. 1815,
TO EASTER TERM, 56 GEO. III. 1816,

BOTH INCLUSIVE.

With Tables of the Cases and Principal Matters.

By WILLIAM PYLE TAUNTON,
OF THE MIDDLE TEMPLE, ESQ. BARRISTER AT LAW.

VOL. VI.

LONDON:

PRINTED BY A. STRAHAN,
LAW-PRINTER TO THE KING'S MOST EXCELLENT MAJESTY;
FOR J. BUTTERWORTH AND SON, 43. FLEET-STREET,
AND J. COOKE, ORMOND-QUAY, DUBLIN.

1818.

JUDGES

COURT OF COMMON PLEAS,

During the Period contained in this VOLUME.

The Right Hon. Sir VICARY GIBBS, Knt. Ld. Ch.J.

Hon. JOHN HEATH, Efq.

Hon. Sir ALAN CHAMBRE, Knt.

Hon. Sir ROBERT DALLAS, Knt.

Hon. Sir JAMES ALLAN PARK, Knt.

Hon. CHARLES ABBOTT, Efq.

Hon. Sir JAMES BURROUGH, Knt.

A

TABLE

NAMES OF THE CASES

REPORTED IN THIS VOLUME.

N. B. The Cases, the Names of which are printed in *Italics*, are printed or cited from MS. Notes.

Moore

ERRATA.

In Vol. IV. Page 555. line 11. *for* " time to plead," *read* " time to declare."

Vol. V. 530. line 24. *for* " Defendant," *read* " Plaintiff."

Table of Cases, page viii. column 2. last line, Croft v. Johnson, *for* " 205." *read* " 319."

Vol. VI. 8. marginal note, line 10., *for* " one which" *read* " one of which."

325. To the King v. Box. Marginal note. " An indictment charged that the prisoner feloniously had falsely made, forged, and counterfeited a certain promissory note for the payment of money which was as follows: ' On demand, we promise to pay Mesdames S. W. and S.D. stewardesses for the time being of the Provident Daughters' Society, held at Mr. Pope's, The Hope, Smithfield, or their successors in office, sixty-four pounds with 5 per cent. interest for the same, value received this 7th day of February, 1815. For F. C. and Co., J. F.' This is a valid promissory note within the stat. 2 G. 2. c. 25., and the conviction was affirmed."

370. Marginal note, line 5., *dele* " though."

449. line 22., *for* "receive," *read* "make," *and for* "from," *read* "to."

464. Marginal note to Abtrsol v. Bristow. "Under an averment that after loading the cargo, the ship sailed on the voyage and was lost, the Plaintiff cannot recover on proof that the ship, before she had half her cargo on board, was driven from her moorings and lost."

527. last line but 6., *for* " Plaintiffs," *read* " Avowants."

528. line 4. *for* " Plaintiffs," *read* " Avowants."
line 12. *for* " Defendant," *read* " Plaintiff."

529. last line but 7., *for* " Defendant," *read* " Plaintiff."
last line but 2., *for* " Plaintiff," *read* " Defendant."
last line, *for* " Defendant," *read* " Plaintiff."

559. line 7. *for* " messuage," *read* " message."

561. line 6. *for* " Plaintiff," *read* " Defendant."

570. line 14. *for* 2 Hen. 6. *read* 23 Hen. 6.

592. line 11. *for* " Plaintiff," *read* " Defendant."
lines 17. and 19., *for* " Defendant," *read* " Plaintiff."

593. line 1. *for* " Plaintiff," *read* " Defendant."

596. line 11. *for* " before the defence of other joint contractors not sued, which used to be pleaded in abatement, was introduced as a defence on *non assumpsit*," *read* " which used to be allowed as a defence on *non assumpsit*, was restricted to be used only as a plea in abatement."

The pages 637. to 652. should be 617. to 632.

A

T A B L E.

OF THE

CASES in HILARY and EASTER Terms, 1815.

* * * Those of which the Names are printed in *Italics* are from Manuscript Notes.

document-

Huguenin

Mitchell

Sidney,

ERRATA.

In Vol. IV. Page 555. line 11. *for* time to plead *read* time to declare.
Vol. V. 530. 24. *for* Defendant *read* Plaintiff.
Table of Cases, page viii. column 2. last line, Croft *v.* Johnson, *for* 205, *read* 319.

A
TABLE

CASES in TRINITY and MICHAELMAS Terms, 1815.

VOL. VI.   b   *that*

: b 2 Crook

b 3

Gernon

two

Robinson

Tasker

Page

A

T·A·B·L·E

OF THE

CASES in Hilary and Easter Terms, 1816.

₊ Those of which the Names are printed in *Italics* are from Manuscript Notes.

Vol. VI.   c   *rupt,*

Everest

Martin

Page

- I -

to

Page

CASES

ARGUED and DETERMINED

IN THE

Court of COMMON PLEAS,

AND OTHER COURTS,

IN

Hilary Term,

In the Fifty-fifth Year of the Reign of GEORGE III.

CLUTTERBUCK, Plaintiff; BRABANT, Deforciant.

Jan. 24.

THE parties having given the cursitor instructions, or a *præcipe*, as it is called, to levy a fine of five messuages, in pursuance thereof five messuages were inserted in the writ of covenant, and the king's silver was paid for five messuages, but four messuages only were inserted in the concord, so that the words " aforesaid messuages" referred to four only. The cyrographer seeing the variance, amended that which was right, by that which was wrong, and erasing " five" in the writ of covenant, and *præcipe*, or instructions for the writ, substituted " four." The party then carried the instruments back to the cursitor, who again erased " five" in the first *præcipe* and writ of covenant, and restored four. The party thereupon applied to the cyrographer to make the like amendment in the concord, who hesitated

Where the concord of a fine by mistake varied in the number of messuages from the writ of covenant and præcipe, *the Court refused to amend it in* fieri *and pass it, as being the agreement of the parties, who were still alive, unless they should all re-acknowledge it after the amendment.*

VOL. VI.   B   sitated

sitated to do it without the direction of a judge of the court. The party then applied to *Gibbs* C. J. at chambers for an order on the cyrographer to amend the *præcipe* to the concord by the first *præcipe* and writ of covenant, who declined to make any order, both because he doubted the power of the Court to order an alteration in the concord, which was the act and agreement of the parties, and also because the fine, being sent into the title with such repeated erasures, might always be a blot on it.

Vaughan Serjt. now moved the Court for the same amendment.

The Court at first inclined to reject the application, observing that it was a very extraordinary blunder, but the parties had dealt for themselves, and had taken on themselves to correct it, instead of coming in the first instance to the Court. The great difficulty which the Court felt, was, whether they had the power to intermeddle with the concord, which was the agreement of the parties; if it had been only a clerical blunder, the Court could correct it; but this was the parties' own act. These difficulties might all be escaped by having a new caption, which would be attended with very little more expence than the amendment. After the parties were dead, the Court could not alter the concord, which was the agreement of the parties; and if the parties were alive, they could all consent to a new caption; and it would be much better for the title that the present motion should fail than succeed. The Court, however, afterwards agreed, that if the parties would re-acknowledge the concord after the amendment, the difficulty would be avoided, and permitted *Vaughan*, whose client preferred having the fine with its erasures to the expence of a new one, to

amend

amend the *præcipe* to the concord, and that after such amendment, and a re-acknowledgment by the parties, the cyrographer might receive and pass it.

Fiat.

PHILLIPS and Another *v.* CHAMPION.

THIS was an action upon a policy of insurance, effected on the 16th of *September* 1808, upon the ship *Active,* at and from *London* to the *Southern* whale and seal fishery, during her stay and fishing, and at and from thence to *London,* until the ship should be arrived back there, with liberty to proceed and sail to and touch and stay at any ports or places, particularly in the Channel, *Madeira,* the *Cape de Verd Islands,* the coast of *Peru, Chili, California, Brazils, Africa, New South Wales, New Holland, Malacca Islands,* the *Cape of Good Hope, St. Helena,* or elsewhere, to load and unload goods, refresh, seek, join, and exchange convoys, or otherwise, and for any and all other purposes whatsoever, without being deemed a deviation, to return two pounds *per cent.* if the ship arrived back at her moorings in the river *Thames* on or before the 16th of *March* 1810. The Plaintiffs averred, first, an average loss of 51*l.* 8*s.* 7*d. per cent.* by perils of the seas off the coast of *New Holland,* and afterwards a total loss by the like cause. The cause was tried at *Guildhall,* at the sittings after *Michaelmas* term 1814, before *Gibbs* C. J.: it appeared that the ship sailed on the voyage insured in *September* 1808. In *June* 1809 she was stranded in *Western Cove,* on the coast of *New Holland:* all her stores and provisions, and 1236 seal-skins, being the whole number which she had then taken, were damaged by sea-water, and landed. The vessel

In an insurance upon a voyage to the *Southern* whale fishery, during the ship's stay and fishing, and at and from thence back to *London,* *semble* that if the ship sends home by another vessel a part of what she has taken, and continues her fishing, the adventure is not ended by her shipping such part for *England.*

And it clearly is not thereby terminated, if the part sent home consisted of damaged skins, which would, if kept on board, have damaged the residue of the cargo.

vessel being repaired for proceeding on her voyage, 817 of these skins were in *October* 1809 sent home from *Sydney Cove* by the ship *Mary Ann*, and the *Active* proceeded in quest of seals for her cargo. It was in evidence, that if any of the damaged skins had been stowed with sound skins, they would have infected and damaged the latter, and that the 817, therefore, could not safely have been taken on board. If they had been in good condition, they would have been put on board the *Active*. They arrived by the *Mary Ann*, and 37*l.* 16*s.* was paid for their freight home; and on sale, they produced a net sum of double that amount. The Defendant relied on the circumstance that some of the produce of the adventure had been shipped for *England*, and had in fact arrived, and produced a small profit, as a criterion that the voyage was thereupon terminated, and that he therefore was not liable for the total loss which afterwards happened. *Gibbs* C. J. was, however, of opinion that the point did not even arise, since they were sent home to prevent injury to the other skins, and, therefore, he would not unnecessarily determine it; though he strongly inclined to think that the sending home a small part of what the ship had taken, in order to make room for more, could not be deemed a termination of the voyage; and under his direction the jury found a verdict for the Plaintiff for a total loss, as well as the average loss.

Lens Serjt, now moved to set aside the verdict and have a new trial; he urged that so soon as any produce of the adventure was sent home, that terminated the policy, on the face of which no other termination of the risk was limited; and it could not be intended that the underwriter was to continue liable during any indefinite number of years that the owners might please to prolong the adventure. He relied on the

clause

clause for return of premium, as a proof that the parties contemplated so early a termination of the adventure, as that the vessel might reach *England* by *March* 1816.

The *Court* was unanimous that there was no possible ground for reviewing the verdict, and

Refused the Rule.

DAND v. BARNES.

THE Plaintiff sued out a common *capias*, tested the 29th of *June* 1814, and returnable on the morrow of *All Souls*, against Sir *Wastel Brisco* Bart., *Joseph Barnes, John Barnes*, and *Joseph Nelson*, and the *English* notice at the foot of the process was directed to them all, and required them to appear " on the third day of *November* 1814," expressing the year in figures.

Best Serjt., for the Defendants, had, on the 26th of *November*, the last day but one of the last term, obtained a rule *nisi* to set aside the service of this process for the irregularity, that the year was in the *English* notice stated only in figures.

Rough Serjt. on this day shewed cause, upon the grounds; first, admitting that, according to *Grojan* v. *Lee, ante*, v. 651., the year ought to be in words at length, yet that the process being returnable on one of the three first general return days of *Michaelmas* term, it was necessary, that if the Defendants would have availed themselves of the irregularity, they should have applied earlier than the last day but one of the

If a Plaintiff joins several Defendants in one common process, one, upon whom it is irregularly served, applying before declaration to set it aside, may entitle his rule and affidavit in a cause of the Plaintiff against himself only.

A party may apply to set aside proceedings for irregularity at any time before the irregular party has taken a further step, if the latter has not, by the delay of the former, been induced to place himself in a worse situation than he would have been in, if the other had come earlier.

B 3   term.

term. For this he relied on a case of *Pearson* v. *Hodgson*, said to have been moved for irregularity in the Court of King's Bench in *Michaelmas* term 1814, where the writ was a *latitat* returnable on the 6th of *November*, and no declaration had been filed, and a motion being made on the 18th of *November* to set aside the process for an irregularity, the Court held that because that motion was not made within four days after the return-day of the writ, and before appearance, it came too late. The delay in this case was much greater. He also took a preliminary objection to the rule, namely, that the rule and the affidavits on which it was obtained, purported to be made in a cause of *Dand* v. *John Barnes*, which was not this cause, inasmuch as there were 14 Defendants in this action. All the parties in a cause, as well Defendants as Plaintiffs, must be named in entitling an affidavit or a rule. So held by Lord *Ellenborough* C. J. *Noel and Others* v. ———, 1 *Smith*, 457. *Acc.* by Lord *Kenyon* C. J. *Owen* v. *Hurd*, 2 *Term Rep.* 643. *Fores* v. *Diemar*, 7 *Term Rep.* 661. *acc.*

Best, contrà, urged, 1st, That it was the established practice in this court, that a party might apply to set aside proceedings for irregularity at any time before the other party had taken a subsequent step in the cause: *Downes* v. *Witherington*, *ante*, ii. 245. And the Plaintiff had taken no step in this case since serving the process. As to the title of the affidavits, it is competent for the Plaintiff to include four Defendants in four several actions in one common *capias;* otherwise in a bailable writ, which distinction is taken in *Jonge* v. *Murray*, 1 *Marsh*. 274.; it must therefore be presumed that the Plaintiff so entitling his rule and affidavit, meant to proceed against *John Barnes* only, and to abandon his action against the others, or else sever in

10   declaring:

declaring: and *John Barnes* might therefore move. If
this were not so, a Plaintiff would be enabled, by suing
out common process against two or more, to put a
Defendant into such a situation that he could obtain
no relief from any irregularity; for according to
the doctrine contended for, he cannot move, unless all the Defendants have been served, and appear,
and apply in concert; and it cannot lie in his power
to know whether the others have been served or not,
and, unless the Plaintiff brings them all into court,
they may not all appear together.

The Court agreed to this doctrine, and instanced the
case of *Richard Roe*, who is joined with the Defendant
in every common process, yet need not appear to warrant a motion by the real Defendant, wherefore they
held that the affidavit and rule were sufficiently entitled. But they thought that the proposition had been
too widely laid down, that the party who complains of
an irregularity, may in all cases proceed to set it aside,
unless the party committing it has taken some second
step; and that the rule must be narrowed to the cases
where the party complaining has not, by lying by, induced
the irregular party to place himself in a worse situation than he would have been in, if the proceedings
had been sooner set aside: but this Defendant in this
case, for any thing that appeared, being entitled to relief
within the rule so narrowed, they held that his application had not come too late, and made the

Rule absolute.

1815.

DAND
v.
BARNES.

1815.

Jan. 25.

HURD v. GIRDLESTONE.

An attorney, grantee of an annuity, preparing the securities, and upon payment of the whole consideration money, retaining his charges thereout, one which is for business never done, does not thereby necessarily avoid the annuity under 17 G 3. c. 26. s. 4.; but it is a question for a jury whether the improper charge was made with intent to get back a part of the consideration money.

THIS was an action of covenant against the surety for an annuity. The defence was, that at the time when the whole consideration-money was paid down, the Plaintiff, who was the grantee, and also prepared the securities as attorney for the grantor, produced and received the amount of his bill of the charges for the same, among which was a charge for searching for incumbrances on the grantor's estates whereon the annuity was secured; which search, it appeared at the trial, never was made. *Gibbs* C. J. left it to the jury, whether there was any collusion or fraud, and whether this charge was made with the intent to get back or retain a part of the consideration-money of the annuity, or whether it was a charge, which indeed ought not to have been made, but was made inadvertently. The jury found a verdict for the Plaintiff.

Lens Serjt. now moved to set aside the verdict and have a new trial. He cited *Broomhead* v. *Eyre*, 5 *T. R.* 597., where it was held that a solicitor preparing the deeds for the purchase of an annuity made with his own money, avoided the grant by taking a commission-fee on the amount. If the grantee takes back any part, on any pretence whatever, it is a retaining within the statute 17 *G.* 3. *c.* 26. *s.* 4., even if he does it inadvertently: but here it was done designedly, and was a deliberate overt act.

GIBBS C. J. The object of the act 17 *G.* 3. *c.* 26. was, that no part of the consideration should be retained, so as that more should be stated in the memorial than was actually paid. The doctrine stated by

16   the

the counsel for the Defendant is, that if an attorney buys an annuity, and after paying the whole consideration-money delivers a bill with charges that cannot be maintained, and the bill is paid, the annuity is void, and that it makes no difference though this be done by mistake. I cannot subscribe to this doctrine. The question is, whether it was by extortion or collusion, and with the intent that a part might be drawn back to the person who advances the money.

HEATH J. The case cited is that of an application to the Court to set aside the annuity; there the Court were to decide the fact as well as the law. Here the fact was left to the jury, and they have found it in favour of the Plaintiff.

CHAMBRE J. It never was meant by the legislature to deprive the party of his property for an act done merely by a mistake. Certainly there were strong circumstances to go to the jury, to shew that this was not a mistake, but they have found that it was a mistake. It was merely a question for the jury.

DALLAS J. The annuity was to be set aside, if the improper charge was founded in fraud. The jury have found it was not founded in fraud, but inadvertence.

Rule refused.

HORNE v. SMITH.

A SUBPŒNÂ was served on *Knight*, a high constable, at his house in *Hampshire*, 24 miles distant from *Winchester*, seven days before the assizes, requiring

The Court will not grant an attachment against a witness for disobedience to a *subpœnâ*, unless it be a clear case of contempt.

requiring him. to attend there upon the trial of this cause as a witness for the Plaintiff. He used contemptuous language of the Plaintiff and the person who served it, and refused to come. At three o'clock on the commission day, a copy of the *subpœná* was again served on him with 1*l*, and again at eight in the evening with 3*l.*, both of which sums he refused to accept, as being too little. There was no public conconveyance from his abode to *Winchester*, he was accustomed to travel on horse-back, but had lent his horse to another to attend at *Winchester* as high constable in his stead, and he omitted to appear on the trial. *Best* Serjt. had in the last term obtained, under these circumstances, a rule *nisi*, for an attachment against the witness; against which *Pell* Serjt. now shewed cause: he cited *Fuller* v. *Prentice*, 1 *H. Bl.* 49. *Chapman* v. *Paynton*, 13 *East*, 16. *n.* and *Bowles* v. *Johnson*, 1 *Bl. Rep.* 37., to shew that when the *subpœná* is served, sufficient must be tendered to bear the witness's expences out and home.

Best in support of his rule. It has not been the practice to tender the whole of the expences when the *subpœná* has been served; nevertheless attachments have been granted in this court. He relied on the witness's injurious expressions, and observed, he had not disaffirmed what the Plaintiff swore, that he believed the witness omitted to come, for the purpose of defeating the Plaintiff of his action. The sum tendered was sufficient for his expences to *Winchester* and back, having regard to the distance.

Per Curiam. It was not necessarily certain that the cause would be tried the first day, and the witness must have sufficient for his subsistence during his probable stay there. It must be a perfectly clear case to call

for

for an attachment, which is an exercise of the Court's extraordinary jurisdiction: and it is not usual to grant it for injurious expressions. This is not a question of extorting an unreasonable sum of money. We are not prepared to say that sufficient money must be tendered with the *subpœna*. Many circumstances may be stated by the witness to make more necessary, such as his health, &c. But in this case the *subpœna* was served seven days before the trial: no sufficient sum was then tendered. It is not pretended that sufficient was tendered till eight in the evening before the day of the trial, which was to be at twelve the next day. The witness had then no manner of conveyance of his own, for he had lent his horse. If the Plaintiff feels he has lost any thing by *Knight's* non-attendance, he may still bring his action.

Rule discharged.

1815.

HORNE
v.
SMITH.

WILKS *v.* ATKINSON.

Jan. 25.

AFTER verdict for the Plaintiff, one objection, upon which *Lens* Serjt. had moved to set it aside, was, that the contract signed by the Defendant, to sell and deliver to the Plaintiff a quantity of rape-oil, for the manufacture of which the Defendant had the seed, but it was not then crushed, was not stamped, and that it did not fall within the exemption contained in the statute 48 G. 3. c. 149. *Schedule, Part* 1. tit. *Agreement*, as an agreement made for or relating to the sale of any goods, wares, or merchandizes.

GIBBS C. J. The facts are, that the Plaintiff, a great dealer in oil, had this, not in oil, but in seed, not then crushed: he enters into an agreement, and,

A contract for selling and delivering oil, not yet expressed from seed in the vendor's possession, is exempted from stamp duty as a contract relating to the sale of goods within the stat. 48 G. 3. c. 149. *Schedule, Part* 1., *Agreement. Exemption.*

as soon as he has made it, he proceeds to perform it, by crushing the seed, and expressing the oil: and the question is, whether this is a contract relating to the sale of goods, wares, or merchandizes. A baker agrees to produce me a loaf to-morrow; he has not the bread, but he has the flour, and is to make it into bread, and deliver it. How often does a butcher contract to deliver meat, when he has not the meat, and the beast is not yet killed. It is out of all common sense to say this is not a contract relating to goods, wares, and merchandizes.

Rule refused.

HOOPER and Another, Assignees of WELLS, v. RAMSBOTTOM and Others.

If the vendor of a leasehold estate delivers the conveyance as an escrow, to take effect on payment of the residue of the purchase money, the property in the title deeds of the estate is so vested in the vendee, that the vendor, obtaining possession of them, and pawning them, confers on the pawnee no right to detain them after tender of the residue of the purchase money.

THIS was an action of trover, brought by the assignees of *Wells*, a bankrupt, for certain title-deeds in the possession of the Defendants. Upon the trial, at the sittings after the last *Michaelmas* term, before *Gibbs* C. J., it was proved that *John Whittle Harvey* had been the owner of a leasehold estate, for the purchase of which *Wells*, the bankrupt, had contracted; and the conveyances were engrossed, and *Wells* paid part of the purchase-money, but 330*l.* remained unpaid; and, as a security, the deeds were delivered only as an escrow to take effect on the payment of the residue, and were left in the hands of *Daniel Whittle Harvey*, (who was the solicitor employed, and was the brother of the vendor,) until *Wells* should pay the rest of the money, whereupon they were to be delivered over to him. *Daniel* suffered *John* to take all the deeds antecedent to the conveyance to *Wells* out of the box in which they were placed, and deposit them with the Defendants, who were *John's* bankers, as security

security for their general balance, amounting to several
thousand pounds; *Wells* became bankrupt: his assignees
claimed to be entitled to the deeds on payment of the
330*l.* which *Wells* was to pay. The Defendants insisted,
they, being ignorant of the sale to *Wells,* were not
bound to give up the deeds till they had the larger
sum repaid them. *Gibbs* C. J. was of opinion, that as
the conveyance to *Wells* had been executed and delivered as an escrow to take effect on delivery of the
residue of the purchase-money, the assignees were
entitled to the deeds on payment of that residue, which
was regularly tendered to the Defendants. The jury
found a verdict for the Plaintiffs.

Shepherd, Solicitor-General, now moved to set it
aside, contending that if any chattel is pledged, no
one has a title to take it out of the hands of an innocent pawnee, without payment of the whole sum for
which it was pledged; and the distinction is taken between property acquired by any means short of felony,
and that which is acquired by felony, *Parker* v. *Patrick,*
5 *Term Rep.* 175.

GIBBS C. J. The case of *Parker* v. *Patrick* does not
apply. There the absolute property in the goods was
obtained by fraud. There may be cases, in which one
person by a gross fraud persuades another to make
him a good title to goods; and however gross the
fraud, it may be that the former owner may have no
right to retake the goods, otherwise than subject to
the pledge. But I hold, that if the goods remain mine,
I may take them, notwithstanding any act whatsoever
which a stranger may do. In the case cited nothing
was considered but the distinction between goods obtained by false pretences, and goods obtained by felony; and the statute 21 *H.* 8. *c.* 11., for restoring goods
obtained by felony, is adverted to: there the former

owner

1815.

HOOPER
. v.
RAMSBOTTOM.

owner had prosecuted to conviction; and obtained possession of the goods; and he contended that, having so done,
he had a right under the statute to have them restored.
There is no ground for granting a rule: if a person sells
land without warranty, the title to the deeds ensures the
title to the land. If there be a warranty, then the seller
is entitled to the custody of the deeds, and the purchaser has his *warrantia chartæ*. These deeds belonged
to ¯*Wells*, afterwards to his assignees, who represent
him. Neither *Daniel* nor *John* had any right over
them, but to hold them until *Wells* had paid the 330*l.*
Wells's assignees have tendered that money. This
comes then to the case, · that the person who is entitled
to land, has a right to the title-deeds of that land.
As to the claim of the Defendants, it matters not that
they had received the goods on a valuable consideration; though there was nothing on the face of such of
the deeds as were deposited with them, which shewed
that there was a title in *Wells*, yet the deeds were deposited by a person who had obtained them by fraud. ·

Rule refused.

Jan 26.

CARRUTHERS *v.* SHEDDON.

A person who
has several inter-
ests in a cargo,
viz. as partner in
7-16ths, as con-
signee of the
whole, and as

THIS was an action upon a policy of insurance
for 5000*l.*, effected by the Plaintiff, as agent,
on coffee, by the ship *Ranger*, at and from ports
of loading in *St. Domingo* to *London*, insured by

having a lien on the whole for advances, may protect them all by one insurance, without
expressing in the policy the number or nature of his interests.
D. and W. being general partners under the firm of D. and Co., and D. and Co. taking
a share with three others in a particular adventure which D. and Co. manage and insure
for the account of D. and Co , it is a latent ambiguity to be explained by evidence,
whether the D. and Co. for whose account the insurance is made means D. and W. only,
or all who are partners of D. in that particular adventure.

order

order and for account of Messrs. *Nathaniel Dowrick*
and Co., to return twenty pounds *per cent.* on short interest. The Plaintiffs in the first count averred interest
in *Nathaniel Dowrick* and *John Way* to the amount of
all the monies insured thereon. They also in eight subsequent counts, otherwise similar, made eight other different averments of interest; whereupon the Defendant
had obtained an order for striking out those eight
counts upon the Defendant's admitting that *N. Dowrick*
and *John Way* were *N. Dowrick* and Co., and consenting
that the Defendant would not take advantage of the fact
that any other person belonged to the firm, if any should
appear at the trial. At the sittings at *Guildhall* after
Michaelmas term 1815, before *Gibbs* C. J., the cause
was therefore tried upon the first count only, upon
the same ground on which it would have stood, if the
record had still contained all the counts, with the nine
separate averments of interest. The evidence was, that
Nathaniel Dowrick and *John Way* alone were general
partners in business, under the firm of *N. Dowrick* and
Co., and that they gave the Plaintiff, who was an insurance broker, the order to effect the insurance in
question. The cargo insured was shipped in consequence of a written agreement, dated in 1810, and
made between *Dowrick* and *Way*, therein mentioned to
trade under the firm of *N. Dowrick* and Co., of the first
part, *T. Dixon* of the second part, *Duncan Hunter* of
the third part, and *James Ronayne* of the fourth part,
which recited that the four parties had agreed to become partners in an adventure of sundry goods, which
Dowrick and *Way* had, on their own separate and personal credit, actually and really purchased and become
responsible for; and had shipped for *Hayti*, to be there
sold, and the proceeds to be invested in goods, and
shipped for *Europe*, and to be sold on the joint account of the four parties, who were to be therein interested,

terested, *Dowrick* and *Way* in 7-16ths, *Dixon* in 4-16ths, *Hunter* in 4-16ths, and *Ronayne* in 1-16th; and the parties thereby stipulated, that each should share profit and loss in those proportions; that *Dowrick* and *Way* should be the agents in *London* for, and have the management in all things of the adventure, pay all demands, and receive all bills and proceeds thereof, and that the other three parties would reimburse *Dowrick* and *Way* their advances with interest, and, upon request, pay all expences in proportion. That *Ronayne* should be agent at *Hayti* for the sale of the outward cargo, and the purchase of the homeward cargo, and should have 20*l.* monthly pay as master of the ship *Nelson*, and 2 *per cent.* commission on the sale of her, and not less than 500*l.* commission in the whole. The invoice of the coffee shipped at *Hayti* on board the *Ranger*, and consigned to *Dowrick* and *Way*, by the executors in that island of *Ronayne*, who died pending the adventure, amounted to 8156*l.* 10*s.* 7*d.* The coffee was lost on the homeward voyage. The amount insured by this and other policies was 6750*l.* *Hunter* had become a bankrupt, and the widow of *Ronayne* had taken out administration here to her deceased husband; and these changes of the parties interested in the whole adventure occasioned the nine combinations of persons in whom the interest was in the omitted counts averred to be. The Defendants had already paid the Plaintiffs 59 *per cent.*, and they now contended that the Plaintiffs were not entitled to recover more, upon the ground that, although the Defendants were bound not to object if some other person might be proved to belong to the firm of *N. Dowrick* and Co., yet that *N. Dowrick* and Co. designated the house of *Dowrick* and *Way* engaged in general partnership, and did not mean all the partners in this particular adventure, of whom *Dowrick* and Co. constituted only one. That the words must

must be understood according to common parlance, and not as including every person who might be secretly concerned with *Dowrick* and Co. in a single transaction: and that therefore the insurance in question, not having by the terms of the contract been made on behalf or account of any but *Dowrick* and *Way*, could not now be transferred or extended for the benefit of other parties; and since the sum already paid covered the 7-16ths which *Dowrick* and *Way* had in the cargo, the action could not be maintained. *Gibbs* C. J. thought, on the evidence, that *Dowrick* and *Way*, who were managers of the whole adventure, meant to insure the interests of all the partners; but left it to the jury, directing them that they should not find the fact to be so, from an opinion that the justice of the case required it, but that they should consider whether in fact, when the insurance was effected, the parties meant the policy to be on the interest of all the adventurers, or upon the interest of *Dowrick* and *Way* only: he further thought that if the insurance was intended to be on the interest of *Dowrick* and *Way* only, they had an insurable interest upon which they might recover under this policy beyond their 7-16th parts, to the amount of all the advances they had made for the benefit of the other partners, and for which they had a lien upon the cargo: he also thought that, as consignees of the cargo, they had an insurable interest to the whole amount, for that a consignee may insure as well as a principal. The jury expressly found, that by the words *N. Dowrick* and Co. in the policy, the parties really meant all the partners in the adventure, and found a verdict for the Plaintiffs for all the residue of the subscription, subject to the permission, which his Lordship reserved to the Defendant, to move to enter a nonsuit.

1815.

CARRUTHERS
v.
SHEDDON.

Accordingly *Lens* Serjt. on this day moved for a rule *nisi*. He urged that if this insurance could prevail, it was capable of being made an instrument of fraud; for if the cargo had arrived safe, the Plaintiffs might have pretended that they meant to insure only the 9-16th parts of *Dowrick* and *V; y*, and they would thereupon have been entitled to a large return of premium for short interest, but in case of a loss they might assert, as they now did, that the policy was designed to protect the whole adventure. It was therefore necessary that the meaning of the contract should be decided by the construction of the instrument itself, which was a question for the Court, not for a jury; the construction of the instrument confined it to the two; for, first the Plaintiff effects the policy generally as agent, and afterwards specifies the particular interest, that of *Dowrick* and Co., which particularizes those two persons only; but if extrinsic evidence were admissible, the agreement for the partnership strongly shewed that *N. Dowrick* and Co., by their own definition meant *Dowrick* and *Way* only. As to any further interest than the 7-16ths, which they might have, although it might be insurable, it was not an interest *ejusdem generis* as the 7-16ths, and if *Dowrick* and *Way* intended to protect two distinct species of interest by one contract, the policy ought so to have specified them; since it had not, they could not recover on both, but were bound at the trial to elect on which species of interest they would recover, and here they had elected their 7-16ths, which were already satisfied.

The Court was unanimous that *Dowrick* and *Way* might protect all their species of interest under one policy, and that it was unnecessary to express in the policy the nature of the several interests which they possessed; nor were they bound to make any election.

And

And after having considered the point, because it had been reserved, the Court all perfectly agreed that the verdict was right.

Rule refused.

WOODROFFE q. t. v. WILLIAMS.

THE Plaintiff, in *Michaelmas* term 55 G. 3., delivered his declaration on the statute for usury, intitled of that term. *Pell* Serjt. had obtained a rule *nisi* to amend by intitling it of *Michaelmas* term 54 G. 3.

Shepherd, Solicitor-General, shewed cause, suggesting that the writ on which the action was commenced was returnable in *Michaelmas* term 54 G. 3. (but neither party had any affidavit, stating the time when the writ was returnable,) and that the Plaintiff's object was, to intitle the declaration within a year after the usury committed: the Court would not permit an amendment in a penal action.

Pell, in support of his rule, urged, that an allegation, which there was in the rule, of the time when the writ was returnable, was evidence of the fact. But if otherwise, yet the memorandum of the declaration was mere form, it was of the Plaintiff's dictation, and the Court would, as of course, alter it to any time the Plaintiff wished. In the present term the Court of King's Bench had amended a misnomer in a Christian name in an action for usury. *Mestaer* v. *Hurst.*

The Court held that the allegation in the rule did not prove the fact: that was the mere suggestion of the party.

The allegations in a rule of court do not prove the facts alleged.

The Court will not alter the memorandum of a declaration in a penal action at the mere instance of the Plaintiff, without a reason shewn.

C 2

1815.

WOODROFFE
v.
WILLIAMS.

party. This application was made on no affidavit whatever. The Plaintiff said the amendment would let him into a case, from which, if the present memorandum stands, he is excluded; the Court could not help that: he had shewn no facts to induce them to let him into that case, and therefore they saw no ground for granting the application.

Rule discharged.

Jan. 3.

. The Court will not decide a motion for security for costs on the merits of the cause.
. Security for costs is not exacted so long as the Plaintiff remains in this country.

CIRAGNO v. HASSAN.

SHEPHERD, Solicitor-General, moved that the Plaintiff, who was a *Greek* sailor on board a *Turkish* vessel of *Smyrna*, whereof the Defendant was master, might give security for costs in this action, which was brought to recover wages for the Plaintiff's labour as a mariner. He would have gone into the circumstances of the case, which, as sworn to, shewed that nothing was due, and that the Plaintiff had been guilty of mutiny, and was about to leave this country. He admitted he had found no case where security had been granted while the Plaintiff remained in this country.

The Court held, first, that they could not decide motions for this purpose according to the merits of the case, and secondly, that security for costs was never exacted on the ground that the Plaintiff was about to go abroad. It was necessary that he should actually have left the country.

Rule refused.

PRIDEAUX, Plaintiff; GIFFORD, Deforciant.   *Feb.* 1.

HEYWOOD Serjt. on a former day in this term
moved that this fine might pass. The concord
was, that " whereas *Nathaniel Gifford* and *Fortune* his
wife hold the tenements aforesaid to him the said *Na-*
thaniel during his life, and after his decease, to her the
said *Fortune* during her life, and the same tenements
after the decease of the survivor of them the said *Na-*
thaniel and *Fortune* are to remain to the use of all and
every, or such one, or more of the children of the said
Nathaniel by the said *Fortune*, and the heirs of the
body of all and every, or any, of the said children, in
such proportions, manner, and form, as the said *Na-*
thaniel and *Fortune* by any deed or deeds, writing or
writings, to be by them jointly executed in the presence of, and attested by two witnesses, shall jointly
limit, direct, and appoint, and in default of such joint
limitation, direction, or appointment, then as the survivor of them the said *Nathaniel* and *Fortune* shall by
any such deed or writing, or by his or her last will, to
be signed and published in the presence of three or
more witnesses, limit, direct, and appoint, and for
want of any such direction, limitation, or appointment,
to the use of the child or children in equal shares, as
tenants in common, and the heirs of his or her or their
body or respective bodies issuing, with cross remainders
in like manner between them; and in default of such
issue, the said tenements will belong to the survivor
of them the said *Nathaniel* and *Fortune*, his or her
heirs and assigns for ever; the said *Nathaniel* and
Fortune have granted to the aforesaid *Neast Grevile*
and *Francis Grevile*, and the heirs of the said *Neast Gre-*

The Court per-
mitted a fine *sur*
concessit to pass,
which comprized
an estate for the
lives of two and
the survivor, and
a contingent re-
version in fee in
the same tene-
ments on the fai-
lure of issue of
the conusors.

vile, the aforesaid tenements with the appurtenances, and all and whatsoever the said *Nathaniel* and *Fortune* have therein, to hold the said tenements with the appurtenances unto the said *Neast Grevile* and *Francis Grevile*, and the heirs of the said *Neast Grevile*, during the lives of the said *Nathaniel* and *Fortune*, and the life of the survivor of them, and also from and after the several deceases of the said *Nathaniel* and *Fortune*, and failure of such child and children of their bodies, and of the issue of such child and children, to whom respectively the said tenements are to remain as aforesaid, and from thenceforth the said tenements wholly to remain to them the said *Neast Grevile* and *Francis Grevile*, and the heirs of the said *Neast Grevile*, for ever. And moreover the said *Nathaniel* and *Fortune* do grant, for themselves and their heirs, that they will warrant against themselves and their heirs to the said *N. Grevile* and *F. Grevile*, and the heirs of the said *N. Grevile*, the tenements aforesaid during the several lives of the said *Nathaniel* and *Fortune*, and the life of the survivor of them, and also the reversion or remainder thereof for ever, after the death of the survivor of them, and such failure of the issue of their bodies as aforesaid. And for this," &c. The cyrographer had objected to the passing of this fine. The Court postponed the consideration of the question until the present day, when the cyrographer, upon notice given him, attended, and

Onslow Serjt., for him, stated the objection to be, that this was an attempt to include two distinct fines, a fine *sur concessit*, and a fine *sur conusance de droit tantum* in the form of one fine. This is not permitted. *Lazenby* v. *Knight* (a); it was there urged

(a) *Barnet*, 216.

that

that a fine was but in the nature of a conveyance, and
the party might have it in what manner he pleased, at
his peril; but the Court held, that that sort of double
fine, *sur concessit*, and *sur conusance de droit tantùm* was
unprecedented; and the party obtained permission to
strike out that part which was *sur concessit*. So far as
appeared, both parts of that fine, as well as of this, related to the same land. The addition of the words
" for ever" made the distinction between the fine *sur*
concessit and the fine *de droit tantùm*. The cyrographer
had in the office no precedent for letting the reversion in
fee pass annexed to the fine *sur concessit*, though that
was properly applicable to the life estate. This was an
attempt to include two conveyances on one stamp, and
it was the officer's duty to guard the revenue. He
prayed costs for the cyrographer.

Heywood, in support of his application, urged that
in *Ludlow* v. *Drummond* (a), the life estate and the
reversion were both conveyed in one fine, and the
law of that case had not been impugned. This was
altogether merely a fine *sur concessit*, by which the
parties purport to convey the estate for life of *Gifford*
and *Fortune* his wife, and also their contingent interest
in fee. The difference between these two species of
fine is, that the fine *sur concessit* states that he granted,
and the fine *de droit tantùm*, is, that he hath acknowledged. It had been questioned whether a fine *sur concessit* passes a fee, but *Heywood* was prepared to argue,
that a fine *sur concessit* passes every interest which a
man has. *Pigot* v. *Earl of Sarum* (b), an hundred and
fifty years since it was perfectly understood what a
fine *sur concessit* was, but it became disused because of
the necessity of suing out execution. *West. Symb.*

(a) *Ante*, ii. 84.　　　(b) *T. Jones*, 69.

part

part 2. *s.* 63. 81. 127. are all precedents in which a reversion in fee is conveyed after a particular estate by a fine *sur concessit.*

Per Curiam. We think this fine ought to be permitted to pass, but no reflection whatever ought to be cast on the officer for the doubts he has expressed: on the contrary, he is entitled to praise, whenever he has any doubts, for bringing them before the Court. Some precedents produced to us now by the officer, so long back as the time of *Gould* J., shew abundantly that it has not been the practice to unite in the fine *sur concessit* the grant of a reversion in fee with that of a particular estate. One of them is, " It appearing that part of the premises are in possession, and part in reversion, it is ordered that the fine be amended by striking out the premises in possession, and letting it stand as to the premises in reversion only, the parties having levied a new fine of the premises in possession;" it appears by this precedent that the parties, having levied a fine of both, viz. of certain part of the premises in possession, and of other part in reverson, entertained doubts whether the fine was good as to both. It is sufficient to say, this was a case where the party himself doubted of the operation of the fine, and came to the Court for the amendment; in two of these instances the fines were of different sorts, one before *Wilmot* J.: he ordered that it should be altered to a fine *sur concessit* only: what the other part of it was, it does not appear. It is true the Court will not permit a fine to pass, when there is something grossly blundering on the face of it, but the Court will not take on themselves to decide here on the operation or goodness of the fine; it is our duty only to see that the fine passes in the usual form; it is at the peril of the party, what is its effect.

Fiat.

BALBI v. BATLEY.

Affidavit to
hold to bail on
promissory notes,
must state that,
the Defendant is
indebted to the
Plaintiff.

BEST Serjt. had obtained a rule *nisi* to discharge
the Defendant out of custody on mesne process,
on a defect in the affidavit to hold to bail, which averred,
that the Defendant was indebted to the Plaintiff on certain promissory notes of the dates and sums therein
stated, and payable at days long since passed, but did
not say that they were given, or payable, or indorsed to
the Plaintiff.

Vaughan Serjt. shewed cause. It may be inferred that
the bills were payable to the Plaintiff, for it is sworn
the Defendant was indebted to the Plaintiff.

Per Curiam. That argument would overthrow all
the cases of enlargement for a defect in the affidavit
that ever were decided.

Rule absolute.

WILSON v. FORSTER.

THIS was an action on a policy subscribed by the
Defendant for 200*l.*, on the ship *Agatha*, valued at
2100*l.*, and freight valued at 900*l.*, from *Liverpool* to
her port of discharge in the *Baltic* and Gulf of *Finland*,
against all risks until the cargo should be safely ware-
housed at the final ports or places of discharge, and at
the free disposal of the consignee. The declaration
averred interest in the Plaintiff, and a total loss of ship
and freight by seizure and arrest of the ship and the
goods she had on board, near *Pillau*, by persons un-
without authority from the assured, who refused to accept the ship or
the assureds who had not abandoned, were not permitted to recover

known,

The seizure
and sale of a ves-
sel by a neutral
state, no sentence
of condemnation
by any compe-
tent court being
shewn, does not
change the pro-
perty.
Therefore, where
in such a case the
master had re-pur-
chased the vessel,
though he acted
repay him the price,
for a total loss.

known, and contained a count for money had and received. The Defendant paid generally into court 110l. At the trial before *Gibbs* C. J. at *Guildhall,* at the sittings after *Easter* term 1814, a verdict was found for the Plaintiff for 200l., subject to a case. The Plaintiff was sole owner of the *Agatha,* which sailed with a cargo of goods, taken in on freight at *Liverpool,* for *Pillau.* In her course she was run down by another vessel, and lost an anchor and cable, and was otherwise damaged. She arrived in *Pillau* roads, and after running upon the bar and increasing her damage, she sailed into *Pillau* harbour, where she was immediately, with her cargo, seized by the officers of the government there; the crew were discharged, and the master, whose residence was at *Pillau,* remained there, but had no command over her, and did not, nor could use any means to recover the possession of the ship on account of his owner until the 1st of *April* 1811, when the maritime court at *Pillau* put up to public sale by auction the ship *Agatha,* detained by the *Prussian* government at *Pillau.* The master at that sale became the purchaser for 552 rix dollars, on payment of which the ship was delivered to him, and he was at liberty to sail with her her from *Pillau* in any direction he thought fit; and he had the command of her in the same manner as before her seizure. The vessel was not then in a sea-worthy state, or capable of prosecuting her voyage in the *Baltic,* or returning to *Great Britain,* without being repaired. The master, being examined as a witness, stated that he recovered possession of the ship by so purchasing her, and that in his judgment it was the most advantageous course that could be taken for his owner, to recover the possession of her by paying that sum at the auction, on which occasion he considered himself as acting as the owner's agent. He had been appointed master by the owner, with the same authority

rity

rity as masters of ships are usually entrusted with.
Having taken possession of her, he caused her to be
repaired, and navigated her safely home to *London.*
The owner had notice that she was arrived in the
Thames, and that the master held her there for him, and
on his account, and was ready to have delivered her
up to him or his agents, if it had been required; and
the owner might then, if he had thought fit, have had
possession of the ship in a perfectly safe and sea-worthy
state. A bottomry bond had been given by the master,
at *Pillau,* for the money with which he had repurchased
the ship, which the owner refused to pay: after the
ship's arrival, that bond was put in suit in the Court
of Admiralty, and the vessel was taken possession of
by the marshal of that court. On the 2d of *December*
1812 a decree of sale was made in favour of the holder of
the bottomry-bond, and on the 21st *January* following
a commission of sale was issued, under and in pursuance of which the ship was sold by public auction at
Hull, and the proceeds of the sale, and the whole of
the homeward freight, were paid over by the registrar
of the Court of Admiralty to the holder of the bottomry-bond under that decree. It was admitted that
the Plaintiff was entitled to a total loss on the freight.

The question for the opinion of the Court was, whether the Plaintiff was entitled to recover a total loss,
or only an average loss upon the ship. If the former,
the verdict was to stand for 90*l.* residue of the 200*l.*,
after deducting the 110*l.* paid into court; if the latter,
the damages were to be reduced to such sum as an arbitrator should ascertain, and if the same should not
exceed 55*l. per cent.*, a verdict was to be entered for
the Defendant.

Lens Serjt., for the Plaintiff, argued that the re-
purchase of the vessel was not an act within the scope
of

1815.

WILSON
v.
FORSTER.

of the master's authority, and that he could not, by constituting himself agent for his owner, bind his owner by an act which the latter refused to ratify. He admitted that an ordinary capture, followed by a recapture, would not divest the property of the ship out of the assured. But in this case the *Prussian* government had by their sentence of condemnation absolutely changed the property, and it was indifferent to the underwriters whether at the sale made under that sentence the master or any other person had been the purchaser. This was distinguishable from the case of *Macmasters* v. *Shoolbred* (a), because there the captors had been a month in possession before the re-sale. This was a completely new title.

Vaughan Serjt., *contrà*, was stopped by the Court.

GIBBS C. J. There is another question here, whether the assured, the ship being restored to them, have not a right to take possession of her? What is there to alter the property? Supposing that she had been condemned by a judgment in any court of *Prussia*, on any fiscal law of that country, it alters the property, but here it does not appear that there is any such judgment; and the mere seizing and selling does not create a forfeiture, nor change the property. Here was no war, and the question is, whether in that case, the ship being taken by violence, and the Plaintiff getting it back, the property is not unchanged. Suppose the assured chose to take to the property, could the master stand out against them, as having bought her under a good title? On the case, as it stands, there appears only an unlicensed seizure of this vessel. The captain purchases her from those who have seized her, and has brought her home: the former owners have a right to say that the ship having

(a) 1 *Esp.* 237.

been

been bought of those who had seized her, still continues their property. I do not know that the ransom here was illegal, so not like the case of *Parsons* v. *Scott* (a). That was illegal by the act of parliament against ransom.

1815.

WILSON
v.
FORSTER.

Feb. 2.

Judgment for the Defendant, subject to the arbitrator's award on the amount of the average costs.

(a) *Ante*, ii. 363.

SUTTON v. CLARKE.

THIS was an action upon the case. The Plaintiff declared, that by an act, 5 G. 3. for repairing and widening a road from *Banbury* to *Lutterworth*, any five or more trustees, or their surveyors, were empowered to cut any watercourses, in, through, or across any lands or grounds, in order to drain, or prevent the roads from being overflowed, making such reasonable

Several tort feasors who unite in an injurious act, may be sued, each one singly.

If a trench cut in the county of *N.* causes the plaintiff's lands to be overflowed in

the county of *W.*, although a statute requires all actions to be brought and tried in the county where the cause of action arises, the action may be brought and tried in *W.*

If a statute directs that an action shall be commenced within six months after the matter or thing for which such action shall be brought, and in consequence of the cutting of a trench a fall of rain causes the Plaintiff's land to be overflowed, first within six months, and again after six months from cutting the trench, whether the action must be brought within six months from the cutting of the trench, or within six months from the perception of the first prejudicial effect, or whether it may be brought within six months from the last injury, *quære*.

One who in the exercise of a public function without emolument, which he is compellable to execute, acting without malice, and according to his best skill and diligence, and obtaining the best information he can, does an act which occasions consequential damage to a subject, is not liable to an action for such damage.

The trustees of a turnpike road, empowered to make watercourses to prevent the road from being overflowed, directed their surveyor to present a plan for carrying off the water of an adjacent brook: he recommended, and on that recommendation they adopted, and caused him to make, a wide channel from the road, gradually narrowing, and conducting the water into the ordinary fence ditches of the plaintiff's land, which were insufficient to discharge it, and his land was consequently overflowed. Held that no action lay against the chairman of the trustees who signed the order for cutting this trench.

satisfaction

satisfaction to the owners or occupiers of such lands or
grounds for the damages they should thereby sustain, as
to any seven or more trustees should seem reasonable;
and that the Plaintiff was possessed of divers closes near
to a road in that act mentioned, in *Hill-morton*, in the
county of *Warwick*, and he being so possessed, on the 10th
of *June* 1812, a certain watercourse had been made and
dug by the Defendant from that road into certain land
near to the Plaintiff's land, under colour of powers and
authorities given by that act, but of so insufficient
breadth, depth, and length, that by means of the narrow-
ness and insufficiency thereof, and of the same not having been continued a sufficient distance from the road,
large quantities of water from time to time flowing to
the same, on 1st *October* 1812, and on divers days
afterwards, had run and flowed in and upon the Plaintiff's lands, and damaged the same, and thereby the
Plaintiff had sustained damage: yet the Defendant,
being one of the trustees, knowing the premises, but
contriving, and wrongfully and injuriously intending to
injure the Plaintiff, on 1st *June* 1813, and from thence
for a long time, wrongfully and injuriously kept and
continued that watercourse or drain of such insufficient
breadth, and depth, and length, and by reason thereof;
and of the watercourse not having been continued a
sufficient distance, on 1st *June* 1813, and on divers
days afterwards, water which had flowed unto and into
that insufficient watercourse, overflowed the same, and
flowed unto, into, and over the Plaintiff's land, and
continued thereon a long time, and thereby damaged
the Plaintiff's corn, turnips, grass, and herbage, and
thereby the Plaintiff sustained damage, whereof the
Defendant afterwards had notice; and although the
Defendant, as such trustee, was requested by the Plaintiff so to do, yet he had not as yet made reasonable
satisfaction to the Plaintiff for the damages, but had re-

fused

fused so to do, contrary to the statute. The second count stated that the watercourse was wrongfully and injuriously made so insufficiently, that by means of the insufficiency thereof, water from time to time flowing to the same, on divers days had run and flowed in and upon the Plaintiff's lands, and that the Defendant, being a trustee, and knowing the premises, wrongfully and injuriously continued the watercourse so insufficiently made, and by reason thereof the water which had flowed to the insufficient watercourse, overflowed the same, and ran over the Plaintiff's land, and occasioned the damage. The third count stated, that the Plaintiff was possessed of closes, and that the Defendant wrongfully and injuriously continued near to them a watercourse so insufficiently and improperly made, that by reason thereof large quantities of water which had run thereto, overflowed the same, and flowed into and over the Plaintiff's closes, and occasioned the damage. The fourth count alleged the Plaintiff's possession of three closes, and that the Defendant wrongfully and injuriously caused and procured large quantities of water to run and flow in, upon, and over those closes, and to continue in and upon the same for a long time, and thereby injured the crops. The Defendant pleaded the general issue. The act contained the power alleged in the declaration, to cut watercourses, and also powers enabling the trustees to purchase lands for widening, turning, or altering any road, and directed the mode in which, when the owners were incapacited to treat, or neglected to treat on the terms of sale, a jury should be impannelled to enquire what damages would be sustained by, and what recompence or satisfaction should be made to such owners, occupiers, or other persons interested, for, or upon account of the taking of such land, grounds, or hereditaments into the roads, or of turning such road into or through any such lands, grounds, or hereditaments;

ments; and after the jury should have enquired and ascertained such damage and recompence, the trustees were to adjudge the sums so assessed, to be paid; and upon payment or tender, the land was to be vested in the trustees. And if any action should be brought against any person for any thing done in pursuance of that act, or in relation to the matters therein contained, such action was to be commenced within six months next after the doing the matter or thing for which such action should be brought, but not afterwards, and was to be brought, laid, and tried in the county where such cause of action should arise, and not in any other county; and the Defendants might plead the general issue, and give the special matter in evidence. The cause was tried at the *Warwick* summer assizes 1814, before *Chambre* J. The case was, that the Defendant was one of the trustees under this turnpike act, and chairman of their meetings. A road in the county of *Northampton*, which led from *Weedon* towards *Lutterworth*, was subject after heavy rains to be flooded by the water of an adjacent brook. The trustees, at a meeting, at which the Defendant presided, ordered a surveyor to examine the spot, and prepare a plan for rectifying this mischief, who accordingly, at a subsequent meeting, made his report, and produced a plan which the Defendant, as chairman, and six other commissioners adopted, and which was accordingly executed in *May* 1812, whereby a cut nine feet wide, and two or three deep, was made from the road through the close of a Mr. *Satchell* in *Northamptonshire*: in its progress through the four next closes, it was narrowed to five feet, and it terminated in an old fence ditch which was not at all widened, and which discharged itself into the fence ditch of the Plaintiff's closes, the width whereof was three feet only: through this cut was turned, first the whole, but afterwards, in consequence of the Plain-

tiff's

tiff's remonstrances, one half only, of the water of the brook, the whole of which had for 50 years preceding discharged itself by another course: the Plaintiff's ditch not being of dimensions adapted to carry off so large a body of water as now passed into it by the new course, the water, after heavy rains, overflowed it, and stagnated on the Plaintiff's land, situate in the county of *Warwick*, and damaged his crops. The first injury was perceived in *October* 1812, within six months after the cutting of the trench, whereupon the Plaintiff had made several applications to the Defendant individually to remedy the mischief, but had never applied to the commissioners collected at any meeting, where alone they were authorized to act. In *May* preceding the trial, the land was again overflowed, and the Plaintiff's crops materially injured; whereupon the present action was brought. No improper motive was imputed to the Defendant, and the Plaintiff himself produced evidence of declarations of the Defendant, that when he ordered the work, he did not foresee the injurious effect. Three objections were made by the Defendant: 1. That the act of the Defendant, of which the Plaintiff complained, was the making the new cut, and that the action not being brought within six months after it was made, was now out of time. To which it was answered, that every continuance of the nusance was a new cause of action, and that the suit was commenced within six months after the last injury sustained.. 2dly, That the action could not be maintained against a single trustee, but that all ought to have been joined who concurred in making the order. 3dly, That the act complained of being an act done by the Defendant within the scope of his power as commissioner, and no malicious motive being either alleged or proved, the action could not be maintained. *Chambre* J. was of opinion, that there was no objection to the form of the action for want of

VOL. VI.   D   parties;

parties; that the clause above stated for making compensation was not applicable to this case, but only to the case of land taken for making roads. The act gave the commissioners a general and unlimited discretion to make watercourses through any lands or grounds for the purpose of turning water from the roads, making satisfaction to the occupiers, and the commissioners, and the Defendant as one of them, had done no more than they were authorized by the statute to do. And it appeared that the trustees had acted under the advice, and according to a plan given them by a surveyor, and were actuated by no improper motive. The action therefore could not be maintained. The Plaintiff ought to have applied for, and might perhaps have obtained from the commissioners, under the discretion which they possessed, a satisfaction. That satisfaction could not be made in the first instance, because the effect was not foreseen. Possibly the Court of King's Bench, on application, would have granted a mandamus to the commissioners to compel them to make a compensation, if they had refused otherwise to do it. He permitted the cause, however, to proceed, and the jury found a verdict for the Plaintiff, upon the injury last sustained, for 10*l.*, with liberty to the Defendant to move to set it aside upon the objections above stated, and such others as might arise upon the matter of law.

Accordingly *Lens* Serjt., in *Michaelmas* term 1814, obtained a rule *nisi* to set aside the verdict and enter a nonsuit, upon the grounds above mentioned, and upon the further grounds, that the act complained of, the cutting of the trench, was committed in the county of *Northampton*, whereas the action was brought in the county of *Warwick*, and was therefore, by this statute, not maintainable: and that if the time of limitation was not to be measured from the cutting of the trench,

yet

;yet at least it was to be computed from the date of the first damage actually sustained in consequence, of the cutting, whereas the action was not brought within six months from that date. Upon the third and principal objection he cited *The Governors and Company of the British Cast Plate Manufacturers* v. *Meredith* (a). [Upon the objection that the other commissioners were not joined in the action, the Court intimated that the rule was universal in actions founded on a tort, that every tort feasor may be sued singly:] the objection to the venue was, upon the argument, abandoned,

Shepherd, Solicitor-General, and *Vaughan* and *Copley* Serjts., shewed cause against this rule. They principally contended that although the trustees had a right to cut drains, they had not a right to cut them so unskilfully and injudiciously as to injure the owners of adjoining lands. They were responsible for any damage occasioned to the subject by the negligent or unskilful exercise of the powers committed to them. If damage ensued, the remedy against them was by action, for the statute had made no provision for compensating the sufferer in such a case, the clause for compensation applying only to the owner of the land through which -the drain is cut, not to the damage thereby occasioned to a neighbour, and the word damage is introduced into the section, only because the taking a part of a close may sometimes materially damage the residue. An action well lies for unskilfully doing that, which being unskilfully done is injurious, though, if it were well done it would not injure. The case in 4 *T. R.* is materially different; first, because a specific power was there given to raise the ground, and the injury was

(a) 4 *Term Rep.* 794.

D 2   directly

directly and necessarily occasioned by the raising it; whereas this is a case of consequential damage occasioned by the negligent exercise of a legal power; 2dly, (upon which *Buller* and *Grose* Justices mainly relied,) there the statute expressly provided the manner of compensation for any injury occasioned by raising the soil. There too, it was expressly found that the line of surface to which the pavement was raised, was necessary and proper, and that any alteration of the inclined surface of the street, less material, was not sufficient to render the strreet safe for carriages passing through. Consequently that action had not for its ground the circumstance that the act was ignorantly, or inartificially, or otherwise improperly done. ' The case of *Leader* v. *Maxon and Others* is differently reported by *Blackstone* (a), and by *Wilson* (b), and although Lord *Kenyon* C. J. in the case in 4 *T. R.* throws some slur on the report of the former, his censure does not apply to the latter, who gives a very material fact, omitted by the former, that the act contained a power to lay out a new strect, with an express prohibition against obstructing the lights or free passage of any person. Therefore it could not be inferred that the commissioners had a power to obstruct the plaintiff's lights in the lanes. So that there was clearly an excess of jurisdiction. And the cutting this trench negligently and inartificially was an excess of jurisdiction in the present case. The power to make watercourses given by the act intends a continued watercourse, which shall conduct the water to its ultimate place of discharge, not a watercourse dammed up at the lower extremity, which shall leave the water in the Defendant's fence-ditch to overflow his land. The Defendant was at least guilty of negligence here, for it required no skill to foresee that the smaller channel could not discharge

(a) 2 *Bl.* 924.   (a) 3 *Wils.* 461.

all

all the water which might enter by the larger channel. In pleading a justification in trespass, it is necessary to shew that the Defendant has done no unnecessary damage: the proof upon the general issue in an action on the case must be the same. But that defence could not be here substantiated: for the Defendant has occasioned unnecessary damage, and the action therefore lies. In the case of *Roberts v. Read* (a), two of the points which arise in this cause were determined: 1. that an action well lay against surveyors of the highway for taking away the soil adjoining to the Plaintiff's wall, by reason of which the wall afterwards fell; and it was never even objected that the action would not lie by reason that the act which produced the damage was an act within the scope of the Defendant's duty; and 2dly, that although more than three months had elapsed since the act, and before the action brought, yet as it was brought within three months after the wall fell, it was, within the meaning of the statute, brought within three months after the thing "done or acted," and "act committed," which are the words of the statute 13 *G.*3. *c.*78. *s.*82. and are fully as strong as the words of this act. If the Defendant's act be so inartificially done that it injures the Plaintiff, it is no discharge to the Defendant that he acted according to the best skill and advice which he had, and that he consulted a surveyor on the manner of doing it. An individual is bound so to restrain the exercise of his rights over his own land, that he may not thereby injure his neighbour, and these trustees must observe the same rule in the exercise of their powers. Even if the principle be, that no action can be maintained against an officer for an injury occasioned by his act, unless the act be malicious, yet there is on this record a sufficient averment of malice, for express malice is not necessary; and it is averred that the Defend-

(a) 16 *East*, 216.

D 3

ant

ant continued the nuisance wrongfully and injuriously, which, in *Drew* v. *Colton* (a) was held equivalent to an averment of malice: and as the jury have found a verdict for the Plaintiff, it must be now intended that the allegation was proved. If the Defendant had rested his case on the absence of malice, he should have gone to the jury upon that point. As to the time of the action, it suffices to bring it within six months after sustaining the damage comprehended in the declaration; for if the Plaintiff had recovered judgment on account of the injury produced in 1812, which might have been small, that would be no bar to an action for an injury sustained in the following year, which might be much greater. It cannot be, that by the Defendant's compensating the first small damage that occurs, he should purchase an indemnity against all future liability; and a jury would not be authorized to give prospective damages. Lord *Ellenborough* C. J. in *Roberts* v. *Read* distinguishes in respect of the time of limitation, between the case of trespass against a custom-house officer for seizing goods (b), and an action on the case for consequential damage; and *Bayley* J. asked, " How was the damage to be estimated before it had actually happened?" It would in the present case be impossible prospectively to estimate all the damage which might, in consequence of the Defendant's act, ever result to the occupiers of this land. It would be most inconvenient, and defeat the attainment of justice, if the action must be brought within six months after the first perceptible effect of the Defendant's act. For instance; the first flood might happen when the land was in grass, and in the beginning of spring, when it would be beneficial rather than injurious, and another might not happen till after the six months elapsed. It is clear therefore,

(a) 1 *East*, 567. n.   (b) G. *ding* v. *Ferris*, 2 H *Bl.* 14.

(to

{to which the Court agreed,) that, if action be the proper remedy, the Plaintiff may bring renewed actions, unless the Defendant can shew that in the first action the Plaintiff may recover prospective damages to all time. And that he cannot do; for *in jure non remota, sed proxima spectatur causa.* There may be cases, as where the Defendant commits an injurious act on my land, in which a jury may possibly be warranted in giving prospective damages, for the Defendant cannot enter my land to redress the mischief: but if the damage be occasioned to me by an act which the Defendant commits on his own land, no prospective damages can be given; for the law intends that he will repair the evil. A jury would not be warranted in presuming that the commissioners would not themselves remedy this evil, before further mischief accrued. The doctrine tends greatly to promote litigation, that the Plaintiff must sue upon the first perceptible injury; and that if, as in this case, he first takes time to expostulate with the Defendant, he loses his remedy. Every repetition of the damage is a fresh nuisance, and will support a fresh action. But the Plaintiff may wave an injury if he will, without thereby giving future impunity,

Lens and *Pell* Serjts. *contrà.* 1. The action is brought too late. This is no nuisance, for if it were, the Plaintiff would have a right to abate it, which he cannot do in this case. Where the injury is done by a private person, it may be waved, but against a public officer, either the party must assert his claim within the limited time from his first perception of the mischief, or rather, the inconveniences which have been urged by the Plaintiff as resulting from that construction, shew the true line to be, that the party is bound to foresee and calculate at the very time of the act of the commissioners, all its consequences, and then instantly to take his remedy. The two parts of the statute must be taken together.

If

If the trench were cut at a time when there was no probability that any flood would happen within six months, yet if there were a probable expectation of a flood at any future and more distant period, the action, if it would lie in any case, would lie in that, and must be brought within the six months, or the remedy lost for ever: at the same time the termor may have the apportioned damages, not for his present loss merely, but for all the mischief to be done within the term, and the reversioner may have his action for all the damage which may happen to the residue of the inheritance. It is very doubtful whether the commissioners could now go through another person's land with a new watercourse, to relieve the Plaintiff's closes: but if they cannot, the termor and the reversioner may in their respective actions recover an entire satisfaction for the whole injury. In *The King* v. *The Justices of Staffordshire* (a) it was determined that where a statute dates from an act done, the Court cannot compute the time of limitation from notice of the act: and here, in like manner, the limitation must be computed from the date of the act, not from its manifesting injurious effects; or at all events it must be computed from the first perception of those effects. Therefore the Plaintiff has not within due time availed himself of the full and speedy remedy which the act gave him, of waiting until it was seen whether any injury were occasioned, and then forthwith suing. *Roberts* v. *Read* is inapplicable, for from the nature of the thing it could not there be foreseen whether the removal of the earth would cause the wall to fall, and until that was seen it would evidently be premature to sue (b). The hardship is mutual of confining to the first

six

(a) 3 *East,* 152.

(b) Upon this part of the argument *Gibbs* C. J. observed, that the case of *Roberts* v. *Read* let the plaintiff loose from the very great difficulty imposed by the words, (which, it might be, were

six months after the act, the option of suing. Unless
the limitation is to take effect, at farthest, from the
commencement of the injury, the liability is perpetual.
An action may be brought for a damage which may
50 years hence be occasioned by this cause. But such
a liability would deter all persons from accepting public
trusts. Secondly, If a person in a public situation does
an act within his jurisdiction, and without malice, even
though it occasion damage to another, no action will
lie; and this, on the general principle that the statute
orders the thing to be done. In the case in *Wilson* the
commissioners grossly exceeded their jurisdiction. In
the case in 4 *T. R.* Lord *Kenyon* C. J. thought, independently of the compensation clause, that the action
would not lie. He says, " If there be no power
(to the commissioners to award satisfaction,) the parties are without remedy, provided the commissioners
do not exceed their jurisdiction." The principle is,
this: that when a party acts as trustee, if the act done
is within his general jurisdiction, it is sufficient, though
he pursue an erroneous mode of executing it. But
here, too, the Defendant is not affected with any personal knowledge of the transaction. A surveyor is
appointed, who performs the work without the interference of the Defendant; and it is an additional hardship, that the Plaintiff selects this one commissioner
only. This is distinguishable from the case put in argument, of the proprietors of waterworks being answerable
for the bursting of one of their pipes, which they might

were very absurd and unjust,) of
making the act done, and not, as
in the statute 21 *Jac.* 2. *c.* 16.,
the cause of action, the criterion
of the time. The Court of
King's Bench had got over that
difficulty, and attained the justice
of the case; he should have had

great difficulty in coming to that
decision, but thought the Court
ought not to recede from it, because it favoured the attainment
of justice. But the Court ultimately refrained from expressing
any opinion upon this very important question.

under

If the trench were cut at a time when there was no probability that any flood would happen within six months, yet if there were a probable expectation of a flood at any future and more distant period, the action, if it would lie in any case, would lie in that, and must be brought within the six months, or the remedy lost for ever: at the same time the termor may have the apportioned damages, not for his present loss merely, but for all the mischief to be done within the term, and the reversioner may have his action for all the damage which may happen to the residue of the inheritance. It is very doubtful whether the commissioners could now go through another person's land with a new watercourse, to relieve the Plaintiff's closes: but if they cannot, the termor and the reversioner may in their respective actions recover an entire satisfaction for the whole injury. In *The King* v. *The Justices of Staffordshire* (a) it was determined that where a statute dates from an act done, the Court cannot compute the time of limitation from notice of the act: and here, in like manner, the limitation must be computed from the date of the act, not from its manifesting injurious effects; or at all events it must be computed from the first perception of those effects. Therefore the Plaintiff has not within due time availed himself of the full and speedy remedy which the act gave him, of waiting until it was seen whether any injury were occasioned, and then forthwith suing. *Roberts* v. *Read* is inapplicable, for from the nature of the thing it could not there be foreseen whether the removal of the earth would cause the wall to fall, and until that was seen it would evidently be premature to sue (b). The hardship is mutual of confining to the first

six

(a) 3 *East*, 152.

(b) Upon this part of the argument *Gibbs* C. J. observed, that the case of *Roberts* v. *Read*   let the plaintiff loose from the very great difficulty imposed by the words, (which, it might be, were

six months after the act, the option of suing. Unless the limitation is to take effect, at farthest, from the commencement of the injury, the liability is perpetual. An action may be brought for a damage which may 50 years hence be occasioned by this cause. But such a liability would deter all persons from accepting public trusts. Secondly, If a person in a public situation does an act within his jurisdiction, and without malice, even though it occasion damage to another, no action will lie; and this, on the general principle that the statute orders the thing to be done. In the case in *Wilson* the commissioners grossly exceeded their jurisdiction. In the case in 4 *T. R.* Lord *Kenyon* C. J. thought, independently of the compensation clause, that the action would not lie. He says, " If there be no power (to the commissioners to award satisfaction,) the parties are without remedy, provided the commissioners do not exceed their jurisdiction." The principle is, this: that when a party acts as trustee, if the act done is within his general jurisdiction, it is sufficient, though he pursue an erroneous mode of executing it. But here, too, the Defendant is not affected with any personal knowledge of the transaction. A surveyor is appointed, who performs the work without the interference of the Defendant; and it is an additional hardship, that the Plaintiff selects this one commissioner only. This is distinguishable from the case put in argument, of the proprietors of waterworks being answerable for the bursting of one of their pipes, which they might.

---

were very absurd and unjust,) of making the act done, and not, as in the statute 21 *Jac.* 2. *c.* 16., the cause of action, the criterion of the time. The Court of King's Bench had got over that difficulty, and attained the justice of the case; he should have had

great difficulty in coming to that decision, but thought the Court ought not to recede from it, because it favoured the attainment of justice. But the Court ultimately refrained from expressing any opinion upon this very important question.

under

prescribed what should be done, in effect prescribed the manner of doing it, because there was no other manner: that, therefore, does not come up to the Defendant's case: here the act prescribes what shall be done, but not the manner of doing it. This case therefore is to be determined on principle alone, and upon principle, we are of opinion that the Defendant is not answerable in this action. This case is perfectly unlike that of an individual, who, for his own benefit, makes an improvement on his own land according to his best skill and diligence, and not foreseeing it will produce any injury to his neighbour: if he thereby unwittingly injure his neighbour, he is answerable. The resemblance fails in the most important point of comparison, that his act is not done for a public purpose, but for private emolument. Here the Defendant is not a volunteer: he executes a duty imposed on him by the legislature, which he is bound to execute. ' He exercises his best skill, diligence, and caution in the execution of it, and we are of opinion that he is not liable for an injury, which he did not only not foresee, but could not foresee. He has done all that was incumbent on him, having used his best skill and diligence. Another point was made on the limitation of the time; but having disposed of the case in favour of the Defendant, and decided that there must be a nonsuit upon the second point, it is unnecessary for us to decide on the other.

Rule absolute.

1815.

PRINCE v. NICHOLSON.

Jan. 23.

JUDGMENT in this case having been given for the Defendant in *Trinity* term last, upon a demurrer to the Defendant's plea *puis darrein continuance* of judgments against the Defendant, as executor, in debt on simple contracts of the testator, recovered since this action commenced, *Shepherd,* Solicitor-General, for the Plaintiff, now prayed to be permitted to withdraw that demurrer, and take judgment of assets *quando acciderint.*

The Court will not amend, to the prejudice of an executor, a judgment which two terms since passed for him on demurrer.

But *The Court* refused the application, because no precedent was cited, and they were aware of none, where a judgment against an executor had been amended to his prejudice after the term in which it was given, and his reliance on this judgment might, in the interval which had elapsed, have materially affected his disposition of the assets.

Rule refused.

SERRA and Others v. WRIGHT.

Feb. 6.

DEBT on bond, the condition of which, on oyer, reciting that *W. Begbie* had been appointed collector of the poor-rates for part of the parish of *St. An-*

Upon bond conditioned that a collector of poor rates shall render an account of

monies received, after general performance pleaded, in assigning a breach that he did not render an account, *semble* that it is necessary to aver that he received monies to be accounted for.

To a voluntary office and not cast by law on the party, it is necessary to aver not only an appointment, but an acceptance by the person appointed.

drew,

1815.

SUTTON
v.
CLARKE.

directly and necessarily occasioned by the raising it;
whereas this is a case of consequential damage occasioned by the negligent exercise of a legal power;
2dly, (upon which *Buller* and *Grose* Justices mainly
relied,) there the statute expressly provided the manner
of compensation for any injury occasioned by raising
the soil. There too, it was expressly found that the
line of surface to which the pavement was raised, was
necessary and proper, and that any alteration of the
inclined surface of the street, less material, was not sufficient to render the strreet safe for carriages passing
through. Consequently that action had not for its
ground the circumstance that the act was ignorantly, or
inartificially, or otherwise improperly done.' The case
of *Leader* v. *Moxon and Others* is differently reported
by *Blackstone* (a), and by *Wilson* (b), and although
Lord *Kenyon* C. J. in the case in 4 *T. R.* throws some
slur on the report of the former, his censure does not
apply to the latter, who gives a very material fact,
omitted by the former, that the act contained a power
to lay out a new strect, with an express prohibition
against obstructing the lights or free passage of any
person. Therefore it could not be inferred that the
commissioners had a power to obstruct the plaintiff's
lights in the lanes. So that there was clearly an excess
of jurisdiction. And the cutting this trench negligently
and inartificially was an excess of jurisdiction in the
present case. The power to make watercourses given
by the act intends a continued watercourse, which shall
conduct the water to its ultimate place of discharge,
not a watercourse dammed up at the lower extremity,
which shall leave the water in the Defendant's fence-
ditch to overflow his land. The Defendant was at
least guilty of negligence here, for it required no skill
to foresee that the smaller channel could not discharge

(a) 2 *Bl.* 924.   (a) 3 *Wils.* 461.

all

all the water which might enter by the larger channel. In pleading a justification in trespass, it is necessary to shew that the Defendant has done no unnecessary damage: the proof upon the general issue in an action on the case must be the same. But that defence could not be here substantiated: for the Defendant has occasioned unnecessary damage, and the action therefore lies. In the case of *Roberts* v. *Read* (a), two of the points which arise in this cause were determined: 1. that an action well lay against surveyors of the highway for taking away the soil adjoining to the Plaintiff's wall, by reason of which the wall afterwards fell; and it was never even objected that the action would not lie by reason that the act which produced the damage was an act within the scope of the Defendant's duty; and 2dly, that although more than three months had elapsed since the act, and before the action brought, yet as it was brought within three months after the wall fell, it was, within the meaning of the statute, brought within three months after the thing "done or acted," and "act committed," which are the words of the statute 13 G. 3. c. 78. s. 82. and are fully as strong as the words of this act. If the Defendant's act be so inartificially done that it injures the Plaintiff, it is no discharge to the Defendant that he acted according to the best skill and advice which he had, and that he consulted a surveyor on the manner of doing it. An individual is bound so to restrain the exercise of his rights over his own land, that he may not thereby injure his neighbour, and these trustees must observe the same rule in the exercise of their powers. Even if the principle be, that no action can be maintained against an officer for an injury occasioned by his act, unless the act be malicious, yet there is on this record a sufficient averment of malice, for express malice is not necessary; and it is averred that the Defend-

(a) 16 *East*, 216.

D 3

ant

ant continued the nusance wrongfully and injuriously, which, in *Drew* v. *Colton* (a) was held equivalent to an averment of malice: and as the jury have found a verdict for the Plaintiff, it must be now intended that the allegation was proved. If the Defendant had rested his case on the absence of malice, he should have gone to the jury upon that point. As to the time of the action, it suffices to bring it within six months after sustaining the damage comprehended in the declaration; for if the Plaintiff had recovered judgment on account of the injury produced in 1812, which might have been small, that would be no bar to an action for an injury sustained in the following year, which might be much greater. It cannot be, that by the Defendant's compensating the first small damage that occurs, he should purchase an indemnity against all future liability; and a jury would not be authorized to give prospective damages. Lord *Ellenborough* C. J. in *Roberts* v. *Read* distinguishes in respect of the time of limitation, between the case of trespass against a custom-house officer for seizing goods (b), and an action on the case for consequential damage; and *Bayley* J. asked, " How was the damage to be estimated before it had actually happened?" It would in the present case be impossible prospectively to estimate all the damage which might, in consequence of the Defendant's act, ever result to the occupiers of this land. It would be most inconvenient, and defeat the attainment of justice, if the action must be brought within six months after the first perceptible effect of the Defendant's act. For instance; the first flood might happen when the land was in grass, and in the beginning of spring, when it would be beneficial rather than injurious, and another might not happen till after the six months elapsed. It is clear therefore,

(a) 1 *East*, 567. n.   (b) *Goding* v. *Ferris*, 2 H Bl. 14.

(to

(to which the Court agreed,) that, if action be the proper remedy, the Plaintiff may bring renewed actions, unless the Defendant can shew that in the first action the Plaintiff may recover prospective damages to all time. And that he cannot do; for *in jure non remota, sed proxima spectatur causa.* There may be cases, as where the Defendant commits an injurious act on my land, in which a jury may possibly be warranted in giving prospective damages, for the Defendant cannot enter my land to redress the mischief: but if the damage be occasioned to me by an act which the Defendant commits on his own land, no prospective damages can be given; for the law intends that he will repair the evil. A jury would not be warranted in presuming that the commissioners would not themselves remedy this evil, before further mischief accrued. The doctrine tends greatly to promote litigation, that the Plaintiff must sue upon the first perceptible injury; and that if, as in this case, he first takes time to expostulate with the Defendant, he loses his remedy. Every repetition of the damage is a fresh nuisance, and will support a fresh action. But the Plaintiff may wave an injury if he will, without thereby giving future impunity.

Lens and *Pell* Serjts. *contrà.* 1. The action is brought too late. This is no nusance, for if it were, the Plaintiff would have a right to abate it, which he cannot do in this case. Where the injury is done by a private person, it may be waved, but against a public officer, either the party must assert his claim within the limited time from his first perception of the mischief, or rather, the inconveniences which have been urged by the Plaintiff as resulting from that construction, shew the true line to be, that the party is bound to foresee and calculate at the very time of the act of the commissioners, all its consequences, and then instantly to take his remedy. The two parts of the statute must be taken together.

D 4 If

If

1815.

SUTTON
v.
CLARKE

If the trench were cut at a time when there was no probability that any flood would happen within six months,
yet if there were a probable expectation of a flood at any
future and more distant period, the action, if it would
lie in any case, would lie in that, and must be brought
within the six months, or the remedy lost for ever: at
the same time the termor may have the apportioned
damages, not for his present loss merely, but for all the
mischief to be done within the term, and the reversioner
may have his action for all the damage which may happen to the residue of the inheritance. It is very doubtful whether the commissioners could now go through
another person's land with a new watercourse, to relieve
the Plaintiff's closes: but if they cannot, the termor
and the reversioner may in their respective actions recover an entire satisfaction for the whole injury. In
The King v. *The Justices of Staffordshire* (a) it was determined that where a statute dates from an act done, the
Court cannot compute the time of limitation from
notice of the act: and here, in like manner, the limitation must be computed from the date of the act, not
from its manifesting injurious effects; or at all events it
must be computed from the first perception of those
effects. Therefore the Plaintiff has not within due time
availed himself of the full and speedy remedy which the
act gave him, of waiting until it was seen whether any
injury were occasioned, and then forthwith suing.
Roberts v. *Read* is inapplicable, for from the nature of
the thing it could not there be foreseen whether the
removal of the earth would cause the wall to fall, and
until that was seen it would evidently be premature to
sue (b). The hardship is mutual of confining to the first

six

(a) 3 *East*, 152.

(b) Upon this part of the argument *Gibbs* C. J. observed,
that the case of *Roberts* v. *Read*

let the plaintiff loose from the
very great difficulty imposed by
the words, (which, it might be,

were

six months after the act, the option of suing. Unless the limitation is to take effect, at farthest, from the commencement of the injury, the liability is perpetual. An action may be brought for a damage which may 50 years hence be occasioned by this cause. But such a liability would deter all persons from accepting public trusts. Secondly, If a person in a public situation does an act within his jurisdiction, and without malice, even though it occasion damage to another, no action will lie; and this, on the general principle that the statute orders the thing to be done. In the case in *Wilson* the commissioners grossly exceeded their jurisdiction. In the case in 4 *T. R.* Lord *Kenyon* C. J. thought, independently of the compensation clause, that the action would not lie. He says, " If there be no power (to the commissioners to award satisfaction,) the parties are without remedy, provided the commissioners do not exceed their jurisdiction." The principle is, this: that when a party acts as trustee, if the act done is within his general jurisdiction, it is sufficient, though he pursue an erroneous mode of executing it. But here, too, the Defendant is not affected with any personal knowledge of the transaction. A surveyor is appointed, who performs the work without the interference of the Defendant; and it is an additional hardship, that the Plaintiff selects this one commissioner only. This is distinguishable from the case put in argument, of the proprietors of waterworks being answerable for the bursting of one of their pipes, which they might,

---

were very absurd and unjust,) of making the act done, and not, as in the statute 21 *Jac.* 2. *c.* 16., the cause of action, the criterion of the time. The Court of King's Bench had got over that difficulty, and attained the justice of the case; he should have had

great difficulty in coming to that decision, but thought the Court ought not to recede from it, because it favoured the attainment of justice. But the Court ultimately refrained from expressing any opinion upon this very important question.

under

1815.

WRIGHT
v.
YLAMANE,
Clerk.

Copley Serjt. on this day shewed cause against this rule. He first applied himself to the case of *Glympton.* The statute 54 *G.* 3. *c.* 54. *s.* 1. gives to the bishop's retrospective certificate the like efficacy, but no greater, than a licence granted before the facts, would have had. The statute 43 *G.* 3. *c.* 84. *s.* 19. enumerates the cases in which the bishop may grant a licence for non-residence; but the circumstance that a spiritual person, having a plurality of benefices, is licensed by one of his diocesans to absent himself from one of them, is not among the causes there enumerated. It is true, that by *s.* 20. the bishop may also licence a non-residence for special causes, and perhaps the performance of the parochial duties of *Llanhydroc* under such circumstances might have been such a cause, but such a special licence is of no avail, unless allowed by the archbishop; this certificate of the Bishop of *Oxford* is therefore in like manner ineffectual, unless allowed by the archbishop, which in this case has not been done. The only other mode in which this certificate can be argued to take effect, is, if a non-residence upon one benefice by virtue of a licence from one bishop, can be considered as an actual residence upon that benefice. But to hold this, would go to the root of all church discipline, since, if a pluralist could obtain a remission of his duties upon one benefice from one lax diocesan, none of the other diocesans to whom he was subject, would have it in their power to enforce the performance of his duties upon any of his other benefices situate within their jurisdiction. So, under the provisions of the stamp acts, it is necessary, if a person had twenty benefices, that he should have twenty distinct licences of non-residence; but if a licence not to reside on one, were considered as an actual residence on that one, only one stamp and one licence would be necessary, and the revenue would be defrauded. He deferred to

5   trouble

trouble the Court with the case of *Oddington*, which embraced the same and other objections, until that of *Glympton* should be disposed of.

Lens, contra, contended that the Bishop of *Oxford's* certificate, referring to the Bishop of *Exeter's* licence and certificate, and thus involving the facts, that there was no parsonage-house on *Llanhydroc,* and that the Defendant had actually performed the duties of that benefice for the period to which the certificate referred, and that the latter diocesan had therefore dispensed with actual residence, was, for the purpose of this action, equivalent to an actual residence at *Llanhydroc* during the same period; and taking it as such, the former certificate was a sufficient ground to support this application; a contemporaneous licence, given in the same terms, and for the same cause, would have been good.

GIBBS C. J. The argument reverts to the question whether the licence so given would not have required the confirmation of the archbishop; and that brings it back to the former question, whether the Defendant has shewn a ground for granting a licence, contained within the 43 G. 3. c. 84. s. 19., and whether the Defendant's residence at *Bodmin*, which is by the bishop's licence, excusing him for his non-residence at *Llanhydroc,* is to all intents and purposes equivalent to a residence at *Llanhydroc,* and puts the incumbent in all respects in the same situation as if he had been corporally resident at *Llanhydroc.* The statute 43 Geo. 3. c. 84. s. 12. subjects a spiritual person to the penalties of that act, who without sufficient cause, as in some of the therein recited acts is specified, or such other sufficient cause as would exempt him from the penalties of those acts, and who shall not have such licence and exemption as in that act is mentioned, shall absent himself from

his

1815.

WRIGHT
v.
FLAMANK,
Clerk.

his benefice, and make his residence and abiding at any ·
other place except at some other benefice, of which he .
may be possessed. The Defendant has the rectory of ,
Glympton : he does not reside on it: that is *primâ
facie* an offence. Has he an excuse? He says, I have
a licence to excuse my non-residence at another of my ·
benefices, *Llankydroc,* and that is equivalent to an ac--
tual residence there. This proposition is not true to · ·
the extent to which it is intended here to be applied.
Look to the purpose of that licence : it is to excuse the
Defendant from non-residence at *Llankydroc,* in respect
of the duties he has to perform there ; but it goes no
further : and if the Defendant wished for an excuse for .
his non-residence at *Glympton,* he ought to have applied
to the bishop of the diocese wherein it lies, for the other
species of licence which is pointed out by my Brother
Copley, as adverted to in the 20th section of the act
43 *G.* 3.: and as he has not done that, he cannot excuse
himself. The rule therefore must be discharged.

Rule discharged...

The case of *Oddington,* which would otherwise have
followed the fate of this, stood over until the present
term, when *Lens* again moved to discontinue as to *Oddington* upon a certificate granted on the 15th of *December* 1814 by the bishop, and confirmed by the archbishop
since the 1st of *July* 1814, viz. on 21st *December,*

The Court referred to *Wynn* v. *Kaye* (a), as having
determined that the limitation of time in the act was
applicable only to the licence, and not to the certificate, and granted a rule *nisi.*

Copley for the Plaintiff stated, that his client conceived that the 4th section applied only to notices of

(a) 5 *Taunt.* 843.

exemption,

exemption, not to all notices, and that the act did not
warrant this application: but he did not, upon further
consideration, find that point tenable, and on this day,
no cause being shewn, the rule was made

1815,

WRIGHT
v.
FLAMANK,
Clerk.

Absolute.

BURTON v. HICKEY.

Feb. 7.

IN replevin, the Defendant avowed for rent arrear;
the Plaintiff demurred. Judgment was thereon
given for the avowant. On the 4th of *January* the
Defendant gave notice of executing a writ of inquiry
on the 12th *January*, which was accordingly executed.
Lens Serjt. had obtained a rule *nisi* for setting aside
the execution of the writ of inquiry with costs, upon
the ground that the notice was insufficient, the statute
17 *Car.* 2. *c.* 7. *s.* 2. requiring fifteen days' notice,

Fifteen days'
notice is re-
quired of the
execution of a
writ of en-
quiry in reple-
vin, after
judgment on
demurrer for
the avowant.

Best Serjt. on this day shewed cause. The writ of
inquiry after judgment on demurrer in replevin, is
given by the 3d section, which prescribes no particular
time for the notice, therefore this notice must fall with-,
in the general rule of reasonable notice, for which eight
days is sufficient. The 2d section, requiring 15 days'
notice, is confined to the case of a writ of inquiry upon
a suggestion after nonsuit in the courts at *Wesminster ;*
and there is a reason for a longer notice in that case,
because in the suggestion the whole facts which constitute the cause of action are stated; it is not a common
inquiry of damages.

Lens, in support of his rule. The two sections
are not separated in the parliament-roll, though they
are in the printed editions of the statutes; the reason
assigned for the supposed distinction is ill founded, for

nonsuit

1815.

BURTON
v.
HICKEY.

nonsuit may be after avowry, and in that case, no suggestion being necessary, there is as little cause for a prolonged notice, as there is after judgment on demurrer. Therefore the same notice is required in the one case as in the other. This is a special enactment for the benefit of the Defendant, and he must take it as it is there given; for before this statute there was no writ of inquiry in replevin, and the statute mentions no other notice than the 15 days; therefore, if this be not the notice intended, no notice at all is necessary. The books of practice treat all the notices to be given of the writs of inquiry under that statute, as subject to the same rule.

GIBBS C. J. We are not furnished with any cases on this subject: it therefore is a matter of practice, and we certainly should abide by the practice which has prevailed. These are not ordinary writs of inquiry, but given by a particular statute; and it seems not unreasonable that the statute having prescribed in one case what the notice shall be, the like practice should, by parity of reasoning, be extended to other cases under the statute. It being a questionable point, the rule ought to be absolute without costs.

Rule absolute.

Feb. 7. BARTRAM, Plaintiff; TOWNE and Another, Deforciants.

The Court will not amend a fine by so increasing the number of acres of the several qualities of land therein comprized, as to comprehend the whole of the premises under each quality.

BLOSSET Serjt. moved to amend this fine, which had passed in the last term, by increasing the quantities comprized, to 40 acres of land, 40 acres of meadow, and

40 acres

40 acres of pasture; it now comprized 30 acres of land, 12 acres of meadow, and 25 acres of pasture. The deed conveyed all that close called *Butt Close*, as now fenced off, containing 25 acres 2 roods 36 perches, without any description of its quality, but it was in fact now pasture, and conveyed another close described as meadow, containing 9 acres 2 roods and 12 perches: the whole, therefore, amounted to 35 acres 12 roods and 8 perches; so that the entire quantity of the estate was in fact greater by 5 acres 2 roods and 8 perches than the quantity comprized in the fine under the name of land, and the quantity which in fact was pasture, was greater by 2 roods and 36 perches than the pasture comprized in the fine. But the parties were desirous to comprize all the acres of which the estate consisted, under each of the descriptions; for, unless it were so, if the quality of the land should be changed, the party would lose his evidence of the identity of the land. It was sworn the whole was in the parish, and was intended to pass. It was for the advantage of the office to insert as many acres as possible: and the party had, in the last term, when the fine was levied, a right to insert so much as he now prayed for: he ought indeed then to have enumerated the whole extent under each quality, but although he had omitted it, the Court would still grant him the same indulgence. He was at all events entitled to amend as to the pasture, which was shorter in the fine than in the deed to lead the uses; for even if it passes by the description of land in the fine, the party is entitled to have also a description of it as pasture, sufficient to cover the whole.

GIBBS C. J. That close of land, the nature of which is not described in the deed, must be taken to fall under the description of land, and the land being 30 acres in the fine, the party has no occasion for any amend-

1815.   amendment of that; if the number of acres in the fine
BARTRAM,   described as land had not equalled the number of acres
Plaintiff, &c, of which that close consisted, the surplus might have
been added. No ground is shewn for increasing the
number of acres either of meadow or pasture; there is
a number of acres of meadow in the fine, sufficient to
cover the number that exists. We cannot, after the
fine is passed, go beyond what the deed to lead the
uses will justify us in. The Court cannot proceed on
the principle, that because the party who conveys 25
acres, might, if he pleased, have put in 30 or 40 acres,
therefore the Court will now raise the number to any
amount he wishes, and which he might formerly have
inserted. The 25 acres of pasture must not be altered
at all.

Blosset took nothing by his motion.

Semble that   *A*SSUMPSIT for non-performance of an agree-
the owner of   ment, dated 3d *May* 1814, whereby the Defendant
land agreeing   agreed to grant to the Plaintiff a lease of a public-
to grant a
lease, does not house in *Drury-lane*, in the occupation of *C. Bingley*,
thereby im-   for 21 years from *Midsummer* 1814. The Plaintiff
pliedly engage agreed to pay 600*l.* for the lease and trade, subject to
that he has a
good title to   70*l.* rent, with a covenant to keep the premises in re-
the fee simple, pair, and other usual covenants, and to take the stock
and that he   in trade by guage and valuation. And the Defendant
will deliver a
written ab-   agreed, on being paid the sum of 600*l.* for the term
stract,   therein, to execute a proper lease, and transfer to the
Plaintiff the licences to sell liquors. The expences of
the lease to be borne in equal proportion between the
parties. And for the performance each bound himself
                                                          to

to the other in 100*l.* penalty. The Plaintiff averred in his first count, that the Defendant had represented to to him that he had good and sufficient authority to grant him a lease for 21 years of the premises, and averred as breach, that at the time of the contract the Defendant had no title. In another count the Plaintiff averred an undertaking by the Defendant to produce an abstract of his title to make such lease, and averred as a breach, that he had not done it. There was also a count for money had and received. Upon the trial of the cause at the sittings after *Michaelmas* term 1814, it was proved that in *May* 1814, the Plaintiff having paid a deposit of 32*l.*, was let into possession. No evidence was given of any promise, either to make a good title, or deliver an abstract. There was a dispute between the attornies of the respective parties who should prepare the lease: the Plaintiff's attorney required an abstract; the Defendant, at a very late period of the dispute, furnished an abstract of a conveyance to himself in 1810 from *Hollingworth*, who was not proved ever to have been in possession of the premises: he objected to deliver any further abstract, on account of the expence, but offered the Plaintiff's attorney permission to inspect, in the Defendant's custody, the earlier abstract by which he had himself purchased, and compare it with the prior deeds, of which offer the other did not avail himself. The Plaintiff contended, that if not entitled to a verdict on the special counts, he might at least recover back the deposit. *Gibbs* C. J. thought that the Defendant was not bound to deliver an abstract under this agreement: he went much on the authority of the case of *Gwillim* v. *Stone* (*a*), which, as it appeared to him, went the whole length of this case. That was an action on the case, and the Plaintiff, in his 1st count,

(*a*) 3 *Taunt.* 433.

declared

declared on an agreement very like the present, and stated as a breach, that the Defendant had not made out or shewn that he had any right to grant to the Plaintiff such a lease as he had agreed to grant. The Court held that the Plaintiff was not entitled to a nonsuit, because the Plaintiff had proved all that he had stated; whereupon the Defendant conceived he was entitled to move in arrest of judgment, because the Plaintiff had shewn no cause of action. The 2d count was for not delivering an abstract; and *Lawrence* J. says, " the alleged agreement to deliver an abstract is all poetry, the mere fancy of the special pleader; there is no trace in the evidence of any such contract." This case then decided; that it was not an implied part of such an agreement to deliver an abstract; if so, the non-delivery of an abstract was no breach of such an agreement; and if the agreement were not broken, on which the money was paid, the Plaintiff had no right to recover back his deposit, as money had and received. Upon this ground his Lordship directed a nonsuit.

Best Serjt. in this term moved for a rule *nisi* to set aside the nonsuit, and have a new trial, on which occasion *Heath* J. instanced the case of leases for three lives, granted some years since in *Devonshire* by a Duchess of *Bolton*, who was mere tenant for life, but assumed to have a power of leasing, and received fines to the amount of 29,000*l.*, nevertheless it had never yet been heard of that a tenant for life was asked to shew his title to lease.

Shepherd, Solicitor-General, now shewed cause. No defect in the title was here imputed or shewn; it was not a case of fraud or concealment; the Plaintiff might have inspected the title if he would, and the title was unquestionably good, therefore the point, whether a lessor is bound to have a good title, did not even arise.
This

This case is distinguishable therefore from that of *Lloyd* v. *Crispe* (*a*), because there the title was clearly bad; if there were any reasonable ground of suspicion, the case would be different. This was merely a question, whether a person engaging to grant a lease, impliedly engaged, there being no express stipulation, to deliver a written abstract of his title to the fee simple. In the case of a contract for the purchase of a fee simple, there is, by the practice of conveyancers, an implied stipulation that the vendor shall make out a good title and deliver a written abstract, but not so upon a contract for granting a lease. No hardship ensues from the rule; for if a person applying for a lease is solicitous about the title, he may make the title and abstract the subject of an express stipulation.

Best, in support of his rule. The weight of authority, as well as of reason, is with the Plaintiff. It is said, there is in this agreement no express stipulation for an abstract: neither is there usually, in an agreement for the purchase of the fee simple of an estate of the largest size; but it is, as much in the one case, as in the other, implied. The Chief Justice truly observed at the trial, that the offer of seeing the abstract is nothing. An attorney would be even liable to an action, who should take on himself upon his own view and judgment to decide on the title to a large estate: he has a right, therefore, to a copy of the abstract, that he may lay it before a conveyancer. If this were a purchase of a freehold interest, there would be no doubt, but that the Plaintiff would be entitled, not only to require a good title, but an abstract which he might take away, and lay before a conveyancer. Here the Plaintiff's attorney, though shewn the abstract, had no opportunity of shewing it to any learned person, or taking it

1815.

TEMPLE
v.
BROWN.

(*a*) *Ante,* v. 249.

awAy.

1815.

TEMPLE
v.
BROWN.

away. A person selling a part, however small, of the property, is bound to give an abstract. A particular interest, as for years, is a part of the estate : this, too, is not an agreement for a lease at rack-rent, but the Plaintiff is to pay 600*l.* for it: he is to have it for 21 years, and to keep the premises in repair. A person taking such a lease as this, is not to be considered as in the case of a common rack-rent tenant. Can it then be said, that though a purchaser has a right to an abstract on the purchase of a single rood of land in fee, yet, that when the whole of a large estate is granted for a long term, leaving in the grantor an interest far less in value than that which the grantee takes, he is to have no abstract? The agreement to grant a proper lease, means not any parchment that the lessor may sign, so that the lessee, after paying hundreds and expending thousands, may be told, " there is no title, that he may go out, and has nothing but his parchment and the lessor's covenant." *White* v. *Fuljanbe* (a), *Waring* v. *Mackreth*, there cited (b), and *Keech* v. *Hall* (c), are in point. In the last, Lord *Mansfield* takes it for granted that a person who takes a lease, has a right to inquire for and examine the title deeds. In the case of *Lloyd* v. *Crispe*, *Mansfield* C. J. was of opinion, that as it was known to both parties that the lease could not be assigned without the licence of the landlord, the party contracting to purchase the assignment took it on himself to obtain the consent of the landlord; but the Court held that the vendor was to obtain that consent.

The Court seeing that this was a question of immense magnitude, at first asked, whether the parties would put it on the record, in the shape of a special verdict; for when Lord Chancellor *Eldon* had said (d), that he would

(a) 11 *Ves.* 341.   (b) *Forrest Exch. Rep.* 137.
(c) *Doug.* 21.   (d) 11 *Ves.* 346, 7.

not

not decide the point in equity, without the aid of the
judges of the courts of law, this Court would be sorry
to take it on themselves to decide it, without affording
an opportunity for a review of their judgment. There
was no doubt of what Lord *Mansfield* says in *Keech* v.
Hall, that a person about to take a lease may refuse to
take it, unless the lessor will satisfy him that he has a
good title, just as any person may refuse to enter into
any agreement whatever, unless on the terms he shall
prescribe.

The Court afterwards considering that the cause had
originated in a dispute between the two attornies, and
that the clients had nothing to gain by the decision of
this momentous question, desired the counsel to consider
what course would be most for the interest of the parties, and adjourned, and the case was never afterwards
argued.

SHIELDS *v.* DAVIS.

Feb. 9.

THIS was an action for freight upon the implied
    contract arising upon the Defendant's acceptance of
certain casks of butter delivered to him by the Plaintiff,
who was the master, but not the owner, of a vessel, under
the bill of lading, which made the delivery conditional
on payment of freight. The defence was, that the
butters were injured by the negligence of the Plaintiff,
and that therefore he could recover nothing. The jury
however found a verdict for the Plaintiff.

If the con-
signee of goods
accepts any be-
nefit by the
carriage, he
cannot defend
himself from
the payment
of freight on
the ground
that the goods
have been da-
maged by the
master in carrying them.

Though the damage exceed the amount of the freight.

The master has a special property in the vessel, and may declare for the freight of
goods as carried in *his* vessel, though he be not owner.

1815.

SHIELDS
v.
DAVIS.

Best Serjt. in this term, moved that either there might be a new trial, or that the judgment might be arrested. The first, upon the ground that the Plaintiff's right to .freight attached only on the safe delivery of the goods, and if, though delivered, they were not safely delivered, he could not recover the freight. He therefore ought to have come to trial prepared to shew that the goods were safely delivered, and consequently the nature of the defence could be no surprize on him. At all events, in this case, where the extent of the damage done to the butter was greater than the whole amount that would have been due for the freight, the Plaintiff could recover nothing. *Farnsworth* v. *Garland* (a). And the reason given by *Chambre* J. in *Temple* v. *Mac Lauchlan* (b), there cited, is, that such a principle prevents multiplicity of actions.

GIBBS C. J. The argument proceeds on the supposition that his delivery of the goods in good condition is a condition precedent to his claim for freight. Consequently, if the master had been in any degree negligent, he could recover no freight at all. He is liable to a cross action.

HEATH J. Here the master has accepted the goods; and the principle is, that if he has received any benefit whatever by the carriage, he cannot set up this defence.

Best grounded his motion in arrest of judgment, as to the first count, upon the circumstance that the words were omitted, which contained the consideration of the Defendant's promise, viz. " that the Plaintiff would deliver the butter." The second count alleged that the Plaintiff had carried and conveyed certain butters to

(a) 1 *Camp. N. P.* 38.   (b) 2 *New Rep.* 141.

be

be delivered for certain freight, whereof the Defendant had notice, and in consideration of the premises, and that the Plaintiff would deliver the butters to the Defendant, the Defendant promised to pay on request, and avers that the Plaintiff confiding, did afterwards deliver the butter to the Defendant, and that the freight amounted to a certain sum. The ground of objection to this count was, that at the time of the supposed promise, the freight was of no amount, for it was to accrue thereafter, but was not then, as yet, in existence, because the delivery had not taken place. In the third count the goods were stated to be carried in the Plaintiff's vessel, and it was objected there was a variance between the evidence and this count, for that the Plaintiff was only the master, and the vessel could not properly be called his.

Shepherd, Solicitor-General, on this day would have shewn cause, but the Court, having called on *Best* to support his rule, held that the second count was to be read, not as a promise to pay that which did not exist, but to pay the freight when it should thereafter become due, and so was good. As to the third count, the master had a special property in the ship, because he had the controul of it, not a mere charge as a servant. He might bring trespass. They were not prepared to say the Plaintiff might not enter his verdict on that count, which stated it to be the ship of the Plaintiff.

> Rule absolute to arrest the judgment on the first count only.

1815.

SHIELDS
v.
DAVIE.

GREEN v. ROYAL EXCHANGE Assurance Com. pany.

ing 318

If, pending an insurance on freight, and a cargo shipped, the vessel becomes incapable of bringing the cargo home, the master is bound, or not bound, to repair her, and earn what he can on the homeward voyage, as a salvage for the underwriters on freight, according as a prudent owner, having regard to the state of his ship, but without reference to any insurance on the freight, would pursue or not pursue that course for his own advantage.

Semble, that an abandonment of freight to the underwriters on freight is impossible and unnecessary.

THIS was an action upon a policy of insurance at and from the ship's port or ports of lading in the *Canary* islands to *London,* to return four *per cent.* if the ship started with convoy and arrived, on freight by the ship *Defiance.* The Plaintiff declared for a total loss by perils of the sea. Upon the trial of this cause at *Guildhall,* before *Gibbs* C. J. at the sittings after *Michaelmas* term 1814, it appeared that the ship, which was of the burthen of 200 tons, took in a full cargo at *Puerta Ventura* for *London,* and proceeded to *Lanzaretto,* where, in consequence of sea-damage, she was obliged to unship her cargo: her state was such, that it would have been impossible to bring her home in that condition, or get her completely repaired there, so as to bring home that cargo. She was therefore surveyed and sold to *Bedford,* who within five or six weeks partially repaired her, and safely brought home in her 96 tons of goods. He sold to the Plaintiff, the master of the *Defiance,* a vessel called the *Ann* of 60 tons, in which the latter brought home some tons of barilla on freight. For the Defendants, it was contended, that the Plaintiff was not entitled to recover a total loss, because there had been no abandonment, and the case of *Parmeter* v. *Todhunter* (a) was cited. *Gibbs* C. J. thought abandonment was not necessary, for he could not understand what was to be abandoned. The ship was fully laden, and as soon as she was laden, it became an insurance on the freight of the particular cargo that was on board a ship, which became incapable of bring-

(a) 1 *Campb.* 541.

ing

ing it home. Nevertheless he reserved the point, subject whereto the jury found a verdict for the Plaintiff.

Shepherd, Solicitor-General, in this term moved for a nonsuit, or a new trial, contending that this was not a total loss, first, because there had been no abandonment; secondly, because if the *Defiance* could not be so repaired as to bring home the whole cargo, she could have been so repaired as to bring home at least as much as *Bedford* actually brought. 3dly, That a part of the voyage having been performed, it was the Plaintiff's duty, upon the failure of this vessel, to have transhipped the cargo into some other vessel to perform the remainder of the voyage for the benefit of the underwriters. (Upon this point the Court intimated, that so very minute a portion of the voyage had in this case been performed before the loss, that the question made could not be considered to arise.) 4thly, That the Plaintiff, instead of selling the vessel, ought to have partially repaired her, and made what freight he could by other goods on the homeward voyage, to be applied in reduction of the loss of the original freight, as a salvage for the underwriters. If the master had power to earn any freight, either with the ship originally intended, or with the cargo by another ship, he was bound so to do. *Everth* v. *Smith* (a). The Court granted a rule *nisi* upon the first ground as a point reserved, and upon the others, which had not been stated at the trial as objections of law, as shewing that the verdict was contrary to the evidence, which went only to prove an average loss.

Lens and *Vaughan* Serjts. on this day shewed cause against the rule. 2 *Marsh. on Ins.* 562. and *Valin*, and *Pothier*, in the passages there cited, all speak of aban-

1815.

GREEN
v.
ROYAL
EXCHANGE
Assurance
Company.

(a) 2 *Maule & Selw.* 278.

F 3

donment

1815.

GREEN

v.

ROYAL
EXCHANGE
Assurance
Company.

donment as applicable only " to the effects insured."
But though freight has of late years been held capable
to be the subject of insurance, it does not fall within
the common category, that there may alike be a partial
or a total loss of the subject insured: it cannot be said
to be effects: it is not a thing which can be saved out
of the general wreck and handed over to the underwriters. There is at no period of the voyage any visible
substantive thing, that can be abandoned. The case of
Parmeter v. *Todhunter* does not explain what there is to
be abandoned upon an insurance on freight, and it is
extremely difficult to discover. In the case of abandonment of ship or goods, if any damage has happened
short of the absolute destruction of the subject matter,
there is the visible and tangible relique of a substance
which has corporeal existence. But that proceeding is
wholly inapplicable to freight. The voyage is totally
destroyed and gone. Abandonment in this case can
only be by giving notice to the underwriters, that by
pursuing a certain course, they may take up an adventure which is suspended, and earn freight which otherwise never will be earned: it could only amount to
this, that the underwriters may, if they please, speculate
on reducing their loss by sending over other vessels to
bring home these goods; but no authorities lay it down
that such a notice is necessary; none countenance the
supposed necessity of abandonment of freight, except
Parmeter v. *Todhunter,* *Thompson* v. *Rowcroft* (a), and
Leatham v. *Terry* (b). In the two last cases there was
an actual declaration of abandonment, and the Courts
put them both upon the plain and intelligible ground
that the assured had received freight, which they had
previously undertaken to give up to the underwriters,
and therefore were bound to pay it over. *Everth* v.

(a) 4 *East,* 34.   (b) 3 *Bos. & Pul.* 484.

Smith

Smith is inapplicable, because that was an insurance on freight generally, and not on the freight of any particular cargo, and the ship earned freight on the voyage, and so, no loss. In *Parmeter* v. *Todhunter* the point arose only incidentally. 2. There is no obligation on the assured to form a new contract for bringing home the goods by another vessel, which is at least equally likely to be productive of expence, as of benefit, to the underwriter. If the assured enters into this speculation, and it fails, and the underwriters disavow the contract, he cannot compel them to adopt it, or to indemnify him for the expences. 3. Neither is there any authority, that where a vessel is incapable of being completely repaired, the assured is compellable partially to repair her, and to make her, instead of a ship of 200 tons, a ship of 96 tons. By what law is the assured bound to enter into a speculation for the benefit of the underwriters, which he would not think it proper to engage in for his own? Why is he to be restrained from selling his vessel, if he finds it most conducive to his interest? The master too had other rights and interests to protect, besides those of the underwriters on freight: the owners of, and underwriters on the goods, might object to the goods being re-shipped by so imperfect a conveyance. The underwriter on the ship might object to the being again exposed to the probable risk of a total loss, after so heavy average losses had been incurred. In *Parmeter* v. *Todhunter* it was never suggested that the assured might have sent home his goods by another ship. The Plaintiff is therefore entitled to recover as for a total loss without any abandonment, but if the Court shall think his right does not extend so far, he is at least entitled to retain his verdict to the amount of the average loss.

The *Solicitor-General*, *Best*, and *Bosanquet* Serjts, *contrà*, contended they were entitled either to a nonsuit

1815.

GREEN
v.
ROYAL
EXCHANGE
Assurance
Company.

on

1815.

GREEN
v.
ROYAL
EXCHANGE
Assurance
Company.

on the want of abandonment, or a new trial. This insurance had not attached on the freight of this specific cargo, and the ship might possibly have earned some other freight home. They were proceeding to recapitulate the grounds on which the motion was made, when

　　· The Court interposing, expressed their opinion that this case ought to be re-considered by the jury. They saw no ground for saying that there ought to be an abandonment in this case; but if the ship had brought home another cargo from the *Canaries*, and earned freight thereon, that would have been a salvage on the freight of her original cargo; for that, when the first cargo was once on board, the policy attached on the freight of that specific cargo; but if the captain, being driven back and unable to proceed with the original cargo, was yet able to proceed with a less cargo, on less freight, of this the underwriter ought to have the benefit. The assured ought to proceed as if he was not insured; and if, not being insured, he for his own profit, in common prudence finds it expedient to repair the vessel and proceed on the voyage, then he ought to do it for the benefit of the underwriters: but he must not sell the ship, which otherwise he might profitably to himself have repaired, and throw the loss on the underwriters. It ought therefore to be left to the jury, whether a prudent man would have sold the ship in these circumstances, or have repaired her, and proceeded with her to earn what she could. The case, therefore, ought to go to a new trial, and the costs of the former trial ought to be costs in the cause.

Rule absolute.

ANONYMOUS.

Feb. 10.

*B*EST Serjt. had no other cause to shew against a rule which had been obtained by *Runnington* Serjt., than a preliminary objection to the admissibility of the affidavit on which the rule was moved, that the Defendant, who swore it, was therein only designated by his name and place of abode, and the predicament of his being Defendant in this cause; whereas *Best* contended that the addition of his degree was necessary; for which he cited the practice of the King's Bench, exemplified in the case of *Jarrett* v. *Dillon* (a). But the Court observed that the reason of that case was, that the rule of Court *Mich.* 15 *Car.* 2. specially required it, but that in this court there was no such rule, and they held that here a Defendant in the cause, making an affidavit, is sufficiently intitled by his place of abode and reference to his quality of Defendant, without stating the additiou of his degree.

It is not necessary that an affidavit made by the Defendant in the cause, stating his abode, and styling him Defendant, should also contain the addition of his degree.

Rule absolute.

(a) 1 *East*, 18.

ROWLITT and Another *v.* ORLEBAR.

Feb. 11.

*B*LOSSET Serjt. moved to amend a fine of *Hilary* term 7 *Geo.* 3. by inserting the parish of *Earl's Barton*, in which a small part of the premises was situated, as being warranted by the deed declaring the uses of the fine, which bore date the 4th *July* 1767. All the parties were dead. In practice, the deed to lead the uses of a recovery commonly precedes the recovery, but

The Court permitted a fine to be amended by the subsequent deed declaring the uses.

1815.

ROWLITT

v.

ORLEBAR.

but the deed declaring the uses of a fine is almost always subsequent to the fine; nevertheless amendments
have been made by the deeds declaring the uses of
fines; and therefore, though their relative dates are not
stated, it may be presumed the deeds were in those
instances subsequent to the fines. *Anon.* 1 *Ld. Raym.*
209., where the learned editor of the 4th edition, in a
marginal note, says, that it is every day's practice in
this court to amend a fine by the deed declaring the
uses; and *Manley* v. *Tattersal* (a). The parties to the
fine and the deed are the same, and the deed recites
the fine, whereby the identity appears.

Fiat.

(a) 4 *Taunt.* 257.

Feb. 11.

SMIDT and Another *v.* OGLE.

This Court
will not stay
proceedings in
an action com-
menced here,
to abide the
event of an
action in the
mayor's court,
where it is
sought to try
in a foreign
attachment the
title to the
same property
which is in
suit here.

CERTAIN persons having commenced three actions
in the mayor's court in *London* against *Smidt* and
Co., and attached them by the debt supposed to be due
to them from *Ogle* (a), and *Smidt* and Co. having also
commenced this action against *Ogle*, to recover what
he was indebted to them, *Vaughan* Serjt. now moved
that all further proceedings might be stayed in this
action till the mayor's court should have determined
whether *Ogle* were or were not indebted to *Smidt* and
Co. in the sum for which they were attached in that
court.

GIBBS C. J. We never can consent to stay proceedings in this court, in order to await the event of

(a) *Ante*, v. 759.

I   a decision,

·a decision in the mayor's court. This is something like the attempt that was made in the case of *Nathans* v. *Giles.* (a)

HEATH J. It is a common law right of the Plaintiff to sue here, and we shall not restrain it.

Rule refused.

(a) 5 *Taunt.* 558.

---

6 May 571.

WOOLCOT v. LEICESTER.

Feb. 13.

B*EST* Serjt. had on a former day obtained a rule *nisi* for entering an *exoneretur* on the bail-piece in this cause, upon the ground that the Defendant had become bankrupt and obtained his certificate.

Shepherd, Solicitor-General, shewed cause, on a surmise that money had been paid to several creditors of the Defendant for signing the certificate, and that after the certificate obtained and before interlocutory judgment signed, the Plaintiff had given the Defendant notice of his intention to contest the certificate, and that if he intended to rely on it, he might plead it *puis darrein continuance*, which he had declined; and the Court would not now relieve him on motion, without giving the Plaintiff an opportunity of trying whether the certificate had been fairly obtained.

The Court directed an issue to try the validity of the certificate, to which *Best*, on behalf of the bail, consented, and the present rule was enlarged until after the trial of that issue, with a stay of proceedings in the ·mean time.

Rule enlarged,

The Court will not exonerate the bail upon the Defendant having become bankrupt and obtained his certificate, without giving the plaintiff an opportunity of trying, by an issue, whether the certificate were fairly obtained.

ung 257.

Smith and Others *v.* Mercer and Another.

The Defendants took a bill, accepted payable at the Plaintiffs', who were the drawee's bankers, and indorsed it to their, the Defendants' agents, to whom the Plaintiffs paid it when due, and seven days after sent it as their voucher to the drawee, who apprized them that the acceptance was forged. Held by three against *Chambre* J. that the plaintiffs could not recover from the Defendants the amount which they had thus paid them on the forged acceptance.

ASSUMPSIT for money had and received, and on the other money counts. At the sittings in *London* after *Michaelmas* term 1814, before *Gibbs* C. J., a verdict was found for the Plaintiffs for 120*l.*, subject to a case: The Plaintiffs were bankers in *London*, with whom *Maurice Evans* kept cash: the Defendants were bankers at *Tunbridge*, and were *bonâ fide* holders, for a valuable consideration, paid by them to *Peter Le Souef*, of a bill of exchange, drawn on 15th *Feb.* 1811, by *Tho. Temple*, at 65 days' date, on *Maurice Evans*, for 120*l.*, payable to the drawer's order, and indorsed by *Temple* and *P. Le Souef.* The bill, when it came to the Defendant's hands, appeared to be thus accepted: " *Smith, Payne*, and *Smiths, Maurice Evans.*" This acceptance was forged. Before the bill was due, the Defendants indorsed the same, and sent it with their indorsement thereon to their corresponding bankers and agents in *London, Spooner* and Co., to be received for them at maturity. Upon the bill being presented by *Spooner* and Co. to the Plaintiffs for payment on the 23d of *April*, when it became due, they immediately paid the amount to *Spooner* and Co., who paid the amount in account to the Defendants; all the parties being at the time equally ignorant of the forgery. The Plaintiffs sent the bill to *Evans* at the usual time, with the other vouchers of payments made for him, and *Evans* immediately returned the same to them, as forged, and refused to allow the payment thereof as a payment made on his account. The Plaintiffs, upon discovering the forgery, on the 30th of *April* 1814, gave notice to the Defendants that the acceptance was forged, and re-

quired

quired the Defendants to repay the money, which they refused to do.

Lens Serjt., for the Plaintiffs. No circumstances of this case take it out of the general rule, that the Plaintiffs have paid to the Defendants a sum of money upon a consideration which has failed, and are therefore entitled to recover it back. The Plaintiffs have done no act tending to give authenticity to this forged instrument, they have merely paid it when it was presented. This case is governed by those, wherein the question was fully considered, of *Jones* v. *Ryde* (a), and *Bruce* v. *Bruce* (b), particularly by the last of them. [*Gibbs* C. J. observed that the latter case could not be used as an authority in this, to the extent intended : it was there held that since the Victualling-office had received the money back from the Bank of *England*, and the Bank of *England* had received it back from the Plaintiffs, the Plaintiffs might recover from the Defendants. The Defendants' argument there was, that the Plaintiff, who had improvidently submitted to a demand which could not have been enforced against him, did not thereby acquire a right to sue the Defendant. The answer given was, that the bill was still to be considered in the light of an unpaid bill, which the Defendant had put off on the Plaintiff as a good bill, but which proved to be forged. There were also some circumstances which made the Court doubt whether that case fell within the general law, and which made it distinguishable from *Price* v. *Neal* (c).] This case also is distinguishable from *Price* v. *Neal*, in which the judgment proceeded on the ground that the Plaintiff had, by his own act in paying the first bill, positively encouraged the Defendant to take the second as genuine,

(a) *Ante*, v. 489.   (b) *Ibid.* 495.
(c) 3 *Burr.* 1354, and 1 *Bl.* 390.

and

1815.

SMITH
v.
MERCER.

and therefore had precluded himself from recovering back the money. But in this case the Plaintiffs are not drawees, nor do they accept the bill, or add any credit to it, for it is not negociated beyond them; they merely pay it when presented, which is far short of saying that it was the acceptance of *Evans;* and their act in paying it, being long subsequent to the Defendants' taking the bill, could have no influence on their minds.

Best Serjt. for the Defendants. The cases of *Jones* v. *Ryde*, and *Bruce* v. *Bruce*, do not conflict with *Price* v. *Neal.* And this case ranges itself with the latter. It was the peculiar duty of the Plaintiffs, as the bankers of *Evans*, to be conversant with his signature. The Defendants had no means of becoming acquainted with his hand-writing. In *Price* v. *Neal*, the judgment of the Court did not turn upon the encouragement given by the Plaintiff to the circulation of the bill, but on the mere fact of his paying it, for the Plaintiff never accepted the first bill, but merely sent his servant, upon notice of the bill being due, to take it up and pay it, which could not operate as an encouragement to the holder's prior act of taking the bill. The case on the second bill, which the Plaintiff actually accepted, was abandoned by the Plaintiff's counsel, and Lord *Mansfield*'s observation, that the Plaintiff had encouraged the Defendant to take it, applies to the second bill only, which is wholly dissimilar to this case. In the report in *Blackstone*, the Court lays stress on the circumstance, most appropriate to the present case, that the Plaintiff is the only person who knows the drawer's hand-writing. There is equal hardship on the Plaintiffs and on the Defendants, but the negligence is in the Plaintiffs, not in the Defendants, and where the negligence is, whether more or less in degree, there the loss ought to fall. The

Court

Court will not measure degrees of negligence; if there be any negligence in the Plaintiffs, they are precluded from recovering; but it is not only some, but an extreme degree of negligence in a banker, not to know the handwriting of his customers. Here then, as in *Price* v. *Neal*, is an admission of the genuineness of the bill by a person competent and required to know the handwriting, and the cases only differ in the immaterial circumstance, that in the one the drawer's, and in the other the acceptor's hand is forged. The person who takes a bill before it is mature, does not, by taking it, recognize it as a genuine bill, nor is it incumbent on him before its maturity to enquire of the payee as to its authenticity; but the person who delivers it over to him, does represent and warrant it to be a genuine bill.

Lens in reply. In *Price* v. *Neal* the Plaintiff's counsel argued for his right to recover on both the bills. It cannot be deemed extreme negligence that every banker's clerk does not know how to discover all forgeries, many of which are not without great nicety and difficulty discerned. In *Jones* v. *Ryde* the forgery was easy to be discovered, for the words " eight hundred" in letters were left unaltered. There was no mode of discovering this till the vouchers were returned to *Evans* by the Plaintiffs. But neither has there been any negligence here, nor have the Defendants lost any thing by the delay; for if this forgery had been sooner discovered, the Defendants would have had no civil remedy against the author of it, for the debt would be merged in the felony. Nothing which the Plaintiffs have done, has deteriorated the condition of the Defendants, wherein is a strong distinction between this case and *Price* v. *Neal*. Here is only the bare act of paying the bill, which is very far short of accepting it, or of representing

ing

ing, for the guidance of another, that it is genuine. It will not therefore militate with the case of *Price* v. *Neal*, to decide this in favour of the Plaintiffs.

Cur. adv. vult.

·On this day the Court delivered their opinions *seriatim.*

DALLAS J. recapitulated the facts of the case, after which he thus proceeded. It is stated in the case that all the parties at the time of payment of the bill were equally ignorant of the forgery; and the question is, on whom the loss ought to fall? And though the facts are not precisely the same, I think the case of *Price* v. *Neal* (a) furnishes a rule which ought to govern the present. The case of *Price* v. *Neal* was in substance this : Two bills had been drawn, the first was only presented when due; the second, drawn some time after the first, was accepted, and paid when due. Both proved to be forgeries as to the hand-writing of the drawer; and the Plaintiff who had paid them, contended, that having paid by mistake, he was entitled to recover back the money from the indorsee, who was an innocent and *bonâ fide* holder. As to the facts of this case, it may be necessary to distinguish, before adverting to the judgment of the Court. The first bill had not derived additional credit from the acceptance, for it had not been accepted; but the second bill had been accepted, and was therefore different in this respect. The action was brought to recover back the amount of both bills. For the Plaintiff, the argument at the bar proceeded on the ground of payment by mistake; but the first bill was said to stand upon ground even stronger than the second, inasmuch as when negociated it had not

(*a*) 3 *Barr.* 1354·, and 1 *Bl.* 390. .

been

been accepted; and therefore was not taken upon the credit of the acceptor. In the judgment of the Court the two bills are also distinguished, but the distinction does not lead to any difference of conclusion; for the Defendant was adjudged to retain as to both, and, as it seems, partly on two grounds; 1st, of neglect in the Plaintiff; 2dly, that supposing no neglect, the loss ought not to be shifted from one innocent man upon another: with the latter ground I shall not interfere upon the present occasion, for the former goes the whole length of reaching this case. And to see that it does, it is only necessary to ask what was the neglect? The answer must be, the having paid when due caution would have prevented such payment. If an acceptor is then bound to know the drawer's hand-writing, is it less the duty of a banker to know the hand-writing of his customer? In degree, it is more so; for he sees it, probably, every day. I consider therefore the payment of this bill as a want of due caution on the part of the Plaintiffs. But to distinguish it from *Price* v. *Neal*, it is said, payment by the bankers, after it became due, did not add to its credit or negotiability: so it was with the first bill in the case of *Price* v. *Neal*; yet this made no difference. Is it however productive of no injury to any of the parties on the bill? Suppose *Smith* and Co. had not paid it, it would have been immediately returned to *Spooner*, and by him to *Le Souef* the indorser, and it might have been recovered, or put in suit. But the effect of the delay has been, to give him an extended credit, and how am I able to say, that his situation in the intermediate time may not have undergone such a change, as to render him incapable of paying what he could have paid upon proper notice and demand. Nor do I think it will be an answer, to observe that nothing of this sort is stated in the case: for the Plaintiffs had no right to cast upon the Defendants the burthen of such proof, which, in point of law, if the fact had existed, and could have made any difference, it was for themselves to produce. The ground, therefore, on which I rest my opinion, and to which I wish to confine it, is the want of due caution in having paid the bill, the effect of which has been, to give time to different parties, which the Plaintiffs were not authorized to do.

CHAMBRE J. I think the Plaintiffs are in this case entitled to recover. The bill appears drawn in the name of *Thomas Temple*, payable to himself or order, directed to *Maurice Evans*, and indorsed by *Temple*. The next indorser is *Peter Le Souef*, and it appears that the bill had the forged acceptance on it when it was in his hands, and in that state he indorsed it, and the Defendants received it from him for a valuable consideration, *bonâ fide* paid to him by the Defendants. The forged acceptance purported to make the bill payable at the Plaintiffs', who were the bankers of the supposed acceptor in *London*. The Defendants, in order to receive the money for which the bill was given, indorsed it, and sent it to their bankers in town, who sent it to the Plaintiffs, and they immediately paid it, under the supposition that they were directed so to do by *Evans*. At what particular period the forgery was committed, and who was then the holder of the bill, is not stated : but it is stated that the parties at the time, meaning, I suppose, the Plaintiffs, the Defendants, and their bankers, were equally ignorant of the forgery. About a week afterwards, the Plaintiffs sent the bill as a voucher to *Evans*, and he, finding out the forgery, refused to allow the payment, and sent back the bill to the Plaintiffs. The Plaintiffs then gave the Defendants notice that the acceptance was forged, and required the money to be repaid. Upon these facts the present action is brought, and it is brought on the general principle that when

7*   money

money not really due is paid by mistake, it is recoverable in this form of action. In this case the money has been paid without any consideration, and under a mistake; and not only under a mistake, but under a representation made to the Plaintiffs by the Defendants, who indorsed the bill with that forged acceptance on it, that the Plaintiffs were required and directed so to pay it, by the person whose agents they were in money transac. tions. Cases undoubtedly may exist, that form exceptions to the general rule. Such are cases respecting bills of exchange, under circumstances wherein the doctrine might produce injurious consequences in that species of negotiation, and particularly where the party claiming restitution has himself, though innocently, given credit to the instrument by his own previous acceptance or indorsement. There the party who wants to recover back his money, has himself given a kind of warranty to subsequent takers, and will not be permitted to recover against those who have innocently received the money claimed to be due on such bills. The case of *Jenys* v. *Fowler* (a) is alluded to both in *Blackstone's* and *Burrow's* reports of *Price* v. *Neal.* That was a case where the acceptor was not permitted to prove the forgery of the bill he had accepted, for the reason given by Lord *Raymond* C. J. that it would be dangerous to negotiable notes. *Blackstone* says, the demand on the accepted bill in *Price* v. *Neal,* was, on the authority of that case, given up by the Plaintiff's counsel, and I cannot well understand why the reasons which relate thereto are introduced into the consideration of the Court on the other bill in *Price* v. *Neal;* but the other part of that case, which relates to the bill not accepted, was there the subject of the decision of the Court, and is relied on in the present case, as an authority for the Defendants. *Blackstone* J. has in his report rather

(a) 2 *Str.* 946.

jumbled

1815.

SMITH
v.
MERCER.

jumbled together the observations applicable to the case on one of the bills with those applicable only to the other. Among other things, the acceptance is relied on as applicable to both. All that he makes the Court say respecting the unaccepted bill, is, " The negligence in the Plaintiff, (who had taken up the forged bill,) is greater than can possibly be imputed to the Defendant." That is a singular subject of calculation. He says, " where the loss has fallen, there it must lie: one innocent man must not relieve himself by throwing it on another." So I should say here. The Defendants have paid their money for that which is of no value; they have thereby sustained a loss, and they ought not to be permitted to throw that loss upon another innocent man, who has done no act to mislead them: and still less ought they to be so permitted, where, instead of being misled by any act of the Plaintiffs, they themselves have given the appearance of authenticity to the instrument by their own indorsement, which was a sort of warranty of its genuineness at a time when the forged acceptance made a part of the instrument. The report of the case in *Burr.* is fuller. It speaks of the liberality of the action for money had and received, and puts the case upon the ground, that the Defendant might conscientiously retain the money, not because it was his, but because he has hold of it without any fraudulent intent. How he can satisfy his conscience by keeping that which is not his, I cannot tell, but it is better not to encourage too far this latitude of conscience. The matter however has been lately discussed and decided in this court in the two cases of *Jones* v. *Ryde* and *Bruce* v. *Bruce.* (Here the learned Judge stated the case of *Jones* v. *Ryde.*) A great part of the doctrine of *Price* v. *Neal* seems in that case to be wholly repudiated by the Court. *Fenn* v. *Harrison* (a) was there

(a) 3 T.R. 757.

cited;

cited; and my Lord Chief Justice says, "it is true, that if he who negotiates a bill does not indorse it, he does not subject himself to that responsibility which the indorsement would bring on him, viz. to an action to be brought against him as indorser, but he does not get rid of that responsibility which arises from his passing off an instrument of no value, and receiving value for it;" and he compared it to the case of paying away forged bank notes. My Brother *Heath* there adverts to what is said by Lord *Kenyon,* that the person paying under such circumstances is entitled to recover back the money, and he refers to *Cripps* v. *Reade* (a); and my Brother *Dallas* refers to the same case, and concurs with the rest of the Court. *Bruce* v. *Bruce* is a still stronger case. There the bill was actually paid, but the Court said they could not distinguish it from the case before decided. It is said in this case the negligence varies it; what was the negligence? How perfect the forgery was, we do not know. Some forgeries will deceive the party whose name is forged. Did the Plaintiffs omit any degree of reasonable diligence which lay within their power? *Evans,* when the bill was sent to him, could not be deceived: he must know: he detected the forgery, and gave immediate notice: where then is the negligence? The bill had done its office, had ceased to be negotiated. It is not like bills which have to go further in circulation. I cannot therefore think this was a case of gross negligence in the Plaintiffs. The situation of the Plaintiffs is extremely material. They are no parties to this bill, neither drawers, acceptors, or payees. They are not purchasers of the bill; they never had any property in it; they are mere servants and agents of the payees; it is, as to them, a payment under a supposed authority, which does not exist. It falls

(a) 6 *T. R.* 606.

within the general principle. My opinion therefore is, that the Plaintiffs are entitled to recover.

HEATH J: I am of opinion that a nonsuit ought to be entered. I agree that this is a case of money paid without consideration, and I agree in the general principle, that money paid without consideration upon an instrument which proves to be of no value, may be recovered back; but there are particular circumstances in this case which materially alter, and take this case out of the general principle. If *Evans* had paid the bill, it is clear he would have been bound. Can an agent be in a better situation than his principal? As between *Evans* and the agent, it may be a question, whether the latter kept within the scope of his authority; but as to the rest of the world, it is the same thing whether it be the act of *Evans* or of his agent. It would be strange, if in an action by *Evans* himself he ought to be nonsuited, and that if the action be by the agent, he should recover. The situation of bankers is most peculiar: they are bound to know the hand-writing of their customers. If the law were otherwise, merchants making their bills payable at their bankers, would have this extraordinary advantage, that if a forgery be imposed on their bankers, the principal would not be the sufferer by it; whereas, if it were imposed on themselves, they must bear the loss, and so would exempt themselves from that liability which would rest on them if they themselves transacted their own business.

GIBBS C. J. I concur in opinion with my Brothers *Heath* and *Dallas*. A narrow and particular ground is with me conclusive on this case. If the acceptance had been genuine, and the Plaintiffs had refused payment, the Defendants had their remedy against the supposed acceptor; or if they failed to obtain the
amount

amount from him, they had their remedy against the
prior parties on the bill. The acceptance carried with
it an order on the bankers of the supposed acceptor to
pay the money: it purported to be an order of *Evans*,
whose bankers the Plaintiffs were. It was incumbent
on them to see to the reality of that order before they
obeyed it; and if, by obeying it, they are sufferers,
they ought not to throw on another a loss accruing
without fault of his. See the circumstances! The Defendants present the bill for payment, and it is paid to
them. The money remained in their hands without
demand made on them for it, from the 23d of *April* to
the 30th of *April*: the forgery being then discovered,
the Plaintiffs demand it back from the Defendants. If
the Plaintiffs had originally refused to pay this money,
the holder would immediately have given notice to the
drawer and to the immediate indorser, which would
have been transmitted to the first indorser and drawer.
In consequence of the bill being paid, the Defendants
continued to have the money in their hands till the
30th of *April*. I think it was then too late for the Defendants to give notice to the prior parties; and by not
having given such notice, they lost their remedy against
those parties. If a person liable on a bill does not
receive notice within a reasonable time, he is discharged for want of such notice. Here *Temple* was
discharged: by whose default? By the Plaintiffs'!
the Defendants, while the bill continued paid, could
not have given notice to him; for the bill was not then
dishonoured; and as the Defendants have lost that opportunity by the negligence of the Plaintiffs, the latter
cannot recover back the money from the former. I
have put the case on the express point that by the acts
of the Plaintiffs the Defendants are put in a worse
situation; but I do not mean thereby to express my
dissent from the larger ground on which the case has

G 4   been

1815.
SMITH
v.
MERCER.

been put by my Brothers *Heath* and *Dallas*; but I think the ground on which I have put it is alone a sufficient answer to all the arguments that have been used, and is sufficient to warrant us in giving

Judgment of nonsuit.

Feb. 13.
May 31.

June 730.

TREMAIN *v.* BARRETT.

SAME *v.* FAITH.

If a witness is *bond fide* sent for from a foreign country for the sake of his testimony in an intended action, though the writ is not sued out until after his arrival, the Plaintiff is entitled in that cause to the costs of bringing him over, his subsistence, and compensation for his loss of time spent here pending the suit for the purposes thereof, and to the costs of his return.
But if the

THE Defendant *Faith* was owner of a vessel, which put into *Halifax*, in *Nova Scotia*, and was there repaired by the Plaintiffs. The Defendant *Barrett*, who was the master, gave the Plaintiffs bills for the amount of their charges, drawn on the Defendant *Faith*, in *London*, which the latter refused to accept. The Plaintiffs' agent in this country thereupon, having previously acquainted the Defendant *Faith* that in the event of his non-payment he should be under the necessity of bringing a witness at *Faith*'s cost from *Nova Scotia* to prove the Plaintiffs' case, upon his refusal, in *August* 1814, wrote to the Plaintiffs to send over a witness, *Lee*, who could prove their demand against the Defendant *Faith*, and *Lee* having arrived on the 2d of *November*, for the sole purpose of proving the Plaintiffs' demand, on the following day an action was commenced against *Faith* for work and labour, and materials furnished, and money paid. But the Defendant *Barrett* also having arrived in *England*, the Plaintiffs' agent sued him on the dishonoured bills, for the

witness being sent for to give evidence in one action, the Plaintiff uses his testimony in another action against a different party, and relaxes his diligence in the first, he is entitled in the second action to the costs only of the witnesses' subsistence and detention for the purpose of the second action, but not of his voyage hither, or of his return.

amount,

amount, with exchange, charges, and interest: and apprizing the Defendant *Faith* that it was not intended to press on the first cause, except for the costs, but expediting the last, recovered therein by the testimony of *Lee*, who was a material and necessary witness therein, a verdict against *Barrett*. He afterwards consented to an order to stay proceedings in the action against *Faith*, upon payment of nominal damages and the costs. The prothonotary first taxed for the Plaintiffs their costs in the action against *Barrett*, and allowed them therein the costs of *Lee's* subsistence and detention here, including his expences, and a recompence for his loss of time, and the costs of his return to *Halifax*, but not of his voyage hither.

1815.

TREMAIN
v.
BARRETT.

Vaughan Serjt., in *Hilary* term 1815, moved that the prothonotary might review this taxation, upon the principle which he conceived to be established by the cases of *Schimmell* v. *Lousada* (a), and *Sturdy* v. *Andrews* (b), that if a witness is brought hither from a foreign country before the writ is sued out, though brought *bonâ fide* for the express purpose of the action, in which he is afterwards examined, yet the costs of his return shall not be allowed. *A fortiori*, they ought not to be allowed in this instance, where the witness was brought to this country for the sole purpose of another cause, viz. against *Faith*, between whom and *Barrett* there was no unity of interest. The same reason which shews that the prothonotary ought not to allow the costs of bringing him hither, operates with equal force against allowing the costs of his return. And even if the witness being found here, and examined in the second cause, the costs of his return ought to be allowed, yet, since he was a witness in two causes, only half those costs at the utmost ought to be allowed in this action.

(a) *Ante*, iv. 695.   (b) *Ibid.* 697.

Blosset

Blosset Serjt. shewed cause *instanter:* he urged that the supposed parity of reason would not discharge the Defendant from the costs of the witness's return; for, he contended, that the Plaintiffs were entitled to receive in this cause the costs also of bringing him hither. The question was, whether a person having resolved in his own mind that he has a clear right of action, and that it is clearly necessary to bring a witness from a distant country to prove it, if in sending for him he anticipates the suing out of the writ, is therefore not entitled to his costs of bringing him, and of his return. This is not, as in *Schimmel* v. *Lousada,* a case where a person has brought the witness hither in order to try whether upon examination he could find ground to support an action. *Mansfield* C. J. in that case proceeded upon the supposed result of inquiries into the practice of the Court of King's Bench as to allowing the costs of a witness coming hither (a), and upon a statement that the costs of his coming are not allowed if the witness come before the suit commenced, but that even in that case the costs of his return are allowed in the King's Bench. *Mansfield* C. J. adopted the former part of the practice, but not approving the distinction, rejected the latter, and held that if nothing was allowed for his coming, neither ought any thing to be allowed for his return. But not only does the practice of the King's Bench as to the costs of return, steadily coincide with the practice now adopted by the prothonotary, but even the practice of that Court as to the costs of coming is the contrary of that which is supposed to have been reported hither in *Schimmell* v. *Lousada;* for to a query put in writing to the master of the King's Bench, " if one who hath a clear right of action, and

---

(a) The prothonotary hereupon stated to the Court, that the enquiry to which the master's answer was given in that case, was, whether the costs of coming were to be allowed, when the witness was brought for the purpose of seeing whether the action would lie.

is determined to sue, before action brought, sends for
a witness from abroad in order to support his cause,
whether he is entitled to the costs of bringing over the
witness," the Master answers in writing, that he is.
In the view taken by the prothonotary, the circumstance of the writ being sued out or not, is immaterial,
for there are many matters necessary to the ultimate
success of the cause, the costs whereof are allowed,
though they are incurred before the writ sued out, as
the preparing of affidavits, of a special declaration, and
perhaps even of the brief for trial; so, of the warrant
of attorney, and of a special original.   Many of the
former distinctions on this subject are now done away.
It formerly was laid down as a general rule, that no
costs of a witness could in any case be allowed, except
for the time during which he was within the reach of a
subpœna.   *Thellusson* v. *Staples*.   *Hagedorn* v. *Allnutt* (a), was one of those anomalous cases.

1815.

TREMAIN
v.
BARRETT.

GIBBS J. observed, that the practice of the Court
of King's Bench as to the costs of the witnesses'
return, was clearly ascertained to be such as was
contended for the Plaintiffs.   The reporter of the
decision in *Schimmell* v. *Losada*, had omitted there to
state one part of the practice in such a case in the
Court of King's Bench, namely, that in that Court the
costs of his return were given.   Their practice was certified to be, that there the costs of bringing a witness
over were not to be allowed, the costs of his detention
were to be allowed, and the costs of his return were to
be allowed; but the Plaintiffs were met by the decision
in this Court, that the costs of sending back the witness
are not here to be given.   This action against *Faith*
for money paid is wholly a different action from the
action against *Barrett* on the bills of exchange.   While
the witness is here, the Plaintiffs, finding *Barrett* here,
sue him on the bills, on which they could not sue *Faith*,

(a) *Ante,* iii. 379.

my / 30

who had not accepted them, and they use the witness who is here, as a witness in that action. The difference between the case of *Schimmell* v. *Lousada* and this case, is, that there the witness was brought for the purpose of that action; here the witness was not brought over with a view to this action against *Barrett*, who was accidentally here, but with a view to the action against *Faith*. The rule therefore must be absolute for the prothonotary to review his taxation, and he must grant costs for the detention of the witness here for the purpose of this action for a reasonable time, which is, (to use the language of the late Chief Justice,) " from the time of its commencement," pending the action, and certainly until the witness could reasonably get out of the country again, but not of his return.

Rule absolute.

In the action against *Faith* the prothonotary afterwards, upon an affidavit that *Lee* was a material and necessary witness in the cause, and the only person who could prove certain of the facts, and that he was expressly sent for, for the purpose of that cause, allowed the Plaintiffs the costs of his voyage to *England*, of his subsistence and detention here, (except of such time for which he had awarded the Plaintiffs the costs of his subsistence and detention in the action against *Barrett*,) and of his voyage back; considering that as the Plaintiff had a clear ground for this action, and had sent for the witness for the express purpose of bringing it, not of judging, (upon which circumstance *Mansfield* C. J. appeared, as well by the report (a) as by a note of that case taken by the prothonotary himself, to have supported the opposite practice in *Schimmell* v. *Lousada*,) whether an action could be brought on his testimony, there was a material distinction between the two cases in that respect.

(a) *Ante,* iv. 695.

Vaughan

Vaughan Serjt. in *Easter* term moved that the prothonotary might review his taxation in the action against *Faith*, contending upon the authority of *Schimmell* v. *Lousada*, and *Sturdy* v. *Andrews*, that inasmuch as the witness was sent for, and landed in this country before the writ was sued out, the costs of his coming and of his return ought not to be allowed, and there was no precedent wherein that practice had prevailed.

GIBBS C. J. It appears that the prothonotary has allowed nothing here, which has been, or could be allowed in any other quarter. If there be a strict and rigid rule that nothing shall be allowed in the costs of a witness who is sent for, for the purposes of a cause, unless the writ is sued out before he is sent for, then, indeed, the prothonotary must review his taxation. We decided the case of *Schimmell* v. *Lousada*, principally on an apprehension that there was a strict and rigid rule in the Court of King's Bench, that nothing was ever allowed for the coming of a witness previously to the writ being sued out; but the prothonotary states to us, that he has spoken to the master in that Court, who does say, that under such circumstances he should have no difficulty in allowing those costs. We think, however, the Defendant may have a rule to shew cause, because the case of *Schimmell* v. *Lousada* seems, as now reported, to run counter to our inclination. Upon the discussion of the case of *Tremain* v. *Barrett*, last term, and upon a note which we received from one of the Judges of the Court at that time, we were induced to doubt whether the rule was exactly that which was proceeded on in the case of *Schimmell* v. *Lousada*, as it is represented in the printed report; and therefore the case should be heard, and time should be taken for making enquiry into the practice of the Court of King's Bench in such case.

Rule *nisi*.

On

1815.   On this day *Gibbs* C. J. reported the practice of the
           Court of King's Bench to coincide with that which
TREMAIN   the prothonotary had in the present instance adopted,
  v.
BARRETT.   and the

                                              Rule was discharged.

Feb. 6.   HENRY GRETTON, ISAAC ANDREWS, JANE HA-
6 868 - 871. 877.   WARD, and GEORGE HAWARD, JAMES HAWARD,
            EDWARD HAWARD, ANN HAWARD, and JANE
Add 948.   HAWARD the Younger, Infants, Plaintiffs;

                              AND

      ELIZABETH HAWARD, GEORGE GARDNER, WIL-
      LIAM HAWARD the Younger, BENJAMIN PAGE,
      WILLIAM WATSON, and ROBERT LANGLEY
      APPLEYARD, Defendants.

Devise to my   THIS was a case directed for the opinion of the
wife *A.* of all   Judges of this Court by Sir *William Grant*, M. R.
my real and   the material parts whereof were as follows:
personal estate,
she first paying   *Searle Edward Haward*, being at the respective times
my just debts   of making his will, and of his death, seised in fee of
and funeral ex-
pences; and   certain freehold messuages at *Charing Cross* and in *Saint*
after her de-   *Martin's Lane, Middlesex*, made his will, bearing date
cease to the
heirs of her   the 18th of *June* 1747, duly executed to, pass freehold
body, share   estates, in the following terms: " I give, devise, and
and share alike   bequeath unto my loving wife *Ann Haward*, all my
if more than
one; and in   real and personal estate of what nature or kind soever,
default of issue   she first paying all my just debts and funeral expences,
to be lawfully
begotten by   and after her decease to the heirs of her body, share
me, to be at   and share alike if more than one, and in default of issue
her own dis-   to be lawfully begotten by me, to be at her own disposal: there
being children   posal;" and he appointed his wife his sole executrix
of the testator
and his wife, held, that the w fe took only an estate for life, with remainder to all
the children as tenants in common in fee.

                                                      and

and residuary legatee. The testator died in 1776, without having revoked or altered his will, leaving *Ann Ha-*
ward his widow, and six children by her, him surviving,
viz. Edward Haward his eldest child, *Ann Haward* the
younger, afterwards *Ann Gardner,* mother of the Defendant *George Gardner,* his second child, the Defendant *Elizabeth Haward* his third child, *William Haward,*
the father of the infant Plaintiffs and of the Defendant
William Haward the younger, his fourth child, *Franois
Haward* his fifth child, and *James Haward* his sixth
child. · *Ann Haward* the widow, upon the death of the
testator, entered into possession of his freehold estates
by virtue of the said devise thereof to her, and continued in the receipt of the rents and profits thereof until
her death. On the 8th of *September* 1807 *Ann Haward*
the widow, by deed of that date, covenanted to levy a
fine *sur conusance de droit come ceo* of the premises, and
such fine was duly levied accordingly as of *Trinity* term
47th *Geo.* 3., and proclamations were duly made thereon; and the fine was, by that deed, declared to enure
to such uses as she the said *Ann Haward* should by
deed or will, signed and published in the presence of
and attested by three or more credible witnesses, limit
or appoint, and in default of, and subject to such limitation or appointment, to the use of herself for life,
sans waste, with remainder to the use of *William Haward* her son, *Elizabeth Haward* her daughter, and
George Gardner her grandson, as tenants in common,
in fee. That fine was passed, and the deed to lead the
uses thereof was executed by the said *Ann Haward*
without the knowledge or consent of *W. Haward* the
son. *Ann Haward* the widow, after the death of *Wm.
Haward* the son, who died in 1809, by her will, dated
the 7th of *August* 1809, signed and published by her in
the presence of and attested by three credible witnesses,
directed, limited, and appointed that the estate devised
to

to her by the will of the testator *S. E. Haward* should thenceforth be and remain, and that the indenture and fine before stated should enure, as to one moiety of parcel of the premises, to the use of her grandson the said *George Gardner*, his heirs and assigns; and as to the remaining moiety of that parcel to the use of *Benjamin Page*, *William Watson*, and *Robert Langley Appleyard*, their heirs and assigns; and as to the residue of the premises, to the use of her daughter the Defendant *Elizabeth Haward*, her heirs and assigns for ever. *Ann Haward* died on the 10th day of *February* 1810, without having revoked or altered her said will, leaving the Defendant *Elizabeth Haward* her daughter and only remaining child, and the Defendant *William Haward* the younger, her grandson, and heir at law as well to her, as to the said *S. E. Haward*, and the infant Plaintiffs, who were also her grandchildren by her son *William Haward*, and the Defendant *George Gardner*, her only other grandchild, her surviving. Upon the decease of the said *Ann Haward*, the said *Elizabeth Haward*, and *George Gardner*, and the said *Robert Langley Appleyard*, on behalf of himself and the said *Benjamin Page* and *William Watson*, respectively entered upon the estate and premises late of the testator *S. E. Haward*, and have ever since received the rents and profits thereof, claiming to be entitled thereto, or to certain parts or proportions thereof respectively, under or by virtue of the will of the said *Ann Haward.* This bill was filed by the Plaintiffs, who were devisees of the said *William Haward* the son, against the devisees named in the will of the said *Ann Haward*, and against *William Haward* the younger, the heir at law, insisting that under *S. E. Haward's* will, she the said *Ann Haward* took only an estate for life in the devised estates, with remainder to the heirs of her body as tenants in common, either in tail, or for life only, ex-

10*   'pectant

pectant upon her decease, and that in either case, whether the respective interests of her children were to be
estates tail in their several shares, or estates for life
only, still *W. Haward* the son, as the heir at law of his
father, the testator *S. E. Haward*, must have taken the
ultimate remainder or reversion in fee in all the shares,
and consequently must have been absolutely entitled to
his own one-sixth part or share devised to him, and to
the shares of such others of the said testator's children
as died without issue in his lifetime. The Defendants,
on the contrary, insisted that the said *Ann Haward*
took an estate tail under the testator's, *S. E. Haward's,*
will, and a question was made between them whether
or not the fine levied by her was effectual to bar that
estate tail; the infant Defendant *William Haward* the
heir at law contending that the said *Ann Haward* took
such estate tail by the gift of her husband, and was
therefore incapable of barring it; and that by force of
the stat. 11th *Hen.* 7. *c.* 20., the fine levied by her was
void. The other Defendant on the contrary contended
that the fine was good, and claimed under the deed declaring the uses thereof, and under the said *Ann Haward's*
will. The questions for the opinion of this Court were,
1st, What estate *Ann Haward* the widow took under
the will of *S. E. Haward* her late husband? 2d, In
case she took an estate tail in the premises devised to
her by her husband's will, whether she did by any fine,
deed, or instrument bar such estate? 3d, In case she
took an estate for life, or an estate tail, and did not bar
the same, then what estate each of her children took
under *S. E. Haward's* will?

   Best Serjt. for the Plaintiffs, who were the devisees
under the will of *William Haward* the son, admitted
that the charge for payment of debts which accompanied the devise to the widow *Ann Haward* would

1815.

GRETTON
v.
HAWARD.

have given her a fee simple, had it not been qualified by the succeeding devise " to the heirs of her body, share and share alike if more than one;" but by those words the devise to her was restricted to a life estate. The words " heirs of the body" might be used either as words of limitation, or of purchase; and in the present instance, they were used as words of purchase, and the terms of the devise, " all my estate," vested in the children an estate in fee simple as tenants in common, expectant on their mother's decease. *Bailis* v. *Gale* (a). The doctrine that heirs of the body might be words of purchase, was recognized by Lord *Hardwicke* in the case of *Bagshaw* v. *Spencer* (b), and by the Court of King's Bench in *Doe, on the demise of Long,* v. *Laming* (c), and *Doe, on the demise of Strong,* v. *Goffe* (d). The words " share and share alike," found in this devise, indicate a clear intention that the eldest issue should not take all, but that the estate should be equally divided amongst all the children, and are therefore inconsistent with an estate tail. Besides the numerous authorities fully considered in *Doe* v. *Goffe,* the case of *Doe, on demise of Gillman,* v. *Elvey* (e), is an authority not only that " issue of the body" might take as purchasers, but that the words " his, her, or their heirs, equally to be divided if more than one," convey an estate in fee to the children as tenants in common. The final clause too, " and in default of issue lawfully begotten by me, to be at her own disposal," shew by the strongest inference, that if the wife had issue by the testator, the land was not to be at her disposal.

Lens Serjt., on behalf of the Defendants *Elizabeth Haward,* and of *Page, Watson,* and *Appleyard,* the de-

(a) 2 *Ves.* 48.
(b) 1 *Ves.* 142.
(c) 2 *Burr.* 1100.

(d) 11 *East,* 668.
(e) 4 *East,* 313.

visees

visees under the will of *Ann Haward* (a), contended that *Ann Haward* the widow took by the devise in her husband's will an estate tail; that she had barred the remainder in tail by her fine, and had well appointed the premises to those Defendants whom he represented. The words " share and share alike," on which the Plaintiffs rely, have in many cases been made to give way to a general intent of the testator, and an estate tail has been decreed notwithstanding them. Lord *Ellenborough* C. J. acknowledges the will in the case of *Doe* v. *Goffe* to be very singular, therefore it establishes no precedent for other cases. In the case of *Doe, d. Candler,* v. *White* (b), a particular intention, though clearly expressed, was made to give way to the general intent of the testator, and the words, " heirs of her body lawfully to be begotten for ever, as tenants in common, and not as joint tenants," did not prevent the ancestor from taking an estate tail. In the case of *Doe* (c), on *demise of Cock,* v. *Cooper,* Lord *Kenyon* C. J. observed, that the general intent of the testator that all the issue of the devisee should inherit before the estate went over, could be fulfilled only by construing the devise to give an estate tail to the first devisee, though there was expressly given him only a life estate, and after his decease to his issue as tenants in common. *Pierson* v. *Vickers* (d) is to the same effect. *Doe* v. *Goffe* does not militate against this construction, for Lord *Ellenborough* C. J. expressly determines the case on the particular circumstances, guarding his judgment by declaring that the decision will not break in upon any of the cases there cited.

(a) *Shepherd,* Solicitor General, appeared for the Defendant *George Gardner,* whose case and question being identical with those of the other defendants, only *Lens* was heard on that side.
(b) 7 T. R. 341.
(c) 1 East, 229.
(d) 5 East, 548.

Secondly,

Secondly, if the widow *Ann Haward* did take an estate tail, she had barred it by her fine, notwithstanding the stat. 11 *H.* 7. *c.* 20., which speaks of the cases, where a woman hath any estate in tail to herself, or to her use, in any hereditaments of the inheritance or purchase of her husband, or given to the husband and wife in tail by any of the ancestors of the husband, or by any other person seised to the use of the husband, or of his ancestors. This statute is confirmed by the stat. 32 *H.* 8. *c.* 36. *s.* 2. This act was made for the protection of the husband; it does not apply to the case where the husband, after marriage, by devise gives an estate to commence after his own decease; nor, as a husband could not at common law convey any estate directly to his wife, could the statute apply to any other than cases of a provision made by the husband before marriage. The disposition too, which the testator has enabled his widow in certain events to make of this estate, is wholly beside the purpose of this statute. In the case of *Foster* v. *Pitfall* (a), it was held that a devise by the husband to the wife in tail, though within the words, was not within the intent of this statute, the meaning of which was, that the wife should not prejudice the heirs of the baron, that the land should not descend to them. *Hughs* v. *Clubb* (b) is a similar decision. *Bro. Abr.* (c) A devise of land by the husband to the wife by his will is not pleadable in bar of dower, for it is a benevolence, and not a jointure, which note, by all the justices; and 6 *Ed.* 6. is cited. This decision is recognized by Lord *Coke* (d), and *Dyer.* (e)

As to the third question, the counsel for all the Defendants agreed that if the widow took only a life estate,

(a) *Cro. El.* 2. S. C. 1 *Leon.* 261.
(b) *Com* 369.
(c) *Bro. Abr.*, *Dower*, 69.

(d) *Vernon's* case, 4 *Co.* 4.
(e) Between *Dennis* and *Statham*, 248.

the

the children of the testator *S. E. Haward* took estates in fee in common.

Blosset Serjt., for the Defendant *Wm. Hayward,* the heir at law of the testator *S. E. Haward,* and of the widow *Ann Haward,* and of three of their sons who had died intestate and without issue, being the eldest son of their eldest son *William,* contended first, that for the reason stated by *Lens,* the widow took an estate tail, and that her fine was inoperative. 'In furtherance of the first of these positions he urged that this was an estate in tail special, viz. to the heirs of her body begotten by the testator *S. E. Haward,* which materially distinguished this case from those cited by *Lens* on the 2d point. The distinction taken between *Doe* v. *Goffe* and *Doe* v. *Cooper* is the material distinction which has governed all the cases, viz. that in the case of *Doe* v. *Goffe,* the event on which the estate is to go over, is not in default of such issue, but if such issue shall depart this life under 21 years; it is quite consistent with this provision, that the word heirs may mean children, and upon the death of some, their shares may consistently go to the others. *Doe* v. *Laming* is entirely consistent with *Doe* v. *Goffe.* He also cited *Counden* v. *Clerke (a).* In *Doe* v. *Elvey,* the question was not, whether the first taker took an estate for life or in tail, but whether the limitation over was a contingent remainder or an executory devise, and the Court, in awarding the postea to the Plaintiff, say, it is immaterial whether the first taker took for life or in tail. As to the 2d point, it was apparent that the sole intent of the statute was to protect the issue in tail of the marriage, so that it might not be in the power of the wife to prevent the land from descending to them. When the statute first passed, it applied, in-

(a) *Hob.* 29.

H 3

deed,

deed, to fewer cases than now exist, but as the new cases arose, of estates tail created by devise of the husband, and otherwise, the statute applied to them. The case in *Bro. Abr.* arose on a question of dower, which is governed by another statute, viz. 27 *H.* 8. *c.* 10. and arose too upon a gift by a stranger to the husband and wife jointly, which, as it was held in (a) *Ward* v. *Walthew,* is not a jointure within the statute 11 *H.* 7. If any of the cases cited are of devises in tail by a husband, the distinction is, that they are devises to the wife in tail general. It cannot be contended that a devise by the husband for the benefit of the issue of any future husband, is a provision for the issue of his own marriage; but in this case the devise is in tail special, which can be beneficial to his own issue only, and to such cases the statute applies. There is no ground for the distinction taken between a devise and any other form of conveyance. The case of *Hughs* v. *Clubb* is very material for this construction; for *Pratt* C. J. determined that "the intent of the statute extends only to cases where the husband settles lands on his wife by way of jointure, to which the issue between them shall be inheritable," and the statute takes notice of a sole estate in the wife, as well as of a jointure.

Best, in reply, mainly relied on the judgment of the Court of King's Bench in *Doe* v. *Goffe.* In that case, as in this, the testator's main intent was, that his children should be provided for, which could be effectuated only by giving his wife an estate for life, not by giving her an estate tail, which would enable her to alienate the property from his children. The principal case materially differs from those cited for the Defendants. If there are children of the testator at any time of the widow's life, her power of disposition over the fee is

(a) *Cro. Jac.* 174.

gone,

gone, the estate vests in the children in fee, and does not remain subject to her appointment in favour of any children whom the widow may have by any other husband. As to the second point, the words of the stat. 11 H. 7. are large enough to embrace not only the modes of conveyance known at the time of passing that statute, but any which have been subsequently invented or created. The words of the statute " aliene, release or confirm with warranty," apply to all species of alienation; and though alienation by will was not then known, yet this is a case within the mischief, and the sound way of interpreting all statutes, is to expound them so as to comprehend all mischiefs that are within their scope. *Hard.* 211. " Things constituted *de novo* have often been construed to be within the meaning of former laws," and he cites several instances, (a) and the Court adjudge accordingly. If therefore the widow took an estate tail, her power of barring it was restrained by the statute, because the entail was special. The case of *Hughs* v. *Clubb,* and the case in *Cro. El.* and 1 *Leon.* were both cases of tail general, and decide nothing on this case, which is of an estate in tail special *ex provisione viri,* for whether it be created by devise or otherwise, is immaterial, and that point is never mooted in either of the decided cases, although it must have been sufficiently obvious.

1815.

GRETTON
v.
HAWARD.

Cur. adv. vult.

The Court afterwards sent to the Master of the Rolls the following certificate:

WE have heard this case argued by counsel, and are of opinion,

1st, That *Ann Haward* the widow took under the will of *Serle Edward Haward* her late husband an

(a) 12 *Eliz. Dyer,* 288. b. 19.; *Bro. Parliament, pl.* 40. and *Bishop of Durham's case,* 12 H. 7. *Plow. Com.* 467.

H 4

estate

estate for life only in the devised premises, and consequently the second question proposed does not arise.

3d, That each of her six children took under the said will a fee simple in remainder expectant upon his mother's life estate, in one undivided sixth part of the said premises, as tenant in common with the other five children."

V. GIBBS.
J. HEATH.
A. CHAMBRE.
R. DALLAS.

END OF HILARY TERM.

CASES

ARGUED and DETERMINED

IN THE

Court of COMMON PLEAS,

AND

OTHER COURTS,

IN

Easter Term,

In the Fifty-fifth Year of the Reign of George III.

Ex parte Corpus Christi College. *April 12.*

BEST Serjt. in the last term moved that Mr. *Fry*; an attorney, who had been employed as the steward of *Corpus Christi* College, *Oxford*, might pay over the sum of 260*l.* of rents which he had received for their use, and might deliver over the court-rolls of the manor of *North Grove*, and all muniments and papers, with costs. The Court, after some hesitation as to their jurisdiction to order the payment of money, granted a rule *nisi* to the whole extent prayed: the rule was drawn

The Court will entertain a summary jurisdiction over one of its officers who is employed as steward of a manor, to make him deliver up court-rolls and muniments of his employer.

And also, as it seems, to compel him to pay over rents received.

An attorney holding over rents received, is not compellable to pay interest on them. *Semble.*

up

up in terms which required that he should pay interest
also on the sums detained.   He had since paid over
the money, but had not paid the costs or interest:
wherefore *Best* now moved to make the rule absolute
as to the residue of the relief prayed.

Per Curiam.   We cannot make Mr. *Fry* pay interest,
nor, according to modern decisions, is it due to him,
and the rule ought not to have been drawn up for payment of interest: but if he does not shew cause, he
must pay the costs.

April 15.   STEVENS *v.* JACKSON.

If a sheriff's
officer, having
arrested a De-
fendant on
mesne process
in his own
house, who is
dangerously
ill, leaves him
there in the
custody of a
follower not
named in the
warrant, until
he is recover-
ed, this is such
a legal custody,
that if an im-
prisonment, of
which this is a
part, be con-
tinued for two
months, it will
constitute an
act of bank-
ruptcy.

THIS was an action brought by the Plaintiff for the
    purpose of trying the validity of a commission of
bankrupt which had issued against him, dated on the
28th of *October;* and at the sittings after *Hilary* term
1815, before *Gibbs* C. J. at *Guildhall,* a verdict was
found for the Defendant, which

   Shepherd, Solicitor-General, now moved to set aside,
upon the ground that the facts proved did not amount
to an act of bankruptcy, which the Plaintiff was
supposed to have committed by lying in prison more
than two months.   The evidence was, that a warrant
having issued, on mesne process, directing *Withers* and
Weldon, two sheriff's officers, to arrest the Plaintiff,
Withers found him in his house dangerously ill, and incapable of being removed to a place of closer custody:
he left the Plaintiff there under the care of *Jones* and
Bretton, two of his followers, with whom the warrant
was left, and who during that time usually had the key

of

of the Plaintiff's house, but sometimes the Plaintiff's own maid-servant had it: after some weeks, the Plaintiff having recovered, was on the 3d of *September* removed, first to a lock-up-house, and thence afterwards to the *Fleet* prison. *Shepherd* objected, first, that *Withers* could not delegate the power of imprisonment to *Jones* and *Bretton*, and that therefore, during the time the Plaintiff was in his own house, he was not in prison; and that as only 55 days had elapsed between the time of his being conducted to the lock-up-house, and the date of the commission, the commission was premature. It was not necessary, he said, to contend that the circumstances amounted to an escape, it sufficed if the Plaintiff had not been continually for two months in legal custody. In the case of *Benton* v. *Sutton* (a), *Eyre* C. J. takes the distinction between the custody of a sheriff's officer and of his follower, though he is not supported therein by either of the other three Judges. There may be cases where humanity requires that the Defendant shall not be instantly removed, but the person left to detain him, must be legally authorized so to do. The warrant to *Withers* and *Weldon* was no authority to *Jones* and *Bretton*. But, at all events, during those times when the Plaintiff's own servant had the key of the house, he was not in legal custody.

GIBBS C. J. One consequence of this doctrine would be, that if a sheriff's officer, having a prisoner in a lock-up-house, should go out and leave the key of his house with his own servant, the prisoner, though continuing in the officer's house, would have escaped. I cannot help thinking this was a legal custody. The warrant certainly would not have authorized *Jones* and *Bretton*

(a) 1 *Bos. & Pull.* 24.

to

to arrest the Plaintiff; but he being arrested, they were sufficiently authorized to detain him. And see who it is that is insisting on the want of authority. The infant bankrupt himself, who has benefited by the officer's humanity!

HEATH J. There is nothing in the point. The Plaintiff was carried to prison in convenient time. Even if he had been a prisoner taken in execution, the circumstances would not have amounted to an escape.

The rest of the Court concurring,

The Rule was refused.

B N C 112

37

LAING v. FIDGEON.

In every contract to furnish manufactured goods, however low the price, it is an implied term that the goods shall be merchantable.

A contract to furnish goods, with a certain latitude as to the price, as saddles at 24l. a 26s. may be described as a contract to furnish them at a reasonable price.

THE Plaintiff declared that in consideration that he would buy of the Defendant divers goods, to wit, (amongst other articles,) 48 saddles, at and for reasonable prices, to be paid by the Plaintiff to the Defendant; the Defendant undertook to sell and deliver to the Plaintiff such quantity of such goods of a good and merchantable quality, and to charge fair and reasonable prices for the same, and averred a breach that the goods delivered were not of a good and merchantable quality. Upon the trial of the cause at *Guildhall* at the sittings after *Hilary* term 1815, before *Gibbs* C. J. the evidence was, that the Defendant having previously sent to the Plaintiff a sample of the saddles that could be furnished at the price aftermentioned, the Plaintiff gave him an order for " goods for *North America*, 3 dozen single flap

16   saddles,

saddles, 24*s.* a 26*s.*, with cruppers, &c." It was proved that the saddles delivered were of very inferior materials and workmanship, and useless and unmerchantable, and they did not correspond with the sample. After verdict for the Plaintiff,

Vaughan Serjt. now moved to set it aside and have a new trial, upon the ground of a variance between the contract averred and the contract proved: for that, first, there was no proof of any contract that the goods should be merchantable; and the price fixed being so low that a good saddle could not be made for that money, the Plaintiff was thereby sufficiently apprized what species of goods he was to expect: there was no warranty in fact, and the law did not, under these circumstances, imply a warranty that the goods were merchantable. In respect to the price, he urged that the proof was, of a contract to sell them at a price varying from 24*s.* to 26*s.*, without reference to the question, whether that price were reasonable; and a reasonable price might much exceed 26*s.* The Plaintiff ought to have declared on a contract to furnish them at 24*s.* or 26*s.*

The Court held, that as to the first objection, although there was no express contract that the article should be merchantable, it resulted from the whole transaction that the article was to be merchantable: the Defendant might have rejected the order, but having accepted it, he ought to furnish a merchantable article. It was objected to the form of the declaration, that it averred a contract to sell at a reasonable price, but that the evidence proved a contract to sell at a stated price. Looking at the order, the Court thought it was not a contract to sell at a stated sum, but at a

price

1815.   price near about those sums; and that it might well be
LAING   described as a reasonable price; and they
  v.   Refused to grant a Rule.
FIDGEON.

April 15.   WILKINSON and Others, Assignees of GWYNNE,
                    a Bankrupt, *v.* CLAY and Others.

If an insurance   THIS was an action for money had and received.
broker debit   Upon the trial of the cause, at *Guildhall*, at the
the under-
writer with a   sittings after *Hilary* term 1815, before *Gibbs* C. J., it
loss, and take   appeared that the Defendants were insurance brokers,
his acceptance
for the balance and had effected for *Gwynne*, who had since become a
of account be-   bankrupt, a policy on the ship *Harriet*, which *Aguilar*,
tween broker
and under-   an underwriter, had subscribed for 500*l.*, and had
writer, pay-   adjusted a total loss thereon; he had not paid the
able at a later money to the Defendants, and his name, though struck
date than the
time when the   off the policy, still remained on the adjustment; but in
loss would be   an account which was current between him and the
payable in
cash, the as-   defendants, the defendants had debited him with the
sured may   amount of this loss, and had with *Gwynne's* know-
maintain an   ledge drawn a bill on him at three months' date, payable
action against
the broker for   to their own order, for 419*l.* 1*s.*, being the general
money had and   balance due to them upon their own account with him,
received.   in which account this debit of 500*l.* was included.
  Though the   The usual period for payment of a loss on a policy is
acceptance was   one month after adjustment. *Aguilar* having become
dishonoured,   a bankrupt, this bill was not paid; and the Defendants
and the broker
never received   proved the then balance of their account, 308*l.* 3*s.*, under
any money.   his commission, and received a dividend thereon which
                 they paid over to the Plaintiffs, who now brought this
                 action for the residue. The jury found a verdict for
                 the Plaintiffs, which

                                                            Best

Best Serjt. now moved to set aside, insisting, first, that as the defendants had never received the money from *Aguilar*, they were not liable for it to the assured; but he, whose name still continued on the policy, or rather on the adjustment, was the person liable; Secondly, that as the Defendants had obtained an acceptance only, and not money, the action for money had and received could not be sustained.

1815.

WILKINSON
v.
CLAY.

The Court held, that inasmuch as there was a loss settled with the underwriter, and a bill of exchange at three months' date accepted for the balance, at a time when the assured was entitled to immediate payment, which was at a month, the Defendants thereby tied up *Gwynne's* hands, which they had no right to do. It was said they took the bill for *Gwynne's* benefit, but if so, they should have transferred the bill to him. The last objection was disposed of in the case of *Andrew* v. *Robinson* (a), cited at the trial.

Rule refused.

(a) 3 *Camp.* 199.

ROGERS *v.* DALLIMORE.

April 16.

IN this cause the Plaintiff had sued out his writ for the purpose of having a cause in court on which to ground an order of reference, and a judge's order to refer having been obtained, the arbitrator in *August* 1814 made his award for 41*l.* in favor of the Plaintiff. He

The Court is not limited by time from setting aside an award founded on a submission by rule of Court in an action pending, where there has been a plain mistake of the arbitrator, although the application be not made in the term next after the making of the award.

But in ordinary cases they will look to the limitation of time given by the stat. 9 & 10 *W. & M. c.* 15. as a rule to guide their discretion as to the time of reviewing awards.

after-

afterwards discovered that he had made a numerical mistake, and that the sum he ought to have awarded was 61l., and he apprized the parties by letter of this mistake, and requested the Defendant to rectify it; upon whose refusal Lens Serjeant was in last *Michael-mas* term instructed to move to set aside the award, but the order of reference not having then been made a rule of Court, he deferred the motion; that rule having been afterwards gotten, he obtained in *Hilary* term last a rule for setting aside the award upon this palpable mistake of the arbitrator.

Best Serjt., in shewing cause against this rule, took a preliminary objection, that the application was too late, for that it ought to have been made in the term next following after the making of the award. The case of *Synge, Executor,* v. *Jervoise* (a), where the Court of King's Bench set aside an award made on an order of reference at *nisi prius,* upon an application in the second term, is but a loose case, but at all events it extends only to orders of reference made at *nisi prius,* and not to other orders of the Judges. The preamble of the statute 9 & 10 *W.* 3. *c.* 15. extends to all references made under any rule of Court; and the jurisdiction which the Court has to set aside awards, is given by that act, and is confined to the period of time therein limited. If the Court does not derive its jurisdiction from that statute, it has no jurisdiction over the subject; for, before that act, the only remedy for any person aggrieved by an award was to file a bill in equity, and if there be any cases not within the statute, that is still the only remedy. It has invariably been considered that the time for setting aside awards is thus limited, and that all these cases were within the statute; *Zachary* v. *Shepherd* (b); and if within the statute, the Plaintiff is too late.

     (a) 8 *East,* 466.   (b) 2 *Term Rep.* 781.

Lens,

Best, in support of his rule, urged that the practice had not been invariable, for the latest case gave a longer time. *Zachary* v. *Shepherd* was inapplicable, for the question there was, whether the operation of the statute was not confined to cases of corruption and undue influence, and it leaves the present question untouched. There was no pretence to say that before the statute, the relief against awards, was confined to suit in equity. This act defines in what particular cases awards made by virtue of that statute only shall be set aside, but it says nothing of other cases. It is confined to cases of corruption; and all the power of the Court to set aside awards upon any other ground, is derived from another source. The Court may refer to the statute, as a rule to guide their discretion in the time of setting aside awards which are not within the act, but they will not adopt it as a positive rule. In this case there is no inconvenience in enlarging the time, for the rule of Court was not obtained till long after the award was made, and the Plaintiff, who as yet has levied nothing, makes this application in his own delay. *Anderson* v. *Coxeter* (a) is treated too lightly, in saying it is not law. It is not decided in *Synge* v. *Jervoise* that references under rules of *nisi prius* are the only cases not comprehended within the statute; but only that they are one exception, any other order of a judge stands on the same foundation as an order of reference at *nisi prius*. No order of a judge, unless made a rule of Court, is a ground of attachment. It is an inaccurate expression to say that an award is made under a judge's order, for in fact it is to the subsequent rule of Court, that it owes all its authority. In *Dubois* v. *Medlycott* (b), it was urged that " the submission being by bond, per statute 9 & 10 *W.* 3. no objection to the award can be made after

(a) 1 Str. 301.   (b) Barnes, 45.

the first term; evidently pointing to the distinction, that if it had been a submission in an action, the motion could have been entertained. And the Court there decide consonantly to the effect which would be obtained by the distinction contended for.

GIBB's C. J. delivered the opinion of the Court.

The Court by no means intend to hold out to parties that applications to set aside awards founded on references which are not made by bond, will be received at any time whatsoever; on the contrary, we think, that in most cases the Court would regulate the exercise of its discretion by the same rule which is prescribed by the stat. of *W.* & *M.* with respect to cases that come under that act; but we do not think that this and similar cases are within the act: we think it does not apply to awards made under the authority of a rule of court made in an action pending. For those awards under orders of *nisi prius*, or of a judge at chambers, derive their authority only from the rule of court which is afterwards made, and therefore they are awards under rules of court. It has been urged for the Defendant, that the Court has no jurisdiction to set aside awards, except under the statute, and that if the Plaintiff applies under the statute, he is out of time. We think otherwise, and that the rule of court which gives superintendance to the arbitrator, gives also to the Court a superintendance over that award, and that the Court have that authority in the present case. The question then is, whether in our discretion we shall interpose in the present instance, this being a case in which it would be too late to apply, if the relief depended on the statute of *W.* & *M.* The merits are clear. The arbitrator himself says he made a mistake, and should have given 61*l.* instead of 41*l.* The counsel for the Plaintiff was instructed to move sooner, but from some circumstance,

　　　　　he

he did not. We think therefore this is a case in which the Court ought to interpose, and consequently the rule must be made absolute, either to set aside the award, or what would be better, to send back the case to the same arbitrator, or to amend the award by altering it to 61*l.* We act on the authority of the case in the King's Bench, supported by that case in *Strange* on which the authority of the former is founded, and we also think that the case in *Barnes* is an authority to the same effect.

Best consented to make the rule absolute to amend the award, by increasing the sum awarded from 41*l.* to 61*l.* without further expence.

Rule absolute.

1815.

ROGERS
v.
DALLIMORE

SMITH *v.* PATTEN.

April 19.

THE Plaintiff's attorney had addressed a letter to the Defendant by the name of *Joseph Patten*, which the Defendant answered, promising payment of the debt, and not complaining of any misnomer: the Plaintiff sued him by the same name, and served him with a notice of declaration, entered an appearance for him, signed interlocutory judgment, and executed a writ of enquiry, the Defendant during these proceedings remaining wholly passive, and having done no other act to countenance them.

Where a Defendant, sued by a wrong name, omits to plead in abatement, and suffers the Plaintiff to proceed to judgment, though he never has appeared to the wrong name, this Court will not interfere to set aside the proceedings.

Best Serjt. had on a former day in this term obtained a rule *nisi* to set aside all these proceedings on the ground that they were a nullity, the Defendant's real

I 2   name.

name being *John* and not *Joseph*; he cited *Greenslade* v. *Prothero.* (a)

Vaughan Serjt. now shewed cause against this rule, relying on the fact that the Defendant had misled the Plaintiff by not noticing the misnomer in the letter addressed to him.

Best, in support of his rule, relied on *Cole* v. *Hindson* (b), distinguishing between a mere irregularity in process, which would not make a sheriff who executed it a trespasser, and a process totally void, as he contended this was; and that therefore laches was in this case no waver.

The Court did not adopt the argument that the Defendant by not noticing the misnomer had misled the Plaintiff, but they decided on the ground that the Defendant might have pleaded the misnomer in abatement, and that not having availed himself of that opportunity, he could not now come to set aside the proceedings. It would be of the worst consequence, if defendants should be permitted, instead of pleading in abatement, to lie by and increase expences, and then to move to set aside the proceedings; they therefore refused to interfere, and

Discharged the rule with costs.

(a) 2 *New Rep.* 132.   (b) 6 *Term Rep.* 234.

(IN THE EXCHEQUER-CHAMBER.)

MITCHELL v. MINIKEN.

April 19.

GASELEE moved for interest on the affirmance in error of a judgment, which the Plaintiff had obtained in an action brought to recover the produce of stock, which the Defendant, holding the Plaintiff's power of attorney enabling him to sell, had sold out without orders, and had applied the produce to his own use. He had for many years regularly paid the amount of the dividends to the Plaintiff, but at length, upon his failing so to do, the fraud was discovered. The jury had in their verdict taken the account between the parties up to the time of the trial, including therein the amount of those dividends which the Defendant had failed to pay: under these circumstances *Gaselee* prayed that the judgement might carry interest on such part of the sum as did not consist of the dividends which were in arrear.

The Court gave interest on affirmance in error of a judgment for the proceeds of stock fraudulently sold out by one holding a power of attorney to sell.

GIBBS C. J. In recent cases in the King's Bench, where there has not been a stipulated time for payment of money, and where a Defendant is bound to repay money merely because he has received it, that Court has not given interest. Nevertheless I remember a case tried at *Exeter* before *Lord Kenyon* C. J., in which a person riding into the *North* of *Devonshire* lost his saddle-bags with three hundred guineas in them, and he who found the money used it in trade, and after twenty years ventured to boast of it, and upon that boast he who lost it founded his action for money had and received, and interest, and the jury, under Lord *Kenyon*'s direction, gave interest for the twenty years, and

I 3   the

1815.

MITCHELL
v.
MINIKEN.

the case never was questioned; but subsequent decisions have restrained this generality. We may presume that in the present instance the jury gave interest, reducing it by the deduction of such dividends as the Plaintiff has received. This is not like the common case, but we think it may be done.

The rest of the Court concurred in granting the
Rule absolute.

(IN THE EXCHEQUER-CHAMBER.)

April 19.   BRUCE *v.* WARWICK.   In Error.

The trading contract of an infant is not void, but he may enforce it at his election.

THIS was a writ of error brought to reverse a judgment of the Court of King's Bench, which was pronounced for the Plaintiff below upon a declaration in *assumpsit*, which stated that the Plaintiff below, an infant, by his next friend complained of the Defendant below for the non-performance of a contract for the sale to the Plaintiff below of the potatoes growing on three acres and a half of ground, and after part performance by the Defendant below, he averred an interruption, whereby the Plaintiff below was not only put to great trouble and expence in and about the digging up of the part of the potatoes so dug up by him, but also thereby he, the Plaintiff below, lost and was deprived of all the profits, benefit, and advantage which might and would otherwise have arisen and accrued to him from the performance of the said promise and undertaking of the Defendant below. The Plaintiff in error assigned for error, that it appeared by the beginning of the declaration, that the Plaintiff below was an infant under the age of twenty-one years, and by the several counts

of

of the declaration, that the contracts whereupon the
Plaintiff below had declared, were trading contracts,
into which an infant was not permitted by the law of
the land to enter, or to sue any one for the breach
thereof.

A. Moore, for the Plaintiff in error, contended that
it appeared by the record that this was a trading
contract, in which the Plaintiff, being an infant, could
not by law engage: for an infant could not by law
be a trader, it not being for his benefit that he
should engage in the risks of trade.   No authority
could be found, that an infant was competent to engage in trade, though he admitted that upon the discussion of this case, the Court below had held that
he was competent so to do. (a) *Ex parte Sydebotham.*
Lord *Hardwick* held that an infant could not be a
bankrupt, and decreed a commission against him to be
superseded; upon the ground, as it may be presumed,
that he was incapable of being a trader. (b) *Ex parte
Moule,* Lord *Eldon,* Chancellor, seems to have doubted
whether a trading during infancy was sufficient to maintain a commission, and he dwells much on the trading,
though far less in degree, which took place after the bankrupt was of full age. *Whywall* v. *Champion* (c). *Lee* C.J.
held that goods sent to an infant who had set up a shop
in the country, could not be recovered for. For the
law will not suffer him to trade, which may be his un-
doing. If no persons can enforce trading contracts
against him, and he can enforce his trading contracts
against those with whom he deals, the consequences
would be, that he might obtain goods on credit to any
extent, and plead infancy as a defence to paying for
those goods, and at the same time may sell those same
goods to others, and enforce payment for them, or may

(a) 1 *Atk.* 146.   (b) 14 *Ves.* 602.   (c) 1 *Str.* 1083.

I 4.

con-

1815.

BRUCE
v.
WARWICK.

contract to sell them to others, and refuse with impunity to complete his contract. *Littleton* (a) says, if any within the age of 21 years be baylife or receiver to any man, &c., all serve for nothing and may be avoided; and Lord *Coke* (b) remarks thereon, One under the age of 21 years shall not be charged in any such account. And in another place (c) he says, an infant or minor is not capable of an office of stewardship of the court of a manor either in possession or reversion. If his infancy would be no bar to his maintaining an action against a lord who had contracted to sell him a stewardship and refused, for not fulfilling his contract, the judgment would award him a compensation for the loss of that, which, if he had obtained, he would be incompetent to perform.

Lawes, contrd, was stopped by the Court.

Gibbs C. J. The court are all of opinion that the judgment of the Court of King's Bench is perfectly right. It has been urged for the Plaintiff in error, that it is incumbent on the Defendant in error to shew that an infant can enter into a trading contract. The general law is that the contract of an infant may be avoided or not, at his own option. As to the case put, the infant could maintain no such action; for he cannot perform the duties of a steward, and the law would not compel the lord to make an unavailing appointment. If he had paid money for such an appointment, we doubt not that he might recover it back. On the whole we are of opinion, that this is in the same case as other contracts made by an infant, which he may either avoid or enforce at his pleasure.

Judgment affirmed.

(a) S. 259.   (b) Co. Litt. 172. a.   (c) Co. Litt. 3. b.

DAVISON and three Others *v.* SAVAGE.

THE declaration stated, that *James Savage* was attached to answer four persons named, of a plea of trespass, and that thereupon the said Plaintiffs, by *A. W.* their attorney, complain, for that the said Defendant, &c. and throughout the residue of the declaration, the Plaintiffs and Defendant were no otherwise described than by the phrase, " the said Plaintiffs," and " the said Defendant." The Defendant demurred specially, and assigned, amongst other causes, that the Plaintiffs had not in their declaration stated or alleged that the said *James* committed the trespasses, but only that the said Defendant committed the same, without stating that the said *James* is the person therein meant by the said words " the said Defendant," or in any part of the said declaration calling, or in any manner describing the said *James* as being a Defendant. The Plaintiff joined in demurrer.

In pleading, it is sufficient, on all occasions after the parties have been first named, to describe them by the terms " the said Plaintiff " and " the said Defendant."

Lens Serjt., in support of the demurrer, urged that upon every occurrence of the parties on the record they ought to be described by their names, not by the terms Plaintiffs and Defendant. It was better to adhere to the usual form in declaring.

The Court intimated a decided opinion that the words " Plaintiffs" and " Defendant" in the record were a sufficient description. *Gibbs* C. J. said, that in a case of *Heaton* v. *Ashdown and Others,* in which there were 26 Defendants, he had, while at the bar about 29 years since, in drawing the pleadings, adopted a like description, naming the first Defendant, and adding the

.words

DAVISON
v.
SAVAGE.

words " and the said other Defendants," and the propriety of it was not even then questioned; and *Chambre* J. held, that the present description was sufficiently clear. Upon the other objections to the declaration the Court offered *Best* Serjt., who was of counsel for the Plaintiffs, leave to amend, which he accepted.

April 21.

WYNN *v.* BELLMAN, Clerk.

A Plaintiff who defers proceeding, in order to await the decision of the Court on a similar question in another cause, will not be relieved on that ground against a rule for judgment as in case of a nonsuit, unless he makes it appear to the Court, in what cause the question will arise, and what the point is to be decided.

IN this action, which was brought to recover penalties for non-residence on the Defendant's benefice, *Blosset* Serjt. had obtained a rule *nisi* for judgment as in case of a nonsuit, against which *Copley* Serjt. now attempted to shew cause, upon an affidavit that the reason why the Plaintiff had not proceeded with greater diligence in this action, was, because he had another action now pending, wherein the same point would occur for the decision of the Court, that would arise in this case; and to avoid expence, he had deferred proceeding, intending to abide in this case by the decision in the other: but his affidavit did not name the other cause, nor state what the point was.

Blosset, in support of his rule, urged that sufficient information was not laid before the Court, to induce them to prolong the cause.

The Court held, that they ought to be apprised what was the cause pending, and what was the point intended to be raised, for they might form respecting it a very different judgment from that of the Plaintiff.

Rule absolute.

SNOW v. TOWNSEND.

THE Plaintiff had been discharged out of prison under the insolvent act, and had under that act assigned to the person who sued him all his property. Many persons were indebted to him before his assignment, and his assignee refusing to 'sue them, he had commenced 'the present action against one of his creditors.

Blosset Serjt. moved that either the proceedings might be staid, upon the ground that the right of suit was now vested in the Plaintiff's assignee only; or else that at least the Plaintiff might give security for costs, which he claimed on the authority of *Webb* v. *Ward*. (a)

The Court will not prevent one who has assigned his property under an insolvent act from suing for a debt due to him before his assignment, the assignee refusing to sue.

Nor will the Court compel the Plaintiff to give security for costs.

Per Curiam. Either the Plaintiff can maintain an action for this debt, or he cannot. If he can, there is no reason why the Court should interfere to prevent him from so doing: if he cannot, it will be matter of defence. As to security for costs, the case cited has been much questioned, and besides, it materially differs from this. There the Plaintiff was suing for the benefit of his assignees, who ought not to be permitted, if unsuccessful, to shelter themselves from costs behind the bankrupt's poverty; here the Plaintiff sues, because the assignee will not sue.

Rule refused.

(a) 7 *Term Rep.* 296.

The memorial of an annuity stated the names of two witnesses as attesting the execution of an annuity-deed, who also attested the execution of a warrant of attorney for further securing the annuity, but that fact was not noticed in the memorial: Held that the names of all the witnesses were sufficiently stated.

A memorial of an annuity-deed stated the contract, and payment of the price, and that for the considerations aforesaid, and for further and better securing the annuity, the grantor demised to J. T. W. upon

IN replevin, the Defendant makes cognizance; and because the Plaintiff, for a quarter of a year ending on 25th December 1813, and from thence until and at the time when, &c., held the place in which, &c., as tenant to Sir J. T. Wheate, Bart. under 800l. a year rent, payable quarterly, for 200l. for a quarter's rent, due on 25th December, he acknowledges the taking. The Plaintiff pleads in bar, in substance as follows: first, that E. Watts Clerk, was rector of the rectories and parish churches of C. and B., and being seised in his demesne as of freehold in right of those rectories in the several places in which, &c. on 26th November 1812, by indenture demised them to the Plaintiff for the term of 12 years, if Watts should so long live and continue rector: that he entered and was possessed; and that the demise in that indenture mentioned and the demise in the cognizance mentioned were the same: that afterwards, on 10th June 1813, by indenture between E. Watts, 1., C. N. A. Humphries, 2., and Sir J. T. Wheate, 3. it was expressed that Watts granted to Humphries for the natural life of Watts, one annuity of 800l. payable as therein mentioned; and it was therein further expressed, that for the better and more effectually securing the payment of that annuity, Watts thereby granted, bargained, sold, demised, and confirmed unto Sir J. T. Wheate, amongst others, the several places in which, &c., for the term of 99 years from the date of that indenture, upon the trusts; and to and for

the trusts in the indenture expressed: Held that it sufficiently appeared for whom J. T. W. was a trustee.

The memorial of an annuity needs not to state the names of the attornies to whom a warrant to confess judgment is given.

If a memorial of an annuity be defective in stating one of several securities, semble that the particular instrument only is void, and not the other assurances.

the

the uses, intents, and purposes, therein expressed and declared. And that for the better securing that annuity, *Watts* then and there executed a certain warrant of attorney, which was executed in the presence of and attested by one *A. B.* and one *J. G.* And that no memorial of that indenture and warrant of attorney was inrolled in Chancery within 20 days of the execution thereof, except a certain memorial, the tenor whereof the plea set forth, and of which the material parts were as follow: A memorial, &c. of an indenture bearing date 10th *June* 1813, made between *E. Watts* 1., *C. N. A. Humphries* 2., and the Rev. Sir *J. T. Wheate* 3., (describing them by their additions,) reciting that *Humphries* had agreed with *Watts* for the purchase of one annuity of 800*l.* to be secured upon the rectories of *C.* and *B.* and the messuages, &c. thereunto belonging, and to be further secured in the manner thereinafter mentioned, and to be payable to *Humphries*, his executors, &c. during the life of *Watts*, for 5200*l.* and that the costs of procuring the money on that security, and of preparing the securities, and of filing a memorial thereof in Chancery should be borne by *Watts*, and that *Humphries* in pursuance of that agreement had in person paid 5200*l.* to *Watts* in person, in bank-notes, it was by that indenture witnessed, that in pursuance and performance of that agreement on the part of *Watts*, and in consideration of 5200*l.* so paid by *Humphries* to *Watts*, *Watts* granted, &c. to *Humphries*, his executors; &c. for the natural life of *Watts*, one annuity of 800*l.* to be charged and chargeable upon the rectories of *C.* and *B.* and the glebe, &c. thereunto respectively belonging, to hold the same annuity of 800*l.* from thenceforth during the natural life of *Watts*, payable quarterly, at the times and with the usual powers and authorities for recovering and receiving the same, therein mentioned. And that it was by that indenture further witnessed,

that

that for the considerations aforesaid, and for the better and more effectually securing the payment of that annuity to *Humphries,* his executors, &c. during the natural life of *Watts,* as also in consideration of ten shillings paid to *Watts* by Sir *J. T. Wheate, Watts,* with the consent and approbation and by the direction of *Humphries,* did grant, bargain, sell, demise, and confirm, unto Sir *J. T. Wheate,* all that and those the rectory of the parish church of *C.* and the rectory of the parish church of *B.,* and the glebe, &c., to hold the same to Sir *J. T. Wheate* for the term of 99 years from the day of the date of that indenture, upon the trusts and to and for the uses, intents, and purposes therein expressed and declared. And also of a warrant of attorney bearing even date with the said indenture, whereby *Watts* authorized certain attornies of K. B. therein named to confess and enter up judgment in that Court, in the penal sum of 10,400*l.* as a collateral security for the payment of the annuity: and that it was by that indenture agreed and covenanted that *Watts* might purchase the annuity for 5200*l.,* and all arrears, on three months' notice; and that on payment thereof, the indenture, rent charge, and annuity should be given up to be cancelled, which indenture, as to the execution thereof, is witnessed by *A. B.* of, &c. and *J. G.* of, &c.; and a memorial thereof is hereby required to be registered pursuant to the act. *E. Watts.* Inrolled, &c. 28th *June* 1813. Which memorial does not nor did contain the names of the witnesses to the warrant of attorney. And that the Plaintiff did not at the said several times when, &c. or at any other time, hold the several places in which, &c. as tenant thereof to Sir *J. T. Wheate,* otherwise than as in the plea is above stated. The Plaintiff, 2dly, pleaded, as before, the seisin of *Watts,* his demise to *E. Watts,* the Plaintiff, the indenture of 10th *June* 1813, and the demise to Sir *J. T.*

Wheate

Wheate therein contained, upon the trusts and to and for the ends, intents, and purposes in that indenture expressed, and the warrant of attorney executed in the presence of and attested by *A. B.* and *J. G.*, and averred that no memorial of the lastmentioned indenture and warrant of attorney, containing the names of all the witnesses to the execution thereof, was inrolled in Chancery within 20 days of the execution thereof according to the statute 17 *Geo.* 3., and that the Plaintiff did not hold the places in which, &c. as tenant thereof to Sir *J. T. Wheate*, otherwise than as in that plea was stated. The Defendant demurred generally to the first plea in bar; and to the second plea he replied, that a memorial of the said indenture and warrant of attorney in that plea mentioned, containing the names of all the witnesses to the execution thereof, was inrolled in Chancery within twenty days of the execution thereof, according to the direction of the act, which memorial he set out, being the same memorial stated by the Plaintiff in his first plea in bar, as by the memorial remaining duly inrolled in the High Court of Chancery, more fully appeared; and the Plaintiff averred that the memorial did duly contain the day of the month, and the year when the indenture and warrant of attorney in the last plea in bar mentioned, bore date, and the names of all the parties, and for whom any of them were trustees, and of all the witnesses, and did truly set forth the annual sum or sums to be paid, and the name of the person and persons for whose life or lives the annuity was granted, and the considerations of granting the same, in manner and form as in and by the statute was required, as by the inrolment of the memorial remaining of record appeared; and this he the Plaintiff was ready to verify by the record, &c.: wherefore, as before, he prayed judgment and a return, &c.

The

The Plaintiff joined in demurrer on the first plea in bar, and demurred generally to the Defendant's replication to the second plea in bar, in which demurrer the Defendant joined.

Lens Serjt., for the Plaintiff, made three objections to the validity of the demise in the annuity deed, founded upon supposed defects in the memorial, namely, first, that the memorial did not set forth the names of the witnesses to the execution of the warrant of attorney; secondly, that the memorial did not set forth the trusts of the demise to Sir J. T. _Wheate_, and thirdly, that the memorial did not state the names of the attornies to whom the warrant to confess judgment was given. Upon the first point, he urged that all the several instruments given to secure an annuity constitute but one assurance in law (a), and a defect in any one of them vitiates all the securities. In the case of _Harte_ v. _Lovelace_ (b), Lord _Kenyon_ C. J. says, "the strong inclination of my opinion is, that any defect in the memorial of one of the deeds will vitiate the whole assurance." The words of the statute are, that "every such deed, bond, instrument, or other assurance, shall be void." The warrant of attorney is doubtless such an instrument as must be included in the memorial. _Hopkins_ v. _Waller_ (c). And in _Howel_ v. _Burton_ (d), it was held that not only the instrument whereby an annuity shall be granted, but all the instruments whereby it shall be in any manner secured to be paid, are within the act. The grantor has not the benefit intended for him by the legislature, if he cannot, by inspecting the memorial, see who were the witnesses attesting each part of the transaction. The grantee cannot disengage himself from the conse-

(a) _Duke of Bolton_ v. _Williams_, 4 _Bro. Ch. Ca._ 310.
(b) 6 _Term Rep._ 476.
(c) 4 _Term Rep._ 463.
(d) 2 _Ves. jun._ 34.

quences

quences of an omission respecting one of his securities, by saying, I do not rest on this instrument. The question is on the meaning of the word "such:" " Such assurance" comprehends all the instruments; for they make together but one assurance. In *Hart* v. *Lovelace* all the instruments were enumerated, and stated to be attested by *W. D.* and *W. M.*, or one of them; yet it was held insufficient, and that the grantor had a right to know from the memorial to which particular instrument each of the persons was witness. The case of *Van Braam* v. *Isaacs* (a) appears to have proceeded on this objection. It is no answer, to say that it appears by other parts of this record that the same persons who were witnesses to the one instrument were witnesses also to the others; that fact ought to appear on the memorial. Where a memorial states an instrument to be attested by four persons, which is attested by two only, the misdescription is fatal (b). Upon the second objection, this case falls not within the principle that it is sufficient if the Court can see for whom the termor is trustee: this memorial leaves it wholly unknown what the trusts may be. Sir *J. T. Wheate* may for some purposes be trustee for the grantor, though for the principal purposes he may be trustee for the grantee. In *Askew* v. *Macreth* (c), though Mr. *Coutts* appeared on the memorial to be a trustee nominated on behalf of the grantee, yet it was held insufficient, because it did not appear for whom he was trustee; for he might be a trustee for the grantor, though nominated by the grantee. In the case of *Leycester* v. *Lockwood* (d), Lord *Ellenborough* C. J. reluctantly held the averment in the memorial that the interest in the 10,000*l.* was conveyed to the trustees upon the trusts in the indenture, men-

(a) 1 Bos. & Pull. 451.
(b) Ex parte Macreth, 2 East, 563.
(c) 1 New Rep. 214.
(d) 1 Maule & Selw. 527. and ante, v. 587.

1815.

BROWNE
v.
ROSE.

tioned, to be insufficient. In the case of *Denn, on demise of Dolman,* v. *Dolman* (*a*), a memorial stating a demise by indenture to have been made, &c. upon the trusts therein mentioned, was in like manner held fatal. So, where a termor was to permit the grantor to hold the premises till default in payment, and thenceforth he was to hold for the grantee, a memorial which averred the trust to be for the grantee was held ill, although the trustee had no act to perform for the benefit of the grantor (*b*). As to the third objection, although a warrant of attorney usually authorizes any attorney of the Court, not named, in addition to those who are named, to enter up judgment, yet those who are named are usually parties to the transaction; they are commonly the attornies of the grantee, and to them the grantor has a right to resort for intelligence respecting the transaction, and their names therefore ought to be set out in the memorial.

Best Serjt. *contrà.* As to the first objection, admitting that the witnesses were insufficiently stated in the memorial, the warrant of attorney alone would be thereby affected; but it has never yet been decided, that where it appears on the record, as here it does, that the same persons are witnesses to the warrant of attorney and to the deed, that is not sufficient. This is distinguishable from all the decided cases. Here the grantor had every information he could want, for he had the names of the witnesses to the warrant of attorney and of the witnesses to the indenture. In *Van Braam* v. *Isaacs* no witnesses appear to have been named in the memorial. In *Hart* v. *Lovelace,* the witnesses were defectively set out, for it did not ascertain any one person in whose presence the deed was executed,

(*a*) 5 *Term Rep.* 641.   (*b*) *Taylor* v. *Johnson,* 8 *Term Rep.* 184.

Watts

Watts v. *Millard* (*a*) is a case strongly favourable to
the grantee, for there the christian name of one of the
witnesses to the warrant of attorney was not set out in
the memorial, yet Lord *Kenyon* C. J. held that there
was no weight in the objection; apparently, not because
the christian name was not necessary in order to identify
the witness, but because (there being several instruments attested by the same person) the witness's name
appeared in another part of the memorial. The act only
requires that the names of all the witnesses shall appear on the enrollment, which is here observed. Where
there is no express decision on the point, the court
will be guided by analogy. The act requires the consideration to be set out, yet it has been held, that if the
consideration be once set out in the memorial of one
out of several deeds, it suffices. So, if the names of all
the witnesses once appear on the memorial, as here
they do, they not be repeated. Next, the defect, if it
be one, invalidates only the single instrument to which
it applies. It is a sufficient penalty on the omission,
that the grantee loses the aid of his judgment, or his
warrant of attorney. The words of the act require no
more. The words " every such" are to be taken distributively, it means every such deed, namely, in the
memorial whereof the requisitions of the act are not
complied with, shall be void; every such bond, with
respect to which they are not observed, shall be void,
every such instrument, with respect to which, &c.,
every other assurance with respect to which, &c. The
argument is not new, that by force of the word " assurance" all the instruments collectively are vitiated, but
the words of the act are, " other assurance," and they
must therefore mean an assurance of which no deed,
bond, or instrument constitutes a part; and the opinion

(*a*) 5 *Term Rep.* 598.

K 2   of

of Lord *Loughborough* Chancellor, in *The Duke of
Bolton* v. *Williams*, on that point, is directly contrary
to the statute. In *Hart* v. *Lovelace*, Lord *Kenyon*, who
was no friend to annuities, acknowledged he was not
prepared to say, whether or not all the instruments
given to secure an annuity must be set aside, merely
because one only is not properly registered. The
Court of King's Bench had before the date of that case
decided that a defect in the memorial vitiated only the
particular instrument (*a*). As to the second point,
enough is set out to disclose to the Court what the
trusts are of the demise to Sir *J. T. Wheate*. It appears that it was made for the consideration of the
price of the annuity and the agreement to grant it, and
that it was intended for the purpose of better securing
the annuity. This therefore shews that the termor is a
trustee for the annuitant; if it had merely been a demise "upon the trusts in the indenture declared," that
would not have sufficed. This is distinguishable from
Leycester v. *Lockwood*; in that transaction there were
trusts for five different parties, the grantor, grantee, and
strangers, and there were no words whence it could be
collected who were all the persons for whom *Lockwood*
and *Aclom* were trustees. In the cases of *Desenfans* v.
O'Bryen, (*b*) and *Bradford* v. *Burland* (*c*), the Court of
King's Bench decided on the ground of an omission in
the memorial of trusts which expressly appeared on the
deed. So in *Dolman* v. *Dolman*, Lord *Kenyon* relied
on the ground that that there were trusts for other purposes after the annuity was satisfied, which subsequent
trusts were not set out; and *Lawrence* J. concurs in
putting the case on the same ground. *Askew* v. *Macreth*
was decided on the point, that *Coutts* was, until default
in payment, a trustee for the grantor, which was not

(*a*) *Ex parte Chester*, 4 *Term.*   (*b*) 3 *East*, 559.
Rep. 694.   (*c*) 14 *East*, 445.

10.*   stated

stated in the memorial, so that the grantor stood in a more advantageous situation than the memorial represented him. In *Taylor* v. *Johnson* there was an express trust to permit the grantor to receive the rents and profits till default, which is still stronger than the case of a resulting trust. Here it does not appear that there was any other trust than for the grantee. But this case has been decided almost in terms, in this Court (*a*). The same case of *Defaria* v. *Sturt* came before the Court of Exchequer; and *Macdonald* C. B. observed, that in *Askew* v. *Macreth Coutts* was a trustee for two, but in the case then before him, there was a trust for one only; and after that was satisfied the trust ceased, and *Graham* B. concurred. Let the question be here asked, which is there put by *Mansfield* C. J., "upon reading the deed, for whom does Sir *J. T. Wheate* appear to be trustee?" The answer is manifest. This decision, then, explains the distinction between the two classes of cases. But if there were a trust for another, the plea ought to have averred it. The plea therefore has not gone far enough to raise the question. As to the third objection, the act does not require the names of the attornies to be set out in the memorial: no case has decided that it is necessary so to do, and the practice is not to set them out. The parties, whose names are by the act required to be stated, mean the principals, not agents. If every person who had any thing to do with the transaction were to be deemed a party, it would have been unnecessary to specify the witnesses in the act. An attorney is no more a party to an annuity transaction, than he is a party in a cause.

Lens in reply. As to the first point, though the memorial contains the names of the persons who in fact

(*a*) *Defaria* v. *Sturt, ante,* ii. 225.

　　　　　　　attested

1815.

BROWNE
v.
ROSE.

attested the execution of the warrant of attorney, yet it does not indicate that fact: the statute requires it should appear on the memorial who are the attesting witnesses. This memorial rather disaffirms than implies their attestation of the warrant of attorney, by confining their attestation to the indenture. The same argument was used in *Van Braam* v. *Isaacs,* but it did not there prevail. In that case the warrant of attorney was actually produced in court, when it appeared attested by the same persons as the indenture. *Hart* v. *Lovelace* is not distinguishable from this case, on the principle, which is, that the memorial must point out to the attention of the reader what witnesses attested each instrument. In *Watts* v. *Millard* the question was wholly different, being only whether a witness who was named, was named sufficiently. *Hodges* v. *Money* (a) is inapplicable. *Ex parte Chester* was decided in Lord *Kenyon's* absence; so that when he suspends his assent to that case, he does not vacillate in his judgment. The case of *Willey* v. *Wheeler* there cited does not appear to corroborate *Ex parte Chester,* and Lord *Loughborough* rejected the last mentioned case. The *Duke of Bolton* v. *Williams* has always been respected as a leading decision. Whatever deeds or instruments the annuitant takes as part of his assurance become a part of his assurance, and he cannot afterwards reject either of them; but if there is a defect in one part, it vitiates the whole. No case has ever yet decided, that one of the securities being defective, any other of them can be enforced. As to the second point, *Lens* admitted that it was sufficient if either the trusts were set out, or if enough appeared on the memorial, from which the court could judge for whom the termor was trustee; but this memorial disclosed neither. Undoubtedly there must have been here a resulting trust for the grantor; and whether re-

(a) 4 *Term Rep.* 500.

sulting,

sulting, or express, it must equally be stated on the memorial. [*Gibbs* C. J. intimated, that there might be a difference between an express trust for the grantor until default in payment, and a resulting trust for the grantor; and therefore even if it were necessary that the memorial should notice the first, it might not be necessary to notice the latter. For suppose that a term was created for securing an annuity payable half yearly, upon an estate which was let at a rent payable quarterly, if there were an express trust for the grantor till default, the trustee would be bound to pay him the first quarter's rent as it was received, whereas, if it were only a resulting trust for the grantor, the trustee might not be warranted in paying over any part of the rents to him until he had seen the first half year's annuity paid.] *Leycester* v. *Lockwood, Lens* agreed, did not govern this case, because there were trusts for strangers to the annuity transaction, newly introduced in performance of a former agreement. In *Defaria* v. *Sturt Macdonald* C. B. does not pursue the decision of the House of Lords in *Askew* v. *Macreth.*

As to the third objection, it is said that the attornies are not parties; if the statute intended to require only the names of the grantor and grantee, it would be nugatory; for it is scarcely possible that in any memorial of the transaction their names should fail to appear: so narrow a construction of the word " parties," therefore, would defeat the purpose of the act, which was to bring into the view of those who might inspect the memorial, the names of all the persons who bore any part in the transaction.

Cur. adv. vult.

GIBBS C. J. now delivered the opinion of the Court.

This is an action of replevin for distraining the goods of the Plaintiff in a certain dwelling-house, and a certain

K 4

tain

tain close. The Defendant makes cognizance as bailiff
of Sir *J. T. Wheate,* and avers that the Plaintiff held
the premises as tenant to Sir *J. T. Wheate,* and that the
rent was in arrear, and he distrained as bailiff to Sir
J. T. Wheate. The Plaintiff pleads, that *Watts* was
seised of the premises in virtue of his rectory, and demised to the Plaintiff, and that he was in possession
under this demise from *Watts,* and that afterwards
Watts granted an annuity to *Humphries,* and that a
memorial thereof was registered; and the plea sets it
out, and that no other memorial was ever registered.
There is a demurrer to this plea. There are two other
pleas in bar, and after stating the securities, they say,
the warrant of attorney was witnessed by *A. B.* and *J. G.,*
and that no memorial was registered according to the
statute. The Defendant replies, that a memorial was
enrolled, and sets it out; but it is not therein mentioned
who are the witnesses to the warrant of attorney; but
by the replication it appears they are the same persons
who witnessed the deed; so that in point of fact, the
person consulting the memorial has the benefit of
access to all persons who were witnesses to any of the
instruments. Three objections are made to this memorial. I take the second objection first, which is presented in the same form, both on the demurrer to the
first plea in bar, and on the demurrer to the replication. The memorial states, that on the 10th of *June*
1813, by indenture between *Watts* of the first part,
Humphries of the 2d part, and Sir *J. T. Wheate* of the
3d part, *Watts* granted to *Humphries* a certain annuity
of 800*l. per ann.* for *Watts*'s life; and for better and
more effectually securing the said annuity, *Watts* granted
and sold the premises to Sir *J. T. Wheate* for the term
of 99 years, upon the trusts and for the purposes therein
expressed and declared. Observe, it states that the more
effectually securing the annuity, was the purpose for
                                                    which

which *Watts* granted and sold to *Wheate* upon the trusts therein expressed; the memorial shews that the conveyance was made on the trusts in the indenture mentioned, having before said, that the term was granted to *Wheate* for the purpose of securing the annuity. The objection is, that it does not appear for whom *Wheate* was trustee, nor what the trusts were. It happens that a case has already been before this Court, and has been decided; and although there may be some little distinction, it is almost in terms the same as this case. [Here his Lordship read the report of *Defaria* v. *Sturt*.] It was objected in that case, that the powers there given, and the manner in which those powers were granted, did not appear; but the Court asked a question, which, if asked here, must be answered in the same manner. Can any one, having read this deed, hesitate to say for whom the termor is trustee? For what is the difference between that case and this? In this, there is one circumstance stronger than in *Defaria* v. *Sturt:* for here it appears that the trustee was nominated by *Humphries*, and was nominated for the purpose in the indenture expressed. It is said, there may be other trusts in the indenture. There may be such: but it lies on the annuitant to shew that there are such other trusts; and that is the difference between this case and that of *Leycester* v. *Lockwood.* It does there appear on the pleadings that there were other trusts in the indenture, which ought to have been expressed in the memorial, and were not. We think, therefore, the present memorial is supported by the case of *Defaria* v. *Sturt*, and is clear of that objection.

Another objection is, that the memorial does not contain the names of the attornies named in the warrant of attorney to enter up judgment. The statute does not require that. (Here his Lordship read the words of the act.) It is impossible to say that the legislature

legislature meant to comprehend them under the description of parties. They are not more parties than the witnesses are; yet the legislature thought it necessary to enact that the witnesses should be named.

The third objection is, that the witnesses to the warrant of attorney are not named in the memorial. On the plea in bar it appears there were witnesses to that instrument, and that they were the same persons who witnessed the deed. The memorial, it is true, does not say they were the witnesses to the warrant of attorney. The statute says, the memorial shall contain the names of all the witnesses. Literally, this memorial does contain the names of all the witnesses, although it does not state that they are the witnesses to the warrant of attorney. If any fraud could result from the omission to state to what instrument these persons were witnesses, I should not favour this construction. But the object of the act is satisfied: when the names of all the witnesses to the transaction are given, the party has all the information that can be given, to enable him by examination of those witnesses to trace out the circumstances. The case of *Orton* v. *Knight* (a) does seem to favour our construction. A witness attested the execution of an indenture by *A.*, *B.*, and *C.* The memorial stated him to be witness to the execution by *A.* and *C.*, but not by *B.*, yet this Court held the memorial good. The Plaintiff's doctrine is, that a defect in the memorial as to any part of the securities avoids the annuity itself. On the hypothesis of those who contend for this doctrine, it must be admitted, that if void against *B.*, the annuity would be void against *A.* and *C.* also; and either the objection is null, and the memorial was good for all three, or else it may be bad for the execution of *B.*, and good for that of *A.* and *C.* So, the warrant of attorney may be bad,

(a) 3 *Bos. & Pull.* 153.

and

and the other securities good. There is indeed a note
of the reporter subjoined to that case, referring to *Van
Braam* v. *Isaacs*, and saying, that when the same witness
attests several instruments, it will not be sufficient if the
memorial only mention their names as witnesses to one.
It does not, however, appear that this point was so decided: that cause of *Van Braam* and *Isaacs* stood over,
and there was some delay, and it does not appear upon
which of the grounds it was ultimately decided. But if it
was so held, and if the objection be good, we are nevertheless of opinion that it affects the warrant of attorney
only; for though it was held in the case of *The Duke
of Bolton* v. *Williams* that a defect in one of the instruments affected all, we cannot think that such was the
intent of the legislature.   We think it was only meant
that the want of the prescribed observances should vitiate the particular security; for on looking into the act,
it appears there may be different memorials of the different deeds, and that the deeds may be executed at
different times; and therefore we think the intent is
that only the particular assurance shall be void, with
respect to which the requisites of the statute are not
complied with.   The demise therefore is valid, and
consequently the distress is good, and the cognizance
must be supported, and the judgment must be entered for

The Defendant.

April 25.   · LUNN *v.* PAYNE.

In debt on bond given to the obligee, conditioned for payment of an annual sum to the wife of the obligor, a breach assigned in non-payment of the annual sum to the obligee is ill.

THIS was an action of debt on a bond given by the Defendant to the Plaintiff in a penalty conditioned that the Defendant should pay to the Defendant's wife, for her separate maintenance, a certain yearly sum during her life, and the Plaintiff alleged as a breach, living the wife, that the sum was in arrear and unpaid to the Plaintiff. After *non est factum* pleaded, and a verdict for the Plaintiff, *Vaughan* Serjt. had obtained a rule *nisi* to arrest the judgment, because the Plaintiff had shewn no breach of the condition.

Lens Serjt. now endeavoured to sustain the declaration, urging that the breach shewed the legal effect of the bond; for payment to the Defendant's wife might be described as payment to the Plaintiff. The claim was his, and the arrears were legally due to him. It might have been, perhaps, more minutely described as a payment to the wife; though that would merely have been to set out the evidence, instead of stating the legal effect of the obligation. The only persons here, between whom a contract could subsist, are the Plaintiff and Defendant. The wife is not a separate person from the Plaintiff with regard to the husband, however the case might be stated if the payment had been stipulated for the benefit of a stranger. The payment by the husband to the wife would be in law a payment to himself. The debt therefore became due to the Plaintiff, and it would be superfluous to add that it became due to the Plaintiff by reason of its not having been paid to the wife on account of the Plaintiff.

Vaughan Serjt., who would have supported his rule, was relieved by

The

The Court. We cannot go with the Plaintiff's counsel, in thinking these arrears were ever due to the Plaintiff at all. Nothing is due to the Plaintiff but the penalty of the bond, and the penalty is due to him by reason of these sums not being paid to the wife.

1815.

LUNN
v.
PAYNE.

Rule absolute.

THISTLEWOOD, qui tam, *v.* CRACROFT and Another.

April 25.

THIS was an action brought upon the stat. 9 *Ann.* *c.* 14. *s.* 2., after the lapse of more than three months, to recover from the Defendants money won by them at play from a third person, and also the treble value thereof. Upon the trial of the cause, at the sittings in *Middlesex* after *Hilary* term 1815, before *Gibbs* C. J., the offence being proved to have been committed in *March* 1812, and the declaration appearing on the record to be of *Hilary* term 1815, in order to shew that the Plaintiff had commenced his action within the year after the offence, he put in evidence a writ sued out the 22d of *February* 1813, returnable on the first return day of *Easter* term. It did not appear to have been returned. *Best* Serjt. for the Defendant, objected, that although that writ was sued out within the year after the offence, yet, *primâ facie*, it appeared that could not be the writ on which the Plaintiff now sued, for that inasmuch as the declaration did not appear to be filed within a year after the writ sued out, it could not be connected with that writ, without shewing the continuances.

Copley Serjt. for the Plaintiff endeavoured to connect the writ and the declaration by the evidence of several rules, giving the Plaintiff time to declare from *Michael-mas*

In a *qui tam* action, if the declaration do not appear on the record to be filed within a year of the writ, it is necessary to connect it with the writ by evidence of the time when the declaration was filed, and shewing the writ to be continued on the roll down to that time.

In the Common Pleas, the placitum being always entitled of the term in or after which the trial takes place, it furnishes no evidence of the date of the declaration.

mas term 1813 to the last day of *Trinity* term 1814, but the first of them was a rule in an action against *Cracroft* only, and none of them were proved to be served, and he abandoned this evidence on the subsequent motion. The jury, however, under the direction of the Chief Justice, found a verdict for the Plaintiff, subject to two questions, the first of which alone was afterwards spoken to, *viz.* whether it was sufficiently shewn that this action was commenced in due time.

Accordingly *Best* Serjt. having on a former day in this term obtained a rule *nisi* to set aside the verdict and enter a nonsuit, upon the authority of several cases (*a*) which he mentioned,

Copley Serjt. now endeavoured to support his verdict, contending that it was sufficient if it were shewn that the declaration was within a year of the writ, and that in such case the proceedings were all regular, for which he relied on *Parsons* v. *King*. It was agreed, that the record in this court did not shew the true date of the declaration, for if a cause was tried in term, the placitum was always entitled of that term; if at the sittings after term, the placitum was entitled of the term preceding the sittings: but that this declaration was filed within a year of the writ sued out, appeared from this circumstance, that if the plaintiff does not declare within the year after the return of the writ, the Plaintiff is out of court, but here the Defendant, by pleading to the declaration, admits that the Plaintiff is not out of court, and, by consequence, admits that he has declared within the year after the writ sued out. In *Harris* v. *Woolford*, the first writ never was returned,

(*a*) *Harris* v. *Woolford*, 6 *Term*   7 *Term Rep.* 6.   *Weston* v. *Four-*
Rep. 627.   *Parsons* v. *King*,   *nier*, 14 *East*, 491,

           though

though it was sued out in time, therefore the proceedings were irregular, and were so held. In *Weston* v. *Fournier* Bayley J. says, " the suing out of the second writ was at least *primâ facie* evidence that the first writ had not been returned. In *Stanway* v. *Perry* (a) both the writs were of the same term, but the production of the second raised a presumption that the first had not been served, and only the first writ being in time, it became necessary to shew its return. *Stanway* v. *Perry* is therefore not adverse to the Plaintiff. There is only one writ in evidence, and the Plaintiff is entitled to say, that is the writ on which he declares, and to make that his *primâ facie* case. If there is another writ in existence, the Defendant may shew it, as was done in *Stanway* v. *Perry*, where the second writ was shewn to exist, and to have been served, and therefore was taken to be the writ declared on; and that writ was clearly out of time, and the first writ was not shewn to have been returned; and therefore the connection between the first writ and the second was wanting. In *Hutchinson* (b) *qui tam* v. *Piper*, the writ was sued out within the year after the offence, but it was not continued on the roll, so as to connect it with the record, which was, as the practice of this court with reference to the time of trial required, entitled of *Hilary* term 1812; and inasmuch as there is a distinction between the practice of the two Courts, and though a Plaintiff in the King's Bench is not out of court for want of declaring until a year after his writ sued out, yet as by the practice of the Common Pleas a Plaintiff is out of court unless he declares within two terms, there was a necessity in that case for shewing continuances to connect the writ with the declaration, if any such necessity exists here; but the Court there held that it was sufficient to produce a

(a) 1 *Bos. & Pull.* 157.   (b) *Ante,* iv. 500.

writ,

writ, upon which the declaration may possibly be founded, without shewing the continuances through which alone it can be founded thereon. The caption of the placitum therefore furnishing in this court no evidence of the time of declaring, the fact is always to be shewn by extraneous evidence. The Plaintiff has given *prima facie* evidence that he declared within the time, and the Defendant has not impugned it.

Best, who was prepared to support his rule, was stopped by the Court.

Gibbs C. J. My Brothers all think it lay upon the Plaintiff to go further in this case. The counsel on both sides have fairly agreed on the rule, and differ only on the evidence necessary to bring the case within the rule. They agree that the merely shewing a writ sued out is not sufficient, unless the Plaintiff connects the subsequent proceedings with the writ. If the declaration was within the usual time of declaration, that would naturally connect it with the writ. At whatsoever distance of time the declaration was delivered, it requires to be connected with the writ by evidence; but the evidence is different in the Court of King's Bench and in this Court. In the Court of King's Bench the record itself proves the date of the declaration by the memorandum at the head: but here the record itself does not prove the date of the declaration, for the placitum is always entitled of the term in which the trial is, or, if the cause be tried out of term, then the placitum is entitled of the term preceding. The Court therefore think, that the Plaintiff must go further, and shew that the declaration was delivered within due time after the writ, and here, since that fact does not appear by the placitum, we think it ought to be supplied by other evidence.

Rule absolute.

STEELE, Demandant; CLENNELL, Tenant;   *April 25.*
BENN, Vouchee.

THE vouchee had instructed his solicitor to suffer a
recovery of all those his free lands in *Brisco*, within
the borough of *Egremont*, in the county of *Cumberland*,
and of all other his lands and hereditaments situate in
the county of *Cumberland*. The solicitor prepared, and
the vouchee executed, a deed to lead the uses, which
conveyed " all those closes called and commonly known
by the name of *Brisco*, or *Brisco* closes, situate within
the parish of *Egremont*, in the county of *Cumberland*,
containing by estimation 50 acres or thereabout, and
then and for some time past let to and occupied by
John Kitchen along with his farm of *Blackhow*. The
recovery was of lands in the parishes of *Cleator* and
Egremont. *Heywood* Serjt. now produced an affidavit
that *Brisco* closes, consisting of 50 acres, except a part
containing 4 acres called *Bigrig Moor*, were situate
within the limits of the borough of *Egremont*, which
circumstance had led to the mistake, but were not
within the parish of *Egremont*, but were within and
parcel of the parish of *St. John*'s: that now and at the
time of executing the deed to lead the uses, they were
in the occupation of *John Kitchen*, along with *Blackhow*
farm; that the whole of the parish of *St. John*'s was in
the county of *Cumberland*; that the parties intended the
premises should pass, and were all alive and consenting
to an amendment, which he prayed might be made,
both in the deed to lead the uses, and in the recovery,
by inserting the parish of *St. John*'s instead of the parish
of *Egremont*. He conceived this application to amend
the deed to be authorized by a preceden in the case of

The Court
cannot amend
a deed.
    Where a
vouchee had,
in his instruc-
tions to suffer
a recovery, and
in the deed to
lead the uses
prepared in
pursuance
thereto, mis-
described the
parish in which
certain closes
were, though
they were de-
scribed in the
deed with truth
and certainty
in four other
circumstances,
the Court re-
fused to sub-
stitute in the
recovery, the
parish in which
the lands lay,
for the parish
named in the
deed and re-
covery.

VOL. VI.   L   *Kinderley*,

Kinderley, Demandant; Domville, Tenant; Bampfylde, Vouchee. (a)

The Court rejecting the first part of the application as absolutely impossible, he confined his prayer to the amendment of the recovery only, urging that the premises sufficiently passed by the deed, being identified by four circumstances in which the deed coincided with the fact, *viz.* in the name of the closes, the quantity of land, the name of the occupier, and their being in the county of *Cumberland,* and a mistake in the additional description of the parish in which they were supposed to be, would not vitiate the conveyance; and as they had well passed by the deed, he prayed that the recovery might be amended pursuant to the fact, by inserting the parish of *St. John's* instead of the parish of *Egremont.*

The Court observed that the closes inserted in the deed were those for which the vouchee himself gave instructions, and if there was any mistake, he had himself mistaken the parish. But suppose that some part of the land was in the parish of *Egremont,* though all might be in *Cumberland,* in the occupation of *Kitchen,* and known by the name of *Brisco* closes; in that case the description of the parish would be restrictive, and that part only would pass by the deed. And they refused the application.

(a) *Ante,* i. 257. In that case it is not stated that there was any application to amend the deed: the entirety of certain tenements in *Chilfroom* was omitted to be specified in the deed; but they nevertheless passed thereby, being comprehended within the description of " all other the hereditaments of the vouchees in the parish of *Chilfroom,*" and *Chilfroom* was already named in the recovery, and the only amendment prayed, as to those premises, was, the increasing the number of messuages, and acres, &c. in *Chilfroom;* which the Court permitted. In the present case, although there were general words in the instructions for the deed, it did not appear that there were in the deed itself any general words that could comprise lands in *St. John's* parish, if they did not pass by the specific description.

1815.

SCHMALING v. THOMLINSON and Others.   *April 29.*

THIS was an action for commission, work and labour, and money paid, brought to recover a compensation for the Plaintiff having shipped and forwarded
a quantity of cocoa for the Defendants from *London* to
Amsterdam, under the following circumstances, as they
appeared upon the trial at the sittings after *Hilary*
term 1815, before *Gibbs* C. J.   In consequence of
Hulletts, the Defendants' brokers in *London*, having
recommended *Aldibert*, *Becker*, and Co. to the Defendants as perfectly safe persons, the Defendants
wrote to *Hulletts*, that although *Aldibert*, *Becker*, and
Co. were unknown to themselves, if they, *Hulletts*,
thought them respectable men, the Defendants would
employ them to transport the cocoa to *Amsterdam*, and
Aldibert undertook to conduct the whole, by the circui-
tous route which the state of *European* commerce then
rendered necessary, and the Defendants knew no one
but *Aldibert*, *Becker*, and Co. in the business. *Aldibert*,
Becker, and Co. employed the Plaintiff, who was indebted to them, to perform the whole business, which
the Plaintiff did, but without any communication had
with the Defendants, and he now looked to the Defendants for payment, whose defence was, that they were
liable to *Aldibert*, *Becker*, and Co., whom alone they
had entrusted, and to no one else.   *Gibbs* C. J. strongly
inclined to think there was no privity between the parties, and that the action would not lie.   The jury found
that the goods were sent as was intended, but that there
was no privity between the Plaintiff and the Defendant,
and a verdict passed for the Plaintiff, subject to an
award as to the amount, and to the opinion of the

A., employed
by the Defend-
ant to transport
goods to a fo-
reign market,
delegates the
entire employ-
ment to the
Plaintiff, who
performs it
without the
privity of the
Defendant :
Held that the
Plaintiff cannot
recover from
the Defendant
a compensa-
tion for such
service.

L 2   Court,

Court, whether under these circumstances the Plaintiff was entitled to recover to any and what extent.

Accordingly, on a former day in this term, *Best* Serjt. obtained a rule *nisi* to set aside the verdict, and enter a nonsuit.

Shepherd, Solicitor-General, and *Lens* Serjt., on a subsequent day, shewed cause. The peculiar state of the commercial world at the time of this transaction, rendered it necessary that the goods should be conveyed by such concealed agents as *Aldibert, Becker,* and Co. might employ; and they having found such an one in the Plaintiff, he forthwith became the immediate agent of the Defendants, and entitled to look to them for payment. This case differs from that of *Cull* v. *Backhouse* (a), cited by the Chief Justice at the trial; for there the Plaintiff was employed to do only a part of the business which the Defendant had commissioned the prime agent to perform; whereas here is a transfer of the entire employment, and the Plaintiff is responsible for the whole to the Defendant, as well as to *Aldibert, Becker,* and Co. At all events the Plaintiff may recover for a certain part of the money, being that which he actually disbursed, and a certain part of the work, being that which he himself actually performed in *England.* It will not follow, that if the Plaintiff may

(a) *Cull* v. *Backhouse,* B. R. Guildhall, sittings after *Hilary* term 1793, before Lord *Kenyon* C. J. That was an action for work and labour, and money paid, brought to recover a compensation for conveying corn from the interior parts of *North America* down to the coast, and the dues paid on shipping it. A person who was commissioned by the Defendant to purchase and ship wheat for him, employed the Plaintiff to bring it down to the coast, and to pay shipping charges, &c., but failed to pay him, whereupon he claimed the amount from the Defendants, who had not at that time paid to their immediate agent any part of the sum due for this service. Lord *Kenyon* C. J. held that the Plaintiff must sue the person who actually employed him, and not the Defendant.

recover, all the persons on the continent, who had any   1815.
share in transporting the goods, may therefore in like
manner recover their respective debts against the De- SCHMALING
fendant; for those persons all acted by the orders of THOMLINSON.
the Plaintiff. He who deals with an agent, believing
him to be a principal, may, when the principal is disco‑
vered, charge the principal.

Adjornatur.

On this day *Gibbs* C. J. relieved *Best* from support‑
ing his rule, and delivered the opinion of the Court.

There is no privity between the Plaintiff and the
Defendants. There was nothing by which the Defend‑
ants could conjecture that the Plaintiff ever would be
introduced to them; nothing by which they should
know that they ever should meet with such a person as
the Plaintiff. The Defendants must, indeed, know that
some persons must be employed under *Aldibert, Becker,*
and Co. to get the goods to *Amsterdam,* but there is
nothing whereby they ever authorized *Aldibert, Becker,*
and Co. to employ any one person to conduct the
whole. An argument was raised by the Solicitor-
General on this ground, that the Defendants must
know that some one would be employed by *Aldibert,*
Becker, and Co.; but he forgets the fact, that another
person introduced *Aldibert, Becker,* and Co. to the De‑
fendants, as the persons who were to conduct the whole,
and there is no pretence that the Defendants ever au‑
thorized them to employ any other to do the whole
under them: the Defendants looked to *Aldibert, Becker,*
and Co. only, for the performance of the work, and
Aldibert, Becker, and Co. had a right to look to the
Defendants for payment, and no one else had that
right: the consequence therefore is, that the Plaintiff
must be nonsuited, and the rule to set aside the verdict
must be made absolute.

May 1.

GREENHILL *v.* MITCHEL.

In opposing a rule for judgment as in case of a non-suit, upon the absence of documentary evidence at the last trial, it is not necessary to state what the evidence is.

VAUGHAN Serjeant having obtained a rule for judgment as in case of a nonsuit, for not proceeding to trial pursuant to notice, *Shepherd,* Solicitor-General, shewed cause upon an affidavit, stating that the plaintiff at the last sittings did not proceed to trial, (which it was his intention to have done,) in consequence of the want of certain documentary evidence, which he was advised by his counsel, just previous to the trial, was necessary to produce in support of his action; not saying what the evidence was. *Vaughan,* in support of his rule, contended that the Plaintiff had not disclosed sufficient matter to the Court, and he compared this to the usual case of opposing the like rule upon the absence of a material witness, whereupon the practice of this Court requires, that the name of the witness should be stated, otherwise the affidavit is insufficient.

But *The Court* held that it was a very short process to give a witness's name, but it might be very complicated to state what the documents were, and they discharged the rule on a peremptory undertaking to try at the sittings after *Easter* term.

Rule discharged.

1815.

The Company of Proprietors of the STAFFORD-   May 1.
SHIRE and WORCESTERSHIRE Canal Navigation
v. The Company of Proprietors of the Navigation from the TRENT to the MERSEY.

THIS was an action of debt for 818*l.* 11*s.* 5*d.* due   A canal act
and of right payable by the Defendants to the Plain-   gave a higher
tiffs for certain rates, duties, and tonnage for and upon   rate of tonnage
for light goods
the carrying of divers goods in divers barges of the De-   than for heavy
fendants, and for the passing and navigating of divers   goods. If a
barges of the Defendants, upon the navigable canal of   jury find that
the Plaintiffs. The Defendants pleaded the general   were heavy
issue, and paid money into court. The cause was   goods when
tried at the last *Stafford* summer assizes before *Dallas* J.   ten years subse-
and a verdict was taken for the Plaintiffs, subject to the   quent consent
opinion of the Court upon a case, and also to a refer-   to consider the
ence as to the amount, if the Court should think the   same species as
Plaintiffs entitled to recover.   light goods,
will not entitle
The case in substance was, that by an act 6th *G.* 3.   the canal com-
the Plaintiffs were incorporated and empowered to make   pany to de-
and maintain a navigable canal, which was afterwards   the toll on
made. By that act, in consideration of the Plaintiffs'   light goods.
charges &c. the Plaintiffs were empowered to demand
for tonnage and wharfage, for all iron, iron stone, coal,
stones, timber, and other goods and commodities whatsoever, which should be carried upon their canal, such
rates or duties as they should think fit, not exceeding
1½*d.* per mile per ton. And for the better ascertaining
the tonnage of timber or wood, 50 feet of round, or
40 feet of square oak, ash, or elm timber, or 50 feet
of fir, or deal, balk, poplar, and other wood, were to be
rated for one ton. By an act, 10 *G.* 3., reciting the
former act, and that some amendments therein were necessary, and some farther and other powers and provisions

L 4   wanting

1815.

STAFFORD-
SHIRE and
WORCESTER-
SHIRE Canal
Company
v.
TRENT and
MERSEY Canal
Company.

wanting for the said navigation, it was enacted that every boat passing through any lock on the navigation with less loading than six tons, should pay the Plaintiffs as a lock due, for the waste of water, 6d. at each lock which such boat should pass through, and also a tonnage rate for six tons of lading, in the same manner as if such boat had actually six tons of loading on board. And for regulating the price of freight to be charged by the owners, or masters, or other persons belonging to any boat, for the carriage of small parcels upon the canal, the Plaintiffs from time to time, at any general assembly, with the consent of the major part of at least 21 commissioners at a general meeting, might make bye laws for fixing the price for the carriage of any parcel not exceeding one cwt. upon the canal, and were from time to time to publish the prices in manner therein mentioned; and a penalty is inflicted on masters of boats for demanding more than the price so ascertained. The same clause enacts, that 60 square feet of light goods shall be deemed and taken to be a ton weight in all parts of the canal, any thing in the recited act contained to the contrary notwithstanding. From 1803 to 1811, inclusive, the Defendants have been carriers navigating boats upon the Plaintiffs' canal, and have carried thereon among other goods, hops, wool, and teazles. The Plaintiffs did not before *October* 1803 charge the tonnage of light goods by measure; they have since that time insisted upon charging all persons in that way, to which the Defendants have refused to submit, and the accounts between them remain unsettled, though some money has been paid. If the Plaintiffs are entitled to charge hops, wool, and teazles by measure, as light goods, then the money paid into court was not sufficient to cover their demand. If they are not entitled so to charge, it was agreed that the sum paid into court

should

should, as far as respected the present action, be deemed sufficient. At the trial, the jury found that at the time of passing the act 10 *Geo.* 3., and prior to ten years ago, hops, wool, and teazles were considered heavy goods, but that within the last ten years, and at the time the charges sought to be recovered in this action were made, hops, wool, and teazles were, according to the custom of the country where the canal lies, light goods. The question for the opinion of the court was, whether the Plaintiffs were intitled to charge at the rate or price of a ton weight, for 60 square feet of the hops, wool, and teazles, carried by the Defendants upon the Plaintiffs' canal.

1815.

STAFFORD-
SHIRE and
WORCESTER-
SHIRE Canal
Company
v.
TRENT and
MERSEY Canal
Company.

Shepherd Solicitor-General, for the Plaintiffs, contended, that upon this finding of the jury, the goods in question were drawn within the meaning of the act, and were to be considered as light goods, and that the Plaintiff might be permitted to recover.

Lens Serjt. for the Defendants, was stopped by the Court.

GIBBS C. J.   The act of 10 *G.* 3. materially varied the interests of this canal company, and the rate of tonnage which they are to receive for light goods: a looser word could not have been used; but we must find some meaning for it.   But it is found, that when the act was passed, these articles were heavy goods, therefore, when the act passed, it was considered by the legislature, that they did not alter the Plaintiffs' rights as to these species of goods; and the Defendants must have considered that their interests were not affected by the act as to these goods; otherwise, perhaps, they would have opposed the bill in parliament.

If

1815.
STAFFORD-
SHIRE and
WORCESTER-
SHIRE Canal
Company
v.
TRENT and
MERSEY Canal
Company.

If an action had been brought a year after the act had passed, the verdict must have been for the Defendants, upon the ground that these were to be rated as heavy goods. What then has since occurred, to alter their rights? That the country has since chosen to consider them as light goods; but that will not affect the interest of the Defendants, who are not bound thereby; and therefore the Plaintiffs are intitled to charge only the price of heavy goods.

Judgment for the Defendants.

May 1.

WEAVER *v.* SESSIONS.

The lessee of a public-house covenanted to buy of the lessor all the mait he should brew into ale or beer, or otherwise use therein, and the lessor covenanted to deliver on request sufficient good, well-dried, marketable malt for the use of the Defendant in the demised premises, and that at a market price, but if the Plaintiff should neglect so to do, the Defendant might purchase of any others. In an action for buying malt of others, a plea that the Plaintiff for a long time would not deliver good malt, but delivered divers quantities of bad malt, whereby the Defendant was in danger of losing his custom, and therefore bought malt of others, was held ill on demurrer.

COVENANT. The Plaintiff declared, that he was a maker of malt for sale, and by indenture demised to the Defendant a certain public house and premises for a term still unexpired, at a certain rent; and the Defendant covenanted that he would from time to time and at all times during the continuance of that demise, buy of the Plaintiff all the malt which the Defendant should brew into ale or beer, or otherwise use and consume in the demised messuage; and the Plaintiff covenanted with the Defendant, that he would, upon every reasonable request of the Defendant, deliver to him a sufficient quantity of good, well dried, marketable malt for the use of the Defendant in the demised messuage, and that, at a market price: but if the Plaintiff should neglect or refuse so to do, the Defendant should and might purchase the same of any other per-

son:

son: that the Defendant entered and was possessed; but that he did not after the demise, and whilst he was possessed of the demised premises, buy of the Plaintiff all the malt which he the Defendant brewed into ale and beer, and otherwise used in the messuage, but neglected so to do; and although the Plaintiff at the several times after mentioned was ready upon every reasonable request to deliver a sufficient quantity of good, well dried, marketable malt, for the use of the Defendant in the demised messuage, and that at the market price, whereof the Defendant at those times had notice, yet that the Defendant, on the first of *October* 1813, and on divers other days, brewed into ale and beer, and otherwise used in the said messuage, divers large quantities, to wit, 1000 bushels of malt, not bought of the Plaintiff, and without requiring the Plaintiff to deliver such malt, or any part thereof, to him. The Defendant acknowledging that he did not after the demise, and whilst he was so possessed, purchase of the Plaintiff all the malt which he brewed into ale and beer, and otherwise used in the said dwelling-house, thirdly pleaded, that the Plaintiff for a long time after making of the said indenture, neglected to deliver to the Defendant a sufficient quantity of good, well dried, marketable malt, for the use of the demised messuage; but instead thereof, contrary to his covenant, delivered to the Defendant divers quantities of bad, ill dried, unmarketable malt, to be brewed into ale and beer, and to be otherwise consumed in the Defendant's demised messuage, by reason whereof the ale and beer became so bad, weak, and unsaleable, that the Defendant was in great danger of losing the custom of many persons who had been accustomed to frequent his house for the purpose of buying his ale and beer; and thereupon the Defendant, in order that he might brew a sufficient quantity of good, strong, and saleable ale and beer for

the

1815.

WEAVER
v.
SESSIONS.

the necessary supply of his customers frequenting the house, did on the said day and on divers other days, as in the declaration was mentioned, buy divers quantities of malt of other persons, and not of the Plaintiff, and did use the same in the demised dwelling-house. The Plaintiff demurred generally.

Best Serjt., who was to have argued this demurrer for the Plaintiff, was stopped by the Court, and *Copley* Serjt. argued it for the Defendant.

GIBBS C. J.. The Defendant is placed in a situation of great difficulty, but he has placed himself in that situation: he has chosen what contract he would enter into, and how he would fortify himself against that covenant to which he is exposed. What is the covenant? On the part of the Defendant, he by this indenture covenanted, that he would from time to time, and at all times during that demise, buy and purchase of the Plaintiff all the malt which he should brew into ale or beer, or otherwise use or consume in the messuage thereby demised; and the Plaintiff covenanted that he would on every reasonable request of the Defendant, deliver to him a sufficient quantity of good, well dried, marketable malt for the use of the Defendant in the messuage thereby demised, and that at a market price; but he goes further, and reserves to the Defendant the liberty of providing himself elsewhere, if the malt be bad; for there is a proviso that if the Plaintiff shall neglect or refuse so to do, the Defendant may purchase the same of any other person. If the Plaintiff sends in bad malt, the Defendant may bring his action of covenant, and may also buy malt of others. The declaration states that the Defendant had used in his malt-house 1000 quarters of malt purchased of others, without requesting the

Plaintiff

Plaintiff to deliver it. The plea is, that while the
Defendant was possessed of the demised premises, for
a long time the Plaintiff refused to deliver a sufficient
quantity of good, well dried, and marketable malt, but
instead thereof delivered divers quantities of bad, ill
dried, and unmarketable malt, and thereupon, that
the Defendant bought of other persons, and not of the
Plaintiff, and did use the same for the cause aforesaid.
This plea does not sufficiently connect the malt purchased, with the orders given to the Plaintiff, so as to
excuse the Defendant for buying of others. The
Defendant ought to have stated, that he did give particular orders to the Plaintiff, and that on his breach
of duly executing them, he bought particular quantities
of others. If we were to hold this plea sufficient, we
must decide that a single breach by the lessor would
release the covenant of the lessee. The argument
urged for the Defendant, is, not that the Plaintiff's
breach destroys the lessee's covenant, but that it suspends its operation until the Defendant receives notice
from the Plaintiff that in future he will send the
Defendant better malt. I cannot accede to this; and
think the plea is defective.

HEATH J. was of the same opinion. This was a
very improvident covenant, but the Defendant is bound
by it.

CHAMBRE J. The covenant is absolute on the one
side: if bad malt is delivered, or none delivered, the
Defendant may sue the Plaintiff: he may also supply
himself elsewhere; but to entitle himself so to do, the
Defendant must shew that he has complied with all
things to be observed by him, that entitle him so to do.
But he only avers that the Plaintiff has sold him bad
malt. A breach by the landlord does not generally
discharge

1815.

WEAVER
v.
SESSIONS.

discharge the covenant of the tenant, nor must it be construed so, because upon these covenants each party has a complete remedy against the other.

DALLAS J. I think each of these parties has a complete remedy, and must resort to the remedy by action on their respective covenants, and that the breach by the Plaintiff of his covenant, is no discharge of the present action.

Judgment for the Plaintiff.

May 2.

POSTLE v. BECKINGTON.

If a Defendant, who pays money into court, afterwards obtains judgment as in case of a nonsuit before the Plaintiff has taken it out, the Plaintiff cannot afterwards have his costs taxed up to the time of paying the money into court.

THIS was an action for goods sold and delivered. The Defendant paid 18*l.* into court. The cause went on to a notice of trial, and was set down for trial at a former sittings for *London.* The Plaintiff withdrew his record. The next term the Defendant ruled him to enter the issue, and afterwards signed a judgment of *non pros.* against him, for not entering the issue. The Plaintiff then took the money out of court, and after the judgment was signed, but before the Defendant had taxed his costs, taxed his costs on the rule for paying money into court. The Defendant taxed the subsequent costs, and on the taxation, the Plaintiff insisted he was entitled to the costs up to the time of paying the money into court, and offered to set them off against the costs of the judgment of *non pros.*, which the prothonotary allowed.

Shepherd, Solicitor-General, now moved, that the prothonotary might review his taxation of costs, insisting, that where a Defendant pays money into court, if the Plaintiff does not take it out before judgment of

non-

non pros., the Plaintiff is not entitled to the costs up to the time of paying the money into court. In the case of *Crosby* v. *Olorenshew* (a), the Court of King's Bench establish this principle, that if the Plaintiff suffers the cause in any way to come to an adverse judgment, he must stand on the same ground, by what means soever he comes to that judgment, as if he had tried the cause, and a nonsuit or verdict had passed against him. The former cases were of a nonsuit at trial; that case says, that upon a judgment as in case of a nonsuit, the Plaintiff shall have the same disadvantage; and so it is here, in the case of a judgment of *non pros.*

1815.

POSTLE
v.
BECKINGTON.

Bosanquet Serjt. shewed cause against this rule in the first instance. The practice in this court is, that unless the Plaintiff proceeds to trial, he is entitled to tax his costs on those counts on which the money has been paid in, and to take the money out of court. Several cases have decided, that though the Plaintiff puts the Defendant in that situation in which he is entitled to move for judgment as in case of a nonsuit, and even if the Plaintiff takes out a rule to discontinue, yet, if he has not actually been to trial, he may have costs for the Plaintiff taxed up to the time of paying the money into court. In this court the practice is more favourable to the Plaintiff than in the Court of King's Bench; for in causes upon policies of insurance, in that court, the short causes are considered as if they were tried, on which the Plaintiff loses the costs; but here, the Court give the Plaintiff the costs on the short causes, though he loses his costs on the cause wherein money has been paid into court, which is actually carried down to trial. *Twemlow* v. *Brock* (b). In *Seaman* v. *Bridge* (c) the Court of King's Bench held, that the Plaintiff was enti-

(a) 2 *Maule & Selw.* 335.   (c) 8 *T. R.* 408.
(b) 2 *Taunt.* 361.

tled

1815.

POSTLE
v.
BECKINGTON.

tled to costs up to the time of paying the money into court, though the Plaintiff had given notice of trial, and by having omitted to countermand it, had entitled the Defendant to judgment as in case of a nonsuit. *Llorck v. Wright* (a), the Plaintiff was held entitled to his costs, though he had twice withdrawn his record, and had since taken out a summons to discontinue on payment of costs. The generality of the rule is exemplified in the cases of *Savage* v. *Franklin* (b), *Davies* v. *Mansell* (c), *Fisher* v. *Kitchingman* (d), and *Bate* v. *Crane* (e). The judgment in *Crosby* v. *Olorenshew* seems to have proceeded on the words of the statute (f) for judgment as in case of a nonsuit. The words of the statute certainly are, that the Defendant shall be entitled to costs in any action where he would upon nonsuit have been entitled to the same. The Plaintiff here, then, though he was liable to a judgment as in case of a nonsuit, was still in a condition to take out the money, and tax costs to the time of paying it in, because he had not previously taxed his costs. Even in the case of judgment as in case of a nonsuit, it is said by *Bayley* J., that if he had taxed his costs before the rule was made absolute, he would have been entitled to them. If the Plaintiff had come hither with a trifling excuse, and given a peremptory undertaking, he would have had an opportunity to get his costs taxed; and there is neither precedent nor principle to deprive him of them.

The Solicitor-General supported his rule. The reason of the Plaintiff's cases is, that the cause is in progress, and by taking the money out then, the Plaintiff shews he does not mean to proceed to judgment: but why has he not costs when a verdict or nonsuit at trial

(a) 8 T. R. 486.
(b) *Barnes*, 280.
(c) *Ibid.* 282.
(d) *Barnes*, 284.
(e) *Ibid.* 287.
(f) 14 G. 2. c. 17. ss. 2, 3.

has

has passed against him? Because he has waited for that which may be the foundation of an adverse judgment, and whenever an adverse judgment takes place he loses his costs.

GIBBS C. J.　The Plaintiff can produce no case in which it has been determined that he is entitled to his costs up to the time of paying the money into court, he not having taken the money out of court until after judgment has been signed against him. What principle, then, can he establish? It has been decided, that where a Plaintiff waits for a verdict against him, or a nonsuit at trial, he loses his costs. That is on the principle, that if he terminates the cause in an earlier stage, he may have costs to the time of paying in the money, but not where he has chosen to await the final issue of the contest. It has been held in the King's Bench that in the case of judgment as in the case of a nonsuit, the Plaintiff is not entitled to his costs. My Brother *Bosanquet* tries to make a distinction between a judgment as in case of a nonsuit, and a judgment of *non pros.* We see no ground for it. So far as any reason can be applied to a case of this nature, we think the decision of the Court of King's Bench on this subject is right, and that the reason of the case requires, that the Plaintiff should not be entitled to his costs; the prothonotary must therefore review his taxation.

Rule absolute.

1815.

May 2.   SHELLY, Plaintiff; MILLER and Wife, Deforciants.

JOHNSON, Plaintiff; same Deforciants.

Fine amended
by substituting
Old B. a lieu
conus. for the
parish of B.,
there being no
such parish.

The Court
are not induced
to amend fines,
by the difficulties raised by
purchasers.

*B*LOSSET Serjt. was permitted to amend two fines by substituting *Old Brentford*, a *lieu conus.* for the parish of *Brentford*, upon an affidavit that there was no such parish as *Brentford*, and that the premises were situate in *Old Brentford*, in the parish of *Ealing;* he referred to *Flower* v. *Bainwright* (a). An objection had been raised to the title by a purchaser on this account, unless the amendment could be made.

Per Curiam. The court will not in the slightest degree be swayed by the difficulties that a purchaser makes, as an inducement to amend the fine: but the amendment is, upon principle, proper to be made.

Fiat.

(a) *Ante,* v. 303.

Buy 726
May 2.

HAGEDORN *v.* LAING.

The Defendant bought
goods by auction, upon the
condition that

*A*SSUMPSIT. The 2d count stated that the Plaintiff, by his auctioneer and agent, caused to be put up to sale by public auction certain goods, to wit, seven they were to be cleared away at the buyer's expence in 14 days, and the price paid on or before delivery: if any lots remained uncleared after the time allowed, the deposit-money should be forfeited, the goods resold, and the loss on resale made good by the present purchaser. The broker gave a bought-note, which allowed 14 days for receiving and delivery: Held that only the buyer had 14 days to deliver, but that the seller was bound to deliver instantly.

Semble. That after a resale of goods by a vendor, as upon default made by the first purchaser, he cannot recover against the first purchaser for goods bargained and sold.

lots

lots of damaged hemp, and one lot of damaged hemp, upon and subject to certain conditions, which this count stated; the second of which was, that the lots were to be cleared away at the buyer's expence in 14 days from the day of sale, and the remainder of the purchase-money must be paid on or before the delivery of the goods. And the third was, that if any lots should remain uncleared after the time allowed, the deposit money should be forfeited to the present proprietors, the lots resold by public or private sale, and the loss (if any), together with interest of money, warehouse-rent, and all charges attending the same, must be made good by the purchaser at the present sale. And the Plaintiff averred that the Defendant was the highest bidder, and was declared the purchaser, at a certain sum of money; and after averring mutual promises to perform all things in those conditions of sale contained, he alleged for breach, that although the Plaintiff afterwards, and during all the 14 days after the Defendant's promise, was ready and willing to deliver the hemp to the Defendant, upon his paying for the same, yet the Defendant did not within 14 days from the day of sale, at the Defendant's expence, clear away the lots, or pay the Plaintiff the purchase-money, or any part thereof, but refused, and the lots remained uncleared after the time limited. And the Plaintiff alleged that he, after the 14 days, resold the goods at a loss, according to and by virtue of the conditions of sale, and that the deficiency, and the charges attending such resale, together with the interest of money, and warehouse-rent, amounted to a large sum, which, by reason of the premises and according to the conditions of sale, the Defendant became liable to pay.   There was also a count for goods bargained and sold to the Defendant. The cause was tried at the sittings at *Guildhall* after *Hilary* term 1815, before *Gibbs* C. J., when it was

M 2   proved

1815.

HAGEDORN
v.
LAING.

proved that the goods were put up to sale on the conditions (annexed to a catalogue of the goods) which are stated in the second count, and that the Defendant was the highest bidder. He applied to take away the hemp immediately after the sale, but it was then in pawn for certain duties, which must be paid before it could be delivered; and he was therefore unable then to obtain it. The broker gave the Defendant a bought note describing the goods as bought of himself, upon the terms, amongst others, that 14 days were to be allowed for receiving and delivery. A particular of the Plaintiff's demand stated that he sought to recover the amount, together with interest, of the loss which had occurred to him upon the resale of the goods in question. On this evidence, (the first count describing a contract which clearly was not proved,) *Best* Serjt. contended, that the Plaintiff could not recover on the second count; that the conditions of sale gave 14 days for the purchaser to take away the goods, but gave no latitude of time to the vendor for delivering them, but that he was bound to deliver instantly, which he had failed to do; that the conditions of sale, and not the bought note, constituted the contract between the parties; that even if the bought note could be called in aid, its true construction did not give the seller 14 days for delivery; but that if it did, the Plaintiff had not declared on that bought note, but on the conditions of sale annexed to the catalogue only. *Shepherd* Solicitor-General, for the Plaintiff, contended, that the seller had 14 days for delivery, as well as the buyer 14 days for taking away the goods. *Gibbs* C. J. thought that the 14 days were allowed to the purchaser as a convenience to him for carrying away the goods, but that the seller was bound to deliver them at the first or any moment of the 14 days; it was impossible that the seller could have till the last moment of the 14 days for delivery, since the

pur-

purchaser, upon not taking the goods away within the
14 days, was to forfeit his deposit. *Shepherd* then resorted to the count for goods bargained and sold, to
which *Best* objected, that as the Plaintiff had taken upon
himself to resell the goods, he had repudiated the sale
to the Defendant, and could not now recover as for
goods bargained and sold; and further, that the particular which the Plaintiff had delivered, confined his
demand to the loss on the resale, and precluded him
from recovering for goods bargained and sold. The
jury found a verdict for the Plaintiff, subject to the
point reserved, whether the Plaintiff, under these circumstances, was entitled to recover.

Accordingly, *Best* in this term obtained a rule *nisi*
to set aside the verdict and enter a nonsuit, relying on
the same construction of the contract on which he had
insisted at the trial.

Shepherd now shewed cause against this rule. He
urged that the resale was no bar to the Plaintiff's recovery for goods bargained and sold, as had been held
by Lord *Ellenborough* C. J. in the case of *Mertens* v. *Ad-
cock* (*a*). The special contract enables the Plaintiff to
resell, so that he does not by the resale repudiate his
contract, and this is a term of the contract which the
law would imply, although it were not expressed;
therefore it is not necessary that it should be specially
declared on, but the Plaintiff may insist on the contract
of goods bargained and sold, although he resorts to a
resale. Whether the seller has or has not sold to any
one else the goods which the purchaser has rejected,
cannot alter the Plaintiff's right to recover for goods
bargained and sold. As to the particular, it only points
out the transaction upon which the Plaintiff's demand

(*a*) 4 *Esp. N. P. Cas.* 251.

M 3

is

is founded; it does not profess to state the technical description of the Plaintiff's right, and to shew on which count he intends to proceed. If indeed it had specified one technical description of the Plaintiff's claim, perhaps it might have been deemed to exclude another technical description of it; as, for instance, if it had stated that the demand was on the count for money lent, perhaps the Plaintiff might be precluded from recovering on the count for money had and received, which he did not particularize; but that was not the case here. The meaning of the bought note is, that the seller should have 14 days for delivering, and the buyer 14 days for receiving the goods.

The Court (b) relieved *Best.* The main question is on the construction of this contract, as it is to be collected from the conditions of sale, and the bought and sold note; and taking the two together, we think it is clear, not that the seller should have 14 days to deliver the goods, but that the purchaser should have 14 days to take them away. He must have a reasonable time, within which he may take them away. The seller may be ready to deliver them at any time. If the purchaser do not take them within the stipulated time, a penalty is inflicted on him; he forfeits his deposit; he is to pay the loss on a resale, and interest on the loss. It is therefore unnecessary to dwell on the other point. I would not unnecessarily differ from Lord *Ellenborough,* but I much doubt, whether this can in any manner be considered as a case of goods bargained and sold. Here is a particular contract, that on paying for the goods, and taking them away at a certain time, the purchaser shall have the goods; but if it be a contract of bargain and sale, it certainly is subject to a condition; for

(a) *Heath* J. was absent on this day, and during the residue of this term.

if

if the purchaser do not take the goods within a certain time, the seller may, by the terms, rescind the contract; he may resell, and if he resells, I think he shews his dissent to the contract of bargain and sale. I throw this out, that I may not seem to have altogether assented to the doctrine that has been contended for, but I think this case must on the merits be decided against the Plaintiff.

Rule absolute.

1815.

HAGEDORN
v.
LAING.

LEIGH v. BERTLES.

May 3.

IN this case the Defendant put in bail to the action on 11th *November.* An exception was entered on the 24th of *November,* but in the mean time the Plaintiff had commenced an action for an escape, in which he recovered. The bail never justified, but the Defendant had nevertheless applied to the filazer to enter on the roll the recognizance of the same bail, which it is the practice of that officer to do, if required; for notwithstanding that the bail are rejected, they still stand as bail in the filazer's book, and though the exception appears on his book, it never appears thereby whether they have justified or not. The sheriff had now sued the bail below on the bail bond, and they had pleaded *comperuerunt ad diem,* whereupon *Best* Serjt. moved for a rule *nisi* to take the bail recognizance off the file, under an apprehension that the bail would prove their issue by the production of this record, against which the Plaintiff could not aver. The Court at first intimated, that the evidence of the recognizance might be met by evidence of the rejection of the bail: they could not perceive for what honest purpose the bail should now enter into this gratuitous undertaking, but

If bail above, who are excepted to and have not justified, afterwards procure their recognizance to be put on the roll, the Court will, at the instance of a Plaintiff suing on the bailbond, cause it to be taken off, that the Defendants may not prove by that evidence the issue of comperuerunt ad diem.

M 4   they

1815.

LEIGH
v.
BERTLES.

they conceived it would be no answer to the bail bond, to shew a recognizance voluntarily entered into, when the sufficiency of the bail had not been allowed by the Court; it was not, however, fit that the sheriff should have to encounter that difficulty, and they granted a rule *nisi*.

Shepherd Solicitor-General now shewed cause against this rule. He contended that the Defendant had done every thing which was incumbent on him, having put in his bail in due time. If the bail did not justify within four days after exception, the sheriff's officer might have treated them as a nullity; but it was by his own neglect that he had subjected himself to the action for the escape, while the Defendant had been guilty of no neglect.

The Court, interposing, observed, that it was not the question there, whether the sheriff had misconducted himself, but whether there was sufficient ground to take off the roll the recognizance of bail, because, standing where it did, it testified a falsehood. The Court thought it ought not to remain. The remedy of the sheriff is by proceeding on the bail bond : if the Defendants, on their plea of *comperuerunt,* give that recognizance in evidence, the sheriff had no opportunity of controverting its truth. The Court therefore thought the rule for taking the recognizance off the roll, ought to be made absolute, because otherwise that record would enable the Defendants to prove at the trial a fact which was not true.

Rule absolute.

WOOD v. BROWN.   *May 3.*

IN this case the Plaintiff declared for a libel written and published concerning him in his trade of a victualler, which he described in his declaration as " purporting that the Plaintiff's beer was of a bad quality and sold by deficient measure, and that his other liquors and the treatment ' of his guests were bad, and that his house, (meaning his public house,) was, from those circumstances, a nuisance, and therefore that another public house was much wanted by the neighbouring inhabitants," and averred special damage. The Defendant demurred generally.

Lens Serjt., in support of the demurrer, cited *Zenobio* v. *Axtell* (a) and *Maitland* v. *Goldney* (b) ; and observed that this was a novel attempt in pleading to declare on a libel, without setting out the very words used.

It is not sufficient to declare that the Defendant published a libel concerning the Plaintiff in his trade, purporting that his beer was of bad quality and sold by deficient measure ; the libel itself ought to be set out.

And it is bad on general demurrer.

Best Serjt., *contrà*, urged, first, That the declaration was sufficient; secondly, that if defective, it was defective in form only, and could not be taken advantage of on a general demurrer. First, It was enough to set out a libel according to its substance. The *Queen* v. *Drake* (c). *Holt* C. J. there says, " you may describe a libel by its sense and meaning ; thus, it is a good information, to shew that the Defendant made a writing, and therein said so and so, translating it into *Latin*. In *Zenobio* v. *Axtell*, the point was but little considered. So, it is sufficient to aver that the Defendant used words imposing the crime of felony. 2dly, The declaration shews an imputation on a tradesman, that he sells bad

(a) 6 *Term Rep.* 162.   (b) 2 *East*, 426.   (c) 2 *Salk.* 661.

goods

1815.

WOOD
v.
BROWN.

goods to his customers, which is a sufficient cause of action: it is substantially shewn, and the not setting out the express words is merely want of form.

Lens in reply. The effect of a libel cannot be set out without any statement of what the libel contains. By this mode of declaring, the Plaintiff deprives the Defendant of the advantage of demurring or moving in arrest of judgment, or bringing a writ of·error; either of which he might do, if the supposed libel, when set out on the declaration, contained no libellous matter. At the time when the *Queen* v. *Drake* was ruled, there was a necessity, which does not now exist, for a departure from this rule so far as to translate the libel into *Latin*, because all pleadings were then in that language. This form of declaration leaves it wholly in the judgment of the Plaintiff himself to determine whether a writing is actionable. The law requires that in the first place the very libel itself should be shewn on the declaration, and after that, the Plaintiff may add what he will by way of *innuendo*.

Cur. adv. vult.

The Court on this day gave judgment for the Defendant, upon the ground that the Plaintiff, by this mode of declaring, withdraws from the Defendant the power of calling for the judgment of the Court on demurrer to the words of the libel, whereas, if he states them upon the record, the Defendant, if he thinks fit, may demur, and bring before the Court the question whether they amount to a libel.

Judgment for the Defendant.

GOODSON *v.* FORBES.　　*May* 5.

SAME *v.* ———.

8/3⊔ 24.

THESE were two actions on a policy of insurance, and the declarations contained also a count upon an award made under a reference by the Plaintiff on the one hand, and all the underwriters on the policy on the other hand. Upon the trial of the cause at the sittings after *Hilary* term 1815, before *Gibbs* C. J., it appeared, that the agreement to refer, and the award, were each written on one stamp: for the Defendant, it was objected, that as many stamps were requisite as there were underwriters. The evidence, however, was admitted, and the jury found a verdict for the Plaintiff, subject to the point reserved.

The several underwriters on the same policy have such a community of interest in the subject insured, that if they all agree to refer the demand of the assured on that policy, one stamp for the agreement to refer, and one stamp for the award, are sufficient.

Best Serjt. in this term moved for a rule *nisi* to set aside the verdict and enter a nonsuit, contending that this case was distinguishable from those that would be cited, because here the award was sought to be used, not between the Plaintiff and all the underwriters in a mass, but between the Plaintiff and this single Defendant, and was therefore more like the case of *Copley* v. *Day* (a), where a lessor made several contracts with several tenants respecting separate lands on the same instrument, and the stamp afterwards affixed was appropriated to one name only, and could not have been applied to any other, and the other contracts were struck out. *Gilby* v. *Lockyer* (b): It was held that separate debts due from two different persons could not be comprized in one affidavit on one stamp. So (c), where four corporations had been

(a) 13 *East,* 241.
(b) 1 *Doug.* 217.

(c) *Rex* v. *Reeks,* 2 *Str.* 716.

admitted

1815.

GOODSON

v.

FORBES.

admitted by one instrument, four separate stamps were required. The Court granted a rule *nisi*.

Shepherd Solicitor-General, in shewing cause against this rule, adopted the language of a recent treatise (*a*), as admirably expressing the principle which was to govern this case. " The distinction established," he said, " was, that if the interest of the parties relates to one thing which is the subject-matter of the instrument, or, in other words, if the instrument affects the separate interests of several, and there is a community of the same subject-matter as to all the parties, there, a single stamp will be sufficient; but where the parties have separate interests in several subject-matters, there ought to be a separate stamp for each party, against whom, or in whose favour, the instrument is offered in evidence." Here, though the interests of all the underwriters are several, they all relate to the same thing, and so the case is distinguishable from *Copley* v. *Day*. If three partners on one side, and their debtor on the other, referred a demand of a debt, though it were agreed that the arbitrator should award in what shares the partners should receive it, that circumstance would not render three stamps necessary. In the case of a debtor compounding with his creditors, one stamp only is necessary. The subject of this insurance is entire: the underwriters do not severally insure specific parts of the goods. There is the same ground for requiring two stamps to a joint and several bond, where the Plaintiff severs in action. He cited the cases of the *Bristol Dock Company* v. *Williams* (*b*), *Baker* v. *Jardine* (*c*), and *Bowen* v. *Ashley* (*d*), This case is wholly distinguishable from *Gilby* v. *Lockyer*.

(*a*) *Phillips's Treatise on the Law of Evidence*, 2d edit 389.
(*b*) *Davis* v. *Williams*, 13 *East*, 232.
(*c*) 13 *East*, 235. *n*.
(*d*) 1 *New Rep.* 274.

Best

Best and *Vaughan* Serjt., in support of the rule, admitted the principle to be as stated, and the propriety of the decisions referred to, but said, they were inapplicable. In all the cases cited, the interests, though separate before, were united by the effect of the agreement, but that was not the case here. In insurance causes a separate stamp for each underwriter is necessary on the consolidation rule, which is an instance in point. In *Bowen* v. *Ashley* the condition of the bond made each obligor answerable for the acts of the others. In the *Bristol Dock Company* v. *Williams*, the object was, to raise one aggregate fund. In a deed of composition the debtor conveys all his property to trustees to make an aggregate fund. Here, neither the submission, which was of several causes of action, (there being here no consolidation rule,) nor the award, which was, that the Defendants, meaning each of them, shall pay 75 per cent., effected any union of interest between the parties. An attachment obtained against one for non-payment, could not be enforced against another of them. Several underwriters cannot be sued in one action; their contracts are several. The case of partners differs, for there, all is bottomed on the same contract.

Cur. adv. vult.

GIBBS C. J. now delivered the judgment of the Court. These causes have stood over for judgment. Each of them was an action on a policy of insurance, with a count in the declaration on an award made by an arbitrator, to whom it was stated at the trial that the parties had referred the matter in dispute. An objection was taken to the Plaintiff's case, that the award produced, and the agreement to refer, had each but one stamp; whereas each of them, it was urged, included the interests of the Defendant, and of all the other underwriters, and comprehended in effect as many separate

1815.

GOODSON
v.
FORBES.

separate agreements and separate awards as there were underwriters on the policy. We think it impossible to decide that, in the present case, more stamps than one were necessary, without disturbing decided cases. It was admitted by the counsel for the Defendant, that in a case of composition by an insolvent debtor with his creditors only one stamp is necessary. There the different creditors have each a separate remedy against the insolvent debtor. They have no joint legal interest; yet it has been always considered that upon such a deed one stamp is sufficient. Such deeds have always been received in evidence without objection; their legality has been acquiesced in on the principle, that all the creditors have a common interest in the joint fund. In the case of *Baker* v. *Jardine*, all the mariners in a vessel conveyed their interest in a prize to an agent. It was objected that they had each a separate interest, and that there ought to be as many stamps as persons interested. It was answered, It is true that when the agent has sold a prize, each claiming his share must assert his claim separately; but they have a community of interest in the joint fund, on the proceeds of which each is hereafter to assert his separate claims; and that community of interest enables them to convey by one deed, with one stamp. Another case arose on the subscription to the *Bristol* Dock, in which a number of persons had subscribed an agreement that each would subscribe the sum set against his respective name. This was an agreement by several for a subscription to one common fund; there it was held that one stamp was sufficient, because though the parties might acquire separate interests, or subject themselves to separate obligations, yet all contributed to one loan, and therefore one stamp sufficed. *Burrough*, of counsel for the Defendant, admitted that he could not distinguish that case from *Baker* v. *Jardine*. In the present case the

agree-

agreement is between the assured and all the underwriters on the policy. All have an equal interest in the matter insured, all being equally interested in the preservation of it; for if it is preserved, none of them are liable. It is true, that in a court of law, on the question whether the assured had a claim on any one underwriter, his claim cannot be mingled with that of either of the others; but it is equally true that all have an equal interest in the question of the liability. Here the parties agree to refer the question, what claims arise. on the policy; and this, we think, is such a community of interest, that one stamp is sufficient. I have omitted to say any thing on the case of *Bowen* v. *Ashley*, in this court, because there was a difference of opinion at the bar respecting the legal effect of that instrument. It was argued by my Brothers *Shepherd* and *Bayley* that each obligor was answerable for the performance of all; now if each was answerable for all, the question did not arise; but the report does not shew how that fact is. [*Best* here stated that he was possessed of a copy of that bond, whereby it appeared that the words were, that each was bound for the others of them.] If that agreement was, that each should be answerable for the other, the subsequent words of the condition, that each should attend the meetings, &c. would refer to and give effect to that agreement; if the agreement was, by each for the act of himself singly, then the subsequent words would not go beyond it. But it is immaterial to the present case, and I have not relied on it.

Rule discharged.

PHILIPSON and BREWER v. CALDWELL.

The Court will not upon motion enable a prisoner to set off in a summary way a debt for which he has obtained no judgment, against the Plaintiff's execution.

J 203.

THE Plaintiffs had recovered a judgment for 143*l.* debt and costs, against the Defendant alone, and had taken him in execution. The Defendant and *Melton* had sued the Plaintiffs for a debt of 115*l.* *Onslow* Serjt. moved that either the Defendant might be permitted to set off this debt against the judgment, as far as it would extend, and pay only the difference to the Plaintiffs, and thereupon be discharged out of the custody of the marshal as to this suit; or else, that he might be permitted to pay 115*l.* into court for the account of himself and *Melton*, and pay over to the Plaintiffs only the residue. He stated that he was instructed that *Melton* would become party to the rule, and he cited *Roberts* v. *Bigg* (a), adopted in *Buller's N. P.* (b), and *Hall* v. *Ody* (c), The Court observed that the case in *Barnes* was very involved : they granted a rule *nisi*, conditionally that *Melton* would become party to the rule.

On this day *Copley* Serjt. appeared for *Melton*, and consented only to the second alternative, viz. that 115*l.* should be paid by the Defendant into court for the use of himself and *Melton*.

Best Serjt. shewed for cause against the rule, that the Defendant and *Melton* had not yet obtained judgment against the Plaintiffs for their debt, and the Court would not try the cause on affidavits.

GIBBS C. J. In all the cases cited where the Court has been desired to relieve the party by way of set-off,

(a) *Barnes*, 146.   (b) 3d edit. 336.   (c) 2 *Bos. & Pull.* 28.

it

it has been the set-off of one execution against another, and it has been at too late a stage of the cause for the party to avail himself of the set-off by way of plea; which here is not the case, and therefore, even supposing *Melton* to be out of the case, there is no instance where the Courts have interfered to establish a set-off against a judgment, when the party might try that question in an action.   The moment this difference between the present case and all the other cases cited appeared, it was too forcible to be withstood.

Rule discharged.

1815.
PHILIPSON
v.
CALDWELL.

SIDNEY, Demandant; HULME, Tenant; AUSTEN and Another, Vouchees.

May 5.

A BARGAIN and sale enrolled to make the tenant to the precipe for suffering a common recovery, conveyed, amongst other premises, the *Cowleaze*, containing 6 acres 3 roods and 31 perches, and a piece of pasture land formerly a part of *Morrice's Ham*, but now thrown into, and forming part of the *Cowleaze*, and containing two roods and 33 perches, and contained the following general words applicable to the whole of the parcels conveyed by the deed, " all which lands and hereditaments are situate in the parish of *Great Canford*, in the county of *Dorset*, and were late and now are in the tenure of *C. Hill*, or his undertenants, and the same form or make the farm commonly called *Knighton Park Farm*." Pursuant hereto a recovery was suffered in *Trinity* term, 53 *Geo.* 3.; of lands in *Great Canford*. It had since been doubted whether the piece of ground, formerly part of *Morrice's Ham*, was not in the parish of *Hampreston*, and not in *Great Canford*. It was sworn that the first vouchee, who was tenant for life, had been

Where a deed to lead the uses of a recovery conveyed land by a minute specific description, and afterwards added a general description of the parish, which was false as to a particular parcel, and the recovery specified that parish only, the Court permitted the parish wherein that parcel lay, to be added in the recovery.

in the seisin of this parcel as part of *Knighton Park Farm*, along with the residue thereof, as parcel of the entailed estate, and that it had been with the rest in the occupation of his tenant *Hill*; that it was situate in *Dorset*; that there was not, at the date of the deed or since, any parcel of *Knighton Park Farm* within the parish of *Great Canford* which answered this description, and that the vouchees intended this piece of land should pass, and the entail thereon be barred. Upon this statement *Bosanquet* Serjt. moved to amend the recovery, by adding the parish of *Hampreston*, upon the authority of *Lambe* v. *Reaston* (a). Though the description of the parish in the deed was false as to this close, the deed contained a sufficiently true description of the close to pass it, notwithstanding the false addition.

The Court referred to the distinction taken in *Dowtie's* case (b), that " if a true certainty had been in the first place, as if he had bargained and sold (the tenements, &c. in the tenure of *Wm. Gardiner* in the parish of *St. Andrew's, Holborn,*) there it was agreed that the tenements shall pass well enough, notwithstanding the addition of the falsity, for *utile per inutile non vitiatur.*" The present case differed from *Dowtie's* in the mode which that distinction required, for here the detailed true description came first. And on the authority of *Lambe* v. *Reaston* they permitted the amendment.

Fiat.

(a) *Ante*, v. 107.   (b) 3 Co. 9.

1815.

(IN THE EXCHEQUER-CHAMBER.)   *May 6.*

HAWKINS *v.* RAMSBOTTOM.   In Error.

THIS was a writ of error brought to reverse a judgment of the Court of King's Bench in an action of *assumpsit* against the Defendant below alone, where the Plaintiff below had in some of the counts of his declaration stated that the Defendant below and one *H. Phillips,* who had since become a bankrupt and obtained his certificate according to the statutes, were indebted to the Plaintiffs below for work and labour, and commission, due to them from the Defendant below and *H. Phillips,* and that the Defendant below and *Phillips,* before he became a bankrupt, promised to pay, and averred a breach, that the Defendant below, and *H. Phillips* before he became a bankrupt, and the Defendant below since the bankruptcy of *Phillips,* had refused to pay; and in other counts they stated that since *Phillips* became a bankrupt, the Defendant below was indebted to the Plaintiffs below for money lent to the Defendant below; and that the Defendant below, since *Phillips* became a bankrupt, promised to pay, and breach that he had not, since *Phillips's* bankruptcy, paid. After judgment by *nil dicit* and a writ of inquiry, the Plaintiff below had final judgment for entire damages. The Plaintiff in error assigned for error, that in the declaration, causes of action were joined, which could not be so by the law of the land; inasmuch as the promises in the seven first counts of the declaration were alleged to have been made by the Defendant below and *H. Phillips* jointly, before *Phillips* became a bankrupt, and the promises and undertakings in the remaining counts were alleged to have been made by the Defendant below only, since *Phillips* became a bankrupt, which could not by the

Counts upon a promise by the Defendant and another, since become a bankrupt and certificated, may be joined in an action against the solvent partner alone, with counts on promises by the Defendant solely since the other became a bankrupt. But the Defendant might plead the joint contract in abatement.

N 2   law

law of the land be joined or included, or sued upon in one and the same declaration. There was also the general assignment of error.

Gifford, for the Plaintiff in error, contended that this was a misjoinder of action. It was clear that if no bankruptcy had intervened, a count stating a promise by the two jointly could not be joined with a count stating a promise by one of the two separately. This is materially distinguishable from the case of a debt due to or from a surviving partner (a), which, it was held, might be set off against a debt due by him in his sole right, for that, by the survivorship, becomes the sole debt of the party sued : here the prior counts having stated a debt due from the Defendant below and the bankrupt, the Defendant below could not set off against that debt a debt due from the plaintiff below to the defendant below only. The inconvenience is, that the bankruptcy is not a discharge of the debt, but only of the person of the bankrupt. Where there were several Defendants (b), and one of them only within reach of process, and the joint contract was pleaded in abatement, one of the judges now on the King's Bench invented a replication, that the other persons jointly liable were in *Scotland*, and had no goods, lands, or property, within the jurisdiction of the Court, by which they might be attached, but the Court held, that the Plaintiff could not by these facts entitle himself to sue on a joint contract, as a several one. Might the Defendant below have pleaded in abatement the joint contract with a traverse of the bankruptcy of *Phillips?* That would be an equally novel attempt. If the Plaintiff below may recover entire damages on this declaration, the Defen-

(a) *Slipper* v. *Stidstone*, 5 *Term Rep.* 493.
(b) *Sheppard* v. *Baillie*, 6 *Term Rep.* 327.

dant

dant below, to whom a right of action would thereby accrue, subsequent to the bankruptcy and certificate of *Phillips*, to sue *Phillips* for contribution, could have no test to distinguish how much of the damages were re- covered in respect of the joint demand, and how much in respect of his separate debt. The rule is the same in tort. If a Plaintiff sues two for a joint tort, he may recover against one for a separate tort; but if he gives evidence of a joint tort, he cannot afterwards pro- ceed to recover in the same verdict further damages for another tort by a single Defendant. The Court of King's Bench have held (*a*) that where one of several joint contractors is a certificated bankrupt, the joint contract may nevertheless be pleaded in abatement, and that a replication that the joint contractor is a bankrupt, and has obtained his certificate, is bad upon demurrer. Yet that declaration and replication together place the Plaintiff exactly in the same situation in which the Plaintiff below places himself by this declaration, viz. that he insists on a joint contract as sole, averring the same excuse as in this case, for not joining in the suit the joint contractor. In the case of *Noke* v. *Ingham* (*b*), it was held that upon the statute 10 *Ann. c.* 15. the pro- per course is, where one of several joint contractors pleads his bankruptcy and certificate, for the Plaintiff to enter a *nolle prosequi* against him, and proceed as to the other.

Curwood for the Defendants in error. There is no misjoinder in the form of action; the only question is, whether there is a misjoinder in the character of the party sued. There is a strong analogy between this case and the case of a partner dying. The liability at-

1815.

HAWKINS
v.
RAMSBOTTOM.
In Error.

(*a*) *Bovill* v. *Wood*, 2 *Maule & Selw.* 23.   (*b*) 1 *Wils.* 89.

N 3   taches

taches alike to the solvent and to the surviving partner. There is a material distinction between the case, where one of several joint creditors, and one of several joint debtors, becomes a bankrupt. In the first case, the assignees of the bankrupt must join in suit; in the other, the debt may be recovered against the solvent partner only. *Bovill* v. *Wood* is in favour of the Plaintiff in error, for it shews that the joint contract ought to be pleaded in abatement, and cannot otherwise be taken advantage of. It is a most material circumstance, too, that it there appeared on the plea, that the bankrupt was still alive, which does not appear on this declaration, so that this is reduced to the case of survivorship, for the continuance of his life cannot be inferred. If the Plaintiff unite in his declaration demands against the Defendant jointly with another, and demands against the Defendant solely, he may recover on both in one verdict, unless the Defendant think proper to plead in abatement as to parcel of the writ, which he may do (a). So, in declaring against a survivor of two partners, it is unnecessary to notice the joint contract (b). *Smith* v. *Barrow*, acc. (c) The question is, whether the Defendant is sued in any other than his personal character; for it may be admitted, that he cannot be sued at once in his personal, and in a representative character: but he is sued in his personal character only, when it is shewn that his partner is discharged by law, by reason of the bankruptcy and certificate. The statutes 10 *Ann. c.* 15. *s.* 3. and 5 *G.* 2. *c.* 30. *s.* 7. speak of discharging the bankrupt from every debt due at the time he became a bankrupt; and the certificate is a bar, not to his liability merely, but a bar to the action, and discharges the debt; and the statute 49 *Geo.* 3. *c.* 121. *s.* 8. prevents the other De-

(a) *Powell* v. *Fullarton*, 2 *Bos.*
& *Pull.* 420.

(b) *Hyat* v. *Hare*, *Comb.* 383.
(c) 2 *Term Rep.* 476.

fendant

fendant from recovering contribution against the bankrupt.

Gifford in reply. It is clear by *Bovill* v. *Wood*, and *Noke* v. *Ingham*, that the bankruptcy is not such a discharge of the debt, but that it is necessary to sue the bankrupt together with the solvent partner. In the case of a joint contract by an infant or a feme covert, it is not necessary to shew they were joint contractors, for their's is no contract, but here it is admitted there did exist a valid contract, but discharged by subsequent matter, and in such case, as well the contract, as the discharge, must be stated. This debt is therefore due from the Plaintiff in error jointly with a party necessary to be sued. It was unnecessary for the Plaintiff in error to plead in abatement, for the joint contract appeared on the record: where the Plaintiff has stated the Defendant's plea, the Defendant need not plead it. There is this distinction between *assumpsit* and debt, that in *assumpsit* the declaration sounds in entire damages, for the whole: in debt there is no incongruity in abating the writ as to a single count, because the demand is severed, and each count carries a specific part. Here the damages being entire on both sets of counts, the judgment is erroneous.

Cur. adv. vult.

GIBBS C. J. on this day delivered the opinion of the Court. After stating the pleadings, he proceeded. These two causes of action are stated separately and expressly on the declaration. It appears on the latter counts, that the Plaintiff proceeds on the express promise of the Defendant only, and upon the first counts, as to the promise of the bankrupt, it is shewn that he is taken out of the way. The omission of one of several joint contractors as a Defendant in *assumpsit*, is

now

now clearly settled to be matter of abatement only, and if it be not so pleaded, the action proceeds as if the promise had been made exclusively by the party sued on the record. A plea in abatement, supposing it available in this case, might therefore be pleaded to the counts on the joint cause of action: the Plaintiff in error having omitted in due season to take that course, which was open to him, has lost the only mode of availing himself of that defence. He has lost that defence to the first class of counts, and has made no defence to the last class of counts. It is now urged that they cannot be joined. Why? It is said, the same plea is not applicable to some counts, which is applicable to others. There is no weight in that objection. In many cases a count on a special contract is joined with money counts; a set-off may be pleaded to the last, which is not applicable to the first. So, here may be a plea of a set-off of joint debts to the first class of counts, and of several debts to the last, and both of them will be good pleas, *reddendo singula singulis*. The plea in abatement was therefore the only way in which the plaintiff in error could have availed himself of the objection to the first counts, and having omitted that opportunity, he has lost the only mode he had of putting forward this answer to that demand, and the Plaintiff below is entitled to judgment. I say nothing on the question, what would be the case, if, before a judge at *nisi prius* the Plaintiff had offered evidence applicable to both demands.

                                   Judgment affirmed,

1815.

SHAWMAN v. WHALLEY.

May 6.

PELL Serjt. moved to discharge the Defendant out of custody on entering a common appearance, upon the ground of a defect in the affidavit to hold to bail, which it is unnecessary to state, because his affidavit disclosed a preliminary objection, namely, that a bail-bond had been given, and bail above had been since put in for the purpose of rendering the Defendant, and they had rendered him. It had been held that after that step, a defendant could not avail himself of irregularity in the (*a*) affidavit to hold to bail.

The Court will not discharge a Defendant out of custody on a defect in the affidavit to hold to bail, after he has given bail to the sheriff, and bail to the action, which last have rendered him.

Per Curiam. We can hardly get over the authority of this case. It shews that the affidavit to hold to bail is part of the process for bringing the Defendant into court, and that the irregularity therein may in due season be taken advantage of, yet it may be waved by any subsequent step; and we think it so desirable to have a conformity of practice between the two courts, that unless it can be shewn that such practice rests on mistake, we shall decide in conformity thereto: we therefore think the application comes too late.

Rule refused.

(*a*) *Dargent v. Vivant,* 1 *East,* 330.

May 6.   HUGUENIN *v.* RAYLEY.

The conditions
of a life insur-
ance required a
declaration of
the state of
the health of
the assured,
and the policy
was to be va-
lid only if the
statement
were free from
all misrepre-
sentation and
reservation ;
the declar-
ation described
the assured as
resident at
*Fisherton
Anger.* She
was then a
prisoner in the
county gaol
there : Held
that it was a
question for
the jury, whe-
ther the im-
prisonment
were a mate-
rial fact and
ought to have
been commu-
nicated.

THIS was an action upon a policy of insurance subscribed by the *Albion* Insurance Company upon the
life of *Elizabeth Swayne.* Upon the trial of the cause
at the *Sarum* spring assizes 1815 before *Dampier* J.
one defence was, that there had been a fraud in effecting the policy by the suppression of a fact which the
contract required the assured to disclose. It appeared
that *E. Swayne,* who had been many years resident in
a house of her own in the parish of *Fisherton Anger,* but
was in *December* 1813 a prisoner for debt in the county
gaol in *Fisherton Anger,* then employed *Mather* to effect
an insurance on her life with the Defendants: one condition of the insurance was, that a declaration should
be made of the state of the health of the life insured,
and *Mather,* reciting that he had proposed on the
behalf of *Elizabeth Swayne* of *Fisherton Anger* an insurance on her life, which had been accepted on the
declaration then following, declared that *E. Swayne* did
not exceed the age of 66 years, and that she was then
resident as above; it was stipulated that the policy
should be valid, only if the statement were free from
all misrepresentation or reservation. For the purpose
of ascertaining the state of her health, *Mather,* by the
direction of the Defendants, called in a physician, who
found the subject in the gaol, which is in a situation
perfectly healthy, confined in a large airy room, well
calculated to preserve the health of its inhabitants.
She was apparently about 60 years of age, a fresh-look-
ing healthy hale woman, making allowances for her
confinement; for confinement makes some difference
in the state of health. He certified that she was in
good health, and he would have noticed on his certifi-

4   cate

cate the fact of her being in jail, had he not been led by the circumstance of *Mather's* speaking of the Defendants by the term " our office," to suppose he was an agent of the Defendants, and that all which he knew would be communicated, for the witness thought it a fact material to the terms of the contract to be communicated. Upon this evidence, *Dampier* J. thought, that *Mather* had by contrivance prevented the physician from stating a fact to the Defendants, which he thought material to the contract, and he therefore stopped the Plaintiff's case, and without hearing the Defendant's case directed a nonsuit.

Best Serjt. in this term obtained a rule *nisi* to set aside the nonsuit and have. a new trial; he urged that the contract did not require any statement respecting the state of the party's liberty, or confinement; the Defendants required precise and particular information respecting certain facts; and the least mis-statement on those facts, would, he admitted, be fatal; but the assured was not bound to disclose facts which were not enquired of, and it would be a dangerous doctrine to encourage; it would render necessary that an assured should furnish the insurers with a minute history of his whole life; there was a manifest distinction between misrepresentation and silence. Some insurance offices required by their contract that every thing should be certified that was material to the risk; but that was not the case here; and therefore, although imprisonment might, as the physician stated, in a slight degree increase the risk, that could not invalidate the contract between the parties : at all events, if the holding back a material fact would avoid the policy, it was a question that ought to have been left to the jury, whether the imprisonment were a material fact, and the Defendant ought to have had the opportunity of bringing evidence

evidence before the jury to shew that it was immaterial. The Court granted a rule *nisi*.

Lens Serjt. now shewed cause against this rule. From whatever cause the concealment originated, if there was a concealment of that which it was important should be known, it avoids the policy. The terms of the declaration induce a belief, that the residence in *Fisherton Anger* was a residence at large there, the physician's evidence is, not only that he thought it important in the construction of the contract, but that, for physical reasons, it was material whether the subject was in prison, and debarred from air and exercise, or not; insomuch, that he saw reason for going beyond the matters expressly required by the proposal, so far to insert the mention of this fact in his certificate, if he had not been misled by the idea that *Mather* was the agent of the Defendants. By the terms " without reservation," the assured was bound to state every thing, which from its nature could possibly bear on the subject. If this fact had been disclosed, the Defendants could have taken medical advice, whether the imprisonment would increase the risk. Unless, therefore, the Plaintiff could prove that this fact could by no possibility increase the risk, (and the nature of things shews the contrary,) it ought to have been communicated, and the Defendants had a right to have it laid before them that they might form their own judgment thereon.

Adjornatur.

On this day the Court relieved *Best* from supporting his rule. They observed that they had examined the documents, and there was nothing express in the terms of the policy which required the imprisonment to be stated, nor was there an omission of the statement of any matter which the office called for: nevertheless, if the imprisonment were a material fact, the keeping it

back would be fatal; but it ought to have been sub-
mitted to the jury, whether the omission of the fact
relied on was or was not a material omission, there-
fore there must be a new trial.

1815.

HUGUENIN
v.
RAYLEY.

- Rule absolute.

JACKSON v. Lord MILSINGTON and Another.   *May 8.*

VAUGHAN Serjt. moved to set aside the judgment
and warrant of attorney which had been given to
secure an annuity, upon four objections: first, that the
Plaintiff had insisted on, as due upon the deed, and re-
ceived from the Defendant, one half-yearly instalment
of the annuity commencing half a year sooner than it
appeared by the deed and memorial that the annuity was
to commence; and as the annuity had in fact been paid as
commencing from an earlier period than the deeds de-
scribed, he contended that the grant of the annuity con-
tained a false descrption of the transaction, and was there-
fore void. Secondly, that the memorial, which stated the
bond to bear date " on or about the 14th of *May*," did
not with sufficient certainty contain the date. Thirdly,
that there was a defeazance to the warrant of attorney,
stipulating for a stay of execution in case of punctual
payment; but that though the memorial directly stated
the warrant of attorney, it did not state the defeaz-
ance; which it had been held necessary to state (*a*).
Fourthly, that the bond bound the heirs of the obligor,
but that the memorial did not state it to be binding
upon the heirs. The Court refused the application
upon the two first grounds, saying that a payment made

Marginal note: Where the grantor of an annuity had, upon a mistaken claim of the grantee, paid a half-yearly instalment for half a year sooner than the deed required it: Held that this did not avoid the annuity.

A memorial describing an annuity-bond as bearing date on or about a day named, states the date with sufficient certainty.

A memorial of an annuity-bond needs not to state that the heirs of the obligor are bound.

A memorial of an annuity-

deed stated a recital in the deed that a warrant of at'orney and a defeazance had been given, which recital shortly set out the defeazance; held that this supplied the place of a substantive memorial of the defeazance.

(*a*) Ex parte *Ansell*, 1 *Bos. & Pull.* 65.

by

by the Defendant in his own wrong, not being made in pursuance of any previous agreement repugnant to the deed, was no breach of the annuity act; and that if the bond bore date the 14th of *May*, that was about the 14th of *May*; if it did not, the false description would be fatal; but it was not stated by the Defendant that the 14th of *May* was not the true date: upon the two last grounds they granted a rule *nisi*.

Best Serjt. on this day shewed cause. The last objection is disposed of by the decision of the Court of Exchequer-chamber upon the case of *Horwood* v. *Underhill*, in error (a). As to the other objection, the deed happens to recite the warrant of attorney and the defeazance also, and the deed, including that recital, is, though unnecessarily, set out at length in the memorial, though there is no separate and substantive memorial of the defeazance.

Vaughan endeavoured to support his rule upon the ground, that a statement of the defeazance in the memorial by way of recital was insufficient.

GIBBS C. J. It would be monstrous to set aside the annuity for such an objection as this. The object of the act is, that the whole transactions should appear on the memorial. It is correctly said by the counsel for the Defendant, and the objection is countenanced by some earlier cases, that the defeazance is not expressly stated, but only by way of recital contained in another memorialized deed; but the recital in the latter is very full. The case cited in 1st *Bos.* & *Pull.* requires that the defeazance shall be stated in the memorial; but it does not say, that a statement by way of recital is not sufficient. Without laying down any general

(a) *Ante*, iv. 346.

prin-

principle to be drawn out of this case, to govern cases which may not resemble it, we think that this defeazance is sufficiently stated to support the annuity.

' Rule discharged.

1815.

JACKSON
v.
Lord MILSING-
TON.

FLETCHER *v.* WELLS.

May 8.

*B*EST Serjt. had on a former day obtained a rule *nisi* to set aside the service of process upon the ground that the *English* notice was irregular in expressing the year in *Arabic* figures instead of words at length. (*a*)

Blosset Serjt. now shewed cause on the preliminary objection that the application was too late, the Defendant having permitted the Plaintiff to execute a writ of inquiry.

Best, in support of his rule, urged, that the line of practice established by the case of *Dand* v. *Barnes* (*b*), was, that so long as the Defendant himself takes no step, he may lie by while the Plaintiff takes any number of steps short of final judgment.

A party who would set aside proceedings for irregularity, must apply instantly after the irregular party has taken the first further step; if he lets him take a second further step, he waves the irregularity.

Per Curiam. The counsel for the Defendant misconceives the rule. It is, that if there has been irregularity, the party suffering is not bound to move to set it aside within any specific time, for he may reasonably suppose that the opposite party will discover his mistake, and abandon his defective proceeding; but if the party guilty of the irregularity takes one step more, which shews that he does not mean to abandon his process, then it is incumbent on the party complaining to apply in-

---

(*a*) See *Eyre* v. *Walsh, post.* 216. (*b*) *Ante,* vi. 6.

stantly

1815.

FLETCHER
v.
WELLS.

stantly to set it aside, for if he takes a step himself, or permits the other party to take a further step, it is a waver of the irregularity. Here the Defendant being served with defective process, was not bound to move to set it aside until after the Plaintiff had shewed that he meant to act on it. The Plaintiff gave notice of declaration, upon which the Defendant ought immediately to have applied; but he lies by until the Plaintiff has executed a writ of inquiry; and therefore he has hereby waved the irregularity.

Rule discharged.

Bing 609

240. May 8.

FENTON v. ELLIS.

An affidavit to hold to bail, stating that the Defendant is indebted to the Plaintiff for goods sold and delivered to the Defendant, not saying by the Plaintiff, is bad.
A supplemental affidavit to hold to bail not allowed.

SHEPHERD Solicitor General had on a former day obtained a rule *nisi* that the bail bond given in this case might be delivered up to be cancelled, upon the ground that the affidavit to hold to bail stated only that " the Defendant was indebted to the Plaintiff for goods sold and appraised to the Defendant," not adding by the Plaintiff, he cited *Eyre* v. *Hulton* (a), and *Taylor* v. *Forbes* (b), which was brought before the King's Bench for the purpose of their reviewing their decision in *Cuthrow* v. *Haggard.* (c)

Best Serjt. now shewed cause: he contended the affidavit was sufficiently certain to support an indictment for perjury, if the Plaintiff had not sold the goods to the Defendant. At least, if this affidavit were insufficient, the Court would permit a supplemental affidavit to be made.

(a) *Ante*, v. 704.
(b) 11 *East*, 316.

(c) 8 *East*, 106.

The

The Solicitor General supported his rule.

The Court said the cases were too strong for the Plaintiff to resist, and they also refused to permit a supplemental affidavit to be made.

Rule discharged. (a)

(a) S. P. *Hyde* v. *Jacob,* C. P., Hil. term 1815, Feb. 7. *Shep-* berd, Solicitor-General, for the Plaintiff.

SAMUEL BAKER and PHŒBE his Wife, and GEORGE EGGLESTON and CATHERINE his Wife, *v.* W. DANIEL, and W. DANIEL the Younger, STEPHEN DANIEL, and JOSEPH DANIEL.

May 8.

IN a writ of partition, the demandants counted that S. *Featherston* being seised in fee, had issue female the Plaintiffs *Phœbe,* and *Catherine,* and *Elizabeth;* that on his decease the lands, being of the nature of gavelkind, which immemorially have been partible between the heirs male, and in default of them among the heirs female, descended in fee to his three daughters as co-heirs female, in default of heirs male; that they entered and were seised; that *Phœbe* intermarried with the Plaintiff *Baker,* and *Catherine* with the Plaintiff *Eggleston,* and the husbands and wives respectively became seised in fee in right of the wives of one-third part; that *Elizabeth* married the tenant *W. Daniel,* and had issue the three other tenants; that on her death, by the custom of gavelkind, *W. Daniel* became seised, as tenant by the courtesy, of one moiety of her purpart for his life, if he lived sole, the reversion in fee being to the three other tenants, to whom the other moiety also descended in fee, and shewed that so the demand-

The count in partition, writ to the sheriff, and his return, amended by striking out words of limitation in tail, where the title stated on the count shewed an estate in fee.

ants and tenants together and without division hold the premises, of the inheritance which was of *S. Feather-ston*, whose co-heirs the said *Phœbe,* *Catherine*, and *Elizabeth* were, whereof to the demandants *S. Baker* and *Phœbe*, in right of the said *Phœbe*, and the heirs of their bodies begotten, it belonged to have one-third part of the premises, and to the demandant *Eggleston* and *Catherine*, and to the heirs male of their bodies lawfully begotten, it belonged to have one other third part, to be divided, to hold to them respectively in severalty. The Defendants not appearing within 15 days after the return of the writ, judgment was entered, that according to the statute partition be made between the demandants and tenants of the tenements aforesaid, (not saying of what estate.) · The sheriff returned an inquisition, wherein he recited a writ commanding him to make partition, and to deliver one equal third part to the demandants *Baker* and *Phœbe*, to be holden to them and the heirs of their bodies, and one-third part to the demandants *Eggleston* and *Catherine*, and the heirs male of their bodies, and the remaining third part to the tenants to be holden in severalty; and after stating the division by metes and bounds, into three equal parts, he returned that he had caused the first-mentioned third part to be delivered to the demandants *Baker* and *Phœbe*, to hold to them and the heirs of their bodies; and the 2dly mentioned equal third part to the demandants *Eggleston* and *Catherine*, to hold to them and the heirs male of their bodies, and the residue to the tenants. And the final judgment was, that the partition aforesaid be holden firm and effectual for ever. .

Lens Serjt. moved to amend the count, and the writ *de partitione faciendâ*, and the sheriff's return, by substituting in each of them " the heirs of *Phœbe*," for
" the

" the heirs of their bodies," and " the heirs of *Catherine*,"
for " the heirs male of their bodies," as the fact was,
and as the title set out in the count warranted.   He admitted that he had found no precedent for amendment
in a writ of partition, but upon principle it was reasonable to be done.   It came within the reason of amendment of fines and recoveries.   Returns made by sheriffs
of writs of seisin in recoveries had been amended (*a*).
So in *Formedon* (*b*), *Scott* v. *Perry*, an amendment had
been made by consent in a real action.   But the ground
on which he relied here, was, that the interlocutory
judgment was correct, for it is not usual to mention in
the judgment what estate the parties are to have.   In
the old precedents (*c*) the sheriff's return in partition
does not notice either the quantity or quality of the
estate which he gives; but the writ to the sheriff and
his return pursued not the judgment of the Court, which
was correct, but the count, which was incorrect; and the
statute (*d*) directs " that in default of appearance within
15 days after the return of the writ of *pone*, or attachment, the Court may proceed to examine the demandant's
title, and quantity of his part and purpart, and accordingly as they shall find his right, part, and purpart to
be, they shall for so much give judgment by default, and
award a writ to make partition, whereby such proportion, part, and purpart may be set out severally."   It
would suffice to strike out the words heirs of their
bodies, and heirs male of their bodies, without inserting
any words.

The Court at first hesitated, whether this did not fall
within their general rule of allowing no amendment in
real actions, and referred to the authorities collected in

(*a*) *Watson*, Demandant; *Lock-*   (*c*) *Rastal, Partition,* 449,
ley, Tenant, 2 *Wils*. 2.   450.
　　(*b*) *Scott* v. *Perry,* 3 *Wils*. 206.   (*d*) 9 *&* 10 *W*. 3. *c*. 31.

a note

1815.

BAKER
v.
DANIEL.

a note of the late Serjt. *Williams* (a).   They also felt a
difficulty in amending the return, which was the act of
the sheriff, not of the Court; but after consideration,
they permitted the amendment, by striking out the
words of entail, so that the writ should stand as a direction to the sheriff to divide the lands generally,
without saying what estate he should give.

Fiat.

(a) 2 *Williams's Saund.* 45. g. *note.*

May 8.

PROTHERO v. THOMAS.

A Plaintiff's
attorney, who,
at the Defend-
ant's request,
puts in bail for
him and after-
wards pays the
debt and costs,
needs not de-
liver a bill a
month before
he sues for the
money so ad-
vanced.

mg 261

THE Defendant being arrested at the suit of *Prosser*,
in which the Plaintiff's father was the attorney, applied to the Plaintiff, who was also an attorney, and not
before employed by the Defendant, and happened to be
in the same house, to know if he could do something
for him; upon which the Plaintiff gave the sheriff an
undertaking to put in special bail, and the defendant
was thereon liberated.   The Plaintiff afterwards put
in special bail, and on enquiry into the nature of the
action, found it expedient for the Defendant, to pay,
and the Plaintiff did pay, the debt and costs; the
latter were not taxed.   The Plaintiff having brought
this action to recover the amount he had so paid,
without making any charge for his own labour therein,
it was, upon the trial at the *Monmouth* spring assizes,
1815, before *Richards* B., objected for the Defendant,
on the authority of *Crowder* v. *Shee* (a), that the
Plaintiff could not recover, because he was an attorney,
and he had not proved the delivery of a bill including
these charges, a month before the action commenced.

(a) 1 *Campb.* 437.

Richards

Richards B. thought this was not a case within the statute (a), and the jury found a verdict for the Plaintiff; which

Pell Serjt. in this term obtained a rule *nisi* to set aside, upon the ground that this was a " disbursement in law," within that act, and being now called on to support it, he maintained that by the Plaintiff having paid the costs of *Prosser's* action, without causing them to be first taxed, he had deprived the Defendant of the opportunity of confining them within reasonable limits: that the Plaintiff had acted as an attorney in this case, was clear, because he had put in bail, and given under-takings, and done other acts, which none but an attorney can do. If a single item in an attorney's bill is of a taxable nature, the whole bill is subjected thereby to taxation.

GIBBS C. J. The case cannot be put ·on other grounds than the counsel for the Defendant has put it on, but this certainly is not a case within the statute. The statute applies to cases where a person employed as an attorney sues to recover a compensation for his labour and skill. This is a case where the Defendant applies to the Plaintiff to pay the debt and costs of an action, in which the Plaintiff and· his partner are attornies for a creditor of the Defendant. It is very true that he thereby gets the costs of that action into his own pocket, but it is not true that the bill of costs therefore might not have been taxed; for if on the bringing this action the Defendant had applied to have had that bill of costs taxed, he certainly might have so done, but this not being an action by the Plaintiff for his fees for business done as an attorney, it was not

(a) 2 *Geo.* 2. *c.* 23. *s.* 23.

O 3   necessary

1815.   necessary for him to deliver his bill a month before
PROTHERO   hand, the rule therefore must be discharged.
v.
THOMAS.   *Shepherd*, Solicitor-General, *contra*.

. *May* 8.   WYNN v. SMITHIES, Clerk.

If a clergyman who has two livings resides within one of the parishes, wherein there is no house of residence, it is a sufficient residence there to exempt him, without licence from the bishop, from penalties for not residing on his other benefice.

No licence is necessary for non-residence in the parsonage-house of a parish wherein there is no such house.

THIS was an action brought to recover penalties from the Defendant for wilfully absenting himself from his rectory of *Little Bentley*, and from his rectory of *St. Martin* in *Colchester*, at various periods stated in the declaration. The cause was tried before *Wood* B. at the last *Essex* spring assizes, when it was proved that during the year 1812 the defendant resided in a house of his own in the parish of *St. Martin*, *Colchester*, (in which parish he had no parsonage-house,) except for a period of four months, calculated at different times within that year, during which four months he was resident in his rectory house of *Little Bentley*. *Wood* B. held that the residence in the Defendant's house in *St. Martin's*, was not only such a residence there as excused the Defendant from penalties for not residing during the same period upon his benefice of *St. Martin's*, but that it also was such a residence as excused him from penalties for not residing during the same period in his parsonage house of *Little Bentley*, and he nonsuited the Plaintiff.

Copley Serjt. in this term obtained a rule *nisi* to set aside the nonsuit; he contended that the residence in the Defendant's house was not, even as to the parish of *St. Martin's*, a sufficient excuse for not residing in the parsonage house of that parish, unless the bishop's licence for that purpose had been previously obtained, which

which had not been done. This, he said, was required by the 43 G. 3. c. 84. s. 19. But even if this were otherwise, the want of a house in *St. Martin's* was only an excuse for non-residence in *St. Martin's*, but the Defendant's abode there was not such a residence on one of his benefices, as would, without the bishop's licence, excuse a non-residence on his other benefice of *Little Bentley*. This had been decided in the case of *Law* v. *Ibbotson* (a), and the doctrine is rather confirmed than narrowed by the subsequent case of *Wilkinson* v. *Allot* (b), where it is treated as an excuse, not as residence. That such was the true construction of the statute against non-residence, appears from the act 54 G. 3. c. 54. which was made to alleviate the state of the clergy, and the indulgence granted, is, that if a pluralist resides nine months within the parish whereof he is beneficed and where he has no house of residence, that shall be deemed such a residence as will exempt him from residing on the benefice where he has a house; this is a legislative exposition of the former statute, and shews that before the late act, either no abode within the one parish would excuse non-residence in the other, or that a whole year's residence in the parish where he had no house was necessary, to exempt him from penalties for not residing on the benefice where he had a house; but in this case the Defendant's residence in *St. Martin's* is of eight months only.

As to the first point, *The Court* held that the gross absurdity of the proposition that the bishop's licence was necessary to excuse a rector living within his parish, from residence in a rectory house which did not exist, was apparent. As to the second point, unless the former act 43 G. 3. plainly made it penal not to re-

1815.

WYNN
v.
SMITHIES.

(a) 5 Burr. 2722.   (b) Cowp. 429. S. C. 5 Burr. 2725.

side

side on that one of the two benefices, where he had a house, they could not find it there enacted by the aid of the subsequent act, made many years after; an act too, which was intended to be remedial, and not to subject the clergy to penalties which did not before exist. They granted however upon the last point a rule *nisi;* and now 'stopping *Best* Serjt. who would have shewn cause,

Called on *Copley* to support it, who relied on *Law* v. *Ibbotson*, as going the whole length of the doctrine he contended for, though he admitted the consequence was that where a clerk has two benefices, on one of which there is no house, it would have been, under the statute of *H.* 8., illegal for him to reside so much as a month in the year in that parish; and *Goodale* v. *Butler* (a) there cited, is to the same purpose. The Defendant takes on himself to determine that, which the law confides to the discretion of the bishop; who may see reason to fix the clerk to residence on the 'benefice where the house is, possibly, for the purpose of keeping up the parsonage house.

GIBBS C. J. In *Law* v. *Ibbotson*, although there was no archidiaconal house, the Court held, that the Defendant's residence within the archdeaconry, in the parish of *Bushey* of which he was rector, was no excuse for his not residing in his parsonage house of *Bushey*. The truth is, the cases of *Law* v. *Ibbotson* and *Wilkinson* v. *Allot* are irreconcileable. To be sure, if one looks at the justice of the case, so far as the term is applicable to this subject, the plaintiff's doctrine is directly counter thereto; for upon the old statute, it would be unlawful for a person who had two livings to reside at all, or, at least, not for a month together, on that which had no

(a) 6 *Rep.* 21.4

house;

house; the evil, indeed, is somewhat qualified by the late statute, but I cannot think a statute which meant generally to divide the residence can bear this construction. This residence on a benefice where there is no parsonage house is not an excuse; it is a residence. Suppose a person were sued for not residing on a benefice on which he has no house, and he defends himself on the ground that he did reside within the parish. His answer would be, he did reside there; no, says the Plaintiff, it is only an excuse for non-residence: but be that as it may, it seems to me that for the same reason for which the statute excuses a clergyman from the penalties of non-residence if he reside in the body of the parish where there is no house, it ought to excuse him from residing in the other parish where there is a house, for he is performing his ecclesiastical duties in the first; and I cannot believe it was not intended to protect him for non-residence in the parish of *B.* where there is a house, by his residence on the parish of *A.* where there is no house: we think therefore that the nonsuit is right, and that the rule must be discharged.

CHAMBRE J. The Defendant has performed all the residence which the nature of the case admits: if there be a house, he must reside in it, if there be none, he must live in the parish. Why is a clergyman who has two livings to consult the bishop on which of them he shall reside, when the law gives him the option to reside on which of them he will? In the case of *Law* v. *Ibbotson* the Court of King's Bench took up the opinion, that the Defendant had nothing to do in his archdeaconry, no duty to perform for it, and therefore that the Defendant ought to reside in his rectory house of *Bushey*: but *Wilkinson* v. *Allott* is a later case, and it completely overrules *Law* v. *Ibbotson.*

DALLAS J. concurring, the

Rule was discharged.

ing 475

475

O In replevin proof of payment of rent to the avowant is *primâ facie* evidence that he is the owner of the land. But in a case where the Plaintiff did not originally receive the possession of the land from the avowant, it is competent to the Plaintiff to rebut the title of the avowant by shewing that he paid rent under circumstances which did not entitle the avowant to the rent.

And such evidence may be given on the issue *non tenuit modo et formâ.*

Semble that tenant in *elegit* may enter by virtue of the writ of *elegit* without ejectment.

THIS was an action of replevin. The defendant avowed for two years' rent due to himself on the 24th of *June* 1814, on a demise of the closes in which, &c., at the rent of 7*l.* 10*s. per ann.* payable half yearly. The Plaintiff pleaded that she did not hold the closes in which, &c. as tenant to the Defendant under the supposed demise thereof, in manner and form as the Defendant had alleged. The Defendant took an issue thereon, which was tried at the *Monmouth* spring assizes 1815, before *Richards* B., to whom it was stated, that the object of this cause was to try the validity of a deed granted by *Price,* a former owner of the land, to Mrs. *Baker.* The Defendant, on whom the issue lay, proved a receipt given by an agent of the Defendant named *Aram* to the Plaintiff, for a year's rent paid by the Plaintiff through the hands of her son to the Defendant, due at *Midsummer* 1812, for one moiety of the *Ty Cooch* farm, the meaning of which was explained to be, that the estate called *Ty Cooch* farm had belonged to *Price,* who had demised it to the Plaintiff at 15*l. per ann.* rent; and afterwards, being indebted to the avowant, had given him a warrant of attorney to confess a judgment, which was docketted in *February* 1810, and the avowant in 1811 sued out a writ of *elegit ;* and the Plaintiff having notice that the sheriff had under that writ taken an inquest and set out the several closes in which, &c. as a moiety of the premises, and returned that he had delivered them to the Defendant, although he the, Defendant had not recovered the premises in ejectment, the Plaintiff had attorned, and paid rent to him for a moiety. The Defendant had also exercised certain acts of ownership, by selling coppice wood standing on the

the farm. The Defendant rested on this case. The
Plaintiff proposed to answer it, by shewing that the
Defendant was not, at the time of her former payment,
or now, entitled to the rent: the Defendant objected,
that by the payment of rent, the Plaintiff had acknowledged himself, the Defendant, to be her landlord, and
was now estopped from contesting his title. *Richards* B. held that the proof of payment of rent made a
good *primâ facie* case for the avowant, but that it was
capable of being answered by other evidence; but reserved the point. Whereupon the Plaintiff answered
this case, by proving that *Price* being indebted to *Sarah
Baker* in 207*l.* for several sums of money, lent in consideration thereof, and of 89*l.* more then paid to him,
which sums together were the full value of the farm, in
1809 conveyed the premises in fee, by deed and fine, to
Mrs. *Baker,* and had paid rent to her before and since
she paid rent to the avowant. The Plaintiff also insisted, that even if this deed were to be postponed to
the *elegit,* the avowant was at most only tenant in common with Mrs. *Baker.* To rebut the evidence of the
prior conveyance, the avowant impugned the supposed
debt to Mrs. *Baker,* as fictitious; that no money passed
from her, and that the conveyance to her was fraudulent, and made only for the purpose of shielding the
possession of *Price.* This suggestion was in some measure fortified by the facts that the deed was all in the
hand-writing of *Price,* who was an attorney; that Mrs.
Baker was his housekeeper, and that she had said, that
she was entitled to one moiety of the value of the wood
which the avowant had sold, thereby seeming to admit
the avowant's title to the other half. The jury, however, giving credit to the deed, found a verdict for the
Plaintiff.

Pell Serjt. in this term moved for a rule *nisi* to set
aside the verdict and enter a nonsuit, upon a supposi-

tion

tion that the plaintiff had insisted at the trial, and that *Richards* B. had accordingly holden, that the proof of payment of rent to the avowant was not *primâ faciè* evidence of his title as lessor, and that he was bound to go into his title upon the issue of *non tenuit modo et formâ*, which was the very mischief, he said, which the statute 11 *G.* 2. *c.* 19. *s.* 22. was intended to prevent. If the plaintiff had meant to contest the avowant's title, he should have pleaded *nil habuit in tenementis.* The Court granted a rule *nisi*, expressly on the point that the avowant was entitled to stand on his proof that the Plaintiff had paid him rent, as sufficient *primâ faciè* evidence to support his avowry, and that unless that case was answered by the Plaintiff, he was not bound to go further.

Shepherd, Solicitor-General, and *Vaughan* Serjt. now shewed cause. They urged that a demise of these specific closes at an entire rent of 7*l.* 10*s.* could not be supported; for the old demise by *Price* having never been determined, was still in force, and the Plaintiff was entitled only to a moiety of the rent of 15*l.* which was reserved for the whole farm, as a tenant in common of that rent: but he was not entitled even to that: before a tenant in *elegit* can claim rent from a lessee of the land, or enter upon the possession of a Defendant who has, before the *elegit*, personally occupied the land, he must not only have the moiety of the land set out by the sheriff by metes and bounds, but must recover judgment in ejectment for that moiety, to entitle him to enter. The sheriff cannot, after he has set it out, give him any possession merely by virtue of the writ of *elegit*, nor can the tenant in *elegit* himself enter by force thereof. If the avowant could by the mere writ entitle himself to the rent, the Plaintiff would be under the hardship of paying rent twice over to two different landlords. Payment of rent works no estoppel; it is only evidence of the title of the payee, but capable of being rebutted. And there is a wide distinction between the case where a tenant has actually received the possession of land from one who has no title, and the case where he has merely attorned by mistake to one who has no title. In the first case, it is not, indeed, competent for the tenant to question his lessor's title, but the estoppel is by his accepting the possession from him, not by the payment of rent. If there be tenant *pur auter vie*, who demises, and *cestui que vie* die, the lessee is not estopped from shewing that the death has determined his demise. So, if payment of rent be obtained by fraud, it may be shewn.

Pell and *Rough* Serjt. in support of the rule. Upon the Judge's report it appears that the question left to the jury was on the validity of the deeds to Mrs. *Baker*, a question which arose only indirectly: and diverted their attention from the principal point in issue, which has never been submitted to the jury, *viz.* whether the Plaintiff held in the manner alleged: that question therefore ought to be tried again. In the case of *Sylli-van* v. *Stradling* (a), a question arose whether the plea of *nil habuit in tenementis* could be pleaded to an avowry and cognizance for rent, Lord *Camden*, who was at first inclined to support it, ultimately agreed with the rest of the Court, that it was taken away by the statute. If, on the issue whether the Plaintiff held in manner and form, she can be permitted to disprove her lessor's title, the title of a landlord may in all cases of avowry for rent come into question, contrary to the intent of the statute 11 *Geo.* 2. There is no pretence to say this rent was paid under a mistake, for the Plaintiff was ac-

(a) 2 *Wils.* 208.

quainted

quainted with all the circumstances. The statute (a) which renders attornments void, contains a particular exception of attornment made pursuant to a judgment at law; and such must be an attornment to a tenant in *elegit*, and others holding under executions.

Gibbs C. J. This case has at different stages presented different forms. As it was moved, I should certainly have thought there ought to be a new trial; for if the avowant had at the trial been told, that the receipt of rent was not *primâ facie* evidence to proceed on, and that he must make out a strict title, I should have thought that he had proved a sufficient case. But it appears that the Judge suffered the Defendant to prove this case, and that he then insisted that the Plaintiff was precluded from disproving the case which he the Defendant had made. The Judge thought the Plaintiff was not precluded from disputing the title of the Defendant, and permitted him to go into evidence for that purpose, which was this. The estate had belonged to *Price*. The Plaintiff had held this estate as tenant to *Price*. When the Plaintiff paid rent to the Defendant, the latter had had an *elegit* against *Price*, had extended the estate, and had a moiety delivered to him by metes and bounds, on which delivery the Defendant would be entitled to the rent of one moiety, and the other would be paid to *Price*. These facts were true, and on them, if they were all, the Defendant would be entitled to the rent of a moiety. It is said, that the avowant had no title, because he had not recovered in ejectment his moiety; but I have no doubt, that the sheriff may deliver the moiety, and enter upon it; except that where the land is under a previous demise, as in this case it is to the Plaintiff, whatever elder term the sheriff finds, he cannot disturb the previous title of the tenant in possession:

(a) 11 Geo. 2. c. 19. s. 11.

all

all he can do is to put the avowant into the state of
landlord: if the land had been in the possession of the
former owner, the sheriff might have delivered actual
possession: where it is in the possession of a tenant,
the sheriff sets it out by metes and bounds, and the tenant is bound thenceforward to pay rent for his moiety
to the tenant by *elegit.* This is a case in which attornment was not necessary before the statute of attornments, because tenant by *elegit* was in by judgment of
law, to whom attornment was not necessary. I am
aware that it has in several places been said, that the
tenant in *elegit* cannot obtain possession without an
ejectment, but I have always been of a different opinion.
There is no case in which a party may maintain ejectment, in which he cannot enter. The ejectment supposes that he has entered; at least, that he has leased
to another, and that that other has entered; and that
the lessor may do it by another, and not enter himself,
is not very intelligible. I would not however consider
the present case as now deciding these points, which I
only throw out in answer to the argument that has been
used. This is a case to which the doctrine does not
apply; for no ejectment could be in this case maintained, there being a tenant who was entitled to retain
the possession. It turned out, that *Price,* being indebted to Mrs. *Baker,* had previously to the avowant's
judgment conveyed the premises to her in satisfaction
of the debt. It is quite clear that Mrs. *Baker* was, after
the execution of this deed, entitled to distrain on the
Plaintiff during her tenantcy for the rent. The avowant contends that because the Plaintiff has once paid
the rent to him, in ignorance of this fact, she is become
irretrievably his tenant. No such law is laid down in
any book. Till the statute of *Anne,* if a lord conveyed
a reversion, by the attornment of the tenant the rent
would pass, though not before attornment; but it never

yet

yet was supposed, that attornment alone, without any conveyance, would carry the rent. Unquestionably the law is not so. It is so plain a proposition, that I did not expect to find any authority for it, nor have I found any case decided on it: but I find a case of *Williams* v. *Bartholomew* (a), where a tenant had paid rent to a remainder man, supposing that the tenant for life had forfeited her estate by a marriage which had been actually solemnized, but it proved to be void, and the tenant was obliged to pay the rent over again to the tenant for life. It was argued, that if the remainder man had distrained and avowed in replevin, the tenant could have made no answer. *Buller* J. says, I see no difficulty in that: the tenant would have proved that his attornment proceeded on the misrepresentation of him who claimed as remainder man, and he might have shewn that the widow was still alive and entitled. The facts which were stated in that case were true, in like manner as all that is stated here by the avowant is true. The payment of rent here raises a presumption that the party receiving it has a good title to the rent; but it is a presumption only, and capable of being rebutted. *Syllivan* v. *Stradling* is rather unnecessarily pressed into this case, though there is much weight in the arguments there urged, and it is certainly settled that the person holding under another by a demise without indenture cannot plead that his lessor *nil habuit in tenementis.* The same doctrine which I now lay down, was held by *Bayley* J. in an ejectment at *Shrewsbury* for cottages, for which rent had been paid to the corporation: the payment of rent was certainly *primá facie* evidence of their title. My Brother *Bayley* held that the Defendants having disclaimed to hold under the corporation, that was equivalent to a notice to quit, and left them at liberty

(a) 1 *Bos.* & *Pull.* 326.

to

to shew who was the real proprietor of the soil. This doctrine must be taken with reference to the subject matter, and to the case in which it is laid down. It was not a case in which the tenants had been originally let into possession by the corporation: if it had been, I should have thought the Defendants never could have disputed the title of the corporation, while they continued in possession; but these were cottages built on the waste, and the corporation claimed to be lords of the manor, and claimed rent; and the tenants, who had at first acquiesced, being afterwards advised of other landlords, disclaimed to hold of the first. I am therefore of opinion that the rule ought to be discharged.

CHAMBRE J. It would be extremely mischievous if the tenants of persons who have property in land, could, by colluding with other persons, and denying their lessor's title, put their landlords on proof of title; many titles resting on possession only. Therefore the law requires that there should be very strong evidence to rebut the case arising from the payment of rent. It ought to be infinitely stronger in a case where the tenant denies the title of the person from whom he received his possession: yet even there, in some cases, as of the land being recovered by a judgment from his lessor, it is competent for a tenant to shew that the lessor's title has ceased. Here the Plaintiff is in possession: the Defendant obtains a judgment and *elegit*, a circumstance very well calculated to mislead the person in possession, and to induce her to recognize the title of the Defendant; but it might be, that this was not a sufficient title; in this case, not this point only came into inquiry, but there was a further inquiry of the validity of a certain deed, whereby the premises were conveyed to Mrs. *Baker*, and that point has been tried twice, in the present action and in another previous action at law (a). I should, on various circumstances of this report, have been as well satisfied if the verdict had been the other way, seeing ground to believe that the deed was intended to cover the possession of the grantor. But after two verdicts, both concurrent, I would not now grant a third trial. One circumstance is that of Mrs. *Baker* claiming one moiety of the wood, under the idea, probably, that the Defendant was entitled under his *elegit* to the other moiety, which could not be, if the deed were good.

DALLAS J. was of the same opinion. The rule is clear, that generally a tenant cannot dispute his landlord's title; but here it comes to this question, whether after a person has been in possession under another lessor, if he is persuaded to attorn under circumstances which do not warrant it, it may not be open to him to prove that the rent was paid without sufficient ground. And I think it is. As to the merits, I shall say nothing; but the case was once tried before me (a), and I saw no ground to impeach the deed.

Rule discharged.

(a) That was an ejectment brought by the avowant to re- cover the premises under this *elegit*, in which he failed.

WARD and Wife v. HUNTER.

A statement by a debtor made to an executor that the testator always promised not to press the Defendant for a debt, is not evidence to prove a promise to pay, made to the testator within six years.

THIS was an action brought by an executrix, for the price of meat sold and delivered by the testator in his lifetime to the Defendant. The declaration averred only promises to pay the testator. The Defendant

4   fendant

fendant pleaded the statute of limitations, and at the
trial of the cause at the last spring assizes for *Rutland*,
the only evidence to take the case out of the statute,
was a note without date, written by the Defendant to
the executrix, in which she said, " the testator always
promised never to distress me for it." After verdict
for the Plaintiff, *Copley* Serjt. had obtained a rule *nisi*
to set it aside and enter a nonsuit, upon the ground
that these words contained no evidence of any promise
made by the·Defendant within six years to pay the
testator.

Lens Serjt. now shewed cause, and insisted that it
was a question for a jury, whether there had not been
a promise made within six years to the testator, who
was proved to have been alive within that time; for if
the Defendant had not acknowledged the debt to him,
and asked for time, the testator would have had no
occasion to promise not to distress her.

Per Curiam, stopping *Copley*. When the Courts
determine that an acknowledgment is evidence of a new
promise then made, it must be of a promise made by a
person competent to make it, and to a person who is
in existence to receive it. We have gone far enough.
Rule absolute.

END OF EASTER TERM.

1815.

WARD
v.
HUNTER.

CASES

ARGUED and DETERMINED

1815.

IN THE

Court of COMMON PLEAS,

AND

OTHER COURTS,

IN

Trinity Term,

In the Fifty-fifth Year of the Reign of GEORGE III.

EDWARDS v. SYMONS.

5 /3 ∠∠ 8 ?/
8 /3 ↲? 238

THIS was a case directed by the Court of Chancery for the opinion of the Judges of the Court of Common Pleas.

Thomas Luce being seised in fee of freehold estates in or near *Saltash,* by his will dated 5th *April* 1794, properly executed and attested for devising freehold estates, and purporting to dispose of all his worldly estate, both real and personal, after bequeathing to four

Devise of a fee-simple estate expectant on the decease of *B.* to trustees and their executors, to receive and apply the rents to the maintenance and advancement of six of the testator's children till the youngest was twenty-one, and then to his said six children and the survivors and survivor of them, their heirs and assigns for ever, as tenants in common : Held that all such devisees as survived the testator took on his decease a vested estate in fee in common.

VOL. VI.   Q   daughters,

daughters, *Mary Rowe, Sarah Trail,* and *Ann,* and *Margaret Luce,* one shilling each, and to his eldest son *James Luce,* one shilling, to be paid when his children should attain their respective ages of 21 years, the testator devised all his freehold, copyhold farm, and lands, called *Luce's* tenements, which he was entitled to upon the death of his mother, to *J. Doidge* and *William Trail,* and their survivor, his executors and administrators, upon trust to receive and apply the rents for the maintenance, education, and advancement of his six children, *John, Thomas, Henry, Francis, William,* and *Elizabeth;* and immediately on *Elizabeth* attaining 21 years, then he devised all his said freehold and copyhold premises to his said six children, and to the survivors and survivor of them, their heirs and assigns, for ever, to hold as tenants in common, and not as jointenants. And he thereby charged all his lands with the payment of his debts and funeral expences. The testator also made a codicil, dated 7th *April* 1794, properly executed and attested for devising freehold estates, and thereby ordered that his daughter *Ann* should share and share alike with his five sons, *John, Thomas, Henry, Francis,* and *William,* and his daughter *Elizabeth,* of the freehold, copyhold lands and premises mentioned in his will, in addition to what he had given her in and by his will. And he thereby confirmed his will in all other parts thereof. The testator died in *February* 1799, without having revoked his will or codicil, leaving *James* his eldest son and heir at law, and his sons *John, Thomas,* and *William,* and daughters *Elizabeth* and *Ann,* five of the devisees named in his will and codicil, him surviving; *Henry,* and *Francis,* the two other devisees, having died in the testator's lifetime. *Thomas Luce* the son, one of the devisees, died in 1800, without issue, and intestate, before the testator's daughter *Elizabeth* attained the age of 21 years, which she

*8   did

did in 1811. The Plaintiff had filed his bill in Chancery for a partition, claiming to be entitled to one-fifth of the devised estate, as having been conveyed to him by *James Luce*, on whom, he insisted, such share descended upon the death of *Thomas Luce* his brother; and the question was, whether *Thomas Luce* the son, had, at the time of his death, any and what estate in reversion in the freehold estate of the testator, or in any and what share or portion thereof, which on the death of *Thomas Luce*, the son, descended on his heir at law.

Lens Serjt. for the Plaintiff, argued that the words when and then, in a will, do not create a contingency on which the estate is to vest, but that where it is provided what shall be done with the rents of the estate in the mean time until a devisee comes of age, and that then he shall take, the estate vests *ab initio* in the devisee, though he cannot assume the management of it until the period directed by the will. This had been determined in several cases; *Doe, on demise of Wheedon*, v. *Lea* (a), which refers to *Goodtitle, on demise of Hayward*, v. *Whitby* (b); and in both of them there is a reference to *Boraston's* case (c). *Rose, on demise of Vere*, v. *Hill* (d), is a still stronger case in point for making this to be a tenancy in common, for there the devise was to them and the survivors and survivor of them, which latter words are not in *Goodtitle* v. *Whitby*. In the case of *Blisset* v. *Cranwell* (e) the reason is assigned for construing it to be a tenancy in common, that it is better for the posterity of the taker that they should have several, than joint estates. In this case, if some of the children had married and had issue, and

(a) 3 T. R. 41.
(b) 1 Burr. 228.
(c) 3 Co. 19a.
(d) 3 Burr. 1881.
(e) 3 Lev. 373.

Q 2

then

then died before *Elizabeth* had attained her full age, if this devise be construed to create a jointenancy, that issue would have been disinherited. *Denn, ex dim. Satterthwaite* v. *Satterthwaite* is in point as to the immediate vesting of the estate. *Thomas Luce,* therefore, upon surviving his father, took a vested interest in common in fee, to which he was entitled in possession upon *Elizabeth* attaining her full age; and upon his death, it passed to his eldest brother *James,* as his heir at law.

Copley Serjt. *contrà.* The only question is, at what particular time the persons to whom this estate is given as tenants in common, are to be the survivors. To refer the survivorship to the time of the decease of the testator has always been held an unnatural construction, because the testator may by new devises provide for the event of any of his devisees dying in his life-time. In the case of *Brown* v. *Bigg* (a), Sir *W. Grant* M. R. says, the general leaning of the Court is against construing the words of survivorship to refer to the decease of the testator, if any other period can be fixed upon, the testator generally supposing the legatee will survive him. In *Hawes* v. *Hawes* (b), cited in the case of *Garland* v. *Thomas* (c), Lord *Hardwicke* adopted this construction. And in *Russell* v. *Long* (d) the Master of the Rolls says, " if all these sisters had not survived their mother, possibly I might have adopted the construction, that the words of survivorship related to the death of the mother and not of the testator, for I think that construction is not to be adopted, if any other can be." This has been the doctrine of Lord *Hardwicke,* and of the present Chancellor and Master of the Rolls in numerous

(a) 7 *Ves.* 286.　　(c) 1 *New. Rep.* 89.
(b) 3 *Atk.* 524.　　(d) 4 *Ves.* 551.

other

other subsequent cases. The words here are strong; the estate is given to trustees, and the survivor, and the executors and administrators of the survivor, in trust to apply the rents to the maintenance and advancement of the testator's six children; and when his daughter *Elizabeth* shall attain 21 years, then he devises all his estates to such persons and the survivors of them, namely, at the time when *Elizabeth* attains 21. In true construction it means those who shall be the survivors when *Elizabeth Luce* attains 21. It was manifestly the testator's intent to disinherit his heir at law, for he gives him 1s. but if one of his other children had died after the testator's decease, and before *Elizabeth* was 21, his part, according to the Plaintiff's construction, would go to the heir, whom the testator intended to disinherit. It was not an improbable event that out of six or seven children some should die; and it is improbable that it was not in the testator's contemplation. Another event indeed is left unprovided for, *i. e.* that if all died before *Elizabeth* were 21, then it would go over to the heir, but that was little probable. Another material circumstance is this, if any one child died before *Elizabeth* was 21, the others were to have the benefit of the rents and profits of his share during that period, it is therefore probable that the testator also meant that the same share should vest absolutely in them by survivorship. Therefore if there is nothing whence to infer the intent of the testator, to what period those words shall refer, it shall refer more naturally to the time when *Elizabeth* attained 21, than to the time of the testator's decease. In *Garland* v. *Thomas* almost all the cases at law, and many cases in equity, are collected. In *Russell* v. *Long* Sir *W. Grant* M. R. impugns the decision in *Lord Bindon* v. *Earl of Suffolk* (a), though he refers with approbation

1815.
EDWARDS
v.
SYMONS.

(a) 1 P. Wms. 95. b.

Q 3

to

to the case of *Stringer* v. *Phillips*(a). Events may be such
that it is immaterial whether the word survivors refers
to one period or another. Many cases have been before the Court, where, though the word " survivor" was
used, the doubt has been whether the devise created a
jointenancy or a tenancy in common; and the Courts
have said, we reconcile it by making it a tenancy in common to a certain period, with survivorship afterwards.
If a sense can be given to both expressions, though apparently repugnant, so that they may be reconciled,
the Court will maintain both. Even in cases where
they cannot be reconciled, the Courts have of late altered the rule of construction, and if a thing be given
in one part of a will to one and in another part to another, instead of holding that the last words shall be
pursued and the first rejected, the Court have said, the
devisees shall take in moieties. The doctrine that the
heir at law cannot be disinherited but by express words
or necessary implication, has been much questioned.
A reasonable implication will suffice: the rule only
throws the *onus* on the devisee.

Lens in reply. No strong intention appears of disin-
heriting the heir: the testator does not shew it by giving
him 1s., for he gives four of his daughters, to whom he
does not devise any thing else, the same sum. Is it to
be supposed that the father was so much set upon dis-
inheriting his heir at law, that if either of the other
children died under 21, leaving issue, he would prefer
that that issue should rather be disinherited, than that
the eldest son and heir at law should have the chance
of taking any thing? It has been urged that the words

(a) 1 *Eq. Cas. Abr.* 292. 1 *P. Wms.* 96. *note.*

" then

" then I give," have the effect of not giving the estate
to vest till then, and that the Court must look to see
who were then the survivors, whereas the clue is to be
sought the other way, and the rule of law is first to be
found, and it will thereby appear who were the survivors. The survivors are the survivors of those in whom
the estate has already vested, and the declaration that
the possession shall be suspended till *Elizabeth* is 21,
suspends the possession only, till that event; and the
effect of what is contended for is, that the estates vested
are to be devested again at her age of 21, and newly
modelled and vested. In none of the cases cited is
maintenance given in the mean time; by giving that
maintenance the testator shews that the estate vests at
his decease. It does not depend on the circumstance
that occurs in several cases, that there is an intermediate estate given to one individual; for in *Boraston*'s
case, where that ingredient was wanting, it was nevertheless held that notwithstanding the words " then and
when" the estate vested. The Court held that the
words " when and then" shewed when the estate should
come into possession, but not when it should vest. It
gives the estate by giving the rents and profits, and
only prescribes a particular course of administration of
them in the mean time. The estate, therefore, vests at
the decease of the testator, and the words " survivors
and survivor" naturally refer to that time.

Cur. adv. vult.

1815.

EDWARDS
v.
SYMONS.

The following certificate was afterwards sent to the
Lord Chancellor:

WE have heard this case argued, and are of opinion
that *Thomas Luce*, the son, had at the time of his death
a fee-simple estate in reversion in one undivided fifth
part of the freehold estate of the said testator, as tenant

Q 4   - in

in common with his said surviving brothers and sisters, and that on the death of the said *Thomas Luce* this estate descended on his heir at law.

V. GIBBS.

J. HEATH.

A. CHAMBRE.

R. DALLAS.

JOHN PHIPPS and THOMAS CHESTER v. PITCHER.

An executor of a testator possessed of real and personal estate, cloathed with a trust to pay debts, and to lay out money for the benefit of the testator's children, and with a power to sell freehold lands in fee, but taking no beneficial interest under the will, is a good attesting witness to the will.

THIS was a case directed by Sir *T. Plumer*, Vice Chancellor, for the opinion of the Judges of this court. *Israel Claringbold* the elder made his will, dated 11th *June* 1811, and thereby, after directing his just debts to be duly paid by his executors, he gave to his wife the use of his dwelling-house and furniture, and 50l. a year to be paid to her out of the rents and profits of his real estates for her life, and he thereby charged and made liable to the payment thereof all his real estates and effects. After the decease of his wife, he gave his son *Israel Claringbould* the use and occupation, rents and profits, of and in all that his said dwelling-house and field thereunto belonging, and in which that house was built, called the Five Acre Field, during his natural life, and after his decease, then the testator devised and bequeathed all the residue and remainder of his real estate and effects, real and personal, to his son *Richard* and daughter *Ann* wife of *William Phipps*, as tenants in common, their heirs, executors, administrators, and assigns, in case such remainder should not exceed 1000l. but in case such remainder should exceed 1000l., then the testator thereby bequeathed the excess above 1000l., unto the

*6   children

children of his son *Israel*, to be laid out and expended upon them in such way as his executors should think fit ; and after stating the sale by him to his son-in-law *William Phipps* of the two bog meadows adjoining the river for the sum of 100*l.*, and his having lodged the said sum of 100*l.* in the hands of the said *William Phipps* for the purpose therein mentioned; and after directing the payment of the said sum of 100*l.* as therein mentioned, the testator thereby appointed the Plaintiffs and the survivor of them, executors and executor of his will. And the testator thereby further willed and ordained, that his executors, or the survivor of them, and the executors and administrators of such survivor, for and towards the performance of his said will, and in order to save money for the payment of his debts, and of all the several legacies and expences attending the performance of the things therein directed and ordered, should and might with all convenient speed after his decease bargain, sell, and alien in fee simple all his freehold lands, houses, and premises, except his dwelling-house and the five-acre field before mentioned ; for the doing, executing, and perfect finishing whereof the testator thereby gave his executors and the survivor of them, and the executors or administrators of such survivor, full power and absolute authority to grant, alien, sell, convey, and assure all the same freehold land and premises to any person or persons and their heirs for ever, in fee-simple, by all and every such lawful ways and means in the law, as to his executors or the survivor of them, or the executors or administrators of such survivor, or his or their counsel should seem fit or necessary. This will was signed and published by the testator in the presence of *Henrietta Rousseau*, *Mary Chester*, and *Thomas Chester*, who signed their names thereto as attesting the execution thereof in the presence of the testator

testator and at his request. *Thomas Chester*, one of the subscribing witnesses, is the same *Thomas Chester* who is named in the said will. The said testator died without having altered or revoked his will, leaving *John Claringbould* and *Israel Claringbould* his heirs in gavel-kind, (and who are still living,) him surviving. The Plaintiffs *John Phipps* and *Thomas Chester* have duly proved the will, and taken upon themselves the execution of the trusts thereof. The testator was at the times of making his will, and of his death, seized in fee-simple of certain lands in the parish of *River*, not being part of the said dwelling-house or five-acre field, or of the said two bog meadows: the personal estate and effects of the testator not specifically bequeathed, were not sufficient for the payment of his debts and legacies, and funeral and testamentary expences; and therefore the Plaintiffs *John Phipps* and *Thomas Chester*, in execution of the trusts of the will, entered into a contract with the Defendant for the sale to him of a piece of land, being part of the testator's real estate, but which did not form part of the dwelling-house or five-acre field, or the said two bog closes; and the question was, whether the Plaintiffs could, as devisees in the will named, or by virtue of any power in them by the will reposed, convey to the Defendant the legal estate and interest in the lands so contracted to be sold to him.

Rough Serjt. for the Plaintiffs, stated that the point intended to be argued was, whether the will were sufficiently attested, *Thomas Chester* the devisee and executor being also a subscribing witness. This case was concluded by the case of *Bettison and Another* v. *Bromley* (a), where the wife of an executor who took no beneficial interest was held to be a good attesting witness, and

(a) 12 *East*, 250.

by

by the cases therein cited of *Fountain* v. *Cook* (a),
Lowe v. *Jolliffe* (b), *Holt* v. *Tyrrel* (c), *Goodtitle*
v. *Welford*. (d)

Best Serjt. *contra.* This case was even in the Court
of Chancery thought distinguishable from the cases
cited. The will gave the executor a right of entry on
the real estate, and if he were to enter, and tresspass
should be brought against him, he must justify under a
will attested by himself. So if the action were brought
against his vendee, he would be liable over, if the
Defendant were ousted, and that would give him such
an interest in the verdict as to render his testimony
inadmissible.

The Court observed, that unless the executor spon-
taneously entered into covenants which rendered him
liable over, his mere execution of the power would not
have that effect, nor would ordinarily be accompanied
with any such covenant: the purchaser would previously examine the title, and would not take under
the execution of a power, unless he were satisfied of its
validity.

The Court afterwards sent to the Vice Chancellor
the following certificate:

We have heard this case argued by counsel, and we
are of opinion that the Plaintiffs can by virtue of the
power in them by the said will reposed, convey to the
said *Joseph Webb Pitcher*, the Defendant, the legal
estate and interest in the said lands contracted to be
sold to him as stated in the case.

V. GIBBS.
J. HEATH.
A. CHAMBRE.
R. DALLAS.

(a) 1 *Mod.* 107. *Anon.*
(b) 1 *Bl.* 365.
(c) 1 *Barn. Rep. K. B.* 12.
(d) 1 *Doug.* 139.

COLLISON v. LETTSOM and WHITTON.

A lessor possessed of considerable freehold and leasehold property lying together, covenanted in a lease of parcel, that if he, his heirs or assigns, should, during the term, have any advantageous offer for the disposing of a certain adjoining freehold parcel, he, the lessor, his heirs or assigns, should not dispose of the same without previously making an offer of that parcel to the lessee, his executors, administrators, or assigns, at five *per cent.* less than that offer. The lessor sold his entire property, including the demised land and the adjoining parcel, for an entire consideration in one entire contract, without offering the parcel to the covenantee: Held that this was no breach of the covenant.

Held that the covenant did not enure to the assignee of the lease, though named.

THIS was a case sent by the Court of Chancery for the opinion of the Judges of this Court. In 1809 the Defendant Dr. *Lettsom* being seised in fee of a share of the manor of *Camberwell*, and of certain messuages, lands, and hereditaments in the parish of *Camberwell*, and possessed of certain leasehold lands there, for the residue of a long term of years, all lying together and adjoining, by indenture dated 12th *Jan.* 1809, demised part of the freehold hereditaments, consisting of a brick messuage, with the yard, garden, coach-house, stables, and paddock used therewith, situate on *Grove Hill*, and containing together about three acres, to *J. Starkey*, his executors, administrators, and assigns, for the term of 28 years, at 100*l.* rent; and the Defendant *Lettsom* thereby for himself, his heirs, and assigns, covenanted with *Starkey*, his executors, administrators, and assigns, that in case he the Defendant *Lettsom*, his heirs, or assigns, should at any time or times thereafter during the term thereby granted, have any advantageous offer or offers made to him or them for the disposing of the land lately fenced off by him from the west side of the premises thereby demised, and adjoining to *Camberwell Grove*, then he the Defendant *Lettsom*, his heirs or assigns, should not dispose of the same, without previously making an offer of the same to *Starkey*, his executors, administrators, or assigns, in writing, at 5*l. per cent.* less than such offer, fourteen days at least before he should accept of the same. In *July* 1810, *Starkey* was duly declared a bankrupt, and the usual assignment was executed to his assignees *Fort*,

Bell,

Bell, and *Stracey*, by the major part of the commissioners. The Plaintiff purchased of the assignees the said leasehold premises, together with certain other leasehold premises which had been *Starkey's*, for a valuable consideration. And by indenture of 3d *Sept.* 1810, *Fort, Bell*, and *Stracey* bargained, sold, assigned, transferred, and set over, and *Starkey*, by their direction, ratified and confirmed to the Plaintiff, his executors, administrators, and assigns, (amongst other property of *Starkey*,) all the premises demised to *Starkey* by the Defendant *Lettsom*, and all their, any or either of their estate, right, title, interest, term and terms of years, property, possession, benefit, claim, and demand whatsoever, of, in, to, or out of the same, and every part and parcel thereof, together with that indenture of lease, to hold for the remainder of the term. On 30th *July* 1812, the Defendant *Lettsom* signed an agreement in writing with the Defendant *Whitton* for the sale to him for the sum of 12,000*l.*, of his share in the manor, and all his real and leasehold estates at *Camberwell*, including the piece of ground the subject of the covenant, and the premises demised to *Starkey* and assigned to the Plaintiff *Collison*, being the same freehold and leasehold estates to which the Defendant *Lettsom* was entitled at the time he granted the lease. Afterwards, in pursuance of that agreement, the Defendant *Lettsom*, by lease and release, dated the 20th and 21st of *November* 1812, and by an indenture of assignment of the last-mentioned date, conveyed and assigned to, or in trust for the Defendant *Whitton*, his heirs, executors, administrators, and assigns, as one entire estate, upon one entire contract, and for one entire purchase money or consideration, all the said freehold and leasehold premises, including the said piece of ground the subject of the covenant for pre-emption. The Defendant *Lettsom* did not previously to the making of such agreement or

convey-

conveyance make any offer in writing or otherwise for the sale of the said piece of land, the subject of the covenant in the lease, to *Starkey*, or to any one on his behalf or account, or to the Plaintiff *Collison*. The Plaintiff, after the agreement for sale was entered into, but before the conveyance was executed, applied to the Defendant *Lettsom*, and claimed the benefit of the covenant, as being the assignee of the term in the premises by and from *Starkey*; and *Whitton*, before the execution of the conveyance to him, was informed of the covenant. The question for the opinion of the Court was, whether under the circumstances of this case, there had been a breach of the covenant on the part of the lessor.

This case was twice argued, first in *Michaelmas* term, last by *Lens* Serjt. for the Plaintiff, and *Blosset* Serjt. for the Defendants; and again, in *Easter* term, by *Shepherd*, Solicitor-General, for the Plaintiff, and *Best* Serjt. for the Defendants. It was stated that the question was worded in the form in which it stands, by the express direction of the Lord Chancellor, in order, if there were a breach, not to occupy the attention of the Court in pointing out who ought to be the parties in the action, which question was much discussed on the first argument; the second argument was confined to the construction of the covenant. For the Plaintiff, it was contended, first, that the sale of the entire estate, including the land which was the subject of the covenant, was a direct breach, for that the meaning of the covenant was, that *Starkey* should have the refusal before any sale of that land should be made to any person whatever: and before the sale the Defendant *Lettsom* ought to have ascertained a specific part of the price as representing that parcel, and offered the land to the Plaintiff at five *per cent.* under that apportioned price. If a covenantor acts contrary to the intention of the

covenant,

covenant, it is a breach, though he do not in direct terms break the covenant, but performs the words of it. Instances are collected by Chief Baron *Comyn* (a). If a covenant be to deliver a recognizance to be cancelled, it is a breach, if he extends it before, though it be afterwards cancelled (b). So, if a brewer covenants to deliver all his grains for the cattle of the Plaintiff, and he puts hops to them before delivery (c). So, if a man covenants to leave all the trees upon the land, and he cuts them down and leaves them there (d). The intent of the present covenant was, that the Defendant *Lettsom* should never sell this piece of land to any one, in any manner, without giving *Starkey* and his assigns the offer of pre-emption, and the sale to *Whitton* is clearly contrary to that intention. It was argued, next, that the Defendant *Lettsom* had committed an indirect breach, because by the sale to the Defendant *Whitton* he had rendered it impossible that he could thereafter perform the covenant, and give *Starkey* the pre-emption. It shall be a breach of covenant, if the covenantor be disabled to perform (e). Tenant (f) in dower of certain land whereon trees were growing had the right of cutting them, and covenanted with the reversioner that he might annually cut 20 trees; the covenantor afterwards destroyed and cut down all the wood, and it was held a breach. So (g) the condition of a bond recited an agreement that the Defendant might cut wood for firebote and hedgebote, without committing waste, and assigned a breach by the obligor by waste in cutting wood, and it was urged the restriction was in the words of the lessor, and not of the

(a) Co. Dig., *Covenant*, E. 2.
Go. Dig., *Condition*, M. 1.
(b) *Robinson* v. *Amps*, T. Ray. 25.
(c) *Griffith* v. *Goodband*, T. Ray. 464. S. C. T. Jon. 191.

(d) *Ibid.*
(e) Co. Dig , *Covenant*, E. 2. Condition, M. 2.
(f) Mo. 18. pl. 65.
(g) *Stevinson*'s case, 1 Leon. 324.

lessee;

lessee; but it was answered, that it was the agreement of the lessee, though the covenant of the lessor, and raised an implied covenant by the lessee, that he would not commit waste. So, the doctrine in *Main's* case (a) confirmed by *Littleton* (b) is applicable: " If a man seised of lands in fee, covenants to enfeoff *J. S.* of them upon request, and afterwards he makes a feoffment in fee of the said lands, now in this case *J. S.* shall have an action of covenant without request." In *Main's* case the Defendant covenanted to make a new lease to *Scott* on surrender of his old lease at any time within *Scott's* life, and he, by fine granted and rendered the same lands to the conusee for 80 years, and it was held a breach, though G. *Scott* had not surrendered. So, if a man have lands for a term of years, and covenanteth to leave them in as good plight as he found them, if he do waste in wood, covenant lieth, (instantly,) for he cannot repair it. (c)

For the Defendant, it was admitted that these authorities were good law, but urged that they were wholly inapplicable, because the present covenant was entirely different, this was not a covenant that the Defendant *Lettsom* only should give the pre-emption; but that he, his heirs or assigns, which means his assignees of the reversion of the piece of land in question, should do it. The parties therefore contemplated two possible events, the one, that the covenantor should avail himself of any opportunity that might occur to him of alienating this piece of land to another person than the covenantee, together with the whole or some other part of his estate, the other, that an offer might occur to him to alienate this particular parcel. The parties intended to provide by this covenant for the latter case only; and that if it should occur, then the covenantee should have the pre-

(a) 5 Co. 21 &c. Res. 2.

(b) Litt. s. 355.

(c) F. N. B. p. 343. I.

emption;

emption; and in order to enlarge the chance that the
covenantee might have an opportunity to buy this piece
of land separately, he stipulates for it, not merely in
case it should occur before the other event, but also,
that in case the other event shall take effect, and the
estate shall pass into other hands, still the Defendant
Lettsom shall procure the alienee to give the Plaintiff
the same pre-emption in case the occasion shall occur.
The parties therefore expressly intended, that the entire estate, or any portion of it, including, and greater
than, that which is the subject of the covenant, should be
alienable in the meantime; and the Defendant *Lettsom*
by the sale of the whole has neither expressly broken
his covenant, nor put it out of his power to pursue one of
the stipulated modes of performance, which the parties
had in view, namely, that if, when the occasion occurred, he did not possess the estate, so as to be able himself to convey to *Starkey*, then his assignee should do it.
When that occasion shall arise of an offer being made
for severing this parcel from the residue at a specific
price, if the then proprietor of the estate cannot be prevailed on by the Defendant *Lettsom* or his representa-
tives to perform the covenant, (for it may be admitted
that although the assignee is named, it does not run
with the land demised, according to the case of the *Mayor
of Congleton* v. *Pattison (a),* because it is to do a thing
collateral to the demised premises, *acc. per Curiam,*)
then there will be a breach; but the sale of the whole
cannot be considered a breach, without striking out of
the covenant the word " assigns;" and the Court is
bound to give effect to every part of the contract. It
was never intended to debar the Defendant from selling
his entire property. In the cases cited of tenant in
dower, *Main's* case, and *Littleton, s. 355.* the Defendants
had disabled themselves. If in the two latter, the covenant had been, that they, or their assigns, should en-

1815.

COLLISON
v.
LETTSOM.

(a) 10 *East,* 130.

feoff, the cases would have been similar to this. *Robinson* v. *Amps*, and *Griffith* v. *Goodband*, were cases of direct fraud upon the covenant. The case cited from *Fitzherbert* is a strong authority for the Defendant, for it is there held, that " although that he pulleth down the houses, the lessor shall not have an action upon his covenant (to leave them in as good a plight as he found them), before the end of the term :" the reason is, that he may within the term have time to rebuild them, and hath not disabled himself. And the intermediate act is no breach.

The *Solicitor-General*, in reply, dissented from the Defendant's construction of the meaning of the covenant, and urged that it must be construed as if the words "heirs and assigns" were not in it. If the parties had meant to restrict the pre-emption to the case where an advantageous offer was made for this parcel alone, they ought so to have expressed it, but otherwise, upon the principle *fortissimè contra proferentem* the words extend to every offer which includes the spot in question, and the vendor ought to have severed this in price from the rest, and by omitting so to do, he has disabled himself.

Cur. adv. vult.

The following certificate was afterwards sent to the Lord Chancellor:

THIS case has been argued before us by counsel, and we are of opinion, that, under the circumstances, there has been no breach of the said covenant on the part of the lessor.

If the covenant be taken in its literal sense, the facts which are stated do not constitute any breach of it, and it does not appear to us with sufficient certainty that the parties intended to provide against such a case as this which has happened.

V. GIBBS.
J. HEATH.
A. CHAMBRE.
R. DALLAS.

1815.

ELLIS v. JOHNSON and Wife.

May 27.

*B*EST Serjt. moved that this fine might pass upon an affidavit that the annexed was a true copy of the copy of the *præcipe* and concord which was in the hands of the clerk of the Chief Justice, and was signed by the parties, the original having been accidentally lost. The parties were alive and consenting.

The Court granted the application, and observed that this was an instance of the utility of the practice recently introduced, that the copy left with the Chief Justice should be signed by the parties as well as the original.

Fiat.

The præcipe and concord of a fine being lost, the Court permitted them to be supplied from the copy thereof, which had been left with the clerk of the Chief Justice, signed by the parties, and the fine to be perfected.

FONSEC v. MAGNAY and Another.

May 28.

*T*HIS was an action against the late Sheriff of *Middlesex* for not arresting upon a writ for 16*l.* returnable on the last return day of *Trinity* term, which had been delivered to the sheriff, and upon which the sheriff had returned *non est inventus.* Upon the trial of the cause at the sittings after *Easter* term 1815, before *Gibbs* C. J., evidence was given that the person of the Defendant was pointed out to an officer named *Owen*, for the purpose of his being arrested under this writ, but that *Owen* did not arrest him. *Owen* had for several years resided at *Portsmouth* and not in *London*, quitting office, and that to make him liable for the default of the officer employed, it was not enough to shew that a warrant was made to the officer, but it must be shewn that the warrant was delivered to the officer, and neglect committed while the defendant was in office.

The sheriffs of the late and present year signed in *No-vember* the return of *non est inventus* on a writ of *Trinity* term. In an action against the late sheriff for not arresting, held that his return related to the day of his

R 2   and

1815.

FONSEC

v.

MAGNAY.

and the evidence to shew that he was an officer employed by the Defendant to execute a warrant on this writ, was an examined copy of the return of the writ, which was made on the 26th of *November*, and signed both by the old and new sheriffs, without any distinction of date, the Defendant having gone out of office on the 26th of *September*. The name of *Owen* was on the warrant, and it was proved to be the practice for officers to whom warrants are committed, to return them to the sheriff with their names thereon, and the Plaintiff offered in evidence this warrant, coming out of the hands of the sheriff, with *Owen*'s name thereon, as an acceptance and acknowledgment by the sheriff of a statement made thereon by *Owen*, that he was the officer employed by the sheriff on that occasion. The Plaintiff also proved, that when the sheriff was ruled to return the writ, he gave express notice of the rule to *Owen*, and he contended on the authority of *Jones* v. *Wood* (a), that the latter evidence was also proof of a recognition of the officer by the sheriff. *Gibbs* C. J. thought that the warrant was evidence of the employment of *Owen* by the sheriff, being received by the sheriff as *Owen*'s return, though it was not made by, but to the sheriff. But *Best* Serjt. for the Defendant, urged that the return of the writ being made on the 26th of *November*, after the Defendant was out of office, did not establish any privity between the Defendant and *Owen*, for the warrant might have been delivered to *Owen* after the Defendant was out of office. *Gibbs* C. J. thought that the old and new sheriffs both joining in the return of *non est inventus*, the return of each was referable to the time of his being in office, and that the Defendant's return therefore only imported that the person to be arrested had not been found before the time when his

(a) 3 *Camp.* 329.

∴

office

office expired, but there was no proof that he ever made a warrant to *Owen* before that time. The new sheriff might have made the warrant to him after his office commenced : his Lordship therefore nonsuited the Plaintiff.

Vaughan Serjt. in this term moved to set aside the nonsuit and have a new trial, relying on *Jones* v. *Wood*.

GIBBS C. J. The original debt is only 16*l.* and therefore if the party is not strictly entitled to a new trial, we should not be disposed to give it him. If I had in any respect misdirected the jury, the Plaintiff would be entitled to a new trial. The sheriff's return on this writ, which he has nothing to do with, except to obey, is, " I have not been able to find the body ;" but he does not thereby assume the truth of any thing contained in the writ; still less does he admit that the name of *Owen* found on the back of the writ was placed there by him. It is urged by the Plaintiff, that the return of the warrant being received by the Sheriff, that acceptance is sufficient to shew that *Owen* was then his officer; but there is no such proof here. The Defendant went out of office in *September*, and there is no return made of the writ till 26th *November :* the return of the warrant then was received in the office, but since the Defendant had then ceased to be sheriff, I do not think it amounts to a recognition by the Defendant, that *Owen* was their officer; therefore even if the sum had been larger, I think the nonsuit was proper.

Rule refused.

TASKER *v.* SCOTT.

The master of ship drew a bill on his owners for supplies for the ship, and wrote on the bill, " If this be not honoured, the holder will insure the amount, and place the premium to the drawer's account." The bill being dishonoured, the holder insured the ship for three months, and declared interest in the bill, which was to be sufficient proof of interest. The ship was lost after the three months: Held that the holder of the bill was authorized to insure for his own benefit, and was warranted in insuring for three months, and that he might recover the premium against the drawer.

THIS was an action for money paid for the use of the Defendant, who was master of a vessel called the *Ocean*, and had drawn in *Canada* on his owners here in favour of *J. Goudie* for 1,990*l.* 13*s.* 1*d.* for supplies for the ship's use, and at the foot of the bill was a printed note, " If the above is not duly honoured, the holder will insure the amount, and place the premium, &c. to my and the ship's account. *J. Scott.*" The bill being presented for acceptance, the drawer, who had then received no advices, declined to accept it, whereon the Plaintiff, to whom the bill had been indorsed by the owners resident in *Scotland,* for the purpose of receiving the proceeds for their use, effected an insurance on the ship *Ocean* for three months, and the interest was declared to be " on the interest in a bill of exchange drawn by the Defendant on Mr. *Bowgfeld* in favour of *J. Goudie,* dated *Quebec,* 10th *June* 1814, being for value received for the use of the ship; and it was agreed that in the event of loss the bill should be considered as sufficient proof of interest, and payment made accordingly." The drawee receiving advices from the drawer, paid the bill, after the insurance was effected, but refused to pay the charges of insurance. The ship was lost after the expiration of the three months. At the trial of the cause at *Guildhall* at the sittings after *Easter* term 1815, *Shepherd,* Solicitor-General, for the Defendant, made four objections to the Plaintiff's recovery. First, That the bill had not been dishonoured. Secondly, That the Plaintiffs were not such holders of the bill as were entitled to sue. Thirdly, That the insurance effected was not only an unavailable, but an

Whether such an insurance be void within stat. 19 *G.* 2. *c.* 37, *quere.*

· I

illegal

illegal contract by the statute 19 *Geo.* 2. *c.* 37. and therefore the premium could not be recovered back. Fourthly, That the authority to effect an insurance was to effect such an insurance as would be useful to the Defendant, and if the Plaintiffs had insured the ship for the voyage, or for a time sufficiently long for the completion of the voyage, the Defendants would have been enabled to receive from the underwriters the value of the ship, whereas the insurance having expired before the loss occurred, the premium had been completely wasted, and the authority given had therefore not been pursued. *Gibbs* C. J. was of opinion with the Plaintiffs upon all the objections. As to the third, his Lordship thought that this was not an illegal, but only an unavailable insurance. The statute says, every such policy shall be void: it does not prohibit the making such. He thought that undoubtedly if an insurance were effected by order of a person who had an interest, that though the insurance were void, yet that he who effected it might recover back the premium from him by whose order he did it. The statute of fines says, *quod finis ipso jure sit nullus :* that does not make the fine illegal; it makes it not even void; only voidable. As to the fourth objection, the Chief Justice thought, that this insurance was not directed nor effected for the security of the owner of the ship, but of him who advanced the money; and the jury found a verdict for the Plaintiffs.

Shepherd, Solicitor-General, now moved to set aside the verdict and have a new trial, relying principally on the two last objections. To shew that this insurance was illegal, as a wagering policy, he cited *Kemp* v. *Vigne;* and on the fourth objection he urged, that if the holder was authorized to effect an insurance, it was his duty to effect a policy for the voyage, so that the

R 4   owners

owners might have the benefit of it, in case the ship were lost. As to the principle upon which it had been supposed that the Plaintiffs might effect this policy, namely, that the holder of the bill wished to have the honorary security of the underwriters, where he had not a legal one, the Plaintiffs were not warranted, in pursuit of that end, in depriving the owners of the resource which they would have had in recovering on this policy, if the ship had been insured absolutely.

GIBBS C. J. There is nothing in either of these objections: the two first are given up; as to the third, a discretion was given to the holder of the bill to insure for his own benefit, and he was to insure according to that discretion as he chose to exercise it, and he has exercised it prudently; as to the fourth objection, on the illegality of the insurance, I desire that the doctrine I lay down may be confined to this particular case: I think the Plaintiffs were entitled to pay the money they paid for the use of the master; this too would clearly be an available security in all cases except the case of a *British* ship, and it is not in proof that the Plaintiffs knew, nor was it incumbent on them to enquire, whether this were a *British* ship or not.

The Court refused the rule on all the grounds.

ANTOINE v. MORSHEAD, Bart.

May 31.

THIS was an action upon five bills of exchange, all drawn by the father of the Defendant, a *British* subject, on the 12th of *September* 1806, while he was detained a prisoner at *Verdun* in *France* during the late war with that country, payable, some to *Tyndall,* some to *Estwicke,* both *British* subjects in like manner detained prisoners there, at one year after date, indorsed to the Plaintiff, who was a *French* subject and a banker at *Verdun,* and accepted by the Defendant. The cause was tried at *Guildhall* at the sittings after *Easter* term 1815, before *Gibbs* C. J., when it was contended on the part of the Defendants, that it would be treason to pay the bills by the statute 34 *G.* 3. *c.* 9. *fs.* 1. 4. *Gibbs* C. J. refused to hear the objection: he did not know to what extent it might be carried, but if it could be supported to its full extent, many of our miserable fellow-subjects detained in *France* must have starved. It was also objected, that this being a contract with an alien enemy, was not merely suspended during the war, but absolutely void; the Chief Justice thought otherwise, and the jury found a verdict for the Plaintiff.

An alien, to whom a bill of exchange, drawn on England by a British subject detained prisoner in France during war, payable to another British subject detained there, is there indorsed by the latter, may sue on it in this country after the return of peace.

Vaughan Serjt. on a former day in this term moved for a rule *nisi* on both these objections, when it being suggested on the part of the Plaintiff, that the statute 34 *G.* 3. *c.* 9. had expired at the peace of 1800 and never been re-enacted, the Court gave time to ascertain that fact, and that being found to be the case, *Vaughan* now moved upon the second objection only, namely, that the indorsement of the bill to an alien enemy was void.

void. For this he cited *Anthon* v. *Fisher* (a), where it is held that no action can be maintained by an alien in the Courts of this country on a ransom bill, because it is a right claimed to be acquired by him in actual war. Lord *Ashburton's* argument in *Ricord* v. *Bettenham* (b), which decision is overruled by *Anthon* v. *Fisher*, is to be called in aid. If a bond be given to an alien enemy, it is good *quoad* the obligor, but void *quoad* the obligee, that is, it enures only for the benefit of the crown (c). And if so of a bond, the law must be the like on a bill of exchange. So is it of contracts of insurance made with an alien enemy. *Flindt* v. *Waters* (d) Lord *Ellenborough* C. J. says the defence of alien enemy may go to the contract itself, on which the Plaintiff sues, and operate as a perpetual bar; though in that case the contracting party having become an enemy after the contract, it was held to be only a temporary suspension of the right to sue, but he shewed a disposition to confirm the cases of *Brandon* v. *Nesbitt* (e), and *Bristow* v. *Towers* (f). No case has decided that a contract made with an alien enemy in time of war may be ever afterwards enforced. Chief Baron *Gilbert* (g) lays it down, that upon the plea of alien enemy the right of the Plaintiff is forfeited to the crown, as a species of reprisal upon the state committing hostility.

GIBBS C. J.   It will not be useless to consider what legal propositions can be deduced from the cases cited on behalf of the defendant, and to try how far they are applicable to the present case.   This is no bill of exchange drawn in favour of an alien enemy, but by one subject in favour of another subject, upon a subject resident here,

(a) *Doug.* 650. note to *Cornu* v. *Blackburne.*
(b) 3 *Burr.* 1734.
(c) *Ro. Abr.,* Alien, B. *pl.* 1. *Danv. Abr.*
(d) 15 *East,* 266.
(e) 6 *T. R* 23.
(f) 6 *T. R.* 35.
(g) *Hist. of Common Pleas,* 205.

the

the two first being both detained prisoners in *France;* the drawer might legally draw such a bill for his subsistence. After the bill is so drawn, the payee indorses it to the Plaintiff, then an alien enemy. How was he to avail himself of the bill, except by negotiating it, and to whom could he negotiate it, except to the inhabitants of that country in which he resided? I can collect but two principles from the cases cited by the counsel for the Defendant, and they are principles on which there never was the slightest doubt. First, that a contract made with an alien enemy in time of war, and that of such a nature that it endangers the security, or is against the policy of this country, is void. Such are policies of insurance to protect an enemy's trade. Another principle is, that however valid a contract originally may be, if the party become an alien enemy he cannot sue. The crown, during the war, may lay hands on the debt, and recover it, but if it do not, then, on the return of peace the rights of the contracting alien are restored, and he may himself sue. No other principle is to be deduced. The first may be laid out of the case, for this was not in its creation a contract made with an alien enemy. The second question is, whether the bill came to the hands of the Plaintiff by a good title? Under the circumstances of this case, not meaning to lay down any general rule beyond this case, I am of opinion that the indorsement to the Plaintiff conveyed to him a legal title in this bill, on which the king might have sued in the time of the war, and he not having so done, the Plaintiff might sue after peace was proclaimed.

HEATH J. was absent.

CHAMBRE J. I am perfectly of the same opinion, and it would be of very mischievous consequence if it were otherwise.

DALLAS J.

1815.

ANTOINE
v.
MORSHEAD.

1815.

ANTOINE
v.
MORSHEAD.

DALLAS J. This is not a contract between a subject of this country and an alien enemy, nor is it a contract of that sort to which the principle can be applied. That principle is, that there shall be no communication with the enemy in time of war, but this is a contract between two subjects in an enemy's country, which is perfectly legal.

Rule refused.

May 31.

REDFORD *v.* EDIE.

Where the Court had given time to one of the bail to justify before a Judge at Chambers in the vacation, a Judge's summons for further time, returnable before the original time had expired, operates as a stay of proceedings.

ONE of the bail in this cause having justified in *Easter* term, time was given to justify the other before a judge at chambers till 15th *May.* On the 12th of *May* a summons for further time to justify was taken out, returnable on the 13th, and the Plaintiff's attorney not then attending, it was twice renewed, pending which, on the 17th, the Plaintiff took an assignment of the bail-bond, and on the 18th sued out writs against the bail. A rule having been obtained to set aside the proceedings against the bail, upon the ground that the summons, having issued before the time to justify the second bail had expired, was a suspension of the Plaintiff's proceedings, the Court this day made the rule absolute. (*a*)

(*a*) The reporter is indebted for this case to a gentleman of the bar of known accuracy.

1815.

MOIR *v.* The ROYAL EXCHANGE ASSURANCE   *June* 1.
Company.

THIS was an action of debt upon a policy of insur- The warranty
ance on the ship *Neptunus* at and from *Memel* to to " depart"
the ship's port of discharge in *England*, free of capture before a certain
day, which is
in the ports and roads of lading, and warranted to de- used by the
part on or before the 15th of *September*. The declara- *Royal Ex-*
change Assur-
tion contained averments that the ship was in good *ance* Company
safety at *Memel*, and afterwards, and before the 15th of in their policies, does not
September, departed for and towards *England* upon mean merely
the voyage, and was lost by perils of the seas. The to break
cause was tried before *Gibbs* C. J. at the sittings after fairly to set
Hilary term 1815, when a verdict was found for the forward upon
Plaintiff, subject to a case, which stated in substance the voyage.
Therefore,
that the *Neptunus* on the 31st of *August* completed her where a ship
lading of a cargo in the port of *Memel*, for *England ;* in complete
she was cleared out at the custom-house at *Memel*, weighed an-
ready to proceed on her voyage, before the 9th of *Sep-* chor with some
tember, on which day, being the first opportunity after, of more fa-
she hove up her anchor, and broke ground from her vourable wea-
station where she had loaded, and got under weigh, ther, but in
half an hour
with intention of proceeding to *England*, the morning was beaten
being calm, and there being some little prospect of a back, and came
favourable change of winds and weather; but before the to anchor
within the bar,
ship had been half an hour under weigh, the sea breeze half a mile
came in strong from the westward, and obliged her to nearer to the
come to an anchor as near the sea, at the *Haff* or river- sea than the
place of load-
mouth, as was consistent with her safety. The ship ing, held that
there lay in perfect sea-readiness, until the first oppor- this was not a
departure
tunity that afterwards presented for sailing, which was within the
on the 21st *September*, when she, with 22 ships more, warranty.
sailed from that port on their respective voyages. No
ship sailed in the interim. The part of the *Haff*, or
situation

situation where the *Neptunus* took in the cargo, is not above a *British* statute mile from the sea mouth : the place where she lay from the 9th of *September* to the 21st is not more than half that distance. There is a bar at the sea mouth about two miles from the town of *Memel,* which is the limit of the port of *Memel.* The *Neptunus* in her voyage on the 4th of *October* sailed from *Hanoe* with convoy for *England,* and was lost. The question was, whether the Plaintiff is entitled to recover ?

Marshall Serjt. for the Plaintiff, contended that the ship had departed before the 15th of *September* according to the mercantile meaning of the word. The intent was, that by the day named the ship should have on board her cargo, and all her clearances, and should get under way, and this was a compliance with the warranty whether the ship were beaten back or not. He admitted that in the case of the same (a) parties in the King's Bench, Lord *Ellenborough* C. J. had held that there was a distinction between the words " depart" and " sail," and that the former meant to get completely out of port; but it was a distinction without a difference. The weighing anchor, and getting to the harbour's mouth, was a departure. If she had been lost before she reached the harbour's mouth, the Defendant would have been liable on a policy " from *Memel,*" though the word " at" had not been inserted : for the risk would have commenced the moment the ship began to move from *Memel.* It is often a question, what is the port, as in *Constable* v. *Noble* (b), *Payne* v. *Hutchinson* (c), *Bond* v. *Nutt* (d), *Thellusson* v. *Fergusson* (e), and *Thellusson* v. *Staples* (f). But

(a) *Mair* v. *Royal Exchange Assurance Company,* 3 *Maule & Selw.* 461.
(b) *Ante,* ii. 403.
(c) *Ante,* ii. 405. *n.*
(d) *Cowp.* 601.
(e) *Doug.* 361.
(f) *Doug.* 366 *n.*

this

this is a stronger case than any of them, for this must be taken to be an insurance from the town of *Memel,* the *caput portus.*

Bosanquet Serjt. *contrà.* The intent of the under-writers in this contract was, to avoid the winter risk of the *Baltic,* which, it is well known, commences on 15th *September.* Upon the construction contended for by the Plaintiff, that *Memel* means the town of *Memel,* the policy never attached, for it is to be gathered from the case, that the ship's station was never so high up the harbour as *Memel,* by a mile, therefore the ship could not depart from *Memel.* The case finds only that when she broke ground, "there was some little prospect" of a favourable change of weather, but that little failing, she could not get over the bar, which is found to be the boundary of the port; in none of the cases referred to was the probability of an effective sailing so feeble as in this. The master here merely changed his situation in the harbour, and put himself in a position to be pre-pared for sailing when occasion offered. But there is a substantial distinction between "depart," which is a relative term, and must mean, to depart from some place; and "sail," and the Plaintiffs purposely, for avoiding the construction which the Courts had put upon the word "sail," have adopted this phrase in all their contracts, at least since 1787, when the question of its meaning was intended to be tried before Lord *Loughborough* C. J. in an action brought against them by *Rogers* (a); but the Plaintiff was nonsuited on the merits. In the grammatical construction of this con-tract the departure must be, from the last antecedent, *viz.* the port and roads of loading, not the town of *Memel* under the word "at." Until 15th *September*

(a) *Park on Insurance,* 6th edit. 442. . *497*

the

the underwriters were liable to sea risks happening in
the port and roads of *Memel,* but after that day, the
ship having not then yet sailed from thence, their liability wholly ceased. So long as the ship lies at any
place, where being, she may be said to be at *Memel,* she
cannot be said to have departed from *Memel.* And
while she lay within the harbour mouth, it might properly be said that she was at *Memel.* In the case between the same parties in the King's Bench, it was
supposed that the vessel had at first broken ground
with a favourable wind, the evidence as to that fact not
having arrived, but even with that advantage for the
Plaintiff, Lord *Ellenborough* was confident that to
" depart" must mean to get clearly out of the port. If
this Court adopts a different construction, they will lay
a ground for fraud; for whenever masters of vessels
foresee any difficulty in sailing, they will shift their
situation in the harbour to evade a similar warranty,
and there will be numerous questions to be tried, whether, when a master broke ground, he had a reasonable
prospect of getting out of the harbour.

Marshall, in reply, reprobated the distinction between " sail" and " depart." To depart is, indeed, a
relative term, but the place of lading is the place
whence the vessel departs, and her progress thence to
the harbour's mouth was a part of her voyage to *England.* He prayed a new trial upon payment of costs,
to ascertain the precise spot where she took in her
cargo.

GIBBS C. J. If this had been a warranty to " sail"
on or before the 15th of *September,* I should have
thought most clearly, on the authority of the cases, and
also without cases, that the ship had " sailed:" for it
has been held that a warranty to have sailed at and

4   from

from *Jamaica* to *London* before the first of *August* means that the ship shall have began her voyage before that time, because a part of her voyage is the getting out from the place in which she is; and if this ship had been warranted to sail before the 15th of *September*, I should have thought she had complied with that warranty; but it seems on the report of the case in 1787, that this company have early adopted a variation in this phrase, whereas all other policies retain that form of warranty to sail. On a warranty to sail, when the ship breaks ground, and gets under way, the warranty is complied with. But this policy will not bear the same construction. To " sail," is to sail on the voyage. To " depart," must be to depart from some particular place. It is said by the counsel for the Plaintiff, that if the ship had got under way at *Memel*, and had been lost on her way to the sea mouth, that would have been a departure. I asked for his authority, but no case was cited. We must therefore construe it upon the reason of the case. It cannot mean a departure from the town of *Memel*. I see not then, what it can mean, except a departure from the port of *Memel*. I can see no other *terminus a quo*, and I think the ship had not departed from the port of *Memel* before the 5th of *September*.

CHAMBRE J. I perfectly agree. What had the underwriters to do with the town of *Memel ?* The meaning of the parties was, to avoid the winter risk. If the other construction were adopted, ships would always move their place in the harbour, to make out a departure. No blame attaches on the conduct of the ship, but I think the warranty is not complied with.

DALLAS J. There are neither the words " port of *Memel*," nor " town of *Memel*," in this policy. It is not a distinction without a difference that is taken between sailing and departing, and the latter word must mean a departure from the port. It is said, there is a commercial meaning to the word. I see not that there is, but I am much struck with the circumstance that this company have deviated from the usual phrase; and the assured seeing a new term proposed, ought to have considered the meaning of it, and known that if he adopted it, he would be bound by it. I am clear that the departure meant a departure from the port of *Memel*, and that this ship had not departed.

Judgment for the Defendants.

A rule was afterwards moved for by previous consent to turn this case into a special verdict, which, in *Michaelmas* term, was discharged by consent.

June 1.

JOHN JOHNSON *v.* LEIGH.

A sheriff cannot justify breaking the inner doors of the house of a stranger, upon suspicion that a Defendant is there, to search for him in order to arrest him on mesne process.

IN trespass for breaking and entering the Plaintiff's house and breaking his inner doors, locks, and hinges, the Defendant justified as sheriff, under a writ of *alias testatum capias* against *Thomas Johnson*, by virtue whereof the Defendant, before the return of the writ, and within his bailiwick, as such sheriff peaceably and quietly entered into the messuage in which, &c. the outer door thereof then and there being open, and there then and there being reasonable and sufficient cause for the Defendant to suspect and believe, and the Defendant suspecting and believing, that *Thomas Johnson* then was in the said messuage, in order to arrest him under that writ, as it was lawful, &c.; and in order to arrest him under that writ, the Defendant

neces-

necessarily made a little noise, &c., and the said
Thomas Johnson not having been taken under the writ,
and the entrance of divers apartments in the dwelling
house being fastened, and there then and there being
reasonable and sufficient ground and cause for the
Defendant to suspect and believe, and the Defendant
suspecting and believing, that *T. Johnson* then was in
those rooms or one of them, the Defendant at the time
when, &c., in order to search for, find, and arrest
T. Johnson by virtue of that writ, necessarily broke
open the said inner doors, locks, and hinges, and in
so doing necessarily a little broke, damaged, and spoiled
the same. The Plaintiff demurred, and assigned for
causes, that although the Defendant had professed to
justify the breaking, &c. of the Plaintiff's doors, locks,
staples, and hinges, yet the Defendant had not by his
plea shewn any sufficient justification or excuse for
such trespasses; and that the Defendant had not
shewn that he demanded or required of any person in
the dwelling house to open the doors of those apartments, or that he demanded or required the key
thereof, or that no person was in the dwelling house,
so as to prevent or preclude the Defendant from so
demanding entrance into the rooms.

The *Court*, stopping *Pell* Serjt., who would have
supported the demurrer, called on *Blosset* Serjt. to
maintain his plea.

Blosset urged that the demurrer admitted that if the
Defendant had previously made the demand and been
refused, though this was the house of another, the
Defendant would have been justified in breaking the
inner door. Lord *Alvanley* C. J. admitted the same
thing in *Ratcliffe* v. *Burton* (a). And in *Hutchison* v.

1815.

JOHNSON
v.
LEIGH.

Birch (*a*), this Court distinguishes between breaking the inner doors and the outer doors, and in *Semayne's* case (*b*), Lord *Coke* says, in many cases the door of a third person may be broken where that of the Defendant himself cannot; for though every man's house is his own castle, it is not the castle of another man. This plea is founded on the case of *Hutchison* v. *Birch*, wherein this Court overturned the reasoning, on which the Court proceeded in *Burton* v. *Ratcliffe*.

GIBBS C. J. In *Hutchison* v. *Birch* the goods were in the house; here the Defendant only avers a suspicion that *T. Johnson* was in the house. I protest that the Court have not decided this point, or dropt in the case of *Hutchison* v. *Birch* any thing which favours the opinion that it may not go abroad to the world, that we have so decided.

Pell cited *Cooke* v. *Birt* (*c*), and the distinction there taken between a stranger's house and the Defendant's, to which the Court agreed.

Blosset was permitted to amend his plea.

(*a*) *Ante*, iv. 619.   (*c*) *Ante*, v. 765.
(*b*) 5 *Co Rep* 92 6*th res.*

THIS was an action brought to recover from the Defendant the moiety of the expences of building a party wall between the adjoining houses of the Plaintiff's testator and the Defendant, which had both been consumed by a fire. At the trial of the cause, before *Gibbs* C. J. it appeared that the Defendant had had a former beneficial term in his house, which had expired before the time of the fire. The Plaintiff's testator had first rebuilt his house, and erected the party wall, and paid the expences of it, and the Defendant afterwards rebuilt his house and finished it in 1811, and therein made use of the Plaintiff's party wall; but the only evidence offered to prove that the Defendant was the owner of the improved rent, was a new lease granted to him by the ground landlord, executed in 1812, whereby, in consideration of the great charge which the Defendant had incurred in rebuilding his house, the lessor demised the site thereof, and the newly erected messuage thereon, to the Defendant for 61 years from *Christmas* 1809, under seven guineas rent. The house was worth 60*l.* per ann. *Vaughan* Serjt. contended that from the contents of this lease the jury might infer a previous agreement in writing by the Defendant to rebuild the house, which would make him the owner of the improved rent, within the principle of the case of *Peck* v. *Wood* (a). *Gibbs* C. J. however was of a different opinion, and directed a nonsuit, which

Vaughan now moved to set aside, contending first, that the retrospective *habendum* made the Defendant

(a) 5 *Term Rep.* 130.

owner

owner of the improved rent at the time of building the
party wall; next, that the mere possession of the house
at the time made him such; and thirdly, that the lease
contained evidence that there had been a previously
subsisting agreement for a building lease from the
ground landlord to the Defendant at the time when he
rebuilt the house. There had been in fact, he said,
such an agreement, which he would produce on another trial.

GIBBS C. J. If the Plaintiff had shewn an agreement for a lease, I think she would have succeeded in
bringing this within the case of *Peck* v. *Wood*. There,
when the premises were built, it was held the Defendant was answerable for half the party wall; but there
the agreement was made while the wall was building. I
cite this only to shew, that under an agreement the
tenant might be esteemed owner of the improved rent,
but we cannot infer an agreement from the facts that
appear to us. Suppose it were the case, that a tenant
from year to year had rebuilt the house, might not the
landlord (though a hard case) turn him out immediately? If you take the lease, you must take it such as
it is, and it only says, in consideration of having rebuilt; it recites no agreement, and on the case the Plaintiff now opens, she must have been nonsuited at the trial,
for the agreement was in writing, and she had it not
there. The mere possession of the house did not make
the Defendant owner of the improved rent.

Rule refused.

*C*OPLEY Serjt. had obtained a rule *nisi* for an attachment for non-payment of a sum of money pursuant to an award, upon the reading of the award and rule of Court for the submission, and upon an affidavit that the deponent saw the arbitrators severally sign and publish their award thereto annexed, and that their names subscribed thereto were of their hands writing, that the deponent had personally served the Defendant with true copies of the award and rule of Court recording the submission, and at the same time shewn him the original award and rule, and demanded the money.

Vaughan Serjt. shewed cause against this rule, upon the ground that the submission by bond, on which the rule for the attachment was drawn up, was conditioned for performance of the award, so as it were made in writing ready to be delivered on or before the first day of *April*, or on or before such other day to which the arbitrators, or any two of them, should think fit to enlarge the time for making their award by indorsement on those presents, with power to make the submission a rule of court, which had been done. The arbitrators reciting in their award, that by memorandums on the bonds, dated the 24th of *March*, and 28th of *April*, the time for making their award was enlarged until the first of *July*, proceeded to award the sum demanded; in witness whereof they thereunto set their hands the 18th of *May* 1815, and the deponent attested the execution thereof, but there was no affidavit that the arbitrators had in fact enlarged the time for making their award beyond the first day of

Where arbitrators have power to enlarge the time for making their award, and have enlarged it, and made their award in the additional time, in order to bring the Defendant into contempt for non-performance of the award, there must be an affidavit that the time has been enlarged, that the award was made within the enlarged time, and that the Defendant has been personally served with notice of those facts.

Semble that the affidavit for an attachment for non-performance of an award, must, contrary to the usual practice, always state the time of execution of the award.

S 4

April,

1815.   *April;* not only ought that fact to appear upon oath,
WOHLENBERG   but it ought also to appear on oath that the fact of en-
v.   largement within the original time was made known to
LAGEMAN.   the Defendant, before he could be punishable for a
contempt of the Court in disobeying the award; and it
is sworn that the office copy of the rule of Court for the
submission, which was served on the Defendant, had on
it no copy of the indorsement on the bonds enlarging
the time.   This point had been twice decided in the
Court of King's Bench, in the cases of *George* v. *Louseley* (a), and *Davis* v. *Vass* (b). It would have been
improper that the officer of the Court should, as was
suggested by the counsel for the Plaintiff on the motion
for the rule, have copied into the rule of submission the
indorsement of enlargement which was on the bond,
for it was not authenticated to that officer by any affidavit, as the bond of submission itself was, for warranting
him in drawing up the rule.

   Copley in support of his rule.   In *George* v. *Louseley*
it did not appear on the award itself, as here it does,
that the arbitrators had enlarged the time for making
their award; so that the award, on the *face* of it, appeared to be made after the authority was expired.   It
is not the ordinary practice, in the affidavit of the execution of an award made for an attachment, to swear
that it is executed on the day of the date, or that
it was ready to be delivered out before the day; but
only that it was executed, the rest is left to be collected
from the date of the award.   [To this the officers of the
Court agreed.]   And on that affidavit of the execution,
the attachment goes.   *Omnia rite acta presumun-
tur.*   Credit is given to the award itself, that it is made
in due time.   Here the arbitrators are to make an

    (a) 8 *East,* 13.   (b) 15 *East,* 97.

award

award before the 1st of *April,* and on the award they re-   1815.
cite that on the 24th of *March* and 28th of *April* they
had enlarged the time; and before the day to which   WOHLENBERG
the time stood enlarged, they award. Admitting that   *v.*
the case of *Davis* v. *Vass* is repugnant to this doctrine,   LAGEMAN.
it is a single case, not in this Court, and not founded in
reason. The instrument is in Court to be inspected; the
Defendant is no party to it, it is the act of strangers.
The Court will look at it, and give credit to it for the
facts therein stated.

GIBBS C. J.   We think that on principle, independently of the authority of those cases, this objection
must be allowed. This is a motion for an attachment
for disobedience to a rule of Court: the Defendant
must have notice that the award was made, and that
he was called on to obey it.   Here is a submission to
an award to be made within a precise time, but which
is to be extended if the arbitrators think fit.   But it
is necessary that the Defendant should have notice
of any extension of the time, and that the award was
made within the extended time.   There is no affidavit
that the Defendant in this case had notice of the extension of the time, or of the award being made within
the extended time.   On the other hand, it is sworn
that the Defendant was served with a copy of a rule
with no indorsement of the enlargement thereon., It
does not appear to us, therefore, that the party charged
with the contempt of the Court had sufficient notice
to bring him within that charge.   We think, on principle, if there were no decided cases on the subject,
this would be so; but we also should be sorry to differ
from the two cases cited.   I do not mean *George* v.
Lousley, but *Davis* v. *Vass* and *Moule* v. *Stawell,* a case
stated in a note to the former.   Those two decisions
are

1815.   are not distinguishable in terms from this. As to the
             argument used for the Plaintiff, that in practice the
WOHLENBERG   affidavit for an attachment never states the date of
   v.   the execution, we see that the ordinary form of affidavit
LACKMAN.   for obtaining an attachment published in the books of
             practice (a) does not state the date of the award, but
             though it does not in terms state that it was executed
             on that day, it may be doubtful whether it might not
             bear that interpretation, and we think it worthy to be
             considered, whether it would not be advisable to alter
             the language of similar affidavits. However, inde-
             pendently of that circumstance, we think, both on
             principle, and on the authority of the decided cases,
             that this objection must be allowed.

                          Rule discharged without costs.

             The award itself, instead of a copy thereof, having
             been annexed by the Plaintiff to the affidavit for the
             attachment, and deposited on the files of the Court,
             the Plaintiff had not the means of shewing the De-
             fendant the award itself upon a further demand; and
             therefore *Copley* now obtained a rule *nisi* that the
             award itself might be taken off the file and delivered
             by the officer to the Plaintiff's attorney, upon an under-
             taking to return it into the office upon a day named.

Though an   *Vaughan* on a subsequent day moved to set aside
arbitrator on   the award, first, on the ground that it was uncer-
a question of
mixed law and   tain; for it awarded that a certain debt of 720l. 9s.
fact has allow- should be paid by the Plaintiff and the Defendant, in
ed transactions
apparently illegal, as premiums of insurance on a voyage to an hostile port, the
Court will not set aside the award.
    An award that two persons shall pay a debt in proportion to the shares which
they held in a certain ship, the ratio of their shares not being a subject of dispute, is
sufficiently certain.

                    (a) *Tidd's Practical Forms*, 235. s. 4.
             I   pro-

proportion to the shares which they severally had held in a certain ship, not ascertaining what those shares were; and the Plaintiff, being a foreigner, was not in law entitled to the benefits of *British* registry, and therefore legally had, and could have, no share in the ship. He also moved on the ground that the arbitrator had allowed in account premiums of insurance on an illegal voyage, namely, to *Rotterdam,* an hostile port. He also urged that usurious commission had been allowed.

GIBBS C. J. We do not think there is any ground for granting this rule. The application is made, first, on the ground that the award is uncertain, in directing that the debt should be paid in proportion to the share in the ship which each formerly had. As it does not appear that it was in dispute between the parties what those shares were, the award is final for all those purposes for which it was intended to be made. There is a dispute about a ship, and the Defendant insists, that, as the Plaintiff was a foreigner, the whole affair was illegal; it may be so, but these were executory matters, and when such are referred, and settled by arbitrators, the Court will never set the award aside. The ground of the insurance also is one which the Court cannot take into consideration. If an arbitrator acts directly against law, the Court will set aside the award; but if, in a matter mixed of law and fact, he mistakes some of the points, they will not therefore set aside an award, *Delver* v. *Barnes* (a). As to the objection, that usurious commission was given by the arbitrators, it was a fact for them to ascertain; we therefore see no reason to grant a rule which ultimately cannot be supported.

Rule refused.

(a) *Ante,* i. 48.

June 7.

MACKIE *v.* LANDON.

Same *v.* LEWIS.

Under the statute 52 G 3. c. 39. s. 11. a master of a vessel who, coming from the *westward* bound to any place in the Thames or Medway, re-fuses to take a pilot on board, is liable to a penalty equal to double the amount of the several sums payable for pilotage from the place where he is bound first to take a pilot on board, to the termination of his voyage.

THIS was an action of debt on the statute 52 G. 3. c. 39. s. 11. and at the trial before *Chambre* J. at the *Kent* Spring assizes 1815, it was proved that the Defendant in his vessel the *John Weston,* of 10 tons bur-then and 14½ feet draft of water, in his course from the *West Indies* came from the *westward* of *Folkstone* bound for a place in the *Thames,* namely, *London,* and that he did not at the time when his ship was discovered to the *westward* of *Folkstone,* or at any time during her course from thence to the line that might be drawn from the buoy of the *Brake* to *Sandown Castle,* hoist an union jack as a signal for a cinque port pilot to come on board, and that during such course he was hailed by a pilot, but while he was coming on board, the Defendant took advantage of a breeze which sprung up, and sailed off from him. The additional penalty of 5*l.* for every 50 tons of her burthen amounted to 10*l.* and the double pilotage was 8 guineas, if, as the Defendant contended, the measure of the forfeiture was to be the pilotage due for the voyage from the *westward* of *Folkstone* to the *Downs,* but the Plaintiff contended, that he was further entitled to double the amount of the pilotage for the re-sidue of the ship's voyage, namely, from the *Downs* to *Gravesend,* which was 22*l.* 16*s.* 9*d.* more. The jury found a verdict for 18*l.* 8*s.* being the double amount of the pilotage from the *westward* of *Folkstone* to the *Downs,* and 10*l.* as the additional penalty of 5*l.* for every 50 tons burthen of the vessel, with liberty to move to increase it to 41*l.* 4*s.* 9*d.* if the Court should be of opinion that the Plaintiff was entitled thereto.

Accordingly

Accordingly *Best* Serjt. in *Easter* term obtained a rule *nisi* to enter the verdict on the 8th count, which warranted the penalties amounting to 41*l.* 4*s.* 9*d.*, contending that though the statute had not said in express terms what were to be the *termini* of the voyage the pilotage whereof was to be the measure of the penalty, it must be intended of all the remaining voyage of the ship during which she was bound to keep a pilot on board.

Shepherd Solicitor-General on this day shewed cause: he contended the measure of the penalty was only the double of the pilotage of that part of the voyage during which by the statute the Defendant was bound to have his flag flying as a signal for a pilot; namely, from the *westward* of *Folkstone* to the *Downs*, at which place the statute made a rest in the voyage, and an alteration in the rates of pilotage; for there the Defendant was entitled to anchor, as was usual, and *non constat* that he would again sail thence for *London* without taking a pilot on board, if he did, it would be a new and distinct offence, for which a separate penalty, namely, the double of the pilotage from the *Downs* to *London*, was enacted. To hold otherwise, would be to give the statute a construction which would inflict very unequal penalties on different offenders for the same offence; for if two ships together came from the *westward* of *Folkstone*, intending to anchor in the *Downs*, the one bound to the *north* of *England*, the other to *London*, and both omitted to take a pilot, the one would incur only the penalty of double the pilotage from the *westward* of *Folkstone* to the *Downs*, while the other would incur the additional penalty of double the pilotage from the *Downs* to *London*. A further circumstance worthy of notice, is, that the pilotage for the two several parts of the voyage is computed on a different principle, viz. that from the *Downs* to *London*, varying according to the depth of

water

water which the vessel draws, while that from the west-ward of *Folkstone* to the *Downs* is a sum certain for vessels of whatever burthen.

Best relied on the words of the statute, as clear, and not to be controuled by inferences to be drawn from the schedule: he was stopped by the Court.

Gibbs C. J. There is no measure by which this penalty can be ascertained, except by the voyage which the ship is about to perform, and which the act directs she shall not perform without a pilot. She is bound to have a flag flying, and to take a pilot on board as soon as she passes *Dungeness*, and if a pilot offers himself, and she refuses to take him on board, he is entitled to recover penalties against the master, and they cannot be measured otherwise than by the sum which the pilot would have been entitled to receive if he had been permitted to perform the duties which the act directs. The Plaintiff is therefore entitled to the larger sum, and the verdict must be transferred from the first count to the eighth.

Rule absolute.

THIS was an action for money had and received, and for interest, brought to recover from the Defendants, who were auctioneers, · the deposit paid by the Plaintiff on being declared the purchaser of certain premises. At the trial of the cause before *Gibbs* C. J. at the sittings after *Michaelmas* term 1814, a verdict was found for the Plaintiff for the deposit without interest, subject to a case, which stated that on 13th *March* 1813, a commission of bankruptcy issued against *M. Price*, on the petition of *Bennett* and Co.; he was declared a bankrupt, and his property assigned to *Jones* and *Mercer*, under whose direction, on 27th *July*, the Defendants put up to sale by public auction part of the bankrupts' copyhold estates: the Plaintiff was declared the purchaser, and according to the conditions of sale paid a deposit of 20 *per cent.* and signed an agreement for payment on the remainder on 30th *August* 1813, on having a good title: an abstract was delivered and approved of on 26th *August* 1813, by the Plaintiff, who afterwards, in in negotiating a loan on the estate, in order to complete his purchase, put the abstract into the hands of a person, who on the 22d of *October* rejected the title, apprising the Plaintiff, that *M. Price* took only an estate for life in the premises, of which the assignees were thereupon informed by the Plaintiff. In *Michaelmas* term 1813, an action was brought by the bankrupt to try the validity of the commission, in which he recovered a verdict at the sittings after that term, upon the ground that the petitioning creditor's debt was not due until some days after the issuing of the commission, and judgment in that action was signed in *Hilary* term 1814.

On

A bankrupt's assignees had contracted for the sale of his copyhold lands, and received a deposit. The commission was afterwards superseded, because, when it issued, the petitioning creditor's debt was not due : Another commission issued upon the petition of another creditor, and the same assignees were chosen : Held that the Plaintiff, having abandoned his contract pending the old commission, might recover back his deposit.

On the 1st of *February* 1814, the Plaintiff abandoned his purchase, and required a return of the deposit with interest. The assignees insisted on the completion of the contract. On the 3d *March* 1814, the commission was superseded, and on the following day a second commission issued directed to the same commissioners, upon the petition of *Chatfield*, upon which *M. Price* was declared a bankrupt. On the 22d *March* 1814, *Jones* and *Mercer* were again chosen assignees under the second commission, and an assignment executed. The writ in the present action was sued out on the 12th of *March* 1814. The Defendants had not paid over the deposit money to the assignees, at the time of bringing the action, nor were the objections (if any) which had been made to the title removed. The question was, whether the Plaintiff was entitled to recover.

Best Serjt., for the Plaintiff, was stopped by the Court.

Copley Serjt., for the Defendants, contended that it was an answer to the action, if the Defendants were enabled at any time before the trial of the cause to make a good title, though acquired by them even since the action commenced; for which he cited *Thomson* v. *Miles* (a). But further, the assignees had at the time of the abandonment the actual legal estate, which they could have transferred.

Per Curiam. We all agree in thinking that at the time the Plaintiff gave the Defendants notice of abandoning his purchase, the contract was at an end: *rebus sic stantibus*, the contract could not have been

(a) 1 *Esp. N. P. Cas.* 184.

performed, because the contract was made with assignees
of a bankrupt, and there was then no valid commission
subsisting: therefore the Defendants had not then a
good legal estate; for to prove that proposition, they
must have begun by proving the petitioning creditor's
debt, which they could not do.

1815.

BARTLETT
v.
TUCHIN.

Judgment for the Plaintiff.

KENT <i>v.</i> YATES.

June 9.

THE Plaintiff having signed judgment for want of a
plea, *Best* Serjt. for the Defendant had obtained a
rule *nisi* to set it aside as premature, contending that
the Defendant was entitled to an imparlance, under the
circumstances, which were these; the writ was returnable on the last return-day of *Easter* term. The Defendant put in bail, but had not perfected them, when
the Plaintiff, on the 25th of *May*, which was after the
essoign-day of *Trinity* term, delivered his declaration
de bene esse, entitled of *Easter* term.

Vaughan Serjt. shewed cause, upon the ground that
the Defendant was entitled to no imparlance; for the
Plaintiff had been guilty of no laches: he could not
declare in chief, because the Defendant had not perfected his bail, and he was not bound to declare *de bene
esse*, as was held here, in the case of *Bailey* v. *Hant-
ler* (a), and in the King's Bench, in the case of *Rolleston*
v. *Scott*. (b)

Best, in support of his rule, admitted that the Defendant was not bound to declare *de bene esse*, but urged,

Where a writ
is returnable
on the last
return-day of
one term, the
Plaintiff, who
is not bound
to declare *de
bene esse*, is
under no com-
pulsion to de-
clare before
the essoign-day
of the next
term; and
therefore the
Defendant is
not entitled to
an imparlance.

(a) 2 Bos. & Pull. 126.   (b) 5 Term Rep. 372.

VOL. VI.   T   that

that if he did so declare, he was bound by the same rules as if he had declared in chief. The practice is well known, that where a writ is returnable upon the last return-day of one term, and the Plaintiff does not declare till after the essoign-day of the suceeeding term, the Defendant is entitled to an imparlance. Another objection is, that the declaration is entitled of the preceding term, though not delivered until after the essoign-day of the following term.

GIBBS C. J. This rule was moved on the ground that the Defendant was entitled to an imparlance. It is now objected, that whether it be so or not, the present judgment, signed for want of a plea, cannot be supported, because there is no declaration which the Defendant need notice. The writ was returnable on the last return-day of *Easter* term; the declaration is entitled of *Easter* term, which is right, being of the term of which the writ is returnable. Generally, when a writ is returnable on the last return-day of a term, unless the Plaintiff declares before the essoign-day of the subsequent term, the Defendant is entitled to an imparlance, but that supposes the Defendant to have done all that is incumbent on him. Here the Defendant had put in bail, but he had not put the Plaintiff in such a situation, that he could declare in chief before the first day of *Trinity* term. The Plaintiff therefore could not have proceeded more expeditiously than he has done, unless he had declared *de bene esse,* which, according to two cases cited, he is not bound to do. The consequence is, that the Plaintiff has not been guilty of negligence, and could not have proceeded more expeditiously, and therefore the rule must be discharged. This rule, I am informed, has been constantly acted on.

HEATH J. The case in *Bosanquet* and *Puller* was decided, overruling the same authority in *Crompton*
which

which is overruled in *Rolleston* v. *Scott.* It is extraordinary that counsel should so often have been misled by it.

CHAMBRE J. A Plaintiff is not obliged to declare *de bene esse*: if he can derive any particular advantage from it, he may declare *de bene esse*: that doctrine has been often held here.

Rule discharged with costs.

---

vid. Searce. &c. dev p. 2

Sir SAMUEL ROMILLY, Knt. *v.* JAMES.   *June 9.*

THIS was an action for money had and received, brought to recover back the deposit paid on a contract for a purchase of lands in fee simple, upon the alleged insufficiency of the title to be derived from *Henry Smith* the son hereinafter mentioned. The cause was tried before *Gibbs* C. J. at the sittings after *Michaelmas* term 1814, when a verdict was found for the Plaintiff, subject to a case, which in substance stated that *T. Smith* by his will dated 26th *September* 1734, duly executed and attested for passing real property, devised to his brother *H. Smith* all his the testator's real estate, subject to the several devises thereinafter expressed. The testator then devised to his brother's son *H. Smith* all his the testator's estate in *Radnorshire*, called the *Meadows* under *Stanmer*, (the premises in question,) to hold to him and his heirs for ever. At the conclusion of the will are these words. " And further, my will is, that in case my brother, and his son my nephew, (meaning the devisees of the

Marginal note: Devise to *H. S.,* my brother's son, to hold to him and his heirs, and in case my brother and his son should happen to die having no issue of either of their bodies, then to *J. Clerk* and his heirs. This is not a defeasible fee-simple in *H. S.* the son, with an executory devise over, but an estate tail.
Whether a devisee in remainder can maintain a writ of intrusion,

Or a writ to be framed on the statute of *Westminster* the 2d in the nature of a writ of intrusion, *quære.*

Devise in fee, with an executory devise over, whether the fine of the devisee in fee shall bar the executory devise over, *quære.*

In a court of law, every title that is not bad, is marketable.

premises in question,) should happen to die, having no issue of either of their bodies, then I devise all my real estate unto my nephew *Josias Clerk* and his heirs." The testator died without having altered or revoked his will, leaving his brother *H. Smith* his heir at law, and his nephew *H. Smith* the younger, only son of *H. Smith* the brother, him surviving. By indenture of 6th *September* 1739, *H. Smith* and *H. Smith* the younger covenanted to levy a fine *sur conusance de droit come ceo* of the premises; which fine should enure to the use of *H. Smith*, and *H. Smith* the younger, and their heirs. On the 1st *September* 1740, at the *Radnor* great sessions, the fine was acccordingly levied, and duly proclaimed. By lease and release of 28th and 29th *June* 1748, between *H. Smith* the younger, 1. *R. Symmonds*, 2. and *R. Hawkins*, 3. (though. *H. Smith* the father was still alive, and his seisin as joint tenant continued,) *H. Smith* the younger, in consideration of 5s. bargained, sold, and released the premises unto and to the use of *R. Symonds* and his heirs, to make him tenant to the precipe in a common recovery of the premises, which, it was declared, should enure to *H. Smith* the younger and his heirs, and which recovery was duly suffered accordingly. *H. Smith* the father died in 1760, and had no other issue than *H. Smith* the son. *H. Smith* the son died in 1779, never having had any issue. *J. Clerk* was living at the death of *H. Smith* the son, and laboured under none of the disabilities mentioned in the saving clauses of the statutes of limitation: he died in 1785, viz. within 30 years from the death of *H. Smith* the son. Neither *J. Clerk* nor his heirs, nor any other person claiming under *Clerk*, ever had the possession of the premises. The question was, whether the Plaintiff was entitled to recover.

Lens

Lens Serjt. for the Plaintiff, contended, first, That H. *Smith* the son took under this will an estate in fee simple, with an executory devise over to *J. Clerk*, in case the two *Smiths*, father and son, died without leaving issue at the time of their decease, and not, as would be contended on the other side, an estate tail. In support of this construction he referred to the cases of *Porter* v. *Bradley* (a), *Weekly* on demise of *Knight* v. *Rugg*, (b), and *Roe* on demise of *Sheers* v. *Jeffery* (c). Secondly, That although the father died before the son, he did not leave issue within the meaning of the will, because at the decease of the survivor of them there was not issue of either left, and therefore the event had occurred upon which the estate was to go over to *Josias Clerk*. Thirdly, That though *Clerk* was barred of his ejectment by the lapse of 20 years since the death of *H. Smith* the younger, yet that a devisee might maintain a writ of intrusion; or if, according to *Co. Litt.* (d) and *Fitzherbert* (e), that writ is confined to the case where tenant for life, or in dower, or by the curtesy, dieth seised of such estate for life, and after their death a stranger doth intrude upon the land, yet, under the statute of *Westminster* the 2d, (f) a devisee may maintain a writ in the nature of a writ of intrusion, which ought to be framed for the use of devisees, so that, since the statute of wills had created the right, a remedy might not be wanting for a right like this, *cadenti sub eodem jure, et simili indigente remedio:* That however is scarcely necessary, for in the case of *Smith* v. *Coffin*, (g) the form of a writ of entry *sur abatement* was altered to enable a bankrupt's assignees to sue. In *Eastman* v. *Baker* (h) a demandant claiming

1815.

ROMILLY, Knt.
v.
JAMES.

(a) 3 *Term Rep.* 143.
(b) 7 *Term Rep.* 322.
(c) Ib. 589.
(d) *Co. Litt.* 277. b.
(e) *F. N. B.* 203.
(f) 13 *Ed.* 1. c. 24.
(g) 2 H. Bl. 444.
(h) *Ante,* i. 174.

T 3

under

under an executory devise, recovered in this Court on a writ of intrusion, without objection; and if *Clerk* might himself maintain the writ, there is no reason why his heir may not. Fourthly, If the devisee over might maintain a writ of intrusion, he was not barred by the lapse of time, by reason of the statute 32 *H.* 8. *c.* 2., in any less period than 50 years of adverse possession, which had not yet elapsed since the death of *H. Smith* the younger, and the possession of the *Smiths* was not adverse, but in aid of the title of *Clerk,* and parcel of the same fee. Lastly, The estate of *Clerk* was not barred by the fine of *H. Smith* the younger, and five years non-claim, for the fine of tenant in fee is wholly inoperative, except that it operates in confirmation of his former estate, this fine was therefore in furtherance and confirmation of the estate of the former tenant in fee, and the estate given by the executory devise is parcel of the same fee, and so is confirmed by the fine, not displaced by it. There is no express decision of this point, but the *dicta* of judges favour this opinion. Lord *Hale* (a) says an estate with five years non-claim must bar an estate precedent to the fine, not subsequent to it. This estate by the executory devise arises after the fine, and a new fine would be necessary to bar it. In *Thomasin* v. *Mackworth* (b), the Court notices (c) *Saffin's* case, and observes, that if the first lessee had been ousted by a disseisor, who had levied a fine, then the second lessee had not been barred by the fine, because his interest then would never have been displaced nor turned to a right. In the present case the fee of *Clerk,* which had never had commencement, was never displaced nor turned to a right by the fine of *H. Smith* the younger. Where the estate is a future,

(a) *Focus* v. *Salisbury, Hardr.*   (b) *Carter,* 82.
400.   (c) 5 *Co. Rep.* 124.

                                                    and

and not an existing estate, there the fine does not bar it.
In *Seymor's* case (*a*), it was resolved that the fine levied
to the bargainee did not make a discontinuance of the
remainder to *John Cheyny,* because it did not touch
or displace his remainder, and no estate of freehold
passed by the fine, but the fine with proclamations
corroborated the estate of the bargainee; and, by the
statutes of 4 *H.* 7. *c.* 24. and 32 *H.* 8. *c.* 36. made his
estate more perdurable, (and gives the reason,) but
if the fine had been levied before bargain and sale
enrolled, it had been a discontinuance. The case
itself is not in point, but it establishes the general proposition, that to give any operation to a fine, it must
be of such a nature as to dispossess some estate.
When a rightful tenant in fee levies a fine, there is no
new estate created, nor displacing of any old estate, all
remains as before. The statute gives no new force to
any fine, it only makes five years non-claim a bar, in the
case where the fine was before calculated to be a bar.

Copley Serjt. *contrà,* argued, first that *H. Smith* the
younger took an estate tail with a remainder over in fee
to *Josias Clerk,* and that the remainder was barred by
the fine and non-claim; next, that if it were an executory devise, the contingency had not happened upon
which the estate was to go over; thirdly, if it had happened, the heir of *Josias Clerk* was barred by the fine
and non-claim; if not, then, fourthly, that he was
barred because he had not entered within 20 years, the
time for an ejectment; and fifthly, that a devisee had
no writ of intrusion, or if he had a writ of intrusion, or
once possessed any legal remedy whatever, he had lost
it by the statutes 32 *H.* 8. *c.* 2. or 21 *Jac.* 1. *c.* 16. according to the nature of the writ; though he contended
that he never had any remedy except ejectment, and had

(*a*) 10 *Co.* 95 *2d Res.* \

T 4   now

1815.

ROMILLY, Knt.
v.
JAMES.

now lost that. He took the 5th objection first. The writ of intrusion will not lie for a devisee. Writs are in the register drawn with great nicety: the writ of intrusion will lie only in three cases, viz. upon the intrusion of a stranger after the death of a tenant for life, tenant in dower, and tenant by the courtesy: this particular writ will not apply to a case of the present description. The power given to the clerks in Chancery to frame new writs, does not apply to enable them to frame writs so widely different as a writ must be which would be framed to meet this case. A proof that there is much difficulty in framing a new writ, is this, that the only instance of this statute having been acted on, is that of the writ *in casu consimili* for remedy in the case of alienation in fee by tenant for life or by the courtesy, which is framed as closely as possible on the model of the writ *in casu proviso*, which extended only to alienation by tenant in dower. If any writ were to be formed for the present occasion, it would be on the model of a formedon, not of a writ of intrusion, for formedon in the reverter lay at common law on an estate conditional, and if formedon in the reverter is taken as the model, the devisee must also take all the consequences of it; and one consequence is, to be barred by 20 years' adverse possession. So that if the Plaintiff has a right to resort to this obsolete statute, for which there is no reason, as he has equal remedy by ejectment, yet he would not advance his case. Another circumstance would prevent the Plaintiff from recovering in a writ of intrusion. In all possessory actions the demandant must count on a seisin within 50 years of him from whom he claims, and it must be an actual seisin. In the construction of the 6th section of 32 *H.* 8. *c.* 2., "actual possession or seisin," the word actual has been holden to apply to both, *Bevil's* case. (*a*). In all the cases the demandant

(*a*) 4 *Co.* 8.√

alleges

alleges the seisin of the person who had the estate an-   1815.
tecedent to the estate for life; thus it will here be necessary to count on the seisin of the devisor, then to   ROMILLY, Knt.
shew the devise for life, and the decease of the tenant   JAMES.
for life, and the intrusion, otherwise the demandant loses
that particular remedy. This is so on a writ of right.
The demandant cannot count, unless he counts on the
seisin of his ancestor within 60 years: he may enter
within 20 years after his title accrues, however distant
be his ancestor's seisin, and how many soever may have
intervened; but the statute 32 *H.* 8. deprives him of
of that particular remedy, unless he can count on the
seisin of the ancestor from whom he claims within 60
years: so here, the heir of *J. Clerk* is barred of a writ or
intrusion, because he cannot count on a seisin of the
devisor within 60 years. 2dly, This is a remainder in
tail by implication, being cut down from a fee-simple by
the devise over to *J. Clerk*. *Denny*, on the demise of *Agar*
v. *Agar* (a). After a devise in fee, " In case my said son
and daughter both happen to die without having any
child or issue lawfully begotten, then I devise the reversion and inheritance to *Richard Agar* and his heirs
for ever;" Lord *Ellenborough* C. J. held it a clear limitation in tail, and *Le Blanc* J. says, it is a known rule
of law in the construction of wills, that if a devise over
can take effect as a remainder, it shall not be taken to
be an executory devise. This will is as nearly similar
in words to that as possible. It was natural to expect
that the father should die before the son, and then the
father's part would come to the son in tail; and therefore why not all in tail? This is a very complicated
event, that the survivor should die without issue. In
Barlow v. *Salter* (b), Sir *W. Grant* M. R. expresses himself strongly; he says it is necessary to decide the

(a) 12 *East,* 253.   (b) 17 *Ves.* 479.

meaning

meaning of the words " in case she dies without issue,"
whether they are to be construed without issue generally, or at the time of the daughter's death.   Ever
since the case of *Beauclerk* v. *Dormer* (a), I think, a different rule has prevailed, and it is now settled that unless there are expressions or circumstances from which
it can be collected that these words are used in a more
confined sense, they are to have their legal signification, viz. death without issue generally." So, that
learned Judge inclines to this construction, unless there
are words strongly inferring the contrary. In *Porter*
v. *Bradley* the word " behind" was relied on. Neither
Porter v. *Bradley* nor *Roe* v. *Jeffery*, therefore, are adverse to the Defendant on this occasion. Having and
leaving issue are synonymous. It could not in this case
mean having had issue; for one of them, the father,
had had issue. It means having issue generally, and
it is necessary for the Plaintiff's purpose to put on the
will a complicated construction, not countenanced by
law, nor founded on this case. But next, if this be
not an estate tail, the contingency has not happened, for the estate is to go over if both shall die
without leaving issue of either of their bodies, this
might have taken place in one event, namely, if the son
had died first without issue. The proposition stated on
behalf of the Plaintiff, is, that a fine operates nothing
where it devests no estate. In *Focus* v. *Salisbury* the
answer was, *partes finis nihil habuerunt*, for he who levied the fine was considered by the Court as a lessee
at will. The case of *Saffyn* v. *Adams* reported in
Croke James (b), occurred in the King's Bench a year
after the case reported in *Coke*, which was in this court,
but it evidently relates to the same property, and there
are the same circumstances, and in *Cro. Jac.* it is held

(a) 2 *Atk.* 308.   (b) 60.

that

that a fine levied before the commencement of a term shall not bar the termor, if claim be made within 5 years after the term comes in *esse ;* but if the possession be not claimed within 5 years after the term comes *in esse,* it is a bar, *Co. Dig.* (*a*). *Acc.* So, here is a fine, the devisee over cannot enter until the contingency happens, but when it happens, then he must enter within the 5 years after the estate commenced, it is true that a fine levied to one with notice of a trust does not bar the trust. This does not apply. So, *Seymor's* case, and many that have been cited, are not in point. The only question in *Seymor's* case was, whether the remainder-man had a right to enter, the fine was connected with the bargain and sale, and all were one conveyance. So, *Margaret Podger's* case (*b*), a grant by copy of court roll to three *successive,* and the fee was conveyed by the lord to the first taker, and he accepted a fine levied by the lord; it was resolved that it did not operate to devest the second life estate: that is not adverse to the Defendant's proposition. Lord *Coke,* on *Saffyn's* case, says, it is within the mischief, and that the construction of the statute of fines ought to be liberal. The second saving in the statute of fines is an answer to the observation made on behalf of the Plaintiff, that a fine does not operate on a future estate, the words of the statute are, by force of any gift in the tail or by any other cause or matter had and made before the fine levied.

Lens in reply. As to the argument that a writ of intrusion will not lie, because that and all other writs are formed with great precision, the statute of *Westminster* the 2d was given for that very purpose, to introduce such modifications as would accommodate them to the occasion. Therefore, though the usual writ avers the

1815.

ROMILLY, Knt.
v.
JAMES.

(*a*) *Co. Dig., Fine,* L. 3.   (*b*) 9 *Co. Rep.* 104.

preceding

preceding tenancy for life, it must be varied to this case of a *quasi* tenant for life. There is no position in the books that the writ of intrusion is confined to those three cases, of tenants for life, in dower, and by the courtesy, though it extends to them. There is no necessity that it should be so restrained, and therefore, though the statute gives no authority to the clerks in Chancery to issue new writs according to their own notions, the Court here would exercise a control over them, and direct what new writs should be framed. The formedon *in reverter* in substance varies much more from this case than does the writ of intrusion. Here is no *forma doni*. This executory devise which now exists is a mode of conferring an estate not then known. Here is a *quasi* tenant for life, for though not originally tenant for life, he is reduced to that by the not having issue. This certainly is neither precisely the case for a writ of intrusion, nor for a formedon; but it is nearer to the first, than to the last. The remedy by ejectment is not, in contemplation of law, one of the remedies looked to, as remaining, because it applies to every possible right of possession. As to the argument, that in the writs of right and of intrusion the demandant must count on the seisin of an ancestor within 60 and 50 years, the intermediate estates are the same estates, not adverse, and he may count on them. It would be very extraordinary, if the length of continuance of the particular interest should impair the remedy of the remainder man. If the Defendant's construction of the 6th section of 32 *H.* 8. is right, that the seisin of the ancestor is to be the actual personal seisin, then, if the first taker lives more than 50 years, the next in remainder is for ever barred: but the seisin of the tenant for life is the seisin of the ancestor. As to the next point, that this is an estate tail, in the case cited of *Denny* v. *Agar*, the estate

†10   was

was plainly not intended to go over, unless all the issue of the son and daughter failed, and that decision does not at all affect this case. Here is no intention and no declaration which can affect the general failure of issue: the testator contemplated the event that both his brother and nephew might die and leave no issue of the survivor. As to the 4th point, on the effect of the fine. Much stress has been laid on the words of the statute, and the counsel for the Defendant admits that no case is found in the books where a mere tenant in fee has levied a fine: but a fine levied by tenant in fee has no more effect than the fine of a mere stranger. It has been argued for the Defendant as if the statute had enlarged the operation of fines, but it merely has effect to change the time of their being a bar. This statute was not made, because fines had not an operation large enough, but to do away the mischiefs of the statute of non-claim. These general words, though they may be large enough to embrace the case, yet are to be restricted to the limitation of time, leaving every thing else exactly where it was. The very nature of barring by a fine, is, that there is an alteration: the whole estate is displaced, which makes it necessary to enter, to do away the new estate. The cases in equity only are, that all who come under a trustee make themselves trustees. *Saffyn's* case in *Cro. Jac.* differs not from that in *Coke*, and is cited in *Thomasin* v. *Mackworth*. The fine did not devest the future interest. The question here is not merely, whether a writ of intrusion can be sustained, but whether the purchaser can hold the land clear of all remedy; for though, if it can be shewn to be a clear legal title, this Court will hold it to be good, yet if it be even doubtful whether or no there be any remedy whatever left open to the heir of the devisee, the Plaintiff is entitled to recover.

1815.

ROMILLY, Knt.

v.

JAMES.

GIBBS

1815.   GIBBS C. J. This case has been exceedingly well
ROMILLY, Knt.   argued, and the Court are much obliged to the counsel
v.   on both sides. We shall consider it; but on one point
JAMES.   I shall now say a word. It is said that the Plaintiff
Ming 390.   will have made out his claim to recover back his deposit,
if a cloud is cast on the title. That is not so in a court
of law; he must stand by the judgment of the Court, as
they find the title to be, whether good or bad; and if it
be good in the judgment of a court of law, he cannot
recover back his deposit. If he had gone into a court of
equity, it might have been otherwise; I know a court
of equity often says, this is a title which, though we
think it available, is not one which we will compel an
unwilling purchaser to take, but that distinction is not
known in a court of law.

Cur. adv. vult.

GIBBS C. J. now delivered the judgment of the Court.
This is an action brought by the Plaintiff for recovering
back a sum of money which has been paid by the
Plaintiff as a deposit on the purchase of an estate, upon
a condition, which the Plaintiff says, has not been performed by the Defendant, because the Defendant undertook to make a good title, which he has failed in
doing. The question was, whether *Henry Smith* the son
in his lifetime had a good title to this estate [His Lordship here stated the case,] and whether his heir can make
a good title to a purchaser. The objection to the title
is, that *Henry Smith* the younger took a fee only defeasible in the event if neither he nor his father should
leave issue behind them, and the counsel for the Plaintiff says, neither of them did leave issue. The Plaintiff
addresses himself to answer the objections he expects,
1st, that there was no good tenant to the *præcipe*, and
he says there is; 2dly, that as to the fine, whatever
remedy *Clerk* and his heirs had is lost. To the objec-

tion

tion that the lapse of 20 years has barred any ejectment
by *Clerk*, he answers, that he may nevertheless have a
writ of intrusion, and to the objection that the writ of
intrusion is only for the case where the adverse possession commences after a tenancy for life, it is answered,
that under the statute of *Westminster* the 2d a similar
writ may be framed; and the Plaintiff truly says, that if
the writ of intrusion lies, the statute of 32 *H.* 8. giving
50 years, the heirs of *Clerk* are not barred. The Plaintiff
meets another objection, namely, that the fine and non-
claim bar the devisee over, by saying, true it is, that
more than five years have elapsed since the title of *Josias
Clerk* accrued; but he says, those statutes do not apply,
for the operation of a fine applies only to estates which
are displaced when the fine is levied, and this is an executory devise, which was not displaced by the fine. The
principal question is, what estate *Henry Smith* the
younger took; for if he was tenant in tail, all other
questions are out of the case: for his fine certainly displaced the estate tail of *Clerk*, and therefore the non-
entry within five years bars. We are of opinion, that
Henry Smith the younger did take an estate tail, and
that renders it unnecessary to give any opinion on the
other points in the case. The will gives a fee to *Henry
Smith* the elder in all which is not afterwards disposed
of: the subsequent clause removes that estate in the
premises before given to *Henry Smith* the elder, and
gives a similar clear estate in fee in the premises
to *Henry Smith* the younger, divesting the estate of
the father; but if *Henry Smith* and *Henry Smith* the
younger die without having issue, then the estate is
given over. This plainly cuts down his estate to an
estate tail; and doing so, it leaves something behind,
which *Henry Smith* may take as part of the residue of
the real and personal estate of the testator; but the
same clause cuts down also the preceding estate in fee

to

1815.

ROMILLY, Knt.
v.
JAMES.

to *Henry Smith* the elder, to an estate tail likewise; *Henry Smith* the younger therefore takes an estate tail, with remainder in tail to his father, remainder in fee to *J. Clerk.* It is urged that this devise does not create an estate tail, but a defeasible fee-simple, with an executory devise over; but we find no authority for supporting that construction. This therefore being an estate tail, *Henry Smith* the younger displaced it by his fine, and the remainder-man is clearly barred by the statute of 4 *H.* 7., and consequently we are of opinion, that the vendor can make a good title.

Judgment for the Defendant.

June 9.

CAREY, Plaintiff; Sir RICHARD BEDINGFIELD and Wife, Deforciant.

Fine of a rent-charge amended by substituting lands out of which it issued, for the premises out of which the fine erroneously described it to issue.

LENS Serjt. moved to amend a fine. A certain rent-charge of 200*l. per ann.* had heretofore issued out of an estate which consisted of the manor of *Drayton,* with the appurtenances, and of certain tythes and commonable rights. By two inclosure acts, 41 *Geo.* 3., and the award made under them, these tythes and common rights were commuted for certain allotments of land, so that after that award the rent-charge ceased to issue out of the tythes and commonable rights, and thenceforth issued out of the manor of *Drayton* and those specific lands, which were allotted. By a deed in 1806, to lead the uses of a fine, Sir *Richard Bedingfield* covenanted to levy a fine of this rent-charge, and in the deed described it as issuing out of the manor of *Drayton,* and out of the specific lands in the parish of *Drayton* on which it was charged, but in the fine itself the ancient description of the rent-charge, such as it was previous to the inclosure act,

was

was retained. *Lens* Serjt. therefore moved to amend the fine, by therein describing the rent-charge as issuing out of the manor of *Drayton* and the several allotments awarded, out of which the rent-charge now issued.

1815.

CAREY,
Plaintiff.

Fiat.

LITTLEWOOD and Another *v.* WILLIAMS, Clerk.

June 9.

THIS was an action for money had and received, and at the trial before *Gibbs* C. J. at the *Middlesex* sittings after *Easter* term 1815, it appeared that the Plaintiffs were, and for five years successively had been, the churchwardens of the parish of *Hendon*, of which the Defendant was, and for three years had been, the vicar; they ought to recover a moiety of fees which had been paid upon the burial of strangers in the church and church-yard of *Hendon* ; they proved by entries in the vestry books, that ever since 1722, a practice had prevailed, that upon the burial of a stranger in the parish, a sum of money was paid, varying in amount, whether he was buried in the church, church-yard, or chancel, one moiety thereof to the vicar, the other moiety to the churchwardens for the use of the poor ; but the amount claimed had been increased by resolutions of the vestry at two several periods since 1722 : one of these resolutions was made in 1757 upon the occasion of a piece of land being purchased by the parishioners, and added to the church-yard, and it was ordered that the clerk should once in a month pay over to the churchwardens the moiety of the fees so received. The Defendant since he had become vicar, had buried several strangers, one of them in the newly purchased

A practice had prevailed during the incumbency of several vicars, that upon the burial of any stranger in the parish of H. certain fees should be paid, of which the vicar took one moiety and the churchwardens the other for the use of the poor. The fees were paid to the sexton, who paid over the moieties to the respective parties. A new vicar refused to accede to this arrangement, he buried several strangers, and procured the sexton, to whom the fees were paid,

to pay over the entire fees to himself: Held that the churchwardens might recover one moiety as had and received to their use.

part of the church-yard, and the sums claimed on their
burial had been paid, as the former practice had been,
by the executors of the deceased, into the hands of the
sexton, who used to distribute them, one moiety to each
party; and the Plaintiffs had not revoked the authority
they had formerly given to the sexton to receive their
moiety. The Defendant, after receiving the moiety of
one such fee, had apprized the sexton, that he meant in
future to claim the whole of the fees paid on the burial
of strangers, but it was not in evidence that he had
communicated his intention to the Plaintiffs. The sexton had paid over to the vicar, who insisted on receiving it, the whole money which he had since received on
this account. The Plaintiffs at first put their claim
upon an immemorial custom, but that being disaffirmed
by the variation in the amount of the fees claimed at
several times, they next rested it upon the ground of a
special agreement between the vicar and the parishioners, but evidence being given of the Defendant's dissent
to the agreement of the former vicars, they were driven
from this ground; they then contended, that whether
the vicar and churchwardens had any right to these
burial fees or not, the one moiety in question of the several fees had never been paid by the executors of the
persons buried as for the Defendant's half, but on the
contrary it had been paid to the sexton, who still continued to be the Plaintiffs' agent, specifically for the use
of the Plaintiffs, and under a demand of right by them;
that sum therefore the Plaintiffs were entitled to recover.
Gibbs C. J. was of that opinion, and the jury, under
his direction, found a verdict for the Plaintiffs for
22*l.* 7*s.* 9*d.* with liberty to move to enter a nonsuit, or,
in case the Court should be of opinion that the Plaintiffs
were entitled to recover the moiety of the fee for burying in the new ground, but not for the residue, then to
reduce the verdict accordingly.

Lens Serjt. in this term having obtained a rule *nisi*,

Vaughan and *Copley* Serjts. shewed cause. They contended, first, that this moiety of the money had been received by the sexton for the use of the churchwardens, whose agent he still continued to be, and not for the use of the vicar. If the Defendant did not chuse to accede to the compact which his predecessors had agreed to, he ought, before the burials, to have given notice to the executors of the deceased, that the fees must be paid to himself only. He ought to have revoked the authority of the sexton to receive for him, and appointed another person agent for himself alone. But further, the vicar is not entitled, either by the common law or canon law, to demand a fee for burying in the church-yard, although such a fee may be due by special custom. *Andrews* v. *Cawthorne* (a). Here was evidence of an immemorial custom for the churchwardens to receive something upon the burial of a stranger, and it is only the increase of the sum that is an innovation; and if the usage exists in fact, it is good in law. In 2 *Sho.* 184. it is said, that in the neighbourhood of *London* the churchwardens are entitled to the money for burying in the church-yard. Inasmuch as every parishioner has a right at common law to be buried in the church-yard of his parish, he has an interest and a right to prohibit strangers from being buried there, and it may be inferred, that when the parishioners purchased the land added to the church-yard, the assent of patron and ordinary was obtained to this arrangement respecting the division of the fees. It is clear that the parishioners can prevent strangers from being buried there, and the vicar, who has the fee simple of the soil of the church-yard, holds it only in trust for the parishioners; and if they agree mutually to re-

(a) *Willes*, 536.

U 2   cede

cede from their respective rights, the vicar permitting the soil to be broken, the parishioners permitting strangers to be buried there, and agree to divide the money which they may receive on this consideration from strangers, it is competent for them so to do.

Lens and *Best* Serjts. in support of the rule. It would be a very different question if this were an action by the churchwarden against the sexton, who was a mere stakeholder, and clearly had no right to the money. But here it has been paid over to the party who claims it, and who, if it is not due to him, would be liable to refund it to the executors of the deceased person, if they were to sue for it. The Defendant never received this as money collected for the use of the Plaintiffs, he has claimed and received it in his own right, and if the moiety does not belong to the Plaintiffs, even though the vicar may not be entitled to it, they cannot recover. The sexton was not the agent of the Defendant: he demanded the money adversely to the sexton. As soon as the money gets into the hands of one who is not an agent, the claimant is put to his mere right. If a person claiming goods as his, gets them out of a carrier's hand, the bailor cannot recover them from him unless he has a better right than the possessor. If neither has a right, *potior est conditio possidentis.* Probably neither of these parties has any right to receive these fees, but if either has a colour, it is the vicar that stands on the better title; because he is the legal owner of the church-yard; not that the vicar can bury whom he pleases in the parish church-yard, but the fee of the soil is in him. It may be, that a burying-place may be so much in request, that the vicar and churchwardens might burthen it with bodies to the exclusion of the parishioners. Therefore both together cannot legally do this to the injury

injury of the others. But it suffices for the Defendant
if neither has a right. The churchwardens have no
pretence to have it but that of an agreement, on which,
even if it existed, there might be a doubt of its legality;
but here the churchwardens and overseers have been
distinctly told by the Defendant, that whatever stranger
is buried here, they shall have no share in the fees.

GIBBS C. J. The counsel for the Defendant has
now stated, and properly, on the part of the vicar, that
he is desirous that these burials should not take place,
and there he takes very magnificent ground, that he
does not approve such arrangements between the vicar
and churchwardens, but I think he has mistaken his
course; and if those were his sentiments, he ought,
instead of laying his hands on the moiety of the churchwardens, to have refused to receive his own. It was
stated by the Defendant's counsel, that the Defendant
gave notice to the churchwardens that he would not
have these burials go on; but that is inaccurately
stated, for the only notice he gave, was, that he should
claim the whole of the fees. His view of the subject
now may be different. At the trial the Plaintiffs'
claim was put on a strict right in the churchwardens
to these fees. The supposed right is, to a fee on
burial: at common law the churchwardens have no such
right whatsoever: it may exist by custom, but the
custom must be immemorial, and invariable. 10s. is
the most ancient payment of which there is any
evidence in this case, it was made in 1723; and when
afterwards a stranger was buried, the churchwardens
claimed the larger sum of 16 guineas; they could ill
have supported that claim by evidence of the payment of 10s. it was therefore found necessary at the
trial to take some other ground, and the Plaintiffs put
it exceedingly well, that there was an agreement, to

U 3   which

which the present vicar had acceded. The evidence did not come up to that. I thought the action might be supported on another point, which, it seems, my Brother *Copley* suggested, and it comes now to the short question, whether the moiety which the vicar has received, is the money of the churchwardens. The counsel for the Defendant has been thundering anathemas against the churchwardens, who, even with the assent of the vicar, shall permit the bodies of strangers to be deposited in their church-yard. If it could be shewn that other parishioners sustained actual inconvenience, it might be different, but if there be not that circumstance, the churchwardens have the discretion lodged with them, to judge of the probability of it; and if out-parishioners chuse to be buried there, or their executors chuse that they shall be, and to pay for it, no law, moral or ecclesiastical, human or divine, prevents them from so doing; and if they had agreed so to do, I am further of opinion that an action might be maintained on that agreement. On the evidence it does not appear that the vicar has ever interfered to prevent the burial of strangers here, on the contrary, he has buried all who have been brought, but he claims the whole burial fee. On what pretence? because, he says, I have prevailed on the sexton to pay it over to me, and the Plaintiffs have no right to it. I am of opinion that the moiety received by the sexton, which used to be received for the use of the churchwardens, was received specifically for them, and that the money in the custody of the sexton was the money of the churchwardens, and that when the vicar prevailed on him to pay over that money, he was prevailing on him to pay over the money of the churchwardens, and therefore the churchwardens have a right to recover it back from him, and consequently the verdict for 22*l.* 7*s.* 9*d.* must stand.

The rest of the Court concurring, the

Rule was discharged.

BROWN v. ROSE.

I N this cause (a) *Vaughan* Serjt. had obtained a rule *nisi* that the Plaintiff might be at liberty to inspect the indenture containing the demise to Sir *J. T. Wheate*, above stated in the pleadings.

Best in shewing cause, urged that there was no pretence and no precedent for such an application. The Plaintiff was at liberty to inspect the memorial of the annuity deed, which was sufficient to inform them of the Defendant's title, and so it differs from the ordinary case of an ejectment.

Vaughan, in support of his rule, urged the hardship which the statute 11 *Geo.* 2. *c.* 19. had laid on the Plaintiff in this respect; for the Plaintiff being tenant in possession of the premises, and being called on to pay rent to an assignee of the reversion, of whose title he knew nothing, would, before that statute, have been furnished with tne requisite information by the pleadings, for the avowant must have pleaded the deed with a *profert in Curiâ*, and the Plaintiff would have been entitled to oyer. The Plaintiff only wished to see what the Defendant's title was, for if he saw a clear title, he would acquiesce and pay the rent; but there was no privity of contract between the parties, and without the desired inspection, either he must acquiesce in a distress which might prove to be illegal, or he might dispute a title which was a good one.

Per Curiam. The argument on which the Plaintiff stands the strongest, is that before the statute of *Geo.* 2.

(a) See ante, 124.

Inspection refused to Plaintiff in replevin of a deed to which he was no party, assigning to the avowant the reversion of the demised premises.

the

1815.

BROWN
v.
ROSE.

the lessor must have set out that deed, and the Plaintiff might have had oyer of it. The difference between this case and the case of an ejectment is, that in an ejectment the situation of the Defendant is not altered by any act of parliament; but here, unless for the statute of *Geo.* 2., the one party must have pleaded the deed with a *profert*, and the other might have had a view of it. That circumstance would not, however, prevent us from compelling the Defendant to shew the deed, if we saw that the justice of the case required it. But here it does not appear that the Plaintiff may not have all the information from the memorial that the justice of the case demands, therefore it is unnecessary for the Court to interpose.

Rule discharged, but without costs.

June 9.

COTTEREL, Plaintiff; FRANKLIN and Wife, Deforciants.

Where a fine comprized only lands lying in the parishes of S. and S., within a larger district, the island of F., the deed so describing the lands, which were in truth within the parish of F. in the same district, the Court refused to amend the fine by inserting also the parish of F.

INDENTURES of lease and release, to lead the uses of a fine, dated in 1720, conveyed a farm and arable and marsh grounds, commonly called or known by the name of the West Part of the new Marsh in *Fowlness,* lying in the parishes of *Little Stanbridge* and *Sutton,* in the county of *Essex,* or any of them, or in any other town or towns to them or any of them next or nigh adjoining. The fine was levied of " 90 acres of land, and 140 acres of marsh, in *Little Stanbridge* and *Sutton."* A deed of later date, made to lead the uses of another fine, conveyed by the same description as in the first deed, and the fine was of the like lands and marsh " in

Semble that by the grant of lands in a vill, only those lands will pass which lie in a vill bearing a different name from the parish.

Little

Little Stanbridge and *Sutton* in the county of *Essex*."
A deed leading the uses of a third fine, purported to
convey the same premises " situate in the parishes of
Little Stanbridge and *Sutton*, in the island of *Fowlness*."
And the fine levied in pursuance thereto comprised
land and marsh " in *Little Stanbridge* and *Sutton*, in the
island of *Fowlness*." It was sworn that all the fines and
deeds related to the same premises, and that *the same premises* (*i. e.* all) were situate in the parish of *Fowlness*, within the island of *Fowlness*, in the county of *Essex*. That
doubts had arisen whether they passed by the description; that the deponent had since 1802 been in possession; that he believed it was the intention of the several
parties to pass premises, and that the lands had ever
since 1720 been enjoyed under the deeds; and that the
omission of the parish of *Fowlness* in the fines was
owing to want of information as to the boundaries of
the several parishes of *Little Stanbridge*, *Sutton*, and
Fowlness,

Shepherd, Solicitor-General, now moved to amend
these several fines by the insertion of the word " *Fowlness*" after the words " appurtenances in."

Per Curiam. That is desiring us to levy a new fine.
The lands conveyed by the deeds are described as
lying in *Fowlness*, in the parishes of *Little Stanbridge*
and *Sutton*, some one or any of them. The fine comprehends only lands in *Little Stanbridge* and *Sutton*;
but though that description will carry all lands in *Fowlness* which are in those two parishes, it will not carry
lands in the parish of *Fowlness*. So that if we were to
grant the amendment, and if you were afterwards to separate the parcels in the fine from the parcels in the
deed, the Plaintiff in an action could recover under
the one, different premises from those which he could
                                                    recover

1815.

COTTEREL,
Plaintiff.

COTTEREL,
Plaintiff.

recover under the other, And as to the argument that the general words "lands in any other town or towns contiguous or near adjoining thereto," include the premises, the parish of *Fowlness* is not a town, neither are these lands sworn to be within a town.

The Court refused the application.

June 13.

MACKENZIE v. MARTIN and Another.

In an action on a recognizance of bail, the bail must be served with process four days before the return of the writ.

In an action against two, not bailable, one Defendant may before declaration well stile his affidavit in a cause of *A.* against *B.*, who is sued with *C.*

*M*ARTIN and *Forbes* were bail to the action for *Aikenhead*, at the suit of the Plaintiff. The Plaintiff commenced an action on the recognizance, and sued out a writ, which was duly served on *Forbes*, but could not be served on *Martin*. That writ was returned, and thereupon the Plaintiff sued out a *capias per* continuance against both, returnable on the 28th day of the month, which was served on *Martin* on the 25th. *Shepherd*, Solicitor-General, had obtained a rule *nisi* to set aside these proceedings against the bail, upon the ground that *Martin* had not been served with the latter process four days before the return of the writ, which in actions on a bail recognizance is necessary.

Best Serjt., in shewing cause, took a preliminary objection, that the Defendant's affidavit was entitled " *Mackenzie* against *Andrew Martin* sued with *Matthew Forbes;*" it ought, he said, either to have been entitled in the original cause, *Mackenzie* v. *Aikenhead*, or in this cause of *Mackenzie* v. *Martin* and *Forbes*. Upon the matter of the rule itself, he objected, first, that the supposed practice that the bail must be served with process four days before the return of the writ had no existence; secondly, that the terms of the rule prayed

too

too much, inasmuch as the writs themselves were not
defective, nor the service of the first writ upon *Forbes*,
but only the service of the last writ on *Martin.*

Shepherd supported his rule, to the limited extent,
confessing that it had through inadvertence been drawn
up in too large terms: he only prayed the relief as to
Martin, but it was impossible the Defendant could be
deceived by it, or laid under the necessity of shewing
cause; for the affidavit shewed that the objection extended only to one; but as to the affidavit, he contended, that inasmuch as *Martin* could not before
declaration, which had not yet been delivered, know
whether the Plaintiff would proceed against one or both
of the bail, he was not incorrect in the title of his affidavit. If it had been entitled in the original cause, this
action on the recognizance being entirely a new proceeding, the title would have been wrong; otherwise,
if it had been an action on a bail bond.

Gibbs C. J. The preliminary objection cannot prevail. The original action is *Mackenzie* v. *Aikenhead.*
This affidavit is entitled in a case of *Mackenzie* v. *Martin*, sued with *Forbes.* So far as the proceedings have
gone, it is a joint action, but when the Plaintiff comes
to declare, doubtless he may sever, and declare against
the Defendants separately, and the Defendant cannot
yet tell, whether the Plaintiff will do so: therefore
I think this affidavit is not improperly entitled as in an
action against *Martin*, who is sued with *Forbes.* The
objection made, that the rule seeks relief for both the
bail, would be decisive, if the Plaintiff were bound by
it; but he is not bound by a misdrawing up of the rule,
but may abandon the surplus. As to the validity of the
objection to the service on *Martin*, the officer reports
that the bail must be served with process in an action
on

on the recognizance of bail four days before the return of the writ: this applies to the process with which the Defendant *Martin* is served; for the writ with which he is served is the first notice he has of the action. If the rule were made absolute in the terms prayed for, both the bail would be relieved. The rule therefore praying relief for both bail, it was of necessity that the Plaintiff should come to shew cause; otherwise more might be obtained against him, than there is any pretence for asking. There were no proceedings on the first writ, which had gone the length of fixing *Martin*. It therefore was necessary for the Plaintiff to sue out a *capias per* continuance for the sake of fixing *Martin*: it was to be served four days before the return: it was served on the 25th, and was returnable on the 28th. The service only was void. *Martin*, the 2d bail, is not then fixed, and *Forbes*, the 1st bail, is fixed by the 1st writ. It follows, that the rule cannot be made absolute as to both, but we will do all that is due; we will set aside the service of the 2d writ against *Martin*, but we do it on the terms of the Defendant paying costs to the Plaintiff, because he has necessarily brought him hither to oppose the rule by which the Defendant has prayed more than he is entitled to.

> Rule absolute, as to setting aside the service of the 2d writ.
>
> Rule discharged, as to the residue.

HUTTON v. EYRE.

THIS was an action of *assumpsit* for money paid by the Plaintiff to the Defendant's use; and it appeared at the trial before *Bayley* J. at the *Lincoln Spring* assizes 1815, that the Plaintiff sought to recover 2788*l.* which he had paid under the following circumstances, with 292*l.* interest. The Plaintiff and Defendant had been partners, as merchants and insurance brokers, and by indenture of 26th *August* 1809, they dissolved their partnership as from the 1st of *January* then next, and mutually covenanted that neither of the partners should after the date of those presents, and before the period fixed upon for the dissolution of this copartnership, either in his own name, or in the name or names of any other person, or in the firm of *Eyre* and *Hutton*, make any purchase of goods in their aforesaid trade or business, or by way of speculation with any other person, so as to bind the other of the parties to such contracts; but that if any purchases of goods were made in the partnership firm, it should be on the private account of the individual party making the same. The Defendant, after executing this deed, contracted five several debts of large amount, after which, on the 27th of *October* 1810, by indenture between the Defendant, 1., two of his creditors, *Todd* and *Lamarche*, 2., and the other creditors whose names were subscribed, 3., the Defendant conveyed all his estate and effects to *Todd* and *Lamarche*, in trust to sell, and out of the proceeds to retain their costs and make a dividend of 5*s.* in the pound among all the creditors who should execute within three months, next to divide the residue of the proceeds among the creditors to the amount of their respective debts, and pay the surplus, if any,

A covenant not to sue one of two joint debtors does not operate as a release to the other.

One joint contractor, who pays money for another under an equitable claim, may recover it from the other as money paid to his use.

any, to the Defendant. And in consideration of the premises, the other parties thereto severally covenanted with the Defendant, that they, their executors or administrators, partners or assigns, or any of them, would not sue, arrest, implead, or prosecute him, his executors or administrators, or his, their, or any of their goods, chattels, lands, or tenements, for or upon account of any debt or sum of money then due or owing to them or any of them, and in case any of the creditors should sue, &c., the Defendant for such debt, that then those presents should be a sufficient release and discharge to all intents and purposes, at law and in equity, to and for the Defendant, his executors, and administrators, and he and they should be and were thereby accquitted, released, and discharged against them the said creditors and every of them, who should sue, &c., and as such might be pleaded by the Defendant. Provided that any creditor who had any security for his debt, or any part thereof, might execute those presents without prejudice to his security, and with the trustees' consent might convert the same security into money, and receive a dividend with the other creditors on so much of the debt as should not be paid out of the produce of that security, with an exception of notes of hand, or other personal security, of the Defendant. The firm of *Hutton* and *Eyre* was a creditor of the Defendant for 1000*l.* on a banking account, and the Plaintiff executed this deed of composition for that sum, and received a dividend thereon, of 5*s.* in the pound, so that he was party to the deed. The five creditors above mentioned executed the deed of composition, and received the like dividend, and afterwards called on the Plaintiff for the residue of their debts, and the Plaintiff paid them. For the Defendant, two points were made at the trial; first, that if the Plaintiff could maintain any action, it ought to be covenant

venant on the deed of dissolution, and not *assumpsit ;*
secondly, that the covenant not to sue, contained in the
Defendant's deed of composition, operated as a release
in law to both the partners, of the five debts, which the
Plaintiff had therefore paid in his own wrong, and consequently was not entitled to recover them back from
the Defendant. *Bayley* J. reserved both the points,
subject whereto the jury found a verdict for the
Plaintiffs.

Vaughan Serjt. in *Easter* term last obtained a rule
nisi to set aside the verdict, and enter a nonsuit.

Shepherd, Solicitor-General, and *Copley* Serjt., in
this term shewed cause against the rule. They cited
Dean v. *Newhall* (*a*), as an authority that a covenant not
to sue one of two creditors does not operate as a release to the other of them. This covenant was framed
upon the authority of that case. The effect of the
covenant is, that it shall in all events operate as an
indemnity to the covenantee, but the remedy by which
he attains that indemnity varies according to circumstances. It is a covenant not to sue the Defendant
separately. If the creditors do sue him separately, he
shall plead the covenant in bar: it is a covenant not
to sue the Defendant jointly; but if the creditors do
sue him jointly, the covenant shall not be pleaded in
bar, but the covenantee shall recover over against the
creditor on his covenant precisely the same sum as he
had lost in the joint action. Another point is, whether
the Plaintiff was bound to plead an abatement: no
rule of law requires that he should: he is not bound
to plead that which is not a just plea. It was the
intent of the deed of composition that the Plaintiff, who
was party to it, should restrain himself from pleading

(*a*) 8 *Term Rep.* 168.

in

in abatement: it was the object of the parties that they might sue the Plaintiff, and it would defeat their object, to make this operate as a release. As to the second point, there was no breach of the Defendant's covenant. It was in the view of both the Plaintiff and Defendant that goods should be purchased in the interval between the date of the deed of dissolution and the 1st of *January,* and that the partnership, though in fact dissolved between the partners, should continue to the world, it was therefore no breach to purchase these goods. ·

Vaughan, contrà, disagreed to the supposed intent of the parties that there should be no plea in abatement. In what state is the Defendant, who after giving up all his effects to pay his creditors, is to be still liable to this action, when he certainly expected to be cleared of all his debts. To find the true construction of the deed, the Court must look to the situation of the Defendant; he was party to a joint contract, and it must be intended that the suit from which he was meant to be released, was the joint suit, for that is the proper remedy on a joint contract. It was the intent of the parties to give the Defendant in effect a release; whether it is called a perpetual bar, or a release, matters nothing. In the case of *Lacy* v. *Kinaston* (a), the distinction is taken. If two be jointly and severally bound, and the obligee covenants with one of them not to sue him, he may nevertheless sue the other, because he might without this covenant sue the one of them without the other; and therefore there being nothing in the covenant to preclude him from that benefit, he has it still left in him. There is much sense in this distinction, and therefore *Dean* v. *Newhall* is

(a) 12 *Mod.* 548. 552. S. C. 1 *Ld. Ray.* 688.

I

inap-

inapplicable to this case, for here the Plaintiff has not the right left of suing the other, he originally had only the power ,of suing both jointly. If a debtor enters into a contract that upon his surrender of all his effects the creditor shall release him, it is a contract which the court will enforce, and favour. It might be hard on the Plaintiff if he should pay 15*s.* in the pound on a debt in which he had no interest; but why does he pay? for if sued, he may set up his character of joint contractor, and desire the Plaintiff to sue them both, for he is only jointly liable; and then the two Defendants may set up the covenant as a bar. The Plaintiff's remedy over against the Defendant, if any, was upon his covenant, and not by an action for money paid but on the covenant. *Toussaint* v. *Martimant* (a). The doctrine of *Ashurst* and *Buller* Js. is, that where the party takes a bond for security, the law will not raise an action of *assumpsit.* Promises in law only exist where there is no express stipulation between the parties. The Plaintiff might perhaps have expressed his covenant more technically, but nevertheless here he may charge the Defendant with purchasing these goods as a breach of this covenant. The Defendant has done the very thing contemplated by this deed; he has so conducted himself as to make the Plaintiff liable who ought not to have been liable, he has done that which he covenanted not to do, and the Plaintiff has a right to charge him on his private account with that which he has done. This cannot be money paid to the use of the Plaintiff. The action for money paid will not lie in any case where he to whose use the money is paid is not bound to pay it. If any action of *assumpsit* would lie here, there ought, at all events, to have been a declaration on an especial *assumpsit*, which possibly

(a) 2 *Term Rep.* 100.

might have been maintained, but the Plaintiff cannot succeed in this action.

Cur. adv. vult.

GIBBS C. J. now delivered the judgment of the Court.

This is an action for money paid: two objections are made to the Plaintiff's recovery; first, that if any thing be due to the Plaintiff, it is not due to him on a parol contract, but in consequence of the breach of a covenant contained in the deed of dissolution of partnership. Next, that if an action for money paid be the correct form, the money was paid unnecessarily by the Plaintiff, and in his own wrong, and therefore cannot be recovered of the Defendant. [Here his lordship fully recapitulated the case.] We think that the first objection cannot avail, for the covenant amounts only to an arrangement, that he who after the dissolution contracts debts for goods, shall pay the money. *Eyre* therefore being bound to pay the money, this money is paid by the Plaintiff, (who was in the firm when the debts were contracted, and, therefore, was jointly liable) for the use of *Eyre*, and we think that notwithstanding this objection, *Eyre* must repay him. Another objection taken by *Eyre*, is, that *Hutton* had in the deed of 1810 a legal answer to those demands, and he having a legal discharge, ought not to have paid the money, and therefore has paid it in his own wrong. *Hutton* replies, that was a covenant not to sue *Eyre*, but it was not a covenant not to sue for joint debts, nor does it operate as a release of joint debts: that if *Eyre* had been sued for a joint debt, his remedy would have been to sue on this covenant against the creditor who sued him. The principle on which the covenant not to sue is held to operate as a release, is to avoid circuity of action; but it goes no further. *Eyre* says it goes much

14   further:

further: it is a release as between me and those to whom I and *Hutton* were jointly indebted, and being a release to me, it is a release to *Hutton*, who was jointly with me obliged for payment of that debt, and he relies on certain authorities, which, however, shew that the rule is not universal, that a covenant not to sue is a release of those, jointly with whom the covenantee may be sued. *Dean* v. *Newhall* is cited. There an issue was joined on the release of another party, with whom the Defendant was jointly and severally bound; and it was contended that a covenant not to sue, and the covenant that those presents should be a sufficient release of the other obligor, would operate as a release to the Defendant who was bound with him; but the Court were of opinion that the rule how far a covenant not to sue should operate as a release, was limited to the parties themselves. Certainly that case in all its parts is not like the present: there the party was jointly and severally answerable to the Plaintiff, who might sue the one obligor without the other: and in the case of *Lacy* v. *Kinaston* in 12 *Mod.* on which that case of *Dean* v. *Newhall* is much founded, it was stated as the reason of the judgment, that the bond being joint and several, the obligee might sue one without the other. The fact is not so here, therefore the same doctrine is not applicable, and we must consider it on principle, whether that law applies to the present case. In the case of a creditor suing a single debtor whom he has covenanted not to sue, it not only promotes the doctrine, which prevails so strongly in the law, of preventing circuity of action, but it falls in with the intent of the parties, to hold that the covenant shall operate as a release; but it is impossible that it should here be in the contemplation of the parties, that in covenanting not to sue *Eyre*, the insufficient debtor, he meant to release *Hutton*, who was sufficient. It

X 2

was

was as easy to insert in the deed a release, as a covenant not to sue, and it would have been shorter; it must be inferred that the parties did not insert a release, because it would release *Hutton* also; but it is this day contended that a covenant not to sue has the same effect. Where the words, by being extended beyond their obvious intent, would, as it seems, go beyond the intent of the party, the Court ought not to put that construction on them. It was urged at the bar, that the creditors might sue *Hutton* alone, and *non constat* that he would plead in abatement; but putting that out of the case, we think the rule that a covenant not to sue operates as a release, applies only to cases where the covenantor and covenantee are single. Another ground on which we found our judgment, is this. Lord *Kenyon* C. J., in *Dean* v. *Newhall,* says, " Even if the Defendant had succeeded here, a court of equity would have given the Plaintiff full relief. I am glad to find by the two cases cited that we are fully warranted in deciding in favour of the Plaintiff on legal grounds." Here, if the Plaintiff had paid this money either under the fear of process of a court of equity, or of a court of law, unquestionably he could have recovered it from the Defendant; and if a court of equity would have restrained the Plaintiff from setting up this covenant as a release, the equitable call on him justified him in paying the money, and gave him this remedy over against the Defendant.

Rule discharged.

1815.

June 14.

Lord SELSEA v. POWELL.

THIS was an action of debt upon the statute of 2 & 3 *Ed. 6. c.* 13. for not setting out tithes; and upon the trial of the cause at the *Sussex Spring* assizes 1815, before *Wood* B., the defence was, that the land on which the crops had grown, whereof the tythe was claimed, were barren lands within the exception in the 5th section of the statute. It appeared in evidence, that the land in question had been parcel of *Stanstead* forest, that it had been covered with timber and underwood: the proprietor had some years since stripped it of the timber, and had now permitted the occupier of the land to grub up the underwood, and had given him the wood for his pains, which was not sufficient in value to repay the expence of grubbing. The land had a few years before been valued at 9*s.* rent per acre, and was then let at 12*s.* 6*d.* per acre. After grubbing the wood, some part of the land had been chalked with chalk raised from the substratum of the same land, but the principal part of the crops were obtained without chalking or any other manure, and without extraordinary labour or expence. The crops in some parts of the land were good, and they were on the whole sufficient to repay all the costs and leave a profit to the farmer. *Wood* B. left the case to the jury, according to that which is laid down by the Court of King's Bench in *Warwick* v. *Collins* (a), to be the proper inquiry, whether the land was of such a nature as to require extraordinary expence either in manure or labour to bring it into a proper state of cultivation. The expence of grubbing was not to be taken into their consideration.

In an action for not setting out tithes, the onus of proving that the land is barren, lies on the Defendant.

The proper test of barrenness within this statute, is, whether the land requires extraordinary expence either in manure or labour to bring it into a proper state of cultivation.

The statute 2 & 3 Edw. 6. c. 13. is a remedial act, and in an action thereon the Court will grant a new trial for a mistake of the jury.

(a) 2 *Maule & Selw.* 362.

X 3

The

1815.
Lord SELKIRK
v.
POWELL.

The jury found a verdict for the Defendant subject to a point respecting documentary evidence, on which the Court, thinking they had not sufficient information of the facts, sent the cause to a new trial without deciding the question.

Shepherd, Solicitor-General, in *Easter* term obtained a rule *nisi* to set aside the verdict and have a new trial, as well on the point reserved, as on the ground that this was not barren land within the statute.

Best Serjt. in the same term, in shewing cause, took a preliminary objection, that this was a penal action, and that where the judge had given no wrong directions to a jury in a penal action, the Court could not grant a new trial upon the ground that the verdict was against evidence. He cited for this proposition *Brook q. t.* v. *Middleton* (a), and *Fonnereau* v. *Bennet* (b), where it is said to have then been the established rule for the last 50 years. The Court adjourned the case to give the Solicitor-General time to examine the authorities touching this objection. On the first day of this term, the Court relieved the Solicitor from arguing this point, as being already decided in the case of *Holloway* v. *Hewett* (c), in which this statute was considered as a remedial, rather than a penal act, and a motion for a new trial was, notwithstanding the same objection, therefore in that instance entertained.

Best now shewed cause against the rule, impugning the judge's direction to the jury to dismiss from their consideration the expence of grubbing the underwood, which he contended the jury were entitled to take into

(a) 10 *East*, 268.
(b) 3 *Wils*. 60.

(c) *Trin.* term 13 G. 3. 10 MSS.
Serjt. *Hill*, p. 339. 2 *Selw. N. P.* 2d edit. 1222.

their

their account. Likewise he urged, that the rule laid down in *Warwick* v. *Collins*, and adopted in the present case, was much too narrow. The statute contemplated two descriptions of land, the one, that which had produced corn within 40 years before, all other land was intended to fall within the exception. The first description did not comprehend the land in question, for nothing in this case shewed that this land had produced corn within that period, or had not been a forest from the beginning of time. It would not be for the interest of the church, that the moment a person undertakes at great expence the cultivation of land, he should be immediately subjected to tithes. It was the interest of the church, as much as of the people, to encourage agriculture.

The Solicitor-General in support of his rule, urged, (and the Court agreed,) that the *onus* of shewing that the land was barren, lay on the defendant. The discussion then passed over to the other point reserved.

Cur. adv. vult.

Gibbs C. J. now delivered the judgment of the Court. This was a question whether the land was barren within the meaning of the statute. The proper inquiry in these cases, is whether the land was of such a nature as required extraordinary expence. My Brother *Wood* left it to the jury whether it were of that description, and the jury found it was. One ground on which a new trial was moved for, is, that the evidence shewed that the land was not of that description: we have looked carefully through the evidence, such as it is reported to us, and we find that there is no ground to say it was barren land. His Lordship then passed to the other point, and concluded by making the rule absolute for a new trial; the costs to abide the event.

Rule absolute.

1815.

Lord SELSEA
v.
POWELL.

X 4

1815.

June 14. **BROWN** *v.* **CRUMP.**

Where the Court, on demurrer, gives leave to amend by stating particularly that which before was stated too generally, the Plaintiff may add new counts, though more than two terms have elapsed from the commencement of the suit, if they contain no new cause of action, but only various specifications of the matter which the Court required to be more particularly stated.

C OPLE Y Serjt. had on a former day, upon this case coming on for argument on a demurrer to the declaration, obtained leave to amend; and the supposed ground of demurrer being, that an allegation of the past and then continuing tenancy of the Defendant in a farm, did not shew a sufficient consideration for a promise to treat the land in a specific manner, he had not only amended the original counts, but had added three new counts, wherein he alleged the same promises, but varied the statement of the consideration. This amendment took place more than two terms after the commencement of the action, and *Best* Serjt. had obtained a rule *nisi* to strike out the three additional counts, upon the grounds, 1. that the Plaintiff was not, by the practice of the Court, allowed to add new counts after the second term from the commencement of the action; and 2dly, that the permission granted by the Court was only to amend the original counts, not to add new ones.

Copley Serjt. shewed cause, upon the ground that the reason of the rule was this, that no new cause of action shall be introduced into the declaration after two terms, because if the Plaintiff does not declare in this Court within two terms after the return of the writ, the Plaintiff is at liberty to sign judgment of *non pros:* but that the reason did not extend to the case where the Plaintiff added no new cause of action, but merely diversified his statement of the grievance already declared on. Secondly, the Court had a discretion as to time; and as this cause had long stood over for argument,

ment, they would see reason to exercise it on the present occasion.

Best endeavoured to support his rule, contending that the Plaintiff had exceeded the limits of the permission granted him by the Court.

GIBBS C. J. The facts are these: the declaration stated that the Defendant was tenant to the Plaintiff, and in consideration thereof undertook to do certain things to a farm. This count was objected, and was defended on the authority of a reported case, *Powley* v. *Walker* (a); and the Court thought that case did not go the length of this, and that it ought to be shewn more particularly on the declaration, what the Plaintiff had done, by which he purchased this promise from the Defendant. The counsel for the Plaintiff says it was necessary to state the consideration of this promise in several different ways; it is, indeed, evident that that which was before unnecessary, may be necessary to be stated in different ways, when we hold it requisite to set out the consideration. These are the facts of the case, and no doubt, if the Plaintiff's counsel had prayed us for liberty to insert those counts, we should have given it. I understand from him that the promise imputed to the Defendant is in all the added counts the same as in the original; and that there is only a difference in the consideration stated. We think that if the undertaking charged on the Defendant is varied in the additional counts, the counts ought to be struck out; but if only the consideration is varied, the Defendant is not entitled to strike them out, and the rule ought to be

Discharged.

(a) *5 Term Rep.* 373.

1815.

June 14.

Bing 152

STREET, Administratrix of JOHN STREET, *v.*
BROWN.

Where two parts of an indenture of charter-party were supposed to have been interchangeably executed, and the part of which the master of the chartered vessel had the custody, was lost at sea with the ship, the Court would not compel the charterer, being sued thereon, to grant inspection and a copy of the other part, for the purpose of the Plaintiff's declaring with certainty.

THIS was an action of covenant on a charter-party made between the Plaintiff's intestate, who was master and part-owner of the vessel, and the Defendant, brought to recover damages for not loading the chartered vessel. The intestate was lost at sea with his vessel, and it was sworn that the deponent was informed and believed that two parts of this charter-party had been executed, and that one part had been delivered to and was in the custody of the intestate, and was on board the ship and lost with him. That the Plaintiffs had applied to the Defendant's attorney for inspection of that part of the charter-party which had been left, and was admitted then to be, in the Defendant's hands, and had been refused; and that the Plaintiff could not safely declare, without that assistance. Upon these facts, *Lens* Serjt. obtained a rule *nisi* that the Plaintiff might be permitted to inspect, and at his own charges to take a copy of the charter-party in the hands of the Defendant, or else that the Defendant's attorney might at the Plaintiff's cost deliver him a copy. He cited *King v. King.* (a)

Shepherd, Solicitor-General, now shewed cause against this application, as being unauthorized by any precedent. He admitted that where one part only of an instrument has been executed and left in the hands of one party, who was in that respect a trustee for the other, the Court has granted inspection, as in *Blakey*

(a) *Ante,* iv. 666.

v. *Por-*

v. *Porter* (a), where there was no counter part of the
lease; and in *King* v. *King* there was only one part of
the indenture; and *Mansfield* C. J. held that the custody
implied a trust to produce, and gave it the effect of a
covenant to produce, in which *Gibbs* J. concurred. So,
in *Bateman* v. *Phillips* (b), where the Court compelled
the production of an unstamped instrument, to be
stamped, there was but one part signed, and it was
wrongfully in the hands of the Defendant. But where
two parts are executed interchangeably, and one party
has lost his part, especially since it is not sworn that
each part is executed by both parties, no such trust
arises; and though it may be a question whether a
court of equity may not aid the Plaintiff, it is very
questionable whether this Court has a summary jurisdiction to give oyer; but if they have it, they have
never yet exercised it, nor will exercise it on this occasion. Upon a bill in equity for a discovery, the Defendant has the opportunity of stating in his answer on
oath such facts as are material in his own favour, an
advantage of which the practice now sought to be introduced, would deprive him.

Lens in support of his rule. The principle of granting inspection in the case where there is only one part,
strengthens the Plaintiff's argument for the production in
this case. The same argument of jurisdiction was urged
in *King* v. *King*, but it was held of no avail. It was
urged in *Bateman* v. *Phillips*, of putting the party to
his bill in equity, that the Defendant might have the
opportunity to tell his own tale; that likewise was overruled; but the principal difficulty, which the Court has
always felt, has been to help the party where there has
been only one part, or the Plaintiff's part has not been

(a) *Ante*, i. 386.   (b) *Ante*, iv. 157.

stamped,

1815.

STREET
v.
BROWN.

stamped, under circumstances, where, from the nature of things, there ought to be two instruments, and where the party by having only one, had defrauded the revenue; but those difficulties do not occur here; and whether it may turn out that this part is executed by both or one of the parties, cannot be seen until the deed is produced. And the missing part is not lost by any negligence of the Plaintiffs, but it was in the situation where it ought most properly to be, on board the ship, and has perished with the ship. This, therefore, is a less strong application than those which are cited; for in *Blakey* v. *Porter* there was no trust for the other, no covenant to produce: there is no omission here, no attempt to make the transaction pass with fewer stamps than the law requires. The jurisdiction is the same in both cases, and in other respects this Plaintiff is in a better condition. This case therefore comes within the principle of *Blakey* v. *Porter*: it may, in the event which has occurred, be considered that the parties are come to the same state, as if there had been but one part originally executed.

GIBBS C. J. The counsel for the application has argued strongly against the jurisdiction of the Court in those cases in which the Courts have granted the inspection; but we must look to the reason of those cases, and not be hurried by them. In *Blakey* v. *Porter* the party covenanted to do certain things, and the deed was to remain in the possession of the covenantor. *Mansfield* C. J. put the case on the ground that the deed was left in the custody of one for the use of both. Afterwards, in *Michaelmas* term (a) 53 G. 3., there was an application for the production of an indenture of lease, executed by both parties, and left in the possession of the Defendant. *Mansfield* C. J. was very averse to

(a) *King* v. *King*, *ante*, iv. 666.

granting

granting the application, and he only proceeds on the
precedent established by *Blakey* v. *Porter*. In both
these cases the ground on which the Court make the
rule, is, that the party holding the deed was a trustee
for the other. I do not put it on the ground, whether
that circumstance gives the Court a jurisdiction, but it
is not this case: here the one party executes a deed, by
which he binds himself, and the other executes a deed,
by which he binds himself, and the one, having lost
his part, calls on the other to produce his: it is like
the case where a man, having given a bond, and kept
a copy of it, the other, losing the bond, applies for a
copy of the copy, we should not grant that. I therefore should be unwilling to establish a new precedent,
though, if there were a case so decided, I cannot say
that I should be unwilling to follow it.

1815.

STREET
v.
BROWN.

Rule discharged.

O'KEEFE *v.* DUNN and Another.

June 14.

THIS was an action brought against the Defendants,
as the drawers of a bill of exchange drawn on *Ricketts*
and Co., at one month after date, payable to *Sinclair*,
and by him indorsed to the Plaintiff, for the non-
acceptance of the bill by *Ricketts*. The Defendant
pleaded, that before the indorsement to the Plaintiff,
and presentment by her for acceptance, the bill was
presented by *Sinclair* for acceptance and refused, and
that the Defendants had no notice given them of such
refusal to accept. After verdict for the Defendant on
the issue joined on a traverse of this plea, *Vaughan*

*The payee of
a bill of ex-
change pre-
sented it for
acceptance,
which was
refused: the
payee did not
give notice to
the drawer,
and indorsed
over the bill
without notice
of the refusal
to accept.
The indorsee*

being again refused acceptance, held, that the indorsee might still *recover on the*
bill against the drawer, notwithstanding the laches of the payee. *By three against*
Chambre J.

Serjt.

1815.

O'KEEFE
v.
DUNN.

Serjt. for the Plaintiff, who at the trial before *Gibbs* C. J. at the sittings at *Guildhall* after *Hilary* term 1815, proved the facts of his declaration as above stated, in *Easter* term obtained a rule *nisi* to enter up judgment for the Plaintiff *non obstante veredicto*, upon the ground that the special plea averring no notice to the Plaintiff of the first dishonour of the bill, was insufficient in law.

Shepherd, Solicitor-General, and *Lens* Serjt., in the same term shewed cause against the rule, maintaining the sufficiency of the plea, for that *Sinclair*, the former holder, by his laches in not giving notice to the drawee of the non-acceptance, had absolutely discharged the drawer; and not with reference to himself only; and that he could not by a subsequent indorsement confer on the Plaintiff a right which he had himself ceased to possess. They cited *Roscow* v. *Hardy*(a), *Blesard* v. *Hirst*(b), and *Goodall* v. *Dolly*. (c)

Vaughan and *Pell* Serjts. in support of the rule, urged that a subsequent holder for a valuable consideration without notice, could not be prejudiced by the laches of the former holder. No person could be safe in receiving an unaccepted bill, if the secret neglect of a former holder might thus destroy its value. The doctrine would give occasion to infinite frauds.

Cur. adv. vult.

The judges on this day delivered their opinions *seriatim.*

DALLAS J. stated the case, and proceeded as follows. Two points seem to be clear, first, that a bill payable

(a) 12 *East*, 434. S.C. 2 *Campb.* 458.   (b) *Burr.* 2670.
(c) 1 *Term Rep.* 712.

at

at a future day, or so many days after date, need not be presented for acceptance, but may be demanded, without such presentment, when due. Secondly, That if, however, presentment be made, and there be a refusal to accept, notice of such refusal ought to be given by the party to whom it was made; and that for want of such notice, as between the drawer and such holder of the bill, the drawer will be discharged; if, therefore, this bill had continued in the hands of *Sinclair* the payee, to whom the refusal to accept was made, and by whom no notice of such refusal was given, the drawer, as to him, would have been discharged; but the action is not brought by *Sinclair*, but by the Plaintiff to whom he had indorsed the bill, and without notice by him to her that the bill had been refused acceptance. The question then will be, whether she can stand in a situation different from that in which he would have stood if he had brought the action. On the part of the Defendants it is argued, that there is no distinction; and this is contended, first, upon the reason of the rule by which the drawer would be discharged against a party knowing of the refusal to accept and omitting to give notice; secondly, on the authority of a decided case, which is said not to be distinguishable from the present. And first, as to the reason of the rule, the drawer is presumed to have effects in the hands of the drawee, and the bill is an order to appropriate so much to the payee or his order. . If, therefore, on presentment the drawer refuse to accept, from the very nature of the transaction, the drawer should have notice, that he may withdraw his effects, or proceed against his debtor, as the case may seem to him to require. But if he have no effects, the reason of the rule fails, and with it the rule; and in such event, notice is not necessary. Now it has been contended, that this rule cannot vary by the shifting of hands, for that the drawer

is

is equally injured by the want of notice, in whatever hands
the bill may be; and further, that when the drawer is
once discharged, his responsibility cannot be revived
by the acts of others independent of him. With respect to the first part of the statement, it may be admitted to be true; but with regard to the latter, it is
begging the question; for the question is, if this responsibility have ever ceased as to a party in the situation of the Plaintiff. Or rather, whether the Defendants have not agreed so to be responsible in the events
which have happened in the present case. The inquiry,
therefore, must be, whether an indorsee for a valuable
consideration, and without notice of any illegality not
making the bill void in its origin, or of any laches in
the course of its circulation, is to be considered as
receiving a bill subject to all that might affect it in the
hands of the payee, or of a previous indorser, or, in
other words, may not the drawer be discharged as to
the payee becoming indorser, and yet continue liable
to his indorsee? The nature of the contract appears to
me to be this: The drawer of a bill payable at a
future day enables the payee, by making the bill payable to him or to his order, to hold out to all the
world, that he will pay the bill, in default of the acceptor, to the party entitled to present it for acceptance
or payment. He does not stipulate for himself that it
shall be presented for acceptance, nor does the law
cast such an obligation on the payee. The drawer,
therefore, must be considered as contented to rest in
ignorance whether it has been accepted or not, till the
bill becomes due. And whether presented or not,
depends upon the casualty of how the holder of the
bill may chuse to proceed. Any party who takes it,
paying a valuable consideration, takes it, then, knowing
that presentment for acceptance is not necessary, and
nothing

nothing appearing upon the face of the bill to shew it to have been presented and acceptance refused. Indeed he has reason to conclude the contrary in every case in which there is no noting for non-acceptance, which noting would be notice on the face of the bill, and under such a circumstance he would act at his peril. Taking it, therefore, before it becomes due, and ignorant of a refusal to accept, he is a purchaser for a valuable consideration, without notice, against a party who has enabled the indorser to put off an instrument, good upon the face of it, and by which, as far as appears, he has contracted to be bound. And considered in this light, I am of opinion, that from the very nature of the contract, he is entitled to notice from the party having knowlege of the refusal to accept, and is dis-charged for want of such notice; but that he must be taken to have stipulated that this rule shall be confined to such party, and not be extended to an innocent and ignorant indorsee. On the reason and convenience of the thing, this doctrine appears to me to be equally supported. It can do no harm to the circulation of bills of exchange, that the holder should be required, when acceptance is refused, to give immediate notice to the drawer, and that the consequence of a neglect to do it should devolve upon himself; but it would greatly clog the negotiability of such securities, if, upon some latent defect, and without any default in himself, every man shall be taught, and so be made to feel, that in the moment of paying the full value of a bill, he may be purchasing that which may turn out to be a mere nullity. This has hitherto been confined to two or three special cases, and ought not, I think, to be further extended; and I will only add, that in what I am now saying, I mean such bills as the genuine pur-poses of commerce require. It may be said, this may be guarded against by ascertaining, before taking the bill, whether it has been refused acceptance or not, and this is certainly possible, but for reasons that must be obvious, would in practice be so inconvenient, as almost to amount to a prohibition to take any unaccepted bill. As to cases in point, I am not aware of any which are directly so, and will consider, therefore, next, how the law stands in these which appear to me to be analogous. And first, in the instance of a bill indorsed over after it becomes due. That it is overdue, and has not been paid, appearing upon the face of it, is notice to the party who takes it, and being therefore out of the common course of negotiability, he is bound to inquire into the cause, and taking it without such inquiry, is subject to all the equities that would have affected it in the hands of former parties. This rests on the ground of knowledge in him, or that which is equivalent to knowledge, a fact amounting to notice, and demanding inquiry; but reverse the fact, and suppose it a taking by indorsement before it became due, he is then an innocent indorsee, without notice of fraud or neglect, and intitled to recover against all those parties, who under the circumstances of the case might be discharged as to each other. A drawer may therefore be released as to the payee, and yet continue liable to the last indorsee. And this appears to me in principle to apply to the present question. It remains only to advert to the case cited from 12 *East*, and though said to be in point, I think it is clearly to be distinguished from the present: the facts were these: the bill had been presented by the *Warrington* bank, and acceptance refused; they gave no notice to the drawer at the time, nor to the party from whom they had taken it; but kept it till due, and then, without notice to the indorser, who was ignorant of these facts, recovered against him, and when he sued the drawer, the drawer was held to be discharged, and

I   the

the indorser to have paid the money in his own wrong, inasmuch as undoubtedly the bank would not have recovered against him. The difference therefore between the two cases is this. In the case cited, the bill had never passed into the hands of an indorsee ignorant of the refusal to accept before the bill became due, and while it was fairly negotiable, but remained till it became due in the hands of those, who, from neglect to give notice, could not recover. Whatever was a discharge to the drawer, was a discharge to the indorser; and the discharged indorser having thought fit to pay, when not liable, could not recover against the drawer what he had paid in his own wrong. In this case the fact is directly the reverse; the bill when becoming due, being in the hands of an innocent holder, and having been taken in a course of fair negotiation during the period that intervened between the refusal to accept and the bill arriving at maturity for payment. For these reasons I am of opinion in every view of the case, that this plea is not a sufficient answer to the action.

CHAMBRE J. dissented from the rest of the Court, and stated the facts on which he grounded his opinion. This was an action by an indorsee against the drawers of a bill of exchange. The bill is dated the 19th *January* 1813, it is drawn by the Defendant on *Rickets* and Co., and is payable in one month to *Sinclair* or order: *Sinclair*, after receiving the bill, and before it was due, presented it to the drawees for acceptance, which they refused: of this dishonour of the bill no notice was given to the Defendant, but *Sinclair* afterwards negotiated the bill by indorsing it over to the Plaintiff, without communicating to her, or any one else, that fact of refusal to accept. When the bill was at maturity, the Plaintiff, being then in possession of it as indorsee of *Sinclair*, presented

it

1815.

O'KEEFE
v.
DUNN.

it for payment, which was also refused, and of this last refusal the Defendant had notice: the question arising from these circumstances is, whether the action is maintainable by the Plaintiff against the drawers, or the drawers, by the laches of *Sinclair*, the holder and owner of the bill at the time of the first presentment and refusal, were compleatly discharged from their responsibility. It is not contended on the one hand, that any negligence is imputable to the Plaintiff personally, or on the other hand, that the Defendants, either by drawing without effects, or by any other circumstance of their conduct, have deprived themselves of any advantage they would otherwise be entitled to by the law of merchants on this subject. As far as appears, the transaction is all fair as between these parties, but the Defendants insist, that the neglect of the actual holder and then sole proprietor of the bill, has wholly discharged the drawers, and left the Plaintiff to seek for redress from *Sinclair*, to whom he has paid the amount of the bill, and who deceived him by a fraudulent concealment. There can be no doubt that a drawer is entitled, equally with an indorser, to notice of the dishonour of the bill, either by non-acceptance or non-payment. Indeed the reason for requiring such notice to the drawer may be stronger than it is for giving it to the indorser. The indorser has nothing at stake but the sum for which the bill is drawn, but the drawer, besides that risk, has, in fair transactions, frequently further effects in the hands of those on whom he draws, and a timely notice, which may assist in enabling him to secure himself, is in such cases of more importance to be given to him, than it is to an indorser. The consequence of the omission of any notice which the law requires in such case, is, that the holder and proprietor, who ought to have given it, loses the security of all prior indorsers and of the drawer.

Here

Here *Sinclair* was the holder and owner. By his neglect his remedy against the drawer was lost! it made an end of the drawer's responsibility at the time; and I am at a loss to discover, by what means, without any act or default of their own, the responsibility can be revived. If *Sinclair* had no right of action against the drawers, how could he by his indorsement under such circumstances transfer a right to another. The case of *Blesard* v. *Hirst*, which was an action by an indorsee against the indorser of a bill of exchange, is an express authority for the necessity of giving notice of a refusal to accept, and Lord *Mansfield's* words are, he (the indorsee) ought to have given notice of this refusal, and not to have concealed it; and by not having given notice has taken the risk upon himself. The indorser is imposed upon, and the person who neglected to give the notice ought to suffer for it. The question is not whether he was obliged to present it for acceptance, he has done so and it was refused. The case of *Goodall* v. *Dolley* expressly confirms the decision in *Blesard* v. *Hirst*, and in both the cases the Defendants had judgment, though in both cases the Defendants had in some degree acknowledged themselves liable to the demand. The case of *Roscow* v. *Hardy* is more expressly in point, where Lord *Ellenborough* C. J., in giving his opinion, says, if the indorsement on the bill be once discharged by the laches of the holder at the time, in not giving due notice of the dishonor of it, their responsibility cannot be revived by the shifting of the bill into other hands. A contrary doctrine would, as it appears to me, be an inlet to fraud; and the effect of the law, which requires a strict observance of its rules in the negotiation of bills, would be completely defeated, if the holder, finding that he had lost his own remedy against the drawer and indorsers, could, by indorsing the bill to another person at any time before the day

Y 3   of

of payment, enable that other person to sue the drawer or prior indorsers, and by so doing indemnify himself at the expence of the party against whom he had lost his own remedy. It is true that innocent parties might be defrauded, while the time of payment is unexpired, and the negotiations apparently regular. So, a man may be defrauded in other transactions; but against whom is he to seek his remedy? against those who have fraudulently obtained his money, and not by destroying the rights of those who have no share in the fraud. The law limits the responsibility of parties to bills of exchange by certain rules for the negotiation of them: I think those rules ought not to be varied by the introduction of new and unnecessary distinctions or exceptions, and that therefore, on the present case, the decision of the Court ought to be in favour of the Defendants.

HEATH J. It is of the greatest importance that the negotiability of bills of exchange should be protected and preserved. In a few cases, such as gaming, usury, and the like, certain statutes make bills void in the hands of an innocent holder, who has his remedy over in another manner; but in other cases the bill is not avoided; even a bill obtained by the grossest fraud is not thereby vitiated. I am not for extending the law beyond the cases already decided. The case of *Roscow* v. *Hardy* proceeded on a very different ground. There the bill was paid without inquiry, and the Defendant had a right to say, " If the *Warrington* bank had sued me, I had a good defence : the Plaintiff had neglected to inquire, and his laches ought not to prejudice the Defendant. In the present case the drawer has failed in his duty; he ought to have had effects in the hands of the drawee, and if he had not, the uttering the bill was a species of fraud. My Brother *Dallas* has ably argued
the

the principles to be deduced from the nature of the contract. I need not therefore enlarge on that ground; but I may observe, that here the Plaintiff does not take the bill merely by virtue of a common law assignment, but also by virtue of the custom of merchants. I am of opinion that the Plaintiff ought to recover.

GIBBS C. J. I am of the same opinion. The distinction has been so well taken by my Brothers *Heath* and *Dallas*, that it is necessary for me to say very little on this case. There are two different species of defence on bills of exchange. The first sort goes to shew that the Defendant is discharged from the claims of all persons whatsoever on that bill; the other sort is directed to shew that the Defendant is discharged as from the claim of a particular person. If a person takes a bill on an usurious stipulation, (I am not speaking of a bill originally made on an usurious consideration, but good in its origin, and passed to an indorsee on usurious consideration,) he cannot sue either the drawer or the acceptor; but if he passes it to the hand of another innocent and ignorant indorsee for a valuable consideration, that person may use it against the person who indorsed it to him. So, he who takes a bill after it has arrived at maturity, takes it subject to all the defences which could have been made by any previous holder; for the bill being unpaid, its date is notice to him sufficient to put him on inquiry; but if he takes the bill before it is due, he takes it not subject to the same infirmity of title, because he then takes it without notice of any suspicious circumstances that may break in upon his remedy against any former holder. This is the general law, but there may be circumstances that may make it otherwise. A holder is not bound to present a bill for acceptance; there is nothing therefore on the face of an

Y 4 unac-

unaccepted bill to awaken a suspicion that it has been presented for acceptance and refused. But it is said, the general law is, that where notice is requisite, if notice be not given, the drawer, and all persons claiming to be entitled to have notice of the dishonour, are discharged. I think that is a begging of the question. If a holder comes to the knowledge that the drawee will not accept, or will not pay the bill when it becomes due, and omits to give notice, he shall never sue the drawer, because his neglect prevents the drawer from using diligence in withdrawing from the drawee the effects which were destined to satisfy the bill; but I am of opinion that if the bill is passed for a valuable consideration without notice of that defect of title, he who so innocently takes the bill is not guilty of any breach of duty towards the drawer, and is therefore not affected by the omission. *Roscow* v. *Hardy* is mainly distinguishable from the present case, in respect that the bill there continued, up to the time of its maturity, in the hands of a holder, who had neglected to give that notice at the time when the bill was first refused acceptance, and the holder, I agree, had thereby, as to his own claim, discharged the drawer. I am of opinion that the circumstance of the bill continuing in the same hand materially differs that case from the present. I therefore think that the present Plaintiff, not having had notice that the bill had been presented for acceptance and dishonoured before she took it, is entitled to recover, notwithstanding the plea that has been put on the record. The rule therefore must be absolute for entering judgment for the Plaintiff *non obstante veredicto.*

Rule absolute.

1815.

UTHWATT v. BRYANT and Others.

June 1.

THIS was a case directed by Sir *Thomas Plumer*, Vice-Chancellor, for the opinion of the Judges o this Court. *William Andrewes* being seised in fee of certain freehold hereditaments in the parish of *Buckingham*, by his will dated 27th *August* 1760, duly executed and attested for passing real estates, devised all his freehold lands, tenements, tythes, hereditaments, and premises in the parish of *Buckingham*, to J. *Millward* and *E. Millward*, their executors and administrators, for a term of 1000 years, in trust to raise 500*l*. by mortgage, (but not by sale,) to discharge his debts, &c. in aid of his personal estate appropriated for that purpose, and subject to that term he devised to his wife all his said freehold lands, tenements, tythes, hereditaments, and premises for her natural life, *sans* waste, and after the determination of that estate, to his son *Temple Andrewes*, and his assigns during his life, *sans* waste, and after that estate to Earl *Temple* and the Rt. Hon. *G. Grenville* and their heirs during the life of *Temple Andrewes*, in trust to preserve contingent remainders, and after the decease of *Temple Andrewes*, to the use of the first and other sons of *Temple Andrewes*, in tail male; and in default of such issue, to the third and other sons of the testator's body begotten and thereafter to be born, (except his son *Henry Uthwatt Andrewes* and his issue male, whom he excepted out of that devise, because an

Devise of all the testator's freehold lands, tenements, tythes, hereditaments, and premises in the parish of B. to trustees for 1000 years, in trust to raise 500l.; and, subject to that term, he devised all his said freehold lands, &c. to the testator's wife for her natural life, sans waste; remainder to his 2d son T. A. for life, sans waste; remainder to trustees to support contingent remainders; remainder to the first and other sons of T. A. in tail male; remainder to the 3d and other afterborn sons of the testator, (except his eldest son,) in tail male; and if the testator should have no third son, or when his son *T. A.*, or any of his sons except *H. U. A.* should succeed to a certain estate entailed on *T. A.* by an uncle, the testator devised his said freehold estate in the parish of *B.* to his daughters *F.* and *C.*, and any other daughters he might thereafter have, to take as tenants in common : *Held that the daughters took a fee.*

estate

estate at *Linford* was left him by his godfather *Henry Uthwatt*, Esq.) successively in tail male, and if the testator should have no third son, or when his son *Temple Andrewes*, or any other of his said sons (except *H. U. Andrewes* and his issue male) in remainder should succeed to an estate in the parish of *Lothbury*, entailed on *Temple Andrewes* by the testator's uncle *Henry Andrewes*, Esq. or either of them then to take, the testator devised his said freehold estate in the parish of *Buckingham* unto his daughters *Frances* and *Charlotte*, and any other daughters he might thereafter have, to take as tenants in common : but in case all such his said children should die in the lifetime of his wife, then he devised all his said freehold estate in the parish of *Buckingham* to his wife and her heirs for ever. And the testator bequeathed to his son *H. U. Andrewes* his diamond ring, with an earnest request that he would assist and provide for his brother and sisters to the utmost of his power when he came to *Linford* estate, and be generous and tender to his mother, whose wisdom in having him named at baptism *H. Uthwatt*, after the testator's friend and relation *Henry Uthwart*, had obtained for him an ample estate; and the testator desired that if the estate at *Lothbury* devised by Mr. *Uthwatt* to his brother *Temple* should be incumbered, he would pay off any such mortgage, as he was so amply provided for, and his brother so little, especially as it was an old family estate. The testator died in *September* 1760 without revoking or altering his will, leaving his widow, *Temple Andrewes* his eldest son and heir at law, and *H. U. Andrewes*, and *Charlotte* and *Frances*, his only other children, him surviving. *Temple Andrewes* died in the lifetime of the testator's widow, without issue; the widow died on 27th *December* 1802, and *Frances Andrewes* is since dead. The question was, What estate *Frances Andrewes* deceased, the testator's daughter, took

took in the freehold estate in the parish of *Buckingham* under the will?

Lens Serjt. for the Plaintiff, contended, that inasmuch as the testator had twice described the subject of this devise by its local description, when he afterwards described it by the term " his said freehold estate in the parish of *Buckingham*," he thereby gave only the same thing which he had given before, namely, his lands, tenements, tythes, and hereditaments in the parish of *Buckingham*. The word estate signified not the quantity of interest, but only local description; and as he had added no words of limitation, the daughters took only an estate for life. The contingency too, on which he intended the estate to go over to his widow, was one which he expected to take place within the compass of a life in being, namely, the decease of his children: for it is highly improbable that the testator should look forward to the failure of issue of all his children, as an event likely to happen during the life of his widow. No case is expressly in point: that which comes nearest to the present, is *Hay* v. *Lord Coventry* (a). No intent is shewn on this will to give the daughters more than an estate for life. Words of inheritance must either be expressed or supplied by necessary inference; but this will afford no ground for such an inference.

Best Serjt. *contra*, argued that the daughters took an estate in fee. The testator shewed in this will great anxiety to exclude the heir at law. In *Ulrich* v. *Lichfield* (b) Lord *Hardwicke*, Chancellor, says, no certain rule is to be laid down for the construction of devises, and cites *Swinburne* (c). It is allowable to call in aid other passages of the will to shew the intent of this

(a) 3 *Term Rep.* 83.
(b) 2 *Atk.* 372.

(c) *Part* 7. *chap.* 1.

clause.

clause. *Hay* v. *Lord Coventry* is inapplicable, for there the word "estate" is not found on which this case turns. The word estate is sufficient to carry a fee. Many circumstances denote that the testator meant to give his daughters a greater estate than for life. The probability of enjoying an estate for life would have been of very little value to these daughters, though they were infants at the time of making the will; for their estate was not to commence until after the death of all the sons, and failure of issue of all the sons. It appears that the testator knew in what terms an estate for life was technically to be given, for he devises to *Temple Andrewes* an express life estate *sans* waste, and where he thinks proper to give an estate for life, he also uses the precaution of interposing a trust to preserve contingent remainders. On two occasions, where he gives less than a fee, he devises by the description of lands and tenements. On the third occasion, when he meant to give a fee-simple, he uses the word estate. The word *said* refers only to the local description of the lands, to shew that he means to give the same subject, but the word estate denotes the quantity of interest he means to give. If his daughters die, living his wife, he gives the wife an express estate in fee. It is not therefore probable that he intended, in case his wife should die before his daughters, to die intestate as to the reversion which was expectant on their supposed life estate. He cited *Roe, on demise of Child,* v. *Wright* (a), *Holdfast* v. *Martin* (b), and *Chichester* v. *Oxendon.* (c)

Lens in reply. The question here is not what answer the testator would have made, if the particular event had been brought before him, but what he has in fact declared. If there be a case unprovided for,

---

(a) 7 *East,* 259.
(b) 1 *Term Rep.* 411.
(c) *Ante,* iv 176.

though

1815.

UTHWATT
v.
BRYANT.

though he has provided for many cases, the heir is not disinherited, whatever might be his personal intent as to the heir. It was first urged that the daughters took a fee, afterwards an estate tail, there not being sufficient ground to maintain the other, but both lie under the same difficulty, that the Court is desired to interpose words which are not found in the will. *Hay* v. *Coventry* was not cited as in point, but because there the same argument was used that the testator did not mean to die intestate; nor does a testator often so mean; but the Court cannot by reason of that intent multiply estates to the extent of the interest or property undisposed of. Nothing is to be inferred from the extent of the testator's knowledge, as shewn by the circumstance that the testator knew how to give estates for life: for he knew also how to give estates in strict settlement, and, in fee, he was not *inops consili*. The three cases last cited for the Defendant do not go beyond the general principle. In *Roe dem. Child* v. *Wright*, were the words *all my estate*, and the question was, whether those words were not to have their full legal import, as well as to designate the land. Those words are not there used by way of reference, but are the first description. The testator gives in the first words that which conveys the interest, and in the following words that which conveys the local description: the conclusion was inevitable. *Holdfast* v. *Marten* goes no further. So, in *Chichester* v. *Oxendon*, " all my estate of *Ashton*," was held to fall within the same principle. The very use of a word of reference, is, to substitute it for the same thing, which was said before, without a new enumeration. The Defendant's argument would add more. It is argued that the word " said" applies to the subject, and the word " estate" to the interest; but the word " said" cannot be so severed as to stand by itself, being a participle. The Court cannot supply another object of reference than that which the party has himself

1815.

UTHWATT
v.
BRYANT.

self intended. The testator certainly meant to exclude his heir in certain events, and has so expressed it, but no further: the word estate would have been sufficient to, have carried a fee, if the other parts of the will would have permitted it; but they repel that inference, and the Defendant's argument stands merely on the words of the clause, and not on the general intent of the will.

Cur. adv. vult.

We have heard this case argued, and are of opinion that *Frances Andrewes*, spinster, deceased, the daughter of the said testator, *William Andrewes*, took an estate in fee-simple in the freehold estate and premises in the parish of *Buckingham* under his will.

V. GIBBS.
A. CHAMBRE.
R. DALLAS.

Mr. Justice *Heath* being absent from indisposition did not hear this case argued.

June 7.

COTTERELL v. APSEY.

One who contracts to build a house, furnishing both timber and labour, cannot recover for the materials on a count for goods sold and delivered, though by reason of a deviation from the original plan, the contract is superseded as to the price.

THE Plaintiff declared in his first count for work and labour, and in his third for goods sold and delivered: his seventh count was on an *insimul computasset.* Upon the trial of the cause at the *Cambridge* spring assizes 1815, before *Heath* J., the Plaintiff proved that he had built a house for the Defendant, furnishing timber and workmanship, for which he claimed to be entitled to 580l. He had entered into a written agreement, that for 350l. he would find all wood and labour

to

to build the house according to a plan given : but some
deviation from the plan had been agreed to and made.
The Defendant had paid him 350*l.*, *viz.* by anterior
payments made generally on account, 188*l.*, and by
payment into court upon the 1st, 3d, and 7th counts,
162*l.* The Plaintiff's witnesses proved that the whole
value of the materials was 290*l.*, and of the workmanship 300*l.* For the Defendant it was submitted, that
the 290*l.* could not be recovered, because there was no
claim in the declaration for materials found, and that no
contract was proved for goods sold and delivered. The
jury found a verdict for the Plaintiff, for 229*l.*, subject
to the point reserved.

Blosset Serjt. having in *Easter* term obtained a rule
nisi to set aside the verdict, and enter a nonsuit,

Pell Serjt. now shewed cause. The Plaintiff having
paid money into Court on the third count, cannot now
contend that there was no contract for goods sold and
delivered, and as the jury have given damages on it, the
Plaintiff is entitled to retain his verdict. The Plaintiff
too, had a right to ascribe the damages recovered to
the account of the labour, which exceeded in amount
the whole verdict, and to consider the money which he
had formerly received, as paid him on the account of
the materials : he might also ascribe the money paid
into court to the count upon the *insimul computasset.*
The objection was *strictissimi juris.*

Blosset, in support of his rule, urged, that although,
where there are distinct subjects of account, the person
who receives money may ascribe it to which account he,
pleases, yet where money is paid, as this was, on one
entire account, arising out of one entire contract, the
person receiving cannot divide the account into several
subjects,

subjects, for the purpose of ascribing the payment to one of them. An entire contract may be, to do several things, as to furnish goods, to build a house, and to perform work and labour, yet it is all one contract. If this demand had been merely for the furnishing of window frames and other distinct articles, the price of them might be recovered as for goods sold and delivered; but, though, if the Plaintiff were permitted to take them distributively, there are goods sold and delivered, and materials found, yet the demand, arising on one contract, cannot be split into several counts, or several actions, and the money paid on one entire account cannot be applied to one part of the contract. The payment of money into court forms no objection to a nonsuit: it has no other effect, than the striking so much money out of the declaration.

Gibbs C. J. This is a very captious objection, and merely technical; but if it is a legal objection, we are bound to give it its effect: and since the pleader or attorney has left out of the count the words " and also for materials found in and about the same building," we think it must prevail. This is, as the Defendant's counsel urges, an entire contract to do several things mixed up together; the Plaintiff professes in his declaration to state those things; and as there is no mention among them of materials, nothing can be recovered on this declaration for that matter. It is immaterial to consider whether the sums paid on account can be applied to the account of materials or not. And since the modern practice in this court does permit the Plaintiff to be nonsuited, although the Defendant has paid money into court, therefore the rule must be absolute for entering a nonsuit.

Rule absolute.

(OLD BAILEY SESSIONS.)

The KING v. BOX.   *May 12.*

THE prisoner was tried and found guilty at the *Old Bailey* session on 10th *April* 1815 before *Chambre* J. upon an indictment which charged that he feloniously had falsely made, forged, and counterfeited a certain promissory note for the payment of money, which was as follows: On demand we promise to pay Messdames *Sarah Wallis* and *Sarah Doubtfire,* stewardesses for the time being of the Provident Daughters' Society, held at Mr *Pope's,* the *Hope, Smithfield,* or their successors in office, sixty-four pounds, with 5 *per cent.* interest for the same; value received this 7th day of *February* 1815.

For Felix Calvert and Co.

£64.   *John Forster.*

Adolphus moved in arrest of judgment, that this was no promissory note, and the case was in *Easter* term argued before the twelve judges. *Adolphus* for the prisoner referred to the definition of a promissory note by *Blackstone* J. (a). That it is a plain and direct engagement in writing, to pay a sum specified at the time therein limited to a person therein named, or sometimes to his order, or often to the bearer at large. The same definition is followed, with little variation, by the authors of several modern treatises (b). So, another (c) eminent writer says, a promissory note may be defined to be a written promise for the payment of money absolutely and at all events. Before bills of exchange

(a) 2 Bl. Com. 467.   (c) Bayley on Bills, 1.
(b) Chitty on Bills, 2d edit.
233. Kyd on Bills.

and promissory notes were in use, merchants raised money on instruments called single bills, the form of which is still extant (a), that bill could only charge the person assigning it, by a special promise indorsed thereon to pay it in case the maker did not pay. The attempt to put promissory notes into circulation was held by Lord *Holt* C. J. (b) as a strange attempt to set up the law of *Lombard Street* above the law of the realm, and he treated them merely as evidence of a debt, like any other letter, but not as creating a debt. The statute 3 and 4 *Ann.* c. 9. made them negotiable, but they owe their whole and only force to that act. This instrument contains no one of the properties of a promissory note. Notes of hand are frequently given to parish officers, and fall into the hands of their successor. That forms no proposition applicable to this case.

Gurney, contrà. This instrument contains a written promise for payment of money absolutely and at all events. This keeps clear of all the cases. No particular form of words is necessary. A promise not to pay (c) may be a good promissory note. If the payees are not rightly described, the misdescription may be rejected, *Brown* v. *Harrowden.* Lord *Kenyon* C. J. says it is not necessary now to consider whether Lord *Holt* were right in so pertinaciously adhering to his opinion before the statute of *Anne,* that no action could be maintained on promissory notes as instruments, but that they were only to be considered as evidences of the debt; but look to the words of the act of *Anne* both in the preamble and enactment: it is observable that the act does not say that a promissory note had no legality, but that it was not assignable by the custom of merchants. This in-

(a) *Postlethwaite's Dictionary of Commerce,* article Bill.

(b) *Clerke* v. *Martin,* 2 Ld. Ray. 757.

(c) 2 *Atk.* 32.

strument

strument before the statute could not be described in an indictment for forgery as any thing but a promissory note; nevertheless the better opinion was, that the forgery of less instruments than deeds was even then an indictable offence. *Ward's* case (*a*). This instrument is in every particular a promissory note.

Adolphus, in reply. No deed is made in which the word "promise" is not introduced; yet a covenant is not a promissory note, neither is this. This may be a bond with an implied condition; a covenant without formalities; but it is not a promissory note. If Lord Holt's opinion in *Clerke* v. *Martin* (*b*) was law, a note had no legal existence whatever; for that was not an action by an indorsee, but by the payee; and Holt C. J. held he might have recovered on the counts on an *indebitatus assumpsit*, upon the evidence contained in this paper; but that he could not recover on it as a special contract by the custom of merchants. The terms of the statute go not merely to the question whether notes were transferable or negotiable, but it puts them generally on the ground of bills of exchange: this wants the simplicity of character of a promissory note, and the judgment must be arrested.

Cur. adv. vult.

LE BLANC J. now delivered judgment. The prisoner was tried at the last session on an indictment for forging and uttering, knowing it to be forged, a promissory note for the payment of money. Several objections to the evidence given to support the indictment were taken, but they were disposed of by the Bench, and the jury found the prisoner guilty. Another objection was taken in arrest of judgment, and argued before all the

(*a*) 2 *Ld. Ray.* 1461. S.C. 2 *Str.* 747.   (*b*) 2 *Ld. Ray.* 757.

judges,

judges, that the instrument in question, such as it is stated in the indictment, was not a promissory note within the statute, so as to be the subject of an indictment for forging, or uttering it, knowing it 'to be forged. The objection to this instrument was founded on this circumstance, that it appears to be made payable to two ladies, describing them as stewardesses of a provident society, or their successors in office; and that this society not being enrolled according to the statute (*a*), this note was not capable to enure to their successors, and was not negotiable. The judges are of opinion that this is, as stated on the indictment, a valid promissory note within the statute of *G.* 2. It is not necessary that such a note should be in itself negotiable, it is sufficient, that it should be a note for the certain payment of a sum of money, whether negotiable or not. And though these ladies were not at the time legally stewardesses, yet it was a description by which they were known at the time; and though they could not legally have successors in office, yet, in case of their decease, their executors and administrators might sue, and they themselves, during their life, might recover on it. Therefore it is an instrument capable of being the subject of forgery, and there is no ground to arrest the judgment; and the Judges are all of opinion that the conviction is right.

(*a*) 33 *G.* 3. *c.* 34.

END OF TRINITY TERM.

C A S E S

ARGUED AND DETERMINED

IN THE

Court of COMMON PLEAS,

AND

OTHER COURTS,

IN

Michaelmas Term,

In the Fifty-sixth Year of the Reign of GEORGE III.

1815.

4 Bing 4

HEWES *v.* MOTT.

DALBY *v.* Same.

Nov. 7.

THE Plaintiffs became the Defendant's bail to the sheriff in an action at the suit of *Field,* and being sued on the bail bond, in *November* 1814, compromised by paying 10*s.* in the pound. On *January* 14th, 1815, the Defendant was declared a bankrupt, and on the 31st *January* was arrested at the Plaintiffs' suit, (the time of commencing which did not appear,) to recover

The Court will not on motion exonerate bail upon the ground that the cause of action for which they are bail, is money paid for their principal,

who is a bankrupt, by his sureties, who therefore might have proved under the commission by 49 *G.* 3. *c.* 121. *s.* 8.

Bail to the sheriff are not sureties within the statute 49 *G.* 3. *c.* 121. *s.* 8.

Z 3

the

the sums they had paid as bail. The Defendant on
13th *May* 1815, obtained his certificate. *Onslow* Serjt.
stated that the Defendant had given bail to the present action, whom he moved to exonerate, on the
ground that under the stat. 49 *G.* 3. *c.* 121. *s.* 8. the
sums paid by the Plaintiffs might be proved under
the commission, and were therefore barred by the certificate. The circumstances therefore furnished a ground
of defence to the Defendant by way of plea, *puis darrein
continuance*, and where that was the case, the Court
would equally, as in the case of a defence by *auditâ
querelâ*, extend a summary relief upon motion.

The *Court* held that the title of the bail to relief was
by no means sufficiently clear to induce them to decide
the case upon an extra judicial motion, thereby leaving
to the Plaintiff no appeal by a writ of error: if the
bail thought they had any ground for it, they must
pursue their regular remedy.

On the 7th of *November*, the Plaintiffs having obtained judgment, the Defendant was rendered to the
Fleet in discharge of his bail, and *Onslow* Serjt. in this
term obtained a rule *nisi* to discharge the Defendant
out of custody, upon a statement that the Plaintiffs
paid the money after the Defendant had become a
bankrupt.

Best Serjt. on a subsequent day shewed cause against
the last-mentioned rule: he contended that the bail
were not, within the act 49 *G.* 3. *c.* 121. *s.* 8., at the
time of the bankruptcy sureties for or liable to any
debt of the bankrupt, they were only bound for his
appearance.

The *Court* interposing, called on *Onslow* to support
his rule, who contended, that though the bond was
con-

conditioned only for the appearance of the Defendant, yet the Court would look to its practical effect, which was to make them liable to the debt, inasmuch as the sheriff's bail have no power to take and render the Defendant; but if he do not appear, the bond is forfeited; and therefore, though they are not in terms sureties for the debt, they are "liable to the debt." The statute intended a liability before the bankruptcy, and a payment subsequent to it, both of which were here found.

GIBBS C. J. The counsel for the Defendant has put this on the only ground on which it could be placed, but we do not think that bail to the sheriff can be sureties for the parties under the meaning of this act. The liability is to the sheriff, and the condition is, for the Defendant's appearance according to the exigency of the writ. Nor is this our opinion only, but we have communicated with the Judges of the Court of King's Bench, and they are of opinion with us, that this is not a suretyship within the meaning of this act, and the rule on both actions must therefore be

Discharged.

HETHERINGTON v. HOBSON.

Nov. 7.

ONE ground on which *Onslow* Serjt. moved to set aside a declaration for irregularity, was, that the notice of declaration did not apprise the Defendant of the amount of the damages laid. The Court, after inquiry of the officers, held that it was unnecessary to mention the damages in the notice of declaration, such a practice never yet having been heard of.

A notice of declaration needs not to state the damages laid.

Rule refused on that point.

Nov. 8.   DAUBUZ *v.* MORSHEAD, Bart.

It is no defence
to an action
on a bill of
exchange, that
the Plaintiff
sues in trust
for an alien
enemy.

THIS was an action upon a bill of exchange for
2020*l.*, drawn by Sir *John Morshead*, Bart. deceased, at *Verdun*, where he had during the late war
been detained by the *French* government, and accepted
by the Defendant, his son, in favour of *Boras Barti*,
and indorsed to the Plaintiff. Upon the trial of the
cause, at the sittings at *Guildhall* after *Trinity* term
1815, before *Gibbs* C. J., one line of defence taken, and
proved, was, that as to all the contents of the bill, except 8*ol.*, the Plaintiff was only a trustee for an alien
enemy. *Gibbs* C. J., without pronouncing what would
become of the money when recovered, and whether the
crown might or might not lay hands on it, thought the
Plaintiff entitled to recover the whole amount, and the
jury accordingly found a verdict for the Plaintiff.

Lens Serjt. now moved to set aside the verdict, and
have a new trial, not impugning the direction of the
Chief Justice, but upon an affidavit that the bill was
given, as to all, except 8*ol.*, for a gaming debt; but
his affidavit stating only information and belief, and
there being evidence that the Plaintiff had by letter
asked for time, and been indulged for several years,
the Court

                                        Refused the rule.

EYRE v. WALSH.

Nov. 8.

VAUGHAN Serjt. moved to set aside a writ of *capias* for a supposed irregularity, which was, that the year was stated in figures; and not in words at length. This had been held fatal in the case of *Grojan* v. *Lee.* (a)

In common process the year needs not to be expressed in words at length.

Per Curiam, The history of that case is, that this Court followed a previous decision of the Court of King's Bench to the same effect (b): but that case has since been overruled. The Judges of both Courts have met, and considered the question, and are of opinion, that it is not necessary that the year should be expressed in words at length.

Rule refused.

(a) *Ante,* v. 651.   & *Selw.* 119; and *Williams* v.
(b) *Pinero* v. *Hudson,* 1 *Maule*   *Say, ante,* v. 652. *n.*

BROOKSBY, Clerk, v. WATTS.

Nov. 8.

THIS was an action brought to recover a sum of money due as a composition for tythes due to the Plaintiff in right of his benefice, and retained by the Defendant. The Plaintiff proved an account settled between the Defendant and himself for the preceding year, whereby it appeared that the Defendant had paid money for the several tythes of that year, which was

A parishioner who has compounded with the parson one year for his tythes, and has not determined the composition, cannot set up as a defence to an

action for the next year's composition-money, that the Plaintiff is *simoniacus.*

sufficient

1815.

BROOKSBY,
Clerk,
v.
WATTS.

sufficient to raise the inference that a composition subsisted, and there was no proof of any notice to determine it. The defence relied on was, that the Plaintiff
had obtained possession of his benefice by simony, to
which he was himself a party. But *Le Blanc* J. rejected the evidence of the simony upon the ground that
there had been a composition for the tythes between the
Plaintiff and the Defendant, which was not yet determined, and the verdict passed for the Plaintiff.

Shepherd, Solicitor-General, now moved to set aside
the verdict, and have a new trial. According to many
authorities, (which the Court relieved him from citing,
as being clear law,) the simony would be an answer to
a suit for tythes in specie, or to an action for not setting
out tythes, and an action for money due upon a composition could not upon principle be distinguished from
the two former. And the principles which governed
the case of *Cook* v. *Loxley,* 5 *Term Rep.* 4. in an action
for the use and occupation of glebe lands, could not be
extended beyond the case of land, to which tythes could
not in all points be assimilated.

GIBBS C. J. I am of opinion that the decision of
the learned Judge was perfectly right, and that the present case is not distinguishable on principle from the
case cited of use and occupation for glebe land belonging to a benefice to which the lessor had been simoni-
acally presented. The Defendant in this action has
undertaken to the Plaintiff, that if he is permitted to
retain his tythes, he will pay the Plaintiff a competent
sum of money in lieu of them. He has been permitted
to retain them, and when he is called upon to pay the
money, he carps at the Plaintiff's title to the tythes.
The answer to the objection, I think, is, that the Defendant has enjoyed the consideration and had the full
benefit

benefit on his side of the contract, and that the Plaintiff is therefore in like manner entitled to claim the benefit of his bargain.

1815.

BROOKSBY, Clerk, *v.* WATTS.

Rule refused.

Ex parte BONNER.   *Nov.* 9.

DURING the whole of *Easter* term 1815 notice had been affixed on the outside of the Court of Common Pleas, and left at the other places directed by the rule of Court of *Trin.* term 31 *G.* 3. of Mr. *Bonner's* intention to apply for admission as an attorney of this court in the ensuing *Trinity* term. Some doubts which had arisen whether the term of his service was sufficient, were solved upon application to a judge at chambers, but not until it was too late for him to obtain his admission in *Trinity* term. *Lens* Serjt. now moved that Mr. *Bonner* might be admitted in this present term, upon that notice, urging that the rule did not require the notice to be affixed during the term immediately previous to the term of admission, and that it had therefore been substantially complied with, by the notice given in *Easter* term.

The notice of intention to apply for admission as an attorney, required by the rule of Court Trin. term 31 G. 3, must be given during the term next immediately preceding the application.

GIBBS C. J. The intent of the rule was, that if any person knew any reason why a person applying to be admitted as an attorney, was improper for that situation, he might have an opportunity of stating it when the objection could be effectual. Any one who wished to oppose this gentleman's admission, would be induced by the notice that was given, to watch for his application during the whole of the then next succeeding term, and finding that no attempt for admission was made,

he

Ex parte
BONNER.

he would conceive the whole matter to be at an end; his vigilance would be eluded, if the gentleman could be admitted in a subsequent term.

HEATH J. It would be a dangerous precedent.

The rest of the Court concurred in

Refusing the Rule.

Nov 9.

ℒ.𝒹.𝒹 *261*.

ROBINSON v. COOK.

If the Plaintiff's counsel acquiesces in the Judge's ruling at the trial, whereby the Defendant takes a verdict without going into his case, the Plaintiff will not be afterwards permitted to move for a new trial on the ground of a misdirection.

A tender of a larger sum, requiring change, is not a good tender of a smaller sum.

A plea of tender of half a year's rent simply, is not supported by evidence of a tender of the half-year's rent, requiring the lessor to get change and pay back the property-tax.

IN replevin, and issue joined on a plea of tender of 12*l*. 10*s*. for half a year's rent, the Plaintiff's evidence before *Dallas* J. at the *Worcester Lammas* assizes 1815, was, that upon the landlord's entering the house with a bailiff, the tenant went up stairs, and returned with two bank notes, of ten pounds, and two pounds, and two guineas, which he laid on a table before the lessor, saying, "There is your rent, take your rent, and give me my change." After a little interval, he produced a receipt for landlord's property-tax, and said that amount must be deducted, and added to the change. The lessor stated no objection to the manner of tender, but after the money had lain an hour on the table, went away without taking it, and his bailiff made a distress. For the Defendant no objection was taken to the sum being partly in bank notes, but it was objected that no tender was proved; first, because the precise sum was not tendered, nor could be had, unless the lessor would give change, which he was not bound to do, *Betterbee* v. *Davis* (a); for if he might be required to

(a) 3 *Campb.* 70.

give

give change for a two pound note, so might he for a note of 50,000*l.*; secondly, that the qualification subjoined to the tender before the lessor had accepted it, made it a tender, not of 12*l.* 10*s.*, as averred by the plea, but of 12*l.* 10*s.* deducting the property-tax, and so a fatal variance. The counsel for the Plaintiff suggesting no other distinction on the first point between the case cited and this, than that there the money was in the hand, and, here on the table, *Dallas* J., thinking the locality of the money immaterial, held both objections valid, in which the Plaintiff's counsel acquiesced, and a verdict passed for the Defendant without the latter going into his case.

Heywood Serjt. now moved to set aside the verdict and have a new trial, upon the ground that the tender of a greater sum was a good tender for the less. *Wade's* case (*a*) had, he said, been misconceived by *Le Blanc* J. in the case cited, for where the tender was of two *Spanish* double pistoles, and five shillings in *Spanish* silver, and the residue only of the 250*l.* in silver, it was impossible that the party should receive the precise sum of 250*l.* without giving change, yet the third resolution is, that if a man tenders more than he ought to pay, the tender is good: for *omne majus continet in se minus,* and the other ought to accept so much as is due to him, *quando plus fit quam fieri debet, videtur etiam illud fieri quod faciendum est. Et in majore summâ continetur minor.*

The *Court* inclined to think both objections good, but peremptorily refused, after the points had been abandoned by the Plaintiff's counsel at the trial, and the Defendant thereby precluded from going into his case, to permit them to be now even mooted; and

(*a*) 5 *Co.* 115. *a.* ✓

Chambre

1815.
ROBINSON
v.
COOK.

Chambre J. observed that the plea stated a tender of the whole; the tender proved was of the whole *minus* the property-tax.

Rule refused.

Confer Tinckler v. *Prentice, ante,* iv. 549.

Nov. 9.

BUFE *v.* TURNER and Others.

The Plaintiff having one of several warehouses, next but one to a boat-builder's shop which took fire, on the same evening, after that fire was apparently extinguished, gave instructions, by an extraordinary conveyance, for insuring that warehouse, then having others uninsured, but without apprizing the insurers of the neighbouring fire. Though the terms of insurance did not expressly require the communication, held that the concealment of this fact avoided the policy.

THIS was an action of covenant brought against the directors of the *Phœnix* Fire Insurance Office upon a policy of insurance, dated the 25th *July* 1814, effected by the Plaintiff on a certain warehouse in *Heligoland.* The policy referred to a letter of the Plaintiff's of 11th *July* 1814, containing the instructions for the insurance and certain conditions to the policy annexed, amongst which was, that if any person should insure his buildings or goods, and should cause the same to be described in the policy otherwise than as they really were, so as the same were charged at a lower premium than was therein proposed, such insurance should be of no force, and that persons insured should give in a particular of their losses, signed, and verified upon oath; and if there appeared any fraud, or false swearing, the claimant should forfeit his claim to restitution or payment. The Defendants, among several pleas, pleaded, 2dly, that immediately before and at the time of the writing the Plaintiff's letter referred to in the declaration, to wit, on 11th *July,* the warehouse in the declaration mentioned, and the merchandizes contained therein, being the premises intended to be insured by the policy, were in imminent peril of being consumed by fire, which the Plaintiff at the time of writing the letter very well knew; that the policy was effected upon the representation contained in the letter, but that the

Plaintiff

Plaintiff fraudulently and deceitfully, and with intent to induce the Defendants to effect the policy, before and at the time of effecting the same, concealed from the Defendants the fact that the premises were in such peril; by reason of which concealment the Defendants averred that the policy was void. The Plaintiff replied, that at the time of writing his letter, he did not know that the premises were in imminent danger of being consumed by fire, and did not fraudulently and deceitfully, and with intent to induce the Defendants to effect the policy, conceal from the Defendants the fact that the premises were in such peril. The Defendants joined issue on this replication. The cause was tried at *Guildhall*, at the sittings after *Trinity* term 1815, before *Gibbs* C. J. It appeared that the Plaintiff was possessed of two warehouses at *Heligoland*, one of which was separated by only one other building from the workshop of *Jasper* a boat-builder, wherein a fire broke out about seven o'clock in the evening of the 11th of *July*. That fire, however, was apparently extinguished in half an hour, and four persons were employed by the Plaintiff, who was a magistrate there, to watch during the night lest the fire should again break out. The Plaintiff on the same evening wrote the letter referred to in the declaration to his agent in *London*, requesting him to effect the insurance against fire for three months, of 400*l.*, upon the Plaintiff's warehouse, No. 1. situate on the *South* quarter of the lower town, between the warehouse of Mr. *John Leader* to the South, and that of Mr. *Nicolaus Peter Krohn* to the North, as also upon the coffee in casks and bags then stored in the same warehouse, value 3500*l.* The mail for *England* was to sail that day, and was then closed; but the Plaintiff procured the master of the packet-boat to take the letter with him, and put it into the post-office at *Cuxhaven*, so that the letter left *Heligoland* at a late hour on the same night,

1815.
BUFE
v.
TURNER.

night, and it reached *England* by the same packet on the 24th, and the Plaintiff's agent, on the following day, effected the policy in question. Early on the morning of the 13th à fire again broke out in the workshop of *Jasper* the boat-builder, and consumed the premises insured. The jury acquitted the Plaintiff of any fraud or dishonest design, the fire being apparently extinguished when he ordered the insurance, but thought that the circumstance of the fire on the 11th ought to have been communicated to the Defendants, who without this information did not engage on fair grounds with the Plaintiff, and for whom, under these circumstances, they gave their verdict.

Lens Serjt. now moved to set aside the verdict and have a new trial, but the Court

Refused the Rule.

Nov. 9.   SMITH v. BROWN,

Where goods, consigned to an agent to be sold on commission by a proprietor who still retains the absolute control over them, have been shipped and dispatched, but are not yet arrived, the consignor, pending the voyage, may, in pleading, still describe the sending them as a thing future and executory.

ASSUMPSIT. The Plaintiff in his first count declared, that in consideration that the Plaintiff would consign to the Defendant at *Bristol* certain deals to be sold by the Defendant for the Plaintiff on commission, the Defendant undertook to sell them, render a just account, and pay over the proceeds, and although the Plaintiff afterwards consigned, and the Defendant received, the goods on the terms aforesaid, and afterwards sold them and received the proceeds, yet the Defendant had not rendered an account, or paid over the proceeds. The second count stated, that in consideration that the Plaintiff would consign to the Defendant at *Bristol* cer-

I   tain

tain deals in the ship *Mary Ann*, in order that the Defendant might dispose of the same for the Plaintiff for
commission, the Defendant undertook, that directly the
Mary Ann should have arrived at *Bristol* with the goods,
he would write to the Plaintiff by the same day's post,
when he, the Plaintiff, might draw a bill of exchange on
the Defendant for 600*l.* on account of the goods, and
would accept the same, or, if it would be any advantage to
the Plaintiff, would get and send to the Plaintiff a short
date banker's bill; that the Plaintiff did afterwards send
the goods to the Defendant at *Bristol* by the *Mary Ann*,
to be sold on commission, that the ship arrived, and the
Defendant received them on those terms, but that the
Defendant did not write to the Plaintiff pursuant to his
undertaking; that thereupon the Plaintiff on 23 *November* drew a bill on the Defendant at two months' sight
for 589*l.* payable to the Plaintiff's order, and presented
it for acceptance, but that the Defendant refused to accept. The third count stated that in consideration that
the Plaintiff would consign the deals to the Defendant
to be sold on commission, the Defendant undertook, so
soon as he should have received the deals, to accept a
bill to be drawn by the Plaintiff on the Defendant for
600*l.* on account of the goods; that the Plaintiff afterwards consigned the goods, and the Defendant accepted them on those terms; that the Plaintiff thereupon
on 23 *November* drew on the Defendant at two months'
sight for 589*l.* to his own order, and presented the bill
for acceptance, which the Defendant refused; the fourth
count alleged that in consideration that the Plaintiff
had consigned to the Defendant at *Bristol* certain goods
to be sold on commission, the Defendant undertook to
accept a bill to be drawn on him by the Plaintiff on account of the goods, or to return such bill within a reasonable time; that the Plaintiff caused the goods to be
delivered to the Defendant, and that the Defendant re-

1815.

SMITH
v.
BROWN.

ceived them on those terms; that the Plaintiff drew on the Defendant on account for 589*l*. and presented the bill for acceptance, which the Defendant refused, nor would he return the bill within a reasonable time. The fifth count averred that in consideration that the Plaintiff had shipped and consigned to the Defendant the goods to be sold for commission, the Defendant undertook, in a reasonable time after he should have received the goods, to accept a bill to be drawn on him by the Plaintiff on account thereof, to wit for 600*l*.; that the Plaintiff caused the goods to be delivered to the Defendant and on 23d *November* drew on him at two months' sight for 589*l*. and presented the bill for acceptance, but although a reasonable time for accepting had elapsed, the Defendant would not accept. The sixth count was for not accounting and paying over the proceeds of the sale. The cause was tried at the sittings after *Trinity* term 1815, before *Gibbs* C. J. at *Guildhall*, when the Plaintiff, who resided in *London*, proved, that being in the habit of employing the Defendant to sell goods for him on commission at *Bristol*, and having received from him information that he had the opportunity of disposing of a cargo there, he shipped the deals to the Defendant by the *Mary Ann*, and on the 31st *October* wrote to him inclosing the invoice and bill of lading amounting to 721*l*., and added, " I want 600*l*., and would thank you to remit me any thing on *London* that would come due about three months. If not, I will draw at that time in manner as before." The Defendant on the 7th of *November* wrote in answer, that the Plaintiff " should not ask him so to do, until the deals were arrived, when the Plaintiff might depend on the Defendant's punctuality, and giving him every support in his power; and that the moment the *Mary Ann* arrived, the Plaintiff might depend on hearing from him." The Plaintiff on the 11th " requested the Defendant

Defendant would inform him, whether he would remit the 600l., or, if the Plaintiff might draw on him for it on the arrival of the vessel. She had sailed from *London* on 2d instant." The Defendant on the 12th rejoined, that "he would, directly the *Mary Ann* arrived, write him by the same post, when the Plaintiff might draw on him; or, if it would be any advantage to the Plaintiff, the Defendant would get him a short date banker's bill." The Plaintiff, in consequence, on the 23d of *November* drew on the Defendant for 589l. payable at two months after sight to the Plaintiff's order. This bill was presented for acceptance on the 24th, but the Defendant, after keeping it till the 10th of *December*, refused to accept it, upon the ground that the Plaintiff had over-drawn his account with them by 503l. 14s. 7d., and for the same reason refused to re-deliver the deals. The *Mary Ann* with the deals arrived at *Bristol* on 4th *December*. After verdict for the Plaintiff, *Best* Serjt. now moved to set it aside, and enter a nonsuit, upon the ground that the evidence of these letters did not prove the contract stated in any one of the counts. As to the promise, that when the *Mary Ann* arrived, the Defendant would let the Plaintiff know when he might draw on him, there was a further act to be done by the Defendant before the Plaintiff could draw on him, namely, to fix the time when the bill should be drawn; and if the Plaintiff complained of any breach in that respect, it ought to have been of his omission to fix that time. Next, if there were proof of a promise to accept any bill, it was not to accept a bill at two months' sight, but a bill at three months from the arrival of the goods in *Bristol*, as was mentioned in the letter of 31st *October*. Next, if there were evidence of a contract to accept a bill at two months' sight from the arrival of the goods in *Bristol*, neither of the counts correctly described the consideration of that contract. For the

A a 2   consider-

consideration in the 2d and 3d counts was described to be, that the Plaintiff would thereafter send the deals, whereas the evidence was, that he had then already sent the deals; there was a material distinction between a consideration executory and executed, and the Plaintiff had before the writing of that letter actually dispatched the vessel from *London* and done every thing which depended on him for delivering the goods to the Defendant. The fourth count averred a promise to accept a bill at two months' sight, for which there was no foundation in the evidence; and to both the fourth and fifth counts it might be objected, that the promise proved was in the alternative, either to accept a bill of exchange, or send a banker's note; and these counts do not state that alternative, which is necessary; for otherwise, if the Defendant had sent a good banker's note, it would have been no answer to the charge contained in these counts, though it would be a complete answer to the justice of the Plaintiff's case.

GIBBS C. J. It requires some attention to the letters, with reference to the declaration, to see whether these objections have or not any foundation. The first objection is, that the Plaintiff has mistaken his course, and sought to have a bill at two months' sight, whereas he is entitled only to a bill at three months, or to a banker's bill. The truth is, the Defendant being a creditor of the Plaintiff's, got the goods into his hands, holding out to the Plaintiff that when he got them he would give him an acceptance; but his true object was, that he might get the goods into his hands, and retain the proceeds towards his debt. This is in evidence; for when the bill is offered for acceptance, the Defendant does not object to the form of the bill, but says, the Plaintiff owes me more money than the amount of the goods. The first objection is, that there is no contract to accept: in

I   answer

answer to the Plaintiff's letter, the Defendant says,
" when the goods come, you may draw on me," which
in all mercantile language means that if the Plaintiff draws, the Defendant will accept the bill. The
2d objection is, that the contract is for accepting a bill
at three months; this originates in a misunderstanding
of the letter of 31st *October*, for the Plaintiff then says,
remit me any thing on *London* that will become due in
about three months. The Defendant's counsel ingeniously transfers this to three months after the arrival of
the deals, but that is not the intent. This is a request
which was never complied with, to send to the Plaintiff
bills due at three months from the date of that letter:
so that the bill which was drawn at two months' sight,
and which, from the date of the arrival of the deals,
would not be due till the 7th of *February*, falls due at a
later period, and is therefore more favourable to the
Defendant than would have been the bills spoken of in
this letter, which were to have only three months to run
from the 31st of *October*. So there is no defect in the
substance of the Plaintiff's request. But it is said, there
is no count which lays the contract as executory on the
part of the Plaintiff. It is, however, clear, that the
Plaintiff is continuing to send these goods, up to the
time when they get into the Defendant's hands; for up
to that time the Plaintiff has the control over them, and
is therefore still sending them. I am by no means clear
that the Plaintiff may not recover on the 5th count, for
the letter says, directly the *Mary Ann* arrives, we will
write you by the same post, when you may draw on us,
or if it would be any advantage to you, we will get you
a short date banker's bill. The option, which it should
be, was for the Plaintiff. But the breach is complete,
by not writing immediately when the cargo arrived, and
giving notice of its arrival. Therefore on all these
grounds we think the verdict may clearly be supported
on one of these counts, and that the rule must be

Refused.

1815.

(IN THE EXCHEQUER-CHAMBER.)

Nov. 11. ——————— *v.* EDMUNDS.

Interest given
on affirmance
of a judgment
in an action on
an attorney's
undertaking to
pay debt and
taxed costs on
or before a day
certain.

On the exe-
cution of a
writ of enqui-
ry, a sheriff's
jury ought to
give interest
in such cases
where the
Courts at
Westminster
would allow
it.

V. *LAWES* moved for interest on the affirmance in error of the judgment which had passed against the Defendant by default in the Court below, in an action upon a special undertaking of the Defendant, who was an attorney, in consideration of the Plaintiff's countermanding notice of trial in a certain cause, to pay on or before the first day of *June* the sum of 64*l.* and the taxed costs of that action. The sheriff's jury on executing the writ of inquiry in this case, had not given interest, and it was their practice never to give interest upon the execution of writs of inquiry, a practice which he conceived, and the Court agreed, to be erroneous.

The Court observed, that the question for their guidance, was not whether the Plaintiff had recovered interest at the trial, but whether he was entitled to recover interest, and upon this instrument they thought he was: it was the province of the Court only to carry on, in aid of the verdict, after the time of the trial, the giving of interest, which the jury cannot give for the subsequent time, because it has not then elapsed; but if the Plaintiff was entitled to take interest at the trial, though the jury did not actually give it him, the Court would give it now; and as the undertaking made the money payable on a precise day, like a note or a bill, they granted the application.

Rule absolute.

CROOK *v.* EYLES.   *Nov.* 16.

IN this action, brought against the warden of the *No action can be regularly commenced against the warden of the Fleet in the time of vacation.* Fleet for an escape, *Shepherd*, Solicitor-General, and in another action brought for the like cause against the same Defendant, *Best* Serjt., had obtained rules *nisi* for setting aside the proceedings as irregular, upon the ground that the bills had been filed in the long vacation, whereas, by the antient practice of the Court, no bill could be filed against the warden and other officers of the Court, except in term time.

Lens and *Vaughan* Serjts. in this case, and in the other *Copley* Serjt., shewed cause against these rules. The practice antiently was, that no action could be commenced either against any officer of the Court, or any prisoner, except in term time, but that practice has long been changed, and the warden stands in no better condition in that respect than other officers of the Court. It was first changed in proceeding against an attorney in the time of vacation, as mentioned by *Buller* J. in the case of *Comerford* v. *Price* (a), and the case of *Lane* v. *Wheat* (b) is express, that a bill might be filed against an attorney in vacation, in a case where it happened to be necessary, in order to save the demand from being barred by the statute of limitations; but in *Waghorn* v. *Fields* (c) the Court positively denied that the practice was confined to that peculiar instance, and ruled that it was general. Upon search in the prothonotary's office it appears that the practice of filing bills against attornies in vacation, has prevailed in this court more than 40 years. The same point was holden

(a) *Doug.* 312.   (c) *5 Term Rep.* 173.
(b) *Ib.* 313. *n.*

A a 4   in

in *Dodsworth* v. *Bowen* (*a*), and that the Plaintiff might entitle his declaration by a special memorandum. In *Heron* v. *Edwards* (*b*) the same doctrine is extended to the case of a prisoner. No case is extant as to the warden, but the reason is as strong, or stronger, as to him; for if no bill can be filed against him in the vacation, a prisoner may be let out of custody on the first day of a vacation, and if he is again found in the custody of the warden before the last day of the vacation, no action can be maintained for the escape; for before an action can be commenced, the Defendant will be provided with his plea of re-taking the prisoner on fresh suit. The Court will not countenance such an use of the warden's privilege. If an escape happens in term time, it is the Plaintiff's own folly if he will not sue immediately, and if a recaption take place before action brought, it is a bar, but otherwise not. It will be said, this advantage is a right of the warden's, but so, it was, as to the statute of limitations, a great advantage to attornies, that if the period of six years ran out during a vacation, they were discharged; but both are incidental advantages, and not to be considered as of that description, which the Court will uphold. There is no evidence that the practice in similar cases is adverse, for during the last 26 years, until the present cases arose, no action has been commenced in vacation time. The same principle will apply in this case, which was held to apply to narrow the privilege of attornies when that question first arose. The Court has jurisdiction to make any new rule for the government of their officer, which the justice of the case requires. The statute 1 *Ric.* 2. *c.* 12. shews that it very early was necessary to keep a strict watch over the conduct of the warden. By the statute 8 & 9 *W.* 3.

(*a*) 5 *Term Rep.* 325.   (*b*) 8 *Term Rep.* 643.

c. 27.

c. 27. s, 6. no retaking on fresh pursuit shall be given in evidence on the trial of any issue in any action of escape against the warden, unless the same be specially pleaded, nor shall any special plea be taken, received, or allowed, unless oath be first made in writing by the warden against whom such action shall be brought, and filed in the proper office of the respective courts, that the prisoner for whose escape such action was brought, did, without his consent, privity, or knowledge make such escape, and if such affidavit shall be false, he shall forfeit 500l. In this case no such affidavit is made, and there is very strong ground to suspect connivance; for the warden went to *Paris* after the prisoner, and brought him back, and had him here before the first day of term. If the practice contended for by the Defendant is to prevail, a person who has the rules of the *Fleet* may, if he thinks proper, take during the vacation a lodging at any of the villages round *London*, and sleep there every night and come back in the day, or he may make a tour on the continent, so long as he returns hither before the end of the vacation; so that when an action for an escape is commenced, in form against the warden, but in substance against the Defendant, who, having the rules of the prison, gives security for his abiding within the rules, and against his sureties, the prisoner's return would, according to *Bonafous* v. *Walker* (a), be a good plea: this practice ought to be checked.

Shepherd and *Best* in support of their rules, observed that it was unnecessary on the present occasion that the Defendant's affidavit should state more than it did. The case must be decided on the general principle. The books of practice say that a bill may be filed against attornies in vacation in *B. R.*, but not so in this court. The Court, it is true, may make new rules

(a) 2 *Term Rep.* 126.

of

of practice for the government of their officers, but they will not make them with a retrospective operation, A strong argument arises from the statute 8 & 9 *W.* 3. *c.* 27. that the legislature were then looking to the then existing practice of filing bills against the warden, which was always done in term only. The 12th section requires the warden to plead in eight days after the bill filed and a rule to plead given, and if he does not plead in three days after the rule is out, the Plaintiff may sign judgment, which, it may be observed, puts the warden in a worse situation than any other Defendant whatsoever: the rule to plead cannot be a rule of the preceding term; it cannot be a rule of the subsequent term. A rule to plead cannot be given but while the Court is sitting to give it; therefore the conclusion is, that the legislature were looking only to the practice of filing bills in term, and intended that they could be filed at no other time. It is true that it was intended to make the proceedings against the warden less dilatory, but it was necessary before that statute, not only to file a bill, but to deliver a declaration, and to call the warden in court, all of which steps took time; but here the statute says that neither appearance, declaration, nor call in court, all of which are necessary in the case of an attorney, shall be necessary in the case of the warden. The unavoidable consequence of that statute, if otherwise interpreted, is, that there must be a new sort of rule to plead, not a rule of court, but a rule made by a judge out of court. It would be incongruous to hold that the statute has created a new sort of proceeding; the inference rather is that the statute alluded only to a rule to plead in term. If, indeed, the prisoner is in custody when the plea is pleaded in term, the Plaintiff has all to which he is entitled.

GIBBS

GIBBS C. J.   The cases decided in the court of King's Bench, and the practice built thereon in this court, at first raised in my mind and the minds of my brethren, some degree of doubt, and I conceived that a bill might be filed against the warden in vacation; but on looking to this statute our doubts are done away. This statute regulates the proceedings in actions against the warden upon the then existing practice.   It would be the greatest injustice, if we were now to alter the practice, leaving the statute to bear against the warden, without his having the advantage of the antient practice.   The enacting part of the 12th section is, it shall be lawful for any person having cause of action against the warden of the *Fleet* prison, upon bill filed in the courts of Common Pleas or Exchequer against the said warden, a rule being given to plead thereto, to be out eight days at most after filing such bill, to sign judgment against the said warden of the *Fleet*, unless he plead to the said bill within three days after such rule is out.   The rule, then, established is, that on filing the declaration, the Plaintiff shall immediately sue out an eight-day-rule, and if the Defendant does not plead in three days after the rule is out, then the Plaintiff is entitled to judgment.   It has been justly observed by the counsel for the Defendant, that a rule must be of some term; the rule for the warden to plead cannot be of the preceding term, for the cause of action had not then existed, nor had any proceedings then been instituted; nor of the subsequent term, for the Plaintiff may obtain judgment before that term commences : therefore the statute clearly proceeds on the supposition, that the practice was confined to declaring in term-time; and it would be the greatest injustice if the practice were now to be changed.   I therefore think the proceedings must be set aside.

HEATH

HEATH J. declared himself of the same opinion. The statute of *W.* 3. was made to advance the action against the warden.

CHAMBRE J. I am of the same opinion, although, but for the statute, I should have been of a different opinion.

DALLAS J. concurred.

Lens then moved to amend the memorandum of the bill, so as to make it appear to have been filed on the first day of the term, on which day it was in fact again brought in and filed.

GIBBS C. J. The Plaintiff must file his bill again. He has chosen to file it again on the first day of this term, and to stand on both his titles. We cannot allow that. He must begin *de novo.*

Rule absolute, but without costs.

STOCK and Others *v.* EYLES.

IN this case, as in the last, a bill for an escape having been filed in the *Trinity* vacation against the warden of the *Fleet, Shepherd* Solicitor-General had obtained a rule *nisi* to set it aside for irregularity.

Bosanquet Serjt. on this day shewed cause. He conceived that the statute 9 & 10 *W.* 3. *c.* 27. contained a material clause, which had not been adverted to on the argument in the preceding case, and which shewed that the practice of filing bills against the warden had not, at the time of passing that act, been confined to term-time,

as the Court had on that argument inferred.   By the
13th section the same rule of practice is established for
declaring against a prisoner in the *Fleet*, as for declaring against the warden, viz. that a rule to plead shall
be given after declaring, to be out in eight days at most
after the delivery of a copy of the declaration, and if the
Defendant do not plead before the rule is out, the Plaintiff may sign judgment. Nevertheless, it is the acknowledged practice in this court, that a declaration may be
filed against a prisoner in the time of vacation, and the
same difficulty would arise in this case, as in the case of
the warden, that if the rule were entitled either of the
preceding or subsequent term, when judgment was to
be signed in the vacation for want of a plea, there would
be an incongruity if the eight days meant eight days to
be accounted in the vacation; but, he said, the meaning
of the statute, in that expression, was, that the rule to
plead should be a rule to plead according to the practice of the court, namely, a rule which should run only
in term time; for a rule to plead is to all intents a proceeding in term; so that the Defendant should have
eight days in bank to plead, which removed the whole
difficulty: therefore, although the bill were filed in vacation, the rule to plead might be entitled as of the last
day of the preceding, or first day of the subsequent
term, and the rule would give the Defendant time to
plead until the eighth day of the succeeding term, and
so the statute would give no facility to the signing
judgment against the warden in vacation.   Lord *Mansfield* C. J. in *Hills* v. *Henrick* (a), states the practice of
this court in respect to prisoners, namely, to file a bill
as of the preceding term, and then to deliver to, or leave
for the Defendant, being in custody, a copy of the declaration as of the preceding term, and to make an affidavit thereof; and the Court pronounced that to be

(a) 2 *Burr.* 1052.

the

the right method for the purpose of charging such a Defendant with a new suit; that is to say, that in the case of a new suit, as this is, the Plaintiff ought to file his declaration in vacation, as of the preceding term; and if this be so against a prisoner, so must it be against the marshal; and, at all events, if such was the practice, on principle it ought not to be narrowed by that statute, which was made to facilitate proceedings against the marshal. The same practice was recognised in *Heron* v. *Edwards* (a); and consequently the Court would, on a review of this statute, see that the supposed inference did not result; for the Court would construe both sections in the same manner, and would be of opinion that this bill was well filed.

The Solicitor-General, in support of his rule, urged that the substance of the Plaintiff's argument amounted only to this, that because with respect to prisoners the Court had altered the practice, therefore they would alter it as to the warden. The one was no consequence of the other. A prisoner and an officer of the court did not stand on the same footing. Before the statute of *William,* a Plaintiff might institute a suit in vacation against a prisoner, but not so against the warden.

The Court interposing, relieved the Solicitor-General from further argument.

GIBBS C. J. If the Court from inadvertence had arrived at a false conclusion on a former day, they would have been glad to be set right; but it seems that this argument goes entirely beside the ground which the Court then took. It was never before disputed, that when the statute of *Wm.* 3. passed, the practice was,

(a) 8 *Term Rep.* 643.

that

that prisoners and officers of the court should be charged
with a declaration only in term-time. The change suggested, was, that as justice might require actions to be
commenced in the time of vacation, the Court would,
by some means, permit Plaintiffs to commence actions,
to prevent the failure of justice: but the Court have in
some cases said, it is only for the furtherance of justice,
and not to interfere with any rights of the parties
against whom the rule is made. When this act passed,
the warden had at common law a defence to actions for
escapes, of fresh suit and retaking; and as the practice
stood before the statute, no action could be commenced
but in term-time. The legislature thought that the
practice should not be altered, and the Court therefore
in the former case were of opinion that no bill could be
filed against the warden except in term-time; and they
were fortified in this conclusion, by finding that no instance could be produced of a bill filed against the
warden in vacation, though there are numerous instances of bills filed against other officers, and against
prisoners. Consequently we held that the practice as
to the warden continued unaltered, and the arguments
which are now urged do not shake our opinion.

HEATH J. I am of the same opinion. It would be
of great injustice to the warden, if the Court should
hold that an action could be commenced against him in
vacation, in consequence of any modern practice which
has prevailed with respect to prisoners and other officers,
of filing a bill in vacation, that practice being, that the
bill may be filed as of the preceding term, the consequence whereof would be to deprive the warden of that
defence which he before had.

CHAMBRE and DALLAS Js. concurring, the rule was
made
                                        Absolute.

Nov. 17.   CAMPION and Others *v.* CRAWSHAY.

The Court will, after judgment by default, refer it to the prothonotary to compute the rent due on a covenant.

But not so in debt on simple contract for rent, or use and occupation.

AFTER judgment by default in an action of covenant, in which no breach was assigned except the nonpayment of rent, *Best* Serjt. now obtained a rule to refer it to the prothonotary to compute the rent due for which final judgment should be signed, instead of sending the case to a writ of inquiry, on the authority of *Byrom* v. *Johnson* (a). He had moved this on a former day, when his affidavit not disclosing whether the action were debt or covenant, nor whether the rent was due on a lease under seal or a parol lease, the Court, contemplating the possibility that it might be the latter, had refused the application.

                                                    Rule absolute.

(a) 8 *Term Rep.* 410.

Nov. 18.   WILLINGHAM *v.* MATTHEWS.

The insolvent debtors' court is such a court as privileges parties and witnesses attending, from arrest, *eundo, morando, et redeundo.*

SHEPHERD Solicitor-General had obtained on a former day a rule *nisi* to deliver up the bail-bond to be cancelled, which had been given by the Defendant, who had been followed by a sheriff's officer and arrested at the Plaintiff's suit, as he was returning from the insolvent debtors' court in *Westminster*, where, at the instance of the Plaintiff, who was his own attorney, he had been attending as a Plaintiff for the purpose of opposing the discharge of *Bragge*, a debtor to himself, but he had not been examined.

                                                    Vaughan

Vaughan Serjt. shewed cause on an affidavit of the officer who took the Defendant, that the Defendant resided in *Crown-street*, *Westminster*, and that when the Defendant left the court, he went to *Tufton-street*, which was not the direct way to *Crown-street*, and in his way passed through *Prince's-street*, and went into a cutler's shop there. It was incumbent on a party privileged by reason of his attendance on a court, to return immediately home, and not to transact his own business by the way.

The Solicitor-General cited *Lightfoot* v. *Cameron* (a) as a much stronger case than this, where the privileged party had unnecessarily remained in court from the morning till five in the afternoon, and had then adjourned to a tavern to dinner. The merely entering a shop on the way, would not destroy the Defendant's privilege.

Per Curiam. No doubt this party ought to be discharged. That this is such a court as privileges parties and witnesses who are attending there from arrest, considering that the Defendants there are debtors against whom judgments have been pronounced in courts of record, and that they are discharged there under the authority of a court erected by the legislature for that purpose, we feel no doubt. If, then, that is the case, never was there a stronger instance, nor one in which justice more demanded the discharge of the Defendant, than the present case. The Plaintiff decoys the Defendant to the court, for there can be no doubt, that to arrest him was one of the Plaintiff's objects: the Defendant does attend the court, is not examined, in his way home, he is arrested. The officer swears the

(a) 2 *W. Bl.* 1113.

Defendant was not going the direct way home. That ought not to be left to be measured by the conscience of the officer. A party is not bound to go the nearest way home; and if he do not abuse the privilege for the purpose of going about other business of his own, of which no evidence appears on these affidavits, we must say that he is entitled to his discharge.

Rule absolute.

FREEN and Another, Assignees of YOUNG, a Bankrupt, v. COOPER.

In an action by the assignees of a bankrupt for a rescue, the Plaintiffs were permitted, after two terms, to amend the declaration, which stated the wrong to be done to themselves, by stating the wrong to be done to the provisional assignees.

Whether the assignees of a bankrupt can sue in tort for a tort committed against the estate of the provisional assignees, quære.

THIS was an action for the rescous of goods distrained upon the estate which had belonged to the bankrupt, for rent due from his tenant, and the declaration stated the distress as made by the Plaintiffs, and alleged the wrong as done to their possession; it was now discovered that the tort had been committed before the assignment to the Plaintiffs, during the time that the effects were vested in the provisional assignees; whereupon *Marshall* Serjt., although two terms had elapsed, now moved to amend by adding other counts founded upon this state of facts.

Best Serjt. shewed cause in the first instance, contending that this amendment was equivalent to an entire new declaration for a new cause of action, which after two terms was not admissible.

Marshall. It is the same cause of action, only differently described.

GIBBS C. J. The rule not to amend after two terms applies only to the adding a count for a new cause of action,

action, because after two terms the Plaintiff is out of court unless he has declared, and cannot declare without a new writ: but here it is only desired to state the same cause of action in a different way, and the rule does not apply. (a)

CHAMBRE J. It is on the Plaintiffs' own risk. I have very great doubt whether the action can be maintained on the amended declaration. This action is in tort, and the tort is committed against the provisional assignees, before the Plaintiffs' estate commenced.

> Rule absolute on payment of costs,
> the Defendant having time given
> him to plead de novo.

(a) See *Brown* v. *Crump*, *ante*, vi. 300.

DOE, on the Demise of THOMPSON, v. PITCHER and Others. (a)

THIS was an ejectment brought to recover a farm called the *Meeting-house* farm in the parish of *Rickmansworth*: on the trial at the *Hertford* spring assizes 1815, before *Chambre* J. a verdict was found for the Defendants, with liberty for the Plaintiff to move to set it aside and enter a verdict for the Plaintiff. The Court, upon the motion, in *Easter* term 1815, directed the facts to be stated in a case, which in substance was, that *Jane Wilson*, being seised in fee of all

A grant of lands in trust perpetually to repair, and, if need be, rebuild a vault and tomb standing on the land, and permit the same to be used as a family vault for the donor and her family, is not a charitable use within the statute 9 G. 2. c. 36.

If there be in a deed one limitation to an use which is a charitable use within the statute 9 G. 2. c. 36., that statute does not therefore avoid other limitations in the same deed, which are not within the act.

(a) See a like case between the same parties in B. R., 3 *Maule &
Selw.* 407.

the

the premises, by lease and release, reciting that the meeting-house and burial ground, parcel, &c. (except the vault and tomb thereinafter mentioned,) had for several years been, and then were used by a society of Quakers, at the rent of 2*l.* 10*s.*, and that the burial vault and tomb over the same, standing upon the burial ground, had been used as a burial vault for the family of the relessor, and that she was desirous that the meeting-house and burial ground, (except the vault and tomb, and the ground next the north side and east end thereof for 6 feet, and all ways thereto in and over the burial ground,) should so long as the society of Quakers should think proper to hold the same under the terms and conditions thereinafter mentioned, be held by them accordingly, as a meeting-house and a burial ground, and the relessor was also desirous that the family burial vault and tomb should for ever be kept in repair for the burial place of the relessor and such of her family as should chuse or require to be interred therein, and for effectuating those purposes, the relessor was desirous of conveying the messuage or farm, and also the meeting-house, burial ground, vault, and tomb, to the uses, &c. thereinafter limited; for effectuating these purposes, and in consideration of 10*s.*, the relessor, according to her estate and interest therein, and as far only as she could or lawfully might, granted and released to *Mavor* and *Smith*, the *Meeting-house* farm, with the several parcels of land thereunto belonging, and also the meeting-house, and burial ground, and burial vault and tomb standing thereon, to hold the same to *Mavor* and *Smith* and their heirs, to the uses, upon the trusts, and for the intents and purposes thereinafter declared, viz. as to the meeting-house and burial ground, except the vault and tomb, and the ground next the north side and east end thereof for six feet, to the use of *Mavor* and *Smith*, their heirs and assigns, so long as the meeting-house and burial ground

(except

(except as excepted) should be used by the society of
Quakers, as and for their meeting-house and burial
ground, and so long as they should pay to *Mavor* and
Smith, their heirs and assigns, the clear yearly rent
of two pounds and ten shillings at *Michaelmas*, and
also should completely repair the meeting-house
and the walls, &c., and fences of the burial ground:
it being the intent of the relessor, and the aforesaid
conditional limitation to the use of *Mavor* and *Smith*
being upon trust, that the meeting-house and burial
ground should thenceforth be held by the society of
Quakers in the same manner as the same had for several
years past been used by them, provided they paid the
yearly rent, and kept the meeting-house and burial
ground in repair as aforesaid; and after the determination of that conditional estate, as to the meeting-house
and burial ground, and from and immediately after the
execution of those presents, as to all other the premises, to the use and behoof of, and as to the yearly
rent of two pounds and ten shillings during the continuance of that conditional limitation, in trust for,
Mavor, his heirs and assigns, subject to the proviso or
condition thereinafter declared; and immediately after
the determination of that conditional estate, to the only
use of, and in trust for *Smith*, his heirs and assigns for
ever. Provided, and it was thereby declared, that the
estate and interest thereinbefore limited, in severalty to
Mavor, his heirs and assigns, of and in the premises,
were so limited upon express condition that he and
his heirs should at all times thereafter repair and maintain the vault and tomb, and all the brick work,
stone work, rails, pales, and fences thereto belonging,
and if need were, should completely and entirely rebuild
the same, agreeably to their present dimensions, and
also should at all times permit the same to be used as a
family burial vault for the interment of the relessor or

any of her family, who might desire, or be required to be interred therein. And in case *Mavor* and his heirs should at any time thereafter neglect to repair, or, if need were, to rebuild the vault or tomb, or should not permit the vault to be used as a family burial vault for the interment of the relessor, or any of her family who might desire or be required to be interred therein, then the use, estate, and interest thereinbefore limited in severalty to *Mavor*, and all benefit and advantage thereof, should thenceforth cease. Provided that *Smith*, and his heirs or assigns, might enter the burial ground to view the condition of the vault and tomb, and of all wants of reparation give notice to *Mavor*, his heirs or assigns, to repair all such decays; and provided that in case the society of Quakers should at any time thereafter, during the trust thereinbefore mentioned for them, and during the lives or life of the relessors *Mavor* and *Smith*, or of the survivors or survivor of them, or within 21 years after the death of the survivor, be desirous of erecting a new meeting-house for their use upon part of the ground thereby released, near the burial ground, instead of repairing the then present meeting-house, then the society might make use of any part of the orchard belonging to the farm, and next adjoining to the west side of the burial ground, so as not to exceed in any part from east to west twenty-five feet from the then present west fence of the burial ground, for the purpose of making commodious ways to the same. And immediately after erecting the same, such new erected meeting-house should be, go, and remain to such and the same uses, upon such and the same trusts, and subject to the same conditions and limitations, as were therein before expressed and declared respecting the then present meeting-house; and then the present meeting-house, and the ground whereon it stood, should thenceforth be, go, and re-

main

main to such and the same uses, &c. as were therein declared concerning the messuage and farm, other than the land whereon the new meeting-house should be erected, freed, and absolutely discharged from the trust therein before declared concerning the society of Quakers. The indentures of lease and release were sealed and delivered by the relessor in the presence of two credible witnesses, more than 12 calendar months before her death, and were duly enrolled in Chancery. The relessor, by her will subsequently made, and duly attested to pass real estates, devised all her freehold property to *G. Thomson,* the lessor of the Plaintiff, in fee, and on the 9th *October* 1810 died without altering or revoking her will, and to the time of her death received the rents of the *Meeting-house* farm, and of the meeting-house and burial ground: *Mavor* since her death had become a bankrupt, and the Defendants were his assignees. The question was, whether the premises in the declaration mentioned passed by the deeds before stated.

Best Serjt. contended that the release of these premises was void, and that they therefore passed by the will of *J. Wilson* to her devisee. It is admitted that the meeting-house, and burial ground did not pass by the deed, because they are given upon uses, which are, within the meaning of the statute 9 *G.* 2. *c.* 36., charitable uses; the third section of which, " absolutely an-" nulling and avoiding all gifts, grants, conveyances, " appointments, assurances, transfers, and settlements " whatsoever of any lands made in any other manner " or form than by that act is directed," vacates not merely the estate which is limited contrary to that act, but the entire deed, and all matters therein contained, and therefore avoids this conveyance of the messuage and farm, and the future use of the present meeting-

B b 4   house,

house, which was intended to arise in case of the erection of a new one.   This construction of the statute is
supported by the case of *Norton* v. *Simmes* (a), where it
is laid down.   " Upon the statute 23 *H.* 6. if a sheriff
" will take a bond for a point against that law, and also
" for a due debt, the whole bond is void, for the letter
" of the statute is so; for a statute is a strict law, but
" the common law doth divide according to common
" reason, and having made that void which is against
" law, lets the rest stand."   But further, the uses
declared of the premises are void, because the reservation of the 2*l.* 10*s.* rent is a limitation for the benefit of the donor, prohibited by this statute, and the
conditional limitation over to *Smith*, a person claiming
under the donor, in case *Mavor* should not repair the
tomb, is also prohibited by the first section.   This too is
not a grant of one part for a legal purpose, and of another
part for a prohibited purpose, but the whole purports to
be conveyed for the prohibited use; it is "for effectuating
the purposes aforesaid," that the deed conveys the meeting-house farm, as well as the meeting-house and the
other premises; and another part of the deed shews that
it was necessary to convey the whole for this purpose;
for the donor has an ulterior object, namely, that if the
Quakers shall elect another spot for a new meeting-
house, they shall be at liberty so to do.   The whole of
the premises is therefore liable to this prohibited use,
until the Quakers have made their election; the whole is
also liable to the repairs of the tomb and vault in case
the rent of 2*l.* 10*s.* be insufficient for that purpose.

Bosanquet Serjt. *contrà*.   It has not been attempted
now, since the decision to the contrary in the King's
Bench (b), to argue that the condition for keeping the
tomb and vault in repair is a charitable use.   Neither

(a) *Hob.* 14.   (b) 3 *Maule & Selw.* 407.

is

is there any ground for the position that because the
farm is conveyed by a deed which does contain a charitable use, the whole is void, either on the words of this
statute, or on general principles. The general principle is, that if any void limitation be mixed up with
good matter, whether against a statute, or against the
common law, the good part stands, the rest is void.
Pigot's case (*a*). But it is said, if there be a statute,
the statute over-rides all. That depends on the words
of the statute. The statute of 23 *H. 6.* declares all
bonds shall be void if not made in a certain form. A
bond is one entire thing, and creates one entire debt.
It is there said the bond shall be void, but this statute
does not say that the deed shall be void, but all gifts,
grants, conveyances, appointments, assurances, transfers, and settlements shall be void, which must be taken
reddendo singula singulis. There are many cases upon
charitable uses in Chancery, but none wherein the whole
settlement has been set aside. The cases which have
been decided on the property-tax acts, are much
stronger than this, the statute is, that all covenants and
contracts for payment of any rent or interest without
allowing the deduction, shall be void ; yet it was held in
Howe v. *Singe* (*b*) that the covenant was only void *pro
tanto.* It would be most mischievous, if a different
doctrine were to prevail. *Adams* and *Lambert's* case (*c*),
on the statute 1 *Ed. 6. c.* 14. which gave to the crown
lands given for superstitious purposes. " If land of the
yearly value of 20*l. per annum* be given upon condition,
or to the purposes following, to find a priest to pray
for souls, and that the priest shall have for his salary 10*l.*,
and to distribute between 20 poor men and women
other 10*l.* yearly for ever for their sustentation, in that
case the king shall have but the 10*l.* limited to the priest,

1815.

DOE
v.
PITCHER.

(*a*) 11 *Co.* 27. *b.*
(*b*) 15 *East*, 443.

(*c*) 4 *Co.* 106. 111.

and

and not the land; but if the same land had been given to find a priest, and for the maintenance of 20 poor men, in that case the king should have all the land." If, then, the limitation of the farm be distinct from the limitation of the burial ground to a superstitious use, there is no pretence for saying that the deed is void. There is no pretence in this case to say that the one is so mixed with the other, that the Court cannot separate them. The deed begins with a general recital of the purposes of the party. The heir at law has recovered the meeting-house and burial ground, inasmuch as the limitation was void as to that, and with it is gone the condition for rebuilding the meeting-house elsewhere. The releasee has this farm subject to repairing the tomb of the settler, which is not a charitable use, and therefore the statute need not be complied with in respect to that limitation; and it is no objection that there is a reservation or limitation over for the benefit of the donor: the first answer is satisfactory, that the repair of the tomb was no charitable use, and therefore no matter whether a condition were affixed to that estate or not. The 2l. 10s. was not reserved out of the farm, nor out of the tomb, but was to be paid by the Quakers out of the meeting-house. It is said there is a limitation to *Smith :* of the farm there is so. But it is no condition applied to the meeting-house: it is no reservation out of the charitable use; it is a condition applied to the limitation of a farm, which the party may well annex to it. A devise for keeping in repair a person's own house, or the fences of his field, is not a charitable use. All the cases respecting charitable uses have been, where some public benefit has been intended, not for the testator's own benefit. A devise (a) of a botanical garden near *Chelsea,* to be kept up for ever, was held a cha-

(a) *Townley* v. *Bedwell,* 6 *Ves.* 194.

ritable

ritable use, because the testator had said in his
will that he thought it would be a public benefit.
The doctrine held in *Durour* v. *Motteux* (a) cannot be
applied to this case. That was a bequest of 1200*l.* to
be laid out in the purchase of lands, part of which were
to be a fund for a perpetual annuity of 10*l. per ann.* to
a minister to preach a sermon once a year to his memory, which the Court held to be a charitable use, and
also to keep his tomb-stone in repair, and the inscrip-
tions legible thereon and upon the stone against the wall
reciting the gift; and the Court held the latter part was
so mixed up with the other that it could not be distinguished, and therefore was void for the whole: but it
never occurred to the Court that the whole was void
because a part was. Even supposing this condition of
maintaining the vault and tomb to be contrary to the
statute, it falls within the principle that the illegal condition is void, and the grant of the land good, for this
not being a case within the statute of *Ed. 6.*, the land
does not go to the king.

Best, in reply. The whole of the limitations are to a
charitable use. *Durour* v. *Motteux* is in point for the
Plaintiff. It is said, this is a selfish use. But the
keeping a tomb for the donor's self and his family, is
not like the keeping up a house for himself and his family: it is the perpetuating an idle vanity, as Lord
Hardwicke expresses it, but it is not therefore the less a
charitable use. The purchasing masses for the soul of
a donor is as selfish as this, yet it does not therefore
cease to be a superstitious use. In *Pigot's* case, where
Lord *Coke* speaks of conditions which are against law,
it must be intended of common law; if they were against
a statute, it would have been so expressed. The coun-

(a) 1 *Ves.* 320.

scl

1815.

DOE
v.
PITCHER.

sel for the Defendant has not impugned the distinction between instruments void by common law and those which are void by statute. *Norton* v. *Simmes* has been recently recognized in *Greenwood* v. *The Bishop of London* (a); and though there was clear simony, the Court held that it only vacated what was simoniacal, and they maintained what was good. The property-tax act does not avoid the whole assurance: it makes void only the " covenant or contract." It is said, if a part be given to superstitious uses, and part not, the first only goes to the king; but that is by reason of the words of the statute, which are, that so much as is given for superstitious uses shall pass to the king. The whole deed therefore is to all intents void. No answer has been given to the second ground. At all events the Plaintiff is entitled to a verdict; for if the use declared of the meeting-house is a charitable use, then the ground destined for a future meeting-house is directly given for a charitable use, and the Plaintiff must recover for that: if otherwise, the society of Quakers may immediately take that land and apply it to that use: but in truth the gift is all one, and the limitations not several but one, and the Plaintiff must therefore recover the whole; at most the uses are several. The preamble of the statute 43 *Eliz. c.* 4. has been mentioned as an enumeration of charitable uses, which contains none for the sustentation of tombs; but the inference is not fair, for that statute is restricted to charitable uses strictly so called, but the preamble of this act shews that it meant to go beyond that line. The mischief intended to be hereby remedied was the rendering property inalienable, to which this grant expressly tends, for the benefit of no person whatever, but only to perpetuate the vanity of this lady and her posterity, which is directly within the mischief.

(a) *Ante,* v. 727.

GIBBS

GIBBS C. J. This is an ejectment brought for the recovery of certain premises in *Hertfordshire*. As to a part of the premises, namely, the meeting-house and burial ground, I am now to take it, that they have been already recovered by ejectment, and that this action is brought for the residue; and the question is, whether the deed be void as to that, by the statute 9 *G.* 2. *c.* 37. It is argued to be void on three grounds. First, if it be void as to part, it is said, it must be void as to the whole. If the objection had been derived from the common law, it is admitted, that would not be the consequence; but it is urged that the statute makes the whole deed void. As the counsel for the Plaintiff puts it, there is no difference between a transaction void at common law, and void by statute: if an act be prohibited, the construction to be put on a deed conveying property illegally, is, that the clause which so conveys it, is void equally, whether it be by statute or common law : but it may happen that the statute goes further, and says that the whole deed shall be void to all intents and purposes; and when that is so, the Court must so pronounce, because the legislature has so enacted, and not because the transaction prohibited is illegal. I cannot find in this act any words which 'make the entire deed void. The words are, " all gifts, grants, conveyances, appointments, assurances, transfers, and settlements whatsoever of any lands, or of any estate or interest therein, shall be absolutely and to all intents void." I think this grant of that interest in land, which by the terms of the grant is to be applied to a charitable use, is void ; but I think the statute makes nothing more void, and that the deed, so far as it passes other lands, not to a charitable use, is good. Therefore that argument fails. The Plaintiff's counsel next insists that the residue of the land is applicable to a charitable use, because the condition is that the donee shall keep in repair a

vault

1815.

DOE
v.
PITCHER.

vault to receive the body of the donor or any of her family. We agree with the Court of King's Bench that this is not a charitable use, and the Plaintiff's counsel seemed to feel the argument that this was not a charitable use, and therefore tried to argue that this was a *quasi* charitable use, and that the statute meant to include all provisions tending to perpetuities. It certainly means to provide against perpetuities in limitations of lands for charitable uses, but it is confined to those uses. It is next urged that the conveyance is void, because it is subject to the right of the society of Quakers, to take any part of the land when they please. It is a sufficient answer, that no part is now appropriated to that purpose, and that that part of the deed being determined to be void by the statute, in which we agree, they never can possess it; there must therefore be

Judgment for the Defendant.

ing. 341.
Nov. 21.

MILLER v. PARNELL.

If a sheriff makes a seizure under a writ of *fieri facias*, though the Plaintiff cannot take the Defendant in execution under a writ of *capias ad satisfaciendum*, till the writ of *fieri facias* is returned, though he abandons the seizure of the goods.

LENS Serjt. had on a former day obtained a rule *nisi* to discharge out of custody the Defendant, who had been taken in execution under a writ of *capias ad satisfaciendum*, upon the ground that the Plaintiff had previously sued out a writ of *fieri facias*, under which the sheriff had seized goods of greater value than the amount of the judgment, which writ was not yet returned.

Best Serjt. on this day shewed cause against the rule, upon the ground that the Plaintiff had not sold the goods taken under the writ of *fieri facias*, but had after some weeks abandoned that process, which he contended that he was at liberty to do, and thereupon to

sue

sue out his writ of *fieri facias*. It was the common
practice, he said, to sue out a writ of *fieri facias* and a
writ of *capias ad satisfaciendum* together. The merely
seizing and abandoning the property, is not such an
execution of the process, as needs delay the issuing of
the second writ till the first is returned.

Lens, in support of his rule, contended that the writ
of *fieri facias*, while unreturned, would always be a sufficient plea for the Plaintiff or the sheriff in trespass for
the seizure of the goods, and that it therefore ought to
be returned, because the Plaintiff ought not in justice
to be furnished at the same time with a legal justification for taking and detaining both the goods and the
body. Even a *testatum fieri facias* to levy the residue,
cannot legally be sued out before the return of the first
writ (a). The Plaintiff is bound first to state to the
Court what he has done under the first writ, and obtain
their permission to abandon it, before he can sue out
the further process.

Per Curiam. No doubt, a Plaintiff having sued out
a writ of *fieri facias*, may, if he pleases, omit to execute
the *fieri facias*, and take out a writ of *capias ad satisfaciendum*, and execute that before the *fieri facias* is returned or returnable. But there is also no doubt that
if the Plaintiff does execute his *fieri facias*, he cannot
have a writ of *capias ad satisfaciendum* till the *fieri facias*
is completely executed and returned. This is a middle
case. So far as the Defendant is concerned, the goods,
to the extent of their value, have been levied; and the
question is, whether the Plaintiff, after taking them,
may change his mind, and sue out a writ of *capias ad
satisfaciendum* without returning his former writ. If

(a) *Coppendale* v. *Debonnaire, Barnes,* 213.

this

any of her family, who might desire, or be required
to be interred therein. And in case *Mavor* and his
heirs should at any time thereafter neglect to repair, or,
if need were, to rebuild the vault or tomb, or should
not permit the vault to be used as a family burial vault
for the interment of the relessor, or any of her family
who might desire or be required to be interred therein,
then the use, estate, and interest thereinbefore limited
in severalty to *Mavor*, and all benefit and advantage
thereof, should thenceforth cease. Provided that *Smith*,
and his heirs or assigns, might enter the burial
ground to view the condition of the vault and tomb, and
of all wants of reparation give notice to *Mavor*, his heirs
or assigns, to repair all such decays; and provided that
in case the society of Quakers should at any time thereafter, during the trust thereinbefore mentioned for
them, and during the lives or life of the relessors
Mavor and *Smith*, or of the survivors or survivor of
them, or within 21 years after the death of the survivor,
be desirous of erecting a new meeting-house for their
use upon part of the ground thereby released, near the
burial ground, instead of repairing the then present
meeting-house, then the society might make use of any
part of the orchard belonging to the farm, and next
adjoining to the west side of the burial ground, so as
not to exceed in any part from east to west twenty-five
feet from the then present west fence of the burial
ground, for the purpose of making commodious ways
to the same. And immediately after erecting the
same, such new erected meeting-house should be, go,
and remain to such and the same uses, upon such
and the same trusts, and subject to the same conditions
and limitations, as were therein before expressed and
declared respecting the then present meeting-house;
and then the present meeting-house, and the ground
whereon it stood, should thenceforth be, go, and re-

4   main

main to such and the same uses, &c. as were therein
declared concerning the messuage and farm, other than
the land whereon the new meeting-house should be
erected, freed, and absolutely discharged from the trust
therein before declared concerning the society of Quakers.
The indentures of lease and release were sealed and
delivered by the releasor in the presence of two credible
witnesses, more than 12 calendar months before her
death, and were duly enrolled in Chancery. The
releasor, by her will subsequently made, and duly
attested to pass real estates, devised all her freehold
property to *G. Thomson,* the lessor of the Plaintiff, in
fee, and on the 9th *October* 1810 died without altering
or revoking her will, and to the time of her death
received the rents of the *Meeting-house* farm, and of
the meeting-house and burial ground: *Mavor* since
her death had become a bankrupt, and the Defendants
were his assignees. The question was, whether the
premises in the declaration mentioned passed by the
deeds before stated.

Best Serjt. contended that the release of these premises was void, and that they therefore passed by the
will of *J. Wilson* to her devisee. It is admitted that
the meeting-house, and burial ground did not pass by
the deed, because they are given upon uses, which are,
within the meaning of the statute 9 *G.* 2. *c.* 36., charitable uses; the third section of which, " absolutely an-
" nulling and avoiding all gifts, grants, conveyances,
" appointments, assurances, transfers, and settlements
" whatsoever of any lands made in any other manner
" or form than by that act is directed," vacates not
merely the estate which is limited contrary to that act,
but the entire deed, and all matters therein contained,
and therefore avoids this conveyance of the messuage
and farm, and the future use of the present meeting-

house, which was intended to arise in case of the erection of a new one. This construction of the statute is
supported by the case of *Norton* v. *Simmes* (*a*), where it
is laid down. " Upon the statute 23 *H.* 6. if a sheriff
" will take a bond for a point against that law, and also
" for a due debt, the whole bond is void, for the letter
" of the statute is so; for a statute is a strict law, but
" the common law doth divide according to common
" reason, and having made that void which is against
" law, lets the rest stand." But further, the uses
declared of the premises are void, because the reservation of the 2*l.* 10*s.* rent is a limitation for the benefit of the donor, prohibited by this statute, and the
conditional limitation over to *Smith*, a person claiming
under the donor, in case *Mavor* should not repair the
tomb, is also prohibited by the first section. This too is
not a grant of one part for a legal purpose, and of another
part for a prohibited purpose, but the whole purports to
be conveyed for the prohibited use; it is "for effectuating
the purposes aforesaid," that the deed conveys the meeting-house farm, as well as the meeting-house and the
other premises; and another part of the deed shews that
it was necessary to convey the whole for this purpose;
for the donor has an ulterior object, namely, that if the
Quakers shall elect another spot for a new meeting-
house, they shall be at liberty so to do. The whole of
the premises is therefore liable to this prohibited use,
until the Quakers have made their election; the whole is
also liable to the repairs of the tomb and vault in case
the rent of 2*l.* 10*s.* be insufficient for that purpose.

Bosanquet Serjt. *contrà.* It has not been attempted
now, since the decision to the contrary in the King's
Bench (*b*), to argue that the condition for keeping the
tomb and vault in repair is a charitable use. Neither

(*a*) *Hob.* 14.   (*b*) 3 *Maule & Selw.* 407.

is

is there any ground for the position that because the
farm is conveyed by a deed which does contain a charitable use, the whole is void, either on the words of this
statute, or on general principles. The general principle is, that if any void limitation be mixed up with
good matter, whether against a statute, or against the
common law, the good part stands, the rest is void.
Pigot's case (*a*). But it is said, if there be a statute,
the statute over-rides all. That depends on the words
of the statute. The statute of 23 *H. 6*. declares all
bonds shall be void if not made in a certain form. A
bond is one entire thing, and creates one entire debt.
It is there said the bond shall be void, but this statute
does not say that the deed shall be void, but all gifts,
grants, conveyances, appointments, assurances, transfers, and settlements shall be void, which must be taken
reddendo singula singulis. There are many cases upon
charitable uses in Chancery, but none wherein the whole
settlement has been set aside. The cases which have
been decided on the property-tax acts, are much
stronger than this, the statute is, that all covenants and
contracts for payment of any rent or interest without
allowing the deduction, shall be void ; yet it was held in
Howe v. *Singe* (*b*) that the covenant was only void *pro
tanto*. It would be most mischievous, if a different
doctrine were to prevail. *Adams* and *Lambert's* case (*c*),
on the statute 1 *Ed. 6. c.* 14. which gave to the crown
lands given for superstitious purposes. " If land of the
yearly value of 20*l. per annum* be given upon condition,
or to the purposes following, to find a priest to pray
for souls, and that the priest shall have for his salary 10*l.*,
and to distribute between 20 poor men and women
other 10*l.* yearly for ever for their sustentation, in that
case the king shall have but the 10*l.* limited to the priest,

(*a*) 11 Co. 27. b.   (*c*) 4 Co. 106. 111.
(*b*) 15 East, 443.

and

the premises, by lease and release, reciting that the
meeting-house and burial ground, parcel, &c. (except
the vault and tomb thereinafter mentioned,) had for
several years been, and then were used by a society of
Quakers, at the rent of 2l. 10s., and that the burial
vault and tomb over the same, standing upon the burial
ground, had been used as a burial vault for the family
of the relessor, and that she was desirous that the
meeting-house and burial ground, (except the vault
and tomb, and the ground next the north side and east
end thereof for 6 feet, and all ways thereto in and over
the burial ground,) should so long as the society of
Quakers should think proper to hold the same under
the terms and conditions thereinafter mentioned, be held
by them accordingly, as a meeting-house and a burial
ground, and the relessor was also desirous that the
family burial vault and tomb should for ever be kept in
repair for the burial place of the relessor and such of
her family as should chuse or require to be interred
therein, and for effectuating those purposes, the relessor
was desirous of conveying the messuage or farm, and
also the meeting-house, burial ground, vault, and tomb,
to the uses, &c. thereinafter limited; for effectuating
these purposes, and in consideration of 10s., the
relessor, according to her estate and interest therein,
and as far only as she could or lawfully might, granted
and released to *Mavor* and *Smith*, the *Meeting-house*
farm, with the several parcels of land thereunto belonging, and also the meeting-house, and burial ground,
and burial vault and tomb standing thereon, to hold
the same to *Mavor* and *Smith* and their heirs, to the
uses, upon the trusts, and for the intents and purposes
thereinafter declared, viz. as to the meeting-house and
burial ground, except the vault and tomb, and the
ground next the north side and east end thereof for
six feet, to the use of *Mavor* and *Smith*, their heirs and
assigns, so long as the meeting-house and burial ground

I   (except

(except as excepted) should be used by the society of

Quakers, as and for their meeting-house and burial ground, and so long as they should pay to *Mavor* and *Smith*, their heirs and assigns, the clear yearly rent of two pounds and ten shillings at *Michaelmas*, and also should completely repair the meeting-house and the walls, &c., and fences of the burial ground: it being the intent of the relessor, and the aforesaid conditional limitation to the use of *Mavor* and *Smith* being upon trust, that the meeting-house and burial ground should thenceforth be held by the society of Quakers in the same manner as the same had for several years past been used by them, provided they paid the yearly rent, and kept the meeting-house and burial ground in repair as aforesaid; and after the determination of that conditional estate, as to the meeting-house and burial ground, and from and immediately after the execution of those presents, as to all other the premises, to the use and behoof of, and as to the yearly rent of two pounds and ten shillings during the continuance of that conditional limitation, in trust for, *Mavor*, his heirs and assigns, subject to the proviso or condition thereinafter declared; and immediately after the determination of that conditional estate, to the only use of, and in trust for *Smith*, his heirs and assigns for ever. Provided, and it was thereby declared, that the estate and interest thereinbefore limited, in severalty to *Mavor*, his heirs and assigns, of and in the premises, were so limited upon express condition that he and his heirs should at all times thereafter repair and maintain the vault and tomb, and all the brick work, stone work, rails, pales, and fences thereto belonging, and if need were, should completely and entirely rebuild the same, agreeably to their present dimensions, and also should at all times permit the same to be used as a family burial vault for the interment of the relessor or

Bb 3   any

any of her family, who might desire, or be required to be interred therein. And in case *Mavor* and his heirs should at any time thereafter neglect to repair, or, if need were, to rebuild the vault or tomb, or should not permit the vault to be used as a family burial vault for the interment of the relessor, or any of her family who might desire or be required to be interred therein, then the use, estate, and interest thereinbefore limited in severalty to *Mavor*, and all benefit and advantage thereof, should thenceforth cease. Provided that *Smith*, and his heirs or assigns, might enter the burial ground to view the condition of the vault and tomb, and of all wants of reparation give notice to *Mavor*, his heirs or assigns, to repair all such decays; and provided that in case the society of Quakers should at any time thereafter, during the trust thereinbefore mentioned for them, and during the lives or life of the relessors *Mavor* and *Smith*, or of the survivors or survivor of them, or within 21 years after the death of the survivor, be desirous of erecting a new meeting-house for their use upon part of the ground thereby released, near the burial ground, instead of repairing the then present meeting-house, then the society might make use of any part of the orchard belonging to the farm, and next adjoining to the west side of the burial ground, so as not to exceed in any part from east to west twenty-five feet from the then present west fence of the burial ground, for the purpose of making commodious ways to the same. And immediately after erecting the same, such new erected meeting-house should be, go, and remain to such and the same uses, upon such and the same trusts, and subject to the same conditions and limitations, as were therein before expressed and declared respecting the then present meeting-house; and then the present meeting-house, and the ground whereon it stood, should thenceforth be, go, and re-

main to such and the same uses, &c. as were therein declared concerning the messuage and farm, other than the land whereon the new meeting-house should be erected, freed, and absolutely discharged from the trust therein before declared concerning the society of Quakers. The indentures of lease and release were sealed and delivered by the relessor in the presence of two credible witnesses, more than 12 calendar months before her death, and were duly enrolled in Chancery. The relessor, by her will subsequently made, and duly attested to pass real estates, devised all her freehold property to *G. Thomson*, the lessor of the Plaintiff, in fee, and on the 9th *October* 1810 died without altering or revoking her will, and to the time of her death received the rents of the *Meeting-house* farm, and of the meeting-house and burial ground: *Mavor* since her death had become a bankrupt, and the Defendants were his assignees. The question was, whether the premises in the declaration mentioned passed by the deeds before stated.

Best Serjt. contended that the release of these premises was void, and that they therefore passed by the will of *J. Wilson* to her devisee. It is admitted that the meeting-house, and burial ground did not pass by the deed, because they are given upon uses, which are, within the meaning of the statute 9 *G.* 2. *c.* 36., charitable uses; the third section of which, " absolutely an-" nulling and avoiding all gifts, grants, conveyances, " appointments, assurances, transfers, and settlements " whatsoever of any lands made in any other manner " or form than by that act is directed," vacates not merely the estate which is limited contrary to that act, but the entire deed, and all matters therein contained, and therefore avoids this conveyance of the messuage and farm, and the future use of the present meeting-

house,

house, which was intended to arise in case of the erection of a new one. This construction of the statute is
supported by the case of *Norton* v. *Simmes* (a), where it
is laid down. " Upon the statute 23 *H.* 6. if a sheriff
" will take a bond for a point against that law, and also
" for a due debt, the whole bond is void, for the letter
" of the statute is so; for a statute is a strict law, *but*
" the common law doth divide according to common
" reason, and having made that void which is against
" law, lets the rest stand." But further, the uses
declared of the premises are void, because the reservation of the 2*l.* 10*s.* rent is a limitation for the benefit of the donor, prohibited by this statute, and the
conditional limitation over to *Smith*, a person claiming
under the donor, in case *Mavor* should not repair the
tomb, is also prohibited by the first section. This *too is*
not a grant of one part for a legal purpose, and of another
part for a prohibited purpose, but the whole purports to
be conveyed for the prohibited use; it is "for effectuating
the purposes aforesaid," that the deed conveys the meeting-house farm, as well as the meeting-house and the
other premises; and another part of the deed shews that
it was necessary to convey the whole for this purpose;
for the donor has an ulterior object, namely, that if the
Quakers shall elect another spot for a new meeting-
house, they shall be at liberty so to do. The whole of
the premises is therefore liable to this prohibited use,
until the Quakers have made their election; the whole is
also liable to the repairs of the tomb and vault in case
the rent of 2*l.* 10*s.* be insufficient for that purpose.

Bosanquet Serjt. *contrà.* It has not been attempted
now, since the decision to the contrary in the King's
Bench (b), to argue that the condition for keeping the
tomb and vault in repair is a charitable use. Neither

(a) *Hob.* 14.   (b) 3 *Maule & Selw.* 407.

is there any ground for the position that because the
farm is conveyed by a deed which does contain a charitable use, the whole is void, either on the words of this
statute, or on general principles. The general principle is, that if any void limitation be mixed up with
good matter, whether against a statute, or against the
common law, the good part stands, the rest is void·
Pigot's case (a). But it is said, if there be a statute,
the statute over-rides all. That depends on the words
of the statute. The statute of 23 *H. 6.* declares all
bonds shall be void if not made in a certain form. A
bond is one entire thing, and creates one entire debt.
It is there said the bond shall be void, but this statute
does not say that the deed shall be void, but all gifts,
grants, conveyances, appointments, assurances, transfers, and settlements shall be void, which must be taken
reddendo singula singulis. There are many cases upon
charitable uses in Chancery, but none wherein the whole
settlement has been set aside. The cases which have
been decided on the property-tax acts, are much
stronger than this, the statute is, that all covenants and
contracts for payment of any rent or interest without
allowing the deduction, shall be void ; yet it was held in
Howe v. *Singe* (b) that the covenant was only void *pro
tanto.* It would be most mischievous, if a different
doctrine were to prevail. *Adams* and *Lambert's* case (c),
on the statute 1 *Ed. 6. c.* 14. which gave to the crown
lands given for superstitious purposes.   " If land of the
yearly value of 20l. *per annum* be given upon condition,
or to the purposes following, to find a priest to pray
for souls, and that the priest shall have for his salary 10l.,
and to distribute between 20 poor men and women
other 10l. yearly for ever for their sustentation, in that
case the king shall have but the 10l. limited to the priest,

(a) 11 Co. 27. b.   (c) 4 Co. 106. 111.
(b) 15 East, 443.

and

and not the land; but if the same land had been given
to find a priest, and for the maintenance of 20 poor
men, in that case the king should have all the land." If,
then, the limitation of the farm be distinct from the limitation of the burial ground to a superstitious use,
there is no pretence for saying that the deed is void.
There is no pretence in this case to say that the one is
so mixed with the other, that the Court cannot separate
them. The deed begins with a general recital of the
purposes of the party. The heir at law has recovered
the meeting-house and burial ground, inasmuch as the li-'
mitation was void as to that, and with it is gone the condition for rebuilding the meeting-house elsewhere. The releasee has this farm subject to repairing the tomb of the
settler, which is not a charitable use, and therefore the
statute need not be complied with in respect to that limitation; and it is no objection that there is a reservation
or limitation over for the benefit of the donor: the first
answer is satisfactory, that the repair of the tomb was
no charitable use, and therefore no matter whether a
condition were affixed to that estate or not. The 2l. 10s.
was not reserved out of the farm, nor out of the tomb,
but was to be paid by the Quakers out of the meeting-
house. It is said there is a limitation to *Smith* : of the
farm there is so. But it is no condition applied to the
meeting-house: it is no reservation out of the charitable
use; it is a condition applied to the limitation of a farm,
which the party may well annex to it. A devise for
keeping in repair a person's own house, or the fences
of his field, is not a charitable use. All the cases respecting charitable uses have been, where some public
benefit has been intended, not for the testator's own
benefit. A devise (a) of a botanical garden near
Chelsea, to be kept up for ever, was held a cha-

(a) *Townley* v. *Bedwell*, 6 *Ves.* 194.

ritable

ritable use, because the testator had said in his
will that he thought it would be a public benefit.
The doctrine held in *Durour* v. *Motteux* (a) cannot be
applied to this case. That was a bequest of 1200*l.* to
be laid out in the purchase of lands, part of which were
to be a fund for a perpetual annuity of 10*l. per ann.* to
a minister to preach a sermon once a year to his memory, which the Court held to be a charitable use, and
also to keep his tomb-stone in repair, and the inscrip-
tions legible thereon and upon the stone against the wall
reciting the gift; and the Court held the latter part was
so mixed up with the other that it could not be distinguished, and therefore was void for the whole: but it
never occurred to the Court that the whole was void
because a part was. Even supposing this condition of
maintaining the vault and tomb to be contrary to the
statute, it falls within the principle that the illegal condition is void, and the grant of the land good, for this
not being a case within the statute of *Ed.* 6., the land
does not go to the king.

Best, in reply. The whole of the limitations are to a
charitable use. *Durour* v. *Motteux* is in point for the
Plaintiff. It is said, this is a selfish use. But the
keeping a tomb for the donor's self and his family, is
not like the keeping up a house for himself and his family: it is the perpetuating an idle vanity, as Lord
Hardwicke expresses it, but it is not therefore the less a
charitable use. The purchasing masses for the soul of
a donor is as selfish as this, yet it does not therefore
cease to be a superstitious use. In *Pigot's* case, where
Lord *Coke* speaks of conditions which are against law,
it must be intended of common law; if they were against
a statute, it would have been so expressed. The coun-

(a) 1 *Ves.* 320.

sol

sel for the Defendant has not impugned the distinction between instruments void by common law and those which are void by statute. *Norton* v. *Simmes* has been recently recognized in *Greenwood* v. *The Bishop of London* (a); and though there was clear simony, the Court held that it only vacated what was simoniacal, and they maintained what was good. The property-tax act does not avoid the whole assurance: it makes void only the " covenant or contract." It is said, if a part be given to superstitious uses, and part not, the first only goes to the king; but that is by reason of the words of the statute, which are, that so much as is given for superstitious uses shall pass to the king. The whole deed therefore is to all intents void. No answer has been given to the second ground. At all events the Plaintiff is entitled to a verdict; for if the use declared of the meeting-house is a charitable use, then the ground destined for a future meeting-house is directly given for a charitable use, and the Plaintiff must recover for that: if otherwise, the society of Quakers may immediately take that land and apply it to that use: but in truth the gift is all one, and the limitations not several but one, and the Plaintiff must therefore recover the whole; at most the uses are several. The preamble of the statute 43 *Eliz. c.* 4. has been mentioned as an enumeration of charitable uses, which contains none for the sustentation of tombs; but the inference is not fair, for that statute is restricted to charitable uses strictly so called, but the preamble of this act shews that it meant to go beyond that line. The mischief intended to be hereby remedied was the rendering property inalienable, to which this grant expressly tends, for the benefit of no person whatever, but only to perpetuate the vanity of this lady and her posterity, which is directly within the mischief.

(a) *Ante,* v. 727.

GIBBS

GIBBS C. J. This is an ejectment brought for the recovery of certain premises in *Hertfordshire.* As to a part of the premises, namely, the meeting-house and burial ground, I am now to take it, that they have been already recovered by ejectment, and that this action is brought for the residue; and the question is, whether the deed be void as to that, by the statute 9 *G.* 2. *c.* 37. It is argued to be void on three grounds. First, if it be void as to part, it is said, it must be void as to the whole. If the objection had been derived from the common law, it is admitted, that would not be the consequence; but it is urged that the statute makes the whole deed void. As the counsel for the Plaintiff puts it, there is no difference between a transaction void at common law, and void by statute: if an act be prohibited, the construction to be put on a deed conveying property illegally, is, that the clause which so conveys it, is void equally, whether it be by statute or common law: but it may happen that the statute goes further, and says that the whole deed shall be void to all intents and purposes; and when that is so, the Court must so pronounce, because the legislature has so enacted, and not because the transaction prohibited is illegal. I cannot find in this act any words which 'make the entire deed void. The words are, " all gifts, grants, conveyances, appointments, assurances, transfers, and settlements whatsoever of any lands, or of any estate or interest therein, shall be absolutely and to all intents void." I think this grant of that interest in land, which by the terms of the grant is to be applied to a charitable use, is void; but I think the statute makes nothing more void, and that the deed, so far as it passes other lands, not to a charitable use, is good. Therefore that argument fails. The Plaintiff's counsel next insists that the residue of the land is applicable to a charitable use, because the condition is that the donee shall keep in repair a

vault

the premises, by lease and release, reciting that the meeting-house and burial ground, parcel, &c. (except the vault and tomb thereinafter mentioned,) had for several years been, and then were used by a society of Quakers, at the rent of 2l. 10s., and that the burial vault and tomb over the same, standing upon the burial ground, had been used as a burial vault for the family of the relessor, and that she was desirous that the meeting-house and burial ground, (except the vault and tomb, and the ground next the north side and east end thereof for 6 feet, and all ways thereto in and over the burial ground,) should so long as the society of Quakers should think proper to hold the same under the terms and conditions thereinafter mentioned, be held by them accordingly, as a meeting-house and a burial ground, and the relessor was also desirous that the family burial vault and tomb should for ever be kept in repair for the burial place of the relessor and such of her family as should chuse or require to be interred therein, and for effectuating those purposes, the relessor was desirous of conveying the messuage or farm, and also the meeting-house, burial ground, vault, and tomb, to the uses, &c. thereinafter limited; for effectuating these purposes, and in consideration of 10s., the relessor, according to her estate and interest therein, and as far only as she could or lawfully might, granted and released to *Mavor* and *Smith*, the *Meeting-house* farm, with the several parcels of land thereunto belonging, and also the meeting-house, and burial ground, and burial vault and tomb standing thereon, to hold the same to *Mavor* and *Smith* and their heirs, to the uses, upon the trusts, and for the intents and purposes thereinafter declared, viz. as to the meeting-house and burial ground, except the vault and tomb, and the ground next the north side and east end thereof for six feet, to the use of *Mavor* and *Smith*, their heirs and assigns, so long as the meeting-house and burial ground

I   (except

(except as excepted) should be used by the society of
Quakers, as and for their meeting-house and burial
ground, and so long as they should pay to *Mavor* and
Smith, their heirs and assigns, the clear yearly rent
of two pounds and ten shillings at *Michaelmas*, and
also should completely repair the meeting-house
and the walls, &c., and fences of the burial ground:
it being the intent of the relessor, and the aforesaid
conditional limitation to the use of *Mavor* and *Smith*
being upon trust, that the meeting-house and burial
ground should thenceforth be held by the society of
Quakers in the same manner as the same had for several
years past been used by them, provided they paid the
yearly rent, and kept the meeting-house and burial
ground in repair as aforesaid; and after the determination of that conditional estate, as to the meeting-house
and burial ground, and from and immediately after the
execution of those presents, as to all other the premises, to the use and behoof of, and as to the yearly
rent of two pounds and ten shillings during the continuance of that conditional limitation, in trust for,
Mavor, his heirs and assigns, subject to the proviso or
condition thereinafter declared; and immediately after
the determination of that conditional estate, to the only
use of, and in trust for *Smith*, his heirs and assigns for
ever. Provided, and it was thereby declared, that the
estate and interest thereinbefore limited, in severalty to
Mavor, his heirs and assigns, of and in the premises,
were so limited upon express condition that he and
his heirs should at all times thereafter repair and maintain the vault and tomb, and all the brick work,
stone work, rails, pales, and fences thereto belonging,
and if need were, should completely and entirely rebuild
the same, agreeably to their present dimensions, and
also should at all times permit the same to be used as a
family burial vault for the interment of the relessor or

B b 3   any

any of her family, who might desire, or be required to be interred therein. And in case *Mavor* and his heirs should at any time thereafter neglect to repair, or, if need were, to rebuild the vault or tomb, or should not permit the vault to be used as a family burial vault for the interment of the relessor, or any of her family who might desire or be required to be interred therein, then the use, estate, and interest thereinbefore limited in severalty to *Mavor*, and all benefit and advantage thereof, should thenceforth cease. Provided that *Smith*, and his heirs or assigns, might enter the burial ground to view the condition of the vault and tomb, and of all wants of reparation give notice to *Mavor*, his heirs or assigns, to repair all such decays; and provided that in case the society of Quakers should at any time thereafter, during the trust thereinbefore mentioned for them, and during the lives or life of the relessors *Mavor* and *Smith*, or of the survivors or survivor of them, or within 21 years after the death of the survivor, be desirous of erecting a new meeting-house for their use upon part of the ground thereby released, near the burial ground, instead of repairing the then present meeting-house, then the society might make use of any part of the orchard belonging to the farm, and next adjoining to the west side of the burial ground, so as not to exceed in any part from east to west twenty-five feet from the then present west fence of the burial ground, for the purpose of making commodious ways to the same. And immediately after erecting the same, such new erected meeting-house should be, go, and remain to such and the same uses, upon such and the same trusts, and subject to the same conditions and limitations, as were therein before expressed and declared respecting the then present meeting-house; and then the present meeting-house, and the ground whereon it stood, should thenceforth be, go, and re-

main

main to such and the same uses, &c. as were therein declared concerning the messuage and farm, other than the land whereon the new meeting-house should be erected, freed, and absolutely discharged from the trust therein before declared concerning the society of Quakers. The indentures of lease and release were sealed and delivered by the releasor in the presence of two credible witnesses, more than 12 calendar months before her death, and were duly enrolled in Chancery. The releasor, by her will subsequently made, and duly attested to pass real estates, devised all her freehold property to *G. Thomson,* the lessor of the Plaintiff, in fee, and on the 9th *October* 1810 died without altering or revoking her will, and to the time of her death received the rents of the *Meeting-house* farm, and of the meeting-house and burial ground: *Mavor* since her death had become a bankrupt, and the Defendants were his assignees. The question was, whether the premises in the declaration mentioned passed by the deeds before stated.

Best Serjt. contended that the release of these premises was void, and that they therefore passed by the will of *J. Wilson* to her devisee. It is admitted that the meeting-house, and burial ground did not pass by the deed, because they are given upon uses, which are, within the meaning of the statute 9 *G.* 2. *c.* 36., charitable uses; the third section of which, " absolutely an-
" nulling and avoiding all gifts, grants, conveyances,
" appointments, assurances, transfers, and settlements
" whatsoever of any lands made in any other manner
" or form than by that act is directed," vacates not merely the estate which is limited contrary to that act, but the entire deed, and all matters therein contained, and therefore avoids this conveyance of the messuage and farm, and the future use of the present meeting-

house, which was intended to arise in case of the erection of a new one. This construction of the statute is supported by the case of *Norton* v. *Simmes* (a), where it is laid down. " Upon the statute 23 *H.* 6. if a sheriff " will take a bond for a point against that law, and also " for a due debt, the whole bond is void, for the letter " of the statute is so; for a statute is a strict law, but " the common law doth divide according to common " reason, and having made that void which is against " law, lets the rest stand."ᴬ But further, the uses declared of the premises are void, because the reservation of the 2*l.* 10*s.* rent is a limitation for the benefit of the donor, prohibited by this statute, and the conditional limitation over to *Smith*, a person claiming under the donor, in case *Mavor* should not repair the tomb, is also prohibited by the first section. This too is not a grant of one part for a legal purpose, and of another part for a prohibited purpose, but the whole purports to be conveyed for the prohibited use; it is "for effectuating the purposes aforesaid," that the deed conveys the meeting-house farm, as well as the meeting-house and the other premises; and another part of the deed shews that it was necessary to convey the whole for this purpose; for the donor has an ulterior object, namely, that if the Quakers shall elect another spot for a new meeting-house, they shall be at liberty so to do. The whole of the premises is therefore liable to this prohibited use, until the Quakers have made their election; the whole is also liable to the repairs of the tomb and vault in case the rent of 2*l.* 10*s.* be insufficient for that purpose.

Bosanquet Serjt. *contrà.* It has not been attempted now, since the decision to the contrary in the King's Bench (b), to argue that the condition for keeping the tomb and vault in repair is a charitable use. Neither

(a) *Hob.* 14.   (b) 3 *Maule & Selw.* 407.

is

is there any ground for the position that because the farm is conveyed by a deed which does contain a charitable use, the whole is void, either on the words of this statute, or on general principles. The general principle is, that if any void limitation be mixed up with good matter, whether against a statute, or against the common law, the good part stands, the rest is void. *Pigot's* case (*a*). But it is said, if there be a statute, the statute over-rides all. That depends on the words of the statute. The statute of 23 *H.* 6. declares all bonds shall be void if not made in a certain form. A bond is one entire thing, and creates one entire debt. It is there said the bond shall be void, but this statute does not say that the deed shall be void, but all gifts, grants, conveyances, appointments, assurances, transfers, and settlements shall be void, which must be taken *reddendo singula singulis.* There are many cases upon charitable uses in Chancery, but none wherein the whole settlement has been set aside. The cases which have been decided on the property-tax acts, are much stronger than this, the statute is, that all covenants and contracts for payment of any rent or interest without allowing the deduction, shall be void; yet it was held in *Howe* v. *Singe* (*b*) that the covenant was only void *pro tanto.* It would be most mischievous, if a different doctrine were to prevail. *Adams* and *Lambert's* case (*c*), on the statute 1 *Ed.* 6. *c.* 14. which gave to the crown lands given for superstitious purposes. " If land of the yearly value of 20*l. per annum* be given upon condition, or to the purposes following, to find a priest to pray for souls, and that the priest shall have for his salary 10*l.*, and to distribute between 20 poor men and women other 10*l.* yearly for ever for their sustentation, in that case the king shall have but the 10*l.* limited to the priest,

(*a*) 11 *Co.* 27. *b.*
(*b*) 15 *East*, 443.

(*c*) 4 *Co.* 106. 111.

and

and not the land; but if the same land had been given to find a priest, and for the maintenance of 20 poor men, in that case the king should have all the land." If, then, the limitation of the farm be distinct from the limitation of the burial ground to a superstitious use, there is no pretence for saying that the deed is void. There is no pretence in this case to say that the one is so mixed with the other, that the Court cannot separate them. The deed begins with a general recital of the purposes of the party. The heir at law has recovered the meeting-house and burial ground, inasmuch as the limitation was void as to that, and with it is gone the condition for rebuilding the meeting-house elsewhere. The relessee has this farm subject to repairing the tomb of the settler, which is not a charitable use, and therefore the statute need not be complied with in respect to that limitation; and it is no objection that there is a reservation or limitation over for the benefit of the donor: the first answer is satisfactory, that the repair of the tomb was no charitable use, and therefore no matter whether a condition were affixed to that estate or not. The 2l. 10s. was not reserved out of the farm, nor out of the tomb, but was to be paid by the Quakers out of the meeting-house. It is said there is a limitation to *Smith*: of the farm there is so. But it is no condition applied to the meeting-house: it is no reservation out of the charitable use; it is a condition applied to the limitation of a farm, which the party may well annex to it. A devise for keeping in repair a person's own house, or the fences of his field, is not a charitable use. All the cases respecting charitable uses have been, where some public benefit has been intended, not for the testator's own benefit. A devise (a) of a botanical garden near *Chelsea*, to be kept up for ever, was held a cha-

(a) *Townley v. Bedwell,* 6 *Ves.* 194.

ritable

ritable use, because the testator had said in his
will that he thought it would be a public benefit.
The doctrine held in *Durour* v. *Motteux* (a) cannot be
applied to this case. That was a bequest of 1200*l*. to
be laid out in the purchase of lands, part of which were
to be a fund for a perpetual annuity of 10*l. per ann.* to
a minister to preach a sermon once a year to his memory, which the Court held to be a charitable use, and
also to keep his tomb-stone in repair, and the inscrip-
tions legible thereon and upon the stone against the wall
reciting the gift; and the Court held the latter part was
so mixed up with the other that it could not be distinguished, and therefore was void for the whole: but it
never occurred to the Court that the whole was void
because a part was.   Even supposing this condition of
maintaining the vault and tomb to be contrary to the
statute, it falls within the principle that the illegal condition is void, and the grant of the land good, for this
not being a case within the statute of *Ed. 6.*, the land
does not go to the king.

Best, in reply.   The whole of the limitations are to a
charitable use.   *Durour* v. *Motteux* is in point for the
Plaintiff.   It is said, this is a selfish use.   But the
keeping a tomb for the donor's self and his family, is
not like the keeping up a house for himself and his family: it is the perpetuating an idle vanity, as Lord
Hardwicke expresses it, but it is not therefore the less a
charitable use.   The purchasing masses for the soul of
a donor is as selfish as this, yet it does not therefore
cease to be a superstitious use.   In *Pigot's* case, where
Lord *Coke* speaks of conditions which are against law,
it must be intended of common law; if they were against
a statute, it would have been so expressed.   The coun-

(a) 1 *Ves.* 320.

sel for the Defendant has not impugned the distinction
between instruments void by common law and those
which are void by statute. *Norton* v. *Simmes* has been
recently recognized in *Greenwood* v. *The Bishop of London* (a) ; and though there was clear simony, the Court
held that it only vacated what was simoniacal, and they
maintained what was good. The property-tax act does
not avoid the whole assurance : it makes void only the
" covenant or contract." It is said, if a part be given
to superstitious uses, and part not, the first only goes to
the king ; but that is by reason of the words of the statute, which are, that so much as is given for superstitious
uses shall pass to the king. The whole deed therefore
is to all intents void. No answer has been given to the
second ground. At all events the Plaintiff is entitled
to a verdict ; for if the use declared of the meeting-house
is a charitable use, then the ground destined for a future
meeting-house is directly given for a charitable use, and
the Plaintiff must recover for that : if otherwise, the
society of Quakers may immediately take that land and
apply it to that use : but in truth the gift is all one, and
the limitations not several but one, and the Plaintiff
must therefore recover the whole ; at most the uses are
several. The preamble of the statute 43 *Eliz. c. 4.* has
been mentioned as an enumeration of charitable uses,
which contains none for the sustentation of tombs ; but
the inference is not fair, for that statute is restricted to
charitable uses strictly so called, but the preamble of
this act shews that it meant to go beyond that line. The
mischief intended to be hereby remedied was the rendering property inalienable, to which this grant expressly tends, for the benefit of no person whatever, but
only to perpetuate the vanity of this lady and her posterity, which is directly within the mischief.

(a) *Ante,* v. 727.

GIBBS

GIBBS C. J. This is an ejectment brought for the recovery of certain premises in *Hertfordshire.* As to a part of the premises, namely, the meeting-house and burial ground, I am now to take it, that they have been already recovered by ejectment, and that this action is brought for the residue; and the question is, whether the deed be void as to that, by the statute 9 *G.* 2. *c.* 37. It is argued to be void on three grounds. First, if it be void as to part, it is said, it must be void as to the whole. If the objection had been derived from the common law, it is admitted, that would not be the consequence; but it is urged that the statute makes the whole deed void. As the counsel for the Plaintiff puts it, there is no difference between a transaction void at common law, and void by statute: if an act be prohibited, the construction to be put on a deed conveying property illegally, is, that the clause which so conveys it, is void equally, whether it be by statute or common law: but it may happen that the statute goes further, and says that the whole deed shall be void to all intents and purposes; and when that is so, the Court must so pronounce, because the legislature has so enacted, and not because the transaction prohibited is illegal. I cannot find in this act any words which make the entire deed void. The words are, " all gifts, grants, conveyances, appointments, assurances, transfers, and settlements whatsoever of any lands, or of any estate or interest therein, shall be absolutely and to all intents void." I think this grant of that interest in land, which by the terms of the grant is to be applied to a charitable use, is void; but I think the statute makes nothing more void, and that the deed, so far as it passes other lands, not to a charitable use, is good. Therefore that argument fails. The Plaintiff's counsel next insists that the residue of the land is applicable to a charitable use, because the condition is that the donee shall keep in repair a

vault

1815.

DOE
v.
PITCHER.

vault to receive the body of the donor or any of her family. We agree with the Court of King's Bench that
this is not a charitable use, and the Plaintiff's counsel
seemed to feel the argument that this was not a charitable use, and therefore tried to argue that this was a
quasi charitable use, and that the statute meant to include all provisions tending to perpetuities. It certainly
means to provide against perpetuities in limitations of
lands for charitable uses, but it is confined to those
uses. It is next urged that the conveyance is void,
because it is subject to the right of the society of Quakers,
to take any part of the land when they please. It is a
sufficient answer, that no part is now appropriated to
that purpose, and that that part of the deed being determined to be void by the statute, in which we agree,
they never can possess it; there must therefore be

Judgment for the Defendant.

ing. 341.
Nov. 21.

MILLER *v.* PARNELL.

If a sheriff
makes a seizure
under a writ
of *fieri facias*,
though the
Plaintiff can-
not take the
Defendant in
execution un-
der a writ of
*capias ad sa-
tisfaciendum*,
till the writ of
fieri facias is
returned,
though he
abandons the
seizure of the
goods.

*L*ENS Serjt. had on a former day obtained a rule *nisi*
to discharge out of custody the Defendant, who had
been taken in execution under a writ of *capias ad satisfaciendum*, upon the ground that the Plaintiff had previously sued out a writ of *fieri facias*, under which the
sheriff had seized goods of greater value than the
amount of the judgment, which writ was not yet returned.

Best Serjt. on this day shewed cause against the rule,
upon the ground that the Plaintiff had not sold the
goods taken under the writ of *fieri facias*, but had after
some weeks abandoned that process, which he contended that he was at liberty to do, and thereupon to
sue

sue out his writ of *fieri facias*. It was the common practice, he said, to sue out a writ of *fieri facias* and a writ of *capias ad satisfaciendum* together. The merely seizing and abandoning the property, is not such an execution of the process, as needs delay the issuing of the second writ till the first is returned.

Lens, in support of his rule, contended that the writ of *fieri facias*, while unreturned, would always be a sufficient plea for the Plaintiff or the sheriff in trespass for the seizure of the goods, and that it therefore ought to be returned, because the Plaintiff ought not in justice to be furnished at the same time with a legal justification for taking and detaining both the goods and the body. Even a *testatum fieri facias* to levy the residue, cannot legally be sued out before the return of the first writ (*a*). The Plaintiff is bound first to state to the Court what he has done under the first writ, and obtain their permission to abandon it, before he can sue out the further process.

Per Curiam. No doubt, a Plaintiff having sued out a writ of *fieri facias*, may, if he pleases, omit to execute the *fieri facias*, and take out a writ of *capias ad satisfaciendum*, and execute that before the *fieri facias* is returned or returnable. But there is also no doubt that if the Plaintiff does execute his *fieri facias*, he cannot have a writ of *capias ad satisfaciendum* till the *fieri facias* is completely executed and returned. This is a middle case. So far as the Defendant is concerned, the goods, to the extent of their value, have been levied; and the question is, whether the Plaintiff, after taking them, may change his mind, and sue out a writ of *capias ad satisfaciendum* without returning his former writ. If

(a) *Coppendale* v. *Debonnaire, Barnes,* 213.

this

this might be, it would confer a power that might be much abused. If the *fieri facias* be returned, there is something to bind the Plaintiff, and to limit for how much he shall have the body, by shewing how much he has already gotten. If a Plaintiff might take goods under a *fieri facias*, and hold them a month, or the greater part of the long vacation, and then change his mind, and say, " I will not sell, but will take the body of the Defendant under a *capias ad satisfaciendum*," it might be the engine of very great oppression. The Plaintiff may, by the practice of the Court, sue out both these processes together, if he will, and may use either the one or the other, as he sees advisable, but by using the *fieri facias* first, he makes his election, and after having so elected, he cannot use the other process, till after the return of the first. We therefore think, that this writ of *capias ad satisfaciendum*, being sued out after the *fieri facias* had issued, and after the sheriff had taken the goods under it, and before its return, cannot be supported.

> Rule absolute, but on the terms
> of bringing no action against
> the sheriff.

1815.

Nov. 21.

FORSTER, Demandant; FORSTER, Tenant;
DARCY BOLTON and Wife, Vouchees.

THE vouchees, who lived in *Canada*, had in this recovery put in their place two persons named, " as
their attornies jointly and severally to gain or lose in a
plea of land," not saying " against *Samuel Forster*," the
Demandant, as they regularly ought to have done; and
upon account of this omission, the officers refused to
perfect the recovery. *Frere* Serjt. now moved to amend
the warrant of attorney, by inserting the words " against
Samuel Forster," upon the authority of the cases of
*Shaw, Demandant; Le Blanc, Tenant; Ramsay and
Wife, Vouchees*(a); and *O'Brien, Vouchee*(b); and the
Court expressing dissent, he was supported by the secondary, who stated, that it had long been the daily
practice of the Court to amend warrants of attorney.
This motion being disallowed, he then moved that the
recovery might pass notwithstanding the omission of
these words, for which he conceived there was sufficient
authority on the face of the instrument. By the practice of this Court, the *præcipe* is engrossed at the head
of the same parchment on which the warrant of attorney is taken, and the *præcipe* is, " command *William
Martin Forster*, that justly and without delay he render
to *Samuel Forster*, &c.;" from whence it may be plainly
collected that the plea of land in which *Darcy Bolton*
and wife make their attornies, is the plea of land against
Samuel Forster in the same instrument above mentioned,
and the warrant of attorney is therefore in its present
state sufficient. Enough appears on the face of it to

The Court will not amend a warrant of attorney, which is the deed of the party.

Where the vouchee's warrant of attorney, in a recovery, omitted in the body of the warrant to express against whom the plea of land was, wherein the attorney was made, but it appeared by the precipe engrossed at the head of the warrant of attorney, who the demandant was, the Court held that the authority must refer to that plea described by the precipe, and permitted the recovery to pass.

(a) *Ante,* iv. 98.   (b) *Ante,* iv. 196.

VOL. VI.   C c   guard

guard against fraud, by rendering it impossible that the parties who executed it should not know by the perusal, what the transaction was, and it plainly appears by the context, that the omission was accidental.

The Court held, as to the proposed amendment, that the cases cited were not well considered, and when they passed, it was not adverted to, that the instrument sought to be amended, was the deed of a party. They could not take on themselves to make it appear that the party had executed a different deed from that which he really did execute. But they allowed the recovery to pass, on the ground on which it was very properly moved by the counsel. The practice of the Court required the instrument to run in that form, containing a recital of the writ, whereby it appeared who were the parties to the plea. They therefore thought the warrant of attorney must be taken to refer to the plea of land, the commencement of which was therein above stated, and that therefore it was in substance a making of an attorney in that plea.

Fiat.

In the case of another recovery moved by *Blosset* Serjt. on the last day of this term, where there was a similar omission in the warrant of attorney to name the tenant against whom the plea of land was, the Court in like manner permitted the recovery to pass, supplying the defect by reference to the *præcipe* at the head of the warrant of attorney.

EVERTH v. HANNAM.

THIS was an action upon a policy of insurance at
and from any port or ports in *Jutland* to *Leith*,
effected in 1814, for 2000*l.* upon the ship, and 1000*l.*
on the freight: and a loss was alleged by seizure by
persons unknown.   Upon the trial of the cause at the
sittings after *Trinity* term 1815, at *Guildhall*, before
Gibbs C. J. it appeared that the vessel was laden with
barley, rye, and oats, and that she was lost, being taken by
the *Swedes.*   The power of *Sweden* was then blockading
Norway, and had notified the blockade to *Great Britain.*
The master of the vessel, being examined as a witness,
stated that the ship was bound for *Leith*, but that she
had, against his will, been driven by a current nearer
to the coast of *Norway* than he intended to have gone,
that he did not intend to go into any port of *Norway*,
and that when he was taken he was steering direct for
Leith.   The Defendants proved a sentence of the
Swedish court of admiralty, condemning the vessel upon
the ground of her having violated the blockade of
Norway, and insisted that was an answer to the Plaintiff's case, being conclusive evidence of the fact, and
that therefore the master's testimony could not be
received to the contrary.   The Plaintiff urged that,
admitting the *Swedish* sentence to be conclusive evidence, it went no further than the point of the breach
of blockade, but did not disprove the master's evidence
that the vessel was bound for *Leith*, which was consistent with the sentence, by supposing that the master
had barratrously carried the ship towards the coast of
Norway, and upon this proof of barratry, the Plaintiff
was still entitled to recover.   The Defendant insisted
that the evidence did not clearly raise the inference of
barratry, but he urged that even if the fact were so, the

C c 2   Plaintiff

*Where the
master of a
vessel, con-
demned for
a breach of
blockade,
swore he was
bound for an-
other destina-
tion, held that
this did not so
disaffirm his
owner's privity
and consent to
the breach of
blockade, as to
enable the
Plaintiff to
recover as for
a loss by bar-
ratry.*

Plaintiff could not recover on this declaration, because there was no count for barratry. A verdict passed for the Plaintiff, subject to three points, which his Lordship reserved, first, whether the sentence conclusively proved a breach of the blockade; secondly, whether the sentence proved the master to have committed an act of barratry; and thirdly, whether the Plaintiff could recover without a count averring a loss by barratry.

Accordingly *Vaughan* Serjt. in this term obtained a rule *nisi* to set aside the verdict and enter a nonsuit, against which

Shepherd, Solicitor-General, and *Best* Serjt. shewed cause: As to the first point, they admitted the sentence was conclusive evidence of the breach of blockade, but that the master's testimony was to be received, so far as it was consistent with it. As to the third point, the existence of a more remote cause of loss, which occasioned the immediate cause alleged in the declaration, cannot be set up to disprove the existence of the immediate cause alleged. *Hodgson* v. *Malcolm* (a). Nor is it necessary to state the remote cause. *Heyman* v. *Parish* (b). If, indeed, the more remote cause were the act of the Plaintiff, than it would be a defence, not because it disproved the allegation of the immediate cause of the loss, but because the Plaintiff could not recover for a damage occasioned by his own act. The immediate cause of the loss here was by seizure occasioned by a breach of blockade, the more remote cause which occasioned the breach of blockade is not proved to have been the act of the Plaintiff: the result of the evidence is, that it was by the act of the master, which is barratry, a risk against which the Defendants insure him. There is sufficient evidence of barratry to warrant the

(a) 2 *New Rep.* 336.   (b) 2 *Campb.* 149.

4   finding

finding of the jury. The declaration shews a sufficient ground of action, and the Plaintiff has proved all his averments.

Vaughan in support of his rule, urged that it was not every deviation from the ship's course that constituted barratry, the master might have broken the blockade through ignorance or unskilful navigation. The declaration was not proved, for it averred that the loss happened while the ship was proceeding on the voyage insured, whereas the evidence was, that she was far out of her destined course when she was seized. But the evidence fails on another ground. It does not necessarily happen that the fact is as the sentence represents it; for the purpose of shewing the ground of condemnation, the sentence is conclusive evidence, but not for other purposes; and it is not to be attended with all the same consequences and inferences as if the fact were true. Therefore the sentence is no evidence that the act of the master was barratrous; and there is no other evidence of barratry in the cause. The whole of the captain's testimony must be taken together, or wholly rejected. But if there were barratry, the Plaintiff could not recover on this declaration, for it gives no notice whatever to the Defendant that he is to prepare to meet a claim founded on barratry.

Cur. adv. vult.

GIBBS C. J. now delivered the opinion of the Court. This is an action on a policy of insurance. The question is, whether the assured, shut out from his right to recover in the first instance by proof of the violation of the blockade, has replaced himself in a situation to recover, by proof that it was the master, and not the Plaintiff, who had been violating the blockade. The Plaintiff started this case, by the master's swearing he

C c 3

was

sel for the Defendant has not impugned the distinction between instruments void by common law and those which are void by statute. *Norton* v. *Simmes* has been recently recognized in *Greenwood* v. *The Bishop of London* (a); and though there was clear simony, the Court held that it only vacated what was simoniacal, and they maintained what was good. The property-tax act does not avoid the whole assurance: it makes void only the " covenant or contract." It is said, if a part be given to superstitious uses, and part not, the first only goes to the king; but that is by reason of the words of the statute, which are, that so much as is given for superstitious uses shall pass to the king. The whole deed therefore is to all intents void. No answer has been given to the second ground. At all events the Plaintiff is entitled to a verdict; for if the use declared of the meeting-house is a charitable use, then the ground destined for a future meeting-house is directly given for a charitable use, and the Plaintiff must recover for that: if otherwise, the society of Quakers may immediately take that land and apply it to that use: but in truth the gift is all one, and the limitations not several but one, and the Plaintiff must therefore recover the whole; at most the uses are several. The preamble of the statute 43 *Eliz. c.* 4. has been mentioned as an enumeration of charitable uses, which contains none for the sustentation of tombs; but the inference is not fair, for that statute is restricted to charitable uses strictly so called, but the preamble of this act shews that it meant to go beyond that line. The mischief intended to be hereby remedied was the rendering property inalienable, to which this grant expressly tends, for the benefit of no person whatever, but only to perpetuate the vanity of this lady and her posterity, which is directly within the mischief.

(a) *Ante,* v. 727.

GIBBS

GIBBS C. J. This is an ejectment brought for the recovery of certain premises in *Hertfordshire*. As to a part of the premises, namely, the meeting-house and burial ground, I am now to take it, that they have been already recovered by ejectment, and that this action is brought for the residue; and the question is, whether the deed be void as to that, by the statute 9 *G.* 2. *c.* 37. It is argued to be void on three grounds. First, if it be void as to part, it is said, it must be void as to the whole. If the objection had been derived from the common law, it is admitted, that would not be the consequence; but it is urged that the statute makes the whole deed void. As the counsel for the Plaintiff puts it, there is no difference between a transaction void at common law, and void by statute: if an act be prohibited, the construction to be put on a deed conveying property illegally, is, that the clause which so conveys it, is void equally, whether it be by statute or common law: but it may happen that the statute goes further, and says that the whole deed shall be void to all intents and purposes; and when that is so, the Court must so pronounce, because the legislature has so enacted, and not because the transaction prohibited is illegal. I cannot find in this act any words which make the entire deed void. The words are, " all gifts, grants, conveyances, appointments, assurances, transfers, and settlements whatsoever of any lands, or of any estate or interest therein, shall be absolutely and to all intents void." I think this grant of that interest in land, which by the terms of the grant is to be applied to a charitable use, is void; but I think the statute makes nothing more void, and that the deed, so far as it passes other lands, not to a charitable use, is good. Therefore that argument fails. The Plaintiff's counsel next insists that the residue of the land is applicable to a charitable use, because the condition is that the donee shall keep in repair a

vault

subject to a reference, which, comprehending all differences respecting rent, embraced the replevin which was the occasion of the Defendant's bond, but it was expressly agreed between the parties, that nothing in their agreement contained should discharge the sureties in the replevin of the 19th of *January* 1814, and that no proceedings should be had in that replevin cause pending the reference. This reference and agreement were entered into without the knowledge of the Defendant. The arbitrators awarded in *July* 1814, that *Shirreff* should pay the rent on the 8th of *August* 1814, and the Plaintiff, under the *cognovit*, on the 7th of *September* entered up judgment, and took in execution the stock of *Shirreff;* and that being insufficient, arrested him for the residue: he was in consequence rendered unable to carry on his farm, and absconded, leaving the Defendant liable on this bond. The Plaintiff had removed the replevin cause into this court by writ of *accedas ad curiam* on the 14th of *April* 1814, gave a rule to declare in replevin on the 25th of *May* 1814, and on the 25th of *January* 1815, and not sooner, signed judgment of *non pros* 'for want of a declaration, issued a writ of *retorno habendo* on the 1st of *February* 1815, and issued a *capias* against the Defendant on the 6th of *June* 1815, returnable in three weeks of the *Holy Trinity.* Upon these facts *Pell* Serjt. had obtained a rule *nisi* to set aside the proceedings in this action, contending that the Plaintiff having by the reference given time to *Shirreff,* had thereby discharged the Defendant and the other surety in the replevin bond.

Best Serjt. now shewed cause. This rule has been obtained upon a supposed analogy to the cases of bail. But the facts are not similar; all the cases where bail have been discharged have proceeded on the ground that the bail are for a time prevented from doing that which they

have

have a right to do. In the case of *Brickwood* v. *Anniss*(a), the Court held that as the bail were not prevented from surrendering their principal, they were not discharged. It is common practice to take a verdict at *nisi prius* subject to a reference, but it never yet was heard of, that by referring a cause, the bail were discharged in a case where there has been a verdict. The bail may be put in a worse situation, and yet not discharged, by the Defendant giving a *cognovit*, for he thereby accelerates execution; but it was nevertheless held in *Hodgson* v. *Nugent* (b) that the bail were not thereby discharged; but independently of that case, which has been questioned, the principle on which the bail are discharged or not discharged by a *cognovit*, is laid down in *Crofts* v. *Johnson* (c) and *Bousfield* v. *Tower* (d), and it does not entitle the Defendant to his present application.

Pell, contrà, urged that that principle did not operate to prevent his making the rule absolute. The agreement of 3d *March* 1814, and all the subsequent proceedings in consequence thereof, took place without the privity of the Defendant, who in consequence of *Shirreff* and the Plaintiff entering into these terms, was deprived of all chance of indemnity. If the replevin cause in which the Defendant was surety, had gone on to judgment in the regular course, probably the present Defendant could in some manner have proceeded against those goods which the Plaintiff in *September* took in execution. If the now Plaintiff had used due diligence, he might have had judgment of *non pros* against *Shirreff* on 30th *May* 1814, whereas the Defendant has no notice of any proceedings till *June* 1815, and in the mean time all the property is swept away,

1815.

MOORE
v.
BOWMAKER.

(a) *Ante,* v. 614.
(b) 5 T. R. 277.
(c) *Ante,* v. 319.
(d) *Ante,* iv. 456.

out

out of which, if the Plaintiff had proceeded with diligence in the replevin suit, the Defendant would have had the opportunity to indemnify himself by an action against the principal.

GIBBS C. J.   The principle was first adopted in the Court of Chancery, that if a creditor gives time of payment to his principal debtor, without giving notice to the surety, the surety no longer remains liable to the debt. The courts of law in late days have acted on the same principle, and applied it to the case of bail; for when the Plaintiff has given time to the principal, the bail are put in a new situation; for as the Plaintiff could not during that time take the Defendant, so neither can the bail, whose right grows out of the Plaintiff's.   But what is the present case? Sureties in replevin cannot at any time take the goods of the Plaintiff and restore them to the avowant.   As to the other part of the case, the agreement between the Plaintiff and Defendant to refer resembles a rule to refer the quantum of damages, and there the bail are answerable for the amount: this has no resemblance to the case where the bail are prevented from rendering the principal, and therefore there is no ground for the application.

Rule discharged.

9 B C 415.   1815.

GERNON *v.* The ROYAL EXCHANGE ASSURANCE.   *Nov.* 24.

THIS was an action on a policy of insurance on sugar
    by the *Mary,* from *Liverpool* to *Calais,* or the ship's
port of discharge in the *British* Channel. Upon the
trial of the cause at *Guildhall,* at the sittings after
Trinity term 1815, before *Gibbs* C. J., the Plaintiff
sought to recover as for a total loss. It appeared that the
ship sailed on 1st *December* 1814, and meeting with tem-
pestuous weather on the 20th, put back into *Liverpool.*
On the same day, one of the owners there resident,
apprized his agent in *London* of her return; and that
it was presumed there would be some damage from the
salt water: this was stated to the Defendants on the 22d,
who begged the assured would act as if they were uninsured. On the 21st, surveyors were employed to
inspect the condition of the sugar, and the master made
a protest. On the 24th, the owners wrote that the
cargo had been discharged, and was about to undergo
a proper survey, and that from present appearances, the
number of chests which had received damage would
not be at all equal to what they had feared, and might
have been expected; and they requested the underwriter's permission to proceed with the cargo to the port
of *Havre,* or to the ship's original destination. The
defendants, transacting no business on the 26th, received this communication on the 27th; they refrained
from making any observation thereon. On the 29th,
the owners wrote, renewing their application for permission to go to a second port, and added, that after
a minute inspection of the sugars, upwards of 290
boxes were found to have received more or less damage,
a number far exceeding what they had at first reason to
be partial, and that the adventure might be pursued.

If a cargo be so much damaged that it is not fit to be sent forward to a market,
the assured may abandon as a total loss.

expect;

An assured is entitled to a reasonable time for acquiring a full knowledge of the state of a damaged cargo, before he is bound to elect, whether he shall aban-don to the underwriters as for a total loss. Where a cargo of sugar da-maged by sea water came into port on 20th December began to be unshipped and examined on 21st, but the assured did not receive the complete re-port of the sur-vey till 7th January, held that an aban-donment on 7th January was made within a rea-sonable time, though the plaintiff had in the meantime con-templated that the loss would

expect; and many of the packages, which the water was supposed not to have actually penetrated, were nevertheless so discoloured by the general humidity, as to be much deteriorated, and it was impossible to say how far the real injury might extend. Under those circumstances, they had advertised the damaged part of the cargo for sale by auction, conceiving that measure to be the best for the Defendants' interest. On 2d *January*, the Defendants being applied to for instructions, declined giving any directions upon the subject of the damaged goods. On the 7th of *January* the owners having obtained a formal protest and certificate of survey, and of the damage of the cargo, sent them to the Defendants, adding, that it appeared by the latter, that the greater part of the cargo was destroyed, and that the whole had suffered deterioration, insomuch that they could not think of sending any part of the cargo forward, and they signified to the insurers their intention of abandoning the whole, and that it would be brought to sale on a day named. Upon the result of the sales, the loss appeared to amount to somewhat more than one-third of the amount insured. The defendants contended, first, that this was in its nature not a total, but only a partial loss; and secondly, that if otherwise, yet the abandonment came too late to convert it to a total loss. His Lordship, pursuing the rule which he had always adopted in similar cases, left it to the jury, whether the cargo was fit to be sent forward to a market; if it was fit to proceed, it ought to be sent on; if it was not, the Plaintiffs had a right to abandon, if they did it in a reasonable time. They ought to have a sufficient time to examine whether it were worth their while to pursue the adventure, and until they had had an opportunity of exercising their judgment, they ought not to be prejudiced. The time taken for communication between *London* and *Liverpool* was to be taken

into

into the account, as prolonging the period necessary
for their election; and he left to the jury the question,
whether the time which the Plaintiff had taken for
making his abandonment, was longer than was sufficient
for ascertaining and judging of the state of the cargo.
The jury found that the sugars were so much deteriorated, that the voyage was not worth pursuing, and
that the assured had abandoned in a reasonable time,
and found a verdict for the Plaintiff for a total loss
minus a sum which the Defendants had paid into court,
to cover a partial loss, subject to the latter question,
which His Lordship reserved, whether the Plaintiffs had
taken a longer time to make their election than the law
allowed them.

Shepherd, Solicitor-General, in this term, obtained on
the authority of *Mitchell* v. *Edie* (a), a rule *nisi* upon
the point reserved, to set aside the verdict, and enter a
verdict for the Defendant. He also moved on the
ground that inasmuch as the deterioration had scarcely
exceeded one-third of the original cost of the cargo, it
was not a case where abandonment could convert the
average loss to a total loss; and he cited *Thompson* v.
The Royal Exchange Assurance (b), and *Anderson* v. *Wal-
lace* (c), but the Court refused to extend the rule to this
point. -

Lens and *Vaughan*, Serjts. shewed cause. They contended that the evidence proved that the plaintiff had
taken no longer time to form his judgment on the propriety of abandoning, than was necessary for that purpose; for it was plain from the correspondence, that
until the 7th of *January*, when the assured first obtained the surveyor's report on the cargo, he was not

(a) 1 *Term Rep.* 608.   (b) 16 *East*, 214.
(c) 2 *Maule & Selw.* 240.

in

1815.

GERSON
v.
The ROYAL
EXCHANGE
ASSURANCE.

1815.

GERNON
v.
The ROYAL
EXCHANGE
ASSURANCE.

in possession of all the necessary information for his guidance. It appears, that up to the date of the preceding letter of the 29th *December*, the assured thought that the voyage was capable of being pursued. There had been the most ample good faith in the Plaintiff's communications with the Defendants, who refused to interfere, and left all to the Plaintiff's discretion and management.   .   *

Best and *Bosanquet*, Serjts., *contra*, stated the rule to be, that as soon as the assured or his agent has a fair opportunity to make up his mind upon the state of the cargo, he shall abandon. *Atwood* v. *Henckill* (a). The Plaintiff had previously, by his letter of the 29th *December*, given the Defendants notice of his election to send forward the part of the cargo that had been preserved, and to sell for the benefit of the Defendants that which was damaged, treating the loss as partial: and he could not afterwards revoke his election. In the case of *Anderson* v. *The Royal Exchange Assurance* (b), it was held that an abandonment of a sunken cargo of provisions must be made on notice of their sinking, not a month after, upon their being fished up and inspected. The Plaintiff is not warranted in withholding his election while he is ascertaining the state of the intended market, or speculating on the rise and fall of prices: neither, while he is pursuing his inquiries, ought he to do any act that can alter the state of the property, or deal with them as if they were his own. There is reason to infer, that pending the delay which intervened between the 20th of *December* and the 9th of *January*, the damage occasioned to the sugars by the sea water had much increased, for want of the Plaintiff's speedy care, and it is unfair that this loss should be thrown on the underwriter. The Defendants'

(a) 1 *Park Ins.* 6 *Ed.* 239.   (b) 7 *East*, 38.

         instructions

instructions to treat the goods as if the Plaintiff was uninsured, must be taken with reference to the Plaintiff's
election to consider this as a partial loss; for if the
Defendants had known it was to be a total loss, they
would themselves have assumed the direction of the sale:
and although on the 29th of *December* the Plaintiff
might not know the precise extent of the injury, he must
have known enough to enable him then to judge of the
propriety of abandonment.

GIBBS C. J. delivered the opinion of the Court. It
is very true that the assured must always elect in the first
instance, whether he will consider a loss as partial, and
take to the property himself, or as total, and abandon
to the underwriter. This is the law in all cases where
the assured has his election by abandoning or not abandoning to treat the loss as total or partial. But it is
equally true, that the first instance means, after the
assured has had a convenient opportunity of examining
into the circumstances which render abandonment expedient or otherwise; because it is on the result of that
examination that he is to make up his mind, whether
he will abandon or not. Let it not be supposed that I
accede to the proposition, that the assured may use this
latitude as an opportunity to judge of the state of the
markets, and as the markets fall or rise, to elect whether
he will abandon or not abandon. He has no right to
govern his conduct by any such rule. The only examination he may make, is into the actual state of the
cargo, to ascertain what is the degree of damage,
without reference to the state of the markets. It is
certainly true that a certain amount of damage was at
first discovered, but the assured did not then think this
cargo so much damaged, but that, as to a considerable
part, the adventure might be pursued; though a part
was necessarily to be disposed of at *Liverpool.* He so
                                        considered

1815.

GERNON
v.
The ROYAL
EXCHANGE
ASSURANCE.

considered on the 24th of *December* ; he so considered it on the 29th, though on the 29th the Plaintiff considered that the loss would be much more extensive than was at first supposed. If the Plaintiff had so treated it, as intending to pursue the adventure, after he knew the full extent of the damage, I should have thought that the abandonment was too late; but on the 29th the assured certainly thought a part of the cargo was in a state to go on. On the ultimate evidence, by the letter of 7th *January*, it appears, and the jury have disposed of the fact, that no part of the cargo was in a state to go on. It was not competent to set up this abandonment on the 7th, if the assurers were fully apprized of the facts on the 29th; but I think it appears from all the circumstances, that they were not so apprized on the 29th, and that the cargo had not then undergone so full an examination as was afterwards made. They ought to have a reasonable and convenient time for their inspection; if they had been dilatory in making their survey, it would have been a very different case: though the Plaintiff ought not to be pressed too closely on this point, yet, if he had been grossly negligent, and had slept over-the business, I think it would have been an answer to the Plaintiff's demand; but here is no unreasonable delay, and therefore we think there is no ground for saying the abandonment was made at too late a period, and the rule for a new trial must be

Discharged.

BROWN v. GARNIER.

*P*ELL Serjt. moved to discharge the Defendant out of custody, on a defect in the affidavit to hold to bail, which stated the Defendant to be indebted to the Plaintiff in 15*l.* and upwards, for the hire of divers carriages of the deponent, hired to and for the use of the Defendant. The Defendant, he said, might have the use, yet not be answerable to the Plaintiff, unless he contracted for them, and they might have been hired by another person, who might be answerable to the Plaintiff, though the Defendant had the use of the carriages. Another objection was, that the affidavit stated the Defendant to be indebted to the Plaintiff for work and labour done for the Defendant, but it did not aver that the work and labour were done at his special instance and request.

Per Curiam. That objection has been held insufficient; and as to the first, " hired to the Defendant" implies a contract, and is equivalent to saying " let to hire to the Defendant," and though hired to the Defendant is not a strictly proper expression, it is not an unusual one.

Rule refused.

An affidavit to hold to bail for the " hire of carriages hired to the defendant," and for " work and labour done for the defendant," not adding at his request, held sufficient.

Nov. 24.

WILLIAMS *v.* MARSHALL.

A licence to export to an hostile country was to continue in force for exporting un-till the 10th of *September.* The ship cleared at the custom-house in *London* on the 9th *September,* and on the 12th received her clearing note at *Gravesend.* No evidence being given by the assured to account for the delay, held that the ship had not ex-ported the cargo before the 10th, and that the in-surance was void.

THIS was an action upon a policy of insurance bearing date in 1809, at and from *London* to *Amsterdam,* then an hostile port, on hides by the ship *Constantia :* it was tried at *Guildhall* before *Gibbs* C. J. at the sittings after *Trinity* term 1815, when it was proved that a licence for the voyage had been obtained from the privy council, which was to continue in force until the 10th of *September* for exporting, and until the 1st of *October* for the ship's return. The defence was, that the voyage was illegal, because the ship did not sail within the time warranted by the licence. The ship cleared on the 9th of *September* at the *London* custom-house, but did not arrive at *Gravesend,* and deliver over the papers necessary to be there produced, until the 12th, on which day the King's searcher proved that he delivered to the master, as is usual, certain cockets received from *London,* and a note with dates, called a clearing note, which is the latest document given to the master, of a vessel outward-bound from *London,* after he has delivered all necessary papers at *Gravesend.* He is not required to sign any document at *Gravesend.* When any drawback of duty is to be repaid to the master on exportation, he cannot entitle himself to the drawback without producing this clear-ing note. *Gibbs* C. J. at first thought it must be con-sidered that the vessel had sailed in due time, for that she had commenced her voyage by dropping down from *London* to *Gravesend,* and licences had of late been liberally interpreted, but upon the evidence given by the searcher of the custom-house, he reserved the point, subject whereto the jury found a verdict for the Plaintiff.

Lens

Lens Serjt. in this term obtained a rule *nisi* to set aside the verdict and enter a nonsuit, against which

Shepherd, Solicitor-General, and *Best* and *Bosanquet*, Serjts. shewed cause. They contended it was not necessary that a vessel should have actually sailed within the time limited by the licence, where it did not appear that she had been deficient in fair diligence, and there was no cause of delay imputed to the Plaintiffs in this case. *Gröning* v. *Crockett* (a), *Goede Hoop, Pieters* (b), *Schroder* v. *Vaux* (c). The principle is thereby established, that if there be no fraud, the ship shall continue to have the benefit of the licence after the time therein mentioned has expired. Even on a warranty to sail before a certain day, if a ship has broken ground, it suffices. To export, simply means to carry out; and if the duties are paid, and the change of place has commenced, there is an exportation. To export cannot mean to convey without the port, for if it did, exportation could not commence, as it is admitted it does, on moving from *Gravesend*, for the port of *London* extends far beyond that limit. No decisions had indeed occurred on the question whether the act of clearing at the custom-house would entitle a ship to the benefit of a licence. It is a very different question, what test the legislature may chuse to fix for entitling parties to a drawback; and there is also a material distinction between the construction of a revenue act, which is to be construed strictly, and of these licences, which are to be construed most liberally; and therefore, even if, on the demurrer now pending in the court of Exchequer in the case of the *King* v. *Poughet*, (which is a suit for the additional duty imposed by the stat. 52 *G*. 3. *c*. 94.

(a) 3 *Campb.* 85.   (c) 3 *Campb.* 84.
(b) *Edwards, Leading Decisions*; 6.

D d 2   on

on all hides in *Great Britain*, and is resisted on the ground that the Defendant's hides were on board ship for exportation, and had passed the custom-house before the day appointed for the operation of the act to take place, although not yet got to *Gravesend*, and were therefore to be considered as already exported,) the decision should be adverse to the subject; that would not govern this case. The appointment of *Gravesend* as the place where certain acts are to be done, is a mere fiscal regulation to prevent fraud, for if the drawbacks were to be paid in *London*, there would be frequent opportunities to re-land the goods, and defraud the revenue. But if the master of a vessel should chuse to relinquish his drawback, it does not appear that there would be any occasion for him to bring to at *Gravesend*, and in that case no limit for the commencement of his voyage can be assigned, except the clearing at the custom-house and breaking ground from *London*. In a case where the vessel, to all appearance, had plainly transgressed her limited time, the *onus* to excuse the delay would be incumbent on the assured; but where the question is on the construction of a doubtful expression, the *onus* lies on the underwriter to shew fraud or laches. And therefore the plaintiff was not called on to account by evidence for the ship's not sooner sailing. In the case of the *Goede Hoop, Pieters,* Sir *W. Scott* called on the underwriters to point out how the assured could be benefited by fraud, where his apparent interest was, as here it is, to use dispatch.

Lens, in support of his rule, urged that the meaning of the word to export, was to convey out of the port, and not simply to carry outwards. There ought not to to be two different meanings given to the word. The embargo, which was taken as a fact in the case of the *Goede Hoop*, materially distinguishes that case from
this,

this, and it was not the underwriter who was to shew the existence, but the assured by that fact shewed the absence of fraud. In cases where an excuse is admissible, the delay is always to be accounted for by the assured, and in this case there is no evidence of the cause of the delay. The moment a ship has exported goods, the drawback is due, therefore a master would be entitled to receive the drawback on breaking ground from *London*, if that were exportation ; but he is not entitled to it till he receives his clearing note at *Gravesend*. The ship had on the 10th done much towards exporting, but more remained to be done. The residue of his argument was stopped by the Court.

GIBBS C. J. I should have been exceedingly glad to find that this licence was substantially complied with. The voyage to be performed was illegal without a licence: one of the terms on which the licence was granted, is, that the goods shall be exported on or before the 10th *September :* these goods were not cleared at the custom-house till the 9th of *September :* the ship had not sailed on the 10th of *September.* On the 12th she was at *Gravesend,* but when she weighed, it does not appear. Whether she was covered by this licence, or not, depends on the question whether she sailed on the 10th. I cannot say, however I may be disposed to favour the Plaintiffs, that the clearing at the custom-house is an exportation. Considerable light is thrown on the question by the fact, that by the regulations, or at least by the practice of this country, the drawback is not paid till after the passing *Gravesend ;* and therefore upon the interpretation, which has prevailed, of those acts of parliament which give a drawback, it appears that ships are not considered as having exported till after passing *Gravesend ;* therefore, with every diposition to favour this action, we cannot say that the Plaintiffs are entitled to recover.

Rule absolute for a new trial, the Defendant admitting the two policies as stated in the declaration.

Nov. 25.

Sir CHARLES MORGAN, Bart. v. EDWARDS and Others.

A lease granted liberty to make levels, pits, and soughs. A declaration in covenant stated it as a liberty to make soughs: held that by the rule *noscitur a sociis*, the Court could discover this to be the word soughs, only mis-spelt, and that it was not a fatal variance.

A declaration described lands demised to be in the parish of *B.* and *M.*: the deed demised lands in the parishes of *B.* & *M.*, the Court held the variance fatal.

Lands in the occupations of *A. B. & C.*, intended of the several occupations of *A. B. & C.*

THIS was an action of covenant for rent on three several colliery leases. Two of the Defendants suffered judgment by default, and the Defendant *Edwards* pleaded *non sunt facta ;* and upon the trial before *Richards*, B. at the *Monmouth* Summer Assizes 1814, a verdict was found for the Plaintiff upon the second and third counts, of the declaration, with liberty for the Defendant to move to enter a general verdict for himself.

Pell Serjt., in *Michaelmas* term, accordingly moved upon the ground of variances affecting the second and third counts, and also moved to arrest the judgment on the third count. The Court directed the points to be submitted to them in the shape of a special case, by which it now appeared, that the second count recited a lease to the Defendants of a colliery, with a grant of " liberty to dig, sink, drive, run, and make pits, shafts, " levels, and sloughs:" the indenture produced to verify this allegation, contained a grant of " liberty to " dig, sink, drive, run, and make pits, shafts, levels, " and soughs." The third count described the premises demised by the indenture therein stated, as being " situate in the parish of *Bedwas* and *Moneytheusloyne*, then in the occupations of *W. Lewis*, *Abraham Edwards*, and

and *Amey Edwards.*" The indenture given in evidence
described the premises as " situate in the parishes of
Bedwas and *Moneytheusloyne*, then in the several occupations of *W. Lewis, Abraham Edwards,* and *Amey
Edwards.*" It was objected that there were two variances
upon this count, for that the declaration described one
parish which bore the conjoint name of *Bedwas* and
Moneytheusloyne, whereas the deed demised lands in two
parishes, one named *Bedwas*, the other named *Moneytheusloyne;* the other was, that upon the declaration, the
land appeared to be in the joint occupation of three joint
tenants, whereas several parts of it were held by three
several tenants.   The Court treated this objection very
lightly.   The covenant alleged in the third count, and
proved, was for payment of the rent, " clear of all
" payments, &c. on account of taxes, &c., whether in
" the nature of property-tax or not," on which the
objection was made in arrest of judgment, that this was
an illegal covenant, and totally void.

Shepherd, Solicitor-General, for the Plaintiff, con
tended, that as it was not necessary to set out the deed,
nor did this declaration purport to give the tenor; the
insertion of the word " slough" was therefore immaterial;
for, as it was here applied, and with reference to this
deed, it was insensible, whether understood of a wound,
or of a quagmire, and did not vitiate; the statement of
the liberty to make soughs, which was intended, was
not necessary to the shewing that the Plaintiff had a
good cause of action for rent, and therefore might safely
be omitted.   As to the second point, it did not necessarily
follow that the words parish of *B.* and *M.* meant that
B. and *M.* were one parish.   Part of the land might
be in the parish of *B.*, and part might be in *M.*   If
premises were described as being in the city of *London*
and *Westminster*, it would be easily understood not to

D d 4   be

be spoken of one city bearing that compound name, but that the latter place was described simply by its name, without stating its character, whether it were a city, borough, parish, vill, or *lieu conus*. It was not necessary to pursue the deed in stating that the demised premises were in a parish, any other adequate description of the land would suffice. As to the third objection, it is disposed of by the cases of *Fuller* v. *Abbott* (a), *Readshaw* v. *Balders* (b), and *Tinkler* v. *Prentice*. (c)

Pell for the Defendants abandoned the third point. As to the second, the word " slough" cannot be rejected ; in many cases even the variance of a letter in misdescribing a contract vitiates the record. The *Queen* v. *Drake* (d), 2d Res. by *Powys* J. *Drewry* v. *Twiss* (e). *Buller* J. lays it down, that a trivial variation in setting out a contract, a record, or any written instrument, is fatal, *Pitt* v. *Green* (f). The Plaintiff declared on a covenant to drain the *Cellar Beer* field, and the covenant in the lease was to drain the *Aller Beer* field, and the variance was held fatal. The Plaintiff describes the demise upon which he claims the rent, as a demise whereby he granted the Defendant permission to commit waste by making " sloughs" in the land, of what utility such a privilege would be to the Defendant, is not now the point to be considered; his answer to the action is, " I never was party to a deed whereby the lessor granted me any such privilege." The variance therefore is fatal. The third count describes all the premises as lying in one parish, called *B.* and *M.*, and the deed proves no demise of any land lying in any such parish of that name, which also is a fatal variance.

(a) *Ante*, iv. 104.   (d) *Salk.* 660.
(b) *Ante*, iv. 59.   (e) 4 *T. R.* 558.
(c) *Ante*, iv. 549.   (f) 9 *East*, 188.

The

The Solicitor-General replied.

GIBBS C. J. As to the second objection, the count which describes the premises to lie in the parish of *Bedwas* and *Moneytheusloyne*, must be taken to mean one parish, which bears that compound name, and the deed being different, it is a fatal variance. Another variance in the second count was relied on, and to judge whether it was fatal, we must weigh its materiality in stating the deed. The Plaintiff does not profess to set out the tenor of the deed, but to state the contract in substance; and if it be mis-described in substance, the objection is fatal. The declaration describes the demise as accompanied with the privilege to make sloughs, and the deed has it soughs: it is urged that these two are different things, and we agree, that if the declaration describes the demise as a letting, accompanied with a privilege of doing something which the deed gives him no privilege of doing, it would be fatal. Suppose the word had been " slough" in the deed, and the tenant had made an artificial quagmire, and the lessor had brought an action of waste for it, and the tenant had justified under the deed, I think the Court would have said, *noscitur a sociis*, and finding this word joined with things which are useful in working mines, and that no such purpose can be attributed to the word slough, in any sense of it, I at least should have said, it is a mis-spelling of the word sough, a thing which is useful for working mines: if so, I think this is not here a fatal variance, and that the verdict may be supported on this count.

CHAMBRE J. It would have been a wasting of the land to have granted licence to make a slough, meaning
a quag-

a quagmire; therefore it cannot be presumed (a) that such is the meaning.

> Judgment for the Defendant on the second count, and for the Plaintiff on the third.

Where two of three joint covenantors suffer judgment by default on counts on several deeds, and the third defends and succeeds on some counts, the Plaintiff cannot hold his judgment on those counts against the other two.

In such case neither party is entitled to costs on the counts on which the Plaintiff fails.

In this case, the other two Defendants having suffered judgment by default on all the counts, the prothonotary taxed full costs for the Plaintiff on all the counts notwithstanding the above decision, conceiving that inasmuch as the three Defendants had jointly become possessed of these leases as devisees of the original lessor, (which was the fact, and was averred in the declaration), the Defendant *Edwards*, who alone defended, would be entitled to recover from the others, in the shape of contribution, the entire costs of those counts, on which, though they had confessed judgment, he had obtained a verdict.

Pell Serjt. in this term obtained a rule *nisi*, that the prothonotary might review his taxation. It was sufficiently hard on the Defendant if he should not be entitled to have costs taxed for him on the two counts wherein the Plaintiff had unnecessarily set out two very long indentures, and had failed; but admitting that the practice of the Court did not entitle him to the costs of those counts, at least the Defendant was not liable to pay costs on them. *Penson* v. *Lee* (b). The Plaintiff cannot now even maintain his judgment against the other two on the counts found for the Defendant *Edwards*. *Porter* v. *Harris*. (c)

(a) But as to the parish, see *Goodtitle* on demise of *Bremridge* v. *Walter*, ante, iv, 671, (which was not cited), contrà; quære necne melius.

(b) 2 *Bos. & Pull.* 330.   (c) 2 *Lev.* 63.

Shepherd, Solicitor-General, endeavoured to support the taxation on the authority of *Norris* v. *Waldron* (*a*), which clearly established the practice of this Court to be, that if the Plaintiff succeeds on one count, he is entitled to the costs of his whole declaration, which was confirmed in *Teasdale* v. *Spicer.* (*b*)

Bell in support of his rule urged, that the practice had been altered in *Penson* v. *Lee*, and was now conformable to the practice of the Court of King's Bench.

Per Curiam. As the practice of this Court is now settled, neither party is entitled to the costs of these counts : the circumstance relied on by the prothonotary does not take it out of the general rule. In tort, the Plaintiff might sustain his judgment against those Defendants who had suffered judgment by default, but in covenant he cannot hold his judgment on these counts against the two. Therefore the third could recover no contribution from them.

The rule must be absolute.

(*a*) 2 *W. Bl.* 1199.   (*b*) 2 *Bos. & Pull.* 51.

An amendment of the Plaintiff's declaration does not necessarily entitle the Defendant to plead *de novo,* but only where the amendment alters the state of the Defendant's case.

IN this action the Plaintiff originally declared, and delivered a particular of his demand, for use and occupation to *October* 1813, and for damages for the mismanagement of a farm, and for carrying off manure, and for the costs of an action against an undertenant for rent, and for interest on the balances, against *Watson* and *Cowlam,* and the Defendants pleaded the general issue: after issue joined, the Plaintiff, upon an unattended summons, obtained an order simply for amending his declaration upon payment of costs, without expressing a permission to the Defendant to plead *de novo.* He then delivered an additional particular for half a year's use and occupation to *May* 1814, to which no objection was made; and having struck out the name of *Cowlam,* who had never appeared, nor been served with notice of declaration, he sent back the issue on 5th *July* 1815, indorsed with notice of trial for the ensuing *Lincoln* assizes, which were on the 15th, and apprized the Defendant's attorney of the nature of the amendment. The Defendant refused to accept the issue so sent back, until the costs of the amendment were taxed and the amendment actually made, and until the Defendant had had an opportunity of pleading *de novo,* if necessary. The Plaintiff again delivered the issue on the 7th, and the Defendant again returned it, and re-delivered on the 10th the amended declaration. On the 8th of *July* the Plaintiff procured the costs to be taxed, and gave notice of trial, and carried down the record. The Defendant, who was under terms of accepting short notice of trial, relying on his right to plead *de novo,* as a matter of course consequent on the amendment, did not appear to defend the cause,

and

and the Plaintiff recovered a verdict. In this term
Shepherd, Solicitor-General, for the Defendant, obtained
a rule *nisi* to set aside the verdict and have a new trial
upon the ground that the trial and notice of trial were
irregular, for that the rule for the amendment was improperly drawn up by the Plaintiff, inasmuch as it did
not contain liberty for the Defendant to plead *de novo*,
to which he was entitled as a matter of right.

Copley Serjt. shewed cause against this rule. He
urged, that the liberty to plead *de novo* was not a
matter of course incident to every amendment, but only
to such as changed the nature of the defence.

GIBBS C. J. agreed that an amendment often was
such as could not render it necessary for the Defendant
to plead *de novo*. He recollected an instance, wherein
Lord *Mansfield* had made an order in *London* for
amending the pleadings in a *quo warranto*, which was
tried at *Dorchester* on the very day after the date of his
order. *Heath* J. observed, that upon attendances before
a judge at chambers, upon a summons to amend, it was
a question continually mooted by the attornies on both
sides, whether the amendment prayed for was, under
the circumstances of the case, such in its nature as to,
entitle the Defendant to plead *de novo*, therefore it was
not necessarily and in all cases attended with that effect.

The Solicitor-General then endeavoured to support
the rule, upon the ground that the Plaintiff never re-
delivered the issue after the amendment made; and the
delivery on the 7th, being before the taxation and payment of costs, put the Plaintiff in no better condition
than the delivery on the 5th. And upon this ground,
the Court made the rule

Absolute.

on all hides in *Great Britain*, and is resisted on the ground that the Defendant's hides were on board ship for exportation, and had passed the custom-house before the day appointed for the operation of the act to take place, although not yet got to *Gravesend*, and were therefore to be considered as already exported,) the decision should be adverse to the subject; that would not govern this case. The appointment of *Gravesend* as the place where certain acts are to be done, is a mere fiscal regulation to prevent fraud, for if the drawbacks were to be paid in *London*, there would be frequent opportunities to re-land the goods, and defraud the revenue. But if the master of a vessel should chuse to relinquish his drawback, it does not appear that there would be any occasion for him to bring to at *Gravesend*, and in that case no limit for the commencement of his voyage can be assigned, except the clearing at the custom-house and breaking ground from *London*. In a case where the vessel, to all appearance, had plainly transgressed her limited time, the *onus* to excuse the delay would be incumbent on the assured; but where the question is on the construction of a doubtful expression, the *onus* lies on the underwriter to shew fraud or laches. And therefore the plaintiff was not called on to account by evidence for the ship's not sooner sailing. In the case of the *Goede Hoop*, *Pieters*, Sir *W. Scott* called on the underwriters to point out how the assured could be benefited by fraud, where his apparent interest was, as here it is, to use dispatch.

Lens, in support of his rule, urged that the meaning of the word to export, was to convey out of the port, and not simply to carry outwards. There ought not to to be two different meanings given to the word. The embargo, which was taken as a fact in the case of the *Goede Hoop*, materially distinguishes that case from

this,

this, and it was not the underwriter who was to shew the existence, but the assured by that fact shewed the absence of fraud. In cases where an excuse is admissible, the delay is always to be accounted for by the assured, and in this case there is no evidence of the cause of the delay. The moment a ship has exported goods, the drawback is due, therefore a master would be entitled to receive the drawback on breaking ground from *London,* if that were exportation; but he is not entitled to it till he receives his clearing note at *Gravesend.* The ship had on the 10th done much towards exporting, but more remained to be done. The residue of his argument was stopped by the Court.

GIBBS C. J. I should have been exceedingly glad to find that this licence was substantially complied with. The voyage to be performed was illegal without a licence: one of the terms on which the licence was granted, is, that the goods shall be exported on or before the 10th *September:* these goods were not cleared at the custom-house till the 9th of *September:* the ship had not sailed on the 10th of *September.* On the 12th she was at *Gravesend,* but when she weighed, it does not appear. Whether she was covered by this licence, or not, depends on the question whether she sailed on the 10th. I cannot say, however I may be disposed to favour the Plaintiffs, that the clearing at the custom-house is an exportation. Considerable light is thrown on the question by the fact, that by the regulations, or at least by the practice of this country, the drawback is not paid till after the passing *Gravesend;* and therefore upon the interpretation, which has prevailed, of those acts of parliament which give a drawback, it appears that ships are not considered as having exported till after passing *Gravesend;* therefore, with every diposition to favour this action, we cannot say that the Plaintiffs are entitled to recover.

Rule absolute for a new trial, the Defendant admitting the two policies as stated in the declaration.

Nov. 25.   Sir CHARLES MORGAN, Bart. v. EDWARDS and Others.

A lease granted liberty to make levels, pits, and soughs. A declaration in covenant stated it as a liberty to make soughs: held that by the rule *noscitur a sociis*, the Court could discover this to be the word soughs, only mis-spelt, and that it was not a fatal variance.

A declaration described lands demised to be in the parish of B. and M.: the deed demised lands in the parishes of B. & M., the Court held the variance fatal.

Lands in the occupations of A. B. & C., intended of the several occupations of A. B. & C.

THIS was an action of covenant for rent on three several colliery leases. Two of the Defendants suffered judgment by default, and the Defendant *Edwards* pleaded *non sunt facta ;* and upon the trial before *Richards*, B. at the *Monmouth* Summer Assizes 1814, a verdict was found for the Plaintiff upon the second and third counts of the declaration, with liberty for the Defendant to move to enter a general verdict for himself.

Pell Serjt., in *Michaelmas* term, accordingly moved upon the ground of variances affecting the second and third counts, and also moved to arrest the judgment on the third count. The Court directed the points to be submitted to them in the shape of a special case, by which it now appeared, that the second count recited a lease to the Defendants of a colliery, with a grant of " liberty to dig, sink, drive, run, and make pits, shafts, " levels, and soughs :" the indenture produced to verify this allegation, contained a grant of " liberty to " dig, sink, drive, run, and make pits, shafts, levels, " and soughs." The third count described the premises demised by the indenture therein stated, as being " situate in the parish of *Bedwas* and *Moneytheusloyne*, then in the occupations of *W. Lewis, Abraham Edwards*,

and

and *Amey Edwards*." The indenture given in evidence
described the premises as " situate in the parishes of
Bedwas and *Moneytheusloyne*, then in the several occupations of *W. Lewis, Abraham Edwards*, and *Amey
Edwards*." It was objected that there were two variances
upon this count, for that the declaration described one
parish which bore the conjoint name of *Bedwas* and
Moneytheusloyne, whereas the deed demised lands in two
parishes, one named *Bedwas*, the other named *Moneytheusloyne ;* the other was, that upon the declaration, the
land appeared to be in the joint occupation of three joint
tenants, whereas several parts of it were held by three
several tenants. The Court treated this objection very
lightly. The covenant alleged in the third count, and
proved, was for payment of the rent, " clear of all
" payments, &c. on account of taxes, &c., whether in
" the nature of property-tax or not," on which the
objection was made in arrest of judgment, that this was
an illegal covenant, and totally void.

Shepherd, Solicitor-General, for the Plaintiff, contended, that as it was not necessary to set out the deed,
nor did this declaration purport to give the tenor; the
insertion of the word " slough" was therefore immaterial;
for, as it was here applied, and with reference to this
deed, it was insensible, whether understood of a wound,
or of a quagmire, and did not vitiate ; the statement of
the liberty to make soughs, which was intended, was
not necessary to the shewing that the Plaintiff had a
good cause of action for rent, and therefore might safely
be omitted. As to the second point, it did not necessarily
follow that the words parish of *B.* and *M.* meant that
B. and *M.* were one parish. Part of the land might
be in the parish of *B.*, and part might be in *M.* If
premises were described as being in the city of *London*
and *Westminster*, it would be easily understood not to

D d 4   be

be spoken of one city bearing that compound name, but that the latter place was described simply by its name, without stating its character, whether it were a city, borough, parish, vill, or *lieu conus*. It was not necessary to pursue the deed in stating that the demised premises were in a parish, any other adequate description of the land would suffice. As to the third objection, it is disposed of by the cases of *Fuller* v. *Abbott* (a), *Readshaw* v. *Balders* (b), and *Tinkler* v. *Prentice*. (c)

Pell for the Defendants abandoned the third point. As to the second, the word " slough" cannot be rejected; in many cases even the variance of a letter in misdescribing a contract vitiates the record. The *Queen* v. *Drake* (d), 2d Res. by *Powys* J. *Drewry* v. *Twiss* (e). *Buller* J. lays it down, that a trivial variation ih setting out a contract, a record, or any written instrument, is fatal, *Pitt* v. *Green* (f). The Plaintiff declared on a covenant to drain the *Cellar Beer* field, and the covenant in the lease was to drain the *Aller Beer* field, and the variance was held fatal. The Plaintiff describes the demise upon which he claims the rent, as a demise whereby he granted the Defendant permission to commit waste by making " sloughs" in the land, of what utility such a privilege would be to the Defendant, is not now the point to be considered; his answer to the action is, " I never was party to a deed whereby the lessor granted me any such privilege." The variance therefore is fatal. The third count describes all the premises as lying in one parish, called B. and M., and the deed proves no demise of any land lying in any such parish of that name, which also is a fatal variance.

(a) *Ante*, iv. 104.   (d) *Salk.* 660.
(b) *Ante*, iv. 59.   (e) 4 *T. R.* 558.
(c) *Ante*, iv. 549.   (f) 9 *East*, 188.

The

The Solicitor-General replied.

GIBBS C. J. As to the second objection, the count which describes the premises to lie in the parish of *Bedwas* and *Moneytheusloyne*, must be taken to mean one parish, which bears that compound name, and the deed being different, it is a fatal variance. Another variance in the second count was relied on, and to judge whether it was fatal, we must weigh its materiality in stating the deed. The Plaintiff does not profess to set out the tenor of the deed, but to state the contract in substance; and if it be mis-described in substance, the objection is fatal. The declaration describes the demise as accompanied with the privilege to make sloughs, and the deed has it soughs: it is urged that these two are different things, and we agree, that if the declaration describes the demise as a letting, accompanied with a privilege of doing something which the deed gives him no privilege of doing, it would be fatal. Suppose the word had been "slough" in the deed, and the tenant had made an artificial quagmire, and the lessor had brought an action of waste for it, and the tenant had justified under the deed, I think the Court would have said, *noscitur a sociis*, and finding this word joined with things which are useful in working mines, and that no such purpose can be attributed to the word slough, in any sense of it, I at least should have said, it is a mis-spelling of the word sough, a thing which is useful for working mines: if so, I think this is not here a fatal variance, and that the verdict may be supported on this count.

CHAMBRE J. It would have been a wasting of the land to have granted licence to make a slough, meaning

a quag-

Nov. 28.

Ex parte NICHOLAS.

The admission of an attorney who has omitted to take out his certificate for one whole year after his admission, is absolutely void, and he must be re-admitted before he can practise.

LENS Serjt. moved that Mr. *Nicholas*, who had been admitted an attorney, but had never practised for himself, nor taken out his certificate, but had for some time acted as an assistant to another gentleman, and then, falling ill, had discontinued practice altogether, might now, being recovered, be permitted to take out his certificate on payment of a small fine.

GIBBS C. J. The statute 37 *G* 3. *c.* 90. *s.* 31., says that every person admitted who shall neglect to obtain his certificate for the space of one whole year, shall be incapable of practising in any of the courts by virtue of his admission, and the admission shall be from thenceforth null and void. Mr. *Nicholas* must therefore be re-admitted.

Rule absolute to re-admit the applicant on payment of 6s. 8d. fine, and on his now taking out his certificate and paying the duty only from the present time.

Nov. 28.

AYRES v. BUSTON.

The Court will not permit a Plaintiff to amend by changing the venue without reasonable ground.

THIS was an action brought to recover the contribution which certain commissioners under an act for inclosing lands in *Bedfordshire*, had awarded to be paid by the Defendant to the expences of the inclosure, and the plaintiff having laid his venue in *Bedfordshire*, *Lens* Serjt. had obtained, upon the reading of the declaration, without affidavit, a rule *nisi* permitting him to amend by changing the venue to *Middlesex*.

Best

Best Serjt. shewed cause against this rule, contending that no sufficient ground was shewn for the application. There was a good reason for trying the cause in *Bedfordshire*, for one part of the award, which would be required in evidence, must be filed with the clerk of the peace of the county, and his affidavit stated that the cause of action arose, and all the witnesses resided, in that county.

Lens in support of his rule. There is nothing local in the action, and justice may be more speedily attained by a trial in *Middlesex*. The Defendant may afterwards change the venue back to *Bedfordshire*, if he can make the usual affidavit. This amendment has been allowed, *Stroud* v. *Tilly* (a), and *Rivet* v. *Cholmondeley* (b). There were two parts of the award, and the other of them was not filed with the clerk of the peace, but was wholly transitory.

Gibbs C. J. The Plaintiff has laid his venue in the county where the cause of action arose, and now desires to amend by removing the venue from that county to *Middlesex*, stating as a reason, that the Defendant may change the venue again on the usual affidavit, and that the Plaintiff cannot then bring it back without an undertaking to give material evidence in *Middlesex*: it is obvious what the effect would be of granting this request: the material evidence in *Middlesex* is the act of parliament for the inclosure. The Plaintiff having originally laid his cause in *Bedfordshire*, the Defendant objects that the Court ought not to remove it, because the cause of action arose in *Bedfordshire*, and the witnesses reside there, which seems a sufficient ground for not changing the venue by allowing this amendment.

Rule discharged.

(a) 2 *Str.* 1162.   (b) 2 *Str.* 1202.

RANDALL *v.* TUCHIN and Another.

26 .

The word estate, used in the operative clause of a will, although referring locality, conveys a fee-simple, unless there is in the will other matter to control that signification.

Devise to *T. C.* of various houses, described by situation, abuttals, dimensions, and occupiers, " all which estates, being copyhold of the manor of *K.*, I devise to *T. C.* for life, and after his decease, to to his son *M. C.*" Devise to *M. P.* of various other houses and premises similarly described, including the

THIS was an action brought to recover from the Defendants the deposit paid them by the Plaintiff, on his being declared the purchaser of certain premises, as money had and received to the Plaintiff's use, and interest. At the trial of the cause before *Gibbs* C. J., at a sittings in this term, a verdict was found for the Plaintiff for the deposit, without interest, subject to a case. The Defendants, who were auctioneers, under the direction of *Jones* and *Mercer,* the assignees of the effects of *Marinus Price,* a bankrupt, put up to sale by auction part of the estates of the bankrupt: the Plaintiff was declared the purchaser of a copyhold dwelling-house and blacksmith's shop, (formerly a stable, situate on the east side of *Fore-street, Lambeth,*) and paid a deposit: he objected to the title, contending that *Marinus Price* took in the premises under the will of *Marinus Coombes,* and the surrender to the use of such will, merely an estate for life. By that will *Marinus Coombes* devised to his nephew *Thomas Coombes* nine dwelling-houses, with sheds, wharfs, and other appurtenances, minutely describing them all separately, by their situation, abuttals, dimensions, and occupiers, " All which estates, being copyhold, and held of the manor of *Kennington*," he devised to *T. Coombes* for his life, and after his decease, to his son *Marinus Coombes.* He also devised to *T. Coombcs* two dwelling-houses, &c.

White Bear public-house, and abutting on the copyhold estate before given, " all which said estates, being copyhold of the manor of *K.,* I devise to *M. P.* for life, and after her decease, to her son *M. P.,* and I order that so long as *W. P.* shall chuse to live in the public-house, and keep the same in good repair, he shall not be charged more than his present rent. And I devise to *M. P.,* the son, all my freehold estate, situate, &c. And I bequeath to *S. G.* and *H.* his wife, and the survivor, the sum of 5*s. per* week out of the estates bequeathed to *M. P.* and *M. P.*" Held that *M. P.* the son took an estate in fee in the copyhold.

situated

situated at *Barnes*, which were copyhold, and held of
the dean and chapter of *Saint Paul's*, for his life, and
after his decease to his son *Marinus Coombes*; also
he devised to his niece *Mary Price*, all that brick
dwelling-house, and a wood four-stall stable, situate on
the east side of *Fore-street*, (the premises in question,)
adding the situation, abuttals, dimensions, and occupiers,
and a warehouse, and thirteen several dwelling-houses,
all minutely designated by a similar description of the
situation, abuttals, dimensions, and occupiers, and several of which were described as "abutting on the copyhold estate thereinbefore bequeathed to *Thomas Coombes*,"
and others as abutting on the copyhold estate of *Terence
Price*; and among them, the *White Bear* public-house
and appurtenances, as the same was in the occupation
of *William Points*; all which said estates, being copyhold, and held of the manor of *Kennington*, the testator
devised to his niece *Mary Price* for her own use, not
subject to the debts, power, controul, or engagements
of her husband, for her life, and after her decease to
her son *Marinus Price*; and he thereby ordered and
directed that so long as *W. Points* should chuse to live
in the *White Bear* public-house, and should keep the
same in good repair, he should not be charged more
than his present rent of fourteen pounds *per ann.* And
also he devised to *Marinus Price* all his freehold estate
situated in *Prince's-street* and *Eagle-and-Child Yard*,
as the same was in the occupation of —— *Beadle*, ——
Cook, and others. And the testator bequeathed to
Samuel Groves and his wife *Hannah Groves*, and the
survivor of them, the sum of five shillings *per week*, to
be paid to them weekly, from and out of the estates bequeathed to his niece *Mary Price*, and her son *Marinus
Price*. The question was, whether *Marinus Price*, the
bankrupt, took a fee-simple or life-estate in the copyholds
under that will.

E e 4

Bosanquet

Bosanquet Serjt. for the Plaintiff, contended that this case exactly coincided with the case of *Doe* on demise of *Bates* v. *Clayton* (a). Whether the word estate shall be descriptive of locality, or of interest, is, as was said by Lord *Mansfield* in *Hogan* v. *Jackson* (b), always a question of construction. It is material here, that the subject which is given to *Marinus Price*, is no other than that which the testator had before given to *Mary Price*; in the devise to her, the words of limitation are distinct from the word estate, the devise being express to her for her life; the word estate then, is, as to her, descriptive of locality, and the same meaning must be sustained when the same subject recurs. *Ibbotson* v. *Beckwith* (c) is the first case where the extended sense is given to the word estate, and a devise of all my estate at *Northwith Close*, was held to mean all my estate in my land at *Northwith Close*. The annuity is no proof that the devisor intended a fee, unless it be a charge on the person of the devisee; but where it is merely a charge on the rents and profits of the estates, as here, it raises no such presumption. *Doe* on demise of *Stevens* v. *Snelling* (d). Lord *Ellenborough* C. J. there explains *Doe* v. *Richards* (e), and says the principle was right, though its applicability to that case might be doubted. This annuity is merely to be paid out of the land. If otherwise, in the case of *Mary* and *Marinus Price* dying before the testator, the annuitants would have lost the bequest. If *Marinus* had died before *Mary*, then, if this annuity be a charge on the person, it would have been a charge on the person of *Mary* only, for *Marinus* would have taken nothing: yet *Mary* has most clearly a mere life-estate. This therefore falls within the principle of *Doe* v. *Mellor* (f).

(a) 8 *East*, 141.
(b) *Cowp.* 306.
(c) *Cas. temp. Talb.* 157.

(d) 5 *East*, 92.
(e) 3 *Term Rep.* 356.
(f) 5 *Term Rep.* 558.

Doe v. *Snelling,* and *Doe* v. *Clarke* (*a*). There are no introductory words here expressive of an intent to dispose of all the testator's interest, and without such, a gift for life with a general devise over, unaccompanied by words of limitation, will not give a fee. *Doe ex dem. Bowes* v. *Blacket* (*b*). *Fawcet's* case (*c*). No inference in favour of a fee can be drawn from the devise of all the testator's freehold estate to *Marinus Price.*

Copley Serjt. *contrà,* contended that *Marinus Price* took an estate in fee. The counsel for the Plaintiff had distinctly stated the principle on which this question was to be decided. He agreed that it made no distinction, whether the land were freehold or copyhold. It is clear that where a person disposes of all his interest he may do it by the word estate. Here the testator bequeaths all his freehold estate to one individual generally, which plainly carries the fee. In many cases it has been held that descriptive words superadded to the word estate, only designate the local situation. If the testator had devised all his copyhold, as he did all his freehold, to one person, he would have said, I give all my freehold and all my copyhold estate to *A. B.,* but when he had to divide the copyholds between *A.* and *B.,* it became necessary to designate the parts by words of distinction; but having first done so, he afterwards uses the words of limitation, and applies the word estate for that purpose. The case of *Uthwatt and Another* v. *Bryant and Another* (*d*) was very similar to the present. That was a devise of his freehold lands for years, remainder for life, remainder in tail, and in default of such issue, then a devise of all the testator's said freehold estate in the parish of *Buckingham* to his daughters, and this Court held that it carried a fee.

(*a*) 2 *New Rep.* 350.
(*b*) *Cowp.* 235.
(*c*) *Vin. Abr. Devise,* Q. 2.
(*d*) *Ante,* vi. 317.

If

If you there substitute for " lands" the word houses, the devise is precisely similar to this. *Doe* v. *Clayton* is not in point; that was a devise to *W. Bates* of all that messuage situate at *Eaton*, with all houses and hereditaments thereto belonging, and all those parcels of land situate in the lordship, precincts, and territories of *Eaton*, now in my own and *G. Blankley's* occupation; and my will is that *W. T. Bates*, when he arrives at the age of 21 years, shall enter upon and enjoy the aforesaid estate, namely, the life-estate before given. The testator could not in the present case mean the estate he had before given, which was a mere life-estate for the life of his niece, therefore the words " all which said estates" must mean his own estate in the houses which he had devised by his will. Whenever he gives a life-estate he gives it in terms. Here are no words of qualification, and it is therefore a fee. But with respect to the charge on the estate, the rule is laid down too narrow by the counsel for the Plaintiff. The rule is, that if the charge may by possibility last longer than the estate given, then the devise gives a fee. *Andrew* v. *Southouse* (a). For if it be a life-estate, then the tenant for life possibly may die before the annuitant, and the annuitant would lose the annuity. In the case last cited, the property is charged and chargeable with the annuity, and in the present case the annuity is to be paid out of the estate, which are equivalent. Lord *Kenyon* C. J. and *Ashurst* J. there held it a fee. It is not therefore necessary that it should be a charge on the person; to make a fee, it suffices if it be a charge on the land, which may last longer than the life-estate. The devises to *Mary* and *Marinus Price* do not therefore, as is said, confer mere life-estates, because if they did so, the annuity might be defeated. It is argued, that

(a) 5 *Term Rep.* 295.

if

if the former takes a life-estate, the latter must also take only a life-estate, the answer is, that the same words must have the same sense in different parts of the will. The words "all which said estates" therefore convey a fee.

Bosanquet in reply. The question merely is, according to Lord *Mansfield,* what the testator meant. After a local description the words "all which estates" referring to it, cannot mean any thing more than the local description before given. It is said that the rule respecting a charge has been stated too narrowly, but that is not so. The case cited for it of *Doe* v. *Snelling,* was subsequent to that of *Andrew* v. *Southouse,* which was considered in the former, and after that consideration, Lord *Ellenborough* lays down the rule in the terms above cited. As to the charge, a mere charge on the lands is much more effectual for the annuitant than a charge upon the interest of the devisees. If the devisee is personally charged, and he is to receive the rents and profits, it gives a fee. *Collier's* case *(a).* In *Doe* v. *Clarke* the charge was to be paid at all events, but admitting that, the question still was, whether the devisee took an interest in fee accordingly as he was or was not personally chargeable.

GIBBS C. J. In this case the testator had much different property to dispose of, partly freehold, but the greater part copyhold: the copyhold part he meant to dispose of to different persons. It was necessary, therefore, in his will to describe the land, in order to keep separate that which he meant for one devisee, from that which he meant for another. The first object of his bounty is *Thomas Coombes :* after devising part of his copyholds to *Thomas Coombes* for life,

(a) 6 Co. 16.

and

and after him to *Marinus Coombes*, he proceeds to make a disposition in favour of his niece *Mary Price*, and her son, his nephew, *Marinus Price*. It was necessary he should distinguish between the property he intended for them, and what he had before given to a different person. He enumerates locally all that he intended for *Mary Price*, and having so done, he goes on to say, " All which said. estates, being copyhold, I give to *Mary Price* for her life, and after her decease, *to* her son *Marinus Price ;* and I hereby order that so long as *William Points* shall chuse to live in the *White Bear* public-house, and shall keep the same in good repair, he shall not be charged more than his present rent of 14*l. per annum:* and also I devise to the said *Marinus Price* all my freehold estate situate in *Prince's-street* and *Eagle-and-Child Yard*, and to *Samuel Groves* and *Hannah Groves*, of *Long-lane*, in the borough of *Southwark*, and the survivor of them, the sum of 5*s. per* week, to be paid to them weekly from and out of the estates bequeathed to my said niece *Mary Price* and her son *Marinus Price*." Now the word estate is here used in the operative part of the devise; not introduced incidentally after the devising part is perfected, but introduced in the devise itself. It is admitted by the counsel for the Plaintiff, that the word estate carries a fee, <u>unless other parts of the will restrain its effect.</u> Formerly a narrower construction prevailed, and it was held that if the former words <u>described locality,</u> the word estate was not descriptive of the quantity of interest, but designated local position : but it is now held, that though the word estate points at a certain house or parish where the estate is situate, yet it shall carry a fee, unless restrained by other parts of the will. It may be, that the signification of the word estate may be restrained, but it lies on the party who seeks to narrow its construction, to shew by what expressions in the will

it

it is restrained. Here the counsel for the Plaintiff
urges, that the testator, after the words of local description, uses the word estate as meaning no more than
what he had before described. The counsel for the
Defendant fairly answers this: he says, the reason why
the testator has enumerated the different houses of his
copyholds, is, because he meant to give some to one
person, some to another: the freehold estate he meant
to give all to one, and therefore says, " I give to *Ma-*
rinus Coombes all my freehold estate;" but that he was
obliged to describe the parts of his copyhold, in order
to shew what was to go to one, and what to another; but
after having enumerated them, he deserts the local description, and takes up the word estate; and it appears
to me that this is a fair explication of the cause of his so
enumerating them, and does not take from the legal
effect of the word estate, nor give it a narrower construction than the law generally gives it.   In the case
of *Doe* v. *Clayton* cited by the counsel for the Plaintiff,
it is observable, that the word estate is introduced,
and when the testator uses it, it there refers to the
estate he had before given, and then the fee-simple
does not pass by the word estate. The counsel for
the Defendant has also referred us to *Uthwatt* v.
Bryant and it does appear to us, that the present
bears a very near resemblance to the case cited.
Here his Lordship stated the devise in that case, (*vide*
ante, 317.): the question was, whether the daughters
took an estate in fee or for life: it was contended there,
that though the gift was conveyed to them by the word
estate, other words qualified it, and gave it a narrower
sense than naturally belonged to the word: what the testator gave was his said freehold estate; and as he had
given his freehold lands for life before, it was contended
that the word estate signified no more than his said freehold lands, but this Court held, that it meant a fee. In
addition

addition to this, other circumstances of the will do certainly furnish a strong reason for saying that " estate," as used by the testator, meant that which the law construes it to mean if not restrained by other words. He gives to *Mary Price* for life, remainder to *Marinus Price*, and his will is, that so long as *W. Points* lives in the public-house and keeps it in repair, he shall not be charged more than 14*l. per annum.* It seems as if the testator contemplated that the two *Prices* were the persons who would have the power of raising the rent which *Points* paid, and it therefore strongly looks as if he meant that their estate should last, at least as long as *Points* had the option of continuing in the public-house. Here is, in addition to this, an annuity to *Samuel* and *Hannah Groves* of 5*s.* a week, and it is clear that the testator contemplated that it was to be paid out of that which he had before given to *Mary Price* and *Marinus Price*, and it therefore shews that he meant a larger estate than for life should pass to them. It is admitted by those who contest it, that the word estate, not being qualified, does carry with it this meaning. We think, looking at the other words of this will, that so far from qualifying this construction, they rather confirm it. It does seem therefore that the property given to *Mary Price* and *Marinus Price*, is given to the latter in fee.

HEATH J. I am of the same opinion. The principle is, that where the word estates is an operative word, it passes a fee, and to try whether it be operative or not, the test is, to strike it out of the will, which test being applied here, the devise becomes nonsense.

CHAMBRE J. No doubt the word estate is large enough to carry a fee: whether it shall do so, is to be collected from the whole will. Nothing on this will shews that the testator meant to die intestate as to any

part

part of his property. When he disposes of his freehold property, he gives his freehold estates, which devise, it is admitted, clearly carries a fee: he uses the same word in his devise to *Mary Price* and *Marinus Price*, and it must therefore carry the same sense. Another strong circumstance is the charge in favour of an old tenant, for whom the testator seems to have had a regard. The charitable donation of 5*s. per* week to two other persons, is a still stronger circumstance. It is next to impossible, that the testator could mean, that on the decease of *Mary Price* and *Marinus Price* it should cease; there is therefore a purpose manifest, to effectuate which, the estate given ought to be a fee; and the words are indisputably large enough, and there is nothing apparent to control them. I therefore am of opinion with my Lord and my Brother *Heath*, that this devise carried a fee, and that the judgment must be for the Defendant. (*a*)

1815.

RANDALL
v.
TUCHIN.

(*a*) *Dallas J.* was absent by reason of indisposition.

Bⁱˡˡⁱⁿᵍ BILLING and Another, Assignees of BURKITT, a Bankrupt, *v.* FLIGHT.

Nov. 28.

THIS was an action of *assumpsit* for money had and received, brought by the assignees of a bankrupt to recover from the Defendant, upon two grounds, a sum paid him by the bankrupt immediately before his bankruptcy. First, that the money was paid for the differences upon stock-jobbing contracts; 2dly, that the *sumpsit* for money had and received, to recover back differences paid on stock-jobbing contracts, and had filed a bill of discovery, to which the Defendant pleaded that the discovery was given by the statute 7 *G.* 2. *c.* 8. *s.* 2. in debt only, the Court permitted the Plaintiffs to amend by changing *assumpsit* to debt after six terms from the commencement of the action.

The statute
7 *G.* 2. *c.* 8. is
a remedial ra-
ther than a
penal act.

Where the
Plaintiffs had
commenced an
action of *as-*

pay-

payment was fraudulent and in contemplation of bank-ruptcy. The money was paid to the Defendant on the 27th of *November* 1813. The Plaintiffs issued a *capias ad respondendum* on the 20th of *April* 1814, and a *capias per continuance* on the 17th of *May,* both within six months after the payment of the money to the Defendant. Rules for time to declare were obtained, and the declaration was served on the 17th of *January* 1815. The Defendant pleaded in *Hilary* term *non assumpsit.* Rule was given to reply, and issue was joined. No notice of trial being given, the Defendant obtained in *Trinity* term last a rule for judgment as in case of a nonsuit, which was discharged on a peremptory undertaking to try at the adjourned sittings after the present *Michaelmas* term, and in default, the Defendant was to be at liberty after the four first days of *Hilary* term to sign judgment as in case of a nonsuit, without further application to the Court, unless the Court should otherwise order. The Plaintiffs had in *August* 1815 filed a bill in equity for a discovery, supposing themselves entitled thereto by the statute 7 *Geo.* 2. *c.* 8. *s.* 2., to which the Defendant pleaded that this action was *assumpsit,* whereas the statute gives the discovery only in an action of debt for money had and received. That plea was still pending. *Shepherd,* Solicitor-General, had therefore obtained a rule *nisi* that the former rule might stand enlarged, on an undertaking to try at the adjourned sittings after *Hilary* term, and that the Plaintiffs might amend their declaration by converting it to an action of debt for money had and received, on payment of costs.

Lens and *Vaughan* Serjts. now shewed cause against the enlargement of the time, upon the ground that the Plaintiff had already been sufficiently indulged with time, and was not entitled to any further delay, having

peremp-

peremptorily undertaken to try at the sittings after the present term. As to the amendment, it was equivalent to enabling the Plaintiff to bring a fresh action, which, after so much delay on their part, was not to be permitted, especially in a penal action. The Court had laid down the rule in *Maddock* v. *Hammett* (a), and *Steele* v. *Sowerby* (b), that where a Plaintiff had been guilty of any delay, the Court would not aid him by amendment.

The Solicitor-General, who would have supported his rule, was stopped by

The Court. This rule has two objects. The one, to get rid of a former rule into which the Plaintiffs were obliged to enter; the other to cure what may, or may not, be a defect in the declaration. The Defendant complains that this action is suspended over him; that is the Defendant's own fault. The statute gives an action, and gives the Plaintiff evidence by the oath of the Defendant, in answer to a bill for a discovery. The Plaintiffs file such a bill, and the Defendant might have enabled them to go on to trial by putting in his answer, instead of putting in a plea; but the Defendant contends that the statute gives a discovery only in a plea of debt, and he therefore refuses to answer the bill, so as to furnish evidence in an action of *assumpsit.* By this act, the Defendant himself delays the Plaintiffs from going on to trial. It is objected by the Defendant's counsel, that to amend the declaration by changing it from *assumpsit* to debt, would be to give the Plaintiff a new cause of action, or at least a new form of action. How the Court of Exchequer will dispose of that plea, we do not yet know, no decision being yet pronounced.

(a) 7 *Term Rep.* 184.   (b) 6 *Term Rep.* 171.

But the amendment would give no new cause of action: it is to be made only by altering a few words in the beginning and a few words in the end of the declaration, and we think the amendment may be made. It has been stated, that this is a penal action; but we do not think it is a penal statute: it is to a certain extent a remedial law.

Rule absolute.

END OF MICHAELMAS TERM.

1816.

Feb. 9.

So, where no bill in equity had been filed for a discovery, the Court permitted the Plaintiffs to amend by converting their declaration from *assumpsit* to debt.

BILLING and Others, Assignees of BURKITT, *v.* POOLEY.

IN this action, which was commenced in *assumpsit* for the like causes as in the preceding case, the Plaintiffs had also in *Trinity* term 1815 discharged a rule for judgment as in case of a nonsuit, upon a peremptory undertaking to try at the sittings after *Michaelmas* term, and they had also prepared a bill in equity for a discovery, but had delayed to file it until they should see the event of their motion for an amendment in the action against *Flight;* and in the mean time they omitted to go to trial. The plea to the bill in equity, that the statute gave a discovery only in an action in debt, not in *assumpsit*, had in the mean time been overruled. The Defendant had again in this term obtained a rule *nisi* for judgment as in case of a nonsuit, for not proceeding to trial pursuant to the Plaintiffs' undertaking; and the Plaintiffs had obtained a rule *nisi* to amend their declaration by converting it to an action of debt.

4

Shepherd,

Shepherd, Solicitor-General, for the Plaintiffs.

Best Serjt. for the Defendant.

GIBBS C. J. The question is not whether we shall make the rule absolute for judgment as in case of a nonsuit upon an application made in the first instance; but this is a rule in a case where a peremptory undertaking has been given, which I am not for disregarding; but the question is, whether any cause has arisen since giving the peremptory undertaking, to prevent the Plaintiff from performing it, and I think he has shewn such cause. In *June,* when he undertook, he was not aware of the objection that would be made to his discovery. Afterwards he became aware of the difficulty, and forbore to file his bill against this Defendant till the objection should be decided. That is a sufficient answer to the rule for judgment as in case of a nonsuit. The next question is, whether we shall permit the Plaintiffs to amend. No ground has been shewn against it except two; the one, that a bill for a discovery did not lie in an action of *assumpsit;* the second, that an action of *assumpsit* would not lie at law. By overruling the plea in equity the first ground is removed, and it is shewn that the amendment is not wanted, but as it cannot possibly be prejudicial to the Defendant to have the amendment, and as there may be a doubt, (I do not say that I have any doubt,) whether the action of *assumpsit* can be maintained on this statute, I think the amendment ought to be allowed on payment of costs.

> Rule for the judgment as in case
> of a nonsuit discharged.
> Rule for amendment absolute.

1814.

The Order of Precedency of the Attorney and Solicitor-General.

In the name and on the behalf of His Majesty.

George P. R.

Order of
Precedency of
the Attorney
and Solicitor-
General before
the King's
Serjeants.

WHEREAS our Attorney and Solicitor-General now have place and audience in our Courts next after the two ancientest of our Serjeants at Law for the time being, and before our other Serjeants at Law, We considering the weighty and important affairs in which our Attorney and Solicitor-General are employed, and on which the Attorney and Solicitor-General of us, our heirs and successors may hereafter be employed, do hereby order and direct that at all times hereafter the Attorney and Solicitor-General of us, our heirs and successors, shall have place and audience as well before the said two ancientest of our Serjeants at Law, as also before every person who now is one of our Serjeants at law, or hereafter shall be one of the Serjeants at Law of us, our heirs or successors, and we do hereby will and require you not only to cause this our direction *to be* observed in our Court of Chancery, but also to signify to the Judges of all our other Courts at *Westminster*, that it is our express pleasure that the same course be observed in all our said Courts.

Given at our Court of *Carlton House* this 14th day of *December*, in the fifty-fourth year of His Majesty's reign.

By command of His Royal Highness the Prince Regent, in the name and on the behalf of His Majesty.

SIDMOUTH.

To the Right Honourable *John* Lord *Eldon*, our Chancellor of *Great Britain*.

CASE

ARGUED and DETERMINED

IN THE

Court of COMMON PLEAS,

IN

Michaelmas Term,

In the Fifty-sixth Year of the Reign of GEORGE III.

EVEREST *v.* GLYN, Bart.

Nov. 24.

THIS was an action of *assumpsit* brought by the steward of the manors of *Ewell* and *Cuddington* for fees due to him upon the admission of the Defendant, who was devisee of his father, the last tenant, to six several tenements, copyholds of inheritance of those manors. Upon the trial of the cause at the *Westminster* sittings after *Trinity* term 1815, before *Gibbs* C. J. the Plaintiff proved that he had prepared drafts of six several instruments of admission to the six several copyholds, and had submitted them to the Defendant's at-

A steward of a manor, is entitled to be paid for admissions of a tenant to several copyholds, only according to a *quantum meruit*, unless certain fees are proved to be due by the custom of his manor.

There is no general custom for all copyholds.

And therefore, although the steward at the tenant's request prepare six several admissions on separate instruments to six tenements, he is not entitled to six times the fees which are due on the first, there being less labour in preparing either of the five last than the first.

VOL. VI.   G g   torney.

torney, who had approved and returned the same, whereupon he engrossed on six several pieces of parchment, with distinct stamps on each, the six separate admissions, which the Defendant accepted, and the Plaintiff now claimed to be paid the same charges for each of them, which he would have made for the admission to a single tenement, had there been only one. He made a charge of two guineas for searching the Court rolls for the admissions of the last tenant, inspecting the award under a recent inclosure act by which certain parcels of some of the copyholds were to be ascertained, examining the rental, in order to fix the fines due to the lord, and making extracts; and upon each of the tenements he charged

	£.	s.	d.
For presenting the last tenant's death -	- 0	2	0
Proclamation for the heir to come in -	- 0	1	0
Presenting and enrolling the will of the devisor - - -	- 1	-	-
Proclamation - - -	- 0	1	0
Admission fee, and by attorney -	- 1	7	8
Enrolling the same - - -	- 1	1	0
Copy of admission, with will set out -	- 1	1	0
Parchment and stamp - - -	- 0	18	c
Respiting fealty - - -	- 0	1	0
Homage and cryer - - -	- 0	7	6
	£6	1	2

Amounting in the whole to 38l. 0s. Evidence was given by stewards of other manors: one gentleman considered that some of these charges were too high, and some too low; but upon the supposition that the Plaintiff was entitled to make the same charges upon each of the admissions, 20l. was insufficient for the whole; 32l. 15s. would have been the reasonable charge. In this computation he allowed upon the admission to the first copyhold three additional charges of 6s. 8d. each,

for

for recording each of the proclamations, and the respite of fealty; and retrenching some other charges, he computed the total fees and charges due on the first admission, at 6*l.* 2*s.* 2*d.* exclusive of the preparatory charges, and for each of the subsequent admissions 4*l.* 18*s.* 2*d.* deeming that the charges for some of the acts, as for instance the proclamations, and presentment of the will, which was made on the first admission, were not necessary to be repeated. Another steward of twelve manors, concurring in the last circumstance, also proved that some of the charges were higher, and some lower than those which he was in the habit of making; but that it was his own practice to comprehend the admissions to any indefinite number of copyhold tenements in one instrument, distinguishing the parcels of each tenement by an *ac etiam,* and inserting for each a separate reddendum, sometimes after the enumeration of the parcels of a single tenement, sometimes after the parcels of all the tenements: that 6*l.* 5*s.* was a reasonable charge for a single tenement, or the first tenement, but that an addition of 8*s.* 8*d.* for the insertion of each additional tenement and quit rent, after the first, together with the cost of the additional stamp for each, and larger parchment, was sufficient. That if six admissions to several tenements were thus combined in one instrument, the sum of 20*l.* which the Defendant had paid into Court, was more than sufficient to cover the Plaintiff's demand. *Gibbs* C. J. in summing up the evidence, having observed to the jury that no evidence was given of any custom of the manor to charge any specific amount of fees, the Plaintiff tendered evidence of a custom of the manor, which the Chief Justice, in that stage of the cause, rejected, as being a new case; and, thinking as he did, that the Plaintiff, by the Defendant's assent, was entitled to make out separate admissions, left it to the jury whether, there being no custom proved for

G g 2   the

the amount of the separate fees, 20l. was a reasonable compensation for preparing the six admissions; but his Lordship reserved this question of law for the Plaintiff, whether, supposing him entitled to make out separate admissions, he was in law entitled to the same fee for each as for the first. If he were, then 20l. was not enough, and the Plaintiff was to be at liberty to enter a verdict for the full amount of his fees on that computation; if he were not, then 20l. was sufficient; it was to be attended to, that the bill for each of the copies comprized many items, and many of the matters charged for were attended with less trouble in the repetition. The jury found that the reasonable compensation due to the Plaintiff would not exceed 20l, and they gave their verdict for the Defendant.

Accordingly *Best* Serjt. on a former day in this term obtained a rule *nisi* to set aside the verdict for the Defendant, and enter a verdict for 10l. for the Plaintiff. He relied on *Attree* v. *Scutt.* (a)

Lens and *Bosanquet* Serjts. now shewed cause. This is merely a question of *quantum meruit ;* the sum paid into court was paid in upon that principle. There is no general law on the subject extending to all copyholds: the Plaintiff's claim, if it stands on any other foundation than a *quantum meruit*, must be governed by the custom of his own particular manor; and in this case there was no evidence of the usage of the particular manor. In the case of *Searle* v. *Marsh*, in *B. R.* *Hilary* term 29 *G.* 3. before Lord *Kenyon* C. J., a question arose whether the several tenements were to be divided by an *ac etiam* or not, and Lord *Kenyon* held that if they might be so divided, it would justify the steward in making a charge for each part.

(a) 6 *East*, 476.

Bower

Bower was for the Plaintiff.   The case was afterwards mentioned to the Court, and Lord *Kenyon* adhered to the rule he had laid down at *nisi prius*, that it depended all on the usage, which was the life and law of the copyhold tenure; and if the usage justified a charge for each *ac etiam*, the charge was good; but that otherwise it stood on a *quantum meruit.*

The Court, interposing, called on

Best to support his rule: he contended that the Plaintiff was entitled to the increased verdict, upon the ground that the Defendant's attorney had approved of each separate draft, and had thereby bound the Defendant to pay for it.   On each copy is an entry of all the matters which entitle the Plaintiff to a fee, the heriot, fine, respite of fealty, and the like.   Therefore the Defendant has not left to the Plaintiff a discretion to make out these admissions in what form the Plaintiff might deem fit, but he has sanctioned their being drawn up in this particular form.   All that the Plaintiff has done, he was required to do by the Defendant. The case cited therefore does not apply.   *Conventio vincit legem & consuetudinem.*   The rule sought to be established by one of the witnesses, would ruin all copyholds.   The advantage of copyhold estates is, that the whole title shall appear on the manor rolls.   But if all the tenements are to be blended in one copy, no good title can appear on the rolls of any manor.   The lord is entitled to distinct fines and heriots, the king to distinct stamps, the steward to his distinct fees.   Here are six fines, six titles, and six rents.   If each do not appear separately, the lord cannot know to what fine and what heriot he is entitled for each, nor can the government ascertain the stamp duties.   It is said, that to do the whole is but one trouble; it is true, that one proclama-

tion

tion only is made in court, but there are six entries of the proclamation, each of which consumes an equal quantity of labour, parchment, and ink. The fee is not regulated by the trouble. If an attorney attends a summons in six policy causes, he is entitled to six fees. But here, indeed, there is six times as much trouble for the six, as there is for the first. If the want of an especial custom had any weight, it is all got rid of by the Defendant's assent. If he meant to put the Plaintiff to his legal right and the custom of the manor, he should not have interfered, but left the Plaintiff to settle his own rolls.

GIBBS C. J. I agree the steward is to be paid for what he does, and also that *conventio vincit legem*, and that if the Defendant agrees that the business shall be done in a particular way, for a particular sum, it shall be paid: the question therefore is, whether there has been a convention that this business was to be done in a particular way, and that the steward was to be paid a particular sum. There have been six separate admissions by the consent of the Defendant's attorney, and the only doubt is, how the steward is to be paid for them. There is no particular stipulation for the price, and therefore the sum due must be determined, either by the custom of that manor, or on a *quantum meruit*. For there is no general law for all copyholds, it can only be the particular usage of each manor, and in this case there is no custom of the manor in evidence; therefore the Plaintiff's right must stand on a *quantum meruit*, and the inquiry must be, in this case, where the Defendant has had six several admissions made out separately on separate stamps, what the Plaintiff is reasonably entitled to receive for the trouble he has had in preparing them: he charges six times as much as for one, but it does not follow that because he is

I   entitled

entitled to his full charge for the first, therefore he is to have six times as much for the six, I therefore asked the witness whether taking the first charge, and adding to it the 8s. 8d. on five other copies, adding also the further charge for the additional drawing, parchment, &c., on the six instruments prepared in lieu of one, adding also the cost of the stamps, the whole amount would exceed 20l., and he did not think it would. I reserved the point whether the Plaintiff had any right in point of law, because he was entitled to charge 6l. for the first copy, therefore to charge the same for each subsequent copy, and the Court are of opinion he has not. As to the *quantum meruit* the jury have disposed of it.

Rule discharged.

CASES

ARGUED AND DETERMINED

IN THE

Court of COMMON PLEAS,

AND

OTHER COURTS,

IN

Hilary Term,

In the Fifty-sixth Year of the Reign of GEORGE III.

Jan. 23.

FAWCETT, Plaintiff; LOWE, Deforciant.

A fine cannot be amended without an affidavit connecting the fine with the deed produced to warrant the amendment.

VAUGHAN Serjt. moved to amend a fine, in which the premises comprized were stated to be in the parish of *Askerton*, by making it pursuant to the deed to lead the uses, which conveyed lands in the manor of *Askerton* in the parish of *Stapleton*, and he prayed that the word "manor" might be substituted for the word "parish:" he moved this upon an affidavit of the commissioner named in the writ of *dedimus potestatem*, that he took the acknowledgment of the deforciant to a fine for passing lands in the manor of *Askerton*, in the barony of *Guildsland*, in the parish of *Stapleton*, and that there was no such parish in exist-

ence

ence as *Askerton*. The Court inquired whether the affidavits stated that the deed which conveyed the lands in the manor of *Askerton*, was the same deed in pursuance whereto the fine was levied; and that fact not being sworn to, they held that they certainly could not permit the amendment without an affidavit stating that the deed produced was the deed in pursuance whereof the fine was levied: without such an affidavit to connect the deed with the fine, wicked persons might make the grossest abuse of these motions.

Vaughan took nothing by his motion.

4 B & C 220

CRAVEN and Another *v.* RYDER.

Jan. 24.

THIS was an action of trover brought to recover the value of certain sugar. It was tried before *Dallas J.* at *Guildhall*, at the sittings after *Michaelmas* term 1815, when the case appeared to be, that the Plaintiffs on 5th *May* contracted to sell to *B. French* and Co. 24 hogsheads of sugar denominated *Hamburgh* loaves, at 108s., free on board a *British* ship, two months being the usual credit on such sales. The Plaintiffs on the 13th *May* sent the sugars by their lighterman alongside a vessel bound for *Hamburgh*, of which the Defendant was master, to be put on board, with an order addressed "to the commanding officer on board, to receive them for and on account of the Plaintiffs;" and when the loading was complete, on 16th *May*, took in exchange from the mate, who happened to have the command, an acknowledgement that the goods were "received on board the *George* for *Hamburgh*, for and on account of the Plaintiffs." The lighterman proved that he had for the last year adopted

A resale of goods by a vendee, and payment to him, does not destroy the vendor's right of stoppage in *transitu*.

this

this more precise form in his receipts, for the express purpose of giving the shipper a command over the goods, till the lighterman's note was, according to the usual course of trade, given up in exchange for the bill of lading. *B. French* and Co. contracted for the resale of the sugars to *Caldas,* and received the price of them; and the Defendant, without the Plaintiffs' privity, on the 15th of *May* signed and delivered to *Caldas,* who had engaged the Defendant's vessel for the voyage, a bill of lading for the sugars, as being shipped by him, deliverable to *Carlo Bene* or his order, at *Hamburgh.* *B. French* and Co. having on the 19th stopped payment, the Plaintiffs, not having been paid for the sugars, reclaimed them, which the Defendant refused to redeliver, on the ground that he had signed a bill of lading in favour of *Caldas,* deliverable to *Carlo Bene,* to whom *Caldas* had resold and consigned them to *Hamburgh,* and had obtained *Bene's* acceptances on the credit of this consignment. The jury found that the receipt given to the Plaintiffs was restrictive, and that nothing had been done by them to alter the right of possession of the goods, and gave their verdict for the Plaintiff.

Lens Serjt. now moved to set aside the verdict and enter a nonsuit. He contended that the moment the Plaintiffs had delivered the goods free on board a *British* ship, their vendees having in the mean time resold to another, the right of stoppage *in transitu* was at an end. There had been an absolute sale by the Plaintiffs to *French,* and an absolute sale by *French* to *Caldas,* and the latter had paid for the goods, and had made a further resale to *Bene.* In *Lickbarrow* v. *Mason* (a), the circumstances of which case are not indeed exactly similar to this, *Buller* J., for whose doctrine he

(a) 6 *East,* 34. *n.*

cited

cited it, lays it down that there is no case, in which, after a resale of goods, and payment of the price, or money advanced on the credit of the goods by the second vendee, there had been a stoppage *in transitu.* Stress was laid on the terms of the receipt, but without reason.   The goods were in a manner received for the Plaintiffs, inasmuch as the receipt was a discharge to the Plaintiffs of their obligation to deliver the goods to *French,* but they were in no other sense received for them: it never was intended that the Plaintiffs should in any event resume the possession. The delivery was complete, and there was no right of stoppage *in transitu.*

GIBBS C. J. Exclusively of the particular form of the receipt for the goods, I take it, the practice is, that the person who is in possession of the lighterman's receipt, is the person entitled to the bill of lading, which ought to be given only to the holder of that receipt. Consequently the holder of that receipt retains a control over the goods at least until he has exchanged the receipt for the bill of lading. My Brother *Dallas,* who tried this cause, had no doubt on the propriety of the verdict, and the jury were still more clear, and thought it was a right which ought not to be questioned.   We should not therefore disturb the verdict unless we could be convinced of the propriety of so doing. *French* and Co. might sell their right again, but the Plaintiffs might refrain from delivering the goods, unless under such circumstances as would enable them to recall the goods if they saw occasion. The Plaintiffs refuse to deliver them, except in exchange for this receipt : they know a bill of lading will be executed before the ship sails, and they know that the bill of lading ought regularly to be executed to themselves. *French* and Co. sell to *Caldas. Caldas* goes to the Defendant, and obtains the bill of lading of these

these goods, but the Defendant signs that bill of lading to *Caldas* in his own wrong, for he ought not to have given the bill of lading but in exchange for the lighterman's note. In this state of . things *French* and Co. became insolvent, and we do not think the right of stoppage *in transitu* is gone. Nor do we mainly rely on the form of the receipt, though it is a circumstance to be considered, but if the receipt had been in the old form, the principle is the same, namely, that the vendors had never yet parted with the control over the goods in that event.

DALLAS J. The jury were clear that the vendors had never parted with the possession of the goods, and I see no reason to disturb the verdict.

PARK J. concurred.

Rule refused.

AUSTIN and Another *v.* DREWE.

An insurance "against all damage which the assured shall suffer by fire on stock and utensils in their regular built sugar-house," does not extend to damage done to the sugar by the heat of the usual fires employed for refining, being accumulated by the mismanagement of the assured, who inadvertently kept the top of their chimney closed.

THIS was an action of covenant on a policy of insurance effected with the Defendant " against all the damage which the Plaintiffs should suffer by fire," on their " stock and utensils in their regular built sugar-house," and the Plaintiffs averred that " their stock and utensils were very much damaged by fire in the sugar-house." The Defendant pleaded that " the stock and utensils were by and through the carelessness, negligence, and improper conduct of the Plaintiffs and their servants, in regulating and managing the fires usually employed in and about the sugar-house, damaged by the smoke arising from such fires, and not from any other cause, without this, that the stock and utensils were damaged by fire in the sugar-house within

16   the

1816.

AUSTIN
v.
DREWE.

the meaning of the policy." The Plaintiffs replied, that the stock and utensils were damaged by fire in the sugar-house, within the meaning of the policy, and the Defendant joined issue on this traverse. Upon the trial of this cause at *Guildhall*, at the sittings after *Michaelmas* term 1815, before *Gibbs* C. J., the evidence was, that the building insured contained eight stories, and in each story, sugar, in a certain state of preparation, was deposited for the purpose of being refined; in order for refining, a certain degree of heat was necessary, and a chimney running up through the whole building formed almost one side of each of the stories, and by means of this chimney heat was communicated to each of the stories. At the top of the chimney, above the 8 stories, was a register, which the Plaintiffs used to shut at night, in order to retain in the chimney and building all the heat they could. They shut it one night, and lighted the fires next day, and they soon afterwards found the building full of smoke and sparks; and on examination they found, that the register, which always ought to be open whensoever the fire was burning, was continued shut down: sparks and smoke had got out into the rooms; the heat had slightly blistered the walls, and considerably discoloured and damaged the sugars. There was much smoke, but the only injury done to the sugars proceeded from heat; the smoke would not have hurt them. There was no fire in the building that ought not to be there, nothing was on fire, that ought not to be on fire, the damage was occasioned by the sparks, heat, and smoke taking a wrong direction. *Gibbs* C. J. directed the jury, that inasmuch as the damage was occasioned entirely by the increased heat, which was produced by keeping the register closed, it was not a loss by fire within the meaning of the policy, but was occasioned by the impro-

.per

per management of the register. The jury found a verdict for the Defendant.

Shepherd, Solicitor-General, now moved for a new trial. The words of the policy are not "excess of fire," or "improper fire," but "damage by fire." The actual flame which proceeded from the grates below, and would, if the register had not been closed, have issued out of that chimney, being confined therein by the register, occasioned the mischief. If actual flame was the cause of the damage, it matters not whether the fire was properly or improperly lighted, but the question is, whether fire occasioned the damage. If any other criterion be taken, it would in many cases of policies against fire introduce nice and intricate questions. It cannot be necessary that the fire, to produce a loss within the policy, should be only such fire as is communicated to some substance not contained in the intended and proper receptacle of fire. Heat may be so intense, as to ignite combustibles without the actual contact of flame. Suppose the intensity of heat necessarily required for any process to be so great, that the fire made in a chimney, though confined there, might ignite neighbouring bodies, it might in that case as well be said, that that was not a damage by fire, because the original fire was contained in its proper receptacle. In the common case of a house on fire, if goods are damaged by the removal, that is a loss by fire within the policy. Put the case of a chimney on fire, there is only the usual quantity of heat below, but the mischief is occasioned by an accumulation of soot in the chimney, yet the insurers would be bound to pay any loss thereby occasioned.

GIBBS C. J. I think it is not necessary to determine any of those extreme questions. In the present case, I
think

think no loss was sustained by any of the risks in the
policy. The loss was occasioned by the extreme mismanagement by the Plaintiffs of their register. I so
directed the jury, and I have no reason to alter the
opinion I then formed.

DALLAS J. I am of the same opinion. The only
cause of the damage appears to me to have been the unskilful management of the machinery by the Plaintiff's
own servants, and it is therefore not a loss within the
meaning of the policy

Rule refused.

FAITH v. PEARSON.

Jan. 25.

THIS was an action of trespass for taking the Plaintiff's ship on her voyage from *Senegal* to *London*,
and carrying her out of the course of her voyage to
Barbadoes, whereby the Plaintiff was subjected to an action on the covenant contained in his charter-party,
and obliged to pay damages, and sustained various
other losses. The Defendant pleaded in justification
that he was commander of a *British* ship of war, the
Bembow, and that he required the master of the Plaintiff's ship to produce a manifest of her cargo, but he
admitted he had none, wherefore he detained the ship
to be dealt with according to law, until at the master's
instance he permitted him to depart; thirdly, that there
was war between *Great Britain* and *America*, and that
he boarded the Plaintiff's vessel to enquire whether she
belonged to an enemy, and having reasonable and probable cause to suspect a part of the cargo to be enemy's
property, namely, *American*, he, in the exercise of his
duty, detained and carried the ship into *Barbadoes* to be

No action lies
against the
commander of
a *British* ship
of war for seiz-
ing and detain-
ing a vessel on
suspicion of
her being hos-
tile prize.

Though he
afterwards dis-
misses her
without libel-
ling her in the
Court of Ad-
miralty.

And though
he detains her
partly on sus-
picion of mat-
ters which are
causes only of
forfeiture if
she is *British*.

dealt

dealt with according to law, until he liberated her at the master's request. Upon the trial of the cause, at *Guildhall*, at the sittings after *Michaelmas* term 1815, before *Gibbs* C. J., it appeared that the Defendant, who was commander of the *Bembow*, a *British* ship of war, hailed the Plaintiff's ship the *John*, in her course from *Senegal* to *London*, and sent an officer on board the Plaintiff's ship, who, having examined the ship's papers, questioned the master, whether he was not an *American*, observing that he and his mate had the appearance of *Americans*, that the ship had *American* canvas and rigging, and appeared to be *American* built, which last was not the case, but she being *British* built, and captured by the *Americans*, had been repaired in *America*, and had on board *American* canvas and cordage. He also inquired whether she had not *African* slaves on board; or had been concerned in that trade, and on his saying the ship was *British*, bound from *Senegal* to *London*, he imputed it as an irregularity that she had not on board a manifest of her cargo from *Senegal*, as required by the statute 26 *G*. 3. *c*. 40. This, though required by the act, in practice is never given to vessels coming from the coast of *Africa*. And the officer caused the Plaintiff's master to go on board the Defendant's ship with his papers. The master having exhibited to the Defendant dispatches from the governor of *Senegal*, which he was carrying to the *British* government, and letters addressed to private persons in *England*, which apparently satisfied the Defendant, was dismissed, and on his return to his own ship the officer quitted her, but soon after came again on board, and more particularly questioned the master; whose answers, though true, not satisfying him, the Defendant detained the vessel, and carried her into *Barbadoes*, where he kept the master and crew prisoners on board her, and took away her stream anchor, by reason of which an *American* ship there ran foul of

her

her, and injured the vessel. After some time the Defendant liberated the master, crew, and vessel, without having instituted any proceedings against her in the Admiralty court. *Gibbs* C. J. held that upon this evidence it must be taken that the Defendant detained her as prize, upon suspicion that she was hostile property. And according to *Le Caux* v. *Eden* (a), no action could be maintained for taking a vessel, where the captors were acting under a belief that she was a subject of prize; and he nonsuited the Plaintiff upon his own case.

Lens Serjt. now moved to set aside the nonsuit and have a new trial. Without questioning the law laid down in the case of *Le Caux* v. *Eden*, he contended that the evidence did not prove that the Defendant took the vessel merely as prize, but that he evidently had detained her on other grounds: namely, first on the want of a manifest, as an irregularity in the ship's papers, admitting her to be *British*, and also on a supposed breach of the laws against the slave trade, neither of which charges, if there had been a foundation for them, was yet any cause for capture as prize, but only for forfeiture; and the Plaintiff was not precluded from trying in this action whether the Defendant was warranted by the facts in detaining the *John* upon those grounds. The putting a prize-master on board was equivocal, for that would have been done equally in the case of prize and forfeiture. It is a strong circumstance for the Plaintiff, that the Defendant never ventures to institute any proceeding in the Admiralty court. Even if a suspicion that the ship was prize, was one of the motives which actuated the Defendant to detain her, yet when the Defendant relies on three or four conjoint causes of detention, the principle of *Le Caux*

(a) *Doug.* 594.

that on the other and partial ground there ought to be a new trial, because this differs from all the cases which have occurred. It is a question of great importance, and I could not have it pass in silence, because I would not have it understood that our judgment proceeds on an opinion that the authority of the case in the Court of King's Bench ought to be deserted. The point first arose in a case in *Willes* exactly resembling this, and the Court granted a new trial. Another case soon after occurred, and *Willes* C. J. with his usual precision, states the four ways in which questions of this sort can be brought before the Court: By motion in arrest of judgment, by motion for an amendment, by motion for a new trial in this court, or by writ of error in a superior court. I state them now, to shew that all the numerous cases cited are applicable to the other modes of objection, and not to a motion for a new trial. He shews clearly that there would be a variance between the *venire* process and the record, on which judgment for the Plaintiff might be arrested for the variance, and the question was, whether a new trial should be granted. Here no amendment is necessary: as the record now stands, no motion in arrest of judgment can be made, nor can the objection be taken on a writ of error. Here every thing is regular on the record, and can be rectified only by a motion for a new trial. That is discretionary with the Court, if justice requires a new trial they will grant it; if not, they will refuse it. It is true that *Willes* C. J. in the second case supported the first, and if there were no other case extant, that would considerably guide our discretion. But it has twice since come before a Court, once before Mr. Baron *Eyre,* and once in the case of *Hill* v. *Yates.* The case before *Eyre* B. was not exactly like the present, but it certainly would have been ground of error. The Court thought it was not a case to

1

give

give relief to the party, and that the verdict, notwithstanding that irregularity, for such it certainly was, ought to
be supported. In *Hill* v. *Yates* it appearred that one
person was returned, and that another served on the
jury. It is impossible to distinguish that case from the
present. The Court in the first instance refused a rule
to shew cause on a general recollection that the case in
Willes had in some later case been overruled. On
a subsequent day Lord *Ellenborough* stated that he
had consulted those judges from whom intelligence might
be obtained, and they were all of opinion that it was discretionary with the Court to grant or to refuse such an
application, and he stated the great inconvenience that
would occur, if such an objection, (which, it is to be
observed, was not taken at the time of the trial,) should
afterwards be made a ground of setting aside a verdict.
It readily will occur to every one how easily such an objection could by a practice be always raised, and therefore how great is the danger of letting it prevail to set
aside a verdict. To that opinion I shall always subscribe, when a case exactly like that occurs; but let it
be remembered that that judgment proceeded mainly on
the ground that the objection came too late: here the
objection was taken, and the Plaintiff's counsel was apprized at the time, that he took the verdict at the peril
of not being able to hold it, and therefore we think that
the eleven jurymen being well summoned, and a twelfth
not being well summoned, and a verdict taken by those
twelve, and the objection being pointed out at the time,
the Court in the exercise of their discretion to grant a
new trial, or not, ought to set aside this verdict, and
that there ought to be a rule absolute for a *venire de
novo*.

The rest of the Court concurred.

Rule absolute.

ABITBOL v. BRISTOW.

THIS was an action upon a policy of insurance on goods at and from *Mogadore* to *London*: it was tried at *Guildhall* before *Dallas* J. at the sittings after *Michaelmas* term 1815, when a verdict was found for the Plaintiff, subject to a point reserved, and *Shepherd* Solicitor-General in this term obtained a rule *nisi* to set aside the verdict and enter a nonsuit, upon the ground that the allegations of the declaration were not proved. The declaration averred that after the loading of the goods on board, on a certain day, the ship with the goods on board departed, and set sail on her intended voyage, and afterwards, and while the ship was in the course of her voyage, they were destroyed by perils of the sea. The evidence was, that before the ship had half her cargo on board, she was driven from her moorings by bad weather and lost.

Best and *Vaughan* Serjts. now shewed cause, contending that enough appeared on the declaration to shew that the goods were loaded, on which the policy had attached, and that a loss had afterwards accrued; and therefore, though the declaration stated more than was necessary, the Plaintiff was entitled to retain his verdict. In *Rhind* v. *Wilkinson* (a) there was an averment of interest at the time of effecting the policy and of the loss; it certainly did not at the time of effecting the policy subsist in the party, but it did subsist at the time of the loss; it was immaterial whether the Plaintiff were or were not interested at the time of effecting the policy, as stated, so long as he was interested at the time of the

(a) 2 *Taunt.* 237.

loss:

cited it, lays it down that there is no case, in which, after a resale of goods, and payment of the price, or money advanced on the credit of the goods by the second vendee, there had been a stoppage *in transitu.* Stress was laid on the terms of the receipt, but without reason. The goods were in a manner received for the Plaintiffs, inasmuch as the receipt was a discharge to the Plaintiffs of their obligation to deliver the goods to *French,* but they were in no other sense received for them: it never was intended that the Plaintiffs should in any event resume the possession. The delivery was complete, and there was no right of stoppage *in transitu.*

GIBBS C. J. Exclusively of the particular form of the receipt for the goods, I take it, the practice is, that the person who is in possession of the lighterman's receipt, is the person entitled to the bill of lading, which ought to be given only to the holder of that receipt. Consequently the holder of that receipt retains a control over the goods at least until he has exchanged the receipt for the bill of lading. My Brother *Dallas,* who tried this cause, had no doubt on the propriety of the verdict, and the jury were still more clear, and thought it was a right which ought not to be questioned. We should not therefore disturb the verdict unless we could be convinced of the propriety of so doing. *French* and Co. might sell their right again, but the Plaintiffs might refrain from delivering the goods, unless under such circumstances as would enable them to recall the goods if they saw occasion. The Plaintiffs refuse to deliver them, except in exchange for this receipt: they know a bill of lading will be executed before the ship sails, and they know that the bill of lading ought regularly to be executed to themselves. *French* and Co. sell to *Caldas. Caldas* goes to the Defendant, and obtains the bill of lading of these

dealt with according to law, until he liberated her at
the master's request.   Upon the trial of the cause, at
Guildhall, at the sittings after *Michaelmas* term 1815,
before *Gibbs* C. J., it appeared that the Defendant,
who was commander of the *Bembow*, a *British* ship of
war, hailed the Plaintiff's ship the *John*, in her course
from *Senegal* to *London*, and sent an officer on board the
Plaintiff's ship, who, having examined the ship's papers,
questioned the master, whether he was not an *American*,
observing that he and his mate had the appearance of
Americans, that the ship had *American* canvas and rigging, and appeared to be *American* built, which last
was not the case, but she being *British* built, and captured by the *Americans*, had been repaired in *America*,
and had on board *American* canvas and cordage.   He
also inquired whether she had not *African* slaves on
board, or had been concerned in that trade, and on his
saying the ship was *British*, bound from *Senegal* to
London, he imputed it as an irregularity that she had not
on board a manifest of her cargo from *Senegal*, as required by the statute 26 *G.* 3. *c.* 40.   This, though required by the act, in practice is never given to vessels coming from the coast of *Africa*.   And the officer caused the
Plaintiff's master to go on board the Defendant's ship
with his papers.   The master having exhibited to the Defendant dispatches from the governor of *Senegal*, which he
was carrying to the *British* government, and letters addressed to private persons in *England*, which apparently
satisfied the Defendant, was dismissed, and on his return
to his own ship the officer quitted her, but soon after
came again on board, and more particularly questioned
the master; whose answers, though true, not satisfying
him, the Defendant detained the vessel, and carried her
into *Barbadoes*, where he kept the master and crew prisoners on board her, and took away her stream anchor,
by reason of which an *American* ship there ran foul of
her

her, and injured the vessel. After some time the Defendant liberated the master, crew, and vessel, without having
instituted any proceedings against her in the Admiralty
court. *Gibbs* C. J. held that upon this evidence it must
be taken that the Defendant detained her as prize, upon
suspicion that she was hostile property. And according
to *Le Caux* v. *Eden* (a), no action could be maintained
for taking a vessel, where the captors were acting under
a belief that she was a subject of prize; and he nonsuited the Plaintiff upon his own case.

Lens Serjt. now moved to set aside the nonsuit and
have a new trial. Without questioning the law laid
down in the case of *Le Caux* v. *Eden*, he contended that
the evidence did not prove that the Defendant took the
vessel merely as prize, but that he evidently had detained her on other grounds : namely, first on the want
of a manifest, as an irregularity in the ship's papers,
admitting her to be *British*, and also on a supposed
breach of the laws against the slave trade, neither of
which charges, if there had been a foundation for them,
was yet any cause for capture as prize, but only for
forfeiture; and the Plaintiff was not precluded from
trying in this action whether the Defendant was warranted by the facts in detaining the *John* upon those
grounds. The putting a prize-master on board was
equivocal, for that would have been done equally in the
case of prize and forfeiture. It is a strong circumstance for the Plaintiff, that the Defendant never
ventures to institute any proceeding in the Admiralty
court. Even if a suspicion that the ship was prize, was
one of the motives which actuated the Defendant to detain her, yet when the Defendant relies on three or four
conjoint causes of detention, the principle of *Le Caux*

(a) *Doug.* 594.

to sell lands for redeeming their land-tax, had agreed to sell to the Defendant all their estate in the premises for 50l. and that the commissioners had agreed to confirm such contract, the said wardein and poore, in consideration of 50l. paid them by the Defendant in discharge of the costs attending the sales made by them for the redemption of their land-tax, the receipt whereof the said wardein and poore thereby acknowledged, and the commissioners, parties thereto, did thereby allow, and of 5s. by the Defendant paid into the Bank of *England,* to be there placed to the account of the commissioners for the reduction of the national debt, under the title, " an account of the sale of the land-tax," as by the receipt of ———— one of the cashiers of the bank, did appear, in exercise of the powers vested in them by the said acts, did by that indenture duly sealed, and delivered, and intended to be enrolled or registered as the law required for the conveyance of estates sold to redeem land-tax, with the consent, &c. of the said commissioners, testified by their signing and sealing that indenture, grant, bargain, sell, and convey, and the commissioners thereby confirmed to the Defendant, the demised premises in that lease specified, and the reversion, and rents, &c. thereof, and particularly the rent reserved by the lease, to hold the same to, and to the use of the Defendant, his heirs and assigns, for ever discharged from all land-tax, reserved rent, and other incumbrances, as by that indenture, duly sealed with the common seal of the Plaintiffs, and with the respective seals of Lords *Auckland* and *Glenbervie,* and duly delivered and signed by them, then remaining duly registered at the land-tax register office, according to the statute, would appear. The Plaintiffs replied to this, that long before the making the indenture in the declaration mentioned, on the 25th of *June,* 41 *Eliz.,* The Right Hon. Rev. Father

in

in God *John Whitegift* Archbishop of *Canterbury*, being
seized in fee in his own right, and to his own use, of
certain houses, &c. in *Croydon*, did by virtue of the
statute 39 *Eliz.* (a) for erecting of hospitals or abiding
and working houses for the poor, by deed dated
25th *June*, 41 *Eliz.* enrolled in Chancery, erect, found,
and establish the said houses, &c. to be an hospital
and abiding place for the finding, sustentation, and
relief, of certain maimed, poor, needy, or impotent
people, to have continuance for ever, which hospital,
and the persons therein to be placed, the founder
thereby incorporated by the name of " The Wardein
and Poore of the Hospitall of the *Holie Trinitie* in
Croydon, of the Foundation of *John Whitegift* Archbi-
bishop of *Canterbury*," and ordained that by the same
name they should be persons capable to purchase lands
not exceeding the value of 200*l.* by the year; by virtue
of which deed and enrolment, and of that act, the
Plaintiffs became incorporated, and had ever since been,
and then were named and called by the last-mentioned
name; and at the time of making the lease, the Plaintiffs
having been so founded, were by virtue of that foundation seized in fee of the premises by that lease demised.
To this plea the Plaintiffs demurred generally.

Best Serjt. for the demurrer contended, first, that
the conveyance by the Plaintiff to the Defendant was
not invalidated by the circumstance that the principal
part of the purchase money was expressed to be paid,
not into the Bank of *England*, but to the Plaintiffs
themselves; and not for redemption of the Plaintiffs'
land-tax, but to reimburse them their costs incurred by
former sales of land for the redemption of their land-
tax. It is true that the grantors, being incorporated
by the statute 39 *Eliz.*, were prohibited from alienating
their land otherwise than in manner warranted by the
acts for redemption of their land-tax. But this applica-

(a) *t. 5. s. 2.*

tion

tion of the money was authorized by the statute 39 G. 3.
c. 6. s. 36. which enables the grantors to raise by sale
sufficient money to pay the expences of the sales, and
that those costs shall be thereout paid before the money
is paid into the bank, or that so much thereof as they
shall deem sufficient, shall be reserved for that purpose;
that sum which is required for the costs, never, indeed,
can be paid into the bank, nor is intended so to be, for
if it were so paid, it could by no authority be drawn out
again and applied to the costs. And the commissioners
allow in the deed that application of the purchase money
as the act requires. But even if there be any informality
in the circumstance, that the commissioners in the deed
express their approbation only of the grant, and not of
the application of the money, yet this is cured by the
statute 42 Geo. 3. c. 116. s. 120., which enacts, that
proof of execution of any deed of sale by the commissioners, parties thereto, shall be sufficient evidence that
the several notices, acts, matters, and things required
by the recited acts or that act to be done by any vendor
previously to any such sale, were duly given, done, and
performed by such vendor pursuant to the directions of
the recited act and that act. The commissioners certify by this deed that this money has been applied to
the purposes for which it is raised. With respect to
the objection that the grant is made by the corporation
by a name other than their true name, and is therefore
void, inasmuch as this was undoubtedly a mistake, and
cannot be avowed by the Plaintiffs as a premeditated
fraud, it is, as a mistake, cured by the statute 54 Geo. 3.
c. 173. s. 12., which confirms deeds that were void for
want of title in the vendors, or " by reason of some
other mistake or inadvertence." But even if no such
act had passed, ancient authorities are not wanting to
shew that this grant is good; though undoubtedly cases
may be cited favourable to the Plaintiffs. Those decisions
are not now, nor ever were they the law of the land; but

conceits

conceits which grew out of the disposition of supporting corporations to an immoderate extent, which prevailed from the beginning of the reign of *Edward* the Sixth to the latter part of the reign of *James* the First. The objection is bottomed on the ground that a corporation has nothing but its name, and that if it do not convey by its name, then it does not at all convey. If this principle were pursued to the utmost extent, then the slightest deviation in a word or a syllable would suffice to avoid a grant. But the spirit of the decisions is, that there must be a material deviation or ambiguity, as for instance, where there are two corporations of one name, and it cannot be known which of them it is. But this corporation is sufficiently designated by the amount of the name that is given. " The Dean and Chapter of *Bristol* made sundry leases, misreciting the name of their corporation, and an intricate case of sundry such leases made of one thing to divers men, wherein the Lord Chancellor (Lord *Ellesmere*) said that it was fit to help such leases in Chancery, being for reasonable time, and upon good consideration. Judges might have done well at the first to have expounded the law so, with averment that they were the same parties, and so was the old law, till now of late: especially where the mistaking arose on their part who kept the evidences, the which the lessees could not see, but must take a lease by the college clerk." There is then the authority of Lord *Ellesmere*, for saying that this was in his time new law. That which has been decided on principles of natural justice is for ever law, but that which is not, though it may prevail as law in our courts for a time, is not law, nor binds the Court. In this case the Chancellor does not hold there is relief in equity because there is no relief at law, but he says, the law ought to be so. *King's Lynn* case (b). Bond to the mayor and burgesses of *Lynn Regis* in com. *Norfolk*. It turned out that the corporation was in-

(a) *Cary*, 24.   (b) 10 *Co.* 122. b. ✓

.corporated

corporated by the name, *majoris & burgensium domini regis, de* Lynn Regis, and although in the bond the words *burgi domini regis* were omitted, it was held good. And herein is cited every previous case, and they are all considered by *Coke* J. And it is ruled, " that when in truth there is but one and the same corporation, leases, grants, &c. made by them ought not to be avoided for such nice and verbal variances, when in substance the true name of the corporation, either by matter expressed, or necessarily implied in the words themselves, appears to the Court: and as to the said case of the hospital of the *Savoy,* it is true that judgment was given in the Exchequer by Baron *Clarke* and Baron *Gent* against the opinion of Sir *Roger Manwood* C. B. *totis viribus.*" But a similar variance is found in the lease to that which is in the deed. The corporation is described in the lease as the wardein and poore of the hospital of the *Holy Trinity* in *Croydon,* in the county of *Surrey,* (which is no part of the name,) of the foundation of *John Whitgift,* (not *Whitegift,* and the former is not *idem sonans* with the latter,) Archbishop of *Canterbury.* This appears by the lease, which is set out on oyer. If the objection be fatal in the deed, it is fatal in the lease, and therefore the Plaintiffs cannot recover.

Bosanquet Serjt. *contrà.* The argument that the Plaintiffs alone know their own founder, is without foundation, for the purchaser was lessee by a lease in which they were rightly named, and the purchaser, not the vendor, prepares his own deeds. The general words used in the statute 54 *G.* 3. *c.* 173. *s.* 12. must apply to grievances *ejusdem generis.* It provides for the cases, first, where the vendor, though seised of the land, is not entitled to convey without some further assurance; or, 2dly, where the lands did not, at the time of the sale, stand limited to the same uses; and, 3dly, where a greater quantity of an estate might have been sold,

than

than was necessary. Such sales are ratified, and, it is declared, shall be as valid as if they had been made in strict conformity to the powers under which they were intended to have effect : but none of them are at all similar or applicable to this case. The nature of the objections is this: as to the land-tax acts, the 3d plea states, in the recital, that an agreement has been entered into for the sale of the premises for 50*l.*, and that the commissioners had agreed to confirm the contract. If this be the contract, it cannot stand, for until the money is paid into the Bank of *England*, no sale takes place, and it proceeds to state that the consideration is 50*l.* paid to the said warden and poor in consideration of the costs and expences attending sales made by the said warden and poor generally, and of 5*s.* paid into the bank. This therefore is a sale made, not for the discharge of the specific expences attending this sale, but for the expences of sales made generally and not under the authority of these commissioners. By the statute 38 G. 3. *c.* 60. *s.* 30. the money is to be paid into the bank, for the redemption of the land-tax, and no more land is to be sold than the commissioners shall certify is fit to be sold. Then came the 39 G. 3. *c.* 6. *s.* 36. which makes it lawful to raise so much money by such sale, as shall be sufficient not only for the purpose of redeeming any land-tax for which such land shall be sold, but also for the purpose of paying and satisfying all such costs and expences as the corporation making any such sale shall incur on account thereof, and that such costs shall be paid out of the purchase money for the said lands, before the same shall be paid into the bank. The 39 G. 3. *c.* 21. enables the king to appoint seven commissioners to execute the act, instead of the general commissioners. This plea does not state that the commissioners, parties to the deed, were privy counsellors, as it certainly ought to do. The 13th section gives to the commissioners only the power to order the payment of such costs and expences attending the sales as they think reasonable, being the same power which the former act gave to the other commissioners. This then is not a mere slip, but an excess of authority. The corporation has sold lands for purposes for which they never were authorized to sell, and as the sale therefore is not warranted by the statutes, the question is, whether this is a good sale at common law. The decisions which have been so lightly treated as new law, were the law of a period when our greatest lawyers lived, and that law subsisted long before the time of *Ed. 6.* and after the time of *James* 1. In the case of *King's Lynn*, Lord *Coke* states the law to be, first, as to these words *idem nomen et non per aliud*, that this word *idem* has two significations, viz. *idem syllabis et verbis*, and *idem re et sensu ;* and the name of a corporation in grants or conveyances need not be *idem syllabis et verbis*, but it is sufficient if it be *idem re et sensu.* Many cases arose about that time in which the struggle was, whether the name varied *litteris et syllabis*, or *rê et sensu* (a). *Nota*, that abbot and convent, dean and chapter, and all other corporations, ought to be named truly by their names of incorporation and foundation, according to the form thereof, without omission of any material part thereof, in all their leases and grants, and in all actions where they are Defendants or Plaintiffs, or otherwise their lease and grant, &c. are void, and also their writ shall abate ; because the name of a corporation is like the name of baptism of a man, which cannot be changed. So, where (b) *Eton* College was incorporated by the name *prepositi et col-*

(a) *New Bendl.* 2., 4 & 5 P.　　(b) *Dyer*, 150., *Eton College & M.*　　　　　　　　　　　　case, *pl.* 85.

legii,

O

legii, a lease which they made by the name *prepositi et sociorum* was held void. So in 10 *Eliz.* the place of which a corporation took its name was omitted, and the grant was held void. In *Croft* v. *Howell* (a) the Cook's company were incorporated by the name *magistrorum sive gubernatorum et communitatis mysteriæ coquorum* London. A lease made by *Jo. Johnson, Mathew Robinson, John Birch,* and *Rafe Isnel,* masters and guardians of the craft or mystery of the cooks of *London,* and the commonalty of the same craft and mystery, was held void. In all the cases the question is whether the variance be material or not, if this be not a material variance, the misnomer cannot hurt. It may be admitted that the cases of abatement of writs stand on a different ground, because the Defendant gives a better writ. *Fanshaw's* case (b), which in 29 *Eliz.* was argued in the Court of Exchequer. Two judges ruled in favour of the misnomer. *Manwood* C. B. thought it not a fatal variance. Upon a writ (c) of error the point was argued by *Coke, Egerton,* and others; then argued by all the judges, and finally compromised. This is cited, not for the decision, but for the authority of *Manwood* C. B. who, as it is said by Lord *Coke,* was *totis viribus contrà,* and for the sound distinctions which he laid down. In *Mo.* 235. he says, " there is no book in the law which avoids the leases or grants of a corporation for a variance in any of these four circumstances, namely, in addition, interposition, omission, or commutation, so that it retain the four first principles of the substance, that is to say, the name of the persons of the house, of the foundation, or dedication, and of the place known before the foundation wherein the house is situate. One of the reasons most particularly applicable to this case, is, that an alteration in the

(a) *Plowd.* 536.   (c) 1 *Leon.* 160. S. C. *Anders.*
(b) *Mo.* 228.   202.

name

1816.

CROYDON
Hospital
v.
FARLEY.

name of a founder is a prejudice to the honour he meant to do himself by including his own name in the name of the foundation, he adds that there had been more points on variances in the names of corporations in the last 42 years than in 400 years before. The various cases on the name of the *Norwich* corporation are in strict conformity to that case. The Dean and Chapter of the Cathedral Church of the *Holy Trinity* of *Norwich* (a) surrendered their possessions to the king, who reincorporated them by the name of " The Dean and Chapter of the Cathedral Church of the *Holy and Undivided Trinity* of *Norwich*, of the foundation of *Edward* the Sixth," and regranted their possessions to them, omitting the words " of the foundation of *Edward* the Sixth." It was contended, and held, that the old name of incorporation remained, and *Herbert* being their founder, they were not bound to keep in the name of *Edward* the Sixth. And in *King's Lynn* case Lord *Coke* says, " There is a great difference between old and new corporations, for old corporations may have several names :" the Plaintiffs, being a new one, can have only one name. In the case of *Heyward* v. *Fulcher* (b), as indeed in all the cases cited for the Plaintiffs, there was a special verdict, and it was found in all of them, that the corporation suing did execute the deed; yet it was held void. Again, the Dean and Chapter of *Norwich* leased, omitting the words " of the foundation of *Edward* the Sixth," and it was held void. So, in a gift to the abbot and nuns of *Sion*, of the foundation of our lord the king, the grant omitting the words " of the foundation of our lord the king," it was held that the omission avoided it. So, *Whitlock* enumerates the name of the founder among the four things that are of the substance of a corporation (c). So, in *Fisher* v. *Bois*(d), a

(a) 3 Co. Rep. 73.
(b) Palm. 491. S.C. W. Jones,
66.

(c) 1 Leon. 126. S.C. Mo.
266 and cit. 10 Co. 125.
(d) Palm. 503.

variance

variance in the name was held fatal; held a hard case, but so decided. *Custodes* for *guardiani* held synonymous; but where it was called *domûs sive collegii de Merton,* instead of *domûs sive collegii scholarium de Merton,* the omission of *scholarium* was held fatal, as a variance in substance. So, where *Eaton* College, incorporated *per nomen præpositi et collegii regalis collegii Beatæ Mariæ de Eaton juxta Windsor,* made a lease, omitting in their name the words " *Beatæ Mariæ*" and the iteration of the word *collegii,* it was held void (*a*).   No authority has been cited overturning these cases.   In the present case there is a variance in substance, and not in immaterial circumstance.   The calling the Archbishop " the most Rev. Father in God," and adding the words " in the county of *Surrey*" in the case, are but circumstance, and as *Manwood* C. B. says, " addition, interposition, omission, or commutation," do not vitiate.   This grant, therefore, is void at common law, and so much varies from the authority of the land-tax acts, that it is not warranted by those statutes.   It does not appear on the record that any other land had been sold for the redemption of the land-tax, upon the sale of which any costs had been incurred.

' *Best* in reply.   The statutes do not warrant the argument that the Plaintiffs have no right to sell land positively for the cost of their sales, but only for the redemption of the land-tax, and to keep back a part of the purchase money for costs, for they enable a vendor to sell to one person to raise money for the redemption, and to another to raise a sum for the costs.   If the Plaintiffs have sold land for the redemption, and kept no part of the purchase money back for their costs, what are they to do, but to sell more for their costs?   It is said, if this be not within the specific object of the act 54 *G.* 3. the general words will not heal it; but the general purport

(*a*) *Jenk.* 214. *case* 54.

K k 3   of

of the act appears by the preamble to this clause, and it shews an intent not to remedy the defect in particular cases only, but to remedy all mistakes. Adopting in the enactment the generality of the preamble, *ipsis verbis:* the only condition is, that the deed be executed *bonâ fide.* It is clear from the mode of the introduction, the remedy is not to be confined to mistakes *ejusdem generis,* but is extended to all mistakes. In a remedial act the Court would carry the relief as far as the mischief extends; even if the words did not reach it. Another objection is, that it does not appear that these noble persons were privy counsellors. But inasmuch as the king has appointed them commissioners, it will be presumed that they have that qualification. The cases cited carry the argument on the misnomer no further than the Defendant's counsel foresaw, and they are all confined to the period before mentioned. They only rule that a misrecital in a material part of the name of corporation vitiates a grant, but what is material is in every case disputed by the Judges. *Manwood* held the dedication of a church a material part, but where the prior of *St. John's* of *Jerusalem* omitted the name of *Jerusalem* in their grant (a), it was held not to be fatal. It is said that the founder has a right to have his name in the grant. It is to be believed that Archbishop *Whitegift* founded his hospital in the hope of a better reward, and that he would rather have concealed his name, if with propriety he could. The question of materiality or immateriality depends on this, whether the grantors can be known by the name, and it is for the Court to judge whether the variance be material or not. It is said the purchaser prepared the deed; that fact does not appear on the record, but if he did, the Plaintiffs executed it, and so gave the name under their common seal. In the *King's Lynn* case the

(a) *Jenk.* 214.

words

words *burgi domini regis*, the founder's name, is omitted,
yet it was held immaterial: as to *Fisher* v. *Bois* no
judgment was there given, but *Fanshaw* compounded.
Heywood v. *Fulcher* was not decided, but it proceeded
on different grounds: the last decision therefore pronounced on this subject is the case of *King's Lynn*, and
that is with the Defendant.   The rule therefore is, and
it is a safe one, that if the corporation is misdescribed
in a grant, and they go on to aver that they are not the
same corporation, that grant ought not to bind them.
The old law, as Lord *Ellesmere* says, was, as it now is:
it must be shewn that it was another corporation: but if
the rule is to stand as settled by those cases, they lay
down no certain criterion what is material or immaterial; it is for the consideration of the Court in each case.
The name of a founder may be important, as the only
means of discriminating two corporations, but here it
is quite immaterial.   If there be no better reason shewn
for inserting his name than to honour him 200 years
after his decease, it is immaterial. (*a*)

GIBBS C. J.   It is certainly true that from the reign
of *Ed.* 6. to the end of the reign of *James* 1. many decisions will be found turning on many nice points, and
many now apparently frivolous objections have been entertained, but it was not because the judges who graced
the bench in those days were inferior, either in intellect
or in learning, to those who now sit on it; in the last, I
fear, they would be found our masters; but it is because
a greater liberality of sentiment now prevails in the decisions of courts of justice.   The present case arises out of
an action of covenant.   Certain persons constituting a
charitable foundation at *Croydon*, have certain property,
part of which consists in land.   At a certain period they
made a lease of part of their land to the Defendant.

1816.

CROYDON
Hospital
v.
FARLEY.

(*a*) See also *Pits* v. *James*, Hob. 124. 2*d Re:.*, and Dr. *Ayray's*
case, 11 *Co.* 18. *b.* ✓

K k 4   They,

They, being generally restrained from alienating their property, are afterwards authorized for certain purposes to dispose of a portion of their land under the acts for the redemption of the land-tax : they profess to sell the reversion of the demised premises in fee to the Defendant, and to convey the reversion to him, and they profess to receive his money for discharging the residue of their land from the land-tax ; but after receiving the money, (how to be applied, I know not, except for the purposes of the charity,) they say, we professed to convey to you by a legal conveyance, but you have been deceived, and you must pay us rent for your land, as if this conveyance had not been made. Their objections are, first, we have conveyed to you by a wrong name; we are the *Wardein and poore* of the *Hospitall* of the *Holy Trinitie* in *Croydon*, of the foundation of *John Whitegift, Archbishop of Canterbury ;* and in the conveyance to you we have omitted to state that we are of the foundation of *John Whitegift, Archbishop* of *Canterbury*, therefore, though we have received your money, we have not sold you the land: the conveyance is void. If this question had occurred for decision at the period of those cases which have been cited, possibly it would have raised considerable doubts, but I subscribe most implicitly to the doctrine laid down by Lord *Ellesmere*, that at that time it was open to the judges, to enquire, whether a grant were the grant of the same corporation; and when I found that it was a deed under the common seal of the same corporation, *pace tantorum virorum*, I should have pronounced the deed good. When I hear that the question is, whether there be a material or an immaterial omission in the name, and it is urged that it is material, because in the omission of the grantor's name the Plaintiffs are wanting in due reverence to the memory of their founder, I agree that they ought to shew their gratitude to their founder ; and I say, that if they, out of that gratitude, were to refuse any gift that shall be offered

1   them

them under a grant wherein that name is omitted, until
the omission were corrected, I think such conduct
could not be blamed: but when they say, for it
is they who use the name, that they have miscalled
themselves, and that therefore the grant is void, I think
them much to be reprehended. On this point, that the
omission of the founder's name is a material omission,
I do think that the *King's Lynn* case does strongly
weigh; for the words *burgi domini regis* imply that it
was, as many others were, a burgh of royal foundation,
and on that ground, as well as others, I should think
the objection now made ought not to have prevailed.
But when I look to the act 54 *G.* 3., and the purposes
for which it was made, it at once sets the question at
rest. That act passed after many conveyances for the
redemption of the land-tax had been made. The recital is, that some sales have been or may be made by
persons not strictly authorized. Observe, this act cor-
rects sales made by persons not strictly authorized to
make them by any means: but it goes on to specify
other cases; by reason that the lands did not at the
time of the sale stand limited to the same uses, or that
a greater quantity of an estate might have been sold
than was necessary, or by reason of some other mistake
or inadvertence, and it then enacts that all such sales
shall be good notwithstanding such mistakes and inad-
vertences. A corporation cannot speak for itself: can
any one for these Plaintiffs unblushingly say that this
omission of the name was not a mistake and inadvertence?
Was it then a trap laid for the purchaser? Next, as to
the land-tax acts themselves; the objection as to the
application of the money resolves itself into this, that
the money was not paid as the act requires, that the act
requires some part of the purchase money to be paid
to the Bank of *England* to the account of the commissioners for the sale of land-tax, and that that which is
the substance is in effect altogether omitted, and that
that

that which is only a permitted application of a part, sweeps away all. There would be much in this objection, if this were the only land sold by the Plaintiffs, but that is not so. The hospital had many farms out at lease, which were subject to the land-tax, and they contract for the redemption of the whole, and it is impossible that they can foresee exactly how much they shall want for the one or the other purpose. They go on selling, and pay into the bank all that they receive, until the last; and at last sell this estate, and appropriate to the costs of their sales, so much of the purchase-money as is necessary, and the small residue of 5s. they pay into the bank. I am of opinion therefore that there is no objection to the title to this land, and that the lessors, having conveyed the reversion to the Defendant, cannot now recover from him the rent which they have granted as incident to that reversion.

DALLAS J. I am of the same opinion. I need not consider whether the corporation is properly named, but I shall confine myself to that general ground, independent of any other, and which supersedes the necessity of considering the others, whereon the counsel for the Defendant relies; that, admitting the defect to exist, the act 54 *Geo.* 3. does cure all mistakes. That this transaction of sale with this corporation took place *bonâ fide*, is not disputed. It was for a valuable consideration; and there is a mistake in the misnomer. The question is, whether it does not fall within the very words of the statute. Both the preamble and enacting clause apply to cure this defect. I am also clear on the other ground, that whether nine or ten sales are made, and the purchase-money paid into the bank first, and the money for the costs paid all together at last, or whether the proportionate costs are retained out of the proceeds of each sale, is quite immaterial. I therefore

fore, on this, as well as on the other point, fully agree with my Lord Chief Justice.

PARK J.   This is a most unrighteous action, and the hospital, whatever their name, have affixed their common seal, and ought not to be heard to aver against it. But independently of that ground, I think the *King's Lynn* case is fully as strong as this, and that the omission of Archbishop *Whitegift's* name is immaterial. But I think the statute is decisive, even if these objections had more weight than they have.   One point I will notice; that the Defendant's counsel properly answered in his reply, that it is not to be expected that the sales will all be made to one man; and therefore, whether that purchase-money which is first received be applied to defray the costs, or that which is received after, it is immaterial.   Therefore the judgment must be

For the Defendant,

LEVETT *v.* KIBBLEWHITE.

Feb. 7.

THE Plaintiff sued out a *capias ad respondendum,* with an *ac etiam* clause in debt, on which the Defendant was arrested for 4000*l.*: by a mistake, his declaration and notice of declaration were in case and not in debt.

Vaughan Serjt. had obtained in this term a rule *nisi* that the Plaintiff might amend the declaration by converting it from a declaration in case on promises, to a declaration in debt, in conformity to the *ac etiam* clause in his *capias ad respondendum,* on payment of the costs of the amendment and of this application.

Best Serjt. had on the other hand obtained a rule *nisi* to enter an *exoneretur* on the bail-piece, upon the ground

Where the Plaintiff had sued out process in debt, and declared in case, and thereby discharged the bail, the Court refused to amend the declaration by altering it from debt to case, so as to hold the bail still liable.

ground that the same mistake entitled the bail to their discharge.

Both rules were now discussed together.

Best and *Onslow* Serjts., for the Defendant, contended that the bail being now discharged, the Court would not make an alteration which should charge them. 2dly, This was not to amend, but to make a new declaration in a new action. The prayer of the rule *ought to have been*, that the Plaintiff might declare anew. This was materially distinguishable from *Billing* v. *Flight* (a), for there were no bail. Where the interests of the bail intervene, the Court has never gone so far as to renew the liability of the bail, if the Plaintiffs have by their own inadvertence discharged the bail from their responsibility.

Vaughan, contrd. The Plaintiff's application is not unusual; it was recently granted in *Billing* v. *Flight.* The amendment alters not the substance of the action. While proceedings are in paper, the Court may make any amendments. It is a constant practice of the Court to amend, even in writs of execution, *a fortiori* in this case.

Gibbs C. J. It certainly is in the discretion of the Court to grant amendments of this sort, or not; and the practice is, where the party has committed a slip, which would prevent his going on and ultimately recovering, the Court has permitted him to amend so much, as not to be precluded from those benefits, which the statute had designed him. Even the case of *Billing* v. *Flight* falls under the same description, for the act of parliament only gives an action in debt, and

(a) *Ante,* vi. 419.

the

the Court of Exchequer doubted whether the Plaintiff
could have the remedy of a discovery except in that
action.   But here, there is no reason as between the
Plaintiff and the Defendant, why the Plaintiff may not
proceed and recover against the Defendant; and the
only object of the amendment here is, that the bail may
be precluded from availing themselves of that discharge,
which the Plaintiff has given him by declaring in case
after he has arrested the Plaintiff in debt.   I am not
therefore inclined to make a precedent in this case, and
consequently the first rule for the amendment must be
discharged, and the rule for exonerating the bail must
be made absolute.

DOE, on the Demise of HATCH, *v.* BLUCK.

IN ejectment for lands in the parish of *Elmly Castle,*
tried at the *Worcester* summer assizes 1814, before
Richards B., a verdict was found for the Plaintiff for
one moiety of the premises, with liberty for the Defendant to move to enter a nonsuit.   On that motion made
in *Michaelmas* term 1814, the Court directed a special
case to be stated, the material parts of which in substance were, that *Joseph Peart* being seised in fee of a
moiety of the premises, in 1720 devised all his free
lands at *Creden* or *Kersoe* to *Elizabeth* his wife for life,
and after her decease, to his son *John Peart* and his
heirs for ever: all the aforesaid lands lying in the parish
of *Elmly Castle,* in the county of *Worcester,* and all his
free lands above mentioned, if it should happen that his
son *John* should die unpossest of them, or without heirs,
he gave them to his daughter *Sarah Peart,* and her
heirs.   The testator died so seised, without altering or
revoking

revoking his will, leaving his wife *Elizabeth*, his son *John*, and his daughter *Sarah* him surviving. By lease and release in 1745, being a settlement previous to the marriage of *John Peart*, *John Peart* conveyed all his lands in *Kersoe* to the use, after the marriage, of himself and his assigns for his life, *sans* waste, remainder to trustees and their heirs during his life, to support contingent uses, remainder to the use of *F. Ward*, his intended wife, for life, *sans* waste; remainder to the use of the heirs of her body by himself; remainder to the use of his own right heir. The marriage took effect, and *John Peart*, the son, continued possessed of the premises so settled till 1747, when he died, leaving his widow *Frances*, and one child, his daughter *Elizabeth*. The widow *Frances* continued in possession, and during such possession, in *Michaelmas* term 1768, a fine was levied, in which she and *Elizabeth* her daughter were deforceants, of all lands in *Kersoe*, wherein *Frances* and *Elizabeth Peart*, or either of them, had any manner of estate of inheritance; and by a deed dated the 6th of *September* 1768, the uses of that fine were declared to be to *Frances Peart* for life; remainder to *Elizabeth Peart* in fee. In 1777 the daughter *Elizabeth* devised the premises to *W. Best* and *J. Wilson*, and their heirs, in trust to permit *W. Hull*, and *Betty* his wife, and the survivor of them, to receive the rents for their lives and the life of the longest liver, expectant after the death of her mother, and then to the use of the first and every other their daughter and daughters in tail female. Proclamations were duly indorsed on the before-mentioned fine, but no other evidence was given of their having been made; and this evidence was objected to by the Plaintiff's counsel, as insufficient to prove the fact of such proclamations having been made. *Elizabeth Peart* the mother died in 1769, and *Elizabeth* the daughter died unmarried in 1799 without altering her will. The De-

     fendant

fendant was in possession of the premises as lessee of
the eldest daughter of *W. Hull* and *Betty* his wife, who
were both dead. *Sarah Peart,* the daughter of *Joseph
Peart* the testator, married *J. Hatch,* by whom she had
one son named *Francis. Sarah Hatch* died in 1776,
and her son *Francis* died in 1810, leaving the lessor of
the Plaintiff his eldest son and heir at law, who was
also heir to *Joseph Peart,* to *John Peart,* and to *Elizabeth Peart* the daughter of *John* and *Frances Peart.*
The question was, whether the Plaintiff was entitled to
recover a moiety or any other part of the premises.

The Court intimating a decided opinion that the
proclamations were not proved,

Lens Serjt., for the Plaintiff, confined his argument to
the point that the word heirs in the will of *Joseph Peart*
could not mean heirs generally, for *John Peart* could
not die without heirs, so long as his sister *Sarah* survived him: it therefore must mean heirs of the body,
and inasmuch as the heirs of the body of *John Peart*
had failed, and the fine, without proclamations, could
not bar by nonclaim, the remainder to *Sarah Peart*
had taken effect.

Best Serjt., for the Defendant, contended that under
this will *John Peart* took either an estate in fee simple,
or no interest at all. It was difficult to understand the
meaning of the word "unpossessed," but the only construction it would bear, was, that if *John Peart* died,
living his mother, the estate should absolutely go over
to his sister. If *John Peart* took no estate, there had
been an adverse possession ever since 1769, which, by
the statutes of limitations, was a complete bar. He
agreed that when a devise over in default of heirs is
given to him who is the real heir, it shewed that the
word heirs meant heirs of the body. But *Sarah Peart*
was

was not necessarily the heir of *John Peart*, for she might have a brother born, and then that brother would be the heir of *John Peart*. Therefore the word heirs was here to be understood according to the ordinary 'import of the word, and then it was a contingent estate to *John Peart*, and the contingency of his surviving the tenant for life not happening, he took no estate at all, and there had been an adverse possession from 1769.

Gibbs C. J. relieved *Lens* from replying. It is clear that this testator never meant that his daughter should take, unless those whom he calls the heirs of his son should fail; and as he gives the next remainder to his daughter, after the failure of heirs of his son, it is clear that he meant a class of heirs, amongst whom the daughter could not be enumerated, for if otherwise, he would be giving a remainder over, which could not take effect, till after the extinction of the person to whom it is given. The first devisee *John Peart* therefore takes an estate tail, with remainder to his sister *Sarah*, and so nothing has been done which bars her right to recover: for the fine levied by *Elizabeth* the daughter of *John* could not bar the remainder over, and the proclamations not being proved, there is no ground for a bar by the five years' non-claim. Therefore the Plaintiff is entitled to recover.

Dallas and Park Js. concurred.

Judgment for the Plaintiff.

Ross, Demandant; WILCHEN, Tenant; WORGE and Wife, Vouchees.

Feb. 9.

THE deed to lead the uses of a recovery conveyed " all the tithes of corn grain, and hay, under the denomination of great tithes," of an extensive estate, the parcels of which it had previously enumerated with great particularity, but did not purport to convey any portion of tithes. The recovery comprized 400 acres of land, 150 acres of meadow, 150 acres of pasture, 150 acres of wood, 50 acres of furze and heath, 50 acres of marsh, and a portion of tithes issuing out of certain lands called *Parker's Croft* and *Spital Hill.*

Vaughan Serjt. moved to amend the recovery, by inserting therein a portion of tithes issuing out of all the parcels of land expressed in the deed to be conveyed; and that not being allowed, he moved to substitute the great tithes of all the lands comprized, and strike out the word " portion" from the recovery.

Where the parties intending to suffer a recovery of the great tithes of near 1000 acres of land, suffered the recovery of a portion of tithes issuing out of only two closes, the Court, with great hesitation, suffered the great tithes of the whole to be added to the recovery, but refused to strike out the portion.

GIBBS C. J. A portion of tithes is a distinct thing of itself; and the " portion of tithes" cannot relate to the tithes of all those lands of which the recovery was suffered: it now turns out the whole is a blunder. Parties to cases involved in such notorious and incomprehensible blunders as these, ought to be very well acquainted with the facts before they come with these applications. I wish it were considered that the amendment of fines and recoveries is not a motion of course, and that it requires at least as much attention as the examination of a title to an estate. This is a very extraordinary mistake; by the deed to lead the uses are conveyed certain lands, and the tithes of all those lands, there is no mention whatever of a portion of tithes: the recovery has a portion of tithes out of certain lands, naming two specific closes, and not out of the rest. This is most incredible, that where a deed declares the use of a recovery of certain premises, into the recovery is thrown a certain portion of tithes, which is not stated in the deed declaring the uses. We cannot strike out this portion of tithes. We do not know that the recoverors have not this portion of tithes, nor what interests we may affect by striking it out. The parties may have since sold this portion of tithes to another. Suppose any person were to come, in the next term, and complain, that in amending this recovery on the affidavit of these deponents, we had revived an entail of this portion of tithes, which he had before purchased, and had paid 1000l. for it. It is with the greatest hesitation that I venture so far as to hold that we may insert the words " all and all manner of tithes of hay, corn, grain, &c. of the land aforesaid," but we think that these words, not being inconsistent with the other, may be added.

Feb. 7.

WOODEN v. MOXON.

Where the sheriff had taken the Defendants on a *capias ad satisfaciendum,* erroneously issued on judgment on a bail-recognizance, and they had paid him the amount of the judgment and costs, whereon he discharged them; and receiving notice that the money belonged to the assignees of a bankrupt, refused to pay it over to the Plaintiff; Held, 1. that the sheriff was guilty of an escape; but, 2. the Court relieved him from the action for an escape, leaving him liable to the counts for money had and received, that the Plaintiff might litigate with him the assignee's right to the money in the sheriff's hands.

THIS was an action commenced against the sheriff of *Hull* for an escape, and also for money which he had received to the Plaintiff's use, under the follow-

ing

ing circumstances. Proceedings had been commenced by *scire facias* against certain bail on their recognizance, and judgment having been obtained against them, and a *capias ad satisfaciendum* issued thereon, the bail were taken, and they paid into the hands of the sheriff the amount of the judgment and costs, whereupon he permitted them to go at large, and on the same day returned on the writ, that he had taken the Defendants, but that he could not legally detain them on a judgment on a bail-recognisance; and he also returned that the money was in the sheriff's hands, but that he had been on the same day served with notice that the money so paid to him was the money, not of the bail, but of the principal, and that the latter had become a bankrupt before he so furnished the money, and that it therefore belonged to his assignees; whereupon the sheriff, being required by the Plaintiff to pay over the money to him, refused so to do, and the Plaintiff had commenced this action for an escape, and for the money so paid to the sheriff.

Blosset Serjt. had on a former day moved, on the authority of *Troughton* v. *Clarke* (a), and a *dictum* in 3 *Salk.* (b) to set aside the proceedings in the present action against the sheriff, on the ground that, as the process against the bail was erroneous, which appeared on the Plaintiff's declaration, there could be no escape: but upon the suggestion of the Court, he took his rule *nisi* to quash the writ of *capias ad satisfaciendum*. In drawing up the rule it was entitled in this cause in which he had originally moved.

Bosanquet Serjt. now shewed cause, first, upon the ground that the rule, relating to proceedings which were not in this action, was wrongly entitled, and that the

(a) *Ante*, ii. 113.   (b) 3 *Salk.* 286.

Court could not meddle with the *capias ad satisfacien-dum* on the present rule. Secondly, The bail had so long lain by, that no relief ought now to be given (a) Thirdly, payment to the sheriff does not satisfy the writ of execution, until it be paid over to the Plaintiff. *Slackford* v. *Austen* (b). If this process were erroneous, the sheriff might refuse to act on it; but having acted on it, and discharged the Defendant, he is liable to an action for an escape, for if he had in the first instance objected to acting on the process, the Plaintiff might have had other process (c). The Plaintiff is at least entitled to his costs, having well commenced his action: but further, the sheriff ought not to be relieved by the Court, unless on the terms of his paying the Plaintiff the money. The present action was commenced a year since, and no motion has been made on the part of the bail for relief. They did not complain. It was, he said, a very important question, whether the assignee were entitled to this money, paid, as it was, under legal compulsion.

Biosset in support of his rule. The bail could not well come hither: they paid the money, and though they paid it on an illegal arrest, they paid no more than they were bound, and compellable by other process to pay. The writ is admitted to be improper. The sheriff, an officer of this Court, out of which an irregular process has issued to him, applies, as it is proper for him to do, to the Court, to have that irregular process set aside. The money paid by the bail remains in the hands of the sheriff for such person as is entitled to it.

GIBBS C. J. As to the objection made to the title of the affidavit, the Court would easily cure that by

(a) *Bayly* v. *Titmass*, *ante*, ii. 114, *n.*

(b) 14 *East*, 468.

(c) Dr. *Drury's* case, 8 *Co.* ✓ 281. *b.*

per-

permitting the sheriff to re-swear his affidavit in the
other cause. I was struck at first with the circumstance
that a year had elapsed, and I coincided with the argument, that after so long lying by and deluding the Plaintiff, the proceedings cannot be set aside. The bail had
nothing to complain of, unless they had chosen to bring
an action of trespass for the arrest. They pay the
money to the sheriff, and, supposing it their own money,
the money belonged to the Plaintiff. But the sheriff
has notice that it is the money not of the bail, but of
the principal, who is become a bankrupt. I think the
sheriff ought to be relieved from the count for an
escape, leaving the Plaintiff still at liberty to pursue
the sheriff on his count for money had and received, on
payment of costs by the sheriff, because the action was
well commenced. The writ of *capias ad satisfaciendum*
is not to be set aside, because it would destroy the
foundation of the action.

Rule absolute to strike the first
count out of the declaration,
on payment of costs.

1816.

WOODEN
v.
MOXON.

NICHOLLS *v.* NEILSON.

Feb. 12.

*P*ELL Serjt. opposed the discharge of an insolvent
debtor, upon the ground that he had been remanded by the insolvent debtor's court, when he had
been brought up thither to obtain his discharge under
the statute 53 *Geo.* 3. *c.* 102. *s.* 7. This Court would

A Defendant
taken in exe-
cution in *Tri-
nity* vacation,
under a writ
of *capias ad
satisfacien-
dum*, return-

able in *Michaelmas* term, applying in *Hilary* term following for his discharge under
33 *G.* 3. *c.* 28. applies in due time.

Though a prisoner has been remanded by the insolvent debtor's court for not
satisfactorily answering, the court in which he is committed will not refuse to inquire into the case on his being again brought up before them.

L l 3

infer

infer from that circumstance, that he had been guilty of a wilful concealment of his effects, and though he did not deny that this Court had a concurrent jurisdiction with that, yet they would so far give credit to the decisions of that Court, that they would not further investigate a question which the other Court had determined. He also contended that the Defendant's present application came too late: the statute 33 *G.* 3. *c.* 5. *s.* 5. he was aware, enabled any debtor " who should neglect to take the benefit of the act 32 *G.* 2. *c.* 28. *s.* 13. within the time limited, and should make it appear to the Court that such neglect arose out of ignorance or mistake, to take the benefit of the acts as if he or she had taken the same within the time limited," but that did not apply to a case where the occasion of the lateness of the application was, that the prisoner had been remanded for wilful concealment. The prisoner was charged in execution on the day after the end of *Trinity* term: and the time given by 32 *G.* 2. *c.* 28. *s.* 13. for the application, is, " before the end of the first term which shall be next after any such prisoner shall be charged in execution."

GIBBS C. J. In the case where the writ of *capias ad satisfaciendum* is returnable in *Michaelmas* term, as this is, we understand from the officer, that a petition in *Hilary* term is always considered as being within the limited time: therefore his application is not too late. On the other point; whatever ground of suspicion there may be against this man, we cannot take the proceedings of the other Court for the foundation of our judgment. It has been determined by the Court of Exchequer, I understand, assisted by the Judges of the Court of King's Bench, that the jurisdiction of the insolvent court does not supersede the jurisdiction of the other courts. The Plaintiff may therefore proceed to put questions to the prisoner.

Upon

Upon his examination, his schedule appearing imperfect, the prisoner was

Remanded.

PARK *v.* HAMMOND.

THE Plaintiff declared that he had employed the
Defendant as his agent to procure an insurance for
1000*l.* on goods of the Plaintiff shipped at *Malaga* by
the *Pearl,* for a part of the voyage from *Malaga* to
Dublin, to wit, from *Gibraltar* to *Dublin ;* and assigned
for breach that the Defendant would not procure such
insurance, but procured an insurance to cover goods
laden at *Gibraltar,* and not at *Malaga :* that the Plaintiff's vessel took in goods at *Malaga,* " to be carried from
Malaga to *Gibraltar,* and thence to *Dublin :*" that the
Plaintiff was interested, the goods lost by an insurable
risk, and the Plaintiff deprived of his expected indemnity.   Another count stated instructions to insure " for
a part of the voyage from *Malaga* to *Dublin,* to wit, from
Gibraltar Bay to *Dublin.*"   Upon the trial of this cause
at *Guildhall,* at the sittings after *Michaelmas* term 1815,
before *Gibbs* C. J., the Plaintiff proved a letter dated from
Malaga, instructing the Defendant " to insure 1000*l.*
on goods shipped on board the *Pearl,* from *Gibraltar*
to *Dublin.*   That the Plaintiff took the risk on himself
from that place to *Gibraltar Bay,* where he should send his
letters on shore."   The vessel sailed with the goods on
board from *Malaga,* and in her course hove to in *Gibraltar Bay,* and sent her letters on shore by a boat from *Al-
gesiras,* and did not touch at *Gibraltar,* but on the same
day proceeded in her voyage, and was lost by striking
on a rock.   The Defendant had effected an insurance

It is gross ne-
gligence in an
insurance bro-
ker, employed
to insure goods
from a certain
point in their
voyage home,
to effect a po-
licy " at and
from" that
point, " begin-
ning the ad-
venture from
the loading
thereof on
board."

L l 4

" on

" on goods by the *Pearl* at and from *Gibraltar* to *Dublin*,
beginning the adventure from the loading thereof on
board at *Gibraltar*," the underwriters not being upon
this policy liable to make good the loss of merchandize
shipped at *Malaga*, refused to pay; and in an action
brought thereon the Plaintiff was nonsuited on this objection. The Defendant communicated the terms of
the policy to the Plaintiff himself, who approved of
them. The Defendant contended that this was not such
crassa negligentia as rendered him liable to pay. The
jury, however, found a verdict for the Plaintiff, which
Copley Serjt. in this term obtained a rule *nisi* to set
aside, on the ground that the decisions in *Spitta Wood-
man* (a), and *Mellish* v. *Allnutt* (b), on the point whereon
the Plaintiff was nonsuited, had been so recently published before effecting the insurance, that the Defendant
was not responsible for not being acquainted with
them.

Shepherd, Solicitor-General, now shewed cause against
this rule. *Gibraltar* and *Gibraltar Bay* are two places
materially distinct. At *Gibraltar* there is only a small
harbour defended by a mole. *Gibraltar Bay* is an extensive bay through which vessels may pass at a great
distance from the shore. The Defendant was sufficiently apprised by the Plaintiff's instructions, that he
only meant to pass through the *Bay*, not to go into
Gibraltar; and that the cargo would be shipped at *Malaga*, not at *Gibraltar*: it was therefore the Defendant's
duty to have effected an insurance on the goods from
Gibraltar Bay, in her homeward course from *Malaga*.
It is sufficiently notorious, that upon an insurance, beginning the risk from the lading on board at *Gibraltar*,
the Plaintiff could not recover against the underwriters

(a) 2 *Maule & Selw.* 106.   (b) *Ante*, ii. 416.

for

for goods laden before the vessel reached *Gibraltar*, and it was a part of the Defendant's duty to be apprised of that point of law.

Copley, in support of his rule, urged that the Plaintiff's instructions were to insure from *Gibraltar*, not from the *Bay*, and they would not have authorized the Defendant to insure from *Gibraltar Bay*. At all events, if, on a nice construction of the letter, it required an insurance at and from *Gibraltar Bay*, yet it was not gross negligence. If the policy had been effected from *Gibraltar Bay*, and the ship had gone into *Gibraltar*, (and the Defendant could not foresee that she would not,) it would have been a deviation which would have discharged the underwriters; the Plaintiff would then have insisted that he had instructed the Defendant to insure from *Gibraltar*, and that he ought to have followed the literal, as now he contends for the constructive orders of the Plaintiff. His directions are to insure from *Gibraltar* to *Dublin*, though he takes on himself the risk from *Malaga* to *Gibraltar Bay*: what was to happen afterwards was no concern of the broker's; he was only to obey those instructions, and insure from *Gibraltar* to *Dublin*.

GIBBS C. J. It is impossible for the case to be put more clearly, or more ingeniously than it is by my Brother *Copley*, but the real neglect of the broker consists in his not stating that the goods were laden at *Malaga*. The Plaintiff states that he does not mean his vessel should go into *Gibraltar*, but should send in his letters from *Gibraltar Bay*. The insurance therefore ought to have applied to the voyage so clearly described in that letter; and it does not. I do not say whether the description of a voyage from *Gibraltar* home, would cover a voyage from *Gibraltar Bay* home; but

but sure I am, that the broker ought not to have precluded, as he has done, the Plaintiff from trying that
question : the broker, however, ought to have known
how to describe that voyage ; but the action is brought
for a different neglect, and I can see no reason to
disturb the verdict.

DALLAS J. concurred.

PARK J. This point having been settled ever since
Robinson v. *French* (a), and down to a late case (b) in
Maule and *Selwyn*, that an insurance to commence from
the loading of goods at a certain point, will not attach
on goods previously laden, no person who undertakes
to insure for others, could be ignorant of it. It is of
very great moment that those who undertake such important business as this, for others who are abroad,
should be acquainted with the proper mode of transacting it ; and if they undertake it without such
knowledge, they are liable to the assured for the consequences.

Rule discharged.

(a) 4 *East,* 130.   (b) *Mellish* v. *Allnutt*, 2 *Maule & Selw.* 106.

KEIR *v.* ANDRADE.

Where an as-
sured, licensed
to export 150
barrels of gun-
powder, which
was prohibited

THIS was an action upon a policy of insurance upon
goods, at and from *London* to *Madeira*, valued at
5000*l.*, to pay average on each package. It was tried
before *Dallas* J. at the *London* sittings after *Michaelmas*

by proclamation, exported 300 barrels: Held that he might recover against the
underwriter the value of the 150 barrels licensed.

term

term 1815, when it appeared that the Plaintiffs had hired and laden the ship *Ann* for the voyage; and that among other goods laden on board were 300 barrels of gunpowder, the exportation of which, at the time of this adventure, was prohibited by a royal proclamation, dated 23d *July* 1814, issued pursuant to the statutes 12 *Car.* 2. *c.* 4., 29 *G.* 2. *c.* 16., and 33 *G.* 3. *c.* 2. *s.* 4. The Plaintiffs gave secondary evidence of a licence obtained, on their own petition, from the king in council, to export 150 barrels of gunpowder on board the ship *Ann*, from *London* to *Teneriffe*, under the usual conditions, and alleged a similar licence to *Wilkinson, Rowlitt,* and Co. to export other 150 barrels; but both the licences had been captured with the ship *Ann*. They offered no evidence to connect the latter licence with themselves, and the petition of *Wilkinson, Rowlitt,* and Co., on which that licence was obtained, prayed for a licence to themselves only by name; nothing in either licence appropriated the permission to any specific parcel of the powder. *Best* Serjt., for the Defendant, contended, that the licence to *Wilkinson* was not in its nature transferable, and therefore, supposing it were proved, it could not be applied to the second 150 barrels, the exportation of which was consequently illegal, and that illegality contaminated the whole adventure, and the whole contract of insurance; and the Plaintiff must therefore be nonsuited. *Dallas* J. thought that the licence, being granted for the exportation of gunpowder in time of war, was to be strictly construed; but he reserved the point, subject whereto the jury found a verdict for the Plaintiffs for the value of the whole cargo.

Best having accordingly obtained a rule *nisi* to set aside the verdict and enter a nonsuit,

Shepherd,

Shepherd, Solicitor-General, and *Lens* Serjt. now shewed cause against the rule. To the extent of 150 barrels of the powder, and the residue of the goods, the Plaintiffs are entitled to recover. The only effect of the statutes is, to confiscate the ship exporting, and the powder illegally exported. It is clear that an innocent stranger might have goods lawfully on board that ship, and recover for them, though the ship be forfeited; and a person who has some confiscable goods on board may also have innocent goods on board, which will neither be forfeited nor liable to penalties; and such goods may be legally insured. The consequences would be most oppressive, if a master of a vessel, who might take out a small excess in quantity of powder above his allowed weight, should forfeit not only the ship and powder, but also all his other goods on board. The voyage is not illegal, though the unlicensed powder is illegally on board. Even though the ship-owner might not insure the ship, if he were conusant of the powder being on board without licence, yet all others who had goods on board, might insure their part of the cargo. The officers of the revenue could have seized no more, nor prosecuted in the Exchequer for more, than that which is not covered by the licence. In several cases in the Court of Admiralty it has been expressly ruled that where a ship has on board certain goods enumerated in a licence, and others not enumerated, the condemnation reaches only the goods not therein enumerated; and it was here determined in *Pieschell* v. *Allnutt* (a), that because the goods belonging to other persons were not forfeited, they were therefore capable of insurance. The 29 *Geo.* 2. *c.* 16. *s.* 2. which makes the powder subject to forfeiture, in its terms makes only the excess the subject of forfeiture, viz. " what-

(a) *Ante,* iv. 792.

ever

ever powder, prohibited by proclamation or order of
council to be exported, shall be shipped or laden for
exportation contrary to such proclamation or order,"
and nothing is incapable of insurance but that which
is liable to be seized. It matters not, that both quantities are comprized in one bill of lading, which also
contains many other articles. The statute 33 *G.* 3.
c. 2. *s.* 4., which imposes forfeiture of the ship, does not
affect this question. Both the licences were to export
in the same ship: and in the bill of lading, as well as on
the casks, 150 of the barrels were marked with the
initials of the Plaintiff's name, and the other 150 barrels
with the initials of *Wilkinson* and *Rowlitt's* name, sufficiently appropriating each licence to a specific parcel.
And it is material that the proclamation now in force
only directs that offending parties shall be liable to the
penalties of the 29 *Geo.* 2. *c.* 16., not mentioning those
of 33 *G.* 3. *c.* 2., and therefore contemplates the milder
penalties only. The licence also requires the additional security to the public of a bond; it does not
follow that the Plaintiffs not only shall lose that for
which they have given no bond, but that also for which
they have given the legal bond.

Best, contrà. The first act on this subject is the
12 *Car.* 2. *c.* 4. *s.* 12. it inflicts no penalty, but enables
his majesty to prohibit the exportation of powder. The
29 *G.* 2. *c.* 16. *s.* 2. for enforcing the former act, directs
that the powder so exported shall be forfeited. By the
act 33 *G.* 3. *c.* 2. *s.* 4. the vessel with her guns, furniture, ammunition, tackle, and apparel, is declared
forfeited, in which the powder shall be laden when
prohibited by proclamation or order in council, and by
the last act, a penalty of 100*l.* is inflicted on the master of the vessel, and also on any other person exporting. It may be admitted, that if the only consequence
had

had been a penalty, it would not have rendered the voyage illegal, but that is not the only consequence of the offence. The former acts remain in full force, and the voyage is declared illegal. The stat. *Car.* 2. renders the act illegal, for it says in terms that the king may prohibit the act; and where a statute prohibits a thing, the doing it is illegal. An insurance cannot be legally effected on a voyage where the very sailing of the ship upon that voyage renders her subject to confiscation, as this is by the statute 33 *G.* 3.; and when penalties are superadded by later statutes, they do not do away the effect of the former acts. *Law* v. *Hodson* (a), was an action for the price of bricks sold, which were of less size than is directed by the statute 17 *G.* 3. *c.* 42. The first section requires that they shall not be less than certain dimensions, and the second section imposes a penalty if they are made less. The Court held that the Plaintiff could not recover. That is not so strong a case as this, for there both clauses stand in the same statute, but here are different acts, of which the first merely declares it illegal, the subsequent acts are for better enforcing, not for repealing the first. The whole of the powder was exported by the Plaintiffs: the numbers on the casks were a mere description of 300 barrels of powder, some having one mark, and some another, therefore, although the Plaintiffs might legally have exported 150 barrels, they have not done it: they have exported 300, and there is no specific part of them which can be designated, for which they have obtained the licence; it is therefore impossible to distinguish which part of this number may be seized as the excess, and which are the barrels whereto the licence applies. The subject is not capable of separation, and if an insurance on one legal and another illegal article be effected, it has never yet been held, that the assured

(a) 11 *East*, 300.

can

can sever it, and protect the legal parts, rejecting the other: the policy is one 'entire contract, attaching at the same instant on the property legally, and the property illegally exported, it is therefore illegal altogether, and the Plaintiff cannot recover for any part. This argument will not, as was urged, involve in forfeiture other exported articles of a description which needs not the aid of a licence; it is true only to this extent, that all goods which require the aid of a licence would be forfeited if a licence were not properly obtained, as in this case. The officers of government may see good reason to permit *A. B.* to export 150 barrels of powder, when they may deem it improper that he should export 300. A licence thus applied is an instrument of fraud. If an officer comes on board, a licence is produced, and the officer cannot know whether it covers all or not.

Cur. adv. vult.

GIBBS C. J. now delivered the opinion of the Court.

This is a question of the illegal exportation of powder as prohibited by certain statutes. By the 12th of *Car.* 2. the king is authorized to prohibit the exportation of powder: a subsequent act, 29 *Geo.* 2., declares forfeited the powder exported without licence. The 33d *Geo.* 3. also forfeits the ship exporting. These are regulations imposed only by the statutes. The powder exported is forfeited, the ship is forfeited, the party is subject to certain penalties, but nothing more. So the law stands. The facts are these. The Plaintiffs, being desirous to export powder, applied for a licence, and obtained a licence to export 150 barrels. I take no notice of what was not proved, and was alleged to excuse the fact of shipping the other 150 barrels. I notice only what was proved, that the Plaintiff had 150 other barrels on board. This is an action on a policy, wherein the Plaintiff claims the value of 150 barrels of

powder,

1816.

KEIR
v.
ANDRADE.

powder, and a loss by capture is proved. The under-writer says, the subject-matter of the insurance was powder, which cannot be exported without licence, that 150 barrels only were licenced, and 300 exported; therefore the whole adventure was illegal, and the insurance illegal for the whole. The Court has no difficulty in dealing with the excess, and declaring that the exportation of it was illegal. But if the 150 licenced barrels were not forfeited, then the exportation of them was legal, and the insurance thereon is also legal. The first 150 barrels could not be seized; they are not forfeited, and the insurance on them is valid. That the first 150 were not forfeited is clear. Then 150 barrels being put on board, to which the licence may be applied, the adding 150 barrels afterwards did not vitiate the application of the licence to the first; and up to the extent of the first 150 barrels, and the other goods, the verdict may be supported; the value of the second 150 barrels must be struck off from the verdict.

Rule absolute to reduce the verdict.

BLEAMIRE v. BARFOOT.

An annuity deed contained a covenant by the grantor to insure a house

THIS was a case directed for the opinion of the Judges of this Court, by Sir *W. Grant* M. R. upon a bill filed in Chancery by the Plaintiff for a specific charged with the annuity, and assigned to a trustee for better securing the payment, upon trust to mortgage and sell in case the annuity were in arrear 40 days, and further, that if the grantor omitted to insure, the grantee might insure, and that the premiums with interest should be a charge on the premises; and that the Plaintiff might raise that money in the same manner as he might raise the annuity by virtue of the trusts aforesaid: Held that a memorial fully noticing the trust for raising the arrears, and noticing the grantor's covenant to insure, and keep insured, and that in default it should be lawful for the Plaintiff to insure and keep insured, "as in the indenture was mentioned," sufficiently stated the name of the trustee, and for whom he was trustee.

performance of the Defendant's contract for the purchase of an annuity, whereof, upon a sale by auction,
the Defendant was declared the purchaser; the Defendant, upon the abstract, objecting against the
Plaintiff's title, that the memorial of the annuity was
defective, inasmuch as it did not sufficiently set forth
a certain covenant to insure and keep insured the premises whereon the annuity was charged, and certain
stipulations in default thereof contained in the annuity
deed. By that deed *E. Angell*, after granting to the
Plaintiff a clear annuity of 37*l.* 10*s.* for three lives, and
the lives and life of the survivors and survivor, for the
better securing payment of the annuity, covenanted that
if the rent were in arrear 20 days, the Plaintiff might
distrain on the premises after mentioned and sell; and
that if it were in arrear 30 days, the Plaintiff might
enter and take the profits; and he assigned to *R. Pigott*,
his executors, &c. a certain leasehold messuage for the
residue of a term of 21 years, in trust to permit
E. Angell, his executors, &c. to receive the rents and
profits until default in payment of the annuity, and in
case the annuity were unpaid 40 days next after any of
the days appointed, then that it should be lawful for
R. Pigott, by and out of the premises assigned, and the
rents, &c. thereof, or by demising and mortgaging, or
selling the same, or by such other means as to him
should seem meet, to raise and levy such sums as
should be sufficient to pay the annuity, and all such
costs, charges, damages, and expences, as *R. Pigott*,
or the Plaintiff, their respective executors, &c., should
sustain by means of the non-payment at the time appointed, or of any remedy or means pursued for the
recovery thereof, and should apply the monies arising
thereupon in payment and satisfaction thereof accordingly: and also should permit *E. Angell*, his executors,
&c. to receive and hold the overplus of the premises,
and the issues and profits thereof, for his own use; and

that during that annuity the messuage thereby assigned should at all times be kept insured in the *Phœnix* or some other insurance office in *London* or *Westminster* at the costs of *E. Angell*, his executors, &c. in a sum not less than 250*l.*; and that if at any time during that annuity, he or they should neglect to insure the premises in that sum, it should be lawful for the Plaintiff, his executors, &c., to insure the same at such sum; and whatever money should from time to time be so advanced by the Plaintiff, his executors, &c. for the making or the continuing such insurance, should be charged on the premises thereby assigned, with interest, and it should be lawful for the Plaintiff, his executors, &c. to raise and satisfy to himself and themselves all such money so to be advanced by him or them, with interest, in such and the same manner as he and they were thereby authorized to raise and satisfy the annuity by virtue of the trusts aforesaid. The memorial enrolled stated, that by the memorialized indenture, *E. Angell* granted to the Plaintiff, his executors, &c. the usual power of distress into and upon the hereditaments therein comprised, for better securing the payment of the annuity in case any part should be in arrear for 20 days, with costs occasioned by the non-payment thereof, and also the usual power of entry into and upon, and perception of rents and profits of the same hereditaments, for better securing the payment of the annuity in case any part should be in arrear for 30 days, with costs accasioned by the non-payment thereof, or by reason of any such entry; and that by the memorialized indenture, for the nominal consideration of 10*s.* *E. Angell* assigned to *R. Pigott*, his executors, &c. the messuage therein described for the residue of the term of 21 years, in trust to permit *E. Angell*, his executors, &c. to receive the rents and profits until default in payment of the annuity; and in case the annuity or any part should be unpaid for

40 days,

40 days, then that it should be lawful for *Pigott*, his executors, &c., by and out of the premises thereby assigned, and the rents and profits thereof, or by demising, and mortgaging, or sale, or by such other ways and means as to him, his executors, &c. should seem meet, to raise and levy such sums as should be sufficient from time to time to pay and satisfy the annuity, or so much thereof as should be unpaid, or such costs, charges, damages, and expences as he, *Pigott*, or the Plaintiff, their respective executors, &c. should sustain by reason of the non-payment, or of any remedy or means pursued for the recovery thereof, and should apply those monies in satisfaction thereof accordingly, and also should permit *E. Angell,* his executors, &c. to receive and hold the overplus of the premises, and the issues and profits thereof; and that *E. Angell* by the memorialized indenture covenanted, that he, his executors, &c. would insure and keep insured the assigned premises, and that in default thereof, it should be lawful for the Plaintiff, his executors, &c. to insure and keep insured the same as therein mentioned.

Lens Serjt., for the Plaintiff, argued that this memorial pursued the requisites of the statute 26 *Geo.* 3. *c.* 17. The act did not require the party to set out covenants, or to set out the trusts themselves. In some cases the grantees, being diffident for whom other parties were trustees, had chosen to set out the trusts, that the Court might thereby see for whom they were trustees, instead of hazarding the grantee's own judgment upon the effect of those trusts; but it was more consonant to the express letter of the act, and equally competent for the grantee, to set forth in the memorial the names of the trustees, and to pronounce for whom they were trustees. In this instance the memorial sets

forth

forth the name of *R. Pigott*, the only trustee, and states for whom he is trustee, namely, under certain circumstances and to a certain extent, for the grantor, and under other circumstances and to a certain other extent for the grantee. It was not necessary to set out with more particularity, than was there used, the covenant that the grantor would keep the premises insured at his the grantor's expence, and that in case of his neglect so to do, the grantee might insure at the grantor's expence, and reimburse himself by the several means of distress and entry, or be reimbursed by his trustee through the medium of a mortgage or sale. He proceeded minutely to examine the several cases of *Leycester* v. *Lockwood* (a), *Defaria* v. *Sturt* (b), *Brown* v. *Rose* (c), *Askew* v. *Macreth* (d), *Mowys* v. *Leake* (e), all of which, so far as they were adverse, he distinguished from the present case, and *O'Callogan* v. *Ingilby* (f), where Lord *Ellenborough* C. J. held it sufficient that the memorial expressed that the deed contained " powers of entry and distress as stated in the indenture," without setting out what those powers were; and said that " the act did not require powers of distress and entry to be stated, except so far as they created a trust." It was unnecessary here even to notice the covenant for insurance, but it certainly was not required to use a greater degree of minuteness than was here found.

Copley Serjt., *contrà*, contended that the earlier cases required that all the trusts of an annuity deed should be memorialized, though he admitted that later decisions had narrowed the requisition to a statement of so much of the trusts, whereby it might fully appear which of the parties are trustees, and for whom they are trustees.

(a) 1 *Maule & Selw.* 527.   (d) 1 *New Rep.* 214.
S. C. in Error, *ante*, v. 587.   (e) 8 *Term Rep.* 416.
  (b) *Ante*, ii. 225.   (f) 9 *East*, 135.
  (c) *Ante*, vi. 124.

By

By the covenant to insure, *Pigott*, whose first trusts extend only to raising money for payment of the arrears of the annuity and costs, and as to all else, both before default and after, his trust was for the grantor, now becomes trustee for a new purpose, namely, that instead of being in the first instance trustee for the grantor until default in payment of the annuity, he is now in the first instance trustee for the grantor, only until default in payment of the annuity, or default in payment of the premiums of insurance by the grantor, which shall first happen: he is next trustee for the grantee, not merely for raising money to pay the arrears of the annuity, but for raising money for payment of the arrears of the annuity and for reimbursement of the premiums of insurance advanced by the grantee; and his ultimate trust for the grantor is narrowed from that which it at first was, a trust of the surplus which remained after payment of the annuity and costs, to the surplus which shall remain after payment of the arrears of the annuity and the premiums of insurance advanced by the grantor, and the costs of each. Therefore, when it is said that this memorial contains the name of the trustee, and for whom he is trustee, the assertion is not *ad idem*. It is true as to the original trusts first expressed; but it is not true as to the trust subsequently engrafted on it; and if it ought to be stated on the memorial that *Pigott* is trustee for the parties in the execution of this latter trust, it is not here sufficiently stated by the words of reference to the deed, " as therein expreffed," for the deed, not being open to those who read the memorial, a reference to the contents of the deed can convey to them no information whatever. *Ex parte Ansell* (a) it was held, that the terms of redemption ought to be memorialized. So

(a) 1 *Bos. & Pull.* 62.

M m 3   in

in *Orton* v. *Knight* (*a*), where the proviso for stay of execution was memorialized with a reference to the deed
for the time and manner thereof, it was held insufficient.
So, in *Cummings* v. *Isaacs* (*b*), and *Denn on demise of
Dolman* v. *Dolman* (*c*), in which last case it was held
by Lord *Kenyon* C. J. that it was necessary to memorialize a trust, " that if the grantor should leave the
kingdom, the grantee should retain, out of the funds in
the hands of the trustee, all the additional expence of
insuring the grantor's life, which might be in the first
instance paid by the grantee;" for that the annuitant
derived an additional benefit therefrom. The case of
Taylor v. *Johnson* (*d*) may be distinguishable from this,
because it perhaps comes within the very words of the
statute; but *Lawrence* J. there broadly states, and the
Court in the case of *Toldervy* v. *Allan* (*e*) held, that
all the trusts which are not mere collateral trusts,
as for payment of rent and taxes, and the like,
ought to be set out in the memorial. To state
that *A.* is trustee for *B.* and *C.* conveys no information : the memorial ought to state *to what extent*
he is trustee for *B.* and to what extent for *C.*, at least
with sufficient particularity to shew the nature of the
transaction. *Denn* v. *Dolman* strongly confirms this doctrine, and the Court there proceeded, not on the defect
that the memorial did not set out the names of the particular creditors for whose benefit the trust was created,
though that defect also there existed, but on the broad
ground that the trusts ought to be set out. *Desenfans* v.
O'Bryen (*f*). The trustee was to permit the grantor to
receive the rents till default, and after default for 60 days
he was to raise the arrears for the grantee by sale, and the
Court held that the omission to memorialize the second

(*a*) 3 *Bos. & Pull.* 153.   (*d*) 8 *Term Rep.* 184.
(*b*) 8 *T.R.* 183.   (*e*) 5 *Term Rep.* 480.
(*c*) 5 *Term Rep.* 643.   (*f*) 3 *East,* 559.

                                                    trust

trust which resulted for the grantor during the 60 days, was fatal. That case is precisely in point; for the memorial did shew, as much as this does, for whom the trustee was trustee, namely, for the grantor till default, and for the grantee after the 60 days; but it failed, because it did not shew the whole extent to which he was trustee for each; and Lord *Ellenborough* there intimates that decided cases bound the Court to require, that all the trusts should be set out; and *Lawrence* J. particularly refers to the judgement of *Eyre* C. J. in the case *Ex parte Ansell*. *Bradford* v. *Burland* (a) is also applicable. In *Leycester* v. *Lockwood*(b), Lord *Ellenborough* C. J. held that the memorial was bad because it did not state all the trusts declared of the sum of 10,000*l.*, and the Court of Exchequer-chamber, upon error brought, unanimously confirmed his opinion. [The Court denied that the judgment of the Exchequer-chamber in that case had coincided with the judgment of the Court below in all its particulars; the Court of Error state that their judgment proceeds on the general ground, that all had not been done in the memoria. which was required; and they point out the particular circumstances in which they coincide with the Court of King's Bench: they proceed mainly on the ground that the Defendant and *Aclom* were by the assignment become trustees for securing the annuity, and that it was not expressed in the memorial for whom they were trustees, but they do not go to the whole extent of the judgment of the Court below.] This doctrine is not impugned by the case of *Defaria* v. *Sturt*, which was decided simply on the principle that it did not appear by any thing before the Court, that other trusts existed, and *Lawrence* J. observes, that the party was not called on to disaffirm the existence of other trusts; and the

(a) 14 *East*, 445.   (b) 1 *Maule & Selw.* 534.

M m 4   *dictum*

dictum there of *Chambre* J. that the act did not require the trusts to be set out, must be understood with the limitation, that it is not necessary to set them out as trusts, but it is necessary to set them out, as the means of shewing for whom either of the parties is trustee, unless that appears by an express declaration of the grantee. *Brown* v. *Rose* falls within the same principle as *Defaria* v. *Sturt.*   There the trusts were set out in the memorial as fully as in the indenture; and the Court held, that if there were other trusts, not stated in the memorial, it was necessary for the party who would impeach the memorial, to shew what they were. But here the existence of further trusts does appear, and the memorial does not shew to what extent *Pigott* is trustee for the grantor, and to what extent for the grantee.

Lens in reply.   The Defendant's argument would reduce to nothing the correction of the law on this subject, supposed to have been attained by the cases of *Defaria* v. *Sturt* and *Brown* v. *Rose.*   In *Askew* v. *Macreth,* it appeared on the face of the deeds, that *Coutts* was a trustee for the grantor, as well as for the grantee, and the name of the grantor was not stated as one for whom he was trustee.   If trusts are so complex that unless they are fully set out the Court cannot judge for whom the parties are trustees, it cannot be sufficient, as in *Brown* v. *Rose* it was held to be, to state them by way of reference, " in manner therein mentioned."   The sounder rule perhaps would be, that the act is not satisfied by setting out the trusts *verbatim* for the judgment of the Court, but is imperative on the grantee to declare in words for whom any of the parties is trustee.   In *Denn* v. *Dolman* the objection was palpable, there was a total omission to pursue the express words of the statute. Money was declared to be

paid

paid to *Griffith* in trust, but it is not said in trust for
whom. *Cummins* v. *Isaacs* is equally distinguishable
from this, the contract for insuring the grantor's life
in case of his going abroad, at the grantor's expence,
was part of the *res gesta*, and it is altogether omitted;
that was not a question whether it would have sufficed
shortly to notice the substance of the 'stipulation. In
Desenfans v. *O'Bryen* the trust during the 60 days is
wholly omitted, for no one could conceive that trust to
be intended under the expression " usual powers of
entry and distress," which would naturally mean an
entry and distress by the annuitant himself. *Bradford* v.
Burland is equally inapplicable, for there a trust during
20 days is entirely omitted. Here *Pigott* becomes a
trustee in no new shape, or new character; there is
only a reference to his former character, which is before
sufficiently memorailized, and the words " as therein
mentioned" enable the enquirer to refer to the grant,
such as it is memoralized, and thereby to see how *Pigott*
is trustee, and for whom he is trustee. This clause creates no trust of which the trustee had not before been
specially named, and the trust set out on the memorial
itself. *Leycester* v. *Lockwood*, as now explained, does
not militate with *Defaria* v. *Sturt* and *Brown* v. *Rose*.
It does not prove that every trust must be set out, nor
that it must appear to what extent the party is trustee.
It is therefore no objection, to say, that the trusts in the
deed are therein more particularly specified than are
the trusts in the memorial, if nothing shews that the
party is trustee for any other person than those whom
the memorial states. It has not been attempted to argue that the grant is vitiated by reason that the memorial omits the amount to be insured, or the stipulation
that the insurance must be effected with a joint company, not with an individual; yet, if every particular

of

of the trust were necessary to be stated, it would be fatal to omit these. This clause extends the trust to another object, but it does not create a trust for another person, and the substance of the statute has therefore been complied with.

Cur. adv vult.

The Court afterwards sent to the Master of the Rolls the following certificate:

Having heard the arguments of counsel in this cause, we are of opinion that the memorial of the annuity is a good and sufficient memorial, as required by law, to make the grant of the said annuity valid.

February 10th, 1816.   V. GIBBS.
                                          R. DALLAS.
                                          J. A. PARK.

MEMORANDA.

IN the last *Michaelmas* vacation Sir *Alan Chambre,* Knt., resigned his office of one of his Majesty's Justices of the Court of Common Pleas.

In the same vacation died *John Heath,* Esquire, one of his Majesty's Justices of the same court.

In the same vacation *James Allan Park,* Esquire, one of his Majesty's counsel, was called to the degree of the coif, and was appointed one of his Majesty's Justices of the Court of Common Pleas, in the room of Sir *Alan Chambre,* Knt. He gave rings with the motto *Qui leges juraque servat.* He soon after received the honour of knighthood.

A little before the end of this term *Charles Abbott,* of the *Inner Temple,* Esquire, was called to the degree

1   of

of the coif, and was appointed to the office of one of his
Majesty's Justices of the Court of Common Pleas, in
the room of *John Heath*, Esquire, deceased.   He gave
rings with the motto *Labore*.

1816.

MEMORANDA.

In this term also died Sir *Henry Dampier*, Knight,
one of his Majesty's Justices of the Court of King's
Bench.

END OF HILARY TERM.

CASES

ARGUED AND DETERMINED

IN THE

1816.

Court of COMMON PLEAS,

AND

OTHER COURTS,

IN

Easter Term,

In the Fifty-sixth Year of the Reign of GEORGE III.

MEMORANDA.

IN the last *Hilary* vacation *George Sowley Holroyd*, of *Gray's Inn*, Esquire, was called to the degree of the coif, and was appointed one of his Majesty's Justices of the Court of King's Bench, in the room of Sir *Henry Dampier*, and gave rings with the motto *Componere legibus orbem*. He soon after received the honour of knighthood.

In the course of the same vacation *James Burrough* of the *Inner Temple*, *Charles Warren*, and *Jonathan Raine*, of *Lincoln's Inn*, *James Scarlett*, and *William Harrison*, of the *Inner Temple*, *James Trower*, *William Cooke*, *Samuel Yate Benyon*, and *William Agar*, of *Lincoln's Inn*, and *John Bell* of *Gray's Inn*, Esquires, were appointed his Majesty's counsel learned in the law; and *Charles Wetherell* of *Lincoln's Inn*, Esquire, received a patent of precedence.

12   In

1816.

MEMORANDA.

In the same vacation died Sir *Simon Le Blanc*, Knt., one of his Majesty's Justices of the Court of King's Bench.

In the course of the same vacation *John Vaughan*, Esquire, Serjeant at Law, her Majesty's Solicitor-General, was appointed one of his Majesty's Serjeants at Law: he was soon after appointed Attorney-General to her Majesty in the room of *George Hardinge*, Esquire, deceased, who was one of his Majesty's counsel, and Chief Justice of the *Brecknock* circuit.

On the second day of *Easter* term, *Charles Abbott*, Esquire, resigned the office of one of his Majesty's Justices of the Court of Common Pleas. He was shortly after appointed one of his Majesty's Justices of the Court of King's Bench in the room of Sir *Simon Le Blanc*, Knight, deceased. And upon that occasion he received the honour of knighthood.

In this term *James Burrough*, Esquire, one of his Majesty's counsel, was called to the degree of the coif, and was appointed one of his Majesty's Justices of the Court of Common Pleas in the room of *Charles Abbott*, Esquire. He gave rings with the motto *Legibus Emendes*.

MOORE and Others, Assignees of SHEATH and Another, *v.* WRIGHT.

May 3.

THE Plaintiffs were the assignees of the effects of Messrs. *Sheath*, who had been bankers, and had become bankrupts, and they brought this action to recover a balance due from the Defendant, who had an account open with the bankrupts, and a credit allowed him, for the balance of that account due to the bankrupts. At the *Lincoln* spring assizes 1816, before *Richards* B. the

Where a person produces notes issued by bankers since become bankrupts, and proves that payments were made to him to that amount in notes of that bank shortly before the bankruptcy, that is evidence to be left to a jury, whether he did not hold these identical notes at the time of the bankruptcy.

Plaintiffs

Plaintiffs proved a balance of 704*l.* due from the Defendant at the time of the bankruptcy. The Defendant proposed to set off notes of *Sheath's* bank, which he produced to the amount of 716*l.*, and proved that various sums had been paid him in notes of that bank by different persons to the amount of 848*l.* at various periods from the 4th to the 27th of *June,* the bankruptcy happening early in *July,* but he did not identify the notes produced to be those which he then received.   For the Plaintiffs, to rebut this evidence, it was proved that the bankrupts on 16th *June* pressed the Defendant, who had then overdrawn his credit, to reduce his balance, that he lived within a very short distance of the bank, so that he might easily lodge there any notes which he had, and that he had discounted with them a bill for 100*l.* a very few days before the bankruptcy. *Richards* B. left the case to the jury upon this evidence, to say whether the notes produced were in the Defendant's possession at the time of the bankruptcy, and they found that they were, and gave their verdict for the Defendant.

Vaughan Serjt. in this term moved to set aside the verdict and have a new trial, contending that it was necessary that the Defendant should identify the notes which were the subject of the set-off, and shew that they were in his hands before the bankruptcy.   The circumstances given in evidence rendered the conclusion extremely improbable which the jury had drawn.

GIBBS C.J. There is no doubt on the law of this case. This is an action brought by the assignees of a bankrupt against a creditor of theirs, who seeks to set off against their claim notes, which, he says, were in his custody at the time of the bankruptcy, and which are in his custody when the action is tried. *Primâ facie*, that is a case for the Defendant, if he follows it with some proof that they were in his custody at the time of the bankruptcy.

ruptcy. Very particular evidence of that fact is not to
be expected, nor that it should be brought quite home to
the time of the bankruptcy. It does appear that the
Defendant did, shortly before the bankruptcy, from
time to time receive notes to the whole amount of the
set-off claimed. On the other side are to be weighed
the probabilities urged by the Plaintiff's counsel, that
the notes were not then in the Defendant's custody;
they were to be put to the jury, and no doubt were ably
put to them, but those arguments having been urged to
the jury, and they having decided on them, there is no
reason to disturb the verdict.

1816.

MOORE
v.
WRIGHT.

The rest of the Court concurred in

Refusing the rule.

BAKER and Others, Assignees of GREGORY, a Bankrupt, *v.* LANGHORN and Another.

May 3.

THIS action was tried at the sittings after *Hilary*
term 1816, before *Gibbs* C. J. It was brought by the
assignees of a bankrupt underwriter, to recover premiums on policies underwritten by the bankrupt for
the Defendant, who was an insurance broker. The
defence was a set-off for a loss, which happened before
the bankruptcy, on the ship *Ulthorne*, on a policy underwritten by the bankrupt, and effected by the Defendants
" as agents, as well in their own names as in the names
of all others whom it might concern." The interest was
in Mr. *Mann.* There had been an adjustment of this
loss between the Defendants and the bankrupt *Gregory*,
but it proceeded on a false supposition that the ship had
been lost when she was not lost, and the adjustment
was therefore struck off; the ship was afterwards
really

Semble that
an insurance
broker cannot
set off against
premiums due
to the assignees
of a bankrupt
on policies un-
derwritten by
the bankrupt,
losses which
occurred before
the bankrupt-
cy, though the
policy was
effected in the
broker's name
as agent.

really lost. It was contended by *Lens* Serjt., that the Defendants, who had no *del credere* commission, not having effected this policy for their own benefit, but as agents for others, were not entitled to set off this loss. And the jury found a verdict for the Plaintiffs.

Shepherd, Solicitor-General, now moved to set aside the verdict and have a new trial, or enter a nonsuit. He contended that the result of the cases was, that where a policy is effected in the name of the assured only, there the broker had no right to set off a loss against premiums due to the underwriter. Here the broker can neither sue, nor prove the debt under a commission, unless the case has additional facts belonging to it, as adjustment, or the like, to enable the broker to sue or set off; it is therefore necessary that something equivalent to payment, as an ascription in account, should take place; but where the broker, as in this instance, effects the policy in his name, there he had a right to set off the loss. *Koster assignees of Swan* v. *Eason* (a). The want of a *del credere* commission could make no difference. The principal, indeed, has always a right to step in, and say, I am the principal, and the underwriter must pay me only. And if it is a hard thing that in the one case the underwriter should be told, when it is against his interest, that he owes the money to the broker, and that in another case the principal should come in, and say, you owe it to me, according as one or the other course is the least beneficial to the underwriter, yet the underwriter submits himself to that hardship, when he underwrites a policy in this form. If the consequence were otherwise, an underwriter might always say, when he underwrites a policy in this form, that he will not be sued by the

(a) 2 *Maule & Selw* 112.

principal

principal for the loss; for the broker owes him more for premiums; but when he underwrites a policy effected in the broker's name, but for the benefit of all interested, he has no right to preclude them of their beneficial interest therein. The broker might, by reason of his right of action, perhaps, release, but the Court would restrain him. Here the brokers would have a right to sue; and if to sue, it follows that they would have a right to prove the loss as a debt to themselves under the commission against *Gregory*, and if they might do that, why may not they also set off, if the principal does not previously step in and prevent it?

GIBBS C. J. The adjustment may be laid out of the case, because after the time when the ship was supposed to be lost, she was seen, and the adjustment was struck off. It is within our memory that the rule has been established, that a broker could in any case set up his right to a loss. We have taken our spring from the case of *Grove* v. *Dubois* (a), and we refer all these distinctions to that case. We suppose that case proceeded upon some principle. I wish I could discover that principle. I think the mistake in *Grove* v. *Dubois* was, to suppose, that he who is only liable in the second instance on the failure of the original debtor, could in any case be considered as the original debtor himself. But in this case it is also to be considered, that an account of these premiums, containing the sum in question, was produced, and exhibited to the Defendant, which he over and over again promised to pay, and there was not, till a very late period in the transaction, any attempt to claim a set-off; and I think the jury may be justified in their verdict on this ground, that the party, who was well acquainted with the facts of his own case,

(a) 1 *Term Rep.* 112.

upon a full knowledge of them, for a long time admitted that he had no claim; and after lulling the other party to sleep, he ought not to be permitted to establish his set-off.

Rule refused.

May 4.

PEWTRISS v. AUSTEN.

A count for a deceit, averring that the Defendant represented to the Plaintiff that his lessor required 150l. premium for a lease, whereas he required only 100l., whereby the Defendant fraudulently obtained from the Plaintiff and converted to his own use 50l., is sufficient.

THE Plaintiff declared, that whereas he had, at the Defendant's request, employed him, (not saying for hire or reward,) to endeavour to obtain for the Plaintiff from *E. Johnson* a new lease of certain premises at a premium, and it thereupon became the Defendant's duty to render to the Plaintiff a true account of the terms on which he had obtained such lease; yet the Defendant, not regarding his duty, falsely and fraudulently represented and pretended to the Plaintiff, that *Johnson* required, and was to be paid, 150l. for granting such lease; whereas he required and was to be paid a much less sum, to wit, 100l., as the Defendant well knew; and the Defendant, by means of his false and fraudulent representation, obtained from the Plaintiff, and converted to his own use, the sum of 50l. After verdict for the Plaintiff, at the sittings after *Hilary* term 1816, before *Gibbs* C. J., *Shepherd*, Solicitor-General, now moved in arrest of judgment, upon the ground that the count did not state that the Defendant obtained from the Plaintiff either the 150l. or the 100l., but only 50l., which must be intended of parcel of the 100l. which the Plaintiff was, on his own shewing, bound to pay. If he had shewn that this 50l. was over and above the 100l., it would have sufficed. But unless the adverb "fraudulently" will supply the place of an averment of fact, the Plaintiff shews no injury sustained.

GIBBS

GIBBS C. J.   It seems to me that there is enough
stated to a common intendment to charge the Defendant.   The declaration states that it was the Defendant's
duty to make as good a bargain with *E. Johnson* as he
could, and to acquaint the Plaintiff with the terms of
the contract; it charges that he represented to the
Plaintiff that *Johnson* was to be paid 150*l.*, whereas he
was to be paid only 100*l.*: there ends the charge of
misrepresentation: what follows is only a statement of
the mischief, which, by that misrepresentation the Defendant was enabled to practise on the Plaintiff.   I
think that the 50*l.* mentioned in this allegation "that the
Defendant thereby fraudulently obtained and converted
to his own use the sum of 50*l.*," must have been the 50*l.*
over and above the 100*l.* which was to be paid to *Johnson*; and I think that, especially after verdict, this is
sufficient; and if these facts had not been proved, the
jury would not have been warranted in the verdict
they found.

DALLAS J.   The allegation that the Plaintiff was
thereby defrauded of 50*l.* sufficiently conveys to my
understanding that proposition which the Solicitor-
General contends must appear on this record, namely,
that by means of the false and fraudulent misrepresentation, damage to the amount of 50*l.* has accrued to the
Defendant.

PARK and BURROUGH Js. concurred in thinking that
the judgment ought not to be arrested.

Rule refused.

1816.

PEWTRISS
v.
AUSTEN.

1816.

5 *Ming* 407

May 6.

TAYLOR *v.* ZAMIRA.

To an avowry for rent, it is a good plea, that before the lessor had any thing in the land, a termor granted an annuity or rent-charge, and granted and covenanted that the grantee might distrain on the premises; that the annuity was in arrear, and the grantee demanded it, and threatened distress; and the Plaintiff paid her the amount of the rent then due to the avowant, and so, nothing in arrear.

IN replevin for taking the Plaintiff's goods in his dwelling-house, the Defendant made cognizance as the bailiff of *H. B. Carpue,* under a demise at 35*l.* rent, payable quarterly, for 8*l.* 15*s.* for a quarter's rent, due 25th *March* 1813. The Plaintiff pleaded, that before that demise, *J. Rideout* being seised in fee of one undivided fourth part of the place in which, &c., and *W. Tothill* being seised in fee of another undivided fourth part thereof, before that demise, on 18th *May* 1802, by two several indentures, the one between *J. Rideout* and *S. S. Still,* and the other between *W. Tothill* and *S. S. Still, Rideout* and *Tothill* severally demised to *Still* their respective undivided fourth parts for two several terms of ninety-nine years: that *Still* entered and was possessed *prout,* and before the demise in the cognizance mentioned, on the 24th *June* 1803, by indenture, *S. S. Still* transferred and set over unto *Henry Still* the said two several undivided fourth parts of the said place in which, &c. for the residue of those terms: that *H. Still* entered and was possessed *prout,* and before the demise in the cognizance mentioned, and before *H. B. Carpue* had any estate or interest in the place in which, &c., on 22d *December* 1807, by indenture between *H. Still,* 1., *Margaret Knowles,* 2., *S. S. Still,* 3., *John Tucker,* 4., and *Mary Knowles, Mary Still* the elder, and *Mary Still* the younger, 5., *H. Still* assigned the said two undivided fourth parts to *J. Tucker* for the respective residues of those terms of ninety-nine years; and *J. Tucker* by that indenture granted to *M. Knowles, M. Still,* and *M. Still* the younger, their survivors and survivor, one annuity, clear yearly rent charge, or annual

nual sum, of one hundred and two pounds, sixteen
shillings, to be yearly issuing, payable, and taken by
M. Knowles during her life, and after her death by
M. Still, for her own sole and separate use, and after
both their deaths by *M. Still* the younger, out of, and
charged upon those two undivided fourth parts of the
·the place in which, &c., payable on the 25th *March*
and the 29th *September :* and for the better securing the
payment thereof, *J. Tucker* granted and covenanted to
·and with *M. Knowles, M. Still,* and *M. Still* the
younger, their survivors, &c. that in case the annuity,
·or any part, should be unpaid by twenty-one days, then
they, their survivors or survivor, unto and upon the mes-
·suages and premises thereby charged, might enter, and
·distrain for the same annuity and all arrears, and the
·distresses there found might take, lead, drive away, and
impound, and in pound detain, until the annuity and all
·arrears and costs attending the distress should be fully
paid; and in default of payment in due time after distress, might appraise, sell, or dispose of such distresses,
or otherwise act therein according to law, in all respects
as landlords are authorized to do in respect to distresses
for rent, to the intent that thereby they respectively
might be paid their annuity, arrears, and costs: that
J. Tucker entered and was possessed *prout,* subject to
such annuity; and that afterwards, and before the time
when, &c., on 29th *September* 1812, a sum of money
exceeding the arrears of rent in the cognizance mentioned, viz. 205*l.* 12*s.* for two half-yearly payments, became due from *Tucker* to *M. Knowles;* and she thereupon, afterwards, and before the time when, &c., on
26th *March* 1813, demanded payment of those arrears
from the Plaintiff, being the occupier of the place in
which, &c., and threatened to distrain upon the Plaintiff's
goods in the said dwelling-house; whereupon the Plaintiff, in order to prevent his goods in the place in which,

&c. from being distrained, before the time when, &c., paid *M. Knowles* 8*l.* 15*s.*, the rent so in arrear as the cognizance alleged, as, and for, and in part payment of the arrears of the annuity so due. And so, no part of the sum of 8*l.* 15*s.* of the rent aforesaid was in arrear to *H. B. Carpue* in manner alleged. To this plea the Defendant generally demurred, and the Plaintiff joined in demurrer.

Vaughan Serjt. in support of the demurrer, contended that this plea was bad, because it amounted in substance to a plea of *nil habuit in tenementis*, and it could not be held good, without virtually repealing the statute 11 G. 2. *c.* 19. Before that act an avowant in replevin for rent was obliged to shew a title in fee, and if his title consisted of many facts, the Plaintiff might traverse either of them; the intent of that act was, not merely to enable the lessor to give his title in evidence on a general allegation of title, but that the title should not be at all put in issue. The mere question on this record, is, whether the Plaintiff held for the term alleged in the cognizance: the interest which the tenant sets up, is not a title subsequently grown, but a prior title, which, if the annuitant had it at the time of the demise, shews that the landlord had then no title. It is a maxim, that a tenant cannot dispute his landlord's title. *Syllivan* v. *Stradling* (a). *Palmer* v. *Ekins* (b). *Parker* v. *Manning* (c) acc. Lord *Kenyon* C. J. says, "The Defendant, who has occupied the premises in question for five years, and taken all the profits of the estate during that period, on being called upon for rent, refuses to pay, because, (he says,) the lessor had no right to confer a title on him. But is this the law? The

(a) 2 *Wils.* 308.
(b) 2 *Str.* 817. S. C. *Lord Raym* 1550.
(c) 7 *Term Rep.* 539.

it

cases cited on behalf of the Defendant do not prove that it is. If, indeed, the Defendant had been evicted, to be sure, he could not have been compelled to pay rent; and he might have pleaded that fact in answer to the Plaintiff's demand." A tenant, indeed, may shew that his landlord's title has expired, but he cannot in any case say, that when his landlord demised, he had no title. In *Palmer* v. *Ekins* it is not added that he evicted. *Sapsford* v. *Fletcher* (a) is mainly distinguishable. Lord *Kenyon's* judgment in that case is perfectly consistent with the Plaintiff's title. There it was held that the tenant might set up a payment to the ground-landlord, made under a threat of distress, But this is no payment for the lessor; this is a disclaimer of his title, it shews that the whole rent, and much more, is due to another; it is bottomed in a denial of his title. It is better that a rare instance should occur, wherein a tenant takes a farm by a bad title, and pays rent twice; for he may, of course, recover it back again, or have a compensation against the other for affirming that he had a good title. At all events this plea is bad, for if this be a payment to the landlord, it may be given in evidence on the general plea, that nothing is in arrear.

Lens Serjt. *contrà* was stopped by the Court.

GIBBS C. J. None of this Court have the least doubt on the point on which the Plaintiff's counsel very properly rested his argument, that *nil habuit in tenementis* is in no case an answer to an avowry for rent, or to an action of covenant for rent; but he was mistaken in the corollary he wished to raise from that proposition. In every plea of eviction there is an averment that the lessor had not a perfect title when he de-

(a) 4 *Term Rep.* 513.

N n 4   mised,

mised, but that fact alone would not suffice; to constitute a plea, to it must be added the fact, that the lessee
was in consequence evicted; the whole is a defence;
the Plaintiff's counsel argues, that because *nil habuit in tenementis* alone is not a defence, therefore it
cannot be a part of any other defence. The question
is, whether the fact, that the tenant was called on by
the annuitant, under a threat of distress, to pay off the
arrears of the annuity, and did pay them off accordingly,
being added to the other fact of the lessor's defect of
title, be not a good plea. *Sapsford* v. *Fletcher* is decisive, that if the Defendant had held land subject to rent
due to a superior landlord, and the tenant had been
threatened with a distress by that superior landlord, he
might pay it, and claim to have it allowed as a payment
to his immediate lessor; and the only difference is, that
there the lessor was personally liable to that rent, here
the land only is shewn to be liable; and if that circumstance made any distinction, we would hear the case
further, but my brothers concur with me, that nothing
can rest on that distinction. Here the case is, that
this land was subject to a burthen in the hands of the
Defendant himself; for before the Defendant demised to
the Plaintiff, the land was subject to a burthen of paying this rent; and it being subject thereto, he let it to
the Plaintiff, as if it were free from that prior burthen,
under a rent payable to himself; and when he calls for
payment, payment is refused, on the ground that he, the
tenant, has paid the burthen to another, from which the
land ought to have been free when the Defendant let it to
him. If he had not paid that burthen, the liability of
the land to it would have been no plea; for then it
would amount only to the plea of *nil habuit in tenementis;*
but when he adds that the annuitant threatened to exercise his right of distress, we think the two facts combined
together do constitute a complete defence.

DALLAS

DALLAS J.   The substantial question is, whether payment to a person who has the first charge on the land, be not payment to the immediate landlord, so as to leave no rent in arrear.   The suggestion that this was a voluntary payment, is disaffirmed by the averment of compulsion, and the payment therefore is equivalent to a payment to the ground-landlord.   Upon the principle, I have no doubt: if there were any, it is decided by *Sapsford* v. *Fletcher.*

PARK J.   I should be sorry if there were any inveterate rule of law, which prevented the Defendant from recovering in this case.   *Syllivan* v. *Stradling* has been relied on, as deciding that *nil habuit in tenementis* is no plea, but this plea is compounded of that fact and other things, and is a good plea.   In a late case (*a*) in this Court, the substance of the Defendant's argument was, that the plea amounted to *nil habuit in tenementis*, but the Court held otherwise.   Here is a compulsory payment under a threat of distress, and in *Sapsford* v. *Fletcher* there was no more.

BURROUGH J. was of the same opinion.   *Carpue*, consistently with the plea in bar, had a good title to create the title under him.   The land was therefore liable to distress; no one can doubt about that.   If premises be liable to a distress, the tenant has a right to pay the charge to which they are liable; and the Defendant having so paid the annuity, has a right to deduct from his rent the sum so paid; and if the payment had exceeded the rent due, it appears to me that he might have brought *assumpsit* against the Defendant for the surplus.   The Plaintiff's counsel felt the difficulty of this case, and therefore took in his argument the course he did.   The judgment must be for the

                                        Defendant.

(*a*) *Rogers* v. *Pitcher*, *ante*, vi. 202.

1816.

TAYLOR
v.
ZAMIRA.

May 8.   WALKER *v.* WILLOUGHBY.

The Court will not discharge a Defendant arrested by a wrong *Christian* name, who has signed that name in dealing with the Plaintiff.

*O*NSLOW Serjt. had obtained a rule *nisi*, on the authority of *Wilks* v. *Llorck* (*a*), to discharge the Defendant out of custody, upon the ground that he had been arrested by the name of *William*, whereas his baptismal name was *Hans William*, which rule

Shepherd Solicitor-General now discharged, upon an affidavit that the Defendant had sent the Plaintiff orders for the goods for which the action was brought, by notes signed *W. Willoughby* only, and that the Plaintiff did not know his name was *Hans*. This evidence, as it would suffice to prove a replication in abatement that he was known as well by the one name as the other, so would it suffice to repel the present application.

Onslow in support of his rule.

                      Rule discharged.

(*v*) *Ante,* ii. 399.

(IN THE EXCHEQUER-CHAMBER.)

May 8.   MARTIN *v.* EMMOTE.   In Error.

Where an entire verdict passes in covenant for liquidated freight,

*U*PON affirmance in error from the Court of King's Bench of an entire judgment in covenant on a charter-party on several breaches, one of which was payable at a certain date after delivery, and for unliquidated damages for detention of the ship, the Court cannot sever them in order to give interest on the freight.

                                     for

for 1500*l.* specifically recoverable as freight, and payable at so many days after delivery which was equivalent to a day certain, and another went to recover a compensation for delay in unloading the ship, beyond the lay days stipulated, *Taddy* moved for interest on the freight, suggesting that the Court could by the aid of the record separate the specific sum of 1500*l.* from the residue of the damages, which were unliquidated. But

1816.

MARTIN
v.
EMMOTE.

The Court held that as the damages were entire, they could not sever them, and refused the application.

HUMPHRIES *v.* WILLIAM WINSLOW.

4 Bing 659

May 8.

THE Solicitor-General had obtained a rule *nisi* to discharge the Defendant out of custody upon the ground that the affidavit made to warrant the arrest was defective, in stating that the Defendant was indebted to the Plaintiff, who was indorsee, on a bill of exchange drawn by *T. Winslow*, not shewing in what relation the Defendant stood to that bill, so as to be thereon indebted.

Affidavit to hold to bail, stating that the Defendant is indebted to the Plaintiff as indorsee on a bill drawn by a stranger, is insufficient.

Best Serjt. endevoured to shew cause; but the Court held the affidavit insufficient, and adhering to their invariable practice of refusing to permit supplemental affidavits to be filed in such case,

Discharged the Rule.

HILL *v.* ROE.

BLOSSET Serjt. moved to justify bail. *Vaughan* Serjt. opposed it on the ground that the Defendant had before given notice of bail, and had since changed his attorney without notice to the Plaintiff or leave of the Court, and had given notice of new bail by a new attorney.

Gibbs C. J. referred to *Macpherson* v. *Rorison* (a), and *Ray* v. *De Mattos* (b), and held the objection fatal; but the Court shewing a disposition to give time for further notice, and for the bail to come up again,

Vaughan waived the objection, and put his questions to the bail.

(a) *Doug.* 217.   (b) 2 *W. Bl.* 1323.

GILLINGHAM and Others, Assignees of HAYWARD, a Bankrupt, *v.* LAING.

THIS was an action of trover brought against the sheriff of *Surry* by the Plaintiffs, who were the assignees under a commission of bankrupt against *Hayward,*

A news-vender, who frequented the Royal Exchange for the purpose of collecting intelligence for a newspaper, appointed a creditor to meet him on the *Royal Exchange,* and afterwards directed a friend, if the creditor inquired there for him, to say he was not there: Held that this was an " otherwise absenting himself," which constituted an act of bankruptcy within the statute 1 *Jac.* 1. *c.* 15. *s.* 2.

So, where he saw a creditor at the theatre, and secreted himself under the stage for the purpose of avoiding him.

ward, to recover the value of certain goods which the Defendant had taken under an execution. The Defendant contested the trading and act of bankruptcy; and at the trial of the cause at the sittings after *Hilary* term 1816 before *Gibbs* C. J. the evidence of the bankrupt being a trader, was, that he purchased the entire daily impression of the *Courier* newspaper, from the printer of that paper, by the quire, at 6*d. per* paper; that his name was registered as the publisher of the *Courier* according to act of parliament; that he sold the papers again for his own benefit, being allowed by the vendor 1*s.* 6*d. per* quire for all that he sold, but that if any remained unsold the loss was the bankrupt's, and he also gave the pressmen directions how many copies should be printed on each day. He was in the practice of sending the papers to customers in the country, and also of selling them to other venders, who retailed them. He was, however, the servant of the proprietors of the paper, liable to dismissal when they pleased, though remunerated for his services by this profit on the papers he sold. He sometimes bought a few copies of other newspapers, but the number was not considerable. The evidence as to the acts of bankruptcy was two-fold; one occasion was, that the bankrupt being at the *Surry* theatre, pointed out some persons, who, he said, were his creditors, and that he must avoid them, and went under the stage for that purpose; one of them was a sheriff's officer who had come thither for the purpose of arresting him, and the bankrupt sent him word that he would call on him on the following day and pay him. The other occasion was, that the bankrupt, being in the habit of frequenting the *Royal Exchange* for the purpose of collecting intelligence for his newspaper, and having appointed certain creditors to meet him there, desired another news-collector, who frequented the exchange, if any of those creditors asked for him, to say that he was not there; and some creditor enquiring there

there for him, the other denied him accordingly. *Gibbs* C. J. had no doubt but that a trading was proved, and refused to reserve that point. His Lordship also thought that what passed at the theatre, and on the *Royal Exchange*, were acts of bankruptcy. He was there, several of his creditors were there; he said they were his creditors, and he avoided them: the jury would consider whether his intent in these acts were to delay his creditors; and as to the point whether this were the sort of absenting himself which could constitute an act of bankruptcy, his Lordship reserved it, subject whereto, the jury, finding that such was the bankrupt's intent, gave their verdict for the Plaintiff.

Shepherd, Solicitor-General, in this term moved for a rule *nisi* upon several points; first that the species of article in which the bankrupt dealt was not such as could constitute him a trader; next, that the amount of his dealing was not sufficient to make him a trader; thirdly, that the profit on his dealing was only a mode whereby his employers paid him a salary as their servant, and that the purchasing the papers, *being only* one commodity, and all bought of his master, was not a dealing by way of merchandize, like the dealing of a trader, who chuses of whom he shall buy his goods; and as for the few which he bought of others, they were too insignificant to constitute a trading: next, that the acts relied on were not acts of bankruptcy.

GIBBS C. J. The Defendant's counsel himself admits that the question resolves itself into three points. As to the first, I have no doubt but that a trading in newspapers is as much a trading as in any other commodity. As to the second, whether a servant buying goods of his master, and selling them out for his own gain, becomes a trader, I have no doubt that he does.

I   As

As to the third, whether there be here a purchase and resale to a sufficient amount, here was a trading to a considerable amount: the bankrupt took the whole impression. We think a man may purchase newspapers of his master to such an extent as to make him a trader within the bankrupt laws: and we think this man did trade to such an extent, and was a trader. The other question, whether the denial on the exchange, and his secreting himself at the theatre, be acts of bankruptcy, is of much greater nicety, and I reserved it to the Solicitor-General, and agree that it ought to be further considered.

ABBOTT J. In considering this case, I have been much struck with the expression in the statute of 1 *Jac.* 1. *c.* 15. "keep his or her house, or otherwise absent himself:" it seems as if the keeping house was one mode of absenting himself, and if so, then the departing from his dwelling-house being also expressly mentioned, the otherwise absenting himself must be by absenting himself from some other place than from his house.

The rest of the Court concurred in granting a rule *nisi* upon the last point, but refused it as to the trading.

Best and *Vaughan* Serjts. now shewed cause against this rule. They contended that in the statute 1 *Jac.* 1. *c.* 15. *s.* 2. "begin to keep his or her house or houses, or otherwise to absent him or herself," the words "otherwise to absent" extend to any mode by which a trader withdraws himself from her presence of his creditors. In the three cases of *Judine* v. *Da Cossen* (a), *Bayly* v. *Schofield* (b), and *Chenoweth* v. *Hay* (c), it had been decided that the absenting himself was not confined to an absence from the dwelling-house.

(a) 1 *New Rep.* 234.
(b) 1 *Maule & Selw.* 338.
(c) *Ib.* 676.

The

The Solicitor-General and *Lens* Serjt. in support of the rule. The going from a counting-house to a country house, as in *Judine* v. *Da Cossen* is very different from the going from one part of the *Royal Exchange* to the other. If this be an act of bankruptcy, a trader who should go down an unusual street in his way home, that he might not pass a creditor's door, would be guilty of absenting himself. An absence from a place of trade might suffice, but this person frequented the *Royal Exchange* not for purposes of trade, but to collect news. A case indeed is cited by *Buller J.* in *Colkett* v. *Freeman* (a) where a person appointed a creditor to come to the house of a friend in *Bridge-Street*, and he would pay him, and when he came, desired the master of the house to deny him; but that is very different, he had made that the place of his abode for that purpose. The meaning of " absenting himself" is not a going away from the place wherever he happened to be. If a man seeing a creditor at the other side of a theatre, or in a church, or a house where he is visiting, quits it to avoid him, or if, going into a coffee-house to collect news, he saw a creditor there, and came out again, or if he refused an invitation to a dinner because he expected to meet a creditor there, would either of these be an act of bankruptcy? What right has a creditor to suppose that his debtor will at all these neutral places be prepared with the means of paying him? If he calls at the debtor's house, he has a right to expect he should there be furnished with money to pay. Suppose a merchant, not liking to meet his creditors, stays at home, and does not go to the *Royal Exchange*, whither he otherwise would have gone, is that an act of bankruptcy? But there is no evidence that the bankrupt did absent him-

(a) 2 T. R. 59.

self

self or ever went away from the *Royal Exchange ;* he only desired the witness to say he was gone, or had not been there; a denial is no part of that branch of the statute which speaks of his absenting himself, and this denial cannot be made evidence of his keeping house. There is therefore no act of bankruptcy committed, either by the denial, or by any absenting himself; no case similar to the present has been found. In all the cases hitherto decided, the otherwise absenting himself, is, as well as the beginning to keep house, and the departing from the dwelling-house, relative to some known place of residence or business. The statute returns after all these general words to the precise term of departing from his dwelling-house, which indicates that the absenting is confined to the narrower scope of some fixed abode, and extends not to every change of place. As to the fact that *Hayward* appointed these creditors to meet him there, and avoided them, there is great difficulty in arguing on that part of the case; it does not however appear, that on withdrawing himself from this place, he went to any place where he was not to be found by his creditors, that he did not go home and remain visible there. As to the transaction at the theatre, it goes no farther than the other. The officer's acquiescence in the message sent, that the bankrupt would call on the following day and pay him, is much the same thing as if he had told him by word of mouth.

GIBBS C. J. The only question now is, whether *Hayward* had committed an act of bankruptcy. It has never been insisted that he had confined himself to his dwelling-house, or departed from his dwelling-house to delay his creditors: the only question made has been, whether he comes within the terms, " otherwise absenting himself," and to look at that question we must see the decisions on the words of the statute of 1 *Jac.* 1

VOL. VI.   O o   *c.* 15.

c. 15. which, following the statute of 13 *Eliz. c.* 7., are, " all persons that shall depart the realm, or begin to keep his or her house or houses, or otherwise to absent him or herself," without saying from whence; and then, having gone through several other acts of bankruptcy, it adds, " or depart from his or her dwelling-house." I cannot think, that by " departing from his or her dwelling-house," the statute means the same thing as by " absenting himself," or means to confine the generality of the former words, to the particularity of the latter. The earlier cases on this statute have not been called to aid; but there have been three important recent decisions, *Chenhoweth* v. *Hay*, *Bayly* v. *Schofield*, and *Judine* v. *Da Cossen*, in which the same objection arose as in this case. In *Chenhoweth* v. *Hay* there was neither an absenting himself from the dwelling-house, nor from any counting-house, or place of business, or trade, of the bankrupt, nor from any place where he had appointed the creditor to meet him. But the Court held that there was an absenting himself within the statutes of *Eliz.* and 1 *Jac.* 1., though he had not departed from his dwelling-house, which *is a distinct* branch of the latter statute. I cite this case, because I think it shews that the learned Judge who tried that cause, thought the statute did not mean an absenting himself from this or that place, but an absenting himself from the presence of his creditor. Now see what this case is. Perhaps *Hayward* was a mere lodger, having no visible place of trade, but there was one place whither he every day resorted to collect news, the *Royal Exchange*. It appears that he had creditors; that they were in the habit of seeing him on the *Royal Exchange*; that he appointed them to meet him there; that they came thither, and that he absented himself from them, desiring a friend to state that he was not there: supposing therefore these words to mean, as I

I   think

think they do, an absenting himself from his creditors, not from a particular place, this is a distinct act of absenting himself. It is not necessary to go minutely into the consideration of the cases of *Bayly* v. *Schofield*, and *Judine* v. *Da Cossen*, though they sufficiently distinguish between a departing from the dwelling-house, and an absenting himself; neither is it necessary to go into the circumstance of the bankrupt's quitting the theatre, though it differs very little from some decided cases. Therefore I think there is no doubt, but that there was an act of bankruptcy committed within the meaning of these statutes.

DALLAS J. As to the trading, there was no doubt; and the bankrupt's frequenting the *Royal Exchange* with intent to pick up news, appears to be a frequenting that place for the purpose of his trade. As to the absenting himself, there is a distinction between the keeping house, otherwise absenting himself, and departing from his dwelling-house, and this is an absenting himself.

PARK J. I was at first struck with the ingenuity of the argument, that the " otherwise absenting himself," meant an absenting himself with reference to his dwelling-house, or to some other particular place; but if that were the construction, this would be an useless provision. And this case comes much within the principle of the case cited by *Buller* J. in *Golkett* v. *Freeman*, therefore I think there is no ground to disturb the verdict.

BURROUGH J. Having been present at the trial of the cause of *Chenoweth* v. *Hay*, and likewise when the rule in that case was moved, and disposed of, it is impossible for me to entertain any doubt on this subject. The rule must be

O o 2   Discharged.

May 13.

YOUNG *v.* WRIGHT and Others.

Where a trader made a fraudulent assignment of his tavern and stock, accompanied with possession, and changed his residence from *Westminster* to *Paddington*, and a commission of bankrupt having issued against him, the assignee brought trespass against the messenger for taking possession of the tavern and goods: Held, 1. that, however fraudulent the deed as against creditors, yet, unless an act of bankruptcy was proved to sustain the commission, the assignee might recover on her possession; 2. that it ought to be left to a jury whether the trader's change of residence was a depart-

THIS was an action of trespass brought by *Mary Ann Young* against the messenger under a commission of bankrupt against *Crowley*, for breaking the Plaintiff's house, which was a tavern in *St. James's-street, Westminster*, and taking away her goods. The Plaintiff's case was, that *Crowley*, who was her brother, and had formerly kept this tavern, had assigned it with his stock and goods to the Plaintiff, that she had taken possession, and that the Defendant afterwards took them as *Crowley's* goods, and as belonging, as such, to the assignees under the commission of bankrupt against *Crowley*. *Crowley*, being called as a witness, swore, that he had entered into an agreement with the Plaintiff, that for 169*l*. she should take the remainder of his term, and take his stock at a valuation. He himself held under an agreement for a lease. He suffered her to make use of his name for a limited time afterwards, on her request. Many persons called for money about that period when *Crowley* was at home; he was seen by those who called. In *December* 1814 he ceased to reside on the premises in question, and went to reside at *Paddington*, which after that time was his home. For the Defendant, it was contended, that all this was a fraud; and that the conveyance was upon a private trust for the bankrupt. On one occasion, of a creditor calling at the tavern to see *Crowley*, the Plaintiff said she did not know where he was, but she undertook that if any letters were left for him, she would convey them. The domestics did in fact all know where he was, but they never told any of the creditors who called for money. A deposition of the Plaintiff's was read, in which she

ing from his dwelling-house with intent to delay his creditors.

gav e

gave a particular account how she had acquired the
money with which she purchased this inn; she said
she had borrowed it of two persons, who, being now
called as witnesses, denied lending her any. *Gibbs*
C. J., stopping the Plaintiff's reply, directed the jury
that it was necessary to prove an act of bankruptcy
in this case, for otherwise, however fraudulent his assignment might be as against creditors, yet the Plaintiff's possession, as against a stranger, enabled her to
maintain this action.   To support a commission of
bankruptcy, an act of bankruptcy must be proved:
he thought none had been proved here. All the denials
of the bankrupt were made in his absence, and there
was no proof of his knowledge of the fact. It did not escape his Lordship's consideration, that those denials were
given by the Plaintiff herself, and that it was she who
said she did not know where *Crowley* was; but the question whether an act of bankruptcy had been committed,
must be tried as if the case of the bankrupt were trying.
The facts were as pregnant with fraud as possible, and
such, that if they were presented by a creditor, the deed
could not be supported for a moment; but there was a
deed regularly executed, transferring the entire property
to this sister, and a stranger coming in, having no connection with the matter, could not, by shewing that all
this was fraudulent, warrant himself in doing what the
Defendants had done.   The jury found that no act of
bankruptcy had been committed, and a verdict passed
for the Plaintiff.

Vaughan Serjt. in this term obtained a rule *nisi* to set
aside the verdict and have a new trial, or enter a nonsuit,
suggesting that *Crowley's* departure from his tavern,
was either, 1. a leaving his house to delay his creditors,
or, 2. an act of "otherwise absenting himself;" and
that these questions had not been put to the jury. He
also

also moved upon the ground that the Defendant, though a stranger, might take advantage of the fraud; but the Court refused to grant the rule on that ground, all agreeing that it could not be supported, and that unless the Defendants could make themselves creditors, and invest themselves with the character of assignees, so as to enable them to avail themselves of the fraud, they could not prevent the Plaintiff from recovering on her possession.

Copley and *Best* Serjts. shewed cause against this rule. To leave to the jury whether *Crowley* moved to *Paddington* with intent to delay his creditors, would be leaving a matter of law to them. It would be of dangerous consequence to leave to a jury every change of a trader's residence, as an act of bankruptcy. It did not appear that *Crowley* had ever told the servants to deny his going to *Paddington*, all his servants knew whither he was gone, and some of the creditors called on him there and saw him; and while the tavern was his home, whenever he was there he was always visible to his creditors. If there were any evidence of an *intent to conceal* himself from his creditors, it would be matter to leave to a jury, but the evidence proves that *Crowley* quitted his house for the purpose of giving possession to his sister under the assignment which was proved to have been made to her. And whether it were void or not as against creditors, it did, as between *Crowley* and the Plaintiff, pass the property to her, and his going to *Paddington* was to give effect to it. It is clear therefore that he did not go to *Paddington* to avoid his creditors, for there is no evidence of any such intent, and there is evidence of another intent, with which he went thither, viz. that he might give effect to this assignment.

Vaughan,

Vaughan, in support of his rule, urged that this supposed assignment being admitted to be a gross fraud, as against the creditors of *Crowley*, no interest passed under it. If all this is bottomed in fraud, it lays a strong foundation for the inference, that when he removed to *Paddington*, he went from home to delay his creditors: besides, the otherwise absenting himself is not merely an absenting himself from his dwelling-house: any absenting himself by a debtor from his creditors would be an act of bankruptcy. A trader may commit an act of bankruptcy by absenting himself from any place whatsoever. Upon the declaration of the Plaintiff herself, she was put in there merely to cheat the world; no money passed. Therefore when *Crowley* went to *Paddington*, this deed being void, he went not to give effect to this deed, but to conceal himself from his creditors. Either he had studiously concealed from the Plaintiff where he was, or if she knew it, he had directed her not to disclose it. If he did not mean to elude his creditors, he would have left word where he was to be found. In *Judine* v. *Da Cossen* (a), where a trader had gone to his country house, &c. to avoid his creditors, it was held an act of bankruptcy. It ought to be left to a jury *quo animo* he went to *Paddington*. The jury are the proper judges of the intent. The law depends on the fact.

GIBBS C. J.   If it had been suggested to me at the trial, that the counsel for the Defendant wished the case to be put to the jury in the way in which it is now presented, I should have so put it to them, but the whole tendency of the evidence was to a different point. This is a case of great importance, of considerable extent of property, and of admitted fraud; there can be

1816.

YOUNG
v.
WRIGHT.

(a) 1 *New Rep.* 234.

O o 4   no

1816.

YOUNG
v.
WRIGHT.

no relief from this verdict if there be not a new trial
granted; therefore I think the case ought to be further
considered.

Rule absolute for a new trial, the
costs of the first trial to abide
the event of the second.

May 17.

DARBY *v.* NEWTON.

Where a trader
shipped goods
for *Cagliari* on
board a general
ship, repre-
sented as sail-
ing with li-
cence and
without con-
voy, and bound
for *Gibraltar,
Cagliari,* and
Majorca,
which had a
licence to sail
without con-
voy to *Gibral-
tar* only, and
sailed from
Gibraltar
without con-
voy or licence,
an officer be-
ing appointed
there to grant
licences under
certain circum-
stances: Held
that an insur-
ance of such
goods by the
shipper was
void.

THIS was an action upon a policy of insurance, at
and from *London* to *Cagliari* in *Sardinia,* with
liberty to touch and stay at *Gibraltar,* and there unload
or load goods, and with or without convoy, upon goods,
to return two *per cent.* of the premium for convoy to
the *Westward,* (not *Irish,*) or three *per cent.* for convoy to *Gibraltar,* and three *per cent.* from *Gibraltar* to *Sardinia,* and arrives. The Plaintiff averred
a loss by capture. Upon the trial of the cause at
Guildhall, at the sittings after *Hilary* term 1816, before *Gibbs* C. J. it appeared that the Plaintiff shipped
his goods on board the *Sybella,* which was put up as a
general ship for *Gibraltar, Cagliari,* and *Majorca,* and
was advertised as having a licence, and as about to
sail without convoy. The ship in fact sailed without
convoy, under a licence from the Lords of the Admiralty to sail from *London* to *Gibraltar,* where she
arrived, and discharged certain other parts of her
cargo. The master then enquired for convoy for the
Mediterranean, and learning that none would be appointed for some time, he solicited from the admiral
stationed at that port, who was authorized by the
admiralty to grant licences, under certain circumstances
which were not defined in the evidence, to sail without
convoy, for a licence to sail to *Cagliari,* which was refused him. He afterwards sailed without licence or
convoy,

convoy, and was captured by a *French* privateer. For
the Defendant two questions were made: 1. That the
licence for *Gibraltar* was not a licence for the voyage;
2. that although the Plaintiff was not privy to any
intention of sailing without a licence for the voyage,
yet as he was aware of the intention to sail without
convoy for the voyage, and inasmuch as no licence
for the voyage was actually obtained, the Plaintiff was
not entitled to recover.   The jury expressed an opinion
that convoy for *Gibraltar* was convoy for the voyage:
they found their verdict for the Plaintiff subject to these
two points, which his Lordship reserved.

Lens Serjt. in this term obtained a rule *nisi* to set
aside the verdict and enter a nonsuit, against which
Shepherd, Solicitor-General, and *Best* Serjt. now shewed
cause.   They endeavoured to distinguish this case
from *Wainhouse* v. *Cowie* (a), on the ground that in this
instance there was an admiral stationed at *Gibraltar*
empowered to grant further licences to sail up the
Mediterranean without convoy; and the assured, who
remained in *England*, had a right to expect that the
master would not violate his duty by sailing without
either licence or convoy from *Gibraltar*, up to which
point he was protected, they said, by the licence obtained for that port.   In *Wainhouse* v. *Cowie*, there was
no officer at *Gibraltar* empowered to grant further
licences; this too, was a voyage to be performed by
stages, first, from *London* to *Gibraltar*, then from
Gibraltar for *Cagliari*, then from *Cagliari* to *Majorca*.
It is not necessary that in the first step a licence should
be obtained for the entire voyage, or co-extensive with
the risk insured; it is to be presumed that the master
will obtain all that is necessary to legalize the voyage,

(a) Ante, iv. 178.

as he proceeds (a).   Upon an insurance to *Jamaica* and
home, it would be sufficient if the ship sailed hence
with a licence or convoy to *Jamaica*, though she had
not previously obtained a licence to return home without convoy.   In *Wainhouse* v. *Cowie*, the voyage was
entire.   This was also distinguishable from *Ingham* v.
Agnew (b), for there was no intention that the ship
should stop at *Gibraltar ;* the master, in fact, was
ordered not to stop there, if he could avoid it; and the
Court decided that case on the ground of fraud.   This
case rather ranged itself under those of *Carstairs* v.
Allnutt (c), and *Wake* v. *Atty* (d).   In the former of these
two, Lord *Ellenborough* C. J. said that the convoy act
was a very penal statute, and to be construed strictly,
and he would not permit the interests of an assured to
be affected by it through the instrumentality of his
agent.   Common sense equally requires, that to vitiate a
policy the assured should be privy and instrumental to
sailing without licence, as it does that he should be
privy and instrumental to sailing without convoy.   The
master legally sailed for *Gibraltar*, and if, after reaching that port, he had sailed thence with convoy for
Cagliari, or obtained from the admiral a further licence
for that port, the statute would have been satisfied, and
the master's neglect to do his duty ought not to prejudice
the Plaintiff.

Lens, who would have supported his rule, was
relieved by the Court.

GIBBS C. J.   I should be extremely glad, if I could
find any ground on which the Plaintiff could escape
the effect of this law.   It is a hard objection to be

(a) *Sewell* v. *Royal Exchange Assurance, ante,* iv. 856. S. P.
Haines v. *Busk, ante,* v. 527.
(b) 15 *East,* 517.   (d) *Ante,* iv. 493.
(c) 3 *Campb.* 497.

taken

taken against him; for he certainly is personally innocent, and what has happened is probably the effect of
mistake, but certainly of no default of his: but I can find
no ground to take him out of the law, which was much
considered in the case of *Wainhouse* v. *Cowie*, and adopted
by the Court of King's Bench in *Ingham* v. *Agnew*. The
fourth section declares that if the assured or any other
party be privy to the sailing without convoy, he forfeits
his policy. By the sixth section, if the assured obtains a
licence, though he knows of the sailing without convoy,
he is protected; but there is this wide difference between
sailing without convoy, and sailing without licence.
If a ship sails without convoy, the assured being
ignorant of her sailing without convoy, he is protected;
but if he knows of her sailing without convoy, not
knowing whether she has a licence or not, he is not
protected, unless she has a licence: his security depends on the fact, whether the ship has a licence for
the voyage or not. Now apply this doctrine to *Wainhouse* v. *Cowie*. (Here his Lordship recapitulated the
facts of that case.) Supposing the licence from this
country were good, the Plaintiff is excused for not
having a licence from *Gibraltar*, for he is not bound to
obtain a licence or convoy from a foreign part, unless
there be an officer there able to grant licences, or a
convoy be sometimes appointed. But the ground of
that judgment was, that the goods were shipped for
Palermo, and a licence was obtained for *Gibraltar*,
without any notice to those who granted it, that the
ship was intended to go further than that port. I
cannot distinguish that case from this. Here the
goods are shipped for *Cagliari*. The owner knows
the ship is to go thither; and though she is to touch
at *Gibraltar*, that makes no difference; for that is not
the ultimate place of her destination, and is a fraud on
the

the government; for though the master intended to *go* to *Cagliari*, he held out to the government that he was going only to *Gibraltar*, and obtained a licence to go without convoy no further than *Gibraltar*, and *non constat*, if the admiralty had known that the vessel was intended to push on to *Cagliari*, that they would have given her a licence to *Gibraltar*. It is said, this is distinguishable, because there was an admiral at *Gibraltar* empowered to grant further licences: to what cases that power was to apply, did not distinctly appear by the evidence: it might be to cases where ships which came with a cargo to *Gibraltar* were to ship there a new adventure for some port further up the *Mediterranean*. But this circumstance renders the assured's case more desperate, for it was the more incumbent on the master to apply there for a second licence. Therefore, though it is very hard that the owner of the goods should suffer by the default of the captain in not applying for a further licence there, yet from these premises I arrive with regret at the conclusion, that the assurance is void.

DALLAS J. I am of the same opinion. It has not been attempted to question the propriety of the decision in *Wainhouse* v. *Cowie*; we therefore assume that *Wainhouse* v. *Cowie* was rightly decided: but it is attempted to distinguish this case from that: I can however find no ground of distinction between the cases. Here the ship had not a sufficient licence for the voyage, but to *Gibraltar* only; and the denial of a further licence by the officer there is in effect a denial to proceed further. In *Wainhouse* v. *Cowie*, the assured supposed there would be, and intended that there should be, a good licence for the voyage; so was it here, and it is not distinguishable on any ground whatsoever.

PARK

PARK J. I am of the same opinion. This case is not distinguishable from *Wainhouse* v. *Cowie.* In *Ingham* v. *Agnew*, it is said, there was fraud. But there was in that case, no fraud *malo sensu;* there was, as *Le Blanc* J. said, a licence for a part of the voyage instead of the whole. It has been ingeniously attempted by the counsel to apply the words privy and instrumental to the case of the licence, as well as to that of the convoy, but the words of the statute do not permit it.

BURROUGH J. In my judgment, to decide this case in favour of the Plaintiff, would be to decide directly contrary to the decision of this Court in *Wainhouse* v. *Cowie*, and also directly contrary to the words and spirit of the statute.

Rule absolute.

KEMP v. POTTER.

May 18.

THIS action was commenced on the 18th *July* 1815, and the Defendant, who was then a bankrupt, on the 21st *July* obtained his certificate. On the 17th of *Nov.* 1815, the Defendant filed a plea of his bankruptcy and certificate. The Plaintiff had within this term exhibited under the commission an affidavit of the debt for which this action was brought; whereupon the Defendant had ruled the Plaintiff to reply, and the Plaintiff had obtained a rule *nisi* to discharge that rule and all subsequent proceedings, with costs, declaring that he abandoned his action, and had made his election to proceed under the commission.

Where the Plaintiff, in an action against a bankrupt, makes his election to proceed under the commission, the Defendant is entitled to have some entry or suggestion, recording the election, put on the record.

Lens Serjt. opposed this rule, contending that the Defendant was entitled to some certain assurance that the action was at an end; the Plaintiff ought to move to discontinue.

Shepherd,

Shepherd, Solicitor-General, in support of the rule, contended that the Plaintiff having made an affidavit for proving his debt under the commission, had thereby given a sufficient proof of his election, after which, by the force of the statute 49 *G.* 3. *c.* 121. the action fell to the ground, and no further proceedings on either side were necessary, or ought to be had. The Plaintiff was under the necessity of making this application; for if he had replied, he would thereby have contravened the statute; if he had not replied, the Defendant would have signed judgment.

GIBBS C. J. The Defendant is not proceeding for costs in this case: for he never can get them. Perhaps he has some reason to complain of the Plaintiff, in that he has commenced his action just at the time when the bankrupt is about to obtain his certificate, and has put him to considerable expence. The Defendant having pleaded, rules the Plaintiff to reply, and this application is made to discharge that rule with costs, and the question is, whether this is not the proper course for the Defendant to take, in order to compel the Plaintiff to give him that satisfaction to which he is entitled; for I think the Defendant is entitled to have some entry or suggestion entered on the record, so that it may appear that the Defendant will be no further troubled in this action; for otherwise the Defendant stands under the apprehension that the action may at some time be proceeded in.

BURROUGH J. It would be very easy to frame such an entry on the record as is suitable to the case, it is only to shew that the Plaintiff has made his election to proceed under the commission.

Rule discharged, but without
costs, there being some colour for the application.

RENALDS v. SMITH.

5 Bin

IN debt on a bail bond, the declaration shewed that the Plaintiff sued out of the King's Court before the Honourable Sir *V. Gibbs*, and others his companions, his Majesty's Justices of the Bench at *Westminster*, a writ of *capias ad respondendum* against *George Smith*: that the sheriff made a mandate thereupon, commanding the high bailiff of the honor of *Pomfret* to take the Defendant, so that the sheriff might have him before his Majesty at *Westminster*, in five weeks from *Easter*, and shews a caption, and a bond to the high bailiff, conditioned for the Defendant's appearance before his said Majesty at *Westminster* in five weeks from *Easter*. The Defendant generally demurred.

Bosanquet Serjt. in support of the demurrer. This was a bond intended to be taken pursuant to the statute 23 *H.6. c.* 9. It was now clear, that all matter on that statute needed not, since the stat. of 4 *Ann. c.* 16. be specially pleaded, but that it was a public act, and any exception in any form of proceeding might be taken on the issue of *non est factum*, or a general demurrer. If a writ required the Defendant's appearance here, and the bond required his appearance elsewhere, it was, by the words of the statute, bad; and the question was, whether an appearance before his Majesty at *Westminster* intended an appearance in this court. His Majesty was in contemplation of law supposed to be always sitting in the court of King's Bench, and it had been ruled that the phrase here used described that court. If it described that court, and also this, the bond was void for ambiguity; but the phrase did not describe this court also.

In

Where, upon a *capias* returnable in the Common Pleas, the sheriff made a mandate to the high bailiff of the honor of *Pomfret*, to take the Defendant, so that the sheriff might have him before his said Majesty at *Westminster* in five weeks of *Easter*, a bail-bond taken with condition for the Defendant's appearance before his said Majesty at *Westminster* in five weeks of *Easter*, was held to describe an appearance in the Court of King's Bench, and therefore void.

9 Bing, 7

In *Jones* v. *Stordy* (a), upon a writ to appear before our Lord the King wheresoever, &c. the bond was to appear before our said Lord the King at *Westminster*. Lord *Ellenborough* C. J. held that was a sufficient description of the court of King's Bench; it meant before the *King* in his court. It appeared not by these pleadings that there was any one word in the bond which would shew that an appearance in this court was intended.

Lens Serjt. *contrà*, urged, that the Defendant's counsel assumed too much, in saying that these words necessarily imported the court of King's Bench. In the case cited it appeared that the court of King's Bench was meant, though there was a mistake in the description. So, though it is not here so distinctly shewn as it might be, that the Defendant was required to appear in this court, yet the appearance before his *said Majesty* is an appearance before his said Majesty in the court out of which the process had issued. If it had been process out of the Exchequer, and the same terms had been used, they would have equally conveyed a requisition to appear before his said Majesty in that court· But there is really no ambiguity in the words. It appears on the record that the high bailiff of the honor is in the mandate sufficiently apprised in what court this appearance was to be, and that the sheriff must have given him notice what the writ was. This is virtually comprised in the averment that the sheriff made a mandate to the high bailiff to take the Defendant, so that the sheriff might have him before his said Majesty, which shews that the mandate must be a call on the high bailiff, pointing out in what court the sheriff was required to have the Defendant's body. But this bond is not conditioned to be void merely if the Defendant

(a) 9 *East*, 55.

appear

appear before his Majesty at *Westminster:* it is not before his Majesty's person, nor in any court *ad libitum,*
but before his said Majesty at *Westminster* in five weeks
of *Easter,* &c. •In *Shuttleworth* v. *Pilkington (a),* which
is the foundation of the case in 9 *East,* the Court say,
there is no set form of words for these bonds, but if in
substance they are to appear according to the design of
the writ, it suffices; and cite *Philips* v. *Philips* in
Scacc. Trin. 3 *G.* 2. In all the cases cited, the writ was
to appear in *B. R.,* and the appearing before his said
Majesty described that court by way of reference, but
without the aid of that reference, *non constat* that the
Court would so have held ; and here the reference is to
another court: his said Majesty at *Westminster,* in this
instance, means his said Majesty in his said court of
Common Pleas.

GIBBS C. J. relieved *Bosanquet* from replying. This
is an action brought by the assignee of a bail bond. To
enable the Plaintiff to support this action, the bond
must be taken pursuant to the statute 23 *Hen.* 6., and
must be assigned according to the statute 4 *Ann. c.* 16.,
and the question is, whether this bond be so taken and
assigned. The writ is a *capias ad respondendum,* returnable in this Court. I dare say, the mandate to the
bailiff recites the writ, though that does not appear on
the record, but it requires the party to appear before
our Lord the King at *Westminster:* and the bail-bond
taken thereon is conditioned that the Defendant appear
before our said Lord the King at *Westminster:* and the
Plaintiff avers for breach, that the Defendant has not
appeared before our said Lord the King at *Westminster.*
With respect to the statute 23 *H.* 6. I should have
some doubt whether this were not a bail-bond taken
according to that statute; for the words of that act are,

(*a*) 2 *Stra.* 1155.

that the prisoners shall appear at the day contained in the writ, bill, or warrant; and this is a bond according to the mandate. But taking the whole record together, I cannot doubt that the bail-bond points out the court of King's Bench as the court in which the Defendant is to appear. I therefore think the demurrer must be allowed.

The rest of the Court concurred in giving
Judgment for the Defendant.

BIRN v. BOND.

May 20.

Where the sheriff had omitted to take a bail-bond, and an action had been commenced for an escape, the Court would not stay proceedings on the terms of the sheriff's charging the Plaintiff in custody in the original action, though the sheriff never was ruled to return the writ, and though the Defendant was charged in custody in several other actions.

BOND and *Barrett* were partners. Actions were commenced against them in *Michaelmas* and *Hilary* terms in several courts for considerable sums. On the 20th of *February* the Defendant *Bond* was arrested in this court for 40*l.* at the suit of *Birn*. On the first day in this term *Bond* was surrendered in the King's Bench, and was removed by *habeas corpus*, and charged with several actions in this court, and in the Exchequer, and in the King's Bench, but not in the action at *Birn's* suit, which was intended, but by mere mistake was omitted. There had been no bail in this action. If the Plaintiff had proceeded to rule the sheriff to return the writ and to bring in the body, he would on the 8th of *May* have been entitled to an attachment, but he sued out no rule to return the writ or bring in the body. But on the 9th he sued out a writ against the sheriff, and commenced an action for an escape in not returning the writ.

Blosset Serjt. on a former day had obtained a rule *nisi* to stay proceedings against the sheriff in that action

for

for an escape, on payment of costs, and on bringing up the body of the Defendant *Bond,* in order to charge him in custody with this action, on the authority of *Allingham* v. *Flower* (a), wherein it was held, that after the commencement of an action of escape against the sheriff, for not taking a bail-bond, if good bail be put in and justified in lieu of bail before put in, who by the practice of the Court were a mere nullity, the Plaintiff cannot recover.

Best Serjt. now shewed cause, upon the ground that the sheriff, having taken the Defendant in this action, had permitted him to go at large, without taking a bail-bond, or perfecting bail for him in due time. It had been settled in the case of *Fuller* v. *Prest* (b), that where the sheriff has omitted to take a bail-bond, he is not entitled to the indulgence of putting in bail for the Defendant, and rendering him. And the Defendant, not being yet in court, is not entitled to be heard. *Webb* v. *Matthew* (c) is also in point.

Blosset in support of his rule. Though the Defendant, being at large till the first day of this term, was at large at a time when the Plaintiff was entitled to call on the sheriff for his return of *cepi corpus,* yet he had not so done; and it was immaterial to the Plaintiff whether the sheriff took a bail-bond, or not, until the Plaintiff should apply to have it assigned to him, which here he had not done. If the Plaintiff had ruled the sheriff to return the writ, the sheriff's mistake would have been rectified as a matter of course. This is a much stronger case for the sheriff than *Allingham* v. *Flower,* for there the Defendant was at large: here he is in custody, though not in this suit.

(a) 2 Bos. & Pull. 246.   (b) 1 Bos. & Pull. 225.
(b) 7 Term Rep. 109.

Gibbs C. J. I do not see how the case of *Allingham* v. *Flower* is consistent with the decisions in *Fuller* v. *Prest* and *Webb* v. *Matthew;* nor do I see how either of the last-mentioned cases is to be distinguished from the present. There the Defendant was at large without the sheriff having taken any bail. Here the Defendant is in custody in other actions, but in this action he is untouched by any process. In that state of things an action is brought against the sheriff for an escape, and what is it that the Court are asked to do? To stay proceedings on payment of the costs of that action, and to permit the Defendant to be charged in custody in this action. How is this case to be distinguished from those? The right to an action for an escape, is a right as well vested as any other right of action, and there is the same reason for denying the sheriff the indulgence prayed for, as there was in the two cases last cited for not allowing the sheriff to put in bail.

Dallas J. concurred in thinking this case was not distinguishable from those of *Fuller* v. *Prest*, and *Webb* v. *Matthew.*

Rule discharged.

Thornton and Another *v.* Simpson and Others.

Under a contract to sell 50 tons of hemp at a price *per* ton, to be shipped from *St. Petersburgh* or *Cronstadt* in *June* or *July*, and the ship's name declared as soon as known; in case the ship should not arrive before 31st *December*, the contract to be void; the seller is not bound to send all by one ship, and having announced more to be coming by one ship than the fact was, he was at liberty to declare the residue to be coming by other ships.

THIS was an action brought to recover damages for not accepting certain hemp according to a contract dated *London*, 5 *April* 1815, which expressed that the

*8   Defendants

Defendants " bought of the Plaintiff 50 tons of *St. Pe-
tersburg* sound clean hemp, of good merchantable quality
at 59*l.* per ton, to be shipped from *St. Petersburgh* or
Cronstadt in *June* or *July* then next, and the ship's
name declared as soon as known. In case the ship
should not arrive before the 31st *December* then next,
that contract was to be void." The Plaintiffs supposing
that on the 30th of *June* 1815, 50 tons of hemp, which
they had intended for the Defendants, were shipped at
St. Petersburgh on board the *Lively*, as they had directed, on the 5th of *September* apprized the Defendants
that the 50 tons of hemp bought in *April* for the Defendants' account were shipped in the *Lively* from *St.
Petersburgh.* It proved, however, that the master had
refused to take on board more than 20 tons out of the
50 tons. ˙ The *Lively* arrived on the 20th of *September*
laden with 44 tons, including these 20, the other 24
being parcels which the Plaintiffs had ordered for other
purchasers. On the 22d the Plaintiffs apprized the
Defendants, that " should the quantity by that ship not
be sufficient, say 50 tons, the Plaintiffs reserved to themselves the option of making up the deficiency on the
Unity or the *Paragon*, both from *St. Petersburgh.*" The
Defendants refused to accept any hemp either by the
Unity or the *Paragon*, neither of which vessels were
then arrived, but required a delivery of 50 tons from
the *Lively*, whereon the Plaintiffs on 29th *September*
sent them an order for 20 tons, and repeated to them,
that " in consequence of that ship's shutting out part of
the hemp intended for her, the remaining 30 tons
would come by the *Paragon.*" The Defendants per-
sisting in their refusal to receive hemp by any other
vessel than the *Lively*, when the *Paragon* arrived, the
Plaintiffs sold at a loss the 30 tons which they had
offered to the Defendants, and now called on them to
make good the deficiency. Upon the trial of the cause

P p 3   at

at *Guildhall*, at the sittings after *Hilary* term 1816, before *Gibbs* C. J., these facts being proved, the Defendants contended that the Plaintiffs were not entitled to recover, upon three grounds: first, that they were entitled upon this contract to receive the entire quantity of 50 tons by one ship; secondly, that the Plaintiffs, having elected the *Lively*, were bound by their election, and could not nominate any other vessel; thirdly, that the Defendants were entitled to all the hemp which did come by the *Lively*. The jury found a verdict for the Plaintiffs, with liberty to move for a new trial.

Lens Serjt. in this term obtained a rule *nisi* to set aside the verdict, and enter a verdict for the Defendants, or a nonsuit, against which

Best Serjt. now shewed cause. Nothing in the contract binds the Plaintiffs to send the hemp by any particular ship, nor to send it all in one ship. The Plaintiffs having given notice, under a mistake, that the whole quantity is coming by a certain ship, as soon as they discover their mistake, apprize the Defendants that it is an error. The hemp is the same, though it arrives by a different ship. No inconvenience results to the Defendant by the change of ships. *Robinson* v. *Touray* (a) is in point, and this, to use Lord *Ellenborough's* expression, is the correction of a corrigible mistake.

Lens and *Blosset* Serjts. in support of the rule, insisted that the meaning of the contract was, that the whole quantity should come by one ship, and not by different ships, and as it had not so come, they were relieved from their bargain. If it were indifferent by what ship it came, it would have been unnecessary to use such haste to announce the ship, or expressly to aver it in

(a) 3 *Camp.* 158.

the

the declaration. So soon as a ship is announced, the
Defendants speculate on the state of the market, and
make their sub-contracts accordingly; at least, the Defendants have a right to the 44 tons which were on
board the *Lively*. *Robinson* v. *Touray* is very distinguishable; Lord *Ellenborough* likens that to a porter
delivering one messuage instead of another. Supposing
the Plaintiffs had a right to reserve a liberty to make
up the residue by the *Unity* or *Paragon*, they have not
done even that : But when the *Lively* arrives, they assume the liberty of making up by the *Paragon* all, except such part of the *Lively's* cargo as they think fit to
deliver to the Defendants, giving the residue of her
cargo to some others. The Plaintiffs were not bound
to declare the ship by any given day, but when they
knew the ship. Having announced that they did know
the ship, they cannot say they did not know her when
they announced her; they might take their own time to
declare, might have waited till she was in port here.
They ought to have given simultaneous notice, that the
other part of the cargo of the *Lively* was intended for
other purchasers, or, by omitting so to do, they appropriated the whole 44 tons to the Defendants.

GIBBS C. J. Three objections are taken to the Plaintiffs' right to recover: 1st, that the Plaintiffs were not
at liberty to send the hemp by more ships than one;
2dly, that after having given notice of the ship that
was bringing the goods, the Plaintiffs were bound by
their election, and could not give notice of another
ship; 3dly, that the Plaintiffs violated their contract
in not giving the Defendants all that came by the
Lively. All these objections stand on different grounds.
As to the 1st question, whether if the Plaintiffs had
in the first instance given notice that half the hemp
was coming by the *Lively*, and half by the *Paragon*,

the

the Defendants could have refused to accept it, I think they could not. The material thing is the time of delivery: it was at all events to be before the 31st of *December*, but by what ships the hemp was to come was immaterial. As to the second question, we must look at the terms of the contract. "The name of the ship," which I have assumed as equivalent to ships, "to be declared as soon as known." In *September*, four months before the delivery must necessarily be completed, the Plaintiffs thought they knew by what ship the hemp was coming, and gave notice, but they were deceived. The question is then, whether the Defendants are not bound by the second nomination, and I think they were. They were not prejudiced, they had taken no steps upon the first notice. As to the third question, I think, whatever part of the 50 tons purchased for the Defendants, the Plaintiffs received by the *Lively*, they were bound to deliver to the Defendants; but whatever part of the 50 tons they did not receive by the *Lively*, they were at liberty to make up out of the *Unity* and *Paragon*. It is true the Plaintiffs had other hemp by the *Lively*, besides the 20 tons, but they had ascribed that other hemp to other purchasers, and the Defendants had no right to say that hemp ought to be delivered to them. I therefore think the rule ought to be discharged.

DALLAS J. In this case there are three questions. As to the 1st, if the words be doubtful, we must look to the substance of the contract, and I think that has been complied with. It is said, that instead of sending the hemp by ship or ships, the Plaintiffs are bound to one ship only. At first they were at liberty to send by any ship, the contract not saying that the goods shall come by the first ship, nor naming any ship; therefore the substance of the contract is, that it need not come

by

by any particular ship. As to the 2d point, I think
the Plaintiffs were at liberty to give the second notice.
As to the 3d, the Plaintiffs having contracted to sell
the other parts of the cargo of the *Lively* to other
persons, did all they were bound to do, in delivering
the 20 tons to the Defendants.

1816.

THORNTON
v.
SIMPSON.

PARK J. was of the same opinion. The Plaintiffs
were at liberty to send the hemp by any ships, so that
it arrived before 31st *December.* As to the 3d point,
the case must be considered as if there were only 20
tons on board this ship, and the contract has been
substantially complied with.

BURROUGH J. concurring, the rule was

Discharged.

STANDLEY, Esquire, *v.* HEMMINGTON.

May 21.

IT having been referred to arbitration to determine
whether a contract subsisted between the Plaintiff
and the Defendant for the purchase of certain allotments of land under an inclosure act, and the arbitrator
having on the 19th of *August* 1815 awarded that such
a contract subsisted, and directed the Plaintiff forthwith to perform the contract, and pay 1652*l.* on the
conveyance of the land by the Plaintiff to the Defendant, the Plaintiff furnished his abstract in *September,*
which on the 1st of *November* was returned with que-
ries; the abstract with answers thereto was re-delivered
on the 11th of *November,* and on the 11th of *December*
the Plaintiff pressed for an early answer. On the 18th
of *January* the Defendant repeated in substance the
same objections. On the 30th of *January* the abstract

Upon an award
to perform a
purchase of
land, and pay
the price upon
conveyance of
the land by the
Plaintiff to
Defendant, the
Defendant is
not in con-
tempt before
tender of a
conveyance
executed, and
demand of the
money, and re-
fusal to accept
and pay.

was

was again sent to the Defendant with answers, and dispatch was requested. A personal demand of performance had on the 11th of *May* been made on the Defendant, and notice that unless he complied in ten days, his silence would be construed as a refusal to perform, and the Court would be moved for an attachment, but he had not yet given any answer.

Lens Serjt. now moved for an attachment for non-performance of this award. The Defendant, he said, being in possession of the allotments, the vendor could get neither his land nor his money, and the usual practice being that the purchaser prepares the conveyances, it was unnecessary for the Plaintiff to tender a deed executed. If any plausible objections had been taken to the title, he would not have asked the Court to try its goodness on affidavits, at least the Court would direct an issue whether the title were good.

GIBBS C. J. I think the Plaintiff must do something more. He might file a bill in equity for a specific performance. The title would then be considered in a court of equity; it is impossible we should try a title here on affidavits. But before the Plaintiff can have an attachment, he must execute and tender to the Defendant a conveyance, and ask for the purchase-money awarded. The modern practice, indeed, has gone thus far, that in an action where the Defendant has dispensed with the Plaintiff's tendering the deed executed, the Plaintiff may nevertheless recover; but even that was a relaxation of the law. *Jones v. Barkley* (a) was the first case that relaxed the rule, which was admirably argued by my Brother *Le Blanc;* but there it was averred he informed the party that he was ready to convey, and

(a) *Doug.* 684.

tendered

tendered a draft of an assignment and release for the
purchaser's approbation, and offered to execute and
deliver the deed pursuant thereto, and the other declared, if the Plaintiff had tendered, he would not accept
it, and that he wholly discharged and exempted the
Plaintiffs from executing the same. In the present case
the Plaintiff could not maintain an action on his agreement, nor on a bond for performance of the award, if
he had such, because he does not shew performance on
his part: I think there is not enough to bring the
party into contempt, and the Plaintiff's much better
course is to apply to a court of equity.

DALLAS J. The Plaintiff does not shew even a refusal by the Defendant, nor whether he has decided on
the objection taken.

The rest of the Court concurring, the
                                 Rule was refused.

HORTON v. MOGGRIDGE.

May 21.

*B*EST Serjt. had obtained a rule *nisi* to discharge the
    Defendant out of custody, upon the ground that
he had been recently discharged under the insolvent
act, and that the present action was brought for an antecedent debt.

Vaughan Serjt. shewed cause against the rule, and
Best endeavoured to support it.

GIBBS C. J. This is an application to discharge the
Defendant from an arrest, on the ground that he has
been discharged under the late insolvent act, which
                                                 frees

A Defendant
may be holden
to bail upon a
promise made
after his dis-
charge under
the insolvent
act, to pay a
debt contract-
ed before his
discharge.

frees him from arrest for all debts contracted before his discharge under that act. There are two questions. The first, whether this falls within one of the exceptions of the act; for the Plaintiff, it is said, if there be any fraud in the Defendant's schedule, this fraud shall be unavailable. This is the substance of the 50th section of the statute, not to give the words; and that it must be open for this Court to see whether those circumstances of fraud exist. The six or seven facts of fraud which the Plaintiff's counsel imputes, have been satisfactorily answered by the Defendant's affidavits; and I do not put the case on that ground; but, 2dly, the Plaintiff says, " my cause of action arose subsequently to the day of the Defendant's discharge, on a promise made since his discharge to pay the antecedent debt." However improvident a person may be in making such a promise, the antecedent debt is a consideration for such subsequent promise. That such a subsequent promise was given, stands not on the affidavit of the Plaintiff alone, but of one *Douglas* with him, and I think the Plaintiff has taken the case out of the operation of the insolvent act, by shewing that his cause of action arose on a promise made since his discharge under that act. The rule therefore must be discharged.

NEALE *v.* NEVILL.
SAVORY *v.* SPOONER.

3 Binz 42.

*P*ELL Serjt. having obtained in the cause of *Neale* v.
　Nevill a rule *nisi* to change the venue from *London*
to *Somerset,* on the usual affidavit, that the cause of
action arose in *Somerset* and not elsewhere,

　Best serjt. now shewed cause, on an affidavit that the
action was partly brought for commission on the sale of
sail cloth, sent, some from *Poole,* and some from *Portsmouth,* to *London* for sale, and partly for goods sold
from the Plaintiff's warehouse at *Bridport* in *Dorset.*

　The Court held that this affidavit answered the application.

Rule simply discharged.

　Pell, on the following day again applied to open this
rule, that the practice might be consistent; he cited
Henshaw v. *Ruttley* (a). The Plaintiff does not in this
case swear, that no part of the cause of action arose in
Somerset, though he swears that part arose in other
counties, and therefore he is not entitled to retain the
venue.

　Best. Supposing that some part of the cause of action
arose in *Somerset,* other parts arising in *Dorset, Poole,*
and *Hants,* the case cited is not applicable: it was
there sworn that the cause of action arose, part in *Kent,*
and part in *London,* but there was no third county.
He hesitated to enter into the usual undertaking to give
material evidence, in order to retain this venue, fearing,
that to satisfy the undertaking in *London,* it must be
evidence that the whole cause of action arose in *London,* and that evidence as to part of the action would
not suffice.

(a) 1 *New Rep.* 110.

The Plaintiff
may retain the
venue where
he has laid it,
on undertaking
to give mate-
rial evidence in
any county, in
which, if the
venue were
laid, the De-
fendant could
not truly make
the usual affi-
davit to change
the venue from
that county.
　Evidence of
any fact ma-
terial to the
cause, though
it go not to
the whole
cause of action,
satisfies the
undertaking
given to retain
the venue.
　When the
cause of action
arises in a fo-
reign country,
the Plaintiff
may retain the
venue without
any undertak-
ing to give
material evi-
dence.

But

But *The Court* held that the undertaking certainly need not go to that extent. Any evidence material to the cause would suffice. *Bearcroft* was permitted to give in evidence a rule of court for paying money into court, as material evidence arising in *Middlesex.*

The Court again discharged the rule on the usual undertaking.

May 24.

SAVORY v. SPOONER.

On the following day, *Onslow* Serjt. having obtained a rule *nisi* in *Savory* v. *Spooner* to change the venue from *London* to *Dorset*, on the usual affidavit that the cause of action arose in *Dorset*, and not elsewhere,

Best Serjt. opposed it, on an affidavit that the action was brought for the price of a threshing machine ordered and made at *Fairford* in *Glocestershire*, and delivered by the Plaintiff on the Defendant's farm in *Dorsetshire.* In this case it was impossible he should enter into the usual undertaking to give material evidence in *London*, as no circumstance connected with the demand had arisen there; but, inasmuch as he had falsified the Defendant's affidavit, he was entitled to retain the venue.

Onslow, in support of his rule, contended, that since on the Plaintiff's own shewing his cause of action did not arise in *London*, to permit him to retain the venue there, would give sanction to an abuse; for he ought to sue where his cause of action arises.

The Court took time to reconsider the case of *Neale* v. *Nevill*, together with this.

GIBBS C. J. now delivered the opinion of the Court. In *Neale* v. *Nevill*, an application was made to change the venue from *London* to *Somerset*, on the usual affidavit.

9*   It

It was opposed on an affidavit that the cause of action arose, partly in the county of *Hants*, partly in the county of *Poole*, partly in *London*, and partly in *Dorsetshire;* in *Savory* v. *Spooner*, the answer to the application made to change the venue from *London* to *Dorset*, on the usual affidavit, was, that the machine, for the price of which the action was brought, was ordered in *Gloucestershire* and sent to *Dorsetshire*, and that the venue was laid in *London*, therefore that was in effect an affidavit that the cause of action did not arise in *London*. The difficulty of determinining what to do in this case, arises from the difference which subsists between the practice of this Court and that of the Court of King's Bench. In the King's Bench, the rule to change the venue is a rule absolute in the first instance. It is granted upon an affidavit that the cause of action arose in the county into which it is sought to change the venue, and not elsewhere, and the venue can only be brought back by the Plaintiff, upon his undertaking to give material evidence in the county in which the venue was originally laid. In this Court the practice is different, and the rule to change the venue is in the first instance a rule *nisi*, and the Plaintiff has an opportunity to shew cause against it, by falsifying the affidavit on which the rule is moved. Still, however, if this were the common case, where the whole cause of action arises in the county in which the venue was originally laid, this Court would not discharge the rule, but on the Plaintiff's undertaking to give material evidence in *London*, if the cause of action arose in *London*. The Court, indeed, in the case of *Collins* v. *Jacob* (a), where the cause of action arose in a county different, as well from that in which the venue was laid, as from that into which the Defendant sought to remove it, permitted the venue to be retained by the Plaintiff without any

(a) 3 *Bos.* & *Pull.* 579.

under-

undertaking to give material evidence. But subsequently, on full consideration by this Court, in the case of *Hunt* v. *Bridgeford* (a), it occurred to the Court, that it was an extraordinary course, that, where the cause of action arose in one county only, being the same where the venue was first laid, they should not discharge the rule unconditionally, but oblige the Plaintiff to give material evidence in the county which he had selected; and that where it arises in several counties, the Plaintiff should have the rule discharged unconditionally. My Brothers *Heath* and *Chambre* doubted. Mr. Justice *Lawrence* speaks of the necessity of requiring an undertaking in general, and the Court took time for consideration. The rule which suggested itself to the good sense of the late Chief Justice *Mansfield* prevailed, and the Court held, that the Plaintiff ought to follow up his affidavit made to retain the venue, by an undertaking to give material evidence in one or other of the counties in which the cause of action arose; and inasmuch as the rule is founded in good sense, and especially when we consider how this Cour was then filled, we think we cannot do better, than to adhere to that rule. Not to limit the expression of the rule to these particular instances, the general rule is this: The Plaintiff, in order to retain the venue, must undertake to give material evidence in that county, from which, if the venue had been laid there, the Defendant, by reason that some part of the cause of action really arose there, would not be entitled to change the venue; that is, in the case where the action arises partly in each of several counties, the Plaintiff shall undertake to give material evidence in one or other of those several counties. The merely swearing that the cause of action arose elsewhere will not suffice, he shall follow up his affidavit with this test of its truth,

(a) *Ante,* i. 259.

that

that if the cause of action does not arise in one or other of the counties in which it is sworn by the Plaintiff that it did arise, the Plaintiff shall be non-suited. In the first of these causes, therefore, the rule is discharged on the Plaintiff's undertaking to give material evidence arising in *London, Dorset, Poole,* or *Hants;* in the other, the rule is discharged on the Plaintiff's undertaking to give evidence arising in *London* or *Gloucestershire.* In a case where it may be proved that the cause of action arises abroad, there the rule must be simply discharged, for it will be impossible to give evidence in any particular county.

1816.

SAVORY
v.
SPOONER.

MORRIS, late Sheriff of GLOUCESTER, *v.* HAYWARD and Others.

May 24.

10 B & 205.

THE Plaintiff declared, that a certain bill had been exhibited in Chancery, by *D. Whatley* against the Defendant *Hayward,* and thereupon, afterwards, the complainant sued out of that Court a writ of attachment directed to the sheriff of *Gloucestershire,* whereby the king commanded him to attach the Defendant *Hayward,* so as to have him before his majesty in Chancery, wheresoever that Court should then be, there to answer to his majesty as well touching a contempt, which it was alleged he had committed against his majesty, as other matters, and to abide such order as that Court should make: that under such writ, the Plaintiff, being sheriff, before the return-day took and arrested the Defendant *Hayward,* and detained him, that the Plaintiff afterwards took bail for the appearance of the Defendant *Hayward* at the return of the writ, according to the form of the statute, and upon that occasion the Defendant *Hayward,* and the other Defendants as bail or

A sheriff may take a bail-bond on an attachment out of Chancery.

But he is not compellable to take bail thereupon.

VOL. VI.   **Q q**   sureties

sureties for him, by their writing obligatory bound
themselves to the Plaintiff, by his name and addition of
sheriff, in 40*l.* under condition for the appearance of
Hayward in the Court of Chancery, in eight days of
St. Hilary, wheresoever that court should then be, there
to answer as well the alleged contempt, as other matters,
and perform and abide such order as that Court should
make in that behalf, at the suit of *Whatley*, and shewed
default made by *Hayward* in appearance according to
the exigency of the writ.

Upon demurrer and joinder, *Onslow* Serjt. for the
Defendant maintained that the sheriff had no power to
bail on attachment of contempt. The words of the
statute 2 *H. 6. c. 9.* are for bailing persons " arrested
by force of any writ, bill, or warrant in any action personal, or by cause of indictment of trespass :" not one
word is there about an attachment of contempt. No
contempt is specifically mentioned on the writ, or the
record; and this Court cannot know how high or how
low the contempt is. They cannot therefore see whether
the sheriff is entitled to take bail. The unlimited
power to bail the highest contempt, is too dangerous a
power to be given to a sheriff. *Bland* v. *Richards* (a).
In an action on a bail bond, taken on an attachment
for a contempt out of chancery, the Court were clear
that the bond was void, for it was not bailable, *Acc.*
1. *Str. Anon.* (b). " On a motion for an attachment the
Chief Justice declared that all the judges on consideration, had resolved that the sheriff could not take bail on
an attachment, but a judge at his chamber might." So, in
Field v. *Workhouse* (c), on an attachment for a contempt
out of this court, the sheriff took a bail-bond, and it

(a) 3 *Leon.* 208.
(b) 1 *Str.* 479.

(c) 1 *Com.* 264.

was held that the sheriff could not bail for a contempt, and that it was not within the words or intent of the statute; and judgment on demurrer was given for the Defendant. In *Bengough* v. *Rossiter* (a), which is cited for the analogy, it being a criminal matter, though not a process of contempt; upon process out of the court of general quarter sessions, a bail-bond was held void. The case of *Studd* v. *Acton* (b), does not directly decide the point, but it was there held that an action would not lie against the sheriff for taking bail. The statute 23 *H.* 6. *c.* 9. gives no such power, and it would be productive of great mischief if it did. The nature of this contempt, for which this attachment issued, is not disclosed. The attachment is in the nature of punishment. The power to bail it, would lead to these mischiefs. The sheriff having no means to know in what sum bail shall be taken, it would lead to those bonds for ease and favor, against which the legislature have attempted to guard; it would lead to extorting excessive bail on the one hand, and to the escape of dangerous criminals on the other. In the case of *Samuel* v. *Evans* (c), a bail-bond taken after the return-day of a writ was held bad, and the Court held that advantage might be taken of it on motion in arrest of judgment; if so, then this defect may be taken advantage of on a general demurrer.

Lens Serjt. *contrà.* There are also authorities to the contrary effect, and the practice is according to them, and has not been of late disputed, though it might be doubted a century since; *Rex* v. *Dawes* (d). It was clearly agreed the sheriff may take a bail-bond upon

(a) 4 T. Rep. 505. 2 H. Bl. 418.
(b) 1 H. Bl. 468.
(c) 2 Term Rep. 569.
(d) 1 Ld. Raym. 722. S. C. Salk. 608.

Q q 2   an

an attachment. So, in *Burton* v. *Low* (a), it was held that a bond to appear to an attachment out of chancery is within the statute. So, Chief Baron *Comyn* lays it down (b), that by the equity of this statute, 23 *H.* 6. *c.* 9. the sheriff may bail upon an attachment out of Chancery, and says, *Semb.* 2 *Vent.* 238., 1 *Vent.* 234. *R. Contr.* 3 *Leon.* 208. The case referred to in 2 *Vent.* is *Lawson* v. *Haddock*, where it is said, "the Court inclined that attachments out of Chancery were within the statute: it is the constant practice for sheriffs to take bail in such cases." As to the argument that it ought to appear what the contempt was, and that because it does not, therefore the sheriff, who cannot know what the contempt was, ought not to be entrusted with the discretion to judge what the amount of the penalty in the bail-bond ought to be, in *Say* v. *Ellis* (c), where the question was, whether a bail-bond was good, taken by a bailiff, whose authority to take it did not appear, upon an attachment out of Chancery for a contempt, the Court do not determine the main point, but say, at all events, the facts sufficient to bring the question before the Court ought to be pleaded, as was done in *Lawson* v. *Haddock*. The sheriff has usually taken the same security, 40*l.* The statute 23 *H.* 6. *c.* 9. does not appear to be confined to actions personal, for it is much wider, and has special exceptions which do not include this case. Though the sheriff has not in this case that guidance, as to the amount, which personal actions afford where a debt is sworn to, yet the sum, which has been regularly taken, was a great sum at the time when it was fixed, and was then sufficient for the purpose. In *Studd* v. *Acton*, which, it is admitted, is not quite in point, the Court say, it may be a question

---

(a) *Sty.* 212. and 234.　　　(c) 2 *W. Bl.* 955.
(b) *Co. Dig.* tit. *Bail,* F. 8.

whether

whether in certain cases the sheriff be not right in taking bail, but that is widely different from being compellable to do it. These cases will be adopted.

Onslow in reply, insisted that none of the cases cited contained any decision adverse to the Defendant. The case in *Ventris* was never decided, as appeared by the reporter himself, and it only stated loose opinions. In *Styles*, notwithstanding what *Roll* C. J. said, the judgment of the Court was in favour of the Defendant. The case of *Rex* v. *Dawes* had not been cited to state the judgment of the Court. If the usage had prevailed for half a century to take bail in 40l., it ought now to be abolished. The case of *Studd* v. *Acton* shewed that the sheriff was not compellable to take bail; and if not compellable, but it was discretionary with him to take bail, it led to all the evils which the stat. 23 *H. 6. c. 9.* meant to remedy. The omission in pleading to state the contempt, was not, as supposed, merely matter of special demurrer; it was a question of substance. The declaration was alone destructive of the Plaintiff's case.

Cur. adv. vult.

GIBBS C. J. now, after stating the pleadings, thus delivered the opinion of the Court.

It appears from this statement, that the sheriff asserts in his declaration, that he had taken the bond in pursuance of the statute. But though it be not according to the statute, yet if the bond be in any manner available, he may so state it. The objection to this bond, is, that the statute 23 *H. 6. c. 9.*, prescribing in what cases the sheriff may take a bail-bond, prohibits the taking a bond in all other cases. We are of opinion this case is not at all touched by the statute 23 *H. 6. c. 9.* The case

Q q 3

was

was very ably argued by my Brother *Onslow,* and we
have considered the authorities which he cited.   The
sheriff's right to take a bail-bond upon this species of
attachment, has repeatedly been recognized by the Court
of Chancery itself, which could never have been, if the
practice had been illegal.   In the case of *Danby* v.
Lawson (a) it appears that in 1700 it was considered as
the established practice of the Court of Chancery, that
the sheriff is to take such bonds, and a distinction in
the amount of the penalty is taken between mesne process and execution.   Lord *Hardwicke* (b) also recognized
the validity of these bonds, and acted on the fact of the
sheriff having taken such a bond, and so the Plaintiff
is not without remedy if the sheriff has him not at the
return of the writ, as he may have a messenger into the
county where the person lives, and he refused process
against the sheriff.   It is impossible Lord *Hardwicke*
could have considered them as illegal, for if he had, he
would have said, it is an aggravation of the sheriff's
offence in not bringing up the body, to attempt to ex-
tenuate it, by saying that he had taken a bond, which
it was highly illegal for him to take.   These bonds,
therefore, must be legal, unless the Court of Chancery
has misunderstood the effect of its own process, which
is not probable.   But in this court also the validity of
these bonds has been recognized.   *Studd* v. *Acton.*
That action was founded on the supposition that the
statute required the sheriff to take a bail-bond in the
case of an attachment: the Court held it was not
within the statute, and Lord *Loughborough's* language
there is remarkable.   The counsel for the Defendant
argued, that if this were not within the statute, and the
bond were not to be given accordingly, the bond could

(a) *Prec. in Chanc.* 110. S.C.   (b) *Amb.* 2 *Atk.* 507.
1 *Eq. Cas. Abr.* 350. *pl.* 4.

not

not be taken at all, and that the statute prohibits all
other bonds. It would be a most extraordinary proposition that there was no bail to mesne process out of
Chancery. In *Bengough* v. *Rossiter* the Court held,
(though the discussion arose on a question of criminal
process,) that the statute extended to actions only. The
judgment of Lord *Loughborough* C. J. is, that " it being
the case of process issuing out of the Court of Chancery,
we think that it does not come within the stat. 23 *H. 6.
c. 9.*, which directs that sheriffs shall let all persons out
of prison by them arrested or being in their custody by
force of any writ, bill, or warrant in any action personal,
which words are confined to actions at law. A subsequent statute, 13 *Car.* 2. *stat.* 2. *c.* 2., which was made
on the same subject, is distinctly confined to actions in
the King's Bench and Common Pleas, and it does not
appear to have been the intent of the legislature to interfere with the process of a court of equity. It is extremely clear, that the usage has been for the sheriff to
take a bail-bond in 40*l.* on an attachment, and it is so
laid down in *Danby* v. *Lawson*." Here, then, is the
judgment of a very able Judge, who had practised all
his life in courts of equity, that the established practice
was to take bail for 40*l.*; and it would be too much for
us to say that all the learned persons who have presided in that court for a century, have been mistaken,
or ignorant of the practice. But Lord *Loughborough's*
judgment does not stop here; he goes on to shew how
the process would be regulated by the Court of Chancery. It is for the Court out of which it issues, to regulate the practice of their own officer. And we are of
opinion that these bonds are neither compellable to be
taken, by the statute, nor prohibited by the statute; but
that they are good at common law; and that whether a
bail-bond shall be taken or not, is in the discretion of

Q q 4

the

1816.

Morris
v.
Hayward.

the sheriff, as regulated by the practice of that Court. We therefore are of opinion that the action on the bond is well supportable, and that the Plaintiff is entitled to judgment.

Judgment for the Plaintiff.

May 25.

The Court will not compel a sheriff to specify in his return to a *fieri facias* the particular goods taken, and the sum for which each article was sold.

WILLETT v. SPARROW.

BEST Serjt. moved that the sheriff of *Norfolk* might amend his return to a writ of *fieri facias* by particularly specifying the goods which he had taken under this levy, on the ground that he had returned only an aggregate sum exceeding 600*l.* and had not specified the several goods which he had sold: it was sworn the bailiff had sold several things of which he had rendered no account, and had wasted the property in a riotous and shameful manner.

Per Curiam. Actions have frequently been brought for such misconduct, and the Plaintiff's best course is by action: if in the course of the action, any misconduct of a criminal sort in the bailiff appears, the Court may then interfere to satisfy public justice, at present no criminal act is shewn; and the Plaintiff has in that course this advantage, that the sheriff is answerable for the act of his bailiff.

Rule refused.

HATCHWELL v. COOKE.

THIS was an action brought against the Defendant, who was master of the *Tortoise* storeship, a vessel taken up for his majesty's service, for the value of a quantity of old silver, shipped by the Plaintiff, through his agent, in *Gibraltar* bay, for the receipt whereof " on board the good ship *Tortoise* S. S., and the delivery to the Plaintiff at *Woolwich*, being paid freight at *Gibraltar*, (the act of God and the king's enemies only excepted,)" the Defendant had signed bills of lading. The silver was stolen out of the master's cabin after the ship had arrived and lain a considerable time at *Woolwich*. Upon the trial of this cause at the *Kent* spring assizes 1816, before *Bayley* J. these facts being proved, and that the letters S. S., for storeship, were painted in large characters on the ship's bows: the defence was, that the Defendant's contract, engaging without previous licence to carry bullion on board a ship in the king's service, was illegal, and prohibited as well by the 18th article of war, set forth in the statute 22 *G.* 2. *c.* 33. *s.* 2., as by the 24th section of the same act. *Bayley* J. reserved the point, subject whereto the jury found a verdict for the Plaintiff.

The master of a storeship in the king's service took in the bullion of a private merchant on freight from *Gibraltar* to *Woolwich*: Held that an action lay against him for the loss of the bullion.

Shepherd, Solicitor-General, in this term obtained a rule *nisi* to set aside the verdict and enter a nonsuit.

Lens, *Best*, and *Copley* Serjts. in this term, in opposing the rule, urged that the decision in *Brisbane* v. *Dacres* (a), did not govern this case. The Defendant there succeeded on the principle that whatever the

Plaintiff

Plaintiff had paid, he had paid with his eyes open. And though something was there thrown out, of the illegality of carrying merchant's bullion in a king's ship, yet it was not the principal ground of their judgment; and besides, this is not an action by the captain of a king's ship to recover freight for bullion so carried. Even if the Defendant had been the captain of a man of war, the statute authorizes him to carry bullion, though not to carry merchandize, and this Court so construed it, in the case of *Hodgson* v. *Fullarton* (a), where the Defendant was captain of a ship of war, yet he was held liable for the value of bullion which he had taken on board, on freight for a private merchant. The practice is inveterate. The *Falmouth* packets daily bring bullion from *Lisbon*, and it never was conceived to be illegal. The Defendant, having received the freight, ought not now to be permitted to say that it is not his duty to convey the bullion in safety. Even if the Defendant had carried merchandize which was not within the exception in the statute, he would only have been liable to a penalty, and it was held in the case of *Keir* v. *Andrade* (b), that a penalty imposed on the master of a vessel does not render the adventure illegal, so far as others are concerned. This contract, in like manner, even if it be illegal to one purpose, may not be illegal to another. But further, the words of the act do not, as has been supposed, render it illegal to carry bullion in a king's ship without a special permission: they are a general exception of " gold, silver, and jewels," not requiring any particular commission, permission, or authority to carry them; the required authority from the admiralty to receive certain things on board, being restricted to the case of other goods and merchandize. There was no evidence in this cause that the Plaintiff's agent understood the meaning of the characters S. S. on the vessel, or was otherwise

(a) *Ante,* iv. 787.   (b) *Ante,* vi. 498.

privy

privy to the fact of her being in the king's service, for a
store-ship bears not the outward appearance of a ship of
war. But even if the shipper knew that this was a
king's ship, yet, if the Defendant either represented
that there was a permission, or that no permission was
necessary, (and if he did neither, the shipper had a
right to presume that the Defendant was furnished
with every necessary permission,) the Plaintiff was not
privy to the illegality; and therefore ought to recover.

The Solicitor-General and *Vaughan* Serjt., in support
of the rule, urged, that though the Defendant might not
be liable to any forfeiture under the statute, yet the
carrying bullion in a king's ship for freight was at
common law illegal, inasmuch as it was a misap-
plication of the king's ship to the Defendant's only
private emolument, and therefore the Plaintiff could
not recover. This principle was much illustrated by a
series of late cases. In *Montagu* v. *Janverin* (a), it was
first decided that in the case of the freight of king's
treasure the admiral had no right to a share of the
captain's freight. In *Brisbane* v. *Dacres*, it was expressly decided that the carrying bullion for freight
was illegal. This store-ship, whether built by his
majesty, or not, being at the time in his service, and
under his control, and commanded by an officer paid
by his majesty, was governed by the same rules as a
ship of war. It must be assumed that the shipper could
understand the meaning of the characters S. S.

Cur. adv. vult.

GIBBS C. J. now delivered judgment.

This was an action against the master of a store-ship
for the loss of a parcel of bullion which he had undertaken to bring home from *Gibraltar*, and which had
not been delivered. The Defendant certainly is answer-

(a) *Ante,* iii. 443.

able

able for not delivering this property, unless it can be shewn that the transaction was an illegal one, and that the Plaintiff participated in that illegality. The Plaintiff was a merchant residing here and acting through his agent at *Gibraltar*. The master of the store-ship takes the bullion on board, signing a bill of lading, whereby he undertakes in the usual course for its safe delivery here, the act of God and the king's enemies excepted, and the Defendant actually receives the freight for it. If this were an illegal transaction, the Plaintiff could not recover for non-performance of a contract that ought never to have been made. As to the illegality, it stands at least on very doubtful ground. The statute 22 *G*.2. *c*.33. refers to the 8 *G*.1. *c*.24. which contains an enactment on the same subject, and the 22 *G*.3. is, that if the master shall receive on board any merchandizes, except gold, silver, and jewels, he shall be liable to certain penalties; and it refers to the 18th article of war. A common man reading that clause would suppose that he might carry gold and silver. I have heard it argued that the master could not put on board bullion except for his majesty. What I said in *Brisbane v. Dacres* has been relied on, as shewing that this transaction was illegal. It was there unnecessary to decide that question; for whether the transaction were legal or illegal, as my Brother *Chambre* said, the effect would be exactly the same; the Plaintiff could not recover; for if it were illegal, he was barred by the illegality; if legal, he was barred, because he had paid the money with his eyes open. That point was very little touched in the case; the private freight being only 20*l*. I took up, rather too hastily perhaps, the opinion that it was illegal, whereas these captains and admirals, who consider their own duties and rights, must be supposed to know something about them. It was quite immaterial to that case, whether the carrying

that

that private treasure was legal or illegal; and I am very glad it is so, because I would not now pronounce that it is illegal. I should have no doubt that it was illegal, if it were not for this statute containing an exception of gold and silver; for it could not be legal that a master should divert a king's ship from its destination, for his own private emolument. It is to be observed also, that that was not an action against a master, for not safely carrying bullion. Whatever may be the duty of a master of a store-ship, and however he may understand those duties, it does by no means follow that the merchant who ships this treasure, is conusant to the same extent. I will take it, that a merchant is bound to be conusant of the law of the land; be it so, he looks into the law of the land, and sees an exception from the statutory prohibition, in favour of gold and silver, and supposes that with respect to any other duty, against which the carrying it may militate, the master has all necessary permission. In *Montague* v. *Janverin*, *Mansfield* C. J. relies much on the heavy responsibility the master takes on him, in receiving a shipment of private bullion, and further, *Hodgson* v. *Fullarton* is an express authority, that under such circumstances the master is liable. For these reasons we think the Plaintiff is entitled to maintain his action, and the rule therefore must be

　　　　　　　　　　　　　　Discharged.

THORNTON and Others v. JONES and Another.　　*May* 25.

THE Plaintiffs in their declaration stated that the Defendants contracted to buy of the Plaintiffs, who at the Defendants' special instance agreed to sell to them, from ship or warehouse before 1st *November:* Held that this was equivalent to a contract to be generally ready for delivery before that day, and need not be specially averred.

A contract for the sale of tallow warranted it to be ready for delivery

　　　　　　　　　　　　　　them,

them, divers, viz. 50 casks of *St. Petersburgh* first sort of yellow candle tallow, at 72*s. per* cwt. to be ready for delivery on or before the 1st day of *November*, to be weighed or taken at the king's scale, with 2lbs. *per* cask draft, and 12lbs. *per* cwt. tare, to be paid for by the acceptance of the Defendants at four months, allowing two months' discount from delivery, and five days' notice to be given before delivery. And after averring mutual promises, they alleged that such 50 casks of tallow, were, before the 1st of *November*, ready for delivery, and the Defendants had five days' notice given them for the delivery thereof, during which five days, and for a long time after, the Plaintiffs were there ready and willing that that the same should be weighed and taken by the Defendants at the king's landing scale, and to have allowed them such draft, tare, and discount, as aforesaid, and requested the Defendants to take and accept the same casks of tallow, and to accept a bill at four months for the price, but that the Defendants did not accept the tallow, or accept that bill, or otherwise pay for the tallow; but wholly refused and neglected, whereby the Plaintiffs lost the profit of their contract, and were obliged to resell the tallow for less, and were put to expences in the warehousing the tallow until resold. Upon the trial of the cause, at the sittings after *Hilary* term 1816, before *Gibbs* C. J., the broker, who sold the the goods for the Plaintiffs, produced a sold note, which corresponded with the contract stated in the declaration in other respects, but, as is their practice, varied from that, and from the bought note, on which the Plaintiffs had accurately declared, in averring that the goods were " warranted to be ready for delivery from ship or warehouse on or before the 1st of *November*." The notice by the Plaintiffs of the tallow being ready, given five days before 1st *November*, was proved, and a tender of the tallow, and of a bill, and a refusal by the

I

Defend-

Defendants to accept either; but for the Defendant it was objected, that the contract proved materially varied from the contract averred: *Gibbs* C. J. was of opinion that a contract to deliver at the king's beam from ship or warehouse, on or before the 1st of *November*, was, in substance, only a general undertaking by the seller to have the goods ready at the day stipulated, i. e. at all events to deliver them from some place or other by the stipulated day. The way to try it, was, would not the obligation on the seller be at all events the same? Suppose the contract had expressed that the goods were to be ready for delivery generally, by having them either on board ship, or in a warehouse, the seller performs his contract. If he had promised to have the tallow ready, above ground or under ground, dead or alive, that would be only an averment of having it ready somewhere or other at that time, and the phrase here used was intended to comprehend every possible place where the goods could then be, and it need not be specially averred. The jury found a verdict for the Plaintiffs.

Shepherd, Solicitor-General, in this term obtained a rule *nisi* to set aside the verdict and enter a nonsuit, or have a new trial, contending that inasmuch as the contract gave an option to one of the parties, probably to the vendor, whether the goods should be delivered from ship or warehouse, it was necessary that, in declaring, the Plaintiffs should aver the option, and shew the election made. All alternative contracts must be so stated. *Penny* v. *Porter* (a). *Shipham* v. *Saunders* (b). The stipulation that the hemp should be weighed and taken at the king's landing scale was very much altered in its consequences, accordingly as one or other branch of this alternative was chosen. For if the goods were to be

(a) 1 *East*, 1.　　(b) 2 *East*, 4. n.

delivered

delivered from ship, they in the ordinary course came on shore to the king's landing scale to be weighed, whereas if they were to be delivered from a warehouse, they had already passed the king's beam, and incurred the additional expence of being brought back thither from the warehouse for delivery.

Best Serjt. now shewed cause against the rule, and relied on the construction given by his *Lordship* to the contract at the trial. The two alternatives comprehended, he said, every possible situation from which the goods could be delivered, and it was therefore unnecessary to aver them. He cited *Barbe q. t.* v. *Parker* (a), and *Whaley* v. *Pajot.* (b)

The Solicitor-General and *Vaughan* Serjt. endeavoured to support the rule. This is not the expression of a general option, for the vendors could not under this contract deliver tallow from their own dwelling-house. A contract to deliver goods from a ship, imports that the goods are not now in this country, and if the vessel never arrives with them, no action lies. *Boyd* v. *Siffkin* (c). And if so, the arrival ought to be specially averred, to shew the Plaintiff's readiness to perform. The buyer also may have insisted on the insertion of these words, because he would not take the goods lying on an open wharf exposed to the sun.

GIBBS C. J. This objection certainly did not go to the merits of the case. The object was, to turn round the Plaintiffs and nonsuit them. If they have not stated the contract correctly, the Defendants are entitled to their nonsuit. But on the best consideration

(a) 1 *H. Bl.* 288.　　　　　(c) 2 *Campb.* 326.
(b) 2 *Bos. & Pull.* 51.

I could

I could give the case at the trial, I thought the contract was substantially well stated. It is put on the true ground by my Brother *Vaughan*; if the statement in the declaration, and the statement in the contract, would not both be satisfied by the same proof, the declaration would not be sufficient; if it would, then the declaration suffices. I was of opinion that this amounted to a contract to be ready for delivery generally. The option in this case is given to the seller, and not to the buyer. If the contract enumerates all possible places of delivery, and gives the seller the option of them, it is the same thing as if it stated the option generally. The case is wholly unlike those that have been cited, except that of *Shipham* v. *Saunders*, there, in neither of the alternative cases averred was the count true. Here the Plaintiff states in his declaration that he contracted to deliver generally, and his contract is, to deliver from one or other of the only places where the goods can possibly be, which is equivalent to a contract for general delivery.

DALLAS J. The counsel for the Defendant have not pointed out that it makes any difference to the purchaser, whether the tallow is delivered from ship, or warehouse; nor was there any difference, for it is to be weighed and taken at the king's landing scale.

PARK J. This rule was granted under an idea that this thing said to be omitted, could have made a difference in the situation of the parties, that has not been shewn.

BURROUGH J. I consider this as a contract to deliver, not from any particular place, but wherever the Plaintiff pleases, therefore the rule must be

Discharged.

May 25.   CLARKE and Wife, RYE and Wife, PROCTOR and Wife, Conusors; BARROW and PENNINGTON, Conusees.

Fine permitted to pass where the Christian name of one party had been interlined after acknowledgment by another party.

L ENS Serjt. moved that a fine might pass under the following circumstances. ' One of the conusors was named in the fine as *Beauchamp Proctor* only, his name being *William Beauchamp Proctor*. This mistake was not discovered until after the acknowledgment of *Rye* and wife was taken, it therefore was not therein noticed by them.   In taking the acknowledgment by the others, it was noticed that the error was corrected in the fine by an interlineation before the acknowledgment. *Rye* and wife were alive, and consenting.

GIBBS C. J.   The other two conusors notice the making of the interlineation before they acknowledged the fine, and a presumption thence arises, which a purchaser would take hold of, that *Rye* and wife acknowledged the fine before the interlineation made; it is therefore worthy of the party's consideration, whether it be not more for their interest to have the fine reacknowledged by *Rye* and wife, than to avail themselves of the indulgence of the Court.

Fiat,

1816.

GODSON, Gent. *v.* GOOD, Administratrix of   *May 25.*
S. GOOD.

THIS was an action of *assumpsit* brought by the
Plaintiff, who was a solicitor, to recover the entire amount of his charges for business done by him in
calling and attending at meetings in the country, and
conducting an opposition in parliament to a bill of the
Leominster canal company, who were indebted to several land owners, through whose property the canal
passed, for land taken, and damages done, and, amongst
them, to the Defendant's husband, who had died intestate,
and who was one of the principal and most active op-
ponents to the bill. The Plaintiff in one set of counts
declared on a retainer by the intestate, and on promises
of the intestate to pay, and in another set of counts he
declared on the retainer of the intestate, and on promises to pay, made by the administratrix, with a count
on an *insimul computasset* with the Defendant as administratrix. The Defendant, in her plea, which, being
generally pleaded, went as well to her own imputed
promises, as to the promises of the intestate, "prayed
judgment of the bill, because the said several supposed
promises, if any, were made by one *W. Smith* and sixteen others, in the plea named, jointly with the intestate, which seventeen persons still were alive, wherefore,
because they were not named, she prayed judgment of
the bill, and that the same might be quashed." The
Plaintiff replied, "that the bill ought not to be quashed,
because the several promises were not made by *W.
Smith* and the other 16 persons jointly with the intestate;" and tendered issue thereon, in which issue the
Defendant joined. Upon the trial of the cause, at the
Worcester spring assizes 1816, before *Holroyd* J. the

R r 2   Plaintiff

Side notes:

If a plea, com-
mencing in
abatement,
shew matter in
bar, and con-
cludes in abate-
ment, it is a
plea in abate-
ment, not in
bar.

And the De-
fendant can-
not, by any
election subse-
quent to the
time of plea
pleaded, con-
vert it to a
plea in bar.

A plea in
abatement, that
the Defendant
jointly with
16 others con-
tracted, im-
ports that the
Defendant
jointly with
16 others, and
no more, con-
tracted.

And if there
were more
joint contract-
ors than the se-
venteen, the
plea is dis-
proved.

Plaintiff proved the resolutions of a public meeting signed by the intestate and above fifty others, declaratory of their intention to compel the canal company to introduce into their projected bill a clause for paying their existing debts, and resolving, that the Plaintiff was chosen their, and each of their attorney for carrying those resolutions into effect; and they thereby agreed with each other, that all expences of such proceedings should be borne and paid by them all, and every one of them, in shares in proportion to the amount of the money due to them respectively from the canal company. The Plaintiff's counsel insisted that the plea, being a plea in abatement, was disproved by the evidence that more persons than the seventeen had contracted, and cited *Abbott* v. *Smith* (a). The Defendant insisted, that though this was, in form, a plea in abatement, it was, in substance, a plea in bar, and destroyed the Plaintiff's right of action, inasmuch as it shewed that the contract was made by the intestate jointly with others, who had survived him, and against whom, therefore, and not against his administratrix, the Plaintiff's remedy survived. *Holroyd* J. permitted the trial to proceed, that the Plaintiff might establish any case that he might have affecting the deceased solely, and the Plaintiff not proving any distinct proportion of his costs payable by the intestate, nor any damages affecting the deceased alone, the learned Judge directed a verdict for the Plaintiff, with 1s. damages, with leave for the Defendant to move to enter a nonsuit.

Shepherd, Solicitor-General, in this term obtained a rule *nisi* to set aside this verdict and enter a nonsuit. He admitted that the plea was not well proved as a plea in abatement, because the purport of it being

(a) 2 *Bl.* 951.   2 *Williams's Saund.* 209. c. *note*

to

to give a better writ, the sense of the proposition that
the contract was made by seventeen, was, that it was
made by seventeen and no others; else the plea did not
give a better writ, or, at least, not a good writ: but he
contended, that inasmuch as matter in bar appeared on
the record, although it were pleaded in the form of a
plea in abatement, it would operate as a plea in bar;
and though, for the reason before given, the plea was
not proved, as a plea in abatement, yet it was proved
as a plea in bar, because the contract was proved to
be made with several persons jointly with the intestate,
against which others the action survived.

Lens and *Copley* Serjts. now shewed cause against
this rule.   They contended, first, that the Plaintiff
might well sustain his verdict on the merits; for he
was entitled by the terms of the contract, which was
several as well as joint, to recover against any one of
the parties thereto not merely a part of the Plaintiff's
demand proportionate to the damage sustained by that
Defendant, but the entire amount of the Plaintiff's
demand.   The act of opposing a bill in parliament
was one entire act, beneficial to each.   The retainer
was general, by each, to do that act, and the Plaintiff
might recover the whole against any one.   And the
proportion in which the several clients were to divide
the burden, was a mere matter of agreement among
themselves.   Next, if this were a plea in abatement,
and if the issue were correctly found for the Plaintiff,
the judgment, upon a denial of fact, which this plea
contains, is not *quòd respondeat ouster*, but *quòd recu-
peret*, for the whole debt; and the Defendant, therefore, was not entitled to a nonsuit.   *Medina* v. *Stoughton* (a).   A precise issue was joined, whether the con-

(a) *Ld. Ray.* 594.

R r 3   tract

tract was signed by seventeen and no others; the burden of proof lay on the Defendant, and her issue was
disproved. She had made, and clearly expressed, her
perfect election to plead this matter in abatement, and
not in bar, and could not now be permitted to wave
her election and avail herself of the matter as a plea in
bar. The plea begins by praying judgment of the
bill: it states matter, which, if true, is matter in abatement, as well as in bar, and it ends by praying judgment of the bill. It may be admitted, that where the
plea begins by praying judgment of the bill, shews
matter in bar, and ends by praying judgment in bar; •
and also, where it begins by praying judgment in bar,
shews matter in bar, and ends by praying judgment in
abatement, it shall be taken as a plea in bar; and so
are the authorities (a); and the reasons for it are plain:
where a Defendant prays two inconsistent judgments,
as he does in either of the two cases put, the Court will
permit him to elect, or, perhaps, will elect for him, the
judgment most beneficial to him. Dilatory pleas are
not favoured in law; and it more conduces to the attainment of justice, to consider an ambiguous plea as
a plea in bar, than in abatement, and to decide the
cause according to the very matter, wherever the Defendant's plea gives an opening so to do; but where
the Defendant asks, both in the beginning and end of
the plea, the same judgment, there the Court will not go
aside to give any other judgment than that which the
Defendant prays. If she had prayed two inconsistent
judgments, the one prayer would destroy the other, and
if the Court can see that the Defendant is entitled to
either of the things prayed for, they will give it. Here
the Court is precluded, by the uniform prayer of judgment in abatement, from giving any other judgment

(a) *Medina* v. *Stoughton*, 1 *Ld. Raym.* 593.

than

than that. The Defendant, throughout her plea, declares her election to plead in abatement, and not in bar; and inasmuch as she has the legal right to plead in abatement if she will, the Court cannot revise her election, and take that to be a plea in bar, which the Defendant elects to plead in abatement. Nor does it vary the case, that the matter so pleaded is matter in bar; if matter which had no effect either in bar, or in abatement, were pleaded with the same introduction and conclusion as this, it would nevertheless be a plea in abatement, though not a good plea: irrelevant matter may, in like manner, be pleaded in bar, and though inoperative as a plea in bar, it would nevertheless be a plea in bar, and not in abatement. It is the form of the plea, and not the tendency or effect of the matter pleaded, that gives the denomination of the plea. Many things may be indifferently pleaded in bar, and in abatement, as, in replevin, property in a stranger, &c. In *Medina* v. *Stoughton* (a), *Holt* C. J. lays it down, that " if a man pleads matter which goes in bar, but begins and concludes his plea in abatement, it will be a plea in abatement; for it is the beginning and conclusion that make the plea," and cites 1 *Sid.* 189, 190. So, in the case from *Siderfin* (b), cited by Lord *Holt*, the converse is good : if matter in abatement be pleaded in a plea which both begins and ends in bar, it is a plea in bar. In *Evans* v. *Stevens* (c) there was a plea of matter in bar, beginning and ending in abatement; and the Court on demurrer held it was a plea in abatement. If it be hard that the Defendant should alone pay the whole of this debt, by reason of a mistake in pleading this plea, yet it is to be considered, that it is she who selects this fact of her case, to put her whole defence on it. It would be a much greater hardship and injustice on the Plain-

(a) 1 *Ld. Raym.* 593.   (c) 4 *Term Rep.* 225.
(b) 1 *Sid.* 189, 190.

tiff,

tiff, if the Defendant, under colour of a plea in abatement, could plead this as a secret plea in bar, for she thereby would be enabled to mislead the Plaintiff. This very same language, used in a plea in bar, and in a plea in abatement, has two different senses. If pleaded in abatement, it means, that the contract was made by seventeen jointly with the intestate, and with no others; the form of the plea therefore allures the Plaintiff to trial, conscious that he can prove that the contract was made by more than seventeen jointly with the intestate, and that, since the Plaintiff puts her case on that issue, he has evidence to prevail thereon: he does produce that evidence, and disproves the Defendant's issue in the sense in which she professes to plead it. It is urged, that as a plea in bar, it is proved, if it appears that there was any joint contractor with the deceased. If the Defendant had had notice that it was intended to be relied on as a plea in bar, he would have come prepared with different evidence to meet that case. The Defendant is also entitled to a verdict on the counts framed on a promise by the administratrix herself, for she does not deny the making such promises; she only avers that the promises which the Plaintiff says were made by her as administratrix, were made by seventeen others jointly with her own intestate in his lifetime, and (impliedly) jointly with herself also, as his administratrix, and who, in his lifetime, as appears by the record, was also his wife. This proposition is impossible, but it is not the less false because it is impossible; and either the Defendant, on whom the *onus* was, gave no evidence on the plea as applied to these counts, or, if the evidence adduced be applied to it, then it does not prove the Defendant's allegation, for she was no party to the resolutions and agreement given in evidence. The case of *Stubbins* v. *Birde* (a), which perhaps may be cited

(a) 2 Mod. 63.

for

for the Plaintiff, is a very loose and ill-reported case, and the judgment of *North* C. J., who there held, that after matter in bar pleaded in abatement, the Defendant had his election whether to treat his plea as a plea in bar, or in abatement, is founded in an utter misconception of the case of *Salkill* v. *Skelton*, which the Chief Justice cites for that doctrine: for in *Salkill* v. *Skelton* it is merely held on demurrer, that " in replevin, (misprinted replication,) for 20 loads of corn, where the Defendant made connusance of taking the corn, as being the property of *J. S.*, and not of the Plaintiff, the Defendant might well pray judgment of the writ, and had his election to conclude his plea in abatement, as the fact there was, or to plead the same matter in bar, and pray judgment of the action:" but not the slightest hint is dropped, that if the Defendant did conclude his plea with a prayer of the one judgment, he had his election to make the Court read it as a prayer for the other judgment, as *North* C. J. is made to suppose; and it is remarkable, that in a short note of the same case of *Stubbins* v. *Birde* (a), it appears, that in the following term it was adjudged that the plea was a plea in abatement, and was good as such.

Shepherd, Solicitor-General, and *Best* Serjt. *contrà.* Whether the plea be a plea in abatement, or in bar, depends on the question whether the matter pleaded be matter in abatement, or matter in bar. If that which is pleaded, is, in truth, matter in bar, though the beginning and end of the plea shew a plea in abatement, this is nevertheless a plea in bar. The present is not a question as to the time of pleading, nor is it a question of the form of pleading, though perhaps, if the Defendant had pleaded these same facts professedly in bar, the plea might have been bad on special demurrer, as

(a) 1 *Mod.* 214, *Major and Stubbins* v. *Birde and Harrison.*

amount-

amounting to the general issue. The plea shews, that the Plaintiff can never by any possibility maintain any action whatever against the Defendant; for, notwithstanding the failure of proof, as it applies to a plea in abatement, if the intestate joined with any one in making the promise, the Defendant is entitled to her verdict and judgment. Every thing that is alleged in the terms of the Defendant's issue, is strictly proved in fact, though not strictly proved in point of law, because she has not done that which by her plea she professes to do, namely, to give the Plaintiff a better writ; but if it be taken as a plea in bar, then it is clear that the matter in bar is sufficiently proved. They referred to the authorities collected by the late Serjt. *Williams* in his note, 2 *Saund.* 209. *b.*, as shewing, that if a plea, which contains matter in bar of an action, concludes in abatement, it is a plea in bar, notwithstanding the conclusion in abatement: and it is there said, that the difference taken by Lord *Holt* in 1 *Sho.* 4. is a mistake of the reporters, so far as relates to the first position, and is contrary to *Littleton.* Whatever be the form, it appears by the plea here pleaded that there is no *cause of action,* and therefore, notwithstanding any mistake in the form of the defence, the Plaintiff shall not recover. In *Medina* v. *Stoughton,* and *Evans* v. *Stevens,* there was a demurrer, whereon the judgment is *respondeat ouster;* but here the judgment would be final; here therefore the Court will not impose that hardship.

GIBBS C. J. This was an action brought by the Plaintiff against the Defendant as the administratrix of her late husband *Samuel Good.* It is an action on a contract, and if the contract were entered into by *Samuel Good* and others jointly, any others of whom are now living, that action cannot be supported, because the action survives against the survivors. The plea is, that the Defendant

. prays

prays judgment of the bill, because *W. Smith* with sixteen others, entered into this contract jointly with the intestate, and therefore the Defendant prays that the bill may be quashed. The plea begins in abatement, and ends in abatement; no part of the form of the plea leaves the Plaintiff ground to suppose that this is any other than a plea in abatement, and the Plaintiff goes down to trial, prepared to meet it as a plea in abatement, and I am not prepared to say that it was not a good plea in abatement; for it has been truly said, that many things may indifferently be pleaded, either in bar, or in abatement. This plea is not proved as a plea in abatement, because, instead of giving the Plaintiff a better writ, it does not give him a better writ; for the others who are named in this plea as having joined in the contract, if sued thereon, would again have a right to plead in abatement that there were other joint contractors, who are not named; therefore, if this be considered as a plea in abatement, the verdict must be against the Defendant. The authorities are not very precise upon this subject; and in such a case, we are glad to find an authority of any considerable judge on the point. I think I can understand the reason of my Lord *Holt's* proposition, namely, that if all which the Defendant asks, is, that the writ may be quashed, the Court can only quash the writ, though some of the Defendant's facts would entitle her to ask more. But if in the one part of the plea, upon an averment of facts which operate in bar, the Defendant prays that the writ may be quashed, and in another part of the same plea prays judgment of the action, the Court will help the Defendant against the irregularity of his plea, and give judgment of the action. We are the more disposed to decide in consonance to this doctrine, because in no case is there any decision directly on the point. And the cases which have been cited by the

Defend-

Defendant's counsel from that most learned and able book of my late Brother *Williams*, have been much misapplied to this case. We therefore think this defence is pleaded in abatement; and that as a plea *in* abatement, it is not proved. If it had been pleaded in bar, I should have had considerable difficulty to say it was proved. The Defendant says, this was a contract made by the intestate and 16 others, and in so stating a contract, I do not feel clear, that the Defendant must not be taken to have said, that it was made by those seventeen alone, and by no others. Before the defence of "other joint contractors not sued," which used to be pleaded in abatement, was introduced as a defence upon *non assumpsit*, if the Defendant shewed in an action on a sole contract, that he had promised jointly with another, the Defendant's issue was proved. This was thought too strict a rule, and was first relaxed in the case of *Rice* v. *Shute* (a); but, before that case, the issue on *non assumpsit* was, whether the Defendant alone promised. Until that case of *Rice* v. *Shute*, if a declaration were, that six had contracted, and the evidence were, that six others had contracted jointly with them, it must always have been held that the contract stated was not proved, unless it were proved that the Plaintiff contracted with six, and six only; and in abatement the question still is, whether the seventeen persons named did alone promise. For this, amongst other reasons, I think the rule must be discharged.

The rest of the Court concurring,

The rule was discharged.

(a) *5 Burr.* 2613.

THIS was an action for money paid, money had and received, for interest of money, and upon an account stated. The four first counts stated, that the Defendants were indebted to, and promised to pay the Plaintiffs. The four next counts stated that the Defendants, being indebted to the Plaintiffs and *R. Beachcroft,* since deceased, promised to pay them and him, but had neglected so to do in *Beachcroft*'s life, or to pay the Plaintiffs since his decease. The four last counts stated that the Defendants and *Beachcroft* in his life, were indebted to, and promised to pay the Plaintiffs, but that the Defendants and *Beachcroft* in his life, and the Defendants since his decease, had neglected so to do. The Defendants pleaded the general issue. The cause was tried at *Guildhall,* at the sittings after *Hilary* term 1816, before *Gibbs* C. J., when a verdict was found for the Plaintiffs for 5000*l.,* subject to the opinion of the Court upon a case, which, in substance, stated, that the Plaintiffs and *R. Beachcroft* deceased, entered into partnership, as bankers in *London,* under a stipulation that the copartners, or any of them, should not, during the continuance of that copartnership, engage or be concerned in banking business, or any transaction, matter, or thing whatsoever, relating thereto, otherwise than upon the account, and for the benefit and advantage of the same copartnership: and in case any of the copartners should at any time misemploy the money or effects of the copartnership, or engage the credit thereof,

The partners in one house of trade cannot maintain an action against the partners in another house of trade, of which one of the partners in the Plaintiffs' house is also a member, for transactions which took place while he was partner in both houses. And that, whether the action be brought in the lifetime of the common partner, or after his decease. But after his decease the surviving partners of the one house may sue the surviving partners of the other house, upon transactions subsequent to the decease of the common partner.

A creditor receiving money without any specific appropriation by the debtor, shall be permitted in a court of law to ascribe his receipt to the discharge of a prior and purely equitable debt, and sue him at law for a subsequent legal debt.

other-

otherwise than in the regular course of their business, or should enter into any other banking establishment, directly or indirectly, or should do, or suffer to be done, any act in breach of those regulations, the partner so offending should immediately forfeit all right and interest in and to the gains and profits of that copartnership, which should thereupon cease and be dissolved with respect to the partner so offending, and for the purpose of his dismission and expulsion therefrom; and the capital belonging to that copartner, and also his share and interest in the gains and profits of the copartnership undisposed of, and all other his property, estate, and interest of in the said capital concern, should be thereupon transferred to him accordingly. The Plaintiffs and *Beachcroft* carried on the business of bankers in *London* in partnership from 1811 until 23d *July* 1813, when *Beachcroft* died. After the execution of the articles, *Beachcroft*, with the consent of the Plaintiffs, became a partner with the Defendants in a banking-house at *Barton*, in *Lincolnshire*, under the firm of *Beachcroft*, *Wray*, and Co., but the Plaintiffs did not themselves become partners in the *Barton* bank, unless they were rendered such by the operation of their articles of partnership, connected with their assent to *Beachcroft* becoming a partner. At *Beachcroft*'s death the *Barton* bank was indebted to the *London* house for the balance of cash receipts and payments, in the sum of 6633*l.* 16*s.* 4*d.* During the life of *Beachcroft*, the *London* house had been in the habit of transmitting weekly to the *Barton* bank an abstract of their account, and every half-year the balance was struck, and the account rendered: the balance only was brought forward in the next weekly account. The same practice was continued after *Beachcroft*'s death. After *Beachcroft*'s death, the Defendants, under the firm of *Beachcroft*, *Wray*, and Co., continued from time to time to make application

I   for

for money to the *London* house: advances of money were made to them by the Plaintiffs, and payments from the Defendants were received by the Plaintiffs, until *January* 1814, when the Defendants relinquished the business at *Barton*: after which time the Plaintiffs made no new advances, except by paying from time to time the outstanding cash notes of the *Barton* bank. Soon after the death of *Beachcroft*, the Plaintiffs transmitted to *W. M. Beachcroft*, his administrator, a general statement, under various heads, of the accounts of the *London* house, to the time of *Beachcroft's* death; in which statement, under the head of " Debtors, in the country ledger, 23d *July* 1813," is the following item, viz. " *Beachcroft, Wray*, and Co., 6633*l.* 16*s.* 4*d.*" On the 5th of *September* 1813, the Defendants wrote a letter to the Plaintiffs, signed *Beachcroft, Wray*, and Co., inclosing a general statement of the accounts of the *Barton* house for *August* 1813, beginning in these words, " We beg to hand you the monthly balance of the *Barton* and *Brig* accounts, to an inspection of which we consider you entitled, both as the surviving partners of the late Mr. *Beachcroft*, and as explanatory of the bad state of our account with you." In the account inclosed the Plaintiffs were stated to be creditors for 11,272*l.* 7*s.* 8*d.* In the beginning of the year 1815, the Plaintiffs transmitted to the administrator of *R. Beachcroft* two statements of accounts of the *London* house, for the purpose of shewing the state of the concerns of the *London* house: the first, continued up to the 30th *July* 1814, and the second, continued to the end of that year. At the end of the former of these statements, under the head " Dr. balances, *June* 30th, 1814," is the following item, viz. " *Beachcroft, Wray*, and Co. 5684*l.* 8*s.* 2*d.*," and at the end of the latter, under the head " Dr. balances corrected from 23d *July* 1813," is the following item, viz. " *Beachcroft, Wray*, and Co. 5882*l.* 5*s.* 4*d.*" Before the

the commencement of the action, the balance due from
the *Barton* house to the *London* house was reduced to
the sum of 4304*l.* 2*s.* 7*d.* The question for the opinion
of the Court, was, whether the Plaintiffs were entitled
to maintain this action against the Defendants. If the
Court should be of opinion that the Plaintiffs were
entitled so to do, the verdict was to be entered for
4304*l.* 2*s.* 7*d.* with interest from the 30th *June* 1815,
to the time of final judgment.

Bosanquet Serjt., for the Plaintiffs, contended that the
clause in the Plaintiffs' partnership articles, coupled with
their assent to *Beachcroft's* becoming a partner in the
Barton bank, had not had, as would be contended by
the Defendants, the effect of rendering all the Plaintiffs
partners in the *Barton* bank. The consequence provided in the articles, in case of any one of the partners
engaging in a new bank, was, that such partner should
cease to continue a partner. If this penalty were incurred by a breach, either it might be waved by the
other partners, or it could not. If it could not, then
the offending partner ceased to be a member of the
Plaintiffs' house, and in that case it was clear that they
did not become his partners in the new firm; but if
they had the power to wave the penalty, as they well
might, inasmuch as it was introduced only for their benefit, and they were free to take advantage of it or not,
it did not therefore follow that their waver of the penalty should make them participators in the act. But
at all events, though, by waving the penalty, they continued to be partners with *Beachcroft* in the *London*
house during his life, that partnership with him ceased
upon his death, and however the connection resulting
from the circumstance of his being a partner in both
houses, might preclude them from maintaining an action
against the *Barton* house during his life, yet after his
                                                    decease,

decease, when that connection no longer existed, the
Plaintiffs were free to apply all sums which they subsequently received from the *Barton* house, to the liquida-
tion of the old balance due at *Beachcroft's* decease from
the *Barton* house to the *London* house, and those receipts would discharge that balance; and for the sums
which the Plaintiffs advanced to the *Barton* house, after
Beachcroft's death, they might indisputably maintain
their present action, the two houses being thenceforth
wholly distinct, and strangers to each other at the time
of the Plaintiffs' making those several last advances.
But further, if *A.*, *B.*, and *C.* are indebted to *A.*, *D.*, and
E., though during the life of *A.*, the one house cannot
sue the other, because *A.* cannot sue himself, yet if *A.*
dies, the debts and credits of each house with relation
to the other survive, and *B.* and *C.* may then sue *D.*
and *E.* for the previous debt. That, if there be two
houses, in each of which some individuals are the
same as in the other, and some different, the one
house may draw bills on the other, and perform all
mercantile transactions distinctly, without making a
common property, is recognized in a court of law by
Eyre C. J. in the case of *Bolton* v. *Puller* (a). The
facts of that case were briefly these. The banking-
house of *Caldwell* and Co. at *Liverpool* consisted of four
partners, *Caldwell*, *Smith*, *Forbes*, and *Gregory*, of
whom *Forbes* and *Gregory* also constituted a distinct
house of trade in *London*. *Bolton* had a banking account with *Caldwell* and Co., and he used in mercantile
business to accept bills, which by his acceptance he
made payable at the house of *Forbes* and *Gregory* in
London, and *Caldwell* and Co. procured *Forbes* and
Gregory to pay these bills for him in *London* at maturity. To enable them so to do, *Bolton* delivered bills
of exchange to *Caldwell* and Co. as his factors, indorsed

(a) 1 Bo:. & Pull. 539.

to them, and they, to enable *Forbes* and *Gregory* to pay the bills when due, indorsed and transmitted these bills to *Forbes* and *Gregory*. Both *Caldwell* and Co. and *Forbes* and *Gregory* became bankrupts, without the latter having paid *Bolton's* acceptances, which he was obliged himself to take up. *Bolton* brought trover against the assignees of *Forbes* and *Gregory* for certain of those bills of exchange which he had delivered to *Caldwell* and Co. to enable the *London* house to meet his acceptances, and which had not yet become due. *Caldwell* and Co. at their failure were indebted to *Bolton*, not he to them; so that they had no lien on the bills; and it was therefore clear that if the bills in the hands of *Forbes* and *Gregory* were to be considered as still remaining in the hands of *Caldwell* and Co., the Plaintiff might recover. *Bolton* had no account with *Forbes* and *Gregory*, but all the transactions with them became items, first, in the account between *Forbes* and *Gregory* and *Caldwell* and Co., and next, in the account between *Caldwell* and Co. and *Bolton*. And the question therefore was, whether the circumstance of *Forbes* and *Gregory* being still partners with *Caldwell* and Co. caused the bills still to be, as it were, in the hands of *Caldwell* and Co., or to be in the like case as if they were in the hands of distinct persons, in which latter case case the Plaintiff would have no right to the bills. *Eyre* C. J. most distinctly lays it down, that the property in those bills might be transferred, and was transferred by the four partners, as *Caldwell* and Co. to two of themselves, as *Forbes* and *Gregory*, and that therefore, notwithstanding the entire privity of the latter, as two of the partners, to the whole transaction, *Bolton* could not recover the bills against the assignees of *Forbes* and *Gregory*. The moment the person is dead who forms the connecting link, the right accrues of suing the others. If an obligor makes one of several joint obligees one of his executors, the obligees cannot sue the obligor's executors, so long as that

14   obligee

obligee who is executor lives; but after his decease, the obligees may sue the other executors. This is the answer to the cases of *Mainwaring* v. *Newman* (a), and *Moffat* v. *Van Millingen* (b), if they are cited for the Defendants, and which cases certainly would furnish an unanswerable objection to the Plaintiffs' recovery, if *Beachcroft* continued alive. There was therefore a good consideration for the credit, which, as it appears by the case, the *Barton* house ascribe to the *London* house, to the amount of 11,272*l.* 7*s.* 8*d.*, for the former were clearly liable in equity to pay as well those sums which had been advanced to them jointly with *Beachcroft*, as those sums which had been advanced to them since his decease. It appears, therefore, by the statements of accounts contained in the case, that after the death of *Beachcroft* the Plaintiffs made new advances, at least to the amount of 4638*l.* 11*s.* 4*d.*, a larger sum than they now seek to recover; and as the payments made by the Defendants in reduction of their balance, are not shewn to have been accompanied with any peculiar appropriation by the Defendants, the Plaintiffs are, according to the case of *Kirby* v. *The Duke of Marlborough* (c), at liberty to ascribe the sums they have so received to the reduction of the balance due in *Beachcroft's* lifetime. That was a very strong case; for when the Defendant entered into a bond of guaranty for future advances to be made by the Plaintiffs to *Cobourn*, to the extent of 3000*l.*, it was not communicated to him that *Cobourn* was then already indebted to them; it was nevertheless held, that the Plaintiffs were at liberty to apply all subsequent payments made by *Cobourn* to the extinction of the old account, and to charge the new advances upon the guarantee.

Best Serjt. *contrà.* Although it was not in the contemplation of the *London* house, that its members were

(a) 2 *Bos. & Pull.* 120.   (c) 2 *Maule & Selw.* 18.
(b) 2 *Bos. & Pull.* 124. *n*

all becoming partners in the *Barton* bank, yet such was the legal effect of their approval of Mr. *Beachcroft's* becoming a partner therein; for by the terms of the articles of partnership none is to enter into any other banking concern except for the benefit of the *London* house: therefore if the Plaintiffs assent to his becoming partner, *Beachcroft* is a trustee for them, and they all become entitled to a share, through the intervention of *Beachcroft*, in the profits of the *Barton* bank, of which it is a necessary consequence, that they all likewise become responsible for the losses of that house; and a community of profit and loss constitutes a partnership. It cannot be otherwise consistently with the case of *Waugh* v. *Carver* (a). But whether all the Plaintiffs were or were not partners in the *Barton* bank, it is clear that *Beachcroft* was a partner after the Plaintiffs' assent, both in the *Barton* bank and in the *London* house; and therefore, during his life, no action could be maintained by the *London* house against the *Barton* house, because the same person cannot be at once Plaintiff and Defendant in the same cause. Neither is any case cited to support the proposition, that the one house may sue the other after *Beachcroft's* decease, for the balance due in his lifetime. The executors of the deceased partner are in equity tenants in common with the survivors of the deceased partner's share. *Hammond* v. *Day* (b), *Brown* v. *Litton* (c). Therefore, though the name of *Beachcroft* no longer appears in the house, the Plaintiffs, who are trustees for his administrator, cannot sue the Defendants, who are equally trustees for his administrator: or, if they could sue at law, after the Plaintiffs have recovered their judgment, the case must go before a court of equity, which would restrain execution. Neither can the Plaintiffs now appropriate the recent payments to the old account

(a) 2 H. Bl. 235.
(b) 5 Ves. jun. 539.

(c) 1 P. Wms. 141.

in

in the manner suggested : for it appears that they have, by the accounts which they are stated in the case to have already rendered, appropriated those payments in a different way, and they cannot now rescind their election. In *Newmarch* v. *Clay* (a) it was held that the payees had not the right to appropriate payments to such account as they pleased, where circumstances indicate that they have been made on a particular account : and here the circumstances shew that the payments made by the *Barton* house since *Beachcroft*'s death, were made to cover the sums advanced by the Plaintiffs since that time.

The Court, stopping *Bosanquet*'s reply, thus delivered their judgment.

This was an action brought by the partners in the house of *Bosanquet* and Company against the Defendants, who belong to the *Barton* bank, for a balance stated to be due to them. The transactions originated during the life of the late Mr. *Beachcroft*, who was a partner in both houses. It is clear that no part of the demand, which accrued to the *London* house upon transactions which took place during the lifetime of *Richard Beachcroft*, and to which therefore he was a party, could ever, either during his life or since his decease, be recovered at law; on this ground, that no legal contract could subsist between him and those connected with him on the one side, and himself with others connected with him on the other side ; the parties could only so far enter into this contract, as to render it available in equity; and as this principle goes to the root of the contract, the same objection to the Plaintiffs' recovery still continues after his decease. This, therefore, shuts the Plaintiffs out of so much of their demand as accrued upon any business transacted before *R. Beachcroft*'s decease and would therefore be excluded by a rest then made in the accounts. The question

(a) 14 *East*, 239.

is, whether, upon other parts of the case, it appears that the Plaintiffs are still entitled to maintain this action. It appears that *Beachcroft* died on the 23d of *July* 1813; that at his decease the balance due from the *Barton* house was 6633*l.* 16*s.* 4*d.*: it also appears, that the sum of 4638*l.* 11*s.* 4*d.* has become due since *Beachcroft's* decease. The sum now sought to be recovered is much less than that sum, and less than the sum due at the time of *Beachcroft's* death. There ought to have been a separation of accounts on *Beachcroft's* decease, which there was not, but the Plaintiffs continued to supply the wants of the *Barton* house, as if *Beachcroft* were still alive; and the Defendants proceed to render weekly accounts, and receive them in return, and to transact business as before. On the 5th *September* 1813, the balance was 11,272*l.* 7*s.* 8*d.*, due to the Plaintiffs from the *Barton* bank: this balance, being so high, shews that considerable transactions had taken place in the interval since the decease of *Beachcroft*, and that the Plaintiffs had advanced to the Defendants since that time considerable sums, to the amount, certainly, of 4638*l.* 11*s.* 4*d.*, being a larger sum than the Plaintiffs now seek to recover. It is said they cannot recover this sum, because, it is argued by the Defendants' counsel, that *Beachcroft* was a partner in both houses, and that either the whole transactions are involved by that circumstance, and the subsequent dealings were had in continuation of the original contract, and that the remaining debt stands on the same footing as the debt due at the death of *Beachcroft*, and is not a legal debt, because *Beachcroft* was a contractor on both sides; or that, at all events, the subsequent payments are to be applied to the subsequent advances, and therefore there is no balance that can be recovered. The Plaintiffs say, we will admit that at the death of *Beachcroft* a sum was due which we cannot recover at law, and that the accounts afterwards went on, as if

Beach-

Beachcroft had not been dead; but in law the transactions preceding the death of *Beachcroft* are of a different description, and raise a different obligation from those which took place afterwards; and though, in fact, the accounts were continued in the same course, yet, of necessity, we may divide them as they should be divided. The Defendants say, nothing is due on this last account, and insist that all the late advances are paid: the Plaintiffs say, monies have been paid, and large sums advanced, since the decease of *Beachcroft,* but they have been paid on the footing of the old account, without any separation of the two periods, the one preceding *Richard Beachcroft's* decease, or the one following it; but all that has been hitherto paid, has been paid without any distinction being made up to this time by those who paid, or by those who received the money; whatever is paid in this general manner, is paid *ad modum recipientis,* and since circumstances now make it desirable for us to appropriate the sums received since *Beachcroft's* decease, we now apply them to that part of our demand, which is, at least, an equitable debt, namely, to the discharge of the sums due to us before his decease, and we seek to recover in this action the remaining part of our demand, and to that part the Defendants have no legal answer, the appropriation being at our option." On this view of the case we think that the Plaintiffs' claim arises out of the advances made since the decease of Mr. *Beachcroft;* and that the Plaintiffs therefore have a right to recover.

DALLAS J. This is quite a plain case. Advances have been made by the Plaintiffs since *Beachcroft's* death, which are now sought to be recovered. There has been no appropriation made by the Defendants of their payments, and the Plaintiffs therefore are entitled to apply them as they now seek to do.

The rest of the Court concurred in giving
    Judgment for the Plaintiffs on the four first counts.

May 27.

TAYLOR and Others *v.* CURTIS.

The expenditure of ammunition, in resisting capture by a privateer, the damage done to the ship in the combat, and the expence of curing the wounded sailors, are not the subject of general average by the law of *England*.

THE Plaintiffs declared, that they were owners of the ship *Hibernia*, which was proceeding upon a voyage from this kingdom to the Island of *St. Thomas*, with a cargo of merchandize upon freight, and that upon the voyage she was attacked by enemies, viz. by persons acting under the authority of the government of the United States of *North America*, who endeavoured to make prize of the ship and cargo, which the master and crew resisted, and thereby, and in the proper and necessary defence of the ship and cargo by the master and crew against those enemies, and in endeavouring to preserve the same from capture, the ship and her furniture were greatly damaged, and the Plaintiffs necessarily and properly expended a large sum in repairing the damage: that the ship and cargo were by such resistance and defence preserved from capture, and afterwards completed her voyage: that when the ship was so attacked, and the damage and expence so occasioned, and during the voyage, the Defendant was the owner of a part of the goods on board of value, and was benefited in respect thereof by the resistance against the attack, and the defence of the ship and cargo, from which the damage and expence accrued, by reason whereof the Defendant, as the owner of such part of the goods, became liable to contribute to that damage and expence in a general average; and in consideration thereof promised to pay so much as he, as such owner, was liable to contribute. The second count stated more generally, that in endeavouring to preserve the ship and cargo from capture, the ship and furniture were greatly damaged, and great loss and expence were necessarily and properly incurred. The 3d count stated,

that

that on the voyage, a part of the ship's furniture, of value, was utterly lost, and other part sustained damage, which loss and damage were occasioned by acts of the master and crew of the ship, properly and necessarily done by them in order to preserve the ship and cargo from capture by enemies, and being thereby wholly lost to the owners thereof, the ship and cargo, were, by the means so used for the general preservation, preserved from capture, and afterwards completed the voyage: that he was during the time that cargo was on board, and of the loss and damage, the owner of a part of the cargo, of value; that he was benefited in respect thereof by those acts of the master and crew; and by reason thereof became liable to contribute to that loss and damage in a general average, and promised to pay, and they averred his proportion, and notice. The 4th count was *indebitatus assumpsit*, for general average payable upon, and in respect of merchandizes of the Defendant, carried in the Plaintiffs' ship the *Hibernia*, from this kingdom to parts beyond the seas. The cause was tried at *Guildhall*, at the sittings after *Michaelmas* term 1816, principally on admissions,' and it appeared that the Plaintiffs were owners of the *Hibernia*, of 6 guns and 22 men. The Defendant was proprietor of goods loaded on board that ship for a voyage from *London* to *St. Thomas*; in the course of which the ship was attacked by an *American* privateer, of 22 guns and 125 men, then hostile; the captain and crew resisted the attack for nine hours, in the course of which the *American* was thrice compelled to sheer off, and as often returned to the combat, but the *Hibernia* ultimately disabled and beat her off, with the loss of two of the *Hibernia's* men killed and several wounded; proceeded to her port of destination, and delivered her cargo in safety to the consignees. The *Hibernia* sustained considerable damage in the engagement,

1816.

Ｔ`TAYLOR`
v.
Ｃ`CURTIS.`

ment, both in her hull and rigging, which were repaired at a considerable expence to the owners. The owners also incurred a further expence in providing medical and surgical assistance for the wounded mariners, and expended in the engagement a considerable quantity of gun-powder and shot, part of the stores and outfit of the ship, and now sued to try the question, whether the Defendant were liable, in respect of his part of the cargo, to contribute to these expences as *general average.* The jury found a verdict for the Defendant, subject *to* a reference as to the amount, but liberty was reserved to the Plaintiffs to move to set aside the verdict, and enter a verdict for the Plaintiffs.

Lens Serjt. in *Hilary* term accordingly moved.

Ｇ`GIBBS` C. J. inclined to grant a rule *nisi*, because two books of high estimation in the profession, but not at present to be cited as authority(*a*), state, that damage sustained in defending the ship, and the healing the wounds of the sailors hurt in a combat, is general average (*b*); they cite no authority. Another treatise (*c*) also, by an author of high character, observes, that there is no authority for this position; that foreign writers differ; that if a ball passes through a bale of goods, the damage rests where it falls; and if so, why is a ball passing through a ship's side to be general average?

Rule *nisi.*

Shepherd, Solicitor General, and *Best* and *Bosanquet* Serjts. shewed cause against this rule. The Plaintiffs

(*a*) *Lens, arguendo.* Books of living authors are not usually to be cited, yet there are such extant, which, in future time, (may that period be long distant!) will be cited as of equal authority with *Emerigon* and *Le Guidon. Lau-*dari *nihil est, nisi ab laudato viro.*

(*b*) *Park on Insurance,* 6 edit. vol. i. 173. *Marsh. on Insur.* 2 edit. vol. ii 535.

(*c*) *Abbott on Merchant Shipping,* 4 edit. 366.

raised

raised their demand on three distinct subjects of damage: first, for the damage done to the hull and rigging of the ship; second, for medical and surgical aid to the mariners wounded in the conflict; third, for ammunition, part of the ship's stores, expended in the engagement. They denied that the Plaintiffs were entitled to recover a contribution by the Defendant to either of these subjects of loss. There was no evidence in the case, of any special custom of merchants to consider these as general average, although a wise policy might frequently have induced individuals to contribute to similar losses. Nor was there any positive ordinance on the subject in the *English* maritime law. The authorities on the point were very few; there were only three decided cases in the *English* law which bore on it. *Birkley* v. *Presgrave* (a), *Covington* v. *Roberts* (b), and *Power* v. *Whitmore* (c). In the case of *Birkley* v. *Presgrave*, a cable and anchor was let go in the river *Thames*, and for saving the ship it became necessary to cut the cable. The act of cutting the cable was a voluntary deliberate act, (which is the distinction taken by *Emerigon*,) for preserving the residue; therefore the case is not applicable; in *Power* v. *Whitmore*, wherein the Court, apparently on better consideration, completely overruled what they had held in *Plummer* v. *Wildman* (d), it was held that where a ship, having suffered in heavy gales, put into port to repair, the wages and provisions of the mariners while she was in port, and the pilotage, and other port-charges, and the expences of her repairs there, were not general average. In *Covington* v. *Roberts*. a ship had struck to a privateer, but the latter could not take possession; the ship therefore crowded sail, and in so doing strained her masts, opened her seams, and carried away

1816.

TAYLOR
v.
CURTIS.

(a) 1 *East*, 220.
(b) 2 *New Rep.* 378.
(c) 4 *Maule & Selw.* 141.

(d) *Plummer* v. *Wildman*,
3 *Maule & Selw.* 482.

her

her mainmast, but escaped; and it was contended this was general average, because the master used such a press of sail in a gale of wind, as he could not have justified in the ordinary course of navigation. Yet it was held to be only a common sea-risk, although it was voluntary, and a matter of judgment, on his part, and it was his duty to do so. So here: the ship is attacked by a privateer; if she can resist, it is the captain's duty so to do; for so doing, he must exercise the means, in that act he expends his powder and ball, but it is not like the throwing goods overboard; he uses it for the very purpose for which he carries it out. If in a dark night he fires signals of distress, there is an expenditure of the ship's powder on an extraordinary occasion to relieve himself from impending distress, but though it is out of the ordinary course of navigation, he only yields to the necessity created by a peril of the sea, of exerting himself to do that duty. The crowding sail, and losing a mast, and the receiving the shot of an enemy, are both consequential on the exertion of escaping the impending evil, yet they are equally voluntary as the expenditure of powder in the combat. The rule as to general average, is, that unless there is a voluntary devotion of some part, it does not constitute general average, if there be that devotion, it entitles him who is the author of that devotion to general average, but if the ship does not go out of the usual duties, course, and practice of her voyage for that purpose, it is not general average. If a ship be attacked by an enemy in the course of her voyage, it is as much a part of the duty of the captain and crew to defend the ship, as it is to pump her if she springs a leak. If in pumping, they broke the pump, that damage would not be called general average. Nothing which does not fall within the ordinary course and duties of the voyage is to be found here. There being then no positive law on the
subject

subject in *England*, how has the subject been treated by writers on general law? The law merchant, indeed, is the law of the civilized world, and the Court would defer to foreign writers on this subject as authorities of weight; but such passages as were found in text writers relevant to the question, rather treated of the positive ordinances of particular countries, than illustrated the general law. And though the latter might in many instances re-enact that which was a principle of general law, they did not necessarily or always agree therewith. But so far as they go, the current of the authorities shews, that the general law is in favour of the Defendant (*a*). *Lege Rhodiâ cavetur, ut si levandæ navis gratiâ jactus mercium factus est, omnium contributione sarciatur, quod pro omnibus datum est;* pointing at the voluntary character of the sacrifice made for the preservation of the whole. And again (*b*), *Si conservatis mercibus, deterior facta sit navis, aut si quid exarmaverit, nulla facienda est collatio, quia dissimilis earum rerum causa sit, quæ navis gratiâ parentur, et earum pro quibus mercedem aliquis acceperit; nam et si faber incudem aut malleum fregerit, non imputaretur ei qui locaverit opus, sed si voluntate vectorum vel propter aliquem metum id detrimentum factum sit, hoc ipsum sarciri oportet.* So, *Cleiracq.*(*c*) *La contribution doit estre des dommages faits ad intra, que ceux qui sont dans len avire ont delibere, qu' ils ont faite et execute par eux mesmes. Mais ce qui vient de dehors, ad extra, comme le dommage cause par les vents, par la tempeste, ou le foudre, ou par les Pillars, c'est tout avarie simple, qui n' entre pas en contribution. Wisbuy,* Article 12. *Valin,* indeed, in his work on the ordinances of the *Hans towns* (*d*), enumerates

---

(*a*) *Dig. lib.* 14. *tit.* 2. *pl.* 1. *De Lege Rhodiâ de jactu.*
    (*b*) *Ibid.*
    (*c*) *Cleiracq, Us et Coustumes*

de la mer. Jugemens d'Oleron. p. 50. *s.* 5.
    (*d*) *Tom.* 2. *liv.* 3. *tit.* 7. *Des Avaries, article* 6.

among

among other heads, average which arises in defending
the ship; and gives the ordinance of the *Hans towns*,
that the expence of the cure is general average, *En
combattant pour eviter d'etrê pris par l' ennemi, sans
distinguer en ce cas, si le matelôt est blessé les armes à la
main, ou s'il n'est qu' en faisant la manœuvre. Mais s'il
est blessè hors le combat en fuisant la service et la manœuvre ordinaire, les frais de ses pansemens & nourriture
ne peuvent passer pour avaries communes, attendu qu'il
n'a pas reçu sa blessure pour le salût commune.* Here,
however, he is not speaking of the common law of
Europe, but of the ordinances of *France* and *Hamburgh*. So, in speaking of the *French* ordinances (*a*),
he says, that the wounds of sailors shall be general
average. *Pothier* also, in his *Traitè des Avaries* (*b*),
is speaking of specific ordinances, and says, that where
the ordinance is that the cure of a wounded sailor is
general average, there the cure of a wounded passenger
is also general average. *Emerigon* (*c*) says, " if the
captain throw goods overboard, or do any other voluntary and necessary act, *ab intra*, which occasions a
beneficial sacrifice, such loss shall be general average.
*Mais si pendant qu'on est engagé dans ce mauvais pas, on
souffre de dehors quelque dommage, soit par la force de
la tempête, soit par le talonage sur le roc, soit par la
canon de l' ennemi, un pareil dommage est avarie simple, parce qu'il est puremeut fatal,* i. e. irremediable, it
must rest where it falls, as a casual or simple loss; and
in a former passage, he says, that the meeting with an
enemy is a sea risk, in like manner as a rock or a storm.

(*a*) P. 165. *article* 6.
(*b*) *Traitè des Avaries*, ii.
421.

(*c*) *Emerigon, p.* 627. *c.* 12.
*Enumeration des Avaries gros-
ses et des avaries simples, s.* 41.
n. 8.

Though

Though *Emerigon* here seems to differ from *Valin*, yet they are reconcileable. In a subsequent sentence he quotes *Le Guidon*, which puts in the rank of simple averages all loss sustained from bad weather, or making water, being struck by cannon shot, or boarded by pirates. (*a*) In the *Hans towns* and *France* there are particular ordinances. In the former, *Si* (*b*) *quis nautarum contra piratas strenuè dimicaverit, et in conflictu fortè debilitationem membrorum passus sit, is sanari et in æqualem contributionem ex navi et bonis præstandam venire debet. Et si ad tantam debilitatem pervenerit, ut sibi de victu ampliùs providere nequeat, tunc ad dies vitæ illi de alimentatione liberâ prospiciatur, aut alia, æqua donatio pro qualitate rei hoc nomine ei offeratur.* By the ordonnance of Louis the XIVth (*c*), *Les pansemens et nourriture du matelot blessè en défendant le navire, sont avaries grosses ou communes.* There being this particular ordinance for wounds of seamen, but none for the wounds of the ship, the two learned writers, *Valin* and *Emerigon*, enquire whether it extends to damage done to the ship. *Valin*, as an inference rising from the ordinance for the wounds of sailors, concludes, first (*d*), confessing all writers are against him, that it does: but he draws another conclusion contrary to the *English* law, for he puts the very case of *Coving-*

(*a*) *Avarie qui concerne la marchandise est empirance, pourriture, degât, mouilleure d'eau, racoutrage, visitation & appretiation, sauvages, & autres semblables choses, si elles procedent par fortune de mer, mauvais temps, ou pour avoir le navire fait eau, touché, abordè par les Pillars, tiré a coups de canon, le tout fait attester & apprecié.*

Guidon de la Mer. Des Avaries, chap. v. *s.* 4.

(*b*) *Kuricke. Jus Maritimum Hanseaticum. Titulus* 14. *De extraordinariâ remuneratione fidelium nautarum, Articulus* 13.

(*c*) *Ordonnance de Louis* 14. *tit.* 7. *Des Avaries, art.* 6.

(*d*) *Valin*, tom. 2. *liv.* 5. *art.* 6. *an finem, p.* 167.

ton

ton v. Roberts (a), and decides it contrary to the decision of this court; so that, from the beginning to the end, Valin, it appears, was proceeding on a ground contrary to this court. Emérigon holds the opposite opinion, and says, that he so decided, as a judge in the French Court of Admiralty. But in both writers, this is only an inference, with respect to the ship, drawn from the French ordinance. In the ordinances of the Hans towns, there is, in like manner, a provision respecting wounded sailors, but none respecting wounds of the ship, and another writer concurs in inferring thence, that it extends not to the ship. Kuricke (b) on the Hanseatic law, who is cited by Emerigon (c), says, armamenta tamen navis et instrumenta in conflictu cum piratis depravata in havariam non veniunt, sed damnum hoc a nauclero et exercitoribus sarciendum est, for which he cites a judgment in the court of Dantzic, 1603. 24 Sept. Plassenburg and others v. Damerau and others. The cure of the wounds of sailors never could be general average by the law of England, because the statute 11 & 12 W. 3. c. 7. s. 11. gives them retribution in another way, by giving power to levy on the owners a sum not exceeding two per cent. on the value of the freight, ship, and cargo. If it had been average in an ordinary way, there would have been no need of these retributions. So, out of the wages of merchantmen, a deduction of six-pence per month is made to provide for hospitals.

Lens and Copley Serjts. in support of the rule. It being habitual with merchants to treat losses of this description as general averages, it may fairly be inferred that the law is such. This case falls within the prin-

(a) Sera demême avarie commune, si faisant force de voiles pour se sauver de la prise, les mâts se rompent, les voiles & cordages sont emportés, &c.

Art. 21. du ch. 5. du Guidon. 2 Valin, Comment 166, 167.
(b) Tit. 14. art. 3. page 73.
(b) Emerigon, tom. 1. 628.

ciples

ciples which have been laid down on the other side. The defence of the ship was a voluntary undertaking to do that on behalf of the ship which should be for the benefit of the whole concern. To the argument, that defence is a duty, and so this loss not a general average, it may be first answered, that this is not a question between the mariners and the owner of the ship, but between the owners of one sort of property, and the owners of another. But further, although it is the duty of the crew to obey the master, no law compels the master universally to fight, but only certain persons, and in certain specified cases. It is not such a part of the public duty of the master and mariners, that it can be considered as a matter of course, that they should enter into the defence of the vessel against such an immense disparity of force; it is no part of their contract, though they deserve high commendation for defending: whatever risk is incurred on this deliberation of the master and men, it is a voluntary sacrifice made by persons who might have abstained from it, if they had thought proper; it is a sacrifice made for the good of the whole, and it proved productive of that good. They did not expend their ammunition for the particular benefit of any part which has remained to themselves alone. The definition of a general average requires that it should be a voluntary sacrifice; but how far is it to be voluntary? Not absolutely so. In cutting away a mast to preserve the ship, you give away that which would be inevitably lost with the rest, if it were not given: so here, all would have been taken, 'but for this voluntary act of fighting. The ship falls in with an enemy, the master deliberates. " If I fight, I shall incur expence in healing the wounded sailors, I shall expend my ammunition, and receive damage to my vessel, but I probably shall save something; and if I do not fight, I assuredly shall lose the whole."

1816.

TAYLOR
v.
CURTIS.

This, then, is clearly a voluntary and deliberate sacrifice of a part for the sake of preserving the rest: it is, 1st, deliberate; 2dly, it is the sacrifice of a part; 3dly, the object and effect of it is to preserve the rest; 4thly, it is *ab intra,* and voluntary. All the required qualities here concur. In *Birkley* v. *Presgrave,* Lord *Kenyon* C. J. says, all those articles which were made use of by the master and crew upon the particular emergency, and out of the usual course, for the benefit of the whole concern, and the other expences incurred, must be paid proportionably by the Defendant as general average: *it is not straining the case,* to say this was an expenditure out of the common course. *Lawrence* J. translates the definition of *Pothier:* he says, that all loss which arises in consequence of extraordinary sacrifices made, or expences incurred for the preservation of the ship and cargo, come within general average, and must be borne proportionably by all who are interested; and that natural justice requires this. Suppose a ship, for the purpose of avoiding an enemy, runs down another vessel, as is sometimes done, by which the first vessel is injured, that is clearly general average. Will the Court then, entertain the nice distinction, that the one way of fighting a vessel is general average, the other not? The only other cases in our common law books not before cited are those of *Dacosta* v. *Newnham,* wherein wages and expences of unshipping a cargo, where the ship had put into port for the general safety, are by *Buller* J. considered as general average, and *Plummer* v. *Wildman,* which is to the same effect: the charges of repairs, powder and shot expended, and the cure of seamen, are in like manner for the benefit of the whole concern. The doctrine of *Mansfield* C. J. in *Covington* v. *Roberts* (a), that it was only a common sea

(a) 2 *Term Rep.* 407.

14

risk,

risk, to put up an unusual press of sail, does not operate against the Plaintiff, that certainly was a common sea risk; but this is not such an one.   A common sea risk is that which does not require the deliberation of the party to determine whether it shall be incurred or not. A case which goes to illustrate the general principle, is that of the *Copenhagen* (*a*), where a question arose concerning the expence of transhipping goods. Sir *W. Scott* J. says, " General average is that loss to which contribution must be made by both ship and cargo; the loss, or expence which the loss creates, being incurred for the common benefit of both, and therefore the expence of that transhipment, or rather of the unloading, seemed to have upon it the character of a general average." That doctrine is applicable to the present case. This is an act done in the hope of saving the ship from a loss which would otherwise be inevitable. This being a voluntary act, as far any of the actors are concerned, must be general average. The stat. *W.* 3., for encouraging seamen to defend the ship, applies not to this case; it does not profess to inquire whether the seamen were entitled to any other compensation or not. Neither does it apply to wounded sailors merely, but it is for giving a reward to the master and the crew generally, as well as to the wounded. Nor is the instance of seamen contributing to hospitals at all analogous.   Therefore the matter is left much at large, to be considered on principle. It is not true that the writers on general law all draw a conclusion in favour of the Defendant. The passage in the *Rhodian* law, on which all the authorities found themselves, is highly favourable to the Plaintiff, where *jactus mercium* is put only as the instance. In *Dobson* v. *Wilson* (*b*), Lord *Ellenborough* C. J. acknowledge-

(*a*) 1 *Robins.* 294.   (*b*) 3 *Campb.* 486.

that

that a jettison to lighten the ship is not the only foundation of general average, but it must arise from that, or something analogous.   The Defendant does not contend that it is literally confined to a *jactus mercium*. This is, in the very terms of the *Rhodian* law, *pro omnibus datum*. The ammunition would not have been destroyed, more than the rest; it would all have been captured together, unless for this exertion against the enemy. *Valin* says, that the damage sustained by the ship and part of the cargo, in fighting to avoid being taken, and the expence of curing the wounded sailors, are the subject of general average. It is said that *Valin* and other foreign jurists, are of little authority on this point, but the more the objection to them, drawn from the assertion that they are treating only of the ordinances of particular countries, is examined, to the less weight will it be found entitled. *Valin* is not a mere commentator on the *French* ordinances, his work was intended as a commentary on the general law of *Europe*; it is known that the ordinance of *Louis XIV.* was a code compiled from the laws of all *Europe*, by order of that monarch; and the plaintiff takes his stand farther back than *Valin*, and says, that ordinance itself is an authority. *Valin* (a) does not say that the repairs of the ship are, by parity of reasoning, from the instance of the cure of the wounded sailors, general average, as is supposed on the other side: he puts several instances, and says, that the repairs of the ship are substantively one subject of general average, though *Kuricke*, *Casa Regis*, and *Carlo Targa* are of a different opinion as to the repairs of the ship. *Pothier* (b), (and a greater authority could not be cited,) agrees with *Valin*. *Kuricke*, in his commentary on the third article of the fourteenth title of the *Jus Maritimum Hanseaticum*, cited above, expressly guards

(a) *Tom. 2. liv. 3. tit. 7. art. 6.*   (b) *Pothier, tom 2. partie 2.
s. 2. art. 144. p. 432.*

against

against the idea, that he was stating this as the law of the *Hans* towns only, and he lays it down as the public and common law of all civilized *Europe* (a). He says, *Hinc est, quod etsi corpora libera in estimationem et contributionem non veniant,* [*de jure civili, l. 2. s. 2. ad l. Rhod. de jact.*] *nihilominus* COMMUNITÈR DE JURE MARIȚIMO STATUATUR, *quod si quis nautarum in pugnâ cum hostibus vel piratis vulneratus, debilitatus, aut occisus fuerit,* tum *id quod interest, seu damnum ex vulneratione, debilitatione, aut nece, resultans, ac porro tota merces, prætensio, vectibilia, et sepultura defuncti, in grossam Havariam, et communem contributionem ex navi et mercibus, pro quarum defensione tot malorum passus est, præstandam veniat:* and he cites for it four different codes. *Jus Marit, Carol. art.* 28. *Philip II. tit. deNaufrag. art.* 2. *Jus Danic. c.* 20. and *Statut. Hamburg. part* 2. *tit.* 14. *art.* 42. *Emerigon* says, it is true, that the meeting an enemy is aperil of the sea, and the subject of particular average only. A loss occasioned by an hostile ship firing on the vessel, before she had time to surrender, or a shot fired after her surrender, would certainly be a peril of the sea; but this is not that case, this is a loss occasioned by the voluntary act of the master and crew, this is not *fatal;* there is no inevitable necessity. The passage *Emerigon* cites from *Le Guidon* does not necessarily suppose an engagement: it even seems not to contemplate an engagement: he speaks of a ship making water, boarded by robbers, receiving a shot, (*tirè a coup de canon,*) which may be in a pursuit, or in order to bring her to; it does not appear that the author's attention was drawn to this case of an engagement, and of wounds received by the ship in her defence. But *Emerigon* (b), and the *French* ordinance, and the *Hans* towns ordinances, and

(a) P. 246.   *p.* 636. *tit. in marg. Matelots*
(b) C. 12. s. 41. *Division* 16. *Blessés.*

T t 3   also

also *Cleiracq*, a great authority on this point, and *Vinnius*, all of whom he cites, all concur as to damage done to the sailors, and only differ as to the damage done to the vessel. *Cleiracq*, in his commentary on the judgments pronounced on the laws of *Oleron* (a), says, *Et si en se defendant, ou combatant contre l' ennemy ou les four-bans, il est mutilè, ou rendu perclus et inhabile a travailler le reste de sa vie, il aura du pain, tant qu' il vivra, aux depens du navire et de la cargaison, et ce'st avarie grosse,* and he cites *Hanze Theut. Art.* 35. *Charles quint, art.* 27. & 28. *Arg. legis secundum Julianum et ibi Barth. et l. cum duobus ss. quidam D. pro socio,* and the following passage from *Grotius. In societate navali adversus pi-ratas utilitas communis est ipsa defensio. Solent estimari naves, et quæ in navi sunt, atque ex his summa confici, ut damna que eveniunt, in quibus sunt et vulneratorum impendia, ferantur a dominis navium et mercium pro parte quam habent in eá summá. Et hæc quidem, quæ diximus hactenus, ipsi juri naturæ sunt consentanea.* (b) *Grotius* here is speaking on the head of contracts, and says, that where no contract subsists, the question ought to be decided by natural justice and natural law. This is à strong confirmation. This and the laws of the *Hans* towns are cited, because they are a commentary on the system, the opinions of legislatures on the question. So, a writer of our own country says, " all extraordinary charges, proceeding from endeavours to preserve the ship and cargo, and the damages resulting from the measures taken for that purpose, constitute and are commonly accounted, a general or gross average, as the ordinance of *Hamburgh* explains it, (No. 981.) of which expences and damages, that ordinance, (No. 983.) particularly enumerates, 1. all

(a) *Cleiracq. Us et coustumes   (b) Grot. De Jur. Bell. et de la mer. Art. 6. pl. 3. p. 31.   Pacis, lib. 2. c. 12. s. 25.*

damage

damage that a ship suffers in her apparel and cargo, in defending her against an enemy, privateer, or pirate; 5. what may be expended in the cure, and extraordinary attendance on either officers or sailors, wounded in defence of the ship; and also, what rewards may be promised by articles to the widows and children of those who may unfortunately lose their lives in the engagement; 6. the extraordinary gratuity which a master may have promised his men, to animate them to a stout defence, or salvage of the vessel (*a*). *Magens* adopts this doctrine as an ordinance of *Hamburgh*; it is therefore, as well the opinion of *Magens*, as of an eminent civilized country. So, another author (*b*), commenting on the 9th article of the laws of *Oleron*, saith, " And in the same manner it is ordained to make an equal contribution for damages sustained by rovers and pirates;" [which must necessarily mean in the defence, as all writers agree that goods captured by pirates are not the subject of contribution;] " the good design of which law, is, to excite every individual mariner and other person in the ship, to do his duty, to which the consideration and apprehension of his own particular risk will not a little contribute." The several parts of this case must be divided, and it is extraordinary, that the legislature of *Hamburgh* made this ordinance contrary to the decision cited by *Kuricke* respecting damage to the ship. *Emerigon* himself, though he denies that the damage to the ship is general average, yet has a separate section in which he calls *matelots blessès* general average. Not a single writer says that seamen's wounds are not general average. As for the expenditure of powder, it comes literally within the term *jactus*: it is thrown overboard, and it is so disposed of for the bene-

(*a*) *Magens on Insurances,*   (*b*) *Treatise on the Dominion*
vol. i. p. 64. s. 57.   of the Sea, 1724, p. 93.

fit

fit of others: it is equally voluntary, as the throwing over of goods for lightening the ship.

Cur. adv. vult.

GIBBS C. J. on this day, after stating the pleadings and the evidence, now delivered the judgment of the Court. The question in this case is, whether the articles on which the Plaintiffs seek to recover, do or do not fall under the denomination of general average, as it is understood by merchants in this country. The doctrine of general average has its origin in the *Rhodian* law, *ut si levandæ navis gratiâ jactus mercium factus est, omnium contributione sarciatur, quod pro omnibus datum est.* Different countries of *Europe* have made different regulations, all professing to be founded on the *Rhodian* law, and differing from each other. The commentators on them have also differed. We have no such regulations in this country, and must therefore expound the law, as it affects this question, upon principle. The losses for which the Plaintiffs seek to recover this contribution, are of three descriptions: first, the damage sustained by the hull and rigging of the vessel, and the cost of her repairs; 2dly, the expence of the cure of the wounds received by the crew in defending the vessel; 3dly, the expenditure of powder and shot in the engagement. Nothing in foreign jurists ought to govern our judgment on these points, unless they have been sanctioned by received principles, decided cases, or the general usage of merchants. But we find none of these lights that might guide us. We have been so long involved in war, that similar circumstances must have been of general occurrence, and similar claims would have been made on the one side, and allowed and submitted to on the other, if they were founded in law: but this has not been the case, these losses must there-

15   fore

'fore be taken not to fall within the description of general average. If, however, it came within the principle, it would equally be due to the Plaintiffs, though this were the first instance in which the claim had been preferred. The measure of resisting the privateer was for the general benefit, but it was a part of the adventure. No particular part of the property was voluntarily sacrificed for the protection of the rest. The losses fell where the fortune of war cast them, and there, it seems to me, they ought to rest. It therefore follows, that these losses were not of the nature of general average, and that the Plaintiffs cannot recover. The rule therefore must be

1816.
TAYLOR
v.
CURTIS.

Discharged.

(IN THE EXCHEQUER-CHAMBER.)

EVERARD <i>v.</i> PATERSON.

10 B+C 210.

May 25.

THIS was a writ of error, brought to reverse a judgment of the Court of King's Bench, which had passed for the Plaintiff in an action of debt, wherein the first count shewed a submission to arbitration, so that the award were in writing, made under the hands of the arbitrators, and ready to be delivered on or before a day named, and averred that the arbitrators, in due manner, and before the day named, duly made their award in writing. The second count was debt on an *insimul computasset.* The Defendant below pleaded that the Plaintiff ought not to maintain his

Where a submission is " so that the award be in writing under the hand of the arbitrator," it must be shewn in pleading that the award is under hand, as well as in writing.

Where entire judgment is given for the Plaintiff

on two counts, one of which is bad, the Court may reverse it as to the first, and affirm it as to the second count.

action,

EVERARD
v.
PATERSON.

action, because he had before recovered judgment on
the same bond: the Plaintiff below replied *nul tiel record*, and, on an issue thereon joined, had judgment.

Nolan, for the Plaintiff in error, made two objections; 1st, that the award was not shewn to be under
the arbitrators' hands; 2dly, that the plea of *nul tiel
record* did not answer the count on the *insimul computasset*, and that the Plaintiff therefore was bound to
have signed judgment on the count which remained unanswered, and his omission so to do was a discontinuance of the whole action. As to the first point, he
urged that the special authority of an arbitrator must
be strictly pursued, and shewn in pleading so to be,
and cited to that effect *Hodsden* v. *Harridge* (a), *Henderson* v. *Williamson* (b), *Thaire* v. *Thaire* (c); and in
the report of that case in *Palmer*, Doddridge J. compared
it to the case of a power to revoke uses by deed under
hand and seal, where a revocation under seal only
would be clearly bad. S. P. *Gerdenfield* v. *Lane* (d). *Scott*
v. *Scott* (e). *Sallows* v. *Girling* (f). *Columbel* v. *Columbel* (g). 1 *Ro. Ab.* (h) *Wright* v. *Wakeford* (i). *Doe ex dem.
Mansfield* v. *Peach* (k). *Doe, on demise of Hodgkiss,* v.
Pearce (l). Upon the second objection, to shew that
when the plea does not answer the whole declaration,
the Plaintiff may and ought to sign judgment by *nil
dicit* for the parts which are unanswered, he cited
Woodward v. *Robinson* (m). *Earl of Manchester* v.

(a) 2 *Williams's Saunders*,
61. G. *note* 3.
  (b) 1 *Str.* 116.
  (c) 2 *Ro. Rep.* 183. and 243.
S. P. *Palm.* 109. and 112.
  (d) *Palm.* 121.
  (e) 1 *Bulst.* 110.
  (f) *Cro. Jac.* 277.

(g) 2 *Mod.* 77.
  (h) 1 *Rol. Abr. Arbitrament,* B.
page 245. *pl.* 25.
  (i) *Ante,* iv. 214.
  (k) 2 *Maule & Selw.* 576.
  (l) *Ante,* vi. 402.
  (m) 1 *Str.* 303.

Vale

Vale (a). *Vincent* v. *Beston* (b). And that if he does
not, but pleads over, it is a discontinuance, and he cannot maintain any judgment at all. *Tippet* v. *May* (c).
[*The Court* expressed a decided opinion that the point
made did not here arise, for the plea did purport to
answer the whole scope of the action, though the matter
pleaded, that the Plaintiff had recovered one half of
his demand, was not an effectual bar to his action for
the other half, and the Plaintiff might have taken advantage of the weakness of the plea upon demurrer,
but if he omitted to demur, he did not thereby discontinue his action.]

    Littledale, contrà, contended that the words " duly,"
and " in due manner," involved the allegation that the
award was made with those formalities which the submission required, and were equivalent to an express
averment that the award was made under the hands of
the arbitrators. If, indeed, the award were not made
in conformity to the submission, it would be no award;
so that the bare allegation that they made their award,
comprised an averment of all the qualities that the award
ought to possess; or, at all events, the omission more
fully to set out the requisites, could only form an objection on special demurrer. It was a test of sufficient
certainty, if an issue could be taken on the allegation;
and an issue joined on a plea of " no award," must
be found for the Defendant, unless the award produced
in evidence possessed all the requisites of the submission,
for it would not otherwise be in due manner made. In
Dudlow v. *Watchorn* (d) an averment that no writ of
capias ad satisfaciendum was " duly" sued out, was

<hr>

(a) 1 *Williams's Saunders*, 28.   (c) 1 *Bos. & Pull.* 411.
note 3.   (d) 16 *East,* 39.
    (b) 1 *Ld. Ray.* 716.

                                 held

held to be satisfied by shewing that no writ of *capias ad satisfaciendum* was sued out in such a manner as the practice of the Court warranted. [*Gibbs* C. J. In *Dudlow* v. *Watchorn* the word *duly* is followed by a reference to the custom and practice of the Court.] It is unnecessary to aver many circumstances, which must nevertheless appear in evidence, being required by law; as, for example, the statute of frauds (*a*), where by the 1st section, leases, by the 3d assignments and surrenders, by the 4th agreements, by the 17th sales of goods, and by the statute 3 & 4 *Ann. c.* 9. *s.* 1. promissory notes, must be made in writing, and under the hand of, or signed by, the parties, yet compliance with the statutes in these particulars need not be averred. *Elliott* v. *Cooper* (*b*). S. P. *Taylor* v. *Dobbins* (*c*), there cited. So, it needs not to be alleged that a bill of exchange was made according to the custom of merchants. *Ereskine* v. *Murray* (*d*). S. P. *Smith* v. *Jarves* (*e*). So, in debt on a bail-bond, it need not be averred that it was assigned according to the form of the statute. *Dawes* v. *Patworth* (*f*). And though, in an anonymous case (*g*), it was once said, that in pleading a will of land, it was necessary to shew that it was executed according to the statute, because a will is wholly the creature of statute, yet it is unnecessary so to do, and the practice is universally contrary. (To which the Court assented.) The authority of the old cases on awards is now much slighted: moreover, in *Thaire* v. *Thaire, Gardenfield* v. *Lane, Columbel* v. *Columbel,* and *Scott* v. *Scott,* it appears that the requisites were not in fact pursued by the award. The case of *Henderson* v. *Williamson* occurred so soon after the statute 4 *Ann. c.* 16, for special demurrers, that the Court may, in their decision on

(*a*) 29 *Car.* 2. *c.* 3.
(*b*) 2 *Ld. Raym.* 1376.
(*c*) 1 *Str.* 399.
(*d*) 2 *Ld. Raym.* 1542.

(*e*) *Ibid.* 1484.
(*f*) *Willes,* 408.
(*g*) *Salk.* 519. *pl.* 17.

a gena general demurrer, have conformed to the earlier cases, though the objection taken, in truth, only went to the form. In *Bowdell* v. *Parsons* (a) the Court of King's Bench held that by this statute an averment of request might be dispensed with, and that the Court should give judgment according to the very right of the cause, by the aid of which right this Court may also affirm the present judgment for the Plaintiff.

Nolan, in reply. The authority of *Doddridge*, the author of *Shepherd's Touchstone*, is of great weight. The case of *The King* v. *Lyme Regis* (b), where the effect of the words " duly elected" underwent much discussion, and it was held that they did not supply the place of an allegation of the circumstances of the election, disposes of the argument raised on the words " duly," and " in due manner:" but, secondly, if the word " duly," standing by itself, would suffice, yet the Plaintiff himself explains what he thereby means, by adding the words " in writing," and thereby impliedly excluding from the award the character of being under the arbitrator's hand. In four of the cases cited the fact how the award is made no otherwise appears than on the pleadings. The case in 1 *Ro. Ab.* 225., is distinct from *Thaire* v. *Thaire*, and is therein cited. Wherever a special authority is created, those who give it, have the right to annex to it their own terms, and a compliance with them is matter of substance, and must be shewn in pleading.

Cur. adv. vult.

On this day GIBBS C. J. delivered the opinion of the Court, that the Plaintiff in error was entitled to reverse the judgment, so far as it respected the first count; but that the Defendant in error was entitled to maintain his judgment on the last count.

(a) 10 *East*, 359.　　　　(b) 1 *Doug.* 79.

May 27.

CRESWELL *v.* PACKHAM.

After judgment for the Plaintiff on demurrer without argument, and general damages assessed, the Court will not permit the Defendant to move in arrest of judgment on the ground that the damages appear to be partly given upon a count which cannot be sustained, because the Defendant had the opportunity of excepting to that count on demurrer.

THE declaration contained three special counts, and the money counts. The Defendant demurred, alleging that the said declaration and the matters therein contained were not sufficient in law. The Plaintiff joined in demurrer, averring that the declaration and the matters therein contained were sufficient. There was no argument, and the judgment was entered generally, that the declaration was sufficient. A writ of inquiry was afterwards executed, evidence was given upon the special counts, and general damages were found.

Heywood Serjt. had on a former day obtained a rule *nisi* to arrest the judgment in this case on certain objections to the special counts.

Best Serjt. in shewing cause, took a preliminary objection, that according to the case of *Edwards* v. *Blunt* (a), no motion in arrest of judgment can be entertained after judgment on demurrer.

Heywood in support of his rule. The case cited is good law, but the reason does not extend to the present case. The reason is, that no one shall be heard to tell the Court that the judgment they have given on mature deliberation is wrong, unless they do it through the solemnities of a court of error; but this motion being made after a writ of inquiry executed, but before final judgment, is not attended with that inconvenience; and the objection on which the motion is grounded could not have been taken advantage of in any earlier stage of the proceedings, for it is this: the declaration containing certain counts which were good, and certain which were

(a) *1 Str.* 426.

bad,

bad, the jury have assessed general damages, for which an entire judgment cannot be supported. But it could not be foreseen before the writ of inquiry executed, that the jury would not assess separate damages on the good counts alone, instead of assessing, as they have here done, general damages upon all the counts: therefore the Defendant could not sooner object.

By *The Court.* The doctrine of that case of *Edwards* v. *Blunt* is, that where the Defendant might, on arguing the demurrer, have availed himself of the exception, he shall not afterwards move in arrest of judgment. The Defendant might have taken this exception, in substance, on the demurrer, for he might have objected to the vitious counts, and having obtained judgment on them, no damages could ever have been assessed thereon. And he is not without remedy by writ of error. It is more convenient to adhere to that practice, than to indulge the Defendant with relief now on motion. Though I am aware of the new view in which the objection presents itself, namely, that judgment cannot be with propriety entered for these general damages; yet it is more convenient to compel parties to come in the first instance with every objection.

Rule discharged.

1816.

May 27.

Fox, Demandant; BEMBOW, Tenant; Earl GOWER and Others, Vouchees.

The Court will not amend a warrant of attorney, because it is the act of the party.

The Court will, on the last day of term, receive no motion either for amending or for passing recoveries.

*H*EYWOOD Serjt. moved to amend the warrant of attorney in this case, by adding after the words " to gain and lose in a plea of land," the words "against *Richard Fox*."

But *the Court* peremptorily refused, as they before had frequently done, to amend a warrant of attorney, which was the act of the party: if the warrant of attorney had the desired effect without amendment, the amendment was unnecessary; if the amendment would alter the effect of the act of the party, the Court ought not to allow it.

Heywood then prayed that it might pass without amendment, it appearing by the *præcipe*, ingrossed at the head of the warrant of attorney, that the plea of land in which the attorney was to be constituted, was between *Richard Fox* and *Bembow*. (a)

But *the Court* persisted in adhering to their rule of not entertaining on the last day of term motions which required such minute and critical attention as those which relate to recoveries, and refused the application.

(a) *Forster*, Demandant, &c. *ante*, vi. 373.

END OF EASTER TERM.

AN

INDEX

PRINCIPAL MATTERS

CONTAINED IN THIS VOLUME.

A

ABATEMENT.

1. WHERE a Defendant sued by a wrong name, omits to plead in abatement, and suffers the Plaintiff to proceed to judgment, though he never has appeared to the wrong name, this court will not interfere to set aside the proceedings. *Smith* v. *Patten. Page* 115

2. If a plea commencing in abatement shew matter in bar, and conclude in abatement, it is a plea in abatement, not in bar. 587

3. And the Defendant cannot, by any election subsequent to the time of plea pleaded, convert it to a plea in bar. *ib.*

4. A plea in abatement that the De-

fendant jointly with 16 others contracted, imports that the Defendant jointly with 16 others, and with no more, contracted. *Page* 587

5. And if there were more joint contractors than seventeen, the plea is disproved. *Godson* v. *Good. ib.*

ABSTRACT,

See TITLE.

ACCEPTANCE,

See BILLS OF EXCHANGE,

ACTION UPON THE CASE,

And see AMENDMENT, 13. PLEADER, IV. 4.

1. Several tort feasors who unite in an injurious act, may be sued each one singly. 29

U u 2. One

2. One who in the exercise of a public function, destitute of emolument, which he is compellable to execute, acting without malice, and according to his best skill and diligence, and obtaining the best information he can, does an act which occasions consequential damage to a subject, is not liable to an action for such damage.   *Page* 29

3. The trustees of a turnpike road, empowered to make watercourses to prevent the road from being overflowed, directed their surveyor to present a plan for carrying off the water of an adjacent brook: he recommended, and on that recommendation they adopted, and caused him to make, a wide channel from the road, gradually narrowing, and conducting the water into the ordinary fence ditches of the Plaintiff's land; which were insufficient to discharge it, and his land was consequently overflowed. Held that no action lay against the chairman of the trustees who signed the order for cutting the trench. *Sutton* v. *Clarke.*   29

ACTION, LIMITATION OF.

1. If a statute directs that an action shall be commenced within six months after the matter or thing for which such action shall be brought, and in consequence of the cutting of a trench, a fall of rain causes the Plaintiff's land to be overflowed, first, within six months, and again, after six months from cutting the trench, whether the action must be brought within six

months from the cutting of the trench, or within six months from the perception of the first prejudicial effect, or whether it may be brought within six months from the last injury, *quære. Sutton* v. *Clarke.*
          Page 29

2. A statement by a debtor made to an executor that the testator always promised not to press the Defendant for a debt, is not evidence to prove a promise made to the testator to pay within six years. *Ward* v. *Hunter.*   211

ACCOUNT,

See PAYMENT. INSURANCE, II. 2.

ADMINISTRATOR,

See EXECUTOR.

AFFIDAVIT,

And see ARBITRATION. PRACTICE, I.

1. It is not necessary that an affidavit made by the Defendant in the cause, stating his abode and styling him Defendant, should also contain the addition of his degree. *Anonymous.*
          73

2. In an action against two, not bailable, one Defendant may before declaration well style his affidavit "in a cause of *A.* against *B.* who is sued with *C.*" *Mackenzie* v. *Martin.*   286

AFFIDAVIT TO HOLD TO BAIL,

And see INSOLVENT, 5.

1. An affidavit to hold to bail on promissory notes, must state that the Defendant

Defendant is indebted " to the Plaintiff." *Balbi* v. *Batley. Page* 25

2. The Court will not discharge the Defendant out of custody on a defect in the affidavit to hold to bail, after he has given bail to the sheriff, and bail to the action, which last have rendered him. *Shawman* v. *Whalley.* 185

3. An affidavit to hold to bail, stating that the Defendant is indebted to the Plaintiff, for goods sold and delivered to the Defendant, not saying " by the Plaintiff," is bad. *Fenton* v. *Ellis.* 192

4. A supplemental affidavit to hold to bail not allowed. *ib.*

5. An affidavit to hold to bail for the " hire of carriages hired to the defendant," and for " work and labour done for the defendant," not adding at his request, held sufficient. *Brown* v. *Garnier.* 389

6. Affidavit to hold to bail, stating that the Defendant is indebted to the Plaintiff as indorsee on a bill drawn by a stranger, is insufficient. *Humphries* v. *Winslow.* 531

AGREEMENT,

See GOODS, CONTRACT FOR SALE OF. LESSOR AND LESSEE, 1. STAMPS. TITLE. VENDOR AND VENDEE.

ALIEN ENEMY.

1. An alien, to whom a bill of exchange, drawn on *England* by a *British* subject detained prisoner in *France* during war, payable to another *British* subject detained there, is there indorsed by the latter, may sue on it in this country after the return of peace. *Antoine* v. *Morshead. Page* 237

2. It is no defence to an action on a bill of exchange, that the Plaintiff sues in trust for an alien enemy. *Daubuz* v. *Morshead.* 332

AMBIGUITY (LATENT),

See EVIDENCE, II. 1.

AMENDMENT OF FINES AND RECOVERIES,

See FINES AND RECOVERIES, AMENDMENT OF.

AMENDMENT.

1. The Court will not alter the memorandum of a declaration in a penal action at the mere instance of the plaintiff, without a reason shewn. *Woodroffe* q. t. v. *Williams.* 19

2. The Court will not amend, to the prejudice of an executor, a judgment which two terms since passed for him on demurrer. *Prince* v, *Nicholson.* 45

3. The Court cannot amend a deed. *Steel, Demandant; Clennel, Tenant; Benn, Vouchee.* 145

4. The count in partition, writ to the sheriff, and his return, amended by striking out words of limitation in tail, where the title stated on the count shewed an estate · in fee. *Baker* v. *Daniel.* 193

5. Where the Court, on demurrer, gives leave to amend by stating particularly that which before was stated too generally, the Plaintiff may add new counts, though more than two terms have elapsed from the commencement of the suit, if

they contain no new cause of action, but only various specifications of the matter which the Court permitted to be more particularly stated. *Brown* v. *Crump.*   **Page 300**

6. In an action by the assignees of a bankrupt for a rescue, the Plaintiffs were permitted, after two terms, to amend the declaration, which stated the wrong to be done to themselves, by stating the wrong to be done to the provisional assignees. *Freen* v. *Cooper.*   358

7. The Court will not permit a Plaintiff to amend by changing the venue without reasonable ground. *Ayres* v. *Buston.*   408

8. The Court will not amend a warrant of attorney, because it is the deed of the party. *Forster, Demandant.* 373. *S. P. Fox, Demandant; Earl Gower, Vouchee.*   632, (misprinted 652)

9. An amendment of the Plaintiff's declaration does not necessarily entitle the Defendant to plead *de novo*, but only where the amendment alters the state of the Defendant's case. *Woodroffe* v. *Watson.* 400

10. The statute 7 *G.* 2. *c.* 8. is a remedial rather than a penal act. 419

11. Where the Plaintiffs had commenced an action of *assumpsit* for money had and received, to recover back differences paid on stock-jobbing contracts, and had filed a bill of discovery, to which the Defendant pleaded that the discovery was given by the statute 7 *G.* 2. *c.* 8. *s.* 2. in debt only, the Court permitted the Plaintiffs, after six terms from the commencement of the action, to amend by changing *assumpsit* to debt. *Billing* v. *Flight.*   **Page 419**

12. So, where no bill in equity had been filed for a discovery, the Court permitted the Plaintiffs to amend by converting their declaration from *assumpsit* to debt. *Billing* v. *Pooley.*   422

13. Where the Plaintiff had sued out process in debt, and declared in case, and thereby discharged the bail, the Court refused to amend the declaration by altering it from debt to case, so as to hold the bail still liable. *Levett* v. *Kibblewhite.*   488

ANNUITY.

And see BOND, *and* REPLEVIN.

1. An attorney, grantee of an annuity, preparing the securities, and, upon payment of the whole consideration money, retaining his charges thereout, one of which is for business never done, does not thereby necessarily avoid the annuity under 17 *G.* 3. *c.* 26. *s.* 4.; but it is a question for a jury, whether the improper charge was made with intent to get back a part of the consideration money. *Hurd* v. *Girdlestone.*   8.

2. The memorial of an annuity stated the names of two witnesses as attesting the execution of an annuity deed, who also attested the execution of a warrant of attorney for further securing the annuity, but that fact was not noticed in the memorial. Held that the names of all

all the witnesses were sufficiently stated.   Page 124

3. A memorial of an annuity deed stated the contract, and payment of the price, and that for the considerations aforesaid, and for further and better securing the annuity, the grantor demised to *J. T. W.* upon the trusts in the indenture expressed. Held that it sufficiently appeared for whom *J. T. W.* was a trustee.   *ib.*

4. The memorial of an annuity needs not to state the names of the attornies to whom a warrant to confess judgment is given.   *ib.*

5. If a memorial of an annuity be defective in stating one of several securities, *semble*, that the particular instrument only is void, and not the other assurances. *Brown* v. *Rose.*   *ib.*

6. Where the grantor of an annuity had, upon a mistaken claim of the grantee, paid a half yearly instalment for half a year sooner than the deed required it, held that this did not avoid the annuity. 189

7. A memorial describing an annuity-bond as bearing date on or about a day named, states the date with sufficient certainty.   *ib.*

8. A memorial of an annuity-bond needs not to state that the heirs of the obligor are bound.   *ib.*

9. A memorial of an annuity-deed stated a recital in the deed that a warrant of attorney and a defeazance had been given, which recital shortly set out the defeazance; held that this supplied the place of a substantive memorial of the de-

feazance. *Jackson* v. Lord *Milsington* and *Another.*   Page 189

10. An annuity deed contained a covenant by the grantor to insure a house charged with the annuity and assigned, for better securing the payment, to a trustee, upon trust to mortgage and sell in case the annuity were in arrear 40 days; and further, that if the grantor omitted to insure, the grantee might insure, and that the premiums with interest should be a charge on the premises, and that the Plaintiff might raise that money in the same manner as he might raise the annuity by virtue of the trusts aforesaid. Held that a memorial fully noticing the trust for raising the arrears, and noticing the grantor's covenant to insure and keep insured, and that on default it should be lawful for the Plaintiff to insure and keep insured, " as in the indenture was mentioned," sufficiently stated the name of the trustee, and for whom he was trustee. *Bleamire* v *Barfoot.* .   504

ARBITRATION.

And see INSURANCE, 6.

1. The Court is not limited by time from setting aside an award founded on a submission by rule of Court in an action pending, where there has been a plain mistake of the arbitrator, although the application be not made in the term next after making the award.   111

2. But in ordinary cases they will look to the limitation of time given by the stat. 9 & 10 *W.* & *M. c.* 15.

U u 3   as

as a rule to guide their discretion as to the time of reviewing awards. *Rogers* v. *Dallimore.*   Page 111

3. Where arbitrators have power to enlarge the time for making their award, and have enlarged it, and made their award in the additional time, in order to bring the Defendant into contempt for non-performance of the award, there must be an affidavit that the time has been enlarged, that the award was made within the enlarged time, and that the Defendant has been personally served with notice of those facts.   251

4. *Semble* that the affidavit for an attachment for non-performance of an award, must, contrary to the usual practice, always state the time of execution of the award. *Wohlenberg* v. *Lageman.*   ib.

5. Though an arbitrator on a question of mixed law and fact has allowed transactions apparently illegal, as premiums of insurance on a voyage to an hostile port, the Court will not on that account set aside the award.   ib.

6. An award that two persons shall pay a debt in proportion to the shares which they held in a certain ship, the ratio of their shares not being a subject of dispute, is sufficiently certain.   ib.

7. Upon an award to perform a purchase of land, and pay the price upon conveyance of the land by the Plaintiff to the Defendant, the Defendant is not in contempt before tender of a conveyance executed, and demand of the money, and re-

fusal to accept and pay.   *Standley* v. *Hemington.*   Page 561

8. Where a submission is, "so that the award be in writing under the hand of the arbitrator," it must be shewn in pleading that the award is under hand, as well as in writing. *Everard* v. *Paterson.*
    645, *perperàm pro* 625

ARREST,

And see AFFIDAVIT TO HOLD TO BAIL. PRACTICE, II.

ARREST OF JUDGMENT,

See JUDGMENT, 6.

ASSIGNEE OF LEASE,

See COVENANT, 3.

ASSIGNEES OF BANKRUPT,

See AMENDMENT, 6. BANKRUPT, III. INSURANCE, VI. 4.

ASSUMPSIT,

See AMENDMENT, 10, 11, 12.

ATTACHMENT,

See ARBITRATION, 4. BAILBOND, 2. PRACTICE, IV. 6. SHERIFF, 4, 5.

ATTACHMENT, FOREIGN,

See FOREIGN ATTACHMENT.

ATTESTATION.

1. A power to appoint by deed or writing under the donee's hand and seal, and attested by two or more credible witnesses, is ill pursued by a will apparently under the testator's

tor's hand and seal, which seal an attesting witness believes was affixed before execution and attestation, if the attestation does not notice the sealing as well as the signing.
Page 402

2 A defective attestation of the execution of a power cannot be supplied by parol evidence of the attesting witness to be given on a trial. *Doe* v. *Pearce.*   402

ATTESTING WITNESSES,

And see ANNUITY.

An executor of a testator possessed of real and personal estate cloathed with a trust to pay debts, and to lay out money for the benefit of the testator's children, and with a power to sell freehold lands in fee, but taking no beneficial interest under the will, is a good attesting witness to the will. *Phipps* v. *Pitcher.*   220

ATTORNEY GENERAL.

Order of precedency of the Attorney and Solicitor General before the King's Serjeants.   424

ATTORNEY,

And see ANNUITY AND NOTICE.

1. The Court will entertain a summary jurisdiction over one of its officers, who is employed as steward of a manor, to make him deliver up Court rolls and muniments of his employer.   105

2. And also, it seems, to make him pay over rents received.   *ib.*

3. An attorney holding over rents received is not compellable to pay interest on them, *semble.* *Ex parte Corpus Christi College.* Page 105

4. The admission of an attorney who has omitted to take out his certificate for one whole year after his admission is absolutely void, and he must be re-admitted before he can practise. *Ex parte Nicholas.*   408

5. The notice of intention to apply for admission as an attorney, required by the rule of Court *Trin.* term 31 *G. 3.*, must be given during the term next immediately preceding the application. *Ex parte Bonner.*   335

ATTORNEY's BILL,

And see ANNUITY, 1.

A Plaintiff's attorney, who, at the Defendant's request, puts in bail for him, and afterwards pays the debt and costs, needs not deliver a bill a month before he sues for the money so advanced. *Prothero* v. *Thomas.*   196

AUCTIONEER.

See GOODS, CONTRACT FOR SALE OF.

AVERAGE GENERAL,

The expenditure of ammunition in resisting capture by a privateer, the damage done to the ship in the combat, and the expence of curing the wounded sailors, are not the subject of general average by the law of England. *Taylor and Others* v. *Curtis.*   608

AVERMENT.

Upon bond conditioned that a collector of poor-rates shall render an account of monies received, after general performance pleaded, in assigning a breach that he did not render an account, *semble* that it is necessary to aver that he received monies to be accounted for. *Serra* v. *Wright.*   Page 45

AWARD,

See ARBITRATION.

―――――――

B

BAIL.

I. *Of the Arrest and the Bail.*
    See *Practice,* I. II.
II. *Proceedings against the Bail or the Sheriff.*
III. *Surrender of the Principal.*
    See *Affidavit to hold to Bail.*
IV. *Discharge by other Means.*

II.

And see SHERIFF.

1. If bail above who are excepted to and have not justified, afterwards procure their recognizance to be put on the roll, the Court will, at the instance of a Plaintiff suing on the bail bond, cause the recognizance to be taken off, that the Defendants may not prove by that evidence the issue of *comperuerunt ad diem. Leigh* v. *Bertles.*   167

2. In an action on a recognizance of bail, the bail must be served with process four days before the return of the writ. *Mackenzie* v. *Martin:*   *Page* 286

IV.

1. The Court will not exonerate the bail upon the Defendant having become bankrupt and obtained his certificate, without giving the Plaintiff an opportunity of trying, by an issue, whether the certificate were fairly obtained. *Woolcot* v. *Leicester.*   75

2. The Court will not on motion exonerate bail upon the ground that the cause of action for which they are bail, is money paid for their principal, who is a bankrupt, by his sureties, who therefore might have proved under the commission by 49 *G.*3. *c.*121. *s.*8.   *Hewes* v. *Mott.*   329

3. Bail to the sheriff are not sureties within the statute 49 *G.*3. *c.*122. *s.*8.   *ib.*

BAIL BOND,

And see SHERIFF.

1. Where, upon a *capias* returnable in the Common Pleas, the sheriff made a mandate to the high bailiff of the honor of *Pomfret,* to take the Defendant, so that the sheriff might have him before his said Majesty at *Westminster* in five weeks of *Easter,* a bail-bond taken with condition for the Defendants' appearance before his said Majesty at *Westminster* in five weeks of *Easter,* was held to describe an

appear-

appearance in the Court of King's
Bench, therefore void. *Renalds*
v. *Smith*.   Page 551
2. A sheriff may take a bail bond on
an attachment out of Chancery.
569
3. But he is not compellable to take
bail thereon. *Morris* v. *Hayward*.
ib.

BANKRUPT.

I. *Of the Bankruptcy and Com-
mission.*
II. *Of the Bankrupt's Rights and
Duties.*
III. *Of the Bankrupt's Estate.*

I.

1. If a sheriff's officer having arrested
a Defendant on mesne process in
his own house, who is dangerously
ill, leaves him there until he is recovered in the custody of a follower not named in the warrant, this
is such a legal custody, that if an imprisonment, of which this is a part,
be continued for two months, it
will constitute an act of bankruptcy.
Stevens v. *Jackson*.   106
2. A servant of the proprietor of a
newspaper, subject to dismissal at
pleasure, who daily directs the
number of copies to be printed,
purchases the whole impression,
retails them, and is paid for his
services by getting 1s. 6d. per quire
on all that he sells, sustaining the
loss which occurs by those copies
which remain unsold, is a trader
within the bankrupt laws.   532
3. A news-vender, who frequented

the Royal Exchange for the purpose of collecting intelligence for
a newspaper, appointed a creditor
to meet him on the Royal Exchange, and afterwards directed a
friend, if the creditor inquired there
for him, to say he was not there.
Held that this was an "otherwise
absenting himself," which constituted an act of bankruptcy within
the statute 1 *Jac.* 1. *c.* 15. *s.* 2.
Page 532
4. So, where he saw a creditor at the
theatre, and secreted himself under
the stage for the purpose of avoiding him. *Gillingham* v. *Laing*. *ib.*
5. Where a trader made a fraudulent
assignment of his tavern and stock,
accompanied with possession, and
changed his residence from *Westminster* to *Paddington*, and a commission of bankrupt having issued
against him, the assignee brought
trespass against the messenger for
taking possession of the tavern and
goods. Held, 1. that, however
fraudulent the deed as against creditors, yet, unless an act of bankruptcy was proved to sustain the
commission, the assignee might recover on her possession; 2. that
it ought to be left to a jury whether
the trader's change of residence
was a departing from his dwelling-
house with intent to delay his creditors. *Young* v. *Wright*.   540

II.

See AMENDMENT, 6. BAIL, IV.
1, 2, 3. INSURANCE, V. PLEAD-
ING, I.

III.

III.

BARRATRY.

BENEFICE.

BILL, DELIVERY OF,

BILLS OF EXCHANGE,

BILLS OF EXCHANGE.

BOND.

BOND,

And see AVERMENT. PLEADING, IV. 2.

1. In debt on bond given to the obligee, conditioned for payment of an annual sum to the wife of the obligor, a breach assigned in non-payment of the annual sum to the obligee is ill. *Lunn* v. *Payne.*
Page 140

2. Upon bond conditioned that a collector of poor-rates shall render an account of monies received, after general performance pleaded, in assigning a breach that he did not render an account, *semble*, that it is necessary to aver that he received monies to be accounted for. *Serra and Others* v. *Wright.* 45

BROKER,

See INSURANCE, VI. AUCTIONEER, 1 GOODS, CONTRACT FOR SALE OF.

BULLION,

See FREIGHT, 7. SHIP, 5.

━━━━━

C

CANAL COMPANY.

A canal act gave a higher tonnage for light goods than for heavy goods. If a jury find that certain goods were heavy goods when the act passed, ten years' subsequent consent of the country to consider the same species as light goods, will not entitle the canal company

to demand for these the toll on light goods. *Staffordshire and Worcestershire Canal Company* v. *Trent and Mersey Canal Company.*
Page 151

CARRIER,

See FREIGHT, 7. SHIP, 5. WORK AND LABOUR, 1.

CASES—*observed on, questioned, explained, or over-ruled.*

Allingham v. Flower, (2 Bos. & Pull. 246.)   556
Blakey v. Porter, (ante, 1. 386.) 304
Bowen v. Ashley, (1 New Rep. 274.)   175
Law v. Ibbotson, (5 Burr. 2722.) 200
Price v. Neal, (3 Burr. 1354. and 1 Bl. 390.)   84
Roberts v. Read, (16 East, 216.)   40. n.
Schimmell v. Lousada, (4 Taunt. 695.)   90

CERTIFICATE,

See CLERGY.

CHANCERY,

See BAILBOND, 2. NEW TRIAL, 2.

CHARITABLE USES.

1. A grant of lands in trust perpetually to repair, and, if need be, rebuild a vault and tomb standing on the land, and permit the same to be used as a family vault for the donor and her family, is not a charitable use within the statute. 9 G. 2. c. 36.   359

2. If there be in a deed one limitation to an use which is a charitable use

use within the statute 9 *G. 2. c. 36.*, that statute does not therefore avoid other limitations in the same deed, which are not within the act. *Doe dem. Thompson* v. *Pitcher.*

Page 359

CHARTER-PARTY,

See DEED, 4.

CHURCHWARDENS,

See CLERGY. MONEY HAD AND RECEIVED, 3.

CLERGY,

And see TITHES.

1. A private act annexed the rectory of *H.* to the deanery of *Windsor*, and recited that the necessary residence on the deanery, and the Dean's attendance on her Majesty, as Registrar of the Order of the Garter, would oblige him to be often absent from *H.*, and the act compelled him to appoint a stipendiary curate constantly resident at *H.* *Semble* that this, without more, conferred an excuse for non-residence at *H.*, although in the subsequent act, 43 *G. 3. c. 84.*, imposing residence on all benefices not therein excepted, this is not enumerated as a ground of exemption or of licence. 48

2. Where a private act "united" and "annexed" a rectory in the diocese of *O.* to a deanery in the diocese of *S.*, and dispensed with any presentation to the Dean, but left institution and induction still necessary, held, that the licence from the Bishop of *O.* for non-re-

· 10

sidence on the rectory was necessary, as well as a licence for non-residence on the deanery from the Bishop of *S.* Page 48

3. Where the defendant had first ruled the plaintiffs to discontinue an action for non-residence. on a notification of exemption, which the plaintiffs had agreed to admit, and traverse the title, held, that the defendant might afterwards have another rule to discontinue as to the same benefice, if he could shew a sufficient ground. *Wright* v. *Legge.* ib.

4. It is no ground within stat. 43 *G. 3. c. 84. s. 19.* for a licence of non-residence upon a benefice in one diocese, that a bishop of another diocese has licensed the incumbent's non-residence on a benefice within that diocese, because he had no house on that benefice, and lived within two miles thereof, and did the duty. 52

5. And a licence granted on that ground would not be valid without the allowance of the archbishop, under *s.* 20. ib.

6. The non residence on one benefice under a licence from the diocesan thereof, is not equivalent to actual residence thereon, so as to excuse the incumbent's non-residence on another benefice. ib.

7. Therefore a bishop's retrospective certificate that he would have granted a licence of non-residence because the incumbent was performing the duties of another benefice, within two miles of which he lived by licence from another diocesan,

cesan, not being allowed by the archbishop, is void. *Page 52*

8. But is good with the archbishop's certificate, though the latter be granted after 1st *July* 1814. *Wright* v. *Flamank.* ib.

9. If a clergyman who has two livings resides within one of the parishes, wherein there is no house of residence, it is a sufficient residence there to exempt him, without licence from the bishop, from penalties for not residing on his other benefice. 198

10. No licence is necessary for nonresidence in the parsonage-house of a parish wherein there is no such house. *Ib. Wynne* v. *Smithies.* ib.

11. A practice had prevailed during the incumbency of several vicars, that upon the burial of any stranger in the parish of *H.* certain fees should be paid, of which the vicar took one moiety, and the churchwardens the other for the use of the poor. The fees were paid to the sexton, who paid over the moieties to the respective parties. A new vicar refused to accede to this arrangement, he buried several strangers, and procured the sexton, to whom the fees were paid, to pay over the entire fees to himself. Held that the churchwardens might recover from the vicar one moiety, as money had and received to their use. *Littlewood* v. *Williams*, Clerk. 277

COMMISSION,
See PRACTICE, 3.

COMMISSION DEL CREDERE,
See INSURANCE, VI.

COMMON RECOVERY,
See FINES AND RECOVERIES, PRACTICE OF PASSING, AND FINES AND RECOVERIES, AMENDMENT OF.

COMPRISE,
And see FINES AND RECOVERIES, PRACTICE OF PASSING, 1.

Semble that by the grant of lands in a vill, only those lands will pass which lie in a vill bearing a different name from the parish. *Cotterel, Plaintiff; Franklin and Wife, Deforciants.* *Page* 284

CONSIGNOR AND CONSIGNEE,
See FREIGHT. INSURANCE. PLEADING, IV. 3.

CONTEMPT,
See ARBITRATION. BAILBOND, 2.

CONVEYANCE,
See DEED. PAWNEE.

CONVOY,
See INSURANCE, I. 8.

COPY,
See FINE, PRACTICE OF PASSING, 2. DEED, 4.

COPYHOLD,
And see STEWARD.

There is no general custom for all copyholds. *Everest* v. *Glyn.* 425

CORPO-

CORPORATION,

See DEED, 5.

COSTS,

See INSOLVENT. PRACTICE, VIII. JURISDICTION. JUDGMENT. COURT OF REQUESTS. 1.

COVENANT,

And see FREIGHT, PRACTICE, V. 3.

1. The lessee of a public house covenanted to buy of the lessor all the malt he should brew into ale or beer, or otherwise use therein ; and the lessor covenanted to deliver on request sufficient good, well dried, marketable malt, for the use of the Defendant in the demised premises, and that at a market price, but if the Plaintiff should neglect so to do, the Defendant might purchase of any others. In an action for buying malt of others, a plea that the Plaintiff for a long time would not deliver good malt, but delivered divers quantities of bad malt, whereby the Defendant was in danger of losing his custom, and therefore bought malt of others, was held ill on demurrer. *Weaver* v. *Sessions.*   *Page* 154

2. A lessor possessed of considerable freehold and leasehold property lying together, covenanted in a lease of parcel, that if he, his heirs or assigns, should, during the term, have any advantageous offer for the disposing of a certain adjoining freehold parcel, he, the lessor, his heirs or assigns, should not dispose of the same without previously making an offer of that parcel to

the lessee, his executors, administrators, or assigns, at five *per cent.* less than that offer. The lessor sold his entire property, including the demised land and the adjoining parcel, for an entire consideration, in one entire contract, without offering the parcel to the covenantee. Held that this was no breach of the covenant. *Page* 224

3. Held that the covenant did not enure to the assignee of the lease, though named. *Collinson* v. *Lettsom.*   *ib.*

4. A covenant not to sue one of two joint debtors does not operate as a release to the other. *Hutton* v. *Eyre.*   289

COURT,

See WITNESS, 4.   BAILBOND, 1.

COURT OF COMMON PLEAS,

See PENAL ACTION, 2.

COURT OF CHANCERY,

See SHERIFF, 4.

COURT OF REQUESTS,

See JURISDICTION.

Although the sum for which a Plaintiff, subject to the jurisdiction of the *London* Court of Requests, sues in a Court at *Westminster,* exceed 5*l.*, yet if he recover a less sum than 5*l.* he is subject to double costs by the statute 39 & 40 G. 3. *c.* 104. *s.* 12. *Younger* v. *Wilsby.*   452

D

DAMAGES,

See ACTION UPON .THE CASE. AND FREIGHT.

DEATHS. 514, 515. 517.

DEBT,

And see AMENDMENT AND ARBITRATION.

A creditor receiving money without any specific appropriation by the debtor, may ascribe it to the payment of a prior and purely equitable debt, and sue him at law for a subsequent legal debt. *Bosanquet* v. *Wray.*   *Page* 597

DECEIT,

See PLEADER, III. 6.   IV. 4.

DEED,

And see PAWNEE, I. 2.   VARIANCE, I, 2.

1. The Court cannot amend a deed. *Steel, Demandant.*   145
2. Inspection refused to Plaintiff in replevin of a deed to which he was no party, assigning to the avowant the reverson of the demised premises. *Brown* v. *Rose.*   283
3. *Semble* that by the grant of lands in a vill, only those lands will pass which lie in a vill bearing a different name from the parish. *Cotterel, Plaintiff.*   ` 285
4. Where two parts of an indenture of charter-party were supposed to

have been interchangeably executed, and the part of which the master of the chartered vessel had the custody, was lost at sea with the ship, the Court would not compel the charterer, being sued thereon, to grant inspection and a copy of the other part, for the purpose of the Plaintiff's declaring with certainty. *Street* v. *Browne.*   *Page* 302

5. A corporation named " The Wardein and Poore of the Hospitall of the *Holie Trinitie* in *Croydon*, of the Foundation of *John Whitegift*, Archbishop of *Canterbury*," conveyed land under the land-tax redemption acts by the name of the " Wardein and Poore of the Hospitall of the *Holie Trinitie* in *Croydon*." The purchaser paid the vendors the purchase-money in discharge of the costs of sales of other lands made by the vendors for the redemption of the land-tax. Held, 1. that the variance in their name was not material; 2. that they might raise money by a latter sale for the costs of former sales; 3. that at all events this was a mistake or inadvertence cured by the statute 54 *G.* 3. *c.* 173. *s.* 12. *Croydon Hospital* v. *Farley.*   467
6. Lands " in the occupation of *A. B.* and *C.*" intended of the several occupations of *A. B.* and *C.* *Morgan* v. *Edwards.*   394

DEFENDANT,

See ACTION UPON THE CASE. AND PRACTICE, II.

DEMUR-

DEMURRER,

See JUDGMENT, LIBEL, PRACTICE,
IV.

DEVISE.

What Estate passes by what Words.

1. Devise to my wife *A.* all my real and personal estate, she first paying my just debts and funeral expences; and after her decease to the heirs of her body, share and share alike if more than one; and in default of issue, to be lawfully begotten by me, to be at her own disposal: there being children of the testator and his wife, held that the wife took only an estate for life, with remainder to all the children as tenants in common in fee. *Gretton and Others* v. *Haward and Others.* *Page* 94

2. Devise of a fee-simple estate expectant on the decease of *B.* to trustees and their executors, to receive and apply the rents to the maintenance and advancement of six of the testator's children till the youngest was twenty-one, and then to his said six children and the survivors and survivor of them, their heirs and assigns for ever, as tenants in common. Held that all such devisees as survived the testator took on his decease a vested estate in fee in common. *Edwards* v. *Symons.* 213

3. Devise to *H. S.*, my brother's son, to hold to him and his heirs, and in case my brother and his son should happen to die having no issue of either of their bodies, then to *J. Clerk* and his heirs. This is not a defeasible fee-simple

in *H. S.* the son, with an executory devise over, but an estate tail. *Page* 263

4. Whether a devisee in remainder can maintain a writ of intrusion, *ib.*

5. Or a writ to be framed on the statute of *Westminster* the 2d in the nature of a writ of intrusion, *quære.* *ib.*

6. Devise in fee, with an executory devise over, whether the fine of the devisee in fee shall bar the executory devise over, *quære.* *Romilly* v. *James.* *ib.*

7. Devise of all testator's free lands at *C.* or *K.* to *E.* his wife for life, and after her decease to his son *I. P.* and his heirs for ever; if it should happen that his son *I.* should die unpossest of them or without heirs, the testator gave them to his daughter *S. P.* and her heirs. Held that *I. P.* took an estate tail, remainder to his sister *S.* *Doe* v. *Black.* 485

8. Devise of all the testator's freehold lands, tenements, tythes, hereditaments, and premises in the parish of *B.* to trustees for 1000 years, in trust to raise 500*l.*; and; subject to that term, he devised all his said freehold lands, &c. to the testator's wife for her natural life, sans waste; remainder to his 2d son *T. A.* for life, sans waste; remainder to trustees to support contingent remainders; remainder to the first and other sons of *T. A.* in tail male; remainder to the 3d and other after-born sons of the testator (except his eldest son) in tail male; and if the testator should

have

have no third son, or when his son *T. A.*, or any of his sons except *H. U. A.*, should succeed to a certain estate entailed on *T. A.* by an uncle, the testator devised his said freehold estate in the parish of *B.* to his daughters *F.* and *C.*, and any other daughters he might thereafter have, to take as tenants in common. Held that the daughters took a fee. *Uthwatt* v. *Bryant.* Page 317

9. The word estate, used in the operative clause of a will, although referring to locality, conveys a fee-simple, unless there is in the will other matter to control that signification. *Randall* v. *Tuchin.* 410

10. Devise to *T. C.* of various houses, described by situation, abuttals, dimensions, and occupiers, " all which estates, being copyhold of the manor of *K.*, I devise to *T. C.* for life, and after his decease, to his son *M. C.*" Devise to *M. P.* of various other houses and premises similarly described, including the *White Bear* public-house, and abutting on the copyhold estate before given, " all which said estates being copyhold of the manor of *K.*, I devise to *M. P.* for life, and after her decease, to her son *M. P.*, and I order that so long as *W. P.* shall choose to live in the public-house and keep the same in good repair, he shall not be charged more than his present rent. And I devise to *M. P.*, the son, all my freehold estate, situate, &c. And I bequeath to *S. G.* and *H.* his wife, and the survivor, the

sum of 5s. *per* week out of the estates bequeathed to *M. P.* and *M. P.*." Held that *M. P.* the son took an estate in fee in the copyhold. *Randall* v. *Tuchin.*

Page 410

DEVISEE,

See DEVISE, 4, 5.

———

E

EJECTMENT,

See DEVISE.

ELEGIT.

Semble that tenant in *elegit* may enter by virtue of the writ of *elegit* without a prior judgment in ejectment. *Rogers* v. *Pitcher.* 202

ENEMY,

See ALIEN ENEMY.

EQUITY,

See PAYMENT. NEW TRIAL, 2.

ERROR,

And see INFANT. INTEREST OF MONEY. JUDGMENT, 6.

The Court gave interest on affirmance in error of a judgment for the proceeds of stock fraudulently sold out by one holding a power of attorney to sell. *Mitchell* v. *Miniken.* 117

ESCAPE,

See SHERIFF.

ESCROW,

See PAWNER.

EVIDENCE,

I. *Of the Competency of the Witnesses.*

II. *Of the Evidence of particular Facts or Averments.*

III. *Secondary Evidence, when admissible.*

I.

See JUDGMENT. WILL.

II.

And see ATTESTING WITNESSES. INSURANCE, III. 5. PLEADING, III.

1. *D.* and *W.* being general partners under the firm of *D.* and *Co.*, and *D.* and *Co.* taking a share with three others in a particular adventure, which *D.* and *Co.* manage, and insure for the account of *D.* and *Co.*, it is a latent ambiguity, to be explained by evidence, whether the *D.* and *Co.*, for whose account the insurance is made, means *D.* and *W.* only, or all who are partners of *D.* in that particular adventure. *Carruthers* v. *Sheddon.* Page 14

2. The allegations in a rule of court do not prove the facts alleged. *Woodrooffe* q. t. v. *Williams.* 19

3. In replevin, proof of payment of rent to the avowant, is primâ facie evidence that he is the owner of the land. 202

4. But in a case where the plaintiffs did not originally receive the possession of the land from the avow-

ant, it is competent to the plaintiff to rebut the title of the avowant, by shewing that he paid rent under circumstances which did not entitle the avowant to the rent. Page 202

5. And such evidence may be given on the issue *non tenuit modo et formâ. Rogers* v. *Pitcher.* ib.

6. A statement by a debtor made to an executor, that the testator always promised not to press the defendant for a debt, is not evidence to prove a promise to pay made to the testator within six years. *Ward and Wife* v. *Hunter.* 210

7. On a warranty of prime singed bacon, evidence is not admissible of a practice in the bacon trade to receive bacon to a certain degree tainted as prime singed bacon. 446

8. Nor of a practice to preclude the purchaser from all remedy, if he does not discover and point out the defect by an early day. *Yates* v. *Pym.* ib.

9. Where proclamations appeared to be duly indorsed on a fine, but no other evidence was given of their having been made, Held, that the proclamations were not proved. *Doe* v. *Bluck.* 485

10. Where a person produces notes issued by bankers since become bankrupts, and proves that payments were made to him to that amount in notes of that bank shortly before the bankruptcy, that is evidence to be left to a jury, whether he did not hold these identical notes at the time of the bankruptcy. *Moore* v. *Wright.* 517

III.

III.

See ATTESTING WITNESSES.

EXECUTION OF POWER,

See ATTESTING WITNESSES.

EXECUTION,

See SHERIFFS. PRACTICE, VI.

EXECUTOR AND ADMINIS-
TRATOR,

See AMENDMENT, 2. ATTESTING
WITNESSES. PLEADING, I.

EXPORTATION,

See INSURANCE, I. 3.

———

F

FELONY,

See FORGERY.

FIERI FACIAS,

See PRACTICE, VI.

FINE.

1. Devise in fee, with an executory devise over: whether the fine of the devisee in fee shall bar the executory devise over, *quære. Romilly* v. *James.*   *Page* 263
2. The proclamations on a fine are not proved by production of the cyrograph. whereon they are indorsed. *Doe on the demise of Hatch* v. *Bluck.*   487

FINES AND RECOVERIES,
PRACTICE OF PASSING,

And see EVIDENCE, II.

1. The court permitted a fine *sur concessit* to pass, which comprized an estate for the lives of two and the survivor, and a contingent reversion in fee in the same tenements, on the failure of issue of the conusors. *Prideaux, Plaintiff; Gifford Deforciant.*   *Page* 21
2. The præcipe and concord of a fine being lost, the Court permitted them to be supplied from the copy thereof, which had been left with the clerk of the Chief Justice signed by the parties, and the fine to be perfected. *Ellis* v. *Johnson.*   231
3. Where the vouchee's warrant of attorney in a recovery, omitted in the body of the warrant to express against whom the plea of land was brought wherein the attorney was made, but by the præcipe engrossed at the head of the warrant of attorney it appeared who was the demandant, the Court held that the authority must refer to that plea described by the præcipe, and permitted the recovery to pass. *Forster, Demandant.*   373
4. The Court will not on the last day of term, receive a motion either for amending or for passing fines or recoveries. *Fox, Demandant.*   652, *perperàm pro* 632
5. Fine permitted to pass, where the christian name of one party had been interlined after acknowledgment by another party. *Clarke*

X x 2   *and*

out an affidavit connecting the fine with the deed produced to warrant the amendment. *Fawcett, Plaintiff.* Page 432

12. Where the parties intending to suffer a recovery of the great tithes of near 1000 acres of land, suffered the recovery only of a portion of tithes issuing out of two closes, the Court, with great hesitation, suffered the great tithes of the whole to be added to the recovery, but refused to strike out the portion. *Ross, Demandant.* 489

13. The Court will not amend a warrant of attorney, which is the deed of the party. *Forster, Demandant; Forster, Tenant; Darcy Bolton, Vouchee.* 373

14. Where the vouchee's warrant of attorney, in a recovery, omitted in the body of the warrant to express against whom the plea of land was, wherein the attorney was made, but it appeared by the præcipe engrossed at the head of the warrant of attorney who the defendant was, the Court held that the authority must refer to that plea described by the præcipe, and permitted the recovery to pass. *ib.*

15. The Court will not amend a warrant of attorney, because it is the act of the party. *Fox, Demandant; Benbow, Tenant; Earl Gower, Vouchee.* 652

16. The Court will not on the last day of term receive any motion either for amending or passing recoveries. *ib.*

FIRE,

See INSURANCE, I. II.

FOREIGNER,

See BILLS OF EXCHANGE.

FOREIGN ATTACHMENT.

The Court will not stay proceedings in an action commenced here, to abide the event of an action in the mayor's court, where it is sought to try in a foreign attachment the title to the same property which is in suit here. *Smith and Another v. Ogle.* Page 74

FORGERY.

An indictment charged that the prisoner feloniously had falsely made, forged, and counterfeited a certain promissory note for the payment of money which was as follows: " On demand, we promise to pay Mesdames *S. W.* and *S. D.* stewardesses for the time being of the Provident Daughters' Society held at Mr. *Pope's, the Hope, Smithfield,* or their successors in office, sixty-four pounds, with 5 *per cent.* interest for the same, value received this seventh day of *February*, 1815. For *F. C.* and *Co., J. F.*" This is a valid promissory note within the stat. 2 *G.* 2. *c.* 25., and the conviction was affirmed. *The King v. Box.* 325

FRAUDULENT SALE,

See BANKRUPT, 5. ERROR.

FREIGHT,

And see INSURANCE, II.

1. If the consignee of goods accepts any benefit by the carriage, he cannot defend himself from the payment of freight on the ground

that the goods have been damaged by the master in carrying them.

Page 65

2. Though the damage exceed the amount of the freight.   *ib.*

3, The master has a special property in the vessel, and may declare for the freight of goods as carried in his vessel, though he be not owner. *Shields* v. *Davis.*   *ib.*

4. If, pending an insurance on freight, and a cargo shipped, the vessel becomes incapable of bringing the cargo home, the master is bound or not bound to repair·her, and earn what freight he can on the homeward voyage as a salvage for the underwriters on freight, according as a prudent owner, having regard to the state of his ship, but without reference to any insurance on the freight, would pursue or not pursue that course for his own advantage.   68

5. *Semble* that an abandonment of freight to the underwriters on freight is impossible and unnecessary. *Green* v. *Royal Exchange Assurance Company.*   *ib.*

6. Where an entire verdict passes in covenant for liquidated freight, payable at a certain date after delivery, and for unliquidated damages for detention of the ship, the Court cannot sever them in order to give interest on the freight. *Martin* v. *Emmote.*   530

7. The master of a storeship in the king's service took in the bullion of a private merchant on freight from *Gibraltar* to *Woolwich.* Held that an action lay against him for the

loss of the bullion. *Hutchwell* v. *Cooke.*   *Page* 577.

G

GOODS BARGAINED AND SOLD.

Semble, that after a re-sale of goods by a vendor, as upon default made by the first purchaser, he cannot recover against the first purchaser for goods bargained and sold. *Hagedorn* v. *Laing.*   162

GOODS, CONTRACT FOR SALE OF,

And see INFANT.

1. A contract for selling and delivering oil not yet expressed from seed in the vendor's possession, is exempted from stamp duty as a contract relating to the sale of goods within the stat. 48 G. 3. c. 149., schedule, part 1., Agreement, Exemption. *Wills* v. *Atkinson.*   11

2. In every contract to furnish manufactured goods, however low the price, it is an implied term that the goods shall be merchantable. *Laing* v. *Fidgeon.*   108

3. A contract to furnish goods with a certain latitude as to the price, as saddles at 24s. or 26s., may be described as a contract to furnish them at a reasonable rate.   *ib.*

4. The Defendant bought goods by auction, upon the condition that they were to be cleared away at the

the buyer's expence in fourteen days, and the price paid on or before delivery; if any lots remained uncleared after the time allowed, the deposit money should be forfeited, the goods resold, and the loss on resale made good by the present purchaser. The broker gave a bought note, which allowed fourteen days for receiving and delivery. Held, that only the buyer had fourteen days to deliver, but that the seller was bound to deliver instantly. *Hagedorn* v. *Laing.*
Page 162

5. On a warranty of prime singed bacon, evidence is not admissible of a practice in the bacon trade to receive bacon to a certain degree tainted, as prime singed bacon. *Yates* v. *Pym.*   446

6. Nor of a practice to preclude the purchaser from all remedy if he does not discover and point out the defect by an early day.   *ib.*

7. Under a contract to sell 50 tons of hemp at a price *per* ton, to be shipped from *St. Petersburgh* or *Cronstadt* in *June* or *July*, and the ship's name declared as soon as known; in case the ship should not arrive before 31st *December*, the contract to be void; the seller is not bound to send all by one ship, and having announced more to be coming by one ship than the fact was, he was at liberty to declare the residue to be coming by other ships. *Thornton* v. *Simpson.*   556

8. A contract for the sale of tallow, warranted it to be ready for delivery from ship or warehouse before

1st *November*. Held, that this was equivalent to a contract to be generally ready for delivery before that day, and need not be specially averred. *Thornton* v. *Jones.*
Page 581

GOODS SOLD AND DELIVERED,

And see AFFIDAVIT TO HOLD TO BAIL, *and* AUCTIONEER.

1. One who contracts to build a house, furnishing both timber and labour, cannot recover for the materials on a count for goods sold and delivered, though by reason of a deviation from the original plan, the contract is superseded as to the price. *Cotterel* v. *Apsey.*   322

2. Where goods consigned to an agent to be sold on commission, by a proprietor who still retains the absolute control over them, have been shipped and dispatched, but are not yet arrived, the consignor, pending the voyage, may, in pleading, still describe the sending them as a thing future and executory. *Smith* v. *Brown.*   340

I and J

ILLEGAL CONTRACT,

See INSURANCE, I. 4. 6, 7.

IMPARLANCE.

Where a writ is returnable on the last return-day of one term, the Plaintiff,

II.

Under an averment that after loading the cargo the ship sailed on the voyage and was lost, the Plaintiff cannot recover on proof that the ship before she had half her cargo on board, was driven from her moorings and lost. *Abitbol* v. *Bristow.*   Page 464

III.

1. In an insurance upon a voyage to the Southern Whale Fishery, during the ship's stay and fishing, and at and from thence back to *London*, *semble*, that if the ship sends home by another vessel a part of what she has taken, and continues her fishing, the adventure is not ended by her shipping such part for *England*. And it clearly is not thereby terminated, if the part sent home consisted of damaged skins, which would, if kept on board, have damaged the residue of the cargo. *Phillips and Another* v. *Champion.*   3

2. The seizure and sale of a vessel by a neutral state, no sentence of condemnation being shewn, does not change the property. Therefore, where, in such a case the master had re-purchased the vessel, though he acted without authority from the assured, who refused to accept the ship or repay him the price, the assureds who had not abandoned, were not permitted to recover for a total loss. *Wilson* v. *Forster.*   25

3. If pending an insurance on freight and a cargo shipped, the vessel becomes incapable of bringing the cargo home, the master is bound or not bound to repair her and earn what he can on the homeward voyage as a salvage for the underwriters on freight, according as a prudent owner, having regard to the state of his ship, but without reference to any insurance on the freight, would pursue or not pursue that course for his own advantage.   Page 68

4. *Semble*, that an abandonment of freight to the underwriters on freight is impossible and unnecessary. *Green* v. *Royal Exchange Assurance Company.*   ib.

5. Where the master of a vessel, condemned for a breach of blockade, swore he was bound for another destination, held that this did not so disaffirm his owner's privity and consent to the breach of blockade, as to enable the Plaintiff to recover as for a loss by barratry. *Everth* v. *Hannam.*   375

6. An assured is entitled to a reasonable time for acquiring a full knowledge of the state of a damaged cargo, before he is bound to elect, whether he shall abandon to the underwriters as for a total loss.   383

7. Where a cargo of sugar damaged by sea-water came into an English port on 20th January, began to be unshipped and examined on 21st, but the assured did not receive the complete report of the survey till 7th January, held that an abandonment on 7th January was made within a reasonable time, though the Plaintiff had in the meantime contem-

contemplated that the loss would be partial, and that the adventure might be pursued. *Gernon* v. *Royal Exchange Assurance.*

Page 383

8. Insurance " against all the damages which the Plaintiffs should suffer by fire" " on stock and utensils in their regular built sugarhouse," does not extend to damage done to the sugar by the heat of the usual fires employed in refining, being accumulated by the extreme mismanagement of the Plaintiffs, who inadvertently kept the top of their chimney closed. *Austin* v. *Drewe.* 436

IV. *See* VI. 2.

V.

1. The warranty to " depart" before a certain day, which is used by the *Royal Exchange Assurance Company* in their policies, does not mean merely to break ground, but fairly to set forward upon the voyage. 241

2. Therefore, where a ship in complete sea-readiness weighed anchor with some little prospect of more favourable weather, but in half an hour was beaten back, and came to anchor within the bar, half a mile nearer to the sea than the place of loading, held, that this was not a departure within the warranty. *Moir* v. *Royal Exchange Assurance.* 241

VI.

1. The several underwriters on the same policy have such a community of interest in the subject insured, that if they all agree to refer the demand of the assured on that policy, one stamp for the agreement to refer, and one stamp for the award are sufficient. *Goodson* v. *Forbes.* Same v. ———.

Page 171

2. After the death of an underwriter, a broker, who has an account open with him for premiums due to the latter, and has had an authority to receive returns of premium for him, and place them to his credit, cannot longer receive or retain any further returns of premium, but is bound to pay over to his executors the amount of all premiums due at his decease, without setting off the returns. *Houstoun* v. *Robertson.* 448

3. It is gross negligence in an insurance broker, employed to insure goods from a certain point in their voyage home to effect a policy " at and from" that point, " beginning the adventure from the loading thereof on board." *Park* v. *Hammond.* 495

4. *Semble*, that an insurance broker cannot set off against premiums due to the assignees of a bankrupt, on policies underwritten by the bankrupt, losses which occurred before the bankruptcy, though the policy was effected in the broker's name as agent. *Baker* v. *Langhorn.* 519

5. If an insurance broker debit the underwriter with a loss, and take his acceptance for the balance of account

count between broker and underwriter, payable at a later date than the time when the loss would be payable in cash, the assured may maintain an action against the broker for money had and received.

Page 110

6. Though the acceptance was dishonoured, and the broker never received any money. . *Wilkinson* v. *Clay.* 110

INTEREST OF MONEY.

1. The Court gave interest on affirmance in error of a judgment for the proceeds of stock fraudulently sold out by one holding a power of attorney to sell. *Mihell* v. *Miniken.* 117

2. On the execution of a writ of enquiry, a sheriff's jury ought to give interest in such cases where the courts at *Westminster* would allow it. 346

3. Interest given on affirmance of a judgment in an action on an attorney's undertaking to pay debt and taxed costs on or before a day certain. ⸺ v. *Edmunds.* 346

4. Where an entire verdict passes in covenant for liquidated freight, payable at a certain date after delivery, and for unliquidated damages for detention of the ship, a Court of error cannot sever them, to give interest on the freight. *Martin* v. *Emmote.* 520

INTRUSION, WRIT OF.

1. Whether a devisee in remainder can maintain a writ of intrusion,

2. Or a writ to be framed on the statute of *Westminster* the 2d in the nature of a writ of intrusion, *quære. Romilly* v. *James.* Page 263

JOINT CONTRACT,
See MONEY PAID, 4.

JUDGMENT,
And see AMENDMENT, INTEREST OF MONEY, PRACTICE, V.

1. A Plaintiff who defers proceedings, in order to await the decision of the Court on a similar question in another cause, will not be relieved on that ground against a rule for judgment as in case of a nonsuit, unless he makes it appear to the Court, in what cause the question will arise, and what the point is to be decided. *Wynn* v. *Bellman,* clerk. 122

2. In opposing a rule for judgment as in case of a nonsuit, upon the ground that certain documentary evidence could not be procured in time for the trial, it is not necessary to state what the evidence is. *Greenhill* v. *Mitchell.* 150

3. Where two of three joint covenantors suffer judgment by default on counts on several deeds, and the third defends and succeeds on some counts, the Plaintiff cannot hold his judgment on those counts against the other two. 398

4. In such case neither party is entitled to costs on the counts on which the Plaintiff fails. *Morgan* v. *Edwards.* 398

5. Although a Plaintiff, subject to the jurisdiction of the *London* Court of Requests,

Requests, suing in a Court at *Westminster*, claims a sum exceeding 5*l.*, yet if he recovers a less sum than 5*l.*, he is subject to double costs by the statute 39 & 40 *G. 3. c.* 104. *s.* 12. *Younger* v. *Wilsby.* Page 452

6. Where entire judgment is given for the Plaintiff on two counts, one of which is bad, the Court may reverse it as to the first, and affirm it as to the second count. *Everard* v. *Patterson.*

645, *perperàm pro* 625

7. After judgment for Plaintiff on demurrer without argument, and general damages assessed, the Court will not permit the Defendant to move in arrest of judgment on the ground that the damages appear to be partly given upon a count which cannot be sustained, because the Defendant had the opportunity of excepting to that count on demurrer. *Creswell* v. *Packham.*

650, *perperàm pro* 630

JURISDICTION,

See INSOLVENT, 4.

JURY.

Where a person not summoned on the jury, was sworn on a jury at *nisi prius* in the name of a person for whom a summons to serve on that jury was delivered, and to whose house he had succeeded; the irregularity being noticed before verdict, the Court awarded a *venire de novo. Dovey* v. *Hobson.* 460

L

LATENT AMBIGUITY,

See EVIDENCE, II. 1.

LEASE,

See DEED. PLEADING, III.

LESSOR AND LESSEE.

Semble, that the owner of land, agreeing to grant a lease, does not thereby impliedly engage that he has a good title to the fee-simple, and that he will deliver a written abstract. *Temple* v. *Brown.* Page 60

LIBEL.

1. It is not sufficient to declare that the Defendant published a libel concerning the Plaintiff in his trade purporting that his beer was of bad quality and sold by deficient measure ; the libel itself ought to be set out. 169

2. And such a declaration is bad on general demurrer. *Wood* v. *Brown.* ib.

LICENCE,

See CLERGY.

LICENCE TO SAIL WITHOUT CONVOY,

See INSURANCE, I. 7.

LICENCE TO TRADE,

See INSURANCE, I. 3.

LIEN,

See INSURANCE, 8.

LIFE-

LIFE-INSURANCE,
See INSURANCE, I. 1.

LIMITATION OF ACTIONS,
See ACTION, LIMITATION OF, AND
EVIDENCE, II. 6.

LOCAL ACTION,
See ACTION ON THE CASE. VENUE.

LORDS' ACT,
See INSOLVENT

———

M

MASTER OF A SHIP,
See FREIGHT. INSURANCE, III. 3.
AND MONEY PAID.

MEMORANDA. 514, 515, 516, 517.

MEMORIAL,
See ANNUITY.

MISNOMER,
See ABATEMENT, 1.   DEED, 5.
PRACTICE, II. 2.

MONEY HAD AND RECEIVED,
And see CLERGY, 11. INSURANCE,
VI. 2. 4.

1. The Defendants took a bill, accepted payable at the Plaintiffs,
who were the drawees' bankers, and
indorsed to their, the Defendants'
agents, to whom the Plaintiffs paid
it when due, and seven days after
sent it as their voucher to the
drawee, who apprised them that the
acceptance was forged. Held by

three against Chambre J., that the
Plaintiffs could not recover from the
Defendants the amount which they
had thus paid them on the forged
acceptance. Smith and Others v.
Mercer and Another.   Page 76

2. A bankrupt's assignees had contracted for the sale of his copyhold
lands, and received a deposit. The
commission was afterwards superseded, because, when it issued, the
petitioning creditor's debt was not
due. Another commission issued
upon the petition of another creditor, and the same assignees were
chosen. Held that the Plaintiff,
having abandoned his contract
pending the old commission, might
recover back his deposit. Bartlett
v. Tuchin.   259

3. A practice had prevailed during
the incumbency of several vicars,
that upon the burial of any stranger
in the parish of H. certain fees
should be paid, of which the vicar
took one moiety and the churchwardens the other for the use of
the poor. The fees were paid to
the sexton, who paid over the
moieties to the respective parties.
A new vicar refused to accede to
this arrangement, he buried several
strangers, and procured the sexton,
to whom the fees were paid, to pay
over the entire fees to himself.
Held that the churchwardens might
recover from the vicar one moiety
as money had and received to their
use. Littlewood v. Williams. 277

MONEY PAID.

1. The master of a ship drew a bill
on

on his owners for supplies for the ship, and wrote on the bill, " If this be not honoured, the holder will insure the amount, and place the premium to the drawer's account." The bill being dishonoured, the holder insured the ship for three months, and declared interest in the bill, which was to be sufficient proof of interest. The ship was lost after the three months. Held that the holder of the bill was authorized to insure for his own benefit, and was warranted in insuring for three months, and that he might recover the premium against the drawer. *Page* 235

2. Whether such an insurance be void within stat. 19 *G*. 2. *c*. 37., *quære*. *Tasker* v. *Scott*. *ib*.

3. One joint contractor, who pays money for another under an equitable claim, may recover it from the other as money paid to his use. *Hutton* v. *Eyre*. 289

N

NAVY,

See SHIP AND FREIGHT.

NEGLIGENCE,

See INSURANCE, VI. 3.

NEUTRAL,

See INSURANCE, III. 2. SHIP, 4.

NEW TRIAL,

And see TITHES.

1. If the Plaintiff's counsel acquiesces in the judge's ruling at the trial, whereby the Defendant takes a verdict without going into his case, the Plaintiff will not be afterwards permitted to move for a new trial on the ground of a misdirection. *Robinson* v. *Cook*. *Page* 336

2. A motion for a new trial, upon an issue directed by a court of equity, must first be made in that court, as well where the point relates to the admissibility of evidence, as on other occasions. *Barker* v. *Nixon*. 444

NOLLE PROSEQUI,

See PRACTICE, IV. 5.

NON-RESIDENCE,

See CLERGY.

NOTICE,

And see ARBITRATION, 3.

1. Fifteen days' notice is required of the execution of a writ of inquiry in replevin after judgment on demurrer for the avowant. *Barton* v. *Hickey*. 57

2. A notice of declaration needs not to state the damages laid. *Hetherington* v. *Hobson*. 331

3. The notice of intention to apply for admission as an attorney, required by the rule of Court *Trin.* term 31 *G*. 3., must be given during the term next immediately preceding the application. *Ex parte Bonner*. 335

4. Where a Defendant was master of a vessel, on board of which he slept, and

and had no other home, he was deemed to be resident where his ship was registered, and that being more than 40 miles from *London*, he was held entitled to 14 days' notice of executing a writ of inquiry.   *Page* 458

5. An undertaking to accept short notice of trial does not entitle the Plaintiff to give short notice of executing a writ of inquiry. *Blaaw* v. *Chaters.*   458

O

OFFICE,

And see ACTION ON THE CASE, 2. 3.

To a voluntary office and not cast by law on the party, it is necessary to aver not only an appointment, but an acceptance by the person appointed. *Serra* v. *Wright.*   45

OFFICER,

See WARDEN OF THE FLEET. FREIGHT, 7. SHIP, 5.

OIL,

See GOODS, CONTRACT FOR SALE OF, 1.

ORIGINAL WRIT,

See PRACTICE, I.

P

PARTNERS,

And see EVIDENCE, II. 1. PLEADING, I.

1. The partners in one house of trade cannot maintain an action against the partners in another house of trade, of which one of the partners in the Plaintiff's house is also a member, for transactions which took place while he was partner in both houses.   *Page* 597

2. And that, whether the action be brought in the lifetime of the common partner, or after his decease.   *ib.*

3. But after his decease the surviving partners of the one house may sue the surviving partners of the other house, upon transactions subsequent to the decease of the common partner. *Bosanquet* v. *Wray.*   *ib.*

PARTY-WALL.

A tenant who rebuilds a house in *London* without a lease or agreement for a lease, and therein makes use of the party-wall of the adjoining house, cannot be sued for half the cost, as owner of the improved rent, though he afterwards obtains, in consideration of the rebuilding, a beneficial lease at a low ground-rent, habendum from a day before the rebuilding. *Taylor* v. *Reed.*   249

PAWNEE.

If the vendor of a leasehold estate delivers the conveyance as an escrow, to take effect on payment of the residue of the purchase money, the property in the title-deeds of the estate is so vested in the vendee, that the vendor, obtaining possession

PAYMENT.

possession of them, and pawning them, confers on the pawnee no right to detain them after tender of the residue of the purchase money. *Hooper and Another*, assignees of *Wells* v. *Ramsbottom and Others*.
Page 12

PAYMENT.

A creditor receiving money without any specific appropriation thereof by the debtor, shall be permitted in a court of law to ascribe his receipt to the discharge of a prior and purely equitable debt, and to sue his debtor at law for a subsequent legal debt. *Bosanquet and Others* v. *Wray*. 597

PENAL ACTION,

And see PILOT. TITHES.

1. In a *qui tam* action, if the declaration do not appear on the record to be filed within a year of the writ, it is necessary to connect it with the writ by evidence of the time when the delaration was filed, and by shewing the writ to be continued on the roll down to that time. 141

2. In the Common Pleas, the *placitum* being always entitled of the term in or after which the trial takes place, it furnishes no evidence of the date of the declaration. *Thistlewood* v. *Craycraft*.
141

PETITIONING CREDITOR,

See BANKRUPT, I.

PILOT.

Under the statute 52 G. 3. c. 39. s. 11. a master of a vessel who, coming from the *Westward* bound to any place in the *Thames* or *Medway*, refuses to take a pilot on board, is liable to a penalty equal to double the amount of the several sums payable for pilotage from the place where he is bound first to take a pilot on board, to the termination of his voyage. *Mackie* v. *Landon*.
Page 256

PLEADING.

I. *Of the Form of Action and Joinder of Actions.*
II. *Of the Parties thereto.*
III. *Of Certainty in Pleading.*
IV. *Of the Manner of Pleading in General.*

I.

And see ACTION ON THE CASE.

1. Counts upon a promise by the Defendant and another, since become a bankrupt and certificated, may in an action against the solvent partner alone, be joined with counts on promises by the Defendant solely since the other became a bankrupt. 179

2. But the Defendant might plead the joint contract in abatement. *Hawkins* v. *Ramsbottom*, in Error.
ib.

3. Counts on promises to a testator, may be joined with counts on promises to an executor, if the damages recovered under the last,

would be assets in the hands of the executor. *Powley* v. *Newton.*
Page 456

II.

1. Several tort feasors who unite in an injurious act, may be sued, each one severally. *Sutton* v. *Clarke.*
29

2. The partners in one house of trade cannot maintain an action against the partners in another house of trade, of which one of the partners in the Plaintiff's house is also a member, for transactions which took place while he was a partner in both houses.
597

3. And that, whether the action be brought in the lifetime of the common partner, or after his decease.
ib.

4. But after his decease, the surviving partners of the one house may sue the surviving partners of the other house, upon transactions subsequent to the decease of the common partner. *Bosanquet* v. *Wray.*
ib.

III.

1. In pleading it is sufficient on all occasions after the parties have been first named, to describe them by the terms, " the said Plaintiff," " and the said Defendant." *Davison* v. *Savage.*
121

2. A lease granted liberty to make levels, pits and soughs: A declaration in covenant stated it as a liberty to make sloughs: held that by the rule, *noscitur a sociis*, the Court could discover this to be the word soughs, only mis-spelt, and that it was not a fatal variance. *Morgan* v. *Edwards.*
Page 394

3. A declaration described demised lands to be in the parish of *B.* and *M.*: the deed demised lands in the parishes of *B.* & *M.*, the Court held the variance fatal.
ib.

4. Lands in the occupations of *A. B.* & *C.*, intended of the several occupations of *A. B.* & *C.*
ib.

5. The words Plaintiff and Defendant, used throughout a declaration, after the parties have been once named, are a sufficient designation of them without their respective names being afterwards expressed in the several counts, and without its being expressly shewn who are the persons designated by the words Plaintiffs and Defendants. *Stevenson* v. *Hunter.*
406

IV.

And see BOND, 2. GOODS, CONTRACT FOR SALE OF, 3.

1. To a voluntary office and not cast by law on the party, it is necessary to aver not only an appointment, but an acceptance by the person appointed. *Serra and Others* v. *Wright.*
45

2. In debt on bond given to the obligee, conditioned for payment of an annual sum to the wife of the obligor, a breach assigned in non-payment of the annual sum to the obligee, is ill. *Lunn* v. *Payne.* 140

3. Where goods consigned to an agent to be sold on commission by a proprietor who still retains the absolute control over them, have been

been shipped and dispatched, but are not yet arrived, the consignor, pending the voyage, may, in pleading, still describe the sending them as a thing future and executory. *Smith* v. *Brown.*   Page 340

4. In an action on a policy of insurance on goods at and from *M.* to *L.*, the declaration averred, that after the loading of the goods on board on a certain day, the ship, with the goods on board, departed and set sail on her intended voyage, and afterwards, and while the ship was in the course of her voyage, they were destroyed by perils of the sea. The evidence was that before the ship had half her cargo on board, she was driven from her moorings by bad weather, and lost. Held, that the Plaintiff was not entitled to recover. *Abithol* v. *Bristow.*   467

5. A count for a deceit, averring that the Defendant represented to the Plaintiff that his lessor required 150*l.* premium for a lease, whereas he required only 100*l.*, whereby the Defendant fraudulently obtained from the Plaintiff and converted to his own use 50*l.*, is sufficient. *Pewtriss* v. *Austen.*   552

6. Where a submission is, " so that the award be in writing, under the hand of the arbitrator," it must be shewn in pleading that the award is under hand as well as in writing. *Everard* v. *Paterson.*   625

PLURALITIES,
See CLERGY.

POWER,
And see ATTESTING WITNESSES.

1. A defective attestation of the execution of a power cannot be supplied by parol evidence of the attesting witness given on a trial.   Page 402

2. A power to appoint by deed or writing under the donee's hand and seal, and attested by two or more credible witnesses, is ill pursued by a will apparently under the testator's hand and seal, which seal an attesting witness believes was affixed before execution and attestation, if the attestation does no notice the sealing as well as the signing. *Doe dem. Hotchki*r v. *Pearce.*   40

PRACTICE,

I. *Relative to Process.*
II. *Arrest, Detainer, Bail, an Appearance.*
III. *Pleadings, and Bill of Particulars.*
IV. *Trial, Inquiry, and Evidence.*
V. *Judgment, and Reference to the Prothonotary.*
VI. *Execution.*
VII. *Staying and setting aside Proceedings.*
VIII. *Costs.*
IX. *Waver of Irregularity.*

L

1. If a Plaintiff joins several Defendant's in one common process, one, upon whom it is irregularly served, applying before declaration to set it aside, may entitle his rule and

affidavit in a cause of the Plaintiff against himself only. *Dand* v. *Barnes.* Page 5

2. In an action on a recognizance of bail, the bail must be served with process four days before the return of the writ. *Mackenzie* v. *Martin.* 286

3. In common process the year needs not to be expressed in words at length. *Eyre* v. *Walsh.* 333

4. No action can be regularly commenced against the warden of the *Fleet* in the time of vacation. *Crook* v. *Eyles.* 347
　　　Stock v. *Eyles.* 352

II.

And see BAIL BOND. INSOLVENT. SHERIFF.

1. If bail above who are excepted to and have not justified, afterwards procure their recognizance to be put on the roll, the Court will, at the instance of a Plaintiff suing on the bail-bond, cause it to be taken off, that the Defendants may not prove by that evidence the issue of *comperuerunt ad diem.* *Leigh* v. *Bartles.* 167

2. The Court will not discharge a Defendant arrested by a wrong *Christian* name, who has signed that name in dealing with the Plaintiff. *Walker* v. *Willoughby.* 530

3. If a Defendant changes his attorney without leave of the Court, and gives notice of new bail, the Plaintiff may prevent them from justifying. *Hill* v. *Roe* 532

4. The Court will not discharge a Defendant out of custody on a defect in the affidavit to hold to bail, after he has given bail to the Sheriff and bail to the action, which last have rendered him. *Shawman* v. *Whalley.* Page 185

III.

And see NOTICE.

1. The Court will not alter the memorandum of a declaration in a penal action at the mere instance of the Plaintiff without a reason shewn. *Woodroffe* q. t. v. *Williams.* 19

2. In a *qui tam* action, if the declaration do not on the record appear to be filed within a year of the writ, it is necessary to connect it with the writ by evidence of the time when the declaration was filed, and shewing the writ to be continued on the roll down to that time. 141

3. In the common pleas, the placitum being always entitled of the term in or after which the trial takes place, it furnishes no evidence of the date of the declaration. *Thistle-wood* v. *Craycraft.* 141

4. Where a writ is returnable on the last return-day of one term, the Plaintiff, who is not bound to declare *de bene esse,* is under no compulsion to declare before the essoign-day of the next term; and therefore the Defendant is not entitled to an imparlance. *Kent* v. *Yates.* 261

5. Where the Court, on demurrer, gives leave to amend by stating particularly that which before was stated too generally, the Plaintiff may add new counts, though more than two terms have elapsed from the commencement of the suit, if they

they contain no new cause of action, but only various specifications of the matter which the Court permitted to be more particularly stated. *Brown* v. *Crump.* Page 300

6. A notice of declaration needs not to state the damages laid. *Hetherington* v. *Hobson.* 331

IV.

1. Fifteen days' notice is required of the execution of a writ of enquiry in replevin, after judgment on demurrer for the avowant. *Burton* v. *Hickey.* 57

2. Inspection refused to a Plaintiff in replevin of the deed, (to which he was no party,) assigning to the avowant the reversion of the demised premises. *Brown* v. *Rose.* 283

3. Where two parts of an indenture of charter-party were alleged to have been interchangeably executed, and the part of which the master of the chartered vessel had the custody was lost at sea with the ship, the Court would not compel the charterer, being sued thereon, to grant inspection and a copy of the other part, for the purpose of the Plaintiff's declaring with certainty. *Street* v. *Brown.* 302

4. An amendment of the Plaintiff's declaration does not necessarily entitle the Defendant to plead *de novo*, but only where the amendment alters the state of the Defendant's case. *Woodroffe* v. *Watson.* 400

5. After demurrer to one count of a declaration, a Plaintiff may enter a

nolle prosequi on that count, and proceed to trial on his other counts. *Bertram* v. *Gordon.* Page 444

6. Where a Defendant was master of a vessel, on board of. which he slept, and had no other home, he was deemed to be resident where his ship was registered, and that being more than 40 miles distant from *London*, he was held entitled to fourteen days' notice of executing a writ of enquiry. 458

7. An undertaking to accept short notice of trial does not entitle the Plaintiff. to give short notice of executing a writ of enquiry. *Blaaw* v. *Chaters.* 458

V.

1. A Plaintiff who defers proceeding, in order to await the decision of the Court on a similar question in another cause, will not be relieved on that ground against a rule for judgment as in case of a nonsuit, unless he makes it appear to the Court in what cause the question will arise, and what is the point to be decided. *Wynn* v. *Bellman,* clerk. 122

2. In opposing a rule for judgment, as in case of a nonsuit upon the absence at the last trial of documentary evidence necessary for the Plaintiff, it is not necessary to state what the evidence is. *Greenhill* v. *Mitchell.* 150

3. The Court will, after judgment by default, refer it to the prothonotary to compute the rent due on a covenant.

4. But not so in debt on simple contract

tract for rent, or use and occupation. *Campion* v. *Crawshay.*

Page 356

VI.

If a sheriff makes a seizure under a writ of *fieri facias*, the Plaintiff cannot take the Defendant in execution under a writ of *capias ad satisfaciendum*, till the writ of *fieri facias* is returned, though he abandons the seizure of the goods. *Miller* v. *Parnell.* 370

VII.

And see STAYING AND SETTING ASIDE PROCEEDINGS.

The Court will not stay proceedings in an action commenced here, to abide the event of an action in the mayor's court, where it is sought to try in a foreign attachment the title to the same property which is in suit here. *Smidt and Another* v. *Ogle.* 74

VIII.

And see JUDGMENT. COURT OF REQUESTS.

1. The Court will not decide a motion for security for costs on the merits of the cause. 20
2. Security for costs is not exacted, so long as the Plaintiff remains in this country. *Ciragno* v. *Hassan.* 20
3. If a witness is *bonâ fide* sent for from a foreign country for the sake of his testimony in an intended action, though the writ is not sued out until after his arrival, the Plaintiff is entitled in that cause to the costs of bringing him over, his subsistence, and compensation for his loss of time spent here pending the suit for the purposes thereof, and to the costs of his return. *Tremain* v. *Barrett. Same* v. *Faith.* Page 88
4. But if the witness being sent for to give evidence in one action, the Plaintiff uses his testimony in another action against a different party and relaxes his diligence in the first, he is intitled in the second action to the costs only of the witness's subsistence and detention for the purpose of the second action, but not of his voyage hither or his return. *ib.*
5. The court will not compel an insolvent to give security for costs, suing for a demand, for which the assignee of his property under the insolvent act refuses to sue. *Snow* v. *Townsend.* 123
6. If a Defendant who pays money into court afterwards obtains judgment as in case of a nonsuit before the Plaintiff has taken it out, the Plaintiff cannot afterwards have his costs taxed up to the time of paying the money into court. *Postle* v. *Beckington.* 158
7. The Court will not compel a Defendant resident abroad to give security for costs, as the price of compelling the Plaintiff, resident abroad, to give the Defendant security for costs. *Baxter* v. *Morgan.* 379

IX.

1. A party may apply to set aside proceedings for irregularity at any time before the irregular party has taken

taken a further step, if the latter
has not by the delay of the former
been induced to place himself in a
worse situation than he would have
been in if the other had come
earlier. *Dand* v. *Barnes. Page* 5
2. A party who would set aside proceedings for irregularity, must apply instantly after the irregular
party has taken the first further
step; if he lets him take a second
further step, he waves the irregularity. *Fletcher* v. *Wells.*   91

PRECEDENCY,
See ATTORNEY GENERAL.

PRESENTATION,.
See CLERGY.

PRISONER,
See SET-OFF.

PRIZE,
And see INSURANCE, III. 2.

1. No action lies against the commander of a *British* ship of war,
for seizing and detaining a vessel
on suspicion of her being hostile
prize.   439
2. Though he afterwards dismisses
her without libelling her in the
Court of Admiralty.   *ib.*
3. And though he detains her partly
on suspicion of matters which are
causes only of forfeiture if she is
British. Faith v. *Pearson.* - -489

PROCEEDINGS,
See STAYING AND SETTING ASIDE
PROCEEDINGS.

PROCESS,
See PRACTICE, I.

PROCLAMATIONS,
See FINE, 2.

PROMISSORY NOTES,
See AFFIDAVIT TO HOLD TO BAIL,
BILLS OF EXCHANGE, AND FOR-
GERY.

PROMOTIONS,
(*And see* ATTORNEY GENERAL,) 514,
515, 516, 517.

PURCHASER,
See VENDOR AND VENDEE.

R

RATE,
See AVERMENT.

RECOGNIZANCE,
See BAIL, II. 1.   PRACTICE, II. 1.

RECOVERY,
See FINES AND RECOVERIES.

REFERENCE,
See ARBITRATION.

RELATION OF TIME,
See SHERIFF, I.

RELEASE,
See COVENANT, 4.

RENT,

See REPLEVIN AND TENDER.

REPLEVIN,

And see DEED, NOTICE. PRACTICE, IV, 1.

1. In replevin, proof of payment of rent to the avowant is *primâ facie* evidence that he is the owner of the land.   *Page* 202

2. But in a case where the Plaintiff did not originally receive the possession of the land from the avowant, it is competent to the Plaintiff to rebut the title of the avowant by shewing that he paid rent under circumstances which did not entitle the avowant to the rent.   *ib.*

3. And such evidence may be given on the issue *non tenuit modo et formâ. Rogers* v. *Pitcher.*   *ib.*

4. A Defendant in replevin does not by giving time to the Plaintiff in replevin discharge the sureties in the replevin bond. *Moore* v. *Bowmaker.*   379

5. To an avowry for rent, it is a good plea, that before the lessor had any thing in the land, a termor granted an annuity or rent-charge, and granted and covenanted that the grantee might distrain on the premises; that the annuity was in arrear, and the grantee demanded it, and threatened distress; and the Plaintiff paid her the amount of the rent then due to the avowant, and so, nothing in arrear. *Taylor* v. *Zamira.*   524

RETURN OF PREMIUM,

See INSURANCE, VI. 2.

ROYAL EXCHANGE ASSURANCE COMPANY,

See INSURANCE, III. 3, 4, 5. V. 1, 2.

S

SALE OF LAND,

See DEED.

SALE BY SAMPLE,

See GOODS, CONTRACT FOR SALE OF.

SALE OF GOODS, WHERE COMPLETE,

See GOODS, CONTRACT FOR SALE OF, AND GOODS SOLD AND DELIVERED.

SALVAGE,

See INSURANCE, III. 3.

SET OFF,

And see INSURANCE, VI. 2. 4.

The Court will not upon motion enable a prisoner to set off in a summary way a debt for which he has obtained no judgment, against the Plaintiff's execution. *Philipson and Another* v. *Caldwell.*   *Page* 176

SHERIFF,

And see PRACTICE, VI.

1. The sheriffs of the late and present year signed in *November the* return of *non est inventus* on a writ

writ of *Trinity* term. In an action against the late sheriff for not arresting, held that his return related to the day of his quitting office; and that to make him liable for the default of the officer employed, it was not enough to shew that a warrant was made to the officer, but it must be shewn that the warrant was delivered to the officer, and neglect committed, while the Defendant was in office. *Fonsec* v. *Magnay*. Page 231

2. A sheriff cannot justify breaking the inner doors of the house of a stranger, upon suspicion that a Defendant is there, to search for him, in order to arrest him on mesne process. *Johnson* v. *Leigh*. 246

3. Where the sheriff had taken the Defendants on a *capias ad satisfaciendum*, erroneously issued on a judgment on a bail-recognizance, and they had paid him the amount of the judgment and costs; whereon he discharged them, and receiving notice that the money belonged to the assignees of a bankrupt, refused to pay it over to the Plaintiff. Held, 1. that the sheriff was guilty of an escape; but, 2. the Court relieved him from the action for an escape, leaving him liable to the counts for money had and received, for the Plaintiff to litigate with him the assignee's right to the money in the sheriff's hands. *Wooden* v. *Moxon*. 490

4. Where the sheriff had omitted to take a bail-bond, and an action had been commenced for an escape, the Court would not stay proceed-

ings on the terms of the sheriff's charging the Plaintiff in custody in the original action, though the sheriff never was ruled to return the writ, and though the Defendant was charged in custody in several other actions. *Birn* v. *Bond*.
      Page 554

5. A sheriff may take a bail-bond on an attachment out of Chancery.
      569

6. But he is not compellable to take bail thereupon. *Morris* v. *Hayward*. *ib.*

7. Where no criminal act is shewn on the part of the bailiff, the Court will not grant a motion that the sheriff should amend his return by particularly specifying the goods sold, he having only made an aggregate return. *Willet* v. *Sparrow*. 576

SHIP,

And see ARBITRATION. GOODS, CONTRACT FOR THE SALE OF. INSURANCE.

1. No action lies against the commander of a *British* ship of war for seizing and detaining a vessel on suspicion of her being hostile prize. 439

2. Though he afterwards dismisses her without libelling her in the Court of Admiralty. *ib.*

3. And though he detains her partly on suspicion of matters which are merely causes of forfeiture if she is *British*. *Faith* v. *Pearson*. *ib.*

4. The seisure and sale of a vessel by a neutral state, no sentence of condemnation by any competent Court

Court being shewn, does not change the property. *Wilson* v. *Forster.*
Page 25

5. Therefore, where, in such a case, the master had repurchased the vessel, though he acted without authority from the assured, who refused to accept the ship, or repay him the price, the assureds who had not abandoned, were not permitted to recover for a total loss. *Wilson* v. *Forster.* ib.

6. The master of a store ship in the King's service took in the bullion of a private merchant on freight from *Gibraltar* to *Woolwich.* Held, that an action lay against him for the loss of the bullion. *Hatchwell* v. *Cooke.* 577

SIMONY,
See TITHES, 4.

SLANDER,
See LIBEL.

SOLICITOR-GENERAL,
See ATTORNEY-GENERAL.

SOLICITOR,
See ATTORNEY.

STAMPS.
See GOODS, CONTRACT FOR SALE OF, I.

1. A contract for selling and delivering oil, not yet expressed from seed in the vendor's possession, is exempted from stamp-duty, as a contract relating to the sale of goods, within the stat. 48 *Geo.* 3. *c.* 149. *Schedule, Part* I. *title Agreement, Exception. Wilks* v. *Atkinson.* 11

2. The several underwriters on the same policy have such a community of interest in the subject insured, that if they all agree to refer the demand of the assured on that policy, one stamp for the agreement to refer, and one stamp for the award, are sufficient. *Goodson* v. *Forbes.* Page 171

STATUTE, CONSTRUCTION OF,
See AMENDMENT.

STATUTE OF LIMITATIONS,
See ACTIONS, LIMITATIONS OF.

STATUTE REMEDIAL,
See AMENDMENT, 10, 11. STOCK-JOBBING. TITHES, 3.

STAYING AND SETTING ASIDE PROCEEDINGS,

And see ABATEMENT. PRACTICE, IX.

1. A party may apply to set aside proceedings for irregularity at any time before the irregular party has taken a further step, if the latter has not by the delay of the former been induced to place himself in a worse situation than he would have been in if the other had come earlier. *Dand* v. *Barnes.*   5

2. A party who would set aside proceedings for irregularity, must apply instantly after the irregular party has taken the first further step; if he lets him take a second further step, he waives the irregularity. *Fletcher* v. *Wells.*   191

3. Where a Defendant sued by a wrong name omits to plead in abatement, and suffers the Plaintiff to proceed to judgment, though he never has appeared to the wrong name, the Court will not interfere to set aside the proceedings. *Smith* v. *Patten.*   113

4. Where the Court had given time to one of the bail to justify before a Judge at Chambers in the vacation, a Judge's summons for further time, returnable before the
              original

original time had .expired, operates as a stay of proceedings.
Redford v. *Edie.*   *Page* 240

STEWARD.

1. A steward of a manor is entitled to
be paid for admissions of a tenant
to several copyholds only according to a *quantum meruit*, unless
certain fees are proved to be due
by the custom of his manor. *Everest* v. *Glyn.*   425
2. There is no general custom for all
copyholds.   *ib.*
3. And therefore, although the steward at the tenant's request prepare
six several admissions on separate
instruments to six tenements, he is
not entitled to six times the fees
which are due on the first, there
being less labour in preparing the
five last than the first.   425

STOCKJOBBING,

See AMENDMENT, 10, 11.

STOPPAGE IN TRANSITU.

A resale of goods by a vendee, and
payment to him, does not destroy
the vendor's right of stoppage *in
transitu.* *Craven* v. *Ryder.*   433

SUGGESTION,

See BANKRUPT, III. 3.

SURETY,

See REPLEVIN. BANKRUPT, IV. 2, 3.

T

TENANT,

See ELEGIT, AND PARTY WALL.

TENDER.

1. A tender of a larger sum, requiring change, is not a good tender of
a smaller sum.   *Page* 336
2. A plea of tender of half a year's
rent simply, is not supported by evidence of a tender of the half year's
rent, requiring the lessor to get
change and pay back the property-
tax. *Robinson* v. *Cooke.*   *ib.*

TITHES,

And see FINES AND RECOVERIES,
AMENDMENT OF.

1. In an action for not setting out
tithes, the *onus* of proving that the
land is barren, lies on the Defendant.   297
2. The proper test of barrenness within this statute, is, whether the land
requires extraordinary expence either in manure or labour to bring
it into a proper state of cultivation.   *ib.*
3. The statute 2 & 3 *Edw.* 6. c. 13. is
a remedial act, and in an action
thereon the Court will grant a new
trial for the mistake of the jury.
Lord Selsea v. *Powell.*   *ib.*
4. A parishioner who has compounded with the parson one year for his
tithes, and has not determined the
composition, cannot set up as a defence to an action for the next
year's composition-money that the
Plaintiff is *simoniacus.* *Brooksby*,
clerk, v. *Watts.*   333

TITLE.

Semble, that the owner of land agreeing to grant a lease, does not thereby impliedly engage that he has a
good

good title to the fee-simple, and that he will deliver a written abstract. *Temple* v. *Brown. Page* 60

TITLE DEEDS.

1. If the vendor of a leasehold estate delivers the conveyance as an escrow, to take effect as a deed on payment of the residue of the purchase-money, the property in the title deeds of the estate is so vested in the vendee, that the vendor, obtaining possession of them, and pawning them, confers on the pawnee no right to detain them after tender of the residue of the purchase-money. *Hooper and Another, Assignees of Wells,* v. *Ramsbottom and Others.* 12

TOLL,

See CANAL COMPANY.

TRESPASS.

See SHERIFFS, AND SHIP.

TRIAL,

See PRACTICE, IV. JURY, 1.

TRUSTEE,

See ACTION ON THE CASE.

———

U and V

VARIANCE,

See PLEADING, III. DEED, 5. INSURANCE, II. 1. TENDER, 2.

1. A lease granted liberty to make levels, pits, and soughs. A declaration in covenant stated it as a liberty to make sloughs: held that by the rule, *noscitur a sociis*, the Court could discover this to be the word soughs, only mis-spelt, and that it was not a fatal variance.
Page 394

2. A declaration described lands demised to be in the parish of *B.* and *M.*: the deed demised lands in the parishes of *B.* & *M.*, the Court held the variance fatal. *ib.*

3. Lands in the occupations of *A. B.* & *C.*, intended of the several occupations of *A. B.* & *C. Morgan* v. *Edwards. ib.*

VENDOR AND VENDEE,

And see STOPPAGE IN TRANSITU. PAWNEE. TITLE.

1. A bankrupt's assignees had contracted for the sale of his copyhold lands, and received a deposit. The commission was afterwards superseded, because, when it issued, the petitioning creditor's debt was not due. Another commission issued upon the petition of another creditor, and the same assignees were chosen. Held that the Plaintiff, having abandoned his contract pending the old commission, might recover back his deposit. *Bartlett* v. *Tuchin.* 259

2. In a Court of law every title that is not bad is marketable, *Romilly* v. *James.* 263

VENIRE DE NOVO,

See JURY.

VENUE,

VENUE,

And see AMENDMENT, 7.

1. If a trench cut in the county of *N.* causes the Plaintiff's lands to be overflowed in the county of *W.*, although a statute requires all actions to be brought and tried in the county where the cause of action arises, the action may be brought and tried in *W.*, *Sutton* v. *Clarke.*
                     Page 29

2. The Court will not, without reasonable ground shewn, permit a Plaintiff to amend by changing the venue. *Ayres* v. *Buston.*   408

3. The Plaintiff may retain the venue where he has laid it, on undertaking to give material evidence in any county, in which, if the venue were laid, the Defendant could not truly make the usual affidavit to change the venue from that county.   564

4. Evidence of any fact material to the cause, though it go not to the whole cause of action, satisfies the undertaking given to retain the venue.   *ib.*

5. When the cause of action arises in a foreign country the Plaintiff may retain the venue without any undertaking to give material evidence. *Savory* v. *Spooner. Neale* v. *Nevill.*   565, 566

USES,

And see FINES AND RECOVERIES, AMENDMENT OF.

1. A grant of lands in trust perpetually to repair, and, if need be, rebuild a vault and tomb standing on the land, and permit the same

---

to be used as a family vault for the donor and her family, is not a charitable use within the statute 9 G. 2. c. 36.   *Page* 359

2. If there be in a deed one limitation which is to a charitable use within the statute 9 G. 2. c. 36., that statute does not therefore avoid other limitations in the same deed, which are not within the act. *Doe* v. *Pitcher.*   *ib.*

W

WARRANT OF ATTORNEY,

See AMENDMENT, 3. 8.   ANNUITY. FINES. AMENDMENT OF DEED.

WARRANTY,

See EVIDENCE, II. 7.

WARDEN OF THE FLEET.

No action can be regularly commenced against the Warden of the Fleet in time of vacation. *Crook* v. *Eyles.*   347

Stock v. *Eyles.*   352

WATERCOURSE.

See ACTION UPON THE CASE.

WILL.

An executor of a testator possessed of real and personal estate, cloathed with a trust to pay debts, and to lay out money for the benefit of the testator's children, and with a power to sell freehold lands in *fee*, but taking no beneficial interest under the will, is a good attesting witness

witness to the will. *Phipps and Another* v. *Pitcher.*   Page 220

WITNESS,

And see WILL. ATTESTING WITNESS.

1. The Court will not grant an attachment against a witness, for disobedience to a *subpœna,* unless it be a clear case of contempt. *Horne* v. *Smith.*   9

2. If a witness is *bonâ fide* sent for from a foreign country for the sake of his testimony in an intended action, though the writ is not sued out until after his arrival, the Plaintiff is entitled in that cause to the costs of bringing him over, his subsistence, and compensation for his loss of time spent here pending the suit for the purposes thereof, and to the costs of his return.   88

3. But if, the witness being sent for to give evidence in one action, the Plaintiff uses his testimony in another action against a different party, and relxaes his diligence in

the first, he is entitled in the second action to the costs only of the witness's subsistence and detention for the purpose of the second action, but not of his voyage hither or of his return. *Tremain* v. *Barrett. Same* v. *Faith.*   Page 88

4. The insolvent debtors' court is such a court as privileges parties and witnesses attending from arrest *eundo, morando, et redeundo. Willingham* v. *Matthews.*   356

WORK AND LABOUR,

See AFFIDAVIT TO HOLD TO BAIL. 5.

1. *A.,* employed by the Defendant to transport goods to a foreign market, delegates the entire employment to the Plaintiff, who performs it without the privity of the Defendant. Held that the Plaintiff cannot recover from the Defendant a compensation for such service. *Schmaling* v. *Tomlinson.*   147

END OF THE SIXTH VOLUME.

Printed by A. Strahan, Law-Printer to His Majesty, Printers-Street, London.

CPSIA information can be obtained
at www.ICGtesting.com
Printed in the USA
BVHW062122051118
532208BV00012B/617/P